Lecture Notes in Computer Science   2857

Edited by G. Goos, J. Hartmanis, and J. van Leeuwen

T0218513

Springer
Berlin
Heidelberg
New York
Hong Kong
London
Milan
Paris
Tokyo

Mario A. Nascimento   Edleno S. de Moura
Arlindo L. Oliveira (Eds.)

String Processing and Information Retrieval

10th International Symposium, SPIRE 2003
Manaus, Brazil, October 8-10, 2003
Proceedings

Springer

Series Editors

Gerhard Goos, Karlsruhe University, Germany
Juris Hartmanis, Cornell University, NY, USA
Jan van Leeuwen, Utrecht University, The Netherlands

Volume Editors

Mario A. Nascimento
University of Alberta
Department of Computing Science
Edmonton, Alberta T6G 2E8, Canada
E-mail: mn@cs.ualberta.ca

Edleno S. de Moura
Universidade Federal do Amazonas
Departamento de Ciência da Computação
Av. Gal. Octavio Jordão Ramos, 3000, 69077-000 Manaus, Brazil
E-mail: edleno@dcc.fua.br

Arlindo L. Oliveira
Instituto Superior Técnico, INESC-ID
Avenida Duque d'Avila, 9, 1000-138 Lisboa, Portugal
E-mail: aml@inesc-id.pt

Cataloging-in-Publication Data applied for

A catalog record for this book is available from the Library of Congress.

Bibliographic information published by Die Deutsche Bibliothek
Die Deutsche Bibliothek lists this publication in the Deutsche Nationalbibliografie;
detailed bibliographic data is available in the Internet at <http://dnb.ddb.de>.

CR Subject Classification (1998): H.3, H.2.8, I.2, E.1, E.5, F.2.2

ISSN 0302-9743
ISBN 3-540-20177-7 Springer-Verlag Berlin Heidelberg New York

Springer-Verlag Berlin Heidelberg New York
a member of BertelsmannSpringer Science+Business Media GmbH

http://www.springer.de

© Springer-Verlag Berlin Heidelberg 2003
Printed in Germany

Typesetting: Camera-ready by author, data conversion by Boller Mediendesign
Printed on acid-free paper   SPIN: 10961155   06/3142   5 4 3 2 1 0

Preface

This volume of the Lecture Notes in Computer Science series provides a comprehensive, state-of-the-art survey of recent advances in string processing and information retrieval. It includes invited and research papers presented at the 10th International Symposium on String Processing and Information Retrieval, SPIRE 2003, held in Manaus, Brazil.

SPIRE 2003 received 54 full submissions from 17 countries, namely: Argentina (2), Australia (2), Brazil (9), Canada (1), Chile (4), Colombia (2), Czech Republic (1), Finland (10), France (1), Japan (2), Korea (5), Malaysia (1), Portugal (2), Spain (6), Turkey (1), UK (1), USA (4) – the numbers in parentheses indicate the number of submissions from that country. In the nontrivial task of selecting the papers to be published in these proceedings we were fortunate to count on a very international program committee with 43 members, representing all continents but one. These people, in turn, used the help of 40 external referees. During the review process all but a few papers had four reviews instead of the usual three, and at the end 21 submissions were accepted to be published as full papers, yielding an acceptance rate of about 38%. An additional set of six short papers was also accepted. The technical program spans over the two well-defined scopes of SPIRE (string processing and information retrieval) with a number of papers also focusing on important application domains such as bioinformatics.

SPIRE 2003 also features two invited speakers: Krishna Bharat (Google, Inc.) and João Meidanis (State Univ. of Campinas and Scylla Bioinformatics). We appreciate their willingness to help with SPIRE's technical program, and also their kindness in providing an invited paper covering the topics of their talks.

On behalf of SPIRE's program and steering committee we thank all authors, reviewers and attendees of this year's symposium. The local arrangements team, headed by Altigran Soares da Silva, also deserves a special acknowledgment. The program committee chair, Mario A. Nascimento, wishes to thank Alberto Laender and Ricardo Baeza-Yates for timely and insightful discussions, as well as for inviting him, on behalf of SPIRE's steering committee, to chair this year's program committee.

As we say in Portuguese: *Bem vindos a Manaus!* (Welcome to Manaus!)

July 2003

Mario A. Nascimento
Program Committee Chair

Edleno S. de Moura
General Chair

Arlindo L. Oliveira
Publications Chair

SPIRE 2003 Organization

General Chair

Edleno S. de Moutra, Universidade Federal do Amazonas, Brazil

Program Committee Chair

Mario A. Nascimento, University of Alberta, Canada

Publications Chair

Arlindo L. Oliveira, Instituto Superior Técnico/INESC-ID, Portugal

Local Arrangements

Altigran Soares da Silva, Universidade Federal do Amazonas, Brazil

Steering Committee

Ricardo Baeza-Yates, Universidad de Chile, Chile
Berthier Ribeiro-Neto, Universidade Federal de Minas Gerais, Brazil
Nivio Ziviani, Universidade Federal de Minas Gerais, Brazil
Arlindo L. Oliveira, Instituto Superior Técnico/INESC-ID, Portugal
Alberto Laender, Universidade Federal de Minas Gerais, Brazil

Program Committee

Alberto Apostolico (Purdue Univ., USA)
Ricardo Baeza-Yates (Univ. de Chile, Chile)
Michael Benedikt (Bell Labs, USA)
Elisa Bertino (Univ. of Milan, Italy)
Nieves Brisaboa (Universidad de A Coruña, Spain)
Edgar Chavez (Universidad Michoacana, Mexico)
Roger Chiang (Univ. of Cincinnati, USA)
Maxime Crochemore (Université de Marne-la-Vallée, France)
Bruce Croft (Univ. of Massachusetts, USA)
Edward Fox (Virginia Tech, USA)
Juliana Freire (Oregon Graduate Institute, USA)
Ophir Frieder (Illinois Institute of Technology, USA)
Pablo de la Fuente (Univ. of Valladolid, Spain)
Norbert Fuhr (Univ. of Duisburg, Germany)
David Grossman (Illinois Institute of Technology, USA)

David Hawking (Australian National Univ., Australia)
Carlos Alberto Heuser (UFRGS, Brazil)
Thomas Roelleke (Queen Mary Univ. of London, UK)
Costas Iliopoulos (King's College London, UK)
Alberto Laender (Federal Univ. of Minas Gerais, Brazil)
Ee-Peng Lim (Nanyang Technological Univ., Singapore)
Dekang Lin (Univ. of Alberta, Canada)
Joel Martin (National Research Council, Canada)
João Meidanis (Univ. of Campinas, Brazil)
Massimo Melucci (Univ. of Padova, Italy)
Alistair Moffat (Univ. of Melbourne, Australia)
Gonzalo Navarro (Universidad de Chile, Chile)
Charles Nicholas (Univ. Maryland, Baltimore County, USA)
Jian-Yun Nie (Univ. of Montreal, Canada)
Arlindo L. Oliveira, (Instituto Superior Técnico/INESC-ID, Portugal)
Gabriella Pasi (CNR, Italy)
Berthier Ribeiro-Neto (Federal Univ. of Minas Gerais, Brazil)
Altigran Silva (Federal Univ. of Amazonia, Brazil)
Marie-France Sagot (INRIA Rhône-Alpes, France)
Fabrizio Sebastiani (CNR, Italy)
Ayumi Shinohara (Kyushu University, Japan)
Amit Singhal (Google, USA)
Dan Suciu (Univ. of Washington, USA)
Jorma Tarhio (Helsinki Univ. of Technology, Finland)
Ulrich Thiel (GMD-IPSI, Germany)
Frank Tompa (Univ. of Waterloo, Canada)
Nivio Ziviani (Federal Univ. of Minas Gerais, Brazil)
Justin Zobel (RMIT, Australia)

External Referees

Alan Watt
Alex Lopez-Ortiz
Ana Cardoso Cachopo
Andrew Turpin
Bruno Pôssas
Carina Friederich Dorneles
Carlos Castillo
Catalina Luiza Antonie
Cecil Eng Huang Chua
Claudine Santos Badue
Claus-Peter Klas
Gudrun Fischer
Guohui Lin
Hannu Peltola

Heikki Hyyrö
Henrik Nottelmann
Hugh E. Williams
Joyce Christina de Paiva Carvalho
Juliano Palmieri Lage
Jussara Marques de Almeida
Kai Großjohann
Kimmo Fredriksson
Juha Karkkainen
Kjell Lemstrm
Laurent Mouchard
Mara Abel
Marco Antonio Pinheiro de Cristo
Miguel R. Penabad

Pável Calado
Reem K. Al-Halimi
Renato Ferreira
Robert Warren
Roberto Grossi
Ronaldo dos Santos Mello
Saied Tahaghoghi

Tomasz Radzik
Takuya Kida
Wagner Meira Jr.
Wong Hao Chi
Yoan J. Pinzon
Zanoni Dias

Table of Contents

Categorization and Ranking

Music Retrieval

Multilingual Information Retrieval

Patterns on the Web

Krishna Bharat

Google Inc.
2400 Bayshore Parkway
Mountain View, CA 94043
Krishna@google.com

Abstract. The web is the product of a planet-wide, implicit collaboration between content creators on an unprecedented scale. Although authors on the web
come from a diverse set of backgrounds and often operate independently their
collective work embodies surprising regularities at various levels. In this paper
we describe patterns in both structural and temporal properties of the web.

1 Introduction

The web, as most people know it now, has been publicly available since 1993 [19].
Despite its youth the web has had perhaps the biggest impact on the ability of individuals and organizations to publish content since Gutenberg's invention of the modern printing press in the 15th century [8].

What makes the web powerful is its ability to remove publishing inertia to the extent that it can transform or displace conventional channels. The lowered bar for entry
encourages publishing by many segments of the population not previously engaged in
authoring content. This increases the volume of communication allowing for phase
effects in social interaction, and also causing new genres of social and commercial
content to be born. The web is fast becoming the de facto repository of everything we
find useful, and a meeting ground for consumers and producers of all sorts. Since the
web is maintained by individuals in a loosely synchronized way it tends to grow or-
ganically. The shape, composition and temporal properties of the web today have
come about, not by design, but by the distributed and accidental collaboration of
millions of human authors. Nonetheless, we observe consistent patterns which illustrate regularities in the way humans tend to create and manage information. We look
at both structural and temporal properties of the web which exhibit patterns, specifically to do with graph structure and online publishing actions.

2 Structural Properties

The web is an interesting data structure to study because it is globally unique, and it
directly affects the accessibility of information on the internet. It is hard to study
because it is continuously changing. Many parts of the web are dynamically gener-

M.A. Nascimento, E.S. de Moura, A.L. Oliveira (Eds.): SPIRE 2003, LNCS 2857, pp. 1-15, 2003.
© Springer-Verlag Berlin Heidelberg 2003

ated and hence potentially infinitely large. Even considering pages that are not dynamically generated (sometimes called the *static web*), mapping the full graph is an engineering challenge.

The graph structure of the web, namely the directed graph with web pages as nodes and hyperlinks as edges, has been a popular subject of research. The first detailed study in this space was conducted by Broder et al [3] in 2000 using web crawl data of 203 million pages and 1.5 billion links from May 1999. By conducting breadth-first scans from random start points they mapped the macroscopic structure of the graph. They discovered that the graph had a massive weakly connected component of size 186 million, which in turn was composed of four parts:

(i) A central strongly connected component of size 55 million (*SCC*)

(ii) An upstream component and (iii) a downstream component,
 both of size 44 million, and

(iv) Other components connected to (ii) or (iii) but unable to reach the SCC or be reached from the SCC by a directed path. These add up to 44 million pages as well.

Before this study it was assumed that much of the web is strongly connected. Personal experience seemed to suggest that most pages were able to reach prominent directories like *Yahoo!* and vice versa. It was surprising to discover that only about 25% of the web exhibited this property. In practice surfers on the web do not try to reach other sites by long paths – instead they use search engines and directories for random access. They jump to a point close to their destination and surf the local neighborhood using local anchor cues. Thus, the reachability properties of the web affect automated surfing (i.e., with robots) more directly than they affect human surfing. Human surfers engage in backtracking within web sites as part of their navigational behavior, often returning to a relevant hub or to the home page of site. This mitigates the effect of running into dead ends by making web sites internally strongly connected for all practical purposes. This suggests that the connectivity between *web sites* is more interesting than studying connectivity between pages directly – if one wants to understand linkage between independently developed web content. In a related study of the web's structural properties at the level of hosts, Bharat et al [1] discovered that 75% of hosts on the web could reach each other by a directed path through other hosts. Specifically, they studied the host graph – a graph in which hosts are represented by nodes and edges signify page level linkage between the end points. Edges have weights corresponding to the number of hyperlinks between pages at the end points. A crawl of 1.29 billion pages in June 2001 was used to generate a host graph with 12.8 million (host) nodes and 395 million edges. The largest strongly connected component was of size 8.5 million.

2.1 Inverse Power Law Distributions

Numerous properties on the web seem to exhibit inverse power law distributions. Some are better explained by a *Zipf-Pareto-Yule* distribution (often abbreviated to *Zipf* distribution), which relates the frequency of an attribute to an inverse polynomial function of its *rank*, for a small exponent. For example, Glassman [10] reported in a study of web caching that the request rate for pages on the web is Zipf distributed.

This was confirmed by Huberman et al [12]. Broder et al [3] discovered that the sizes of strong and weakly connected components in the page graph of the web obey power laws with an exponent of roughly 2.5. Kumar et al [16] report that the fraction of web pages with indegree i is proportional to $1/i^{2.1}$. Broder et al confirm this behavior for both in and out-degrees on the page graph, which were found to have exponents of 2.09 and 2.72 respectively. Fig. 1 shows that the distribution of indegrees is better explained by the Zipf distribution than the general power law distribution.

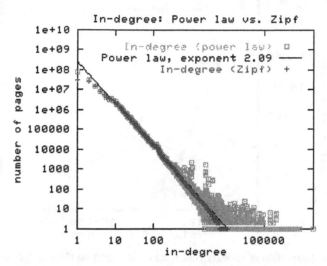

Fig. 1. In-degrees of pages on the web are Zipf distributed (Reproduced with permission from Broder et al [3])

In our work [1] we found similar effects at the level of web sites (i.e., on the host graph). Specifically, based on the June 2001 host graph mentioned earlier in this section, we found that the fraction of hosts with i incoming hyperlinks from pages on other hosts (weighted indegree) is proportional to $i^{1.62}$ and the fraction of hosts with i hyperlinks to pages on other hosts (weighted outdegree) is proportional to $i^{1.67}$. These are shown in Fig. 3 and Fig. 4 respectively. Further, we investigated the distribution of inlinks and outlinks for subgraphs of the host graph – specifically, subgraphs restricted to top level domains such as '.com' or '.jp'. The distributions in these subgraphs were also Zipfian, with the exponent increasing in proportion to the size of the domain.

2.2 Country Linkage

Our study of the host graph included an examination of the linkage between country domains. In all cases self-linkage, i.e., linkage between hosts in the same country was dominant. Linkage across country domains was influenced strongly by geographical proximity and language affinity. We found that language affinity tends to outweigh geographical proximity. The strongest example of this is Brazil's top linkage to Portugal, and Portugal's to Brazil. Spain doesn't appear in Portugal's list of closely

4   Krishna Bharat

linked countries until position 5, despite its strong geographical connection to Portugal. There is also a strong English language affinity among US, UK, Australia, and New Zealand. Examples like this support the intuition that linkage on the web is strongly influenced by shared language.

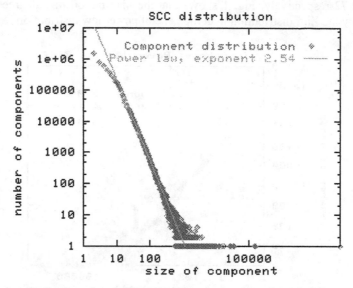

Fig. 2. The size distribution of strongly connected components on the web follows a power law (Reproduced with permission from Broder et al [3])

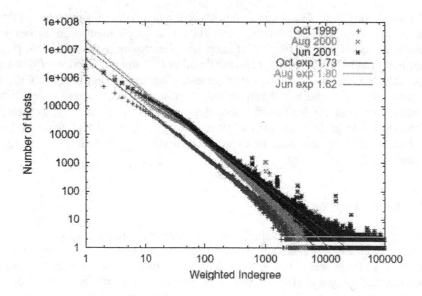

Fig. 3. The number of incoming hyperlinks to a host exhibits a Zipf distribution

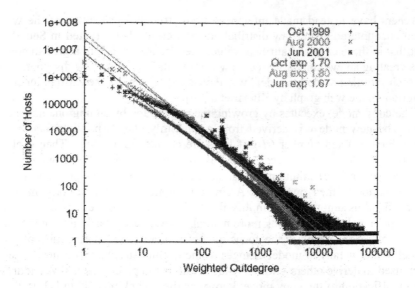

Fig. 4. The number of outgoing hyperlinks from a host exhibits a Zipf distribution

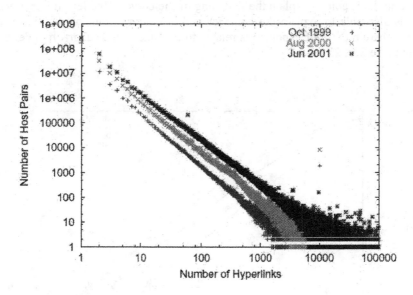

Fig. 5. The number of hyperlinks between distinct pairs of hosts on the web is Zipf distributed

2.3 Evolutionary Models

The best way to study growth on the web is to observe changes between successive snapshots of the web. However, such snapshots are hard to compute and align. Researchers have instead made inferences from structural properties of the web. The often encountered power law distributions of web attributes (listed in Sec. 2.1) suggest that in these cases the attribute values seen frequently afford a growth advantage, thus creating an evolutionary process which results in a power law distribution. Based on such intuition a "copy model" was developed to explain the Zipfian indegree distribution on the web graph by Kumar et al[16].

The copy model executes by growing the page graph by adding one new node at a time. The new node v is derived from a randomly chosen previous node u in two steps. First, a fixed number (d) of links are copied from u to v. Then each link is considered in turn and replaced with a link to a random existing node with probability α. This captures the intuition that authors on the web consult previous web pages before authoring their own links. A single reference page and a constant outdegree are artificial assumptions to simplify the analysis. Given more realistic assumptions the graph may be made to look more natural, without necessarily improving the indegree distribution, which is the focus of the simulation. A shortcoming of the copy model is that it fails to model changes to the outlink structure of a node after it has been used to derive others – which tends to happen in practice. This was addressed in our modification of the copy model known as the "relink model" in [1]. In the relink model instead of always adding a new node, with probability β an existing node may be extended with d more links. In all other respects it resembles the copy model. The relink model is able to explain the flattening of the curve to the left in Fig. 1 and Fig. 3. It is also able to explain the behavior within country domains mentioned previously, wherein the Zipf exponent is related to the size of the subgraph under consideration (see Sec. 2.1).

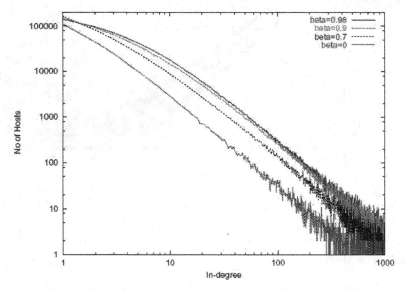

Fig. 6. Indegree distributions predicted by the "relink model" on the host graph show a flattening to the left of the curve

2.4 Applications

Understanding the graph structure of the web is an interesting intellectual pursuit. However, linkage analysis of the web has practical applications as well. The best known of these attempts have been to use accessibility analysis in the *Pagerank* [7] algorithm, and co-citation analysis in the *HITS* algorithm [5] and variants [2] for ranking of web pages. Knowledge of distributions of edges in the web graph have guided the data structures used to compress it, such as the compression models employed by Randall et al [17] in advanced versions of *Compaq*'s *Connectivity Server*. Finally, co-citation has been used a signal in identifying similar pages (or sites) to a given page (or site). Dean and Henzinger [6] used a *HITS* like co-citation analysis on the graph surrounding the given node to find similar pages. They compared the performance with ranking by co-citation coupling and found the former approach to be more effective. At the host graph level Bharat et al [1] used a *tf.idf* inspired approach to find related hosts to a given host. A host's set of terms are the hosts which link to it (*back hosts*). The edge weight of a back host is its *term frequency*. The outdegree of a back host is used as the term's *document frequency*. A ranked list of related hosts computed by this algorithm is shown in Table 1 for the query *www.airfrance.com*.

Table 1. Related hosts mined from the host graph for the host *www.airfrance.com*

Rank	Score	URL
1	70.25	www.lufthansa.com
2	52.21	www.klm.com
3	29.47	www.british-airways.com
4	18.21	www.swissair.com
5	14.18	www.iberia.com
6	12.25	www.britishairways.com
7	10.00	www.aircanada.com
8	9.95	www.aa.com
9	7.96	www.singaporeair.com
10	6.37	www.ual.com

3   Temporal Characteristics of Publication

Web publishing is a largely asynchronous activity. Authors publish content as and when they see fit. However, the link structure between pages can imply a weak temporal dependency, since the act of link creation establishes a causal relationship between two pages. A link between pages *A* and *B* usually implies that the author of page *A* saw (a version of) page *B* before the link was created. It is weak because all the linkage implies is that the last version of page *A* was *not* created before the first version of page *B*. The absence of explicit temporal information in the web graph makes it problematic to study the evolution of the web retrospectively. The age and growth characteristics of web content can be established from snapshots of the web, such as the crawls of the web available at major search engines and research institutions such as the *Internet Archive* (*www.archive.org*). In particular, the *Wayback Machine* [13] provides online access to old snapshots of the web.

An exception to the asynchronous nature of the web is the systematic recording of real world events by web logs (tracking by individuals) and news sources (tracking by agencies). This has been referred to as the "living web" [4]. The living web updates in a time sensitive way and is driven by human judgment. In contrast, many other parts of the web change dynamically as well but are updated by machines (e.g., product prices, calendar entries, weather information, stock quotes). Unlike news sites and web logs which evolve based on human judgment, updates to data attributes as in the examples above tend to be executed in an automated way that makes them relatively uninteresting to study. For example, by monitoring a weather site's activity we can estimate its update frequency (say 15 minutes), but there is nothing deeper to be learned from the analysis since there is no human input.

Next we describe how temporal update patterns in the living web may be detected and exploited.

Fig. 7. Screenshot of Google News (*news.google.com*). Articles from 4,500 newspapers worldwide are fetched, clustered and ranked in real time to form a meta-newspaper. Ranking is done on the basis of *freshness* and *global editorial interest* in the story.

3.1 Online News

The best known example of real-time temporal correlation between news streams on the web is the *Google News* service (http://news.google.com/). In the English language version of the service (shown in Fig. 7) 4,500 web sources of news content are crawled continuously to fetch news articles as they are published. The HTML content thus fetched is processed to extract the text of individual articles. Articles within a certain time period (at present 3 days) are grouped to form news clusters corresponding to individual stories in the news. The articles within each cluster constitute multiple, independent accounts and analyses relating to the same events in the news by individual newspapers. Although the news sources contributing to the cluster may be unaware of the other articles on the subject, text clustering and temporal proximity allows a unifying semantic linkage to be inferred between them in real time.

In a conventional newspaper the layout is determined by editors based on a *subjective* assessment of the importance and novelty of stories in the news. In the *Google News* service, the same determination is done *objectively* by a ranking algorithm based on measurable properties of the clusters formed by stories in the news. Specifically, *freshness* – measurable from the age of articles, and *global editorial interest* - measurable from the number of original articles published worldwide on the subject, are used to infer the importance of the story at a given time. If a story is fresh and has caused considerable original reporting to be generated it is considered important. The final layout is determined based on additional factors such as (i) the fit between the story and the section being populated, (ii) the novelty of the story relative to other stories in the news, and (iii) the interest within the country, when a country specific edition is being generated.

Country specific editions (e.g., Fig. 8) can be generated by additionally factoring in *regional editorial interest* and evaluating the geographical classification of news stories. In the interests of diversity sources from around the world will still be shown. However, local articles will be preferred for lead position. This helps for three reasons: (a) local sources tend to be locally popular and usually represents the regional viewpoint, (b) the titles tends to be phrased in a locally intelligible way, and (c) the page tends to download fast since the server is local.

The German edition (shown in Fig. 9) operates on the same principle as the English edition, demonstrating the scalability of the paradigm across languages.

There are several implications to being able to cluster and rank the world's news output in real time using computers. Like a seismograph for news, the system can detect and log world events of all magnitudes thus creating a historical record for research. Second, by performing the editorial interest analysis described above computers can rank all stories by importance on an absolute and objective scale. This allows the resulting newspaper's layout to be made provably unbiased and deterministic, unlike newspapers in the real world which are open to accusations of editorial bias and selective coverage. Lastly, by bringing together multiple sources in a single place, the user interface encourages readers to read more viewpoints (as in the examples shown in Fig. 10). This increases the understanding individuals have of controversial subjects and furthers the cause of democracy.

World »

Celebrations Greet India, Pakistan Peace Buses
Reuters - 5 minutes ago
WAGAH, India-Pakistan border (Reuters) -
Sobbing relatives hugged each other in
emotional reunions in India and Pakistan as
bus services between the nuclear rivals resumed after an 18-
month freeze due to a military ...
Euphoria as India, Pak, restore road links The Hindu
India and Pakistan resume bus link Guardian
Times of India - Hindustan Times - BBC News - Sify -
and 146 related »

The Hindu

Mourners delay twin's burial
CNN Europe - 40 minutes ago
TEHRAN, Iran -- The burial of Iranian
conjoined twins Ladan and Laleh Bijani has
been delayed until Saturday because of the
number of mourners trying to pay their
respects in their hometown.
Mourners pay respect to twins parents
Atlanta Journal Constitution
Hundreds pay their respects to parents of Iranian twins
MSNBC
Channel News Asia - News24 - irib - The Hindu -

CNN Europe

U.K. »

Prince concerned at Diana fund crisis
Reading Chronicle - 55 minutes ago
The Prince of Wales is understood to be
concerned over the crisis surrounding the
memorial fund set up in honour of his former wife.
INTERVIEW - Thousands threatened by Diana fund freeze
Reuters AlertNet
Diana fund charities 'facing crisis' BBC News
Cambridge Evening News - icWales - Glasgow Evening
Times - Creditman - and 191 related »

BBC News

Blair should quit, warns Short
Reading Chronicle - 55 minutes ago
Former Cabinet minister Clare Short has
warned that Tony Blair should quit as Prime
Minister before things got "ever nastier".
Quit before it gets nasty, Blair told BBC News
Short warns Blair to quit Ananova
The Scotsman - MSNBC - Hi Pakistan - Arutz Sheva -
and 16 related »

BBC News

Plan to recognise adopted genders
Guardian - 1 hour ago

Fig. 8. A country-specific edition for UK (*news.google.co.uk*) based on geographical classification and country-specific ranking.

International »

Al-Qaida-Sprecher im Iran inhaftiert
Die Presse - vor 20 Stunden gefunden
Kuwait bestätigte die Festnahme von Abu
Gheith, Sprecher des Terrornetzwerks. Der Iran
hatte dies bislang stets dementiert.
Kuwait bestätigt Haft von Al-Qaida-Sprecher in Iran
Neue Zürcher Zeitung
Kuwait: El-Kaida-Sprecher im Iran verhaftet Rheinische Post
Zisch - eBund - und 6 ähnliche Artikel »

Die Presse

Britische Abgeordnete fühlen sich von Regierung getäuscht
Frankfurter Rundschau -
vor 10 Stunden gefunden
Die britische Regierung glaubt nach Angaben
des Fernsehsenders BBC nicht mehr daran, dass in Irak
Massenvernichtungs-waffen gefunden werden - sie waren das
Hauptargument von Premierminister Tony Blair für die Invasion
Iraks. Blair ist inzwischen davon ...
Zweifel in Großbritannien über Iraks Massenvernichtungswaffen
Reuters Deutschland
London rechnet nicht mehr mit Fund von
Massenvernichtungswaffen Spiegel Online
Donaukurier (Online) - eBund - Die Presse - Netzeitung -
und 105 ähnliche Artikel »

Deutsche Welle

Deutschland »

Linden-Boulevard wird umgebaut
Berliner Morgenpost - vor 10 Minuten gefunden
Stadtentwicklungssenator Peter Strieder (SPD) hat sich gestern
mit den Verkehrsexperten der rot-roten Koalition auf den
umstrittenen Umbau des Boulevards Unter den Linden geeinigt.
Demnach soll die auf 12,7 Millionen Euro veranschlagte
Baumaßnahme bis ...
Linden-Boulevard wird nun doch für 12,7 Millionen Euro
umgebaut Die Welt
Bald nur noch eine Spur Unter den Linden Berliner Zeitung

Italiens Botschafter beschwört die Gemeinsamkeiten
Spiegel Online - vor 1 Stunde gefunden
Alles halb so schlimm, wiegelt der italienische Botschafter in
Berlin ab. Die Beschimpfungen und Urlaubsabsagen der
vergangenen Tage werden nach Ansicht von Silvio Fagiolo keine
negativen Auswirkungen auf die deutsch-italienische
Freundschaft haben. "Ich ...
Beziehungen zu Berlin nicht belastet Netzeitung
Italienischer Botschafter sieht Beziehungen zu Berlin nicht
belastet Yahoo! Nachrichten
Frankfurter Rundschau - Märkische Allgemeine - OWL-Online -
und 27 ähnliche Artikel »

Fig. 9. A screenshot of the German edition of *Google News* (*news.google.de*).

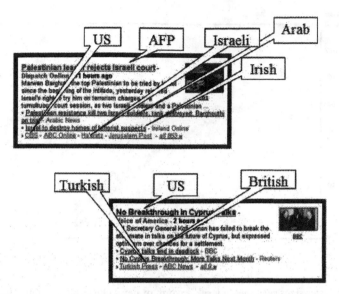

Fig. 10. Clusters juxtapose multiple viewpoints giving readers a broad coverage of issues.

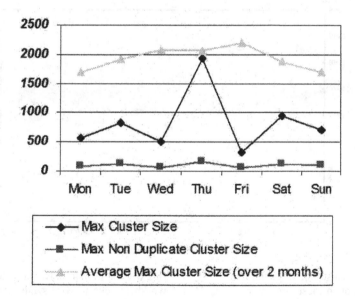

Fig. 11. The size of the biggest story of the day, as measured by maximum cluster size, is shown plotted against the day of the week for one particular week (Jun 30 – Jul 6, 2003), counting both (a) all articles in cluster and (b) all distinct articles in a cluster. The size of the biggest story depends on the day of the week and ongoing events. The Friday dip in the above case was due to a public holiday in the United States. Since there is much inter-week variability we also show (c) the daily maximum cluster size averaged over 2 months (May and June 2003).

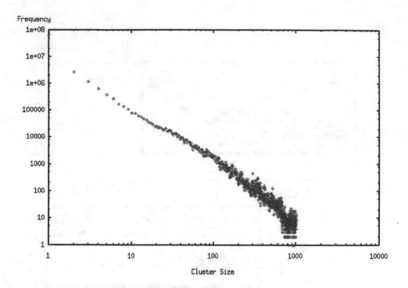

Fig. 12. Cluster sizes seen over a week's worth of news clustering are Zipf distributed

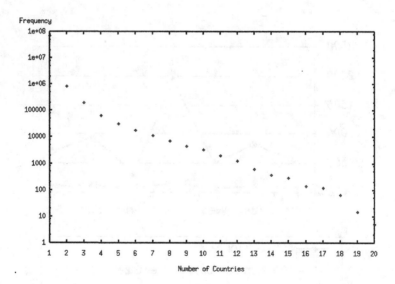

Fig. 13. The distribution of the number of countries with *original* articles on a story is log-linear. Although most large stories are reported worldwide due to wire syndication original articles on any given story tend come from relatively few countries.

3.2 Web Logs

Web logs (commonly called "blogs") are the modern equivalent of a personal home page. Unlike home pages which evolve by revision, blogs evolve by the addition of new postings in an append-only fashion. Individual postings are immutable. The postings typically contain links to external content which they comment on (e.g., news stories, other blog entries). In some cases they resemble personal journal entries and record the author's thoughts and experiences during a period of time. The postings are typically shown in reverse chronological order, with older postings moving to an archive. They have unique identifiers (also known as *Permanent Links* or *Permalinks*) for reference since a posting's location will change as it ages. Permalinks are URLs that identify an archive page and a position within it where the posting is present. Since postings carry timestamps, which are usually inserted by authoring software in a stylized format, their age can be accurately established. *Blogger* (www.blogger.com) and *Movable Type* (www.movabletype.com) are examples of services that support blogging (the act of maintaining a blog). *Blogger* provides a hosted solution whereas *Moveable Type* provides software to be run on a server owned by the customer.

Since blogs are updated asynchronously polling is the best strategy to monitor their evolution in real-time. For non real-time analysis given a crawl of the web the evolution of blogs can be reconstructed since most postings have timestamps. *Weblogs.com* (http://www.weblogs.com/) provides a non-exhaustive list of links to blogs that have recently changed. They effectively make updates synchronous by requiring *bloggers* (authors of blogs) to send notifications as new entries are added via SOAP and XML-RPC.

The best known examples of services providing real-time analysis of web logs are *Daypop* (www.daypop.com) [4], *Blogdex* (blogdex.net) [9], and *Technorati* (www.technorati.com) [18]. All three crawl blogs and links referenced by blog entries (e.g., news articles) and use citation analysis to highlight interesting topics. *Daypop's* most popular feature is the "Top 40" page which lists the most frequently referenced links found on blogs weighted by recency. Similar features are provided by *Blogdex's* and *Technorati*. *Daypop* further refines the list to show the most popular news articles and posts linked to by bloggers. This is an example of activity in one portion of the web (namely blogs) providing a ranking signal over another portion of the web (namely news content). The ranking of news stories on *Daypop* can differ significantly from that seen on *Google News* because the former counts explicit citations from authors of blogs, whereas the latter estimates importance based on implicit publishing decisions made by editors. Also, Daypop ranks individual news articles whereas *Google News* ranks stories in the news by identifying the numerous articles that make up the story. Daypop also provides trend analysis in the form of their *Word Bursts* feature. Like Google's *Zeitgeist* [11] which tracks trends in Google search queries, the *Word Bursts* feature detects memes in blog coverage by computing word sequences whose frequency has risen significantly in the coverage seen. *Google Zeitgeist* lists are posted weekly, whereas *Daypop's* *Word Bursts* are updated continuously.

Some recent work in understanding the evolution of blogs was reported by Kumar et al [15]. To study blogs the authors developed the notion of a "time graph", which is a directed graph with timestamps on edges. This was computed for the blog graph - a graph in which web logs are nodes and directed edges represent one or more hyperlinks between postings in the blogs corresponding to the end points. The graph was constructed by crawling a set of known blogs and inferring timestamps from stylized date markers in the text of the postings. Communities were identified in the undirected version of the blog graph in a two step process. Interconnected triples (K_3 cores) were used as seeds in an expansion process to form subgraphs, which they considered to be individual communities. Given a core, the expansion process incrementally added new nodes that had a threshold linkage to the existing set of nodes in the community, where the threshold was raised as the community grew in size. Once a maximal subgraph had been computed as described it was extracted from the graph. The time graph representation of each community derived from the blog graph was then analyzed to detect bursts. Specifically, they counted the number of new blog links created between members during each week, and identified bursts of activity that were significantly higher than the base rate of link addition. Plotting the growth of community sizes and activity bursts over time they detected a dramatic increase in the growth rate of both at the end of 2001. The reasons for this are unknown.

4 Conclusion

In this paper two aspects of the web which demonstrate interesting patterns were considered – patterns in the graph structure (a relatively mature topic) and patterns in the way independent publishing of time-sensitive content happens (a relatively new area of research). In both cases insight was found by surveying data at a web scale. Other aspects of the web exhibit regularities as well but were not covered. The distribution and linkage of topics on the web exhibits patterns which are influenced by the activities of the underlying communities. *Community extraction* is an active area of research and has applications in ranking. So is pattern learning for information extraction on web sites generated automatically from databases – also known as *site wrapping*. *Mirror detection* by detecting isomorphic linkage and overlapping URL namespaces has been studied as well. As new genres of content (e.g., web logs) are born they bring with them a pattern of collaboration which leaves a unique signature, providing opportunities for research, and sometimes resulting in useful applications.

Acknowledgements

The *Google News* service described in Sec 3.1 was the work of a team of talented *Googlers* whose contributions I would like to gratefully acknowledge. These include Kerah Pelczarski, Jeff Dean, Anurag Acharya, Ben Polk, Brian Rakowski, Michael Curtiss, Marissa Mayer, Michael Schmitt, Jenny Zhou, Scott Hess, Vijay Boyapati, Srdjan Mitrovic, Eileen Rodriguez, Debbie Frost, Daniel Lemin, and Nate Tyler. The host graph was constructed and analyzed with the help of fellow researchers at Google: Monika Henzinger, Bay-Wei Chang and Matthias Ruhl (visiting from *MIT*).

References

1. Bharat, K., Chang, B., Henzinger, M., and Ruhl, M.: Who Links to Whom: Mining Linkage between Web Sites. Proceedings of the 2001 IEEE International Conference on Data Mining (ICDM), http://www.henzinger.com/monika/mpapers/hostgraph.ps (2001) 51–58
2. Bharat, K. and Henzinger, M.: Improved algorithms for topic distillation in hyperlinked environments, Proceedings of ACM SIGIR (1998)
3. Broder, A., Kumar, R., Maghoul, F, Raghavan, P., Rajagopalan, S., Stata, R., Tomkins, A. and Wiener, J.: Graph Structure in the Web. 9th WWW Conference, Netherlands http://www9.org/w9cdrom/160/160.html (2000)
4. Chan, D.: Daypop – About Page, http://www.daypop.com/info/about.htm (2003)
5. Chakrabarti, C., Dom, B., Gibson, D., Kleinberg, J., Raghavan, P, and Rajagopalan, S.: Automatic resource compilation by analyzing hyperlink structure and associated text, Proceedings of 7th International WWW Conference (1998)
6. Dean, J. and Henzinger. M.R.: Finding Related Web Pages in the World Wide Web. In Proc.of 8th International WWW Conference (1999).
7. Brin, S. and Page, L.: The Anatomy of a Large Scale Hypertextual Web Search Engine, In Proc. of 7th International WWW Conference (1998)
8. Briggs, A., Burke, P.: A Social History of the Media: From Gutenberg to the Internet. Polity Press (2001)
9. Blogdex - About Page: Media Lab., MIT http://blogdex.net/about.asp (2001)
10. Glassman, S.: A Caching Relay for the World Wide Web. In Proc. of 1st International WWW Conference (1994).
11. Google Inc.: Google Zeitgeist http://www.google.com/press/zeitgeist.html
12. Huberman, B., Pirolli, P., Pitkow, J. and Lukose, R.: Strong regularities in World Wide Web surfing, Science. 280 (1998) 95-97
13. Internet Archive: The Wayback Machine (2001) http:/web.archive.org/collections/web.html
14. Kleinberg, J., Kumar, S.R., Raghavan, P., Rajagopalan, S. and Tomkins, A.: The web as a graph: Measurements, models, and methods. Proceedings of ICCC (1999)
15. Kumar, R., Novak, J., Raghavan, P., and Tomkins, A.: On the bursty evolution of blog-space. WWW (2003) 568-576
16. Kumar, S. R., Raghavan, R., Rajagopalan, S., Sivakumar, D., Tomkins, A., and Upfal, E. Stochastic models for the web graph. In Proc. Conference on Foundations of Computer-Science (FOCS) (2000)
17. Randall, K., Stata, R., Wickremesinghe, R., Wiener, J.L.: The Link Database: Fast access to graphs of the Web.: Proceedings of the Data Compression Conf. (2002)
18. Sifry Consulting: Technorati – Help. http://www.technorati.com/resultshelp.html (2002)
19. World Wide Web Consortium: A Little History of the World Wide Web http://www.w3.org/History.html (2000)

Current Challenges in Bioinformatics

João Meidanis

[1] Scylla Bioinformatics, Estrada Unicamp-Telebrás, km 0,97, P.O.Box 6123,
13084-971 Campinas, Brazil
meidanis@scylla.com.br
[2] University of Campinas, Institute of Computing, P.O.Box 6176,
13084-970 Campinas, Brazil
meidanis@ic.unicamp.br,
http://www.ic.unicamp.br/~meidanis

Abstract. My purpose in this text is to highlight some of the most important challenges in the area of Bioinformatics, drawing from several sources. The field is already pretty large and becoming more so. Therefore the selection of challenges presented here will tend to focus on topics I am more familiar with, with only brief mentions of topics I do not know in depth. The challenges vary in scope and motivation: some are broad, abstract while others are specialized to a given topic. Some are biologically motivated, others are nice as computer science problems. Also, I tried to show the dependencies among the challenges in order to get a global picture of the area. A basic knowledge on the principles of computational biology is assumed.

1 Introduction

In Physics, we know how to predict the behavior of solids (hence we are able to construct tall buildings and long bridges), the behavior of waves (hence we are able to communicate through fiber optics), and of the atoms (hence we are able to use nuclear energy).

In Chemistry we know less. We are able to predict the outcome of some mixtures of substances, we know how to make dyes, plastic, and how to process petrol. We know a lot about molecules, but still cannot predict the macroscopic behavior of a substance from its molecules, even for something as simple as water.

In Biology we know even less. There are few, if any, general, quantitative theories. Most of the knowledge is in the form of "lists of facts." For every rule there are exceptions. We know the basics about cells, but we do not know how cells differentiate in a multicellular organism. We can control some diseases, but many others still defy our knowledge. The attempts at biological pest control have seen success stories, but also formidable failures. "Biology is a mess", a phrase I once heard from a distinguished bioscientist, conveys well the amount of work still needed.

It seems like Biology is in the stage that Chemistry was a while ago, and that Chemistry is in the stage that Physics was a while ago. On the other hand,

M.A. Nascimento, E.S. de Moura, A.L. Oliveira (Eds.): SPIRE 2003, LNCS 2857, pp. 16–27, 2003.

Computer Science is, like Mathematics, a helper science. It finds applications in Physics and Chemistry, but mainly related to "number crunching." Although "number crunching" applications do exist in Biology, genomics brought combinatorial problems to the scene. DNA and protein sequences, the conveyors of information in living cells, have a strong combinatorial appeal.

But Computer Science and Biology have one important thing in common. Software is easier to generate than concrete objects like cars and buildings, so we are seeing the appearance of very large, very complex software systems. I dare say that the complexity of software systems today exceeds, or is about to exceed, the complexity of any other artifact produced by humans, and as such is approaching the complexity of living cells, being nonetheless still far from it.

So, apart from the combinatorial problems, a new kind of challenges related to managing complexity, more closely related to Software Engineering, appears when Computer Science touches Biology. I will try and comment on challenges of both kinds, and the relationship among them.

It is hard to understand complex systems. The human mind seems to have a limited capacity in the number of details it can handle. One approach to deal with complex systems is to try and extract the essential aspects, the most important for a given goal, and to design models to predict just those aspects. It is more or less like projecting a multidimensional vector into a given subspace. To describe the entire system in a meaningful way, many such projected, integrated views are necessary. We will see how this is being done, for instance, in protein classification.

The rest of the paper is organized as follows. Section 2 presents the major challenges as seen by biologists. Section 3 presentes the major challenges as seen by computer scientists. Section 4 presents more specialized areas, which can be seen as providing building blocks for the major challenges. We conclude with perspectives in Section 5.

2   Bioinformatic Challenges as Seen by Biologists

I will begin trying to capture what people primarily trained as bioscientists see as challenges. I am not a bioscientist myself, so I will draw from other sources. Collins and colleagues from the US National Human Genome Research Institute wrote about the future of genome research, and cite Computational Biology as an important resource, but do not enter in specifics [4]. At a bioinformatics conference in 2002, EBI's Ewan Birney, MIT's Chris Burge, and GlaxoSmithKline's Jim Fickett gave an impromptu roundup of the future challenges for the field. They came up with the "Ten Most Wanted," listed below. Highlighting in boldface is mine.

- Precise, predictive model of **transcription** initiation and termination: ability to predict where and when transcription will occur in a genome
- Precise, predictive model of RNA **splicing**/alternative splicing: ability to predict the splicing pattern of any primary transcript in any tissue

- Precise, quantitative models of signal **transduction** pathways: ability to predict cellular responses to external stimuli
- Determining effective protein:DNA, protein:RNA and protein:protein **recognition codes**
- Accurate ab initio **protein structure prediction**
- Rational **design** of small molecule inhibitors of proteins
- Mechanistic understanding of **protein evolution**: understanding exactly how new protein functions evolve
- Mechanistic understanding of **speciation**: molecular details of how speciation occurs
- Continued development of effective gene **ontologies** - systematic ways to describe the functions of any gene or protein
- **Education**: development of appropriate bioinformatics curricula for secondary, undergraduate and graduate education

These challenges are in general of a high difficulty, i.e., they are likely to require many years, decades, or even more time of combined effort from many groups around the world to be satisfactorily solved. The first six challenges will probably be solved with the aid of large amounts of data collected in the laboratories, analyzed manually or semi-automatically to generate curated data which will serve as "benchmarks" for hypothesis testing. Protein evolution and speciation (a topic in species evolution) are much more abstract. It is even hard to formulate them as input/output problems (a favorite format for computer scientists). One key issue here is to find ways of *measuring evolution*. Gene ontologies fall more into the domain of understanding a complex system via projections. The education challenge is of a completely different kind. It deals with dissemination of knowledge rather than with the generation of new knowledge.

Figure 1 is an attempt to link together these challenges. Each challenge is seen as a "black box", represented as a rectangle containing an abbreviated description of the challenge (based on the bold terms in their statements above), which can transform certain types of knowledge into others. Pieces of knowledge consisting of catalogs of various objects occurring in Nature are depicted as phrases without boundaries. Ovals delimit main bodies of knowledge, "knowledge on proteins" and "knowledge on biological processes". Therefore each challenge has "inputs" and "outputs" and together they form a knowledge network where the ultimate goal is to understand biological processes. I included a "translation" box to complete the network but this is not a challenge as it is relatively well understood. Challenges "protein evolution" and "speciation" where depicted as some kind on enhancers of the knowledge about proteins and biological processes, respectively, drawing information from them and giving back improved information. The "education" challenge permeates everything.

3   Bioinformatic Challenges for Computer Scientists

I will now try and capture what people trained primarily in Computer Sciences perceive as challenges in the field of Bioinformatics. I will start with very broad, practical issues and them proceed to more specialized ones.

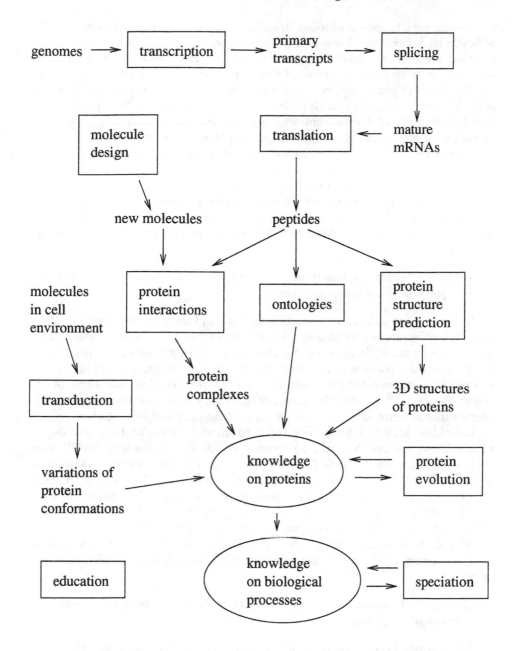

Fig. 1. Relationship among challenges. Each challenge is represented as a rectangle and can transform certain types of knowledge into others. Catalogues of natural objects are depicted as phrases without boundaries. Ovals delimit main bodies of knowledge. The challenges form a knowledge network where the ultimate goal is to understand biological processes. The "translation" box which is not a challenge since it is relatively well understood. The "education" challenge permeates everything.

Having been in charge of many Brazilian Genome projects, and now as CEO of Scylla Bioinformatics, I acquired certain impressions as to what the real issues are that need to be solved if we want to fully explore the amount of genomic data that is being generated today. I was glad to observe that these impressions are for the most part confirmed and substantiated by the testimony before the NSF Advisory Committee on Cyberinfrastructure of Gene Myers [12], a leading, world-renowned bioinformatician, who as vice-president of Celera Genomics had to deal with much more data and complex problems than myself.

According to Myers, current hardware is adequate. The problem is software. Software for data storage and sharing, software for parallel flows on computer grids, and, perhaps more significantly, software for writing software.

Better information management technologies are needed. The challenge is to find models and develop flexible data mining capabilities that can deal with huge sets, semi-structured data, experimental error, and integration of loosely coupled data.

Challenge 1 (Information management) *Create novel, paradigm-breaking systems for information management.*

Relational databases are the success that we all know, but for bioinformatics they lack some important characteristics. The entries have to be single-valued, and in biology many times we need multi-valued fields, for instance, when classifying a protein according to an ontology. Changing the schema is painful, and is an operation that researchers would like to do more often than, say, in commercial applications. The query language, SQL, is very basic and to write complex queries that execute efficiently can be very challenging and not intuitive.

Individual attempts have been made to alleviate some of these problems, with relative success, but still an integrated solution is needed. AceDB is a database specifically designed for biological data, and implements multi-valued fields as default [6]. It also has its own query language. The SRS (Sequence Retrieval System — see [20] for a recent development) provides capabilities to search multiple databases and goes a long way solving the integration problem. Perhaps that is the limit of what we can do with current technology.

The XML standard is an advance, but data grows too much with it, and it lacks semantics. Graham [7] points out that XML looks a lot like LISP, only not as prolix.

Challenge 2 (Parallelism) *Design expressive control systems for distributed, heterogeneous computing.*

Some issues become more apparent when we examine an application, for instance, data mining. Data mining can be loosely defined as a type of search where you do not really know in advance what you are looking for, but you can recognize when you stumble into something interesting. So you try many search approaches, each time learning from the previous one and producing improved searches, until you are satisfied with the result. If each approach requires a modification of the software, or of the database schema, as it often does, then we have a bottleneck if people who use the tools are not the same that make the tools. A real revolution would occur when biologists are able to make their own tools and modify existing tools in a fast and effective way.

Challenge 3 (Programability) *Improve the programmability of computers.*

This challenge is a very general one and it is also important in a variety of other fields. As such, bioinformatics may benefit from advances in other fields, but it may also contribute to its solution, since in bioinformatics many users with no specific formation in computer science need to use computers in very sophisticaded ways.

4   The Specialized Challenges

Up to now we have focused in relatively abstract, broad challenges. But as we try and solve a big challenge, we often need to break it apart into a number of more detailed, specialized problems, some of which can still be difficult enough to keep researchers busy for many years. These specialized problems are just as important as the large ones. They are the bricks with which we can construct a tall building. Although they can be attacked by individual researchers or groups independently of the context, it is beneficial to know the context so that we can modify the challenge into a similar, more easily solvable one, but that is still useful in the context that motivated it.

In this section I mention some of the areas containing specialized in Computational Biology that would hopefully attract the interest of computer scientists, and can contribute toward solving the main challenges. This is but a small sample of the existing areas, whose choice was influenced by my own personal experience.

The starting point for this part will be the book written by Setubal an myself in 1997 [17]. This is an introductory textbook where the basic techniques and background are presented, divided by areas of interest. However, new developments spurted the appearance of new areas, or reshaped significantly old areas in the last years, and I will comment on some of those.

I made the decision of still keeping the discussion at a higher level, not going down to the precise definitions of problems, but rather commenting on the area in a more general form. I had to do that because otherwise this text would have become exceedingly long. I intend however to keep updating it until it reaches this stage. One undesirable effect of this decision is that the text is not autocontained, and readers are expected to be familiar with the basic notions of computational biology, as explained in ours or other textbooks in the area.

4.1   Sequence Comparison

Pairwise sequence comparison is a relative well-solved problem in the community. Everybody seems to be happy with the existing algorithms, although of course people are always looking for faster implementations or approaches (see, for instance, the recent work by Myers and Durbin on accelerating the Smith-Waterman algorithm [11]). Score matrices have also apparently stabilized with the BLOSUM matrices (BLOSUM50 is the default in Fasta align, BLOSUM62 the default in BLAST). There is also a pretty stable agreement around gap parameters (gap open ranging from 10 to 12, gap extend from 0.5 to 3). Fasta align, Emboss align, BLAST, and SeqAln all use default values in these ranges.

One challenge that appeared in the last decade or so and is still with us is the matter of aligning long sequences. It is known that when one applies the standard alignment algorithms to a pair of very long sequences, for instance, genome size sequences, the resulting optimal alignment may contain long contiguous regions of very bad score, which is balanced in the final score by very long, very good flanking regions. This should in fact be reported as two very good alignments, dropping the bad part in between, and not as a single, longer alignment [1].

Other challenges here include multiple sequence alignment, and comparisons between genomic DNA and cDNA, and between DNA and protein sequences.

4.2 Fragment Assembly

Fragment assembly is one of the oldest problems in bioinformatics, because since the very beginning of DNA sequencing technology researchers wanted to reconstruct genome pieces larger than read length. The Institute for Genomic Research (TIGR) maintains an interesting page with the history of the "largest contig published so far" [9]. Current champion is human chromosome 14 with over 87 million base pairs.

Besides the traditional overlap-layout-consensus paradigm, which is still the norm in production work, both sequencing by hybridization and the Eulerian method have appeared as alternatives. Software package EULER by Pevzner and colleagues is a promising tool that explores these alternatives [16, 15].

4.3 Physical Mapping

To study long chromosomes in certain ways it is necessary to clone pieces of them, and to be able to map back these clones in the longer sequence. Physical mapping of DNA motivates several interesting combinatorial problems, both in the digest and hybridization versions. We refer the reader to the collection of open problems organized by Pevzner and Waterman [14], where several digest problems are mentioned, some of them still open.

In the absence of experimental errors the hybridization version is equivalent to the consecutive ones property for (0,1) matrices. PQR trees can be used to solve the problem in this case, and recently an almost linear time algorithm was presented to construct the PQR tree corresponding to a matrix [19]. Although PQR trees can pinpoint subsets of probes where experimental errors might have occurred, it is not clear how to solve the practical problem with errors.

4.4   Phylogenetic Trees

Phylogenetic trees are diagrams that describe the evolution of a set of species from a common ancestor of them all. It is related to the protein evolution challenge cited earlier, only here entire organisms are compared. The construction of phylogenetic trees is an old problem, but it gained additional momentum with the advent of high volumes of molecular data. Sequences of several species can be aligned and each column can be viewed as a character. Alternatively, distances can be computed from sequences and used as input for the tree construction algorithms.

It is often the case that the use of different methods and/or inputs for the same set of species yields different trees. One important problem is to combine various trees for the same species into a tree that is potentially better, in the sense that it has a higher probability of reflecting the real evolutionary scenario.

4.5   Genome Rearrangements

Genome rearrangements refer to the study of large transformations in a genome, such as the reversal of a large contiguous region, or a translocation between two chromosomes. Weights are given to a set of allowed operations and the goal is to compute, given two genomes, a series of operations that transforms one into the other with minimum total weight. This minimum weight can be used as a measure of distance for phylogenetic tree calculations.

This topic is relatively recent in bioinformatics, compared to others mentioned here. It received a lot of attention when the reversal problems for signed and unsigned (gene orientation known or not know, respectively), were proved polynomial time solvable and NP-hard, respectively, in the mid 90s [8, 3]. The proofs were rather involved, and many people have worked on these problems, simplifying proofs, improving algorithms, and trying to solve the open problems. The transposition operation has been resisting researcher's efforts for many years. The difficulty of this problem seems to extend to problems involving transposition as one of the operations as well.

To apply the genome rearrangement distance in real instances we need to solve the issues of duplicated genes, and genes appearing in just one of the genomes, either by fixing a one-to-one mapping between the sets of genes that will be considered, or by including gene duplication, creation, and deletion in the operation set. This problem is related to genome comparison (Section 4.6).

4.6   Genome Comparison

Genome comparison has many applications. It can be used to predict genes, because of gene conservation among species, or to measure the differences and produce input for phylogeny construction. The first challenge is to know which genes in one genome correspond to which genes in the other. Sometimes a gene in genome A does not correspond to any gene in genome B, and sometimes it corresponds to more than one. If a gene is present in many genomes, it can be used to try and establish the evolutionary relationship between them, as ribosomal RNA has been [13]. This can be done using phylogenetic tree building techniques, but the challenge here is that using different genes we often end up with different trees, and we have to find a consensus of them all (Section 4.4). Of course some genes may be bad candidates for tree building, for instance, because they were acquired by horizontal transfer rather than by vertical inheritance.

Genome comparison can be seen as a collection of techniques that includes long sequence comparison, genome rearrangements, and others and is useful in gene prediction and phylogenetic tree construction.

4.7 Micro-array Experiments

This topic is among the newest in the scene, and it is getting a tremendous amount of attention. In a micro-array experiment we have a fixed set of (usually) DNA probes printed on a rectangular array. The quantity of such probe sequences can be of the order of thousands. Each probe is part of a gene that we are interested in. An RNA preparation containing messenger RNAs extracted from live tissue is then put in contact with the array. Those that hybridize (that is, have sequence complementary with) a probe will be caught in the array and this can be measured with the help of fluorescent dyes. Repeating the experiment with RNA preparations under several different conditions allows researchers to find out which of the array genes are expressed under which conditions, and how much they are expressed.

The key computational issue here is to cluster genes with similar expression patterns and use this information to draw conclusions on these genes. Hierarchical clustering (UPGMA) with the complement of the correlation coefficient seems to be the most widely used method in practice. Datta and Datta [5] compared several clustering methods and concluded that a divisive clustering method known as Diana [10] performs well in most cases, although other methods may outperform it depending on the data set and on the performance metric used.

The work of Spellman and colleagues [18] on yeast genes whose expression is regulated by the cell cycle has been very influential. One of the reasons is that the authors of this pioneering paper put together a web site where all the data can be retrieved. As a result, almost all papers on the subject use this data as a benchmark.

Since the output produced by laboratory instruments used in microarray experiments is in form of images, there is also the computational task of interpreting these images and generate the intensity values.

4.8 Protein Classification

The goal here is to predict the function of a given protein sequence, in general a previously unknown sequence obtained by translating a predicted gene in a high-throughput genome sequencing project, where the problem is also known as genome annotation. The definition of this problem is complicated because the meaning of "function" of the protein is far from clear. The function of a protein can be very complex and multiple. Also, proteins are sometimes formed by two or more subunits, which are peptides translated from different genes. The SWISS-PROT database [2] is a key reference: an entry in this database is full of relevant information about the protein and contains links to several other web resources where a researcher can obtain even more information on the molecule.

With the plethora of genome projects around, and the need to annotate the data generated at a fast pace, automatic annotation becomes essential. Gene ontology (www.geneontology.org) is an initiative that aims at helping protein annotation by providing a standard vocabulary plus a classification of proteins or gene products into three orthogonal hierarchies:

- molecular function
- biological process
- cellular component (location)

For instance, a protein can have "transcription factor activity" as molecular function, "polarity of the adaxial/abaxial axis" as biological process, and "nucleus" as its cellular component. Each of these descriptions use controlled vocabulary and are in fact lower nodes in a hierarchy.

The hierarchies are not tree-like but rather the kind that permits a node to have more than one parent. It is therefore a connected, directed acyclic graph (DAG) with a single source.

5 Perspectives

We attempt to illustrate the relations between these problem areas using Figure 2. Each area is viewed as the development of a set of techniques to help obtain data on three main domains: genomes, annotation, and evolution. The arrows indicate which areas are used by which other areas, offering a view that complements that of Figure 1.

The interconnections make clear the symbiosis between Biology and Computer Sciences. For computer scientists who want to work with bioinformatics, here is an advice: do not isolate, form interdisciplinary groups with bioscientists. Try to comprehend what "keeps them awake at night," i.e., the main issues in their research. Try to build a relationship where everyone is at the same time user and designer of the computing systems produced. Biologists *are* learning computer science at a fast pace.

For most of the problems, there are still not enough benchmarks. Work together to put those in place. It is an advance to at least specify their format, even if data will be filled in the future.

Quantify. Biologists are not very much used to think in numeric terms, but that is a necessity in the current state of affairs. With the advent of genomics, Biology is turning more and more into an exact science.

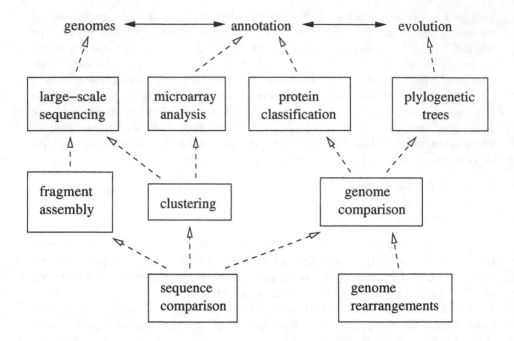

Fig. 2. Relationship among specialized problem areas in bioinformatics. The arrows indicate dependencies: an arrow from area B to area A means that A uses methods from B, or that problems in A create subproblems belonging to B. This diagram provides a view that complements that of Figure 1.

References

[1] Abdullah N. Arslan, Ömer Egecioglu, and Pavel A. Pevzner. A new approach to sequence comparison: normalized sequence alignment. *Bioinformatics*, 17:327–337, 2001.

[2] Boeckmann B., Bairoch A., Apweiler R., Blatter M.-C., Estreicher A., Gasteiger E., Martin M.J., Michoud K., O'Donovan C., Phan I., Pilbout S., and Schneider M. The SWISS-PROT protein knowledgebase and its supplement TrEMBL in 2003. *Nucleic Acids Res.*, 31:365–370, 2003.

[3] A. Caprara. Sorting permutations by reversals and Eulerian cycle decompositions. *SIAM Journal on Discrete Mathematics*, 12(1):91–110, February 1999.

[4] Francis S. Collins, Eric D. Green, Alan E. Guttmacher, and Mark S. Guyer. A vision for the future of genomics research. *Nature*, 422:835–847, Apr 2003.

[5] S. Datta and S. Datta. Comparisons and validation of statistical clustering techniques for microarray gene expression data. *Bioinformatics*, 19:459–466, 2003.

[6] Richard Durbin and Jean Thierry-Mieg. A *C. elegans* database. Documentation, code and data available from http://www.acedb.org.

[7] Paul Graham. *ANSI Common Lisp*. Prentice Hall, 1995. ISBN 0133708756.

[8] S. Hannenhalli and P. A. Pevzner. Transforming cabbage into turnip: Polynomial algorithm for sorting signed permutations by reversals. *Journal of the ACM*, 46(1):1–27, January 1999.

[9] The Institute for Genomic Research. World's longest contiguous DNA sequence. www.tigr.org/tdb/contig_list.shtml, Jul 2003.

[10] L. Kaufman and P. J. Rousseeuw. *Fitting Groups in Data. An Introduction to Cluster Analysis.* Wiley, New York, 1990.

[11] G. Myers and R. Durbin. A table-driven, full-sensitivity similarity search algorithm. *Journal of Computational Biology*, 10(2):103–117, 2003.

[12] Gene Myers. Testimony for NSF Advisory Committee on Cyberinfrastructure. https://lapp1.cise-nsf.gov/rhilderb/index.htm, Jan 2002.

[13] G.J. Olsen and C.R. Woese. Ribosomal RNA: a key to phylogeny. *FASEB Journal*, 7:113–123, 1993.

[14] P. A. Pevzner and M. S. Waterman. Open combinatorial problems in computational molecular biology. In *Proceedings of the 3rd Israel Symposium on Theory of Computing and Systems*, pages 158–163. IEEE Computer Society Press, 1995.

[15] P.A. Pevzner and H. Tang. Fragment assembly with double-barreled data. *Bioinformatics*, Suppl 1:S225–233, 2001. Special ISMB 2001 issue.

[16] P.A. Pevzner, H. Tang, and M.S. Waterman. An Eulerian path approach to DNA fragment assembly. *Proc. Natl. Acad. Sci. USA*, 98(17):9748–9753, Aug 2001.

[17] J. C. Setubal and J. Meidanis. *Introduction to Computational Molecular Biology.* PWS Publishing Company, 1997. ISBN: 0-534-95262-3.

[18] Spellman et al. Comprehensive identification of cell cycle-regulated genes of the yeast *Saccharomyces cerevisiae* by microarray hybridization. *Molecular Biology of the Cell*, 9:3273–3297, 1998. Web site with complementary material: http://genome-www.stanford.edu/cellcycle.

[19] Guilherme P. Telles. *An almost-linear time algorithm for PRQ trees and a scheme for clustering of expressed sequences of sugarcane.* PhD thesis, Istitute of Computing, University of Campinas, Campinas, Brazil, 2002. In Portuguese.

[20] E.M. Zdobnov, R. Lopez, R. Apweiler, and T. Etzold. The EBI SRS server — New features. *Bioinformatics*, 18(8):1149–1150, Aug 2002.

What's Changed? Measuring Document Change in Web Crawling for Search Engines

Halil Ali and Hugh E. Williams

School of Computer Science and Information Technology, RMIT University
GPO Box 2476V, Melbourne 3001, Australia
{hali,hugh}@cs.rmit.edu.au

Abstract. To provide fast, scalable search facilities, web search engines store collections locally. The collections are gathered by crawling the Web. A problem with crawling is determining when to revisit resources because they have changed: stale documents contribute towards poor search results, while unnecessary refreshing is expensive. However, some changes — such as in images, advertisements, and headers — are unlikely to affect query results. In this paper, we investigate measures for determining whether documents have changed and should be recrawled. We show that content-based measures are more effective than the traditional approach of using HTTP headers. Refreshing based on HTTP headers typically recrawls 16% of the collection each day, but users do not retrieve the majority of refreshed documents. In contrast, refreshing documents when more than twenty words change recrawls 22% of the collection but updates documents more effectively. We conclude that our simple measures are an effective component of a web crawling strategy.

1   Introduction

Web search is a mainstream information finding method: it is ubiquitous in the home, business, and educational environments for discovering answers to information needs. All web users are familiar with the simple, easy-to-use interfaces of search engines that are used for entering bag of words or ranked queries, and equally familiar with the ten-results-per-page summaries that are returned as responses. However, despite their apparent simplicity, web search engines are complex applications that deal with staggering query loads, numbers of documents, and concurrent users.

To support fast searching, search engines manage documents as a centralised collection that is gathered from the Web using a web crawler. A web crawler retrieves resources that are submitted by users (who may be internal maintainers of the search engine or external authors of web resources), processes those resources and extracts hypertext links, and continues the process. The resources to be retrieved are maintained in a priority queue.

The aim of the crawling process is to retrieve as much of the Web as possible while keeping the collection current and minimising the resources used in the process. Crawler efficiency is important: network bandwidth is expensive, careful

M.A. Nascimento, E.S. de Moura, A.L. Oliveira (Eds.): SPIRE 2003, LNCS 2857, pp. 28–42, 2003.
© Springer-Verlag Berlin Heidelberg 2003

rules are needed to avoid traps where a crawler continually revisits the same resource, and resources should only be revisited when there is a likelihood they have changed. Crawler accuracy or effectiveness is paramount: only resources that have been visited can be searched and resources should be up-to-date to meet users' information needs.

In this paper, we consider part of the web crawling problem. After crawling to establish a collection, resources need to be recrawled periodically so that the stored copy is refreshed to match the actual web-based resource. One possible approach to establishing when to recrawl resources is to manually or automatically classify pages based on their content or URL; for example, a list of well-known news sites might be manually maintained, and all resources within the list recrawled every 12 hours. Another approach is to retrieve a resource twice and to find how much a document has changed to establish a recrawl frequency. We focus on elements of the latter approach in this paper but, in practice, both approaches may be applied and we plan to consider this in the future.

A well-known technique for establishing when to recrawl a resource is to inspect the expiry and last modified information in the web resource HTTP headers. However, as we discuss later, this information is only present in around 32% of the documents in our collection (this is in marked contrast to the observations of others discussed in Section 2). Another approach is to compute the past change in a resource and use this to decide whether a document has changed enough to warrant recrawling. We explore this idea in this paper by investigating whether the number of bytes added or removed from a document is a good indicator of interesting change and, if so, how many bytes of change is significant enough to impact on search results. We extend the idea for words, and also investigate the impact of removing HTTP headers, document markup, and common words prior to computing change.

Our results show that these simple metrics are excellent predictors of changes that affect search results. For example, our parameterised bytes change measure SIZE is typically only 1% less accurate than refreshing all documents that change by any amount, while crawling 30% less data; this accuracy difference is unlikely to be perceived by the search engine users. Our scheme is also 5%–10% more accurate than refreshing documents that are predicted to change using HTTP headers. We conclude that our simple change metrics are an effective component of a web crawling refresh strategy. In addition, we recommend our accuracy evaluation approach as a benchmarking method for determining crawler accuracy.

2   Background

In this section, we present a background on web crawling, how the Web changes, observing document change, and HTTP headers and HTML markup.

2.1   Web Crawling and Web Change

The change rate of documents on the web has previously been considered as part of a web crawling strategy.

Cho and Garcia-Molina [1] investigate web page change and how it affects crawling strategies. In their work, they studied 720,000 pages over a four month period to determine how the Web evolves. The implications of their results were then used to determine the features of an effective crawling technique. They found that more than 20% of all pages changed on a daily basis, and that .com pages were much more dynamic than those in other domains. They also found that more than 40% of pages had a lifespan of more than four months, 70% for more than 1 month, and less than 10% of pages less than one week. From this study, they concluded that web page change follows a Poisson distribution and use this in their crawling techniques.

Their work does not consider in detail the problem of determining web resource change from document content. Rather, their crawler uses a simple checksum to determine whether pages have changed. It then examines the history of the changes to determine how many times the crawler detected that the page changed [2] and uses this in its scheduling strategy. It is possible that our development of novel crawling strategies could incorporate the outcomes of this work and, in particular, the use of URLs in estimating initial change rates.

Edwards et al. [3] describe an incremental crawler that considers crawl strategies for maintaining collection freshness. Unlike much other work — but similarly to our work described in Section 3 — their design does not make assumptions about the statistical nature of changes in web pages. Instead, it adapts to actual change rates that are detected as part of the crawling process. Specifically, they propose partitioning change frequencies into 256 buckets of different priorities and handling separately documents that change very rapidly. Their scheme measures document change using *shingles*, which we describe further in Section 2.2. A limitation of their work is that the experimental results are simulated.

Brewington et al. [4] have also investigated how the web evolves. They made daily observations of 100,000 pages over a period of seven months and then estimated the rate web search engines need to revisit the pages to keep them up to date. They found that to maintain a 95% probability that a page taken at random is no more than one day old, a web crawler must re-index at least 94 million pages per day (or have a reindexing period of 8.5 days), under the assumption that the total Web is 800 million pages in size.

Of relevance to our work were the observed statistics for documents. They found that most web pages were modified during the span of US working hours, and modification frequency peaked in files that were approx 4kB–5kB in size and that had less than two or three images. They also found that 4% of pages that were observed six times or more changed on every observation and 70% of these had no timestamp, while 56% of pages observed six times or more had no change. However, their work did not investigate the types or significance of changes in a search context.

2.2   Measuring Document Change

Liu et al. [5] describe a large scale web page monitoring and reporting tool. Their technique allows users to specify web pages that they want monitored, and the type of changes they want reported. In particular, the following types of change can be detected:

- Content Update: Any update on a page
- Content Insertion: Increase in size (above a threshold)
- Content Deletion: Reduction in size (above a threshold)
- Link Change: New or removed HTML links
- Image Change: New or removed images
- Word Change: New words added or existing words removed
- Phrase Update: Detect changes to specific phrases
- Phrase Deletion: Detect removal of specific phrases
- Table Change: Detect changes to specific tables
- List Change: Detect changes to specific lists
- Arbitrary Text Change: Identify any changes in specified fragments
- Keyword: Detect addition/removal of selected keywords

We have implemented several of these schemes in our work as change metrics in Section 3, and investigated these in a web crawling and search context.

The work of Edwards et al. discussed in the previous section computes *shingles* [6] for each document, and uses these in determining document change rates. A shingle is the set of all overlapping contiguous word sequences of length l extracted from each document. Similarity or *resemblance* between documents is then computed by measuring the number of shingles in the intersection between a document version in the collection and its actual web based version. We experiment with alternative approaches to determining document change and test these on actual web data in Section 5. Shingles have also been used in other web crawlers [3].

2.3   HTTP Headers and HTML Markup

Web resources that are indexed by search engines typically contain two components: HTTP headers and the resource content. HTTP headers specify information that includes the date the document was returned, the web server, the HTML document length, and the document content type. Of particular use for web crawling are the headers `Last-Modified`, `Date`, and `Expires` that we discuss next. The resource content is often marked-up using HTML, although it may also be another content type such as Adobe PDF format, PostScript, or a proprietary text format. When HTML is used, the markup specifies the HTML recommendation, the document character set (which could alternatively have been specified in the HTTP headers), and the structure of the document; we focus on HTML resources in this paper.

The `Expires` HTTP header explicitly indicates the date at which the document should be recrawled. When used correctly, this header solves the recrawl problem, that is, it indicates a validity period for the document version and an exact date for recrawling. However, as we show experimentally later, it is an unreliable tool: many web servers do not provide the header and, when it is provided, it is often set to a past time. Setting the `Expires` header to a past time helps ensure a document is not cached by user agents such as web browsers and proxy caches.

The Last-Modified and Date headers are often provided. As we discuss later in Section 3, if two versions of a document are available, then past document changes can be used as a predictor of a future change. In this context, the time interval between the current retrieval — specified in the Date header — and the most-recent change to the document — specified by the Last-Modified header — can be used as inputs to a predictive function [4] to decide when the document is likely to change. We would expect that this approach would be effective when the time between retrieval of document versions is short.

Wills and Mikhailov [7] have examined the accuracy of headers and their implications for caching. They found that more than 9% of resources did not change despite a change in the Last-Modified header, and 0.3% of resources had changed when the header had not. They also found that in 14%–18% of cases no Last-Modified header was available; in contrast, we found only 32% of the documents we use in Section 5 contained these headers.

In addition to studying change and HTTP headers, Wills and Mikhailov investigated actual document change. They found that many document changes were predictable, that is, the same lines in the HTML markup often changed as, for example, banner advertisements were rotated. This is consistent with our motivation and conclusions that document content needs to be analysed to determine the importance of change in web documents.

3   Using Document Change in Web Crawling

In this section, we propose simple measures for determining whether to recrawl web resources. We focus on measures that are efficient to compute: our measures can be calculated during the normal process of indexing, that is, no additional document processing is required. In addition, we assume that each web resource has been retrieved twice, that is, we are able to determine how much a document has changed and use this as a predictor of significant future change. In practice, as discussed in the introduction, a recrawl frequency needs to be determined after the first time a document has been retrieved.

Our aim is to identify schemes that can use past document change as an effective predictor of future document change. With each scheme s, we compute a function $C_s(d_i, d_{i+1}, \alpha)$ that evaluates to 0 or 1 for a change threshold α and two versions of document d that have been retrieved at time intervals i and $i+1$. A value $C_s(d_i, d_{i+1}, \alpha) = 1$ indicates document d has changed by more than α under scheme s and should be recrawled, while $C_s(d_i, d_{i+1}, \alpha) = 0$ indicates that no change has occurred or it is less than the threshold α. We make two simplifying assumptions: first, when $C_s = 1$ we assume that sufficient resources are available to recrawl document d in the next time interval $i + 2$; and, second, we assume only binary values for C_s, that is, a priority for recrawling is not available.

An implementation of the function $C_s(d_i, d_{i+1}, \alpha)$ is effective if it is able to identify document changes that will affect the accuracy of the search engine. We discuss how the impact on search engine accuracy is measured in Section 4. Moreover, the function $C_s(d_i, d_{i+1}, \alpha)$ is efficient if it minimises the number of resources that are retrieved to those that affect effectiveness. We quantify efficiency in Section 5 by measuring the number of megabytes of data retrieved in a given time interval, and consider it relative to the extremes of recrawling all documents with any change and not recrawling.

We propose three schemes that we experiment with later in Section 5. These are as follows:

1. ALL — retrieve all documents at time $i + 2$ that have changed between time intervals i and $i + 1$, that is, any document version d_{i+1} that is not bytewise identical to d_i is recrawled. In this scheme, $\alpha = 0$
2. SIZE — retrieve all documents at time $i + 2$ that have changed by more than α bytes in size between time intervals i and $i + 1$
3. WORD — retrieve all documents at time $i + 2$ that have changed by more than α words between time intervals i and $i + 1$.

As discussed in Section 2, we also experiment with the use of the HTTP headers Expires and Last-Modified (which we refer to as HEADERS). We also experiment with no recrawling, which we refer to as NONE.

We use the ALL and NONE schemes as ceiling and floor benchmarks for performance respectively. The ALL scheme shows the maximum achievable accuracy when all past changes are used to predict future change, that is, all other schemes will always retrieve either the same set of documents or a subset. Because of this, ALL crawls the maximum number of resources per time interval. In contrast, NONE shows the effect on search accuracy of not refreshing the collection. We do not propose using ALL or NONE in practice.

The SIZE scheme is an approximation of ALL but any changes that do not affect size by more than α bytes are ignored. Moreover, even when $\alpha = 0$, document changes can occur that are not detected: for example, a changing date, page number, or HTML colour attribute may not affect the size of the document. Because it is less sensitive to change, we expect that for low values of α the SIZE scheme will be effective. In addition, because SIZE can be computed from file size, it is particularly efficient to evaluate.

The WORD scheme is sensitive to single byte changes, but not to more than one change per word. In this context, change is defined as substitution, deletion, or insertion of a word, that is, α defines the number of such elementary changes that must occur for a document to be crawled. This is a different form of robustness to change to the SIZE scheme: a multi-byte change in a currency amount, a counter, or a page footer may be only a one word change. The WORD scheme therefore matches an intuitive understanding of what constitutes change. Words are defined as strings of alphanumeric characters that may include hyphens or apostrophes; all other characters are non-words and define boundaries between adjacent words [8].

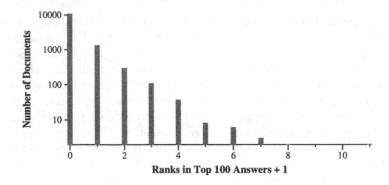

Fig. 1. Skewed ranking of collection documents in response to 50 queries. The graph shows on the x-axis the number of times a document appears in the top 100 responses to the 50 queries, while the y-axis shows the number of documents with that frequency. For example, over 1,300 documents appear once in the top 100 answers for the 50 queries

In our basic implementations of SIZE and WORD, we consider all resource content including HTTP headers and HTML markup. We have also experimented with removing headers, markup, and removing both. Our rationale for removing headers is based on our observation in preliminary experiments that these frequently contribute to recrawling of documents that have not changed in their content. For example, header tags such as `Date: Wed, 23 Apr 2003 22:08:08 GMT` reflect the time of retrieval and not the document content but are updated at each retrieval. Our rationale for removing markup is based on observations that changes in it rarely affects document content and that markup is rarely indexed by search engines.

4   A Measurement Framework for Web Crawling

An obvious measure of the accuracy of a recrawling strategy is to record the success and failure rate for revisiting documents. For example, after using a scheme to decide whether to recrawl each document in the collection, the prediction success may be recorded in a confusion matrix that tabulates *successes* and *failures*. A success is where a document that was predicted to change was retrieved and had changed, or where a document was predicted not to change and had not changed. Failures are where a document was predicted to not change but did change, and where a document predicted to change and was retrieved but had not changed. The sum of the values in the matrix is the number of documents in the collection.

For a search engine, we argue that this measure does not accurately reflect the performance of a recrawling strategy. Similarly to the use of terms in queries [9] and word occurrences in text [8], we have observed that the frequency of appearance of documents as highly-ranked answers is skew. That is, a subset of the documents in the collection are often returned as answers to a stream of queries, while the majority of documents are rarely returned. Figure 4 shows this effect for the collection and queries we use in our experiments in Section 5. For our set of 50 queries, over 10,000 of our 12,348 documents are never ranked in the top 100 responses. In contrast, 20 of the documents appear 5 times or more, and 1 document appears in answers to 11 queries. We have observed similar access frequencies in larger collections in unpublished results.

Skewed ranking of documents suggests two principles for recrawling. First, recrawling documents that are returned as answers to queries is important, while recrawling unaccessed documents is unnecessary. Second, that a complete recrawling strategy should include document access frequencies, an idea we plan to explore in the future.

Returning to our first observation, we propose a novel measurement framework for web crawling that considers its impact on search performance. Specifically, we determine the answers that would have been returned as the top 1,000 ranked responses if the collection were entirely up-to-date, and then measure how these results are affected when the collection is formed from a recrawling strategy. This process of forming a collection is similar in spirit to the TREC experimental testbed [10]: for a set of queries, a set of known answers are stored, and techniques can be evaluated by measuring how accurate they are in returning the set of known answers. We explain this process below.

We determine the correct answers that would be returned if a collection was up-to-date using four steps. First, we crawled and recrawled a document collection at three time intervals i, $i+1$, and $i+2$ to form three collections D_0, D_1, and D_2 respectively. Second, we extracted fifty queries from a well-studied Excite search engine log [9]. Third, we ran the queries using our search engine on the D_2 collection retrieved at time $i+2$. Last, for each query we stored as the relevant answers either the top 1,000 ranked responses or the number of ranked responses returned, whichever is less. In this way, the performance of our search engine with a perfect recrawling strategy for the time interval is known. (Further details on the collection, queries, and search engine are provided in Section 5.)

We can now evaluate the performance of our recrawling schemes proposed in Section 3. Using the document collections D_0 and D_1 crawled at time intervals i and $i+1$, we can compute the change measure $C_s(d_i, d_{i+1}, \alpha)$ for all documents in D_1. For documents where $C_s = 1$, we update the collection D_1 so that the document version d_{i+2} replaces d_{i+1} to form document collection D_2'. Having derived our new collection based on a recrawl strategy, we run our queries on the D_2' collection and record the top 1,000 responses (or the number returned if this is less).

To express the effectiveness of each recrawl scheme, we compute the standard Information Retrieval measures of *recall* and *precision* [11] by comparing the results returned from search D_2' to the correct results from searching D_2. In our scheme, a correct answer is one that has the same URL. That is, we view a match as correct even if the page has changed, as long as the correct URL is identified.

Equation 1 shows that recall measures the fraction of the correct answers that were returned in the top 1,000 results (or as many as are returned).

$$\text{Recall} = \frac{\text{Correct Answers Returned}}{\text{Total Correct Answers}} \ . \tag{1}$$

In contrast, Equation 2 shows that precision measures the fraction of the answers that were correct.

$$\text{Precision} = \frac{\text{Correct Answers Returned}}{\text{Total Answers Returned}} \ . \tag{2}$$

In the situation where 1,000 relevant answers are stored and 1,000 answers are returned, recall and precision are the same.

We summarise the recall and precision results using two well-known measures used in the TREC evaluation framework. First, we present *average precision* (AVP), where the precision values at each of eleven recall intervals from 0% to 100% are averaged, and an overall macroaverage computed for all queries. Second, we present *precision-at-10* (P@10), which is the precision after 10 answers have been inspected, again macroaveraged over all queries. The P@10 measure is particularly suited to measuring search engine effectiveness since it quantifies the accuracy in returning answers on the typical first web page of results.

5   Results

In this section, we present the results of using the schemes discussed in Section 3 to predict when resources should be recrawled. Our experiments were carried out using our public domain search engine LUCY[1] that implements a variant of the Okapi BM25 ranking function [12]. Queries were evaluated as ranked queries, and no stopping, stemming, or other techniques were used. We begin this section by describing the collection and queries we used in our experiments.

Collection and Queries

Our document collection is derived from web resources retrieved by staff and students of the CS department at RMIT University. We obtained a proxy cache log of around 50 Mb that lists around 300,000 web resources retrieved by several hundred user agents over a two day period, and used this to guide the retrieval of documents to form a collection. Because of its size, the number of user agents, and observed diversity, we believe that this proxy log represents a realistic source of documents that would form part of a search engine collection.

To develop a collection from the list of web resources in the proxy cache log, we carried out the following process:

---

[1] The Lucy search engine is available from http://www.seg.rmit.edu.au/

1. We extracted all URLs that were successfully retrieved (those that had a
   2xx HTTP response code) and had a `Content-Type` (a MIME type) of
   `text/html`; our search engine indexes only HTML documents, and recrawl
   schemes for other document types — such as PDF, PostScript, RTF, and
   proprietary formats — are outside the scope of this paper
2. We removed any query strings from URLs so that the base URL was retrieved. Our rationale is that the URLs dynamically generated pages can be
   extracted from web pages during a crawl process, but that these are not necessarily the same URLs as would be found in a proxy log; we therefore chose
   to omit dynamically generated pages from these experiments. For example,
   the URL:
   `http://www.google.com/search?hl=en&q=richmond`
   becomes:
   `http://www.google.com/search`
3. We then removed duplicate URLs, and selected every fifth URL to give a
   list of around 14,000 URLs
4. We then retrieved the HTTP headers for each URL to ensure the resource
   was able to be found (that is, to ensure a **2xx** HTTP response code was still
   possible), and deleted any URLs that were no longer accessible
5. For the remaining URLs, we retrieved the HTML page and HTTP headers
   and stored these as a "day one" collection
6. Each day for fourteen further days, we repeated the retrieval process and
   stored the HTML and HTTP headers; using this approach, the minimum
   time interval we were able to experiment with was one day
7. For any URL that was not able to be retrieved on all fifteen days, we removed
   the resource from our fifteen collections. We also removed any page that
   contained explicit or offensive terms using the script used to filter the TREC
   VLC collection [13].

After completing this process, our collection consisted of fifteen copies — one
each from fifteen consecutive days — of 12,348 documents. Its total size on day
one was 126 Mb.

In our experiments, we used fifty queries extracted from a well-studied query
log from the Excite search engine [9]. To ensure that the queries had answers in
our collection, we selected the first 50 queries that returned at least 500 answers
and had at least 10 answers that contained all of the query terms; these heuristics
were chosen based on empirical observation with the aim of finding queries that
had relevant answers in our collection.

Efficiency and Effectiveness

Table 1 shows the overall effectiveness and efficiency of selected recrawl change
detection schemes. The results are shown for predicting which documents to
crawl on the third of three consecutive one day intervals, that is, documents
are crawled on days one and two, and predictions using our recrawl schemes
are used to decide which documents to retrieve on day three. We performed the

Table 1. Overall results of the change determining schemes over one day intervals. Collections crawled on days one and two are used to predict document changes on day three. Effectiveness is shown as average precision (AVP) and precision-at-10 (P@10) relative to the actual day three collection. Efficiency is reported as Mb of data crawled on day three.

				Prediction Scheme			
Measure	NONE	ALL	HEADERS	SIZE		WORD	
				$\alpha = 5$	$\alpha = 20$	$\alpha = 5$	$\alpha = 20$
AVP	91.86	97.96	93.71	96.73	96.42	97.76	97.37
P@10	93.80	96.80	95.00	95.60	95.60	96.40	96.00
Data Crawled	—	56	19	34	29	46	34

same experiment with days twelve, thirteen, and fourteen and found the same relative results; we report these results briefly in Table 4. All document content — including headers and markup — is used in the change detection process.

The results show that our schemes are efficient and effective. Without recrawling for just one day, the staleness of documents results in the AVP and P@10 falling to 91.86% and 93.80% respectively. For the SIZE scheme, recrawling documents that have changed in size by more than $\alpha = 20$ bytes improves the accuracy of AVP by almost 5% and P@10 by almost 2%. Alternatively, using SIZE has a less than 2% impact on the measures compared to recrawling all documents that have changed; it is unlikely that this change is significant or would be perceived by users. Moreover, using SIZE, the data crawled is only around 50% of all documents that have changed or 23% of the collection overall.

Interestingly, the WORD scheme is more effective and as efficient as the SIZE scheme. For $\alpha = 20$, the accuracy is marginally better than the SIZE scheme with $\alpha = 5$ while crawling the same amount of data. We believe that the WORD measure works well because it is less susceptible than SIZE to recrawling documents with multibyte changes in header components, page footers, and advertisement URLs. As WORD can be computed as documents are indexed, it works well for a web search engine.

Not surprisingly, using the `Expired` and `Last-Modified` headers alone is ineffective, and using either header exclusively is worse still. With both headers, the accuracy is less than 2% better than not recrawling at all. We therefore conclude that our WORD strategy should be used in preference.

The SIZE Scheme Table 2 shows detailed results of the SIZE scheme. We show different thresholds for detecting change — shown as the α parameter — and two simple variants: first, we experimented with detecting only *decreases* in file size; and, second, we experimented with detecting only *increases*. Our rationale for experimenting with unidirectional change was motivated by the work of Liu et al. [5]. All experiments use one day intervals and the days one, two, and three collections.

Table 2. Results of SIZE schemes using the same parameters as in Table 1. The variations "Decrease" and "Increase" show the effect of prediction when only decreases or increases of file size are considered. Values for changes of $\alpha = 5$ and $\alpha = 10$ are shown in Table 1

Measure	Change		Decrease			Increase		
	$\alpha = 0$	$\alpha = 10$	$\alpha = 0$	$\alpha = 10$	$\alpha = 20$	$\alpha = 0$	$\alpha = 10$	$\alpha = 20$
AVP	96.73	95.60	94.33	94.31	94.05	94.22	94.20	94.19
P@10	95.60	96.70	94.40	94.40	94.40	95.20	95.20	95.20
Data	40	32	20	17	15	21	16	14

Table 3. Results of WORD schemes using the same parameters as in Table 1. Values for $\alpha = 5$ and $\alpha = 20$ are shown in Table 1

Measure	$\alpha = 10$	$\alpha = 50$	$\alpha = 100$	$\alpha = 250$	$\alpha = 500$
AVP	97.40	97.18	96.77	95.65	95.18
P@10	96.00	95.80	95.80	95.40	95.20
Data	41	27	22	14	9

Perhaps unsurprisingly, our results show that detection of any file size change is more effective than unidirectional change. In addition, our results show the predictable trend that small reductions in the amount of data crawled come at the expense of reductions in accuracy. Overall, we recommend values of α that are in the range 10–50, with the ideal value likely to be dependent on the collection. As noted in the previous section, we prefer the WORD for production implementations.

The WORD Scheme Table 3 shows detailed results for the WORD scheme for different threshold values of the α parameter. All experiments use one day intervals and the days one, two, and three collections.

Our results reinforce the effectiveness and efficiency of the WORD approach. The efficiency of WORD is impressive: for example, for WORD with $\alpha = 100$ and SIZE with $\alpha = 0$, the WORD scheme retrieves only around half of the data crawled by SIZE with the same effectiveness. Even with $\alpha = 500$, WORD is only around 2% less effective than crawling ALL documents, while retrieving only 16% of the data; moreover, it is still more effective than HEADERS — which retrieves twice as much data — and over 3% on average better than no crawling (NONE). The WORD scheme is an effective and efficient scheme for finding significant changes in documents.

Removing Headers, Markup, and Common Terms Table 4 shows the results of selective filtering of document components using the WORD scheme with $\alpha = 20$. *Stopping* [11] is the process of removing around 700 common and uninformative English words — such as "the", "of", "while, and "meanwhile"

Table 4. Results of WORD schemes with $\alpha = 20$ over one day intervals using different document components. "All" uses HTTP headers, HTML markup, and document text. "Stopping" uses all components but removes 700 common words. "No Headers" uses all components except HTTP headers. "Text Only" does not include HTTP headers or HTML markup. Collections crawled on days twelve and thirteen are used to predict document changes on day fourteen. Effectiveness and efficiency measures are described in the caption of Table 1

Measure	All	Stopping	No Headers	Text Only
AVP	97.20	97.17	97.20	96.79
P@10	95.80	96.40	95.80	95.40
Data	29	29	29	20

Table 5. Results of ALL, NONE, and WORD schemes with $\alpha = 20$ for different time intervals. Effectiveness is measured relative to the ideal final collection

Measure	One Day			Three Days			Seven Days		
	ALL	NONE	WORD	ALL	NONE	WORD	ALL	NONE	WORD
AVP	97.96	91.86	97.37	98.93	93.26	98.37	97.75	86.82	96.39
P@10	96.80	93.80	96.00	98.60	96.40	98.40	96.20	93.20	95.60
Data	56	—	34	65	—	45	67	—	45

— prior to comparing document changes. *No headers* is the removal of HTTP headers. *Text only* refers to the removal of both HTTP headers and HTML markup. Stopping is not applied with the latter two schemes.

We had expected that uninteresting change may have been filtered using these approaches, leading to more efficient recrawling with the same effectiveness. However, the effect is almost the opposite: crawling efficiency is unchanged for "stopping" and "no headers", while effectiveness is marginally reduced. For "text only", the efficiency is improved at the expense of a small accuracy loss. We therefore conclude — based on the inspection of our results — that the WORD scheme alone is sufficient to discover interesting change, and that HTTP headers and HTML markup aids in this process.

Other Recrawl Intervals So far in this section, we have shown only results with one day intervals. Table 5 shows the effect of varying this to three and seven day intervals for the ALL, NONE, and WORD schemes; WORD is again shown with $\alpha = 20$ only.

Not surprisingly, as interval lengths increase more document change occurs, and the number of megabytes of data recrawled by the ALL and WORD schemes increases. Interestingly, the change over seven days is only slightly more than that over three days, an observation that is partly inconsistent with the work described in Section 2. We plan to further investigate these variations by experimenting with other, larger, more heterogeneous collections. However, the important trend is the relative performance of our WORD scheme to the ALL approach over all time intervals.

6 Conclusions

Web crawling is essential to maintaining an up-to-date and complete document collection at a web search engine. In this paper, we have proposed simple measures to determine when document content has changed and will affect the search process. Our schemes are based on comparing document versions, and will form an important component of an overall recrawling strategy.

Our results show that the use of the number of words that change in a document is a practical tool for guiding document recrawling. For example, if documents copies are desired to be at most one day older than their web-based originals, then a word scheme is less than 1% less effective than recrawling all documents that have changed in any way, while recrawling 40% less data. In contrast, using HTTP headers is less than 2% better than not recrawling at all. We conclude that our word-based schemes are an effective and efficient tool for guiding web recrawling for web search engines.

Our schemes are only part of a recrawling strategy and other alternatives are possible. We plan to investigate the use of automatic document categorisation and its use in predicting recrawl frequency. We also plan to investigate ongoing trends for large collections, that is, how a priority queuing strategy and longer histories of document recrawls can be used to guide efficient and effective querying. Last, we plan to investigate the relative performance of document shingles to our schemes.

Acknowledgements

This work was supported by the Australian Research Council.

References

1. J. Cho, H. Garcia-Molina: The Evolution of the Web and Implications for an Incremental Crawler. In A.E. Abbadi, M.L. Brodie, S. Chakravarthy, U. Dayal, N. Kamel, G. Schlageter, K.-Y. Whang (editors): Proceedings of 26th International Conference on Very Large Data Bases, Morgan Kaufmann, Cairo Egypt (2000) 200–209
2. J. Cho, H. Garcia-Molina: Estimating Frequency of Change. Stanford University, Computer Science Department, Nov. (2000)
3. J. Edwards, K.S. McCurley, J.A. Tomlin: An adaptive model for optimizing performance of an incremental web crawler. Proceedings of the Tenth International World Wide Web Conference, ACM Press, Hong Kong Hong Kong (2001) 106–113
4. B.E. Brewington, G. Cybenko: How dynamic is the Web?. Proceedings of the 9th international World Wide Web Conference on Computer Networks 33(1–6), Amsterdam Netherlands (2000) 257–276

5. L. Liu, C. Pu, W. Tang: WebCQ: Detecting and delivering information changes on the Web. Proceedings of the International Conference on Information and Knowledge Management (CIKM), ACM Press, McLean Virginia (2000) 512–519
6. A. Broder, S. Glassman, M. Manasse, G. Zweig: Syntactic clustering of the Web. Proceedings of the 6th International World Wide Web Conference, Santa Clara California (1997) 391–404
7. C.E. Wills and M. Mikhailov: Towards a better understanding of Web resources and server responses for improved caching Computer Networks, 31(11–16), (1999) 1389-1286
8. H.E. Williams, J. Zobel: Searchable Words on the Web. International Journal of Digital Libraries, (to appear)
9. A. Spink, D. Wolfram, B. J. Jansen, T. Saracevic: Searching the web: The public and their queries. Journal of the American Society for Information Science 52(3), (2001) 226–234
10. D. Harman: Overview of the second text retrieval conference (TREC-2). Information Processing & Management 31(3), (1995) 271-289
11. I.H. Witten and A. Moffat and T.C. Bell: Managing Gigabytes: Compressing and Indexing Documents and Images. Morgan Kaufmann Publishers, Los Altos CA, 94022, USA, second edition (1999)
12. S.E. Robertson, S. Walker: Okapi/Keenbow at TREC-8. In E.M Voorhees, D. Harman (editors): Proceedings Text Retrieval Conference (TREC), National Institute of Standards and Technology, Washington (1999) 151–162
13. D. Hawking and N. Craswell and P. Thistlewaite: Overview of TREC-7 Very Large Collection Track. The Eighth Text REtrieval Conference (TREC 8), National Institute of Standards and Technology Special Publication 500-246, Washington DC (1999) 91–104

Link Information as a Similarity Measure in Web Classification

Marco Cristo[1,2], Pável Calado[1], Edleno Silva de Moura[3], Nivio Ziviani[1], and Berthier Ribeiro-Neto[1]

[1] Federal University of Minas Gerais, Computer Science Department,
Belo Horizonte — MG, Brazil
{marco, pavel, nivio, berthier}@dcc.ufmg.br
[2] Fucapi, Technology Foundation, Manaus — AM, Brazil
[3] Federal University of Amazonas, Computer Science Department,
Manaus — AM, Brazil
edleno@dcc.ufmg.br

Abstract. The objective of this paper is to study how the link structure of the Web can be used to derive a similarity measure between documents. We evaluate five different measures and determine how accurate they are in predicting the subject of Web pages. Experiments with a Web directory indicate that the use of links from external pages greatly increases the quality of the results. Gains as high as 45.9 points in F_1 were obtained, when compared to a text-based classifier. Among the similarity measures tested in this work, co-citation presented the best performance in determining if two Web pages are related. This work provides an important insight on how similarity measures can be derived from links and applied to Web IR problems.

1 Introduction

The World Wide Web has become a main focus of research in information retrieval (IR). Its unique characteristics, like the increasing volume of data, the volatility of its documents, or the wide array of user's interests, make it a challenging environment for traditional IR solutions. On the other hand, the Web provides ground to explore a new set of possibilities. Multimedia documents, semi-structured data, user behavior logs, and many other sources of information allow a whole new range of IR algorithms to be tested. This work focuses on one such source of information widely available in the Web: its link structure.

It is possible to infer two different meanings from links between Web pages. First, if two pages are linked, we can assume that their subjects are related. Second, if a page is pointed by many other pages, we can assume that its content is important. These two assumptions have been successfully used in Web IR for tasks like page ranking [1, 2, 3], finding site homepages [4], and document classification [5, 6, 7, 8, 9].

In this work we evaluate how the link structure of the Web can be used to determine a measure of similarity between documents. We experiment with five

M.A. Nascimento, E.S. de Moura, A.L. Oliveira (Eds.): SPIRE 2003, LNCS 2857, pp. 43–55, 2003.

different similarity measures and determine how accurate they are in predicting the subject of Web pages. We argue that a good similarity measure will be able to accurately determine if two Web documents are topic-related. Thus, we expect that such measure will be effective in classifying documents into a set of pre-defined categories.

To validate this assumption, tests were performed using a *kNN* classifier on a Web directory containing approximately 44,000 documents. Experiments show that the use of links from pages outside the directory greatly increases the quality of the results. Among the similarity measures considered in this work, the co-citation measure presents the best performance in determining if two pages are related.

These measures have never been directly compared in a Web environment and the results shown here provide an important insight on how they perform. Since they are simple to compute and use highly available information, we expect them to be applicable to several other Web related problems, such as Web document clustering [10, 11], finding similar pages [12], or building visual retrieval systems [13].

2   Related Work

The issue of document similarity is of central importance to Information Retrieval. Although the most widely used measure up to today is still the *cosine similarity* in the *vector space model* [14], it is known that using different approaches will influence retrieval effectiveness. For this reason, many alternatives have been proposed. Tombros and van Rijsbergen [11], for instance, show that a similarity measure that depends on the users queries may lead to better results in document clustering. In [15], Zhang and Rasmussen show that the traditional cosine similarity measure can be improved, when combined with a distance measure. And, for detecting changes in Web pages, Flesca and Masciari [16] propose a similarity measure that compares not only text, but also HTML trees.

Using link information as a way of finding related Web documents has also been proposed. One example is the Companion algorithm [17], which we describe in Sect. 3.4, where links are used to determine a set of pages related to a given initial page. He et al. [10] use link information to assign weights the edges of a graph representing hyperlink structure. Graph partitioning algorithms are then used to split the set of pages into clusters. In a work more similar to ours, three measures of linkage similarity are compared to a human evaluation of similarity between Web pages [12]. The authors come to quite different conclusions, however, mainly due to the collection used— a set of academic sites from the U.K. This collection has a very different link structure where, for instance, many of the pages link to each other, a phenomena that we cannot expect in a Web directory (or the Web in general [18]).

In this paper, we evaluate the linkage similarity measures by applying them to a classification algorithm. Several other works in the literature have reported the successful use of links as a means to improve classification performance.

Using the taxonomy presented in Sun et al. [19], we can summarize these efforts in three main approaches: hypertext, link analysis, and neighborhood.

In the hypertext approach, Web pages are represented by context features, such as terms extracted from linked pages, anchor text (text describing the links), paragraphs surrounding the links, and the headlines that structurally precede the sections where links occur. Yang et al. [20] show that the use of terms from linked documents works better when neighboring documents are all in the same class. Similarly, Furnkranz et al. [21], Glover et al. [22] and Sun et al. [19] achieved good results by using anchor text, and the paragraphs and headlines that surround the links.

In the link analysis approach, learning algorithms are applied to handle both the text components in Web pages and the linkage among them. Slattery and Mitchel [6] exploit the hyperlink topology using a HITS based algorithm [2] to discover test set regularities. Joachims et al. [7] studied the combination of support vector machine kernel functions representing co-citation and content information. By using a combination of link-based and content-based probabilistic methods, Cohn et al [8] improved classification performance over a content-based baseline. Fisher and Everson [9] extended this work by showing that link information is useful when the document collection has a sufficiently high link density and the links are of sufficiently high quality.

Finally, in the neighborhood approach, the document category is estimated based on category assignments of already classified neighboring pages. Chakrabarti et al [5] showed that co-citation based strategies are better than those using immediate neighbors. Oh et al [23] improved this approach by using a filtering process to select the linked documents.

Our method is based on the link analysis approach, but it differs from previous works in the fact that our focus is not build a link based classifier, but to analyze what linkage similarity measures could be best used by a link based classifier. We evaluate a set of different approaches to extract information from the links and determine which ones provide the best results.

3   Linkage Similarity Measures

To determine the similarity of subject between Web pages we used five different similarity measures derived from their link structure: co-citation, bibliographic coupling, Amsler, Companion with authority degrees, and Companion with hub degrees. The first three were introduced in bibliometric science, as measures of how related two scientific papers are [24, 25, 26]. In this work, we evaluate how they perform when applied to the Web environment, where we assume that links between Web pages have the same role as citations between scientific papers. The Companion algorithm was proposed by Dean and Henzinger [17], as a method to find Web pages related to each other. Here, we use it to provide a value of similarity between documents. We now describe in detail each of the proposed linkage similarity measures.

3.1 Co-citation

Co-citation was first proposed by Small [26] as a similarity measure between scientific papers. Two papers are co-cited if a third paper has citations to both of them. This reflects the assumption that the author of a scientific paper will cite only papers related to his own work. Although Web links have many differences from citations, we can assume that many of them have the same meaning, i.e., a Web page author will insert links to pages related to his own page. In this case, we can apply co-citation to Web documents by treating links as citations. We say that two pages are co-cited if a third page has links to both of them.

To further refine this idea, let d be a Web page and let P_d be the set of pages that link to d, called the *parents* of d. The co-citation similarity between two pages d_1 and d_2 is defined as:

$$cocitation(d_1, d_2) = \frac{P_{d_1} \cap P_{d_2}}{|P_{d_1} \cup P_{d_2}|} \tag{1}$$

Equation (1) tells us that, the more parents d_1 and d_2 have in common, the more related they are. This value is normalized by the total set of parents, so that the co-citation similarity varies between 0 and 1. If both P_{d_1} and P_{d_2} are empty, we define the co-citation similarity as zero.

3.2 Bibliographic Coupling

Also with the goal of determining the similarity between papers, Kessler [24] introduced the measure of bibliographic coupling. Two documents share one unit of bibliographic coupling if both cite a same paper. The idea is based on the notion that paper authors who work on the same subject tend to cite the same papers. As for co-citation, we can apply this principle to the Web. We assume that two authors of Web pages on the same subject tend to insert links to the same pages. Thus, we say that two pages have one unit of bibliographic coupling between them if they link to the same page.

More formally, let d be a Web page. We define C_d as the set of pages that d links to, also called the *children* of d. Bibliographic coupling between two pages d_1 and d_2 is defined as:

$$bibcoupling(d_1, d_2) = \frac{C_{d_1} \cap C_{d_2}}{|C_{d_1} \cup C_{d_2}|} \tag{2}$$

According to (2), the more children in common page d_1 has with page d_2, the more related they are. This value is normalized by the total set of children, to fit between 0 and 1. If both C_{d_1} and C_{d_2} are empty, we define the bibliographic coupling similarity as zero.

3.3 Amsler

In an attempt to take the most advantage of the information available in citations between papers, Amsler [25] proposed a measure of similarity that combines both co-citation and bibliographic coupling. According to Amsler, two papers A and B are related if (1) A and B are cited by the same paper, (2) A and B cite the same paper, or (3) A cites a third paper C that cites B. As for the previous measures, we can apply the Amsler similarity measure to Web pages, replacing citations by links.

Let d be a Web page, let P_d be the set of parents of d, and let C_d be the set of children of d. The Amsler similarity between two pages d_1 and d_2 is defined as:

$$amsler(d_1, d_2) = \frac{(P_{d_1} \cup C_{d_1}) \cap (P_{d_2} \cup C_{d_2})}{|(P_{d_1} \cup C_{d_1}) \cup (P_{d_2} \cup C_{d_2})|} \tag{3}$$

Equation (3) tell us that, the more links (either parents or children) d_1 and d_2 have in common, the more they are related. The measure is normalized by the total number of links. If neither d_1 nor d_2 have any children or parents, the similarity is defined as zero.

3.4 Companion

On a different approach, the Companion algorithm was proposed by Dean and Henzinger in [17]. Given a Web page d, the algorithm finds a set of pages related to d by examining its link structure. Companion is able to return a degree of how related each page is to d. This degree can be used as a similarity measure between d and other pages.

To find a set of pages related to a page d, the Companion algorithm has two main steps: (1) build a vicinity Graph of d and (2) compute the degrees of similarity. In step 1, pages that are linked to d are retrieved. We build the set $\mathcal{V}$, the vicinity of d, that contains the parents of d, the children of the parents of d, the children of d, and the parents of the children of d. This is the set of pages related to d.

In step 2 we compute the degree to which the pages in $\mathcal{V}$ are related to d. To do this, we consider the pages in $\mathcal{V}$ and the links among them as a graph, called the vicinity graph of d. This graph is then processed by the HITS algorithm [2]. The HITS algorithm returns the degree of *authority* and *hub* of each page in $\mathcal{V}$. Intuitively, a good authority is a page with important information on a given subject. A good hub is a page that links to many good authorities. In practice, the degrees of authority and hub are computed recursively: a page is a good hub if it links to many good authorities and a good authority if it is linked by many good hubs.

Once HITS is applied, we can choose to use the degree of authority or hub (or a combination of both) as a measure of similarity between d and each page in $\mathcal{V}$. We define the similarity between d and any page that is not in $\mathcal{V}$ as zero. In this work we experimented with the Companion algorithm using either the authority or the hub degree in isolation as a similarity measure.

For a more detailed description of the Companion and HITS algorithms, the reader is referred to [17] and [2], respectively.

4   The *kNN* Classifier

The measures described in Sect. 3 can be used to calculate the similarity between any two Web documents. To be useful, these measures should be able to
correctly determine if two Web pages are on the same subject. In order to test
this assumption, we applied them in a Web classification task.

To evaluate the linkage similarity measures, we used a strategy based on
a nearest neighbor classifier. This classifier assigns a category label to a test
document, based on the categories attributed to the k most similar documents
in the training set. The most widely used such algorithm was introduced by
Yang [27] and is referred to, in this work, as *kNN*. The *kNN* algorithm was chosen
since it is simple, efficient, and makes a direct use of similarity information.

In the *kNN* algorithm, to a given test document d is assigned a relevance
score $s_{c_i,d}$ associating d to each candidate category c_i. This score is defined as:

$$s_{c_i,d} = \sum_{d' \in \mathcal{N}_k(d)} similarity(d, d') f(c_i, d') \tag{4}$$

where $\mathcal{N}_k(d)$ are the k nearest neighbors (the most similar documents) of d in the
training set and $f(c_i, d')$ is a function that returns 1 if document d' belongs to
category c_i and 0 otherwise. Traditionally, documents are represented by vectors
of term weights and the similarity between two documents is measured by the
cosine of the angle between them. Term weights are computed using one of the
conventional TF-IDF schemes [28], in which the weight of term t in document d
is defined as:

$$w_{d,t} = (1 + \log_2 f_{t,d}) \times \log_2 \frac{N}{f_t} \tag{5}$$

where $f_{t,d}$ is the number of occurrences of t in document d, N is the number
of training documents, and f_t is the number of training documents containing
t. Based on the computed scores, we determine the top ranking category and
assign it to the test document. This text-based version of the *kNN* classifier was
used in our experiments as the baseline for comparison.

To test the linkage similarity measures, (1), (2), (3) and the values returned
by the Companion algorithm were used in place of the cosine similarity in (4).
This allowed us to test all measures under the same set of conditions, and evaluate how accurate they are in predicting the subject of Web pages.

5   Experiments

5.1   The Test Collection

We performed experiments using a set of classified Web pages extracted from
the Cadê Web directory [29]. This directory points to Brazilian Web pages that
were classified by human experts. To obtain the content of the classified pages we

used a database composed of Brazilian Web pages, crawled by the TodoBR [30] search engine.

We constructed two sub-collections using the data available on Cadê: Cade12 and Cade188. Cade12 is a set of 44,099 pages labelled using the first level categories of Cadê (Computers, Culture, Education, Health, Internet, News, Recreation, Science, Services, Shopping, Society, and Sports). Cade188 is a subset of Cade12, without the pages originally classified in the first level category. Thus, Cade188 corresponds to a set of 42,004 pages relabelled using the second level categories of Cadê (Biology, Chemistry, Dance, Music, Schools, Universities, etc.). Each Web page is classified into only one category. Figures 1, 2, and 3 show the category distributions for these collections. Notice that the two collections have skewed distributions. In Cade12, the three most popular categories represent more than 50% of all documents. The most popular category, *Services*, has 9,081 documents while the least popular, *Shopping*, has 715 documents. In Cade188, 50% of the documents are in just 10% of the categories. The most popular category, *Society:People*, has 3,675 documents while the least popular, *Internet:Tutorials*, has 24 documents. Cade12 and Cade188 have vocabularies of 192,580 and 168,869 unique words, respectively, after removing stop words.

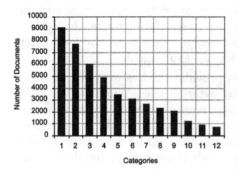
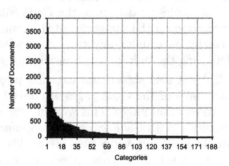

Fig. 1. Category distribution for Cade12.

Fig. 2. Category distribution for Cade188.

Information about the links related to the Cadê pages was also extracted from the TodoBR collection. TodoBR provides 40,871,504 links between Web pages (an average of 6.9 links per page). We extracted from this set all the links related to the pages of our two experimental sub-collections.

Table 1 summarizes the link data obtained. It was divided into two types: the *internal links*, which are links between pages classified by Cadê, and the *external links*, which are links where the target or the source page is in TodoBR, but not in the set of pages classified by Cadê. This distinction is important to verify whether the external information provided by TodoBR can be used to improve the results.

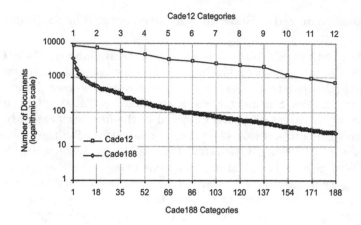

Fig. 3. Compared distributions for Cade12 and Cade188.

We call *hierarchy pages* those that belong to the Cadê site itself and are used to compose the directory hierarchy. For instance, the Cadê Science page, which links to science related sites. As can be seen, hierarchy pages represent a great part of the internal links in the Cadê collection. Since hierarchy pages provide information on the categories of the remaining pages (for instance, the Science hierarchy page links only to science related pages), they were not used when calculating the link information measures for our experiments.

Table 1 also shows that external pages provide a rich source of link data. About 96% of the Cadê pages are linked by external pages while less than 4% link to external pages. This was an important reason for using Cadê in our experiments. With Cadê we can obtain information about external links extracted from TodoBR and verify how useful this information can be during the classification process. This is only possible because Cadê is a subset of TodoBR, which is a large collection containing most of the link information available in Brazilian Web pages. This is not the case with most other classification collections where, in order to obtain more link information, it would be necessary to collect a huge amount of Web pages, or to have access to another search engine database, as we did with TodoBR.

Statistics	Whole Cadê	Cadê without Hierarchy Pages
Internal Links	45,548	3,830
Links from external pages to Cadê pages	570,404	570,337
Links from Cadê pages to external pages	7,584	5,894
Cadê pages with no in-links	2,556	1,625
Cadê pages with no out-links	40,917	40,723

Table 1. Link statistics for the Cadê collection.

5.2   Methodology and Evaluation

To perform the experiments, we used 10-fold cross validation [31]. Each dataset was randomly split in ten parts, such that in each run, a different part was used as a test set while the remaining were used as a training set. This split on training and test sets was the same in all experiments. The final results of each experiment represent the average of the ten runs.

To make sure that the results for conventional *kNN* are not biased by an inappropriate choice of parameters, different feature selections were conducted, using term frequency and information gain [32]. To each number of features, different values for k were tested. The best performance parameters were $k = 30$, feature selection by information gain, and using 15,000 features.

The performance of the presented methods was evaluated using the conventional precision, recall and F_1 measures [33]. Precision p is defined as the proportion of correctly classified examples in the set of all examples assigned to the target class. Recall r is defined as the proportion of correctly classified examples out of all the examples having the target class. F_1 is a combination of precision and recall in a way that gives them equal weight. F_1 is defined as:

$$F_1 = \frac{2pr}{p+r} \tag{6}$$

To compute the final F_1 values, we used macro-averaging and micro-averaging. For macro-averaging, recall, precision, and F_1 scores were first computed for individual categories and then averaged over all categories. For micro-averaging, the decisions for all categories were counted in a joint pool. Since the datasets used in the experiments are single label per document, micro-averaged recall, precision and F_1 are the same. Thus, the micro-averaged scores will be referred to as just micro-averaged F_1.

5.3   Experimental Results

Table 2 shows the F_1 figures for five different similarity measures obtained for the Cade12 and Cade188 collections: Amsler, bibliographic coupling, co-citation, Companion using authority degrees, and Companion using hub degrees. Only internal links were considered. As a baseline for comparison we show the results for the *kNN* classifier using the TF-IDF weighting scheme, as explained in Sect. 4.

We observe that all the results were below the baseline values. By considering only internal links, much of the link structure information of the collection is lost. In fact, as shown in Table 1, about 98% of the link information in the collection comes from external pages. This lack of information does not allow us to draw any definite conclusions.

When we make use of external links, however, results are much improved. Table 3 shows the F_1 figures for the Cade12 and Cade188 collections using both internal and external links. The figures for Amsler, co-citation, and the Companion algorithm using authority degrees are well above the baseline, showing

kNN Similarity Measures	Cade12		Cade188	
	$macF_1$	$micF_1$	$macF_1$	$micF_1$
Amsler	**16.02**	**22.44**	4.83	**8.87**
Bibliographic Coupling	15.12	21.79	3.95	8.31
Co-citation	15.31	21.81	4.67	8.55
Companion authority	15.88	22.12	**4.89**	8.50
Companion hub	15.31	22.10	4.64	8.50
TF-IDF (baseline)	35.61	37.26	22.08	23.33

Table 2. Macro-averaged and micro-averaged F_1 measures obtained with the kNN classifier in Cade12 and Cade188 collections, using different similarity measures. Only internal links were used.

gains as high as 36.9 and 45.9 points in micro-averaged F_1, for the Cade12 and Cade188 collections, respectively. On the other hand, bibliographic coupling and the Companion algorithm using hub degree are still below the baseline.

kNN Similarity Measures	Cade12		Cade188	
	$macF_1$	$micF_1$	$macF_1$	$micF_1$
Amsler	79.08	74.02	78.74	67.32
Bibliographic Coupling	15.12	22.08	4.10	8.55
Co-citation	**79.25**	**74.12**	**78.80**	**69.24**
Companion authority	74.88	70.44	73.68	63.51
Companion hub	22.46	25.45	9.91	11.40
TF-IDF (baseline)	35.61	37.26	22.08	23.33

Table 3. Macro-averaged and micro-averaged F_1 measures obtained with the kNN classifier in Cade12 and Cade188 collections, using different similarity measures. External and internal links were used.

These results can be explained. Since most of the links are *from* external pages *to* pages in the collection, i.e., they are from parents of the pages in the collection, we can expect measures that make use of parents to perform the best. Thus, co-citation, which uses the intersection of the sets of parents benefits greatly from such information. The same happens for the Companion algorithm using authority degrees and for the Amsler similarity. These last two, however, suffer from the fact that they also rely on children pages, which are not so widely available.

All measures show better absolute results for the Cade12 collection. This is due to the fact that the Cade12 link per class distribution is much more balanced. The number of links among documents of the same class amounts to 22.7% of the total number of internal links for Cade12, whereas it is only 10.1% of the total number of internal links for Cade188. However, the gain relative to the baseline was higher for the Cade188 collection. This happens because the kNN classifier tends to perform worst in collections where the class distribution is very skewed, which is the case of Cade188, as shown in Sect. 5.1.

6   Conclusions

In this paper, we compared five different similarity measures based on link structure. Experiments show that, in order to have sufficient information for expressive results, pages external to the test collection must be used. Also, we observe that most external pages are parents of the pages in the collection, i.e., they have a link to the pages in the collection. For this reason, the co-citation similarity measure obtained the best results. Other measures, such as the Amsler similarity and the Companion algorithm using authorities, also show good results but are, however, affected by the fact they use out-link information, which is much scarcer.

We expect the most popular pages in the Web to be those with a high number of in-links [1,2]. These pages will also be the most interesting for Web directories, where it is preferable (and easier) to populate the hierarchy with a reasonable set of highly referenced sites, instead of a huge set of obscure pages. Thus, similarity measures that make use of in-link information are expected to be the most appropriate. This conclusion is reinforced by that fact that, although most Web pages have very few links (or no links at all), those that are highly linked have much more in-links than out-links.

The difference between results using internal or external link information also confirms that the effectiveness of the proposed measures depends highly on the link structure, as also stated in [9]. Thus, on subsets of the Web with a very different link structure, similarity measures other than co-citation may show a better performance.

Although in this work we are only evaluating link-based similarities, the contents of Web pages is a valuable source of information and should not be disregarded. The combination of content and link-based information has been shown to yield good results [3, 7], and we intend to pursue it in future work. Experiments were already initiated where the linkage similarity measures here tested are combined with content-based information. Preliminary results show that this can lead to further improvements.

Since the measures here presented were shown effective in determining the subject of Web pages, we can expect them to perform well in other IR tasks where document similarity is an important concept, such as, finding similar pages, Web page clustering, information filtering, among others. Experiments with these tasks are left for future work.

7   Acknowledgements

This work was supported in part by the I3DL project—grant 680154/01-9, the GERINDO project—grant MCT/CNPq/CT-INFO 552.087/02-5, the SIAM project—grant MCT/FINEP/CNPq/PRONEX 76.97.1016.00, by CNPq grant

520.916/94-8 (Nivio Ziviani), and by MCT/FCT scholarship grant SFRH/BD/-4662/2001 (Pável Calado).

A special thanks goes to Marcos André Gonçalves, for his good ideas and help in tuning up the classification algorithms.

References

[1] Brin, S., Page, L.: The anatomy of a large-scale hypertextual Web search engine. In: Proceedings of the 7th International World Wide Web Conference, Brisbane, Australia (1998) 107–117

[2] Kleinberg, J.M.: Authoritative sources in a hyperlinked environment. Journal of the ACM (JACM) **46** (1999) 604–632

[3] Calado, P., Ribeiro-Neto, B., Ziviani, N., Moura, E., Silva, I.: Local versus global link information in the Web. ACM Transactions On Information Systems **21** (2003) 42–63

[4] Hawking, D., Craswell, N.: Overview of TREC-2001 Web track. In: The Tenth Text REtrieval Conference (TREC-2001), Gaithersburg, Maryland, USA (2001) 61–67

[5] Chakrabarti, S., Dom, B.E., Indyk, P.: Enhanced hypertext categorization using hyperlinks. In: Proceedings of the ACM SIGMOD International Conference on Management of Data, Seattle, Washington, USA (1998) 307–318

[6] Slattery, S., Craven, M.: Discovering test set regularities in relational domains. In: Proceedings of ICML-00, 17th International Conference on Machine Learning, Stanford, California, USA (2000) 895–902

[7] Joachims, T., Cristianini, N., Shawe-Taylor, J.: Composite kernels for hypertext categorization. In: Proceedings of ICML-01, 18th International Conference on Machine Learning, Williamstown, Massachusetts, US (2001) 250–257

[8] Cohn, D., Hofmann, T.: The missing link - a probabilistic model of document content and hypertext connectivity. In Leen, T.K., Dietterich, T.G., Tresp, V., eds.: Advances in Neural Information Processing Systems 13, MIT Press (2001) 430–436

[9] Fisher, M., Everson, R.: When are links useful? Experiments in text classification. In: Proceedings of the 25th annual European conference on Information Retrieval Research, ECIR 2003, Pisa, Italy (2003) 41–56

[10] He, X., Zha, H., Ding, C.H.Q., Simon, H.D.: Web document clustering using hyperlink structures. Computational Statistics & Data Analysis **41** (2002) 19–45

[11] Tombros, A., van Rijsbergen, C.J.: Query-sensitive similarity measures for the calculation of interdocument relationships. In: Proceedings of the 10th International Conference on Information and Knowledge Management CIKM, Altlanta, Georgia, USA (2001) 17–24

[12] Thelwall, M., Wilkinson, D.: Finding similar academic Web sites with links, bibliometric couplings and colinks. Information Processing & Management (2003) (in press).

[13] Olsen, K.A., Korfhage, R.R., Sochats, K.M., Spring, M.B., Williams, J.G.: Visualization of a document collection: the VIBE system. Information Processing & Management **29** (1993) 69–81

[14] Salton, G., McGill, M.J.: Introduction to Modern Information Retrieval. McGraw-Hill (1983)

[15] Zhang, J., Rasmussen, E.M.: Developing a new similarity measure from two different perspectives. Information Processing & Management **37** (2001) 279–294

[16] Flesca, S., Masciari, E.: Efficient and effective Web change detection. Data & Knoweledge Engeneering **46** (2003) 203–224

[17] Dean, J., Henzinger, M.R.: Finding related pages in the World Wide Web. Computer Networks **31** (1999) 1467–1479 Also in Proceedings of the 8th International World Wide Web Conference.

[18] Kumar, S.R., Raghavan, P., Rajagopalan, S., Sivakumar, D., Tomkins, A., Upfal, E.: The Web as a graph. In: Proceedings of the 19th Symposium on Principles of Database Systems, Dallas, Texas, USA (2000) 1–10

[19] Sun, A., Lim, E.P., Ng, W.K.: Web classification using support vector machine. In: Proceedings of the Fourth International Workshop on Web Information and Data Management, McLean, Virginia, USA, ACM Press (2002) 96–99

[20] Yang, Y., Slattery, S., Ghani, R.: A study of approaches to hypertext categorization. Journal of Intelligent Information Systems **18** (2002) 219–241

[21] Furnkranz, J.: Exploiting structural information for text classification on the WWW. In: Proceedings of the 3rd Symposium on Intelligent Data Analysis (IDA-99), Amsterdam, Netherlands (1999) 487–498

[22] Glover, E.J., Tsioutsiouliklis, K., Lawrence, S., Pennock, D.M., Flake, G.W.: Using Web structure for classifying and describing Web pages. In: Proceedings of WWW-02, International Conference on the World Wide Web, Honolulu, Hawaii, USA (2002)

[23] Oh, H.J., Myaeng, S.H., Lee, M.H.: A practical hypertext catergorization method using links and incrementally available class information. In: Proceedings Of The 23rd Annual International ACM SIGIR Conference on Research and Development in Information Retrieval, Athens, Greece (2000) 264–271

[24] Kessler, M.M.: Bibliographic coupling between scientific papers. American Documentation **14** (1963) 10–25

[25] Amsler, R.: Application of citation-based automatic classification. Technical report, The University of Texas at Austin, Linguistics Research Center, Austin, Texas, USA (1972)

[26] Small, H.G.: Co-citation in the scientific literature: A new measure of relationship between two documents. Journal of the American Society for Information Science **24** (1973) 265–269

[27] Yang, Y.: Expert network: Effective and efficient learning from human decisions in text categorization and retrieval. In: Proceedings of the 17th Annual International ACM SIGIR Conference on Research and Development in Information Retrieval, Dublin, Ireland (1994) 13–22

[28] Salton, G., Buckley, C.: Term-weighting approaches in automatic text retrieval. Information Processing & Management **24** (1988) 513–523

[29] : The *Cadê?* Web directory. (http://www.cade.com.br/)

[30] : The TodoBR search engine. (http://www.todobr.com.br/)

[31] Stone, M.: Cross-validation choices and assessment of statistical predictions. Journal of the Royal Statistical Society **B36** (1974) 111–147

[32] Mitchell, T.: Machine Learning. McGraw-Hill (1997)

[33] Yang, Y., Liu, X.: A re-examination of text categorization methods. In: Proceedings of the 23rd Annual International ACM SIGIR Conference on Research and Development in Information Retrieval, Berkeley, California, USA (1999) 42–49

A Three Level Search Engine Index Based in Query Log Distribution*

Ricardo Baeza-Yates and Felipe Saint-Jean

Center for Web Research
Department of Computer Science
Universidad de Chile
Blanco Encalada 2120, Santiago, Chile
{rbaeza,fsaint}@dcc.uchile.cl

Abstract. Queries to a search engine follow a power-law distribution, which is far from uniform. Hence, it is natural to adapt a search engine index to the query distribution. In this paper we present a three level memory organization for a search engine inverted file index that includes main and secondary memory, as well as precomputed answers, such that the use of main memory and the answer time are significantly improved. We include experimental results as well as an analytical model.

1 Introduction

Given the rate of growth of the Web, scalability of search engines is a key issue, as the amount of hardware and network resources needed is large, and expensive. In addition, search engines are popular tools, so they have heavy constraints on query answer time. So the efficient use of resources can improve both scalability and answer time.

The query distribution in a search engine follows a very biased distribution, namely a power or Zipf's law, which allows to organize a search engine index such that memory is used well and answer time is improved. For this, we just have to analyze the search engine query log. For example, we can leave the part of the index that is really queried in main memory and the rest in secondary memory. This is surely done by all search engines. In addition, very common queries can be precomputed, such that the answer time is faster.

In this paper we present an inverted file organization that has three levels: precomputed answers, main and secondary memory indexes. Our analytical model is based on real search engine data which also shows the improvements obtained. We show for example, that by using half the index in main memory we can answer 80% of the queries, and that using a small number of precomputed answers we can improve the query answer time on at least 7%. Part of our analysis shows that there is almost no correlation between query word frequency and Web page word frequency, at least in our context. This implies that what people search is different from what people write.

There are few papers that deal with the use of query logs to improve search engines, because this information is usually not disclosed. The exceptions deal with caching the

---

* We wish to thank the helpful comments of the reviewers.

M.A. Nascimento, E.S. de Moura, A.L. Oliveira (Eds.): SPIRE 2003, LNCS 2857, pp. 56–65, 2003.

index and/or the answers [7,4,3] or consider query clustering for ranking or similar goals [2,8]. Precomputed answers can be considered as static caching of answers, but they are conceptually different because precomputed answers could have better quality, for example with manual intervention (e.g. main links related to a query as in Yahoo!). Storing part of the index in main memory can be considered as static caching of inverted lists, but in practice is not the same because current search engines must have large portions of the index in main memory to achieve fast answer time. In the sequel, we consider that our scheme and caching are orthogonal. That is, we can devote part of the main memory to do dynamic caching of the answers and of the inverted lists that are in secondary memory. Similarly, we can use compression.

In section 2 we present basic concepts related to query distributions and inverted files. In section 3 we described the data used and the query log analysis. In section 4 we present the analysis for a two level memory organization for the index, while in section 5 we add precomputed answers to it. In section 6 we present a simple analytical model and its analysis, including the sensibility of our solution. We finish with some concluding remarks and future work.

2   Preliminaries

2.1   Zipf's Law

The Zipf's law was introduced in the late 40's to describe several empirical observations such as the distribution of population of cities or the frequency of words in English written text [9]. If F_i is the frequency of the i-th most frequent event, we have that $F_i \sim \frac{1}{i^\alpha}$ where α is a constant, and the parameter of the distribution. In a log-log graph, α is the slope (without the sign) of the line. In the case of words, this means that there are few very frequent words (usually called stop words) and many unusual words. Perhaps, due to this distribution, the number of distinct words in a text (vocabulary) does not grow linearly, but follows a sublinear curve of the form $N = O(T^\beta)$ (Heaps' law), with T the total number of words, and β around .5 for English text [1] and a bit larger for the Web (around 0.6).

2.2   Inverted Files

The main components of an inverted file are the vocabulary or list of unique words and the posting file which holds the occurrences in the text of each word in the vocabulary. For each word we basically have a list of pointers to Web pages plus some additional information that is used for ranking the results. The exact implementation depends on the retrieval model used and if we want to use full addressing (for example to answer sentence queries) or just point to Web pages to save space. As the words in the text are not uniform, the posting file has few long lists as well as many more short lists. For more details see [1].

Due to the Heaps' law, we can assume that the vocabulary always fits in main memory. In practice, the vocabulary of a large search engine has several million of words that will point to hundred millions of Web pages. Due to the constraints imposed by concurrent access to search engines, the inverted file should be in main memory (RAM), but as is too large, part of the index will be in secondary memory (disk), with the subsequent loss in query answer time.

3   Query Log Analysis

For our experimental results we use about 800 thousand pages from a local search engine. In this set of pages we find $T = 151, 173, 460$ words, from which $N = 2, 067, 040$ were unique (vocabulary). The average length of a word in the vocabulary is $\bar{x} = 8.46$. The number of documents where a word appears follow a Zipf's distribution as seen in Figure 1 (the model is fitted in the main part of the graph).

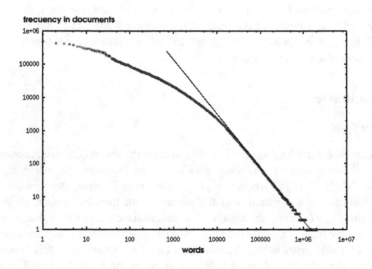

Fig. 1. Words in the vocabulary vs. their number of occurrences in Web pages.

The query set, from the same search engine, considers a two month log of 2001 which consists in 777,351 queries containing 738,390 words, where the unique words are $C = 465, 021$. Figure 2 shows that the frequency of query words also follow a Zipf's law, with a parameter $\alpha = 1.42$. This is larger than the parameter 0.59 obtained in [4], perhaps due to language and cultural differences. We used single word queries because on average each query had 1.05 words. That is, queries with more than one word were less than 4% of them. Nevertheless, our analysis is also valid for phrases and with a few changes for Boolean queries.

The standard correlation among the frequency of a word in the Web pages and in the queries is 0.15, very low. That is, words in the content of Web pages follow a Zipf's distribution which is very different from the distribution of the query words, as is depicted in figure 3 (any correlation would show as a pattern in the figure.)

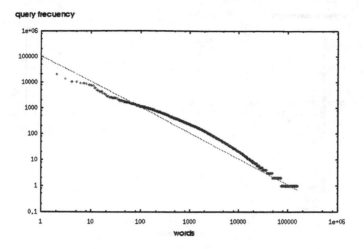

Fig. 2. Sorted frequency of query words in a log-log scale.

4 Zipf Helps

In this section we show a simple memory model for a search engine which uses efficiently main memory, improving scalability. As few words are queried frequently, what is important is the growth of the most queried subset of words, rather than the growth of the vocabulary on the Web pages. Let M be the available memory. We assume that always the vocabulary fits in main memory (as it grows sublinearly, is a small percentage of the inverted file). So we have the vocabulary and part of the lists will be in main memory. The rest of the word lists will go to secondary memory.

Recall that N is the number of words of the vocabulary and let L_i be the number of documents where the i-th word appears, where the words $1..N$ are ordered by decreasing query frequency. For each word in the vocabulary we need to store the word itself (let x_k be the length of the k-th word) and a pointer to the corresponding occurrence list (say 4 bytes). In each list element, we need at least an integer to a Web page identifier plus information for ranking purposes (for example, the frequency of the word in the Web page). Let b be the number of bytes per list element, which depends on the exact implementation of the inverted file. Hence, the average space needed by the inverted file, in bytes, is:

$$E = \sum_{k=1}^{N}(4 + x_k + bL_k) = \underbrace{(4 + \bar{x})N}_{V} + b\sum_{k=1}^{N} L_k$$

where $\bar{x}$ was the average length of the vocabulary words, and V the space needed by the vocabulary. Notice that by using $\bar{x}$ we are assuming independence between the word length and the query word frequency. In fact, for our data, the correlation is -0.02, almost nothing.

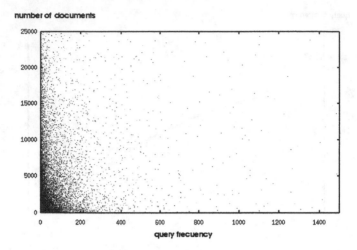

Fig. 3. Number of occurrences of word queries vs. number of documents that contain each word.

If $E \leq M$ everything fits in RAM. However, when $E > M$, part of the inverted file must be stored on disk. We could assume that memory paging and disk buffering will improve the access time, but we do not have control of this. Most inverted files use a hashing table for the vocabulary, which implies a random order for the words. If we put in this order the lists of the inverted file until we run out of main memory and the rest on disk, many words that are frequently queried (because the correlation is small) will have to go to disk. The optimal arrangement would be to store in main memory the subset of query words that maximizes the total frequency and still fits in memory. The rest of the word lists would go to secondary memory. Formally, we have to find the variables $i_1, ..., i_p$ such that they maximize the sum of the query frequencies of the words $i_1, \cdots, i_p$ with the restriction that $V + b \sum_{j=1}^{p} L_{i_j} \leq M$. The optimal solution will depend on each data set.

As the distribution is so biased, a nearly optimal solution is to put in main memory the lists of the most frequent query words that fit in it. Let p be the largest number of words in the vocabulary such that $V + b \sum_{j=1}^{p} L_j \leq M$. Then, the lists of the p most queried words will be in main memory. This heuristic is not optimal because there will be a few cases where would be better to replace a word with a large posting list with two or more words with overall lists of similar size or smaller but at the same time larger total query frequency. Nevertheless, we show next that this solution is quite good.

Using our data, Figure 4 shows the difference between the heuristic (curve below) and a random order (curve above, basically a diagonal). In the x axis we have the portion of query words that have their list in main memory. The y axis shows the portion of the index that must be in main memory to reach that proportion of queries. The vertical line at the end are the words that are never queried. The gap in the diagonal line are two of the most frequently queried words which in our heuristic are at the beginning (the dots of the graphs are plotted in multiples of 100 words). From this example we can see that

- To reach 100% of the queries, we only need to have 80% of the index in main memory. This is because more than 75% of the words are never queried (but have short posting lists).
- To reach 50% of the queries we only need 20% of the index in memory.
- With 50% of the index in memory, we can answer 80% of the queries.

Hence, this simple heuristic reduces the usage of memory in at least 20% without increasing the query answer time.

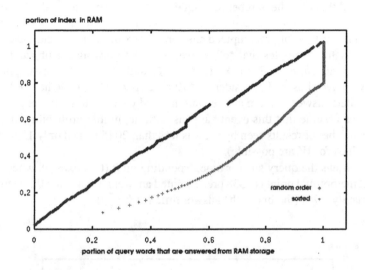

Fig. 4. Query frequency vs. memory: random order and our heuristic.

5 Improving the Query Answer Time: Precomputed Answers

If we have precomputed answers for the most frequent queries, answer time is improved as we do not have to access the index. However, more memory with respect to the index information of these words might be needed, decreasing the value of p and increasing the search time for other words. This implies that there is an optimal number of precomputed answers. We call the precomputed answers a cache memory, although is in main memory.

In our data, with only 2000 precomputed answers we can resolve 20% of the queries. On the other hand, to answer 50% of the queries we need around 100 thousand precomputed answers, which is too much space.

Assume that each precomputed answer needs W bytes of memory (for example, 80 URLs with the text context and other attributes such as size and date). Then we must have:

$$kW + V + b \sum_{i=k+1}^{p+k} L_i \leq M \tag{1}$$

where the words $k + 1$ to $p + k$ have their lists stored in main memory. We want to find k and p that optimize the query answer time. Hence we have three sections of memory: precomputed answers, index in memory, and index in disk, that depend on k.

The query answer time is given by

$$t_a = \frac{\beta_1 \sum_{i=1}^{k} F_i + \beta_2 \sum_{i=k+1}^{p+k} F_i + \beta_3 \sum_{i=p+k+1}^{C} F_i}{\sum_{i=1}^{C} F_i} \tag{2}$$

where we recall that C is the number of unique words in the queries and F_i is the query frequency of the i-th word. In addition, β_1, β_2, and β_3 are constants that represent the relative answer time of precomputed answers, index in memory, and index in disk, respectively. In the examples that follow we use the following set of values: $M = 400Mb$, $W = 40Kb$, $b = 8$, $\beta_1 = 1$, $\beta_2 = 5$, and $\beta_3 = 50$. This implies $V = 24.56Mb$. We have chosen W considering 512 bytes per URL, so we have 80 URLs in the precomputed answer. If more answers are needed we have to go to the inverted file in disk and we assume that this event happens with negligible probability. In practice the average number of results seen by users is less than 20 [5,6] and only 12 in our data (but other values for W are possible).

Figure 5 shows the query answer time depending on k (this fixes p), where we can observe that the optimal point is 1338 precomputed answers, improving the answer time in approximately a 7% (the line is the answer time for $k = 0$).

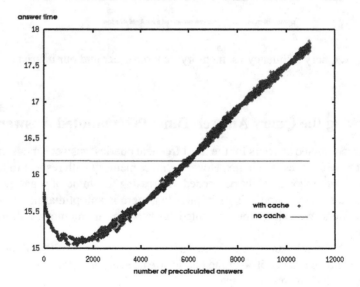

Fig. 5. Query answer time in function of the number of precomputed answers.

6 Analysis

Recall that the query distribution follows follows a Zipf's law. If F_i is the query frequency of word i, then $F_i = \frac{R}{i^\alpha}$ where $R = C/\sum_{j=1}^{C} F_j$ is a normalization constant such that $\sum F_i$ equals the total number of queries. Hence, the number of queries that will be answered by the index in main memory when $k = 0$ is

$$R\sum_{i=1}^{p} \frac{1}{i^\alpha} \leq R \int_{1}^{p+1} \frac{1}{x^\alpha} dx = R \frac{(p+1)^{1-\alpha} - 1}{1-\alpha}$$

Because we assume that the length of the lists L_i is independent of the query frequency (because of the low correlation), we can approximate the average list length by $E(L_i) = \frac{T}{N} = \gamma$ where we recall that $T = \sum_{i=0}^{N} L_i$ is the total number of words in the Web pages and N is the size of the vocabulary. In our data, $\gamma = 73.1$. Hence, we will use the following approximation for equation (1): $M = kW + V + 8p\gamma$. From here we solve p:

$$p = \frac{(M - kW - V)}{8\gamma} = \frac{(M-V)}{8\gamma} - \frac{W}{8\gamma}k$$

Clearly $k \leq (M-V)/W$, because we cannot use more than the available memory (that is, p cannot be negative).

We can optimize equation (2) by using the Zipf's law for the query distribution (notice that the fitted model holds beyond the most frequent k queries)

$$t_a = \beta_1 R \sum_{i=1}^{k} \frac{1}{i^\alpha} + \beta_2 R \sum_{i=k+1}^{p+k} \frac{1}{i^\alpha} + \beta_3 R \sum_{i=p+k+1}^{C} \frac{1}{i^\alpha}$$

Approximating the summations with integrals, and replacing p we have

$$t_a R/C = \beta_3 \int_{x=1}^{C} \frac{dx}{x^\alpha} - \Delta_{21} \int_{x=1}^{k} \frac{dx}{x^\alpha} - \Delta_{32} \int_{x=1}^{(M-V+(b\gamma-W)k)/b\gamma} \frac{dx}{x^\alpha} + O\left(\frac{1}{k^\alpha}\right)$$

where $\Delta_{21} = \beta_2 - \beta_1$ and $\Delta_{32} = \beta_3 - \beta_2$. Then

$$t_a R/C = \beta_3 \frac{C^{1-\alpha}}{1-\alpha} - \Delta_{21} \frac{k^{1-\alpha}}{1-\alpha} - \frac{\Delta_{32}}{(b\gamma)^{1-\alpha}} \frac{(M-V+(b\gamma-W)k)^{1-\alpha}}{1-\alpha} + O\left(\frac{1}{k^\alpha}\right)$$

The first term is constant while the second term decreases as k increases. The third term also decreases with k if $W \leq b\gamma$. Hence, the optimal k is the maximum possible value, that is $k = (M - V)/W$. However, in practice $W > b\gamma$ and the third term increases with k until reaches its maximal value $(M-V)/W$ (and $p = 0$). In this case the optimal value is

$$k \approx \frac{(M-V)}{W + b\gamma \left(\left(\frac{(\beta_3-\beta_2)(W/b\gamma-1)}{(\beta_2-\beta_1)} \right)^{1/\alpha} - 1 \right)}$$

By replacing the values used in the example of the previous section, k is 3791 (and $W > b\gamma = 585$ bytes). This is an over-estimation of the experimental value because the Zipf's distribution is accurate for the main part of the data but not for the most frequent queries (which are above it). Notice that the maximal value for k is over 9600, so the result is still good and not far from optimal. In fact, for our experimental data the query time is still improved by a 5% (see Figure 5).

Let analyze now which parameters of the optimal value of k can change. We can change W by using more or less memory per URL or storing more or less URLs per answer. Is clear that if W decreases, k increases and viceversa. If we improve secondary memory access time k also increases. However, if we improve the index search time then k decreases, as the precomputed answers are less competitive. If M decreases (grows) then k decreases (grows). Finally, γ grows over time because the text size grows faster than the vocabulary size. In fact, using Heaps' law, $\gamma = O(T^{1-\beta})$ where $\beta \approx 0.63$ (see Section 2.1). In our experimental data $\gamma \approx 0.048T^{0.37}$. Using this fact, we will consider $M - V$ to be constant as V increases slowly (the results do not change due to this assumption). Figure 6 shows how the optimal k changes as γ grows (recall that the maximal value is W/b).

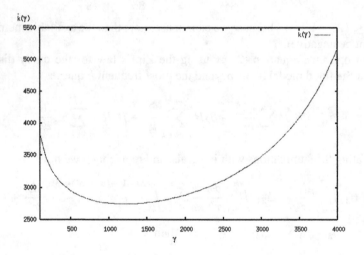

Fig. 6. Variation of optimal k as γ grows.

Notice that k decreases for $\gamma < 1203.99$ as γ grows and after that k increases. In our data γ is on the left hand side of the minimal point and hence k decreases until T is more than 5 thousand times larger than at the beginning. In our case that implies more than 4 billion pages, so in practice k will decrease slowly as the number of Web pages increases (k can reach a minimal value of 2744 which is not far from 3791 so we could use a fixed k without much penalty).

7   Concluding Remarks

We have shown, backed by real empirical data, that memory usage and query answer time can be optimized considering a three level memory organization: a cache of pre-computed answers and part of the inverted index in main memory, and the rest of the index in secondary memory. Our experimental data may seem small compared to the size of the Web. However, it is significantly large in statistical terms. Also our analytical model has the collection size as a parameter, so can be extrapolated to larger subsets of the Web, as we have already shown.

We have also shown the sensitivity of the optimal value using a simple model based in a power-law for the query distribution. An adaptive solution can be implemented based on those results by tracking the total number of words to vocabulary size ratio, which changes slowly as Web pages are added, changed or deleted. In addition, further study is needed to see how the solution changes as the query distribution changes. Other simple on-line algorithms could use adaptive heuristics in a list of most frequent queries (a few thousand). The model of these cases are simple extensions of the model presented here.

Future work includes to find the approximation factor for our heuristic, which in practice should be close to 1, and the complexity of finding the optimal solution. Another extension is adapt the model for more complex queries (two or more words with Boolean operations), but these are less frequent [5,6]. Finally, further study is needed to combine our strategy with other techniques as dynamic caching and compression.

References

1. Ricardo Baeza-Yates, and Berthier Ribeiro-Neto. *Modern Information Retrieval*, ACM Press/Addison-Wesley, England, 513 pages, 1999.
   URL: http://sunsite.dcc.uchile.cl/irbook/.
2. Doug Beeferman, and Adam Berger. Agglomerative clustering of a search engine query log, Proceedings on the 2000 Conference on Knowledge Discovery and Data Mining (Boston,MA), pages 407-416, Aug. 2000
3. Evangelos P. Markatos. On Caching Search Engine Query Results. In Proceedings of the 5th International Web Caching and Content Delivery Workshop, May 2000.
4. Patricia Correia Saraiva, Edleno Silva de Moura, Nivio Ziviani, Wagner Meira, Rodrigo Fonseca, and Berthier Ribeiro-Neto. Rank-preserving two-level caching for scalable search engines, In Proceedings of the 24th annual international ACM SIGIR on Research and development in information retrieval, New Orleans, LA, p.51-58, September 2001.
5. Craig Silverstein, Monika Henzinger, Hannes Marais, and Michael Moricz. Analysis of a Very Large AltaVista Query Log. *SIGIR Forum* 33(3), 1999.
6. Amanda Spink, Bernard J. Jansen, Dietmar Wolfram, and Tefko Saracevic. From E-Sex to E-Commerce: Web Search Changes. *IEEE Computer* 35(3): 107-109 (2002).
7. Y. Xie, and D. O'Hallaron, Locality in Search Engine Queries and Its Implications for Caching, Infocom 2002.
8. Dell Zhang, and Yisheng Dong. A Novel Web Usage Mining Approach For Search Engine.*Computer Networks*, 2003.
9. George Zipf. Selective Studies and the Principle of Relative Frequency in Language, Harvard University Press, Cambridge, MA, 1932.

Row-wise Tiling for the Myers' Bit-Parallel Approximate String Matching Algorithm

Kimmo Fredriksson*

Department of Computer Science, PO Box 111,
University of Joensuu, FIN-80101 Joensuu
kfredrik@cs.joensuu.fi.

Abstract. Given a text $T[1..n]$ and a pattern $P[1..m]$ the classic dynamic programming algorithm for computing the edit distance between P and every location of T runs in time $O(nm)$. The bit-parallel computation of the dynamic programming matrix [6] runs in time $O(n \lceil m/w \rceil)$, where w is the number of bits in computer word. We present a new method that rearranges the bit-parallel computations, achieving time $O(\lceil n/w \rceil (m + \sigma \log_2(\sigma)) + n)$, where σ is the size of the alphabet. The algorithm is then modified to solve the k differences problem. The expected running time is $O(\lceil n/w \rceil (L(k) + \sigma \log_2(\sigma)) + R)$, where $L(k)$ depends on k, and R is the number of occurrences. The space usage is $O(\sigma + m)$. It is in practice much faster than the existing $O(n \lceil k/w \rceil)$ algorithm [6]. The new method is applicable only for small (e.g. DNA) alphabets, but this becomes *the fastest algorithm* for small m, or moderate k/m. If we want to search multiple patterns in a row, the method becomes attractive for large alphabet sizes too. We also consider applying 128-bit vector instructions for bit-parallel computations.

1 Introduction

Approximate string matching is a classical problem, with applications to text searching, computational biology, pattern recognition, etc. Given a text $T[1 \ldots n]$, a pattern $P[1 \ldots m]$, and a threshold k, we want to find all the text positions where the pattern matches the text with at most k differences. The allowed differences are the following edit operations: substitution, deletion or insertion of a character.

The first dynamic-programming-based $O(mn)$ time solution to the problem is attributed to [11]. Many faster techniques have been proposed since then, both for the worst and the average case. The first efficient and practical method is the $O(nk)$ expected time algorithm [12]. This was improved to take only $O(n \lceil k/\sqrt{\sigma} \rceil)$ time on average [2], where σ is the size of the alphabet. For large alphabets this is the fastest algorithm based on dynamic programming. For small alphabets the bit-parallel $O(n \lceil k/w \rceil)$ expected time algorithm [6], where w is

---

* The work was partially developed while the author was working in the Dept. of CS, Univ. of Helsinki. Partially supported by the Academy of Finland.

M.A. Nascimento, E.S. de Moura, A.L. Oliveira (Eds.): SPIRE 2003, LNCS 2857, pp. 66–79, 2003.

the number of bits in computer word (typically 32 or 64), is in practice the fastest. A few years earlier a $O(nm \log(\sigma)/w)$ algorithm was obtained [13], but this is not competitive anymore.

Besides the dynamic programming based methods, there are a myriad of filter based approaches [7]. The filters can work extremely well for small k/m and large alphabets, but the computational biology applications (searching DNA) do not fall into this category. The filtering algorithms are based on simple techniques to quickly eliminate the text positions that cannot match with k differences, and the rest of the text is verified using some slower algorithm. The filter based methods invariably use the dynamic programming based algorithms for verification.

We propose a modified version of the $O(n \lceil k/w \rceil)$ algorithm [6], that runs in $O(\lceil n/w \rceil (L(k) + \sigma \log_2(\sigma)) + R)$, expected time, where $L(k)$ depends k, and R is the number of occurrences, and show that in practice this can be much faster than its predecessor, and in fact becomes the fastest algorithm for small m or large k/m.

2   Preliminaries

Let Σ be an alphabet of size σ, and the *pattern* $P[1..m]$ and the *text* $T[1..n]$ be two strings over Σ. We are interested in finding the positions j, such that the edit distance between P and a suffix of $T[1..j]$ is at most k with $0 \le k < m$, for some fixed value of k.

This problem can be solved using dynamic programming. The well-known recurrence [11] for filling the dynamic programming matrix E is as follows:

$$E_{i,0} = i$$
$$E_{0,j} = 0$$
$$E_{i,j} = \min\{E_{i-1,j-1} + \delta(i,j), E_{i-1,j} + 1, E_{i,j-1} + 1\},$$

where $\delta(i,j)$ is 0, if $P[i] = T[j]$, and 1 otherwise.

The matrix can be filled in $O(nm)$ time. The matrix needs also space $O(nm)$, but it is easy to see that if the matrix is filled column-wise, then only one column need to be kept in memory at a time, reducing the space complexity to just $O(m)$.

After the matrix is filled, the values $E_{m,j} \le k$ indicate that there is an occurrence of P with at most k differences, ending at text character $T[j]$.

More efficient variation of this algorithm is given in [12], requiring only $O(nk)$ expected time. The key observation is that in the expected case it is enough to compute only the first $O(k)$ rows of each column j to guarantee that there cannot be an occurrence ending at position j.

One of the properties of the matrix E is that the adjacent (horizontal, vertical or diagonal) values can differ at most by ± 1:

$$\Delta h_{i,j} = E_{i,j} - E_{i,j-1} \in \{-1, 0, +1\}$$
$$\Delta v_{i,j} = E_{i,j} - E_{i-1,j} \in \{-1, 0, +1\}$$
$$\Delta d_{i,j} = E_{i,j} - E_{i-1,j-1} \in \{0, 1\}$$

It is clear that these vectors fully define the matrix E, and any value $E_{i,j}$ can be obtained e.g. as follows:

$$E_{i,j} = \sum_{h=1}^{j} \Delta v_{i,h}.$$

In [6,4] it was shown how to compute the vectors $\Delta h, \Delta v, \Delta d$ bit-parallelly, in time $O(n \lceil m/w \rceil)$, where w is the number of bits in a computer word. Each vector is $\Delta h, \Delta v, \Delta d$ is now represented by the following bit-vectors:

$$hp_{i,j} \equiv \Delta h_{i,j} = +1$$
$$hn_{i,j} \equiv \Delta h_{i,j} = -1$$
$$vp_{i,j} \equiv \Delta v_{i,j} = +1$$
$$vn_{i,j} \equiv \Delta v_{i,j} = -1$$
$$d_{i,j} \equiv \Delta d_{i,j} = 0$$

The values of these vectors can be computed very efficiently using boolean logic. The following logical equivalencies exist:

$$hp_{i,j} \equiv vn_{i,j-1} \text{ OR NOT}(vp_{i,j-1} \text{ OR } d_{i,j})$$
$$hn_{i,j} \equiv vp_{i,j-1} \text{ AND } d_{i,j}$$
$$vp_{i,j} \equiv hn_{i-1,j} \text{ OR NOT}(hp_{i-1,j} \text{ OR } d_{i,j})$$
$$vn_{i,j} \equiv hp_{i-1,j} \text{ AND } d_{i,j}$$
$$d_{i,j} \equiv (P[i] = T[j]) \text{ OR } vn_{i,j-1} \text{ OR } hn_{i-1,j}$$

These vectors can be computed using bit-wise logical operations, bit shifts and additions, w vector elements in $O(1)$ time, leading to a $O(n \lceil m/w \rceil)$ time algorithm. The comparison $(P[i] = T[j])$ can be implemented parallelly using preprocessed table of bit masks. For correctness and more details, refer to [6,4].

3   Rearranged Bit-Parallelism

For short pattens, i.e. for $m \ll w$, many bits of the computer word are effectively wasted, due to the column-wise computation of the matrix. Therefore we suggest that the matrix is computed row-wise, resulting in $O((m + \sigma \log_2(\sigma)) \lceil n/w \rceil + n)$ time, where the $\sigma \log_2(\sigma)$ term comes from preprocessing, and therefore in practice works only for small alphabets. This is relatively straight-forward. The algorithm itself does not change, only the initialization of some vectors. The same technique has been utilized before, although in different contexts, in [5,3]. This row-wise computation can be seen as the column-wise computation if the roles of P and T are transposed, i.e. P is seen as the text, and T as the pattern. The initial boundary conditions of the dynamic programming matrix are therefore transposed as well.

The complete algorithm is shown in Alg. 1. We use C programming language like notation for the bit-wise operations: OR: $|$, AND: $\&$, XOR: $^\wedge$, NOT: $\sim$, shift to left with zero fill: $\ll$, and shift to right with zero fill: $\gg$. The preprocessing is as in the original algorithm, besides that we preprocess T, not P.

Alg. 1 RowWise(n, eq, P, m). Row-wise computation of the dp matrix.

Input: n, eq, P, m
Output: $E_{m,j}, \; j \in \{1..n\}$

```
1        for r ← 1 to ⌈n/w⌉ do
2            vp[r] ← 0
3            vn[r] ← 0
4        for i ← 1 to m do
5            cp ← 1
6            cn ← 0
7            for r ← 1 to ⌈n/w⌉ do
8                x ← eq[P[i]][r] | cn
9                d ← ((vp[r] + (x & vp[r])) ^ vp[r]) | x | vn[r]
10               hp ← vn[r] | ∼(vp[r] | d)
11               hn ← vp[r] & d
12               x ← (hp ≪ 1) | cp
13               vp[r] ← (hn ≪ 1) | cn | ∼(x | d)
14               vn[r] ← x & d
15               cp ← hp ≫ (w − 1)
16               cn ← hn ≫ (w − 1)
17       d ← m
18       for r ← 1 to ⌈n/w⌉ do
19           d ← BlockScore(d, (r − 1)w, vp[r], vn[r])
```

Alg. 2 BlockScore(d, pos, vp, vn). Compute scores for one block.

Input: d, pos, vp, vn
Output: $E_{m,j}, \; j \in \{pos + 1..pos + w\}$

```
1        for i ← 1 to w do
2            d ← d + (vp & 1) − (vn & 1)
3            vp ← vp ≫ 1
4            vn ← vn ≫ 1
5            output pos + i, d
6        return d
```

The algorithm needs $O(\lceil n/w \rceil)$ space to store the vp and vn vectors. Note however, that the order of the two nested loops can be changed, so that vp and

vn need only $O(1)$ space. In this case the carry bits cp and cn should be stored for all m rows (see Alg. 5). The eq table needs $O(\sigma)$ entries.

The computation of the matrix takes only $O(\lceil n/w \rceil m)$ time now. However, there are two problems. First, the preprocessing of T (used as the pattern) takes $O(\sigma \lceil n/w \rceil + n)$ time with the standard method. For small alphabets we can apply bit-parallelism in the preprocessing phase to bring it down to $O(\sigma \log_2(\sigma) \lceil n/w \rceil)$. The second problem is, that after computing the matrix, obtaining the scores from the last row still takes $O(n)$ time. There is not much one can do for this, as the output is of size $O(n)$. In the k-differences problem the maximum distance is restricted to be $\leq k$. In this case, the last row can be evaluated faster bit-parallelly.

4   Preprocessing

The preprocessing algorithm evaluates a bit-vector $eq(c)_j$ for each character $c \in \Sigma$. This is needed for parallel computation of Δd vectors, i.e. to perform the comparisons $P[i] = T[j]$ parallelly. The value of the bit $eq(c)_j$ is 1, iff $T[j] = c$, and 0 otherwise. These vectors are easy to compute in time $O(\min\{m, \sigma\} \lceil n/w \rceil + n)$ (or in time $O(n)$ for fixed σ). The $O(\min\{m, \sigma\} \lceil n/w \rceil)$ time is required to initialize the bit-vectors to 0. This is required only for the characters that actually occur in P. Setting the bits requires $O(n)$ additional time.

For small alphabets we can do better. First consider binary alphabets. For $\sigma = 2$ each character of T requires only one bit, and we store the string in the natural way, packing w characters to one machine word. Now, by definition, $eq(1) = T$, and $eq(0) = \text{NOT } eq(1)$. Hence the preprocessing is not needed, and we can use T in the place of eq, see [10].

Consider now $\sigma = 4$. This has a very important application in DNA searching. In fact, this can be seen as the main application of the algorithm, the filter algorithms do not perform very well on small alphabets and for the relatively high error levels that are typical on DNA searching. On the other hand, the filters work quite well for large alphabets and small error levels typical for applications in ASCII natural language [7].

DNA alphabet requires only two bits of storage per symbol. We keep T in compressed form, and preprocess that representation. Let the codes for the four possible DNA characters A, C, G, T be as follows: A=0, C=1, G=2, T=3. These codes are in binary 00, 01, 10, 11, respectively (least significant bit *rightmost*). However, note that real DNA may have other characters too, namely IUB/IUPAC codes that are standard degeneracy symbols for nucleotide strings. This brings the alphabet size up to 15, which requires 4 bits.

Let T be a string of bits encoding a DNA sequence using the codes given above. We interpret T as an integer. E.g. $T = 00\,10\,01\,11\,00\,10\,10\,01$ encodes the string "CGGATCGA". The eq vectors are easy to compute from this compressed representation. We interpret T as an unsigned integer. Now, to compute which positions have character C, for example, we use bit-wise operations to check if the low bit is 1, and the high bit is 0. This is done by shifting the bits one upon the other and using bit-wise logic: $eq'(1) = \text{NOT}(T \gg 1) \text{ AND } T$. Similarly we obtain

$$eq'(0) = \text{NOT } (T \gg 1)\text{AND NOT } T = 01\ 00\ 00\ 00\ 01\ 00\ 00\ 00$$
$$eq'(1) = \text{NOT } (T \gg 1)\text{AND} \qquad T = 00\ 00\ 01\ 00\ 00\ 00\ 00\ 01$$
$$eq'(2) = \qquad (T \gg 1)\text{AND NOT } T = 00\ 01\ 00\ 00\ 00\ 01\ 01\ 00$$
$$eq'(3) = \qquad (T \gg 1)\text{AND} \qquad T = 00\ 00\ 00\ 01\ 00\ 00\ 00\ 00$$

The vectors eq' are 'fat' versions of eq, each bit in eq is padded with one zero bit in eq'. We convert eq' to eq with look-up tables with 2^q precomputed entries. Each machine word packs $w/\log_2(\sigma)$ symbols, there are σ entries in eq, and processing each entry takes $\log_2(\sigma)$ bit-wise operations; hence the preprocessing time is now $O(2^q + \sigma(\log_2^2(\sigma) \lceil n/w \rceil + \lceil n/q \rceil))$.

There is even more efficient way to preprocess the DNA alphabet. If the low and high bits of w consecutive characters are stored in two different words, then the zero padding problem and the need for the look-up tables disappear. Let integer T^l store the low bits, and T^h the high bits. Now eq can be computed as follows:

$$eq(0) = \text{NOT } T^h\text{AND NOT } T^l = 1\ 0\ 0\ 0\ 1\ 0\ 0\ 0$$
$$eq(1) = \text{NOT } T^h\text{AND} \qquad T^l = 0\ 0\ 1\ 0\ 0\ 0\ 0\ 1$$
$$eq(2) = \qquad T^h\text{AND NOT } T^l = 0\ 1\ 0\ 0\ 0\ 1\ 1\ 0$$
$$eq(3) = \qquad T^h\text{AND} \qquad T^l = 0\ 0\ 0\ 1\ 0\ 0\ 0\ 0$$

The preprocessing cost is now $O(\sigma \log_2(\sigma) \lceil n/w \rceil)$, because we do not waste bits, and the look-up table is not needed. For the rest of the paper we asssume that this latter method is used. The compression is straight-forward, and the compressed file is reduced to only 25% of its original size.

The same approach for computing eq is possible for other alphabets, and without the compression, using just the bits of the corresponding ASCII codes, but the method is more complex and slower. Alg. 3 shows the code to preprocess T in the general case, where T is coded with $\lceil \log_2(\sigma) \rceil$ separate bit vectors. The algorithm runs in $O(\lceil n/w \rceil \sigma \log_2(\sigma))$ time.

The method is still useful for large alphabets, if we want to search several patterns (*dictionary matching* problem). In this case, the preprocessing of the text has to be done only once. It is also possible to rearrange the search code (with or without dictionary matching) such that only $O(\sigma)$ space is required for eq table. This is achieved by processing each block of w columns for all patterns before moving to the next block. In this method the preprocessing has to be merged with the search code.

5   The k-Differences Problem

Alg. 1 can be adapted for the k differences problem. That is, we allow only at most k edit operations. In this case the distance computations of Alg. 2 can be optimized. This can be done with look-up tables [8,3]. Consider two bit vectors v and u, each of length q. The vector v represents the increments and u the

---

Alg. 3 Preprocess$(T^1, ..., T^{\lceil \log_2(\sigma) \rceil})$. Preprocessing eq.

Input: $T^1, ..., T^{\lceil \log_2(\sigma) \rceil}$
Output: eq

```
1        for i ← 1 to σ do
2            eq[i] ← ~0
3        for j ← 1 to ⌈log₂(σ)⌉ do
4            b ← ~0
5            for i ← 1 to σ do
6                eq[i] ← eq & Tʲ ∧ b
7                b ← ~b
8        return eq
```

---

decrements as in the representation of the matrix vectors. We precompute for each possible pair of values of v, u, the total increment S and the minimum value M. Let v_i denote the ith bit of v, then:

$$S(q)_{v,u} = \sum_{i=1}^{q} v_i - u_i, \quad M(q)_{v,u} = \min\left\{ \sum_{i=1}^{j} v_i - u_i \mid 1 \le j \le q \right\}.$$

Preprocessing of $S(q)$ and $M(q)$ takes $O(q2^{2q})$ time, and they take $O(2^{2q})$ space[1]. Using S and M it is possible to compute the distances that are $\le k$ in $O(n/q+R)$ expected time, where R is the number of occurrences. Alg. 4 shows the code. The total time of Alg. 1 with the call to **BlockScore** (Alg. 2) substituted with a call to **BlockScore-k** (Alg. 4) takes now $O(\lceil n/w \rceil m + \lceil n/q \rceil + R)$ expected time. So we use such q that

$$\lceil n/q \rceil = O(\lceil n/w \rceil m).$$

This holds for $q = O(w/m)$, which shows that very small q is enough in practice for all but very small m. This requires additional $O(q2^{2q})$ time preprocessing. It does not dominate as far as $q2^{2q} = O(\lceil n/w \rceil m)$, that is, for $m = \Omega(w/\log_2(n))$. For very small m we can use $q = \varepsilon w/m$ for some constant $0 < \varepsilon < 1$ to reduce the space complexity while keeping the same time complexity. The total time can therefore be made $O(\lceil n/w \rceil (\sigma \log_2(\sigma) + m) + R)$ including the fast preprocessing.

This can be clearly improved. The algorithm in [12] runs in $O(nk)$ expected time, and its bit-parallel version in $O(n \lceil k/w \rceil)$ expected time [6]. We would like to obtain $O(\lceil n/w \rceil k)$ expected time algorithm.

The well-known method proposed in [12] works as follows. The algorithm computes column wise the values of $E_{i,j}$ only up to row $i \le \ell_j$, where $\ell_1 = k + 1$ (i.e. the pattern mismatches), and

---

[1] In fact, only $O(3^q)$ space would suffice, as it is not possible that both v_i and u_i equal to 1. Albeit this would permit larger q in practice, it would also require (slow) hashing to index $S(q)$ and $M(q)$.

Alg. 4 BlockScore-k(d, pos, vp, vn). Computing distances $d \leq k$.

Input: d, pos, vp, vn

Output: $E_{m,j} \mid E_{m,j} \leq k$, $j \in \{pos + 1..pos + w\}$

```
1       h ← (1 ≪ q) − 1
2       for i ← 1 to ⌈w/q⌉ do
3           v ← vp & h
4           u ← vn & h
5           if d + M(q)_{v,u} ≤ k then
6               compute all q distances wrt v, u
7               output possible occurrences
8           d ← d + S(q)_{v,u}
9           vp ← vp ≫ q
10          vn ← vn ≫ q
11      return d
```

$$\ell_j = \max\{i \mid E_{i,j-1} \leq k + 1\}.$$

The last relevant row of column j is therefore ℓ_j. This is because the search result does not depend on the elements of the matrix whose exact values are greater than $k + 1$, and the last relevant row ℓ_{j+1} for the next column $j + 1$ can be at most $\ell_{j+1} \leq \ell_j + 1$.

After evaluating the current column of the matrix up to the row ℓ_j, the value ℓ_{j+1} is computed, and the algorithm continues with the next column $j + 1$. The evaluation of ℓ_j takes $O(1)$ amortized time, and its expected value is $O(k)$, and hence the whole algorithm takes only $O(nk)$ time.

The problem with this approach is that since we compute w columns of E in parallel, we would need the maximum of the values $\ell_{j..j+w-1}$, but we cannot compute this from $\ell_{j-w..j-1}$. Instead, we take the following approach.

Let ℓ'_j denote the last relevant row for a *block* j of w contiguous columns, i.e. the definition is

$$\ell'_j = \max\{\ell_h \mid (j-1)w \leq h \leq jw - 1\}.$$

Let $\ell'_1 = k$. We first compute bit-parrallely the Δ vectors for the current block j of columns up to row ℓ'_j. During this process the score s is updated explicitly only for the first column of the current block. We then evaluate the minimum distance $s + M(w)_{vp,vn}$ of the row ℓ'_j of the block j. If $s + M(w)_{vp,vn} \leq k$ we continue to the next row of the current block, and keep computing the blocks and their minimum entries $s + M(w)_{vp,vn}$ until for some row i it happens that $s + M(w)_{vp,vn} > k$. At this point it is safe to stop evaluating the rows. If i was equal to m, then there is at least one occurrence for the current block. In this case the occurrences are checked using similar method as in Alg. 4 (by using $S(q)$ and $M(q)$). The minimum value for a given block is evaluated similarly. After the current block is computed up to row i, we compute ℓ'_{j+1}. This can be done exactly as in the original algorithm. We decrease i as long as the score for the last column of the current block is $> k$. This is easy to implement using the last bits of the Δh vectors. The complete algorithm is given in Alg. 5, and Fig. 1 illustrates the computation.

In practice we have found that it is faster to just set $\ell'_{j+1} = i$, skipping the more elaborate computation of ℓ'_{j+1}. In this case we set $\ell'_1 = k+1$, compute the Δ vectors only up to row $\ell'_j - 1$, and correspondingly require that $s + M(w)_{vp,vn} \le k + 1$. In effect, we can decrease ℓ' values only by one, that is $\ell'_{j+1} \ge \ell'_j - 1$. In both versions it is possible that $\ell'_{j+1} = \ell'_j + w$. This simpler version is in practice faster, because the more pessimistic ℓ'_{j+1} values computed are in fact more accurate in practice. Hence the complex **if-then-else** structure of the inner loop is usually executed only once or twice.

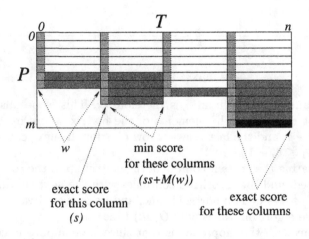

Fig. 1. Computation of the dynamic programming matrix with $w \times 1$ blocks. The bit positions shown in light gray correspond to the exact score accumulation (s) of line (21) in Alg. 5. The dark gray areas correspond to the area of minimum score computation of line (27). Finally, the black area shows the positions that need the exact score computed for score values $\le k$ (line (35) in Alg. 5).

By using the same argument as in [12], we can see that updating ℓ takes still $O(\lceil n/w \rceil)$ total amortized time. Hence the expected running time of Alg. 5, including preprocessing, is $O(\lceil n/w \rceil (\sigma \log_2(\sigma) + L(k)) + \lceil n/q \rceil + R)$, where R is the number of occurrences. $L(k)$ denotes the expected value of the variable ℓ' for the simple version of updating ℓ'. The running time then becomes $O(\lceil n/w \rceil (\sigma \log_2(\sigma) + L(k)) + R)$ for $q = \varepsilon w / L(k)$.

For the accurate updating method and for $w = 1$ it is known that $L(k) = O(k)$ [2]. It is obvious that $L(k)$ must grow as w grows, but in Sec. 7 it is shown experimentally that at least up to $w = 128$ this growth is negligible compared to the increased parallelism. It seems clear that $L(k) = O(k + w)$, as $\ell_{j+1} \le \ell_j + 1$,

Alg. 5 Approximate string matching allowing k errors.

Input: n, eq, P, m

Output: $E_{m,j} \mid E_{m,j} \leq k, \ j \in \{1..n\}$

```
1       for i ← 1 to m do
2           cp[i] ← 1
3           cn[i] ← 0
4       ℓ ← k
5       ℓ' ← ℓ
6       for r ← 1 to ⌈n/w⌉ do
7           vp ← 0, vn ← 0
8           i ← 1
9           s ← 0
10          eq ← Preprocess(Tˡ[r], Tʰ[r])
11          do
12              x ← eq[P[i]] | cn[i]
13              d ← ((vp + (x & vp)) ^ vp) | x | vn
14              hp ← vn | ~(vp | d)
15              hn ← vp & d
16              x ← (hp ≪ 1) | cp[i]
17              vp ← (hn ≪ 1) | cn[i] | ~(x | d)
18              vn ← x & d
19              cp[i] ← hp ≫ (w − 1)
20              cn[i] ← hn ≫ (w − 1)
21              s ← s + (hp & 1) − (hn & 1)
22              if i < ℓ then
23                  i ← i + 1
24              else
25                  ss ← s − (vp & 1) + (vn & 1)
26                  if i < m then
27                      if ss + M(w)_{vp,vn} ≤ k then
28                          i ← i + 1
29                          if i > ℓ' then
30                              cp[i] ← 1
31                              cn[i] ← 0
32                      else
33                          break
34                  else
35                      BlockScore-k(ss, (r − 1)w, vp, vn)
36                      break
37          while i ≤ m
38          ℓ' ← i
39          ss ← S(w)_{vp,vn}
40          while ss > k
41              ss ← ss − cp[i] + cn[i]
42              i ← i − 1
43          ℓ ← i
```

and therefore $\ell_{j+w} \leq \ell_j + w$. However, we conjecture that $L(k) = O(k + f(w))$, where $f(w) < w$.

As an implementation detail, note that the algorithm can be optimized somewhat, the line (21) can be removed, as the value of s is not needed for the first $O(L(k))$ iterations. This requires that the line (25) should be replaced with slightly more complex expression.

The preprocessing space is reduced to just $O(\sigma)$, as the preprocessing is embedded directly into Alg. 5. The eq values are needed only for the current block r, and the previous values can be discarded. This also improves the locality of reference, and can speed-up the algorithm in practice. We use this method in our implementation.

6   Vector Instructions

Many recent processor have so called multimedia or vector instructions. These SIMD (single instruction, multiple data) instructions can be used to parallelize serial code. For example, the SSE2 instruction set found in Intel Pentium4 processors can work with 128 bits in single instruction, making it possible to compute sixteen 8 bit, eight 16 bit, four 32 bit, or two 64 bit (and for some instructions, one 128 bit) results in a single step[2]. Intel icc and GNU gcc[3] C/C++ compilers provide intrinsics (built-in functions that translate to one machine instruction) to work with 128 bit quantities. In C++ it is easy to overload standard arithmetic and bit-wise operators so that the translate to the intrinsics[4]. This allows to use exactly the same code for standard 32 bit operations and for the 128 bit operations, so that the programmer does not have to worry about the SSE2 implementation details. The only obstacle is the addition and shift instructions, which work at most in two 64 bit quantities, but this can be simulated with few 64 bits instructions. We have done just that, to provide the algorithm with $w = 128$.

7   Experimental Results

We have implemented the algorithms in C/C++, compiled using icc 7.0 with full optimizations. The experiments were run in 2GHz Pentium 4, with 512MB RAM, with Linux 2.4.

We compared the performance of the new algorithm against the original method BPM [6], ABNDM/BPA [10] (their implementation), and EXP [9] (their implementation). The implementation of ABNDM/BPA has hand optimized special versions for $k = 1..5$. Our implementation of BPM requires that $m \leq w$, and

---

[2] Other vector extensions are e.g. AMD's 3DNow!, DEC's MVI, Sun's VIS, Motorola's AltiVec, and MIPS's MDMX.

[3] For GCC (3.3, 3.4 prerelease) the intrinsics are currently broken, see http://gcc.gnu.org/bugzilla/show_bug.cgi?id=10984.

[4] In fact, e.g. Intel provides a C++ class that does this, and comes with their C/C++ compiler.

hence is more efficient than the general method would be without this limitation. Our algorithm does not have such restriction. We experimented with Alg. 5 for $w = 32$, and $w = 128$. We used the simpler update formula for ℓ', see Sec. 5.

We experimented with randomly generated (uniform Bernoulli model) DNA of length 64Mb. The tests were run for various m and k. We also examined the performance for different w, namely for values 8, 16, 32, 64, and 128. The native word size of the machine is 32 bits, while the 64 bit data type (unsigned long long) is simulated by the compiler using 32 bit instructions. The 128 bit version uses the Intel SSE2 instructions, overloaded on the standard C/C++ arithmetic and bit-wise operators. The cases $w = 8$, $w = 16$ and $w = 64$ were included as a curiosity, and to study the effect of w in the average value of ℓ (the last row evaluated for a block of w columns) in Alg. 5. Fig. 2 shows the experimental values. In [1] the theoretical bound (for $w = 1$) $L \leq k/(1 - e/\sqrt{\sigma}) + O(1)$ (for $w = 1$) was proved. They also experimentally verified that the expression is very close $0.9k/(1 - 1.09/\sqrt{\sigma})$. We plot that curve in Fig. 2 too.

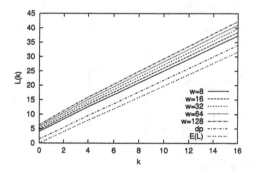

Fig. 2. The average value $L(k)$ of ℓ for different k. The pattern length was 64, and $\sigma = 4$. DP is for the $O(nk)$ expected time algorithm, and $E(L)$ denotes the predicted curve. The other curves are for our algorithm with different choices of w.

The timings are reported in Fig. 3. All the times include all preprocessing and file I/O. Our algorithms use compressed files and corresponding preprocessing method. The timings are reported for $q = 8$. Note that in the case of $m \leq 32$ we used the native 32 bit data type in implementing the Myers' algorithm. For the case $32 < m \leq 64$ we used the simulated 64 bit data type provided by the compiler. In this case the algorithm would probably be much faster if implemented using the (more complex) $O(n \lceil k/w \rceil)$ method. The implementation of ABNDM/BPA did not allow pattern lenghts of 32 or 64, and therefore they are not included in the experiments.

The results show that our new algorithm is very fast, in fact the fastest for moderate k. ABNDM/BPA could eventually become faster as the pattern length grows, as it is able to skip characters, but is only applicable for $m \leq w$.

However, the results are somewhat architecture dependent. We also compared our method against ABNDM/BPM [5], but it wasn't competitive. This was somewhat surprising, as they report excellent times in [5], but they run the experiments in different architecture (Alpha EV68). Our new algorithm is simple to implement, and has relatively few branches. The heavy pipelining of the current CPUs suffer from branching.

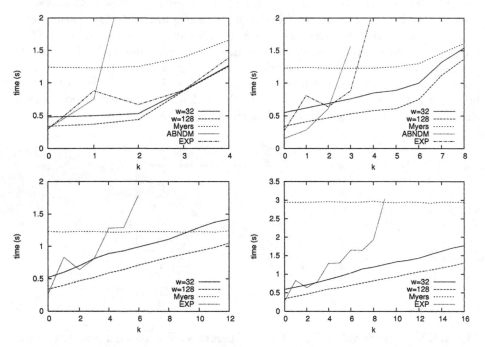

Fig. 3. Comparison of the methods for different k. From left to right, top to bottom, the pattern lengths are respectively 8, 16, 32, and 64. The times are in seconds.

In conclusion from the figures it is clear that the algorithm benefits much more on the increased parallelism than it loses for computing more of the dynamic programming matrix. The algorithm with $w = 128$ is not four times faster than with $w = 32$. There are several reasons for this. When w grows, larger portion of the matrix is evaluated. In both cases we used the same value for q (8, fixed in our current implementation), altough we should use larger q for larger w. Finally, the SIMD instructions are relatively slow, preventing the full expected speed-up. Although the SIMD instructions allow four times more bits (and larger register pool) than the integer instructions, they have also almost that much larger latency. This might improve in future.

8   Conclusions

The new arrangement of the bit-parallel computations of the dynamic programming matrix utilize the bits of computer word more economically, yielding faster approximate string matching algorithm for small patterns or for small number of allowed differences. The new algorithms work well in practice too.

References

1. R. A. Baeza-Yates and G. Navarro. Faster approximate string matching. *Algorithmica*, 23(2):127–158, 1999.
2. W. I. Chang and J. Lampe. Theoretical and empirical comparisons of approximate string matching algorithms. In A. Apostolico, M. Crochemore, Z. Galil, and U. Manber, editors, *Proceedings of the 3rd Annual Symposium on Combinatorial Pattern Matching*, number 664 in Lecture Notes in Computer Science, pages 175–184, Tucson, AZ, 1992. Springer-Verlag, Berlin.
3. K. Fredriksson and G. Navarro. Average-optimal multiple approximate string matching. In *Proceedings of the 14th Annual Symposium on Combinatorial Pattern Matching (CPM 2003)*, LNCS 2676, pages 109–128, 2003.
4. H. Hyyrö. Extending and explaining the bit-parallel approximate string matching algorithm of Myers. Technical report A2001-10, Department of Computer and Information Sciences, University of Tampere, 2001.
5. H. Hyyrö and G. Navarro. Faster bit-parallel approximate string matching. In *Proceedings of the 13th Annual Symposium on Combinatorial Pattern Matching (CPM 2002)*, LNCS 2373, pages 203–224, 2002.
6. G. Myers. A fast bit-vector algorithm for approximate string matching based on dynamic programming. *J. Assoc. Comput. Mach.*, 46(3):395–415, 1999.
7. G. Navarro. A guided tour to approximate string matching. *ACM Computing Surveys*, 33(1):31–88, 2001.
8. G. Navarro. Indexing text using the ziv-lempel trie. In *Proceedings of the 9th International Symposium on String Processing and Information Retrieval (SPIRE 2002)*, LNCS 2476, pages 325–336. Springer, 2002.
9. G. Navarro and R. Baeza-Yates. Very fast and simple approximate string matching. *Information Processing Letters*, 72:65–70, 1999.
10. G. Navarro and M. Raffinot. Fast and flexible string matching by combining bit-parallelism and suffix automata. *ACM Journal of Experimental Algorithmics (JEA)*, 5(4), 2000. http://www.jea.acm.org/2000/NavarroString.
11. P. H. Sellers. The theory and computation of evolutionary distances: Pattern recognition. *J. Algorithms*, 1(4):359–373, 1980.
12. E. Ukkonen. Algorithms for approximate string matching. *Inf. Control*, 64(1–3):100–118, 1985.
13. A. H. Wright. Approximate string matching using within-word parallelism. *Softw. Pract. Exp.*, 24(4):337–362, 1994.

Alternative Algorithms
for Bit-Parallel String Matching

Hannu Peltola and Jorma Tarhio

Department of Computer Science and Engineering
Helsinki University of Technology
P.O. Box 5400, FIN-02015 HUT, Finland
{hpeltola, tarhio}@cs.hut.fi

Abstract. We consider bit-parallel algorithms of Boyer-Moore type for exact string matching. We introduce a two-way modification of the BNDM algorithm. If the text character aligned with the end of the pattern is a mismatch, we continue by examining text characters after the alignment. Besides this two-way variation, we present a simplified version of BNDM without prefix search and an algorithm scheme for long patterns. We also study a different bit-parallel algorithm, which keeps the history of examined characters in a bit-vector and where shifting is based on this bit-vector. We report experiments where we compared the new algorithms with existing ones.
The simplified BNDM is the most promising of the new algorithms in practice.

1 Introduction

Searching for occurrences of string patterns is a common problem in many applications. Various good solutions have been presented during years. The most efficient solutions in practice are based on the Boyer-Moore algorithm [2]. We consider several Boyer-Moore modifications applying bit-parallelism for exact string matching.

Three of our algorithms are based on the Backward Nondeterministic DAWG Matching (BNDM) algorithm by Navarro and Raffinot [8,9]. The BNDM algorithm itself has been developed from the Backward DAWG Matching (BDM) algorithm [3]. BNDM is a fascinating string matching algorithm. The nice feature of BNDM is that it simulates a nondeterministic automaton without explicitly constructing it.

The first of our algorithms is a two-way modification of BNDM. We call it Two-way Nondeterministic DAWG Matching or TNDM for short. If the text character aligned with the end of the pattern is a mismatch, BNDM scans backwards in the text if the conflicting character occurs elsewhere in the pattern. In such a situation TNDM will scan forward, i.e. it continues by examining text characters after the alignment.

In addition to TNDM we consider two other variations of BNDM. The first one has lighter shift computation than BNDM. This algorithm is called Simplified BNDM or SBNDM for short. The second one is a technique to handle

M.A. Nascimento, E.S. de Moura, A.L. Oliveira (Eds.): SPIRE 2003, LNCS 2857, pp. 80–94, 2003.
© Springer-Verlag Berlin Heidelberg 2003

long patterns with BNDM. This variation is called Long BNDM or LBNDM for short.

After a shift, most algorithms of Boyer-Moore type forget totally the examined text characters of the previous alignment. We present a new algorithm, which maintains a bit-vector telling those positions where an occurrence of the pattern cannot end in order to transfer information from an alignment to subsequent alignments. We base shifting on this bit-vector. The problem of computation of shift reduces to searching for the rightmost zero in a bit-vector. This algorithm is called Shift-Vector Matching or SVM for short.

Although SVM is a kind of brute force approach, it is surprisingly efficient, because it fetches less text characters than other tested algorithms.

Navarro and Raffinot [9, p. 14] also use the method of searching for a certain bit in a bit-vector describing the state of the search. However, they consider only one alignment at a time and they initialize the bit-vector for each alignment. In SVM we initialize the bit-vector only once and so we are able to exchange information between alignments. SVM searches only for complete matches and does not recognize substrings of the pattern like BNDM.

We tested the algorithms with English, DNA, and binary texts on several machines.

We measured numbers of fetched characters and execution times.

No algorithm was the best in every individual test.

However, the simplified BNDM is the most promising of the new algorithms in practice.

2   Two-Way Variant of BNDM

Let us consider TNDM, our first modification of BNDM, in detail. Let a *text* $T = t_1 \cdots t_n$ and a *pattern* $P = p_1 \cdots p_m$ be strings of an alphabet Σ. Let us consider the first comparison of an alignment of the pattern: t_i vs. p_m. There are three cases:

1. $t_i = p_m$;
2. $t_i \neq p_m$ and t_i occurs elsewhere in P, i.e. there exists $j \neq m$ such that $t_i = p_j$;
3. t_i does not occur in P.

The new algorithm works as BNDM in Cases 1 and 3, but the operation is different in Case 2, where the standard BNDM continues examining backwards until it finds a substring that does not occur in the pattern or it reaches the beginning of the pattern. TNDM will scan *forward* in Case 2. Our experiments indicate that this change of direction will decrease the number of examined characters. In a way this approach is related to Sunday's idea [10] for using the text position immediately to the right of an alignment for determining shift in the Boyer-Moore algorithm.

In Case 2, the next text characters that are fetched are not needed for checking a potential match in the BNDM algorithm, but they are only used for computing the shift. Because $t_i \neq p_m$ holds, we know that there will be a shift forward anyway before the next occurrence is found. The idea of TNDM is to examine text characters forward one by one until it finds the first k such that the string $t_i \cdots t_k$ does not appear in P or $t_i \cdots t_k$ forms a suffix of P. In the former case we can shift beyond the previous alignment of the pattern.

Checking whether the examined characters form a suffix of the pattern, is made by building the identical bit-vector as in BNDM, but in the reverse order. Note, that the bit-vector is built with AND operations which are commutative. So we can build it in any order—especially in the reverse order. Instead of shifting the bit-vector describing the state, we shift the bit-vectors of characters. Thus if we find a suffix, we continue to examine backwards starting from the text position $i - 1$. This is done by resuming the standard BNDM operation.

We use the following notations. The length of a computer word is denoted as w. A bit mask of s bits is represented as $b_s \cdots b_1$. The most significant bit is on the left. Exponentiation stands for bit repetition (e.g. $10^2 1 = 1001$). The C-like notations are used for bit operations: "|" bitwise (inclusive) OR, "&" bitwise AND, "~" one's complement, "<<" bitwise shift to the left with zero padding, and ">>" bitwise shift to the right with zero padding. For the shift operations, the first operand is unsigned and the second operand must be non-negative and less than w.

The pseudo-code of TNDM for $m \leq w$ is shown as Algorithm 1. It is straightforward to extend the algorithm for longer patterns in the same way as BNDM, see [9]. Because BNDM is a bit-parallel implementation of BDM, it is possible to make a two-way modification of BDM.

To be able to resume efficiently examining backwards, i.e. jumping in the middle of the main loop of BNDM, we preprocess the possible values of the variable *last* of BNDM for the suffixes of the pattern. With *last*, BNDM keeps track of the starting position of the next potential occurrence P. By updating the state vector in a clever way during the forward phase, we keep it ready for the backward phase.

In preprocessing the values of *last* are computed with the BNDM algorithm as if there were a full occurrence of the pattern in the text. Algorithm 2 shows the pseudo-code where the values of *last* are stored in the array *restore*. We demonstrate the execution of TNDM with an example in Table 1.

Our experiments indicate that TNDM examines less characters than BNDM on the average. There are two reasons for that. Let $t_i \cdots t_k$ be the string examined during the forward phase.

- When $t_i \cdots t_k$ is a suffix of P, we shift the pattern to that suffix. The suffix need not to be reexamined for a possible match ending at t_k. (If BNDM finds a prefix $t_h \cdots t_i$, that prefix may be reexamined for a possible match starting at t_h.)
- If $p_1 \neq p_m$ and $t_i = p_1$ hold, TNDM may make a shift one position longer than BNDM.

It is not difficult to find examples where TNDM examines more characters than BNDM. However, there is always a dual case where the situation is vice versa. Basically BNDM searches for a substring $t_h \cdots t_i$ and TNDM for

---

Algorithm 1 TNDM.

$\mathbf{TNDM}(P = p_1 p_2 \cdots p_m, T = t_1 t_2 \cdots t_n)$

        /* Preprocessing */

1. **for** $c \in \Sigma$ **do** $B[c] \leftarrow 0^m$

2. **for** $j \in 1 \ldots m$ **do** $B[p_j] \leftarrow B[p_j] \mid 0^{j-1} 1 0^{m-j}$

3. Init_shift$(P, restore[])$

        /* Searching */

4. $epos \leftarrow m$

5. **while** $epos \leq n$ **do**

6. $i \leftarrow 0;\ last \leftarrow m$

7. $D \leftarrow B[t_{epos}]$

8.   **if** $(D\&1) = 0$ **then** /* when $D \neq B[p_m]$, */

9.   **do**   /* forward scan for suffix of pattern */

10. $i \leftarrow i + 1$

11. $D \leftarrow D\&(B[t_{epos+i}] << i)$

12.   **until** $D \neq 0^m$ **and** $D\&10^i = 0^m$

13.   **if** $D = 0^m$ **then** /* already $last \leftarrow m$ */

14.   **goto** Over

15. $epos \leftarrow epos + i;\ last \leftarrow restore[i]$

16.   **do** /* variation of BNDM */

17. $i \leftarrow i + 1$

18.   **if** $D\&10^{m-1} \neq 0^m$ **then**

19.   **if** $i < m$ **then** $last \leftarrow m - i$

20.   **else** report an occurrence at $epos - m + 1$; **goto** Over

21. $D \leftarrow D << 1$

22. $D \leftarrow D\&B[t_{epos-i}]$

23.   **until** $D \neq 0^m$

24.   Over:

25. $epos \leftarrow epos + last$

Algorithm 2 Initialization of the array *restore*.

Init_shift$(P = p_1 p_2 \cdots p_m, restore[])$

1. $D \leftarrow 1^m$

2. $last \leftarrow m$

3. **for** $i \leftarrow m$ **downto** 1 **do**

4. $D \leftarrow D\&B[p_i]$

5.   **if** $D\&10^{m-1} \neq 0^m$ **then**

6.   **if** $i > 0$ **then** $last \leftarrow i$

7. $restore[m - i + 1] \leftarrow last$

8. $D \leftarrow D << 1$

Table 1. Simulation of TNDM. $P =$ ATCGA; $T =$ GCATCATGATCGAATCAG$\cdots$; Bit-vectors B: $B[\text{A}] = 10001$, $B[\text{C}] = 00100$, $B[\text{G}] = 00010$, $B[\text{T}] = 01000$. The last fetched character has been underlined.

Text window	Line	D	i	epos	last	Explanation
GCAT**C**ATGA$\cdots$	8	00100	0	5	5	The lowest bit is 0; continue to line 9.
GCAT**C**ATGA$\cdots$	12	00000	1	5	5	$D = 0$; leave the loop and proceed with lines 13, 14, 24, 25, and 5–.
$\cdots$ATGA**T**CGAy$\cdots$	8	01000	0	10	5	The lowest bit is 0; continue to line 9.
$\cdots$ATGA**T**CGAA$\cdots$	12	01000	1	10	5	$D \neq 0$ **and** $D\&10 = 0$; continue to line 9.
$\cdots$ATGA**T**CGAA$\cdots$	12	01000	2	10	5	$D \neq 0$ **and** $D\&100 = 0$; continue to line 9.
$\cdots$ATGA**T**CG**A**A$\cdots$	12	01000	3	10	5	$D \neq 0$ **and** $D\&1000 = 1$; leave the loop and continue to lines 13, and 15–.
$\cdots$ATCG**A**A$\cdots$	16	01000	3	13	4	A suffix is found; *epos* and *last* are updated; the scanning direction changes.
$\cdots$ATCG**A**A$\cdots$	18	01000	4	13	4	$D\&10000 = 0$; not interesting, proceed with lines 21, 22, and 23.
$\cdots$A**T**CGAA$\cdots$	23	10000	4	13	4	$D \neq 0$; proceed with lines 16, 17, and 18.
$\cdots$**A**TCGAA$\cdots$	18	10000	5	13	4	$D\&10000 = 1$; something interesting! A prefix or a match?
$\cdots$AT**G**ATCGAA$\cdots$	20	10000	5	13	4	$i = m(= 5)$; the else branch reports an occurence at 9; continue to lines 24, 25, and 5–.
$\cdots$AAT**C**AG$\cdots$	8	10001	0	17	5	The lowest bit is 1; continue from line 16 with BNDM.
$\cdots$AAT**C**AG$\cdots$	18	10001	1	17	5	$D\&10000 \neq 0$; a prefix or a match?
$\cdots$A**A**TCAG$\cdots$	19	10001	1	17	4	$i < m(= 5)$; it was a prefix, update *last*.
$\cdots$**A**ATCAG$\cdots$	23	00000	1	17	4	$D = 0$; continue to lines 24 and 25.
$\cdots$**C**AG$\cdots$	25	00000	1	21	4	$D = 0$; continue to line 5.

a substring $t_i \cdots t_k$ which do not appear in P. Depending on the proportion $(k - i)/(i - h)$ either algorithm has gain.

Further enhancements. If the last character examined does not occur in P while scanning forward, we are able to shift pattern entirely over it. This can be done by adding the following line to TNDM:

13.5   **if** $B[t_{epos+i}] = 0$ **then** $last \leftarrow i + m$

This test is computationally light, because after a forward scan only t_k of $t_i \cdots t_k$ can be missing from the pattern. The test clearly reduces the number of fetched characters.

However, the test is beneficial only for alphabets large enough. In Section 5 we call TNDM with this test TNDMa.

In TNDM we scan forward when t_i is not p_m and t_i occurs elsewhere in P. This can be generalized as follows. If the backward phase has encountered $v = t_h \cdots t_i$ such that v is not a suffix of P but v appears elsewhere in P, we will scan forward starting from t_{i+1}. We expect this modification would improve TNDM a bit in the case of small alphabets.

Implementation remarks. Note that on lines 9–12 the algorithm may address at most $m-1$ characters past t_n, the last character of text. This can be prevented by adding the following test on line 8:

8.   **if** $(D\&1) = 0$ **and** $epos + m - 1 \leq n$ **then**

The other possibility is to ignore spurious suffix and change line 13 in the following way:

13.   **if** $D = 0^m$ **or** $epos + i > n$ **then**

and allow references to $t_{n+1}, \ldots, t_{n+m-1}$. The third solution is to store to t_{n+1} a stopper character, e.g. null, which do not appear in any pattern.

If the interesting bits do not use the whole word i.e. $m < w$, then one has to be careful with tests like '$D \neq 0^k$'. As the result of a shift some set bits may move beside the interesting area of bit-vector, and tests cannot be simplified to form '$D \neq 0$'. If the interesting bits are located on that edge in the shifting direction, the uninteresting bits fall off during shift. Navarro and Raffinot use this trick successfully in their implementation of BNDM. In the pseudo-code of TNDM, all tests with 0^m can be simplified without extra masking.

Complexity. We consider only patterns than are at most w characters long. The preprocessing time is $O(m + |\Sigma|)$. The worst case complexity of TNDM is clearly $O(nm)$. The average case complexity of BNDM (and BDM) is $O(n \log_{|\Sigma|} m/m)$. It is not difficult to see that the same is true for TNDM.

3 Other Variations of BNDM

3.1 SBNDM

When BNDM finds $t_h \cdots t_i$ which is a match or do not appear in P, there are two options for shifting. Let j be the smallest index such that $h < j \leq i$ holds and $t_j \cdots t_i$ is a prefix of P. Then the next alignment starts at t_j. If there is no such prefix, then the next alignment starts at $i + 1$.

In SBNDM we shift as in BNDM in the case of a match. But if $t_h \cdots t_i$ do not appear in P, we skip the examining of prefixes and set $h + 1$ to be the start position of the next alignment. Naturally this reduces the average length of shift, but on the other hand the innermost loop of the algorithm becomes simpler. Our experiments show that SBNDM is most often faster than BNDM.

The pseudo-code of SBNDM is shown as Algorithm 3. The table B is initialized as in BNDM and TNDM. In the case of a complete match, the shift is s_0, which is easy to precompute as $restore[1]$, see Alg. 2. In other words, s_0 equals to $m - x$ where x is the length of the longest prefix of P, which is also a suffix of P.

Note that it is possible to leave out the test of j on line 8, because D becomes always zero after m bitwise shifts, but this version will need to examine one extra character after each match (immediately to the left of a match).

Algorithm 3 Simplified BNDM.

$\mathbf{SBNDM}(P = p_1 p_2 \cdots p_m, T = t_1 t_2 \cdots t_n)$

1.   initialize B and s_0
2. $pos \leftarrow 0$
3.   **while** $pos \leq n - m$ **do**
4. $D \leftarrow 1^m; j \leftarrow m$
5.   **do**
6. $D \leftarrow (D << 1)\&B[t_{pos+j}]$
7. $j \leftarrow j - 1$
8.   **until** $D = 0^m$ **or** $j = 0$
9.   **if** $D \neq 0^m$ **then**
10.   report an occurrence at pos
11. $pos \leftarrow pos + s_0$
12.   **else** $pos \leftarrow pos + j + 1$

3.2   LBNDM

Navarro and Raffinot [9, p. 12] introduced also a method of searching for patterns longer than w. They partitioned the pattern in consecutive subpatterns. All the subpatterns have w characters except possibly the rightmost one which gets the remaining characters. The leftmost subpattern is searched with the standard BNDM algorithm. Only when the match of the leftmost subpattern is found, the rest of an alignment is examined. The maximum shift is w.

We introduce another approach called LBNDM for long patterns. LBNDM is able to make shifts longer than w. The pattern is partitioned in $\lfloor \frac{m}{k} \rfloor$ consecutive parts, each consisting of $k = \lfloor \frac{m-1}{w} \rfloor + 1$ characters. The $m - k \lfloor \frac{m}{k} \rfloor$ remaining character positions are left to either end of the pattern (or to both ends). This division implies k subsequences of the pattern such that the ith sequence takes the ith character of each part. The idea is to search first the superimposed pattern of these sequences so that

only every kth character is examined. This filtration phase is done with the standard BNDM algorithm. Each occurrence of the superimposed pattern is a potential match of the original pattern and thus must be verified.

Note that the shifts of the LBNDM are multiples of k. To get a real advantage of shifts longer than

in the approach of Navarro and Raffinot,

the pattern length should be at least about two times w.

On the other hand, this implies $k \geq 3$,

which on DNA data turns out to be quite high. In the case of a small alphabet a feasible solution could be to use q-grams instead of single characters, see [7].

4   Shift-Vector Matching

One problem of Boyer-Moore type algorithms is that they do not remember the tried text positions of previous alignments. When the shift is shorter than the pattern length m, some alignments of the pattern may be tried in vain. In the following we will introduce an algorithm with partial memory. The key idea is simple: We maintain a bit-vector, called a *shift-vector*, which tells those positions where an occurrence of the pattern can or cannot end. This approach makes it possible to base shifting on this shift-vector and to manage without any shift table.

While moving the pattern forward and shifting the shift-vector, the old knowledge of already handled positions goes off from the shift-vector. Then the bit corresponding to the end of the pattern must be the highest or the lowest bit. We chose the lowest one, because then masking on some processors is slightly faster. (Often the fastest way to load the specific bit-mask 1 to a register is loading the constant 1 with some instruction, which is not referring to the memory.) This decision implies that the shifting direction is to the right. The new bits entering to a bit-vector during a bitwise shift are zeros, and therefore it is natural to use the convention where zero denotes a text position not yet rejected.

In preprocessing we create bit-vectors representing the characters of an alphabet. These bit-vectors have the zero bit on every position where that character occurs in the pattern, and one elsewhere. So the characters that do not appear in the pattern have the bit-vector $0^{w-m}1^m$. Note that the essential parts of these vectors are complements of those used in TNDM.

We keep track of possible end positions of the pattern in the shift-vector S. It is simply updated by taking OR with the bit-vector corresponding to text character aligned with last character of the pattern. If the lowest bit in S is one, a match cannot end here and we can shift the pattern. The length of the shift is simply got by searching the lowest zero bit in S which is above the lowest position. In addition to shifting the pattern, we also shift bits in S with the same number of positions to the right.

If the lowest bit in S is zero, i.e. p_m has been found, we have to continue checking for the match. Our first implementation had a classical pairwise comparison of pattern and text characters. In addition, S was updated with all characters that were fetched during verifying of alignments. Of course the scope of text characters is relative to the end of pattern. To correctly update S with bit-vectors of text characters, that are aligned with pattern, their values have to be shifted to the right depending how far the are from the end of pattern: $S \leftarrow S \mid (C[t_{epos-j}] >> j)$. Because the lowest bit remains zero as long as a mismatch has not been found, we could remove the pairwise comparison. Text characters that are on the left-hand side of alignment give less information for shifting than those, which are close to the right end of alignment. That is why we chose to check, if there is a match, in the reverse order, i.e. from right to left.

The pseudo-code of SVM for $m \leq w$ is shown as Algorithm 3. To our knowledge, this approach of shifting has not been studied before. The function BSF scans the bits in the operand bit-vector starting from lowest bit and searches

---

Algorithm 4 SVM.

$\mathbf{SVM}(P = p_1p_2 \cdots p_m, T = t_1t_2 \cdots t_n)$

   /* Preprocessing */

1. **for** $c \in \Sigma$ **do** $C[c] \leftarrow 1^m$
2. **for** $j \in 1 \ldots m$ **do** $C[p_j] \leftarrow C[p_j] \& 1^{j-1}01^{m-j}$

   /* Searching */

3. $epos \leftarrow m;\ S \leftarrow 0$
4. **while** $epos \leq n$ **do**
5. $S \leftarrow S \mid C[t_{epos}]$
6. $j \leftarrow 1$
7.   **while** $(S\&1) = 0$ **do**
8.   **if** $j \geq m$ **then**
9.   report an occurrence at $epos + 1 - m$
10.   **goto** Over
11. $S \leftarrow S \mid (C[t_{epos-j}] >> j)$
12. $j \leftarrow j + 1$
13.   Over:
14. $last \leftarrow \mathrm{BSF}(\tilde{\ }(S >> 1)) + 1$
15. $S \leftarrow S >> last$
16. $epos \leftarrow epos + last$

---

for the first set bit. The function returns the number of zero bits before first set bit. In the end of this section we discuss various implementation alternatives of BSF.

We demonstrate the execution of SVM with an example in Table 2. After a long shift, the shift-vector S becomes zero or almost zero. Then the subsequent shift is more likely shorter. Fortunately after a short shift, there will normally be several ones in S, and so the subsequent shift will likely be longer again. E.g. after reading G on the second row of the example, S becomes full of ones enabling a full shift of 5 positions.

In SVM there is an obvious trade-off between the number of fetched characters and searching for a set bit in the shift-vector. The run times depend on the relative speed of these functions. It is straightforward to extend this algorithm for longer patterns.

Complexity. Let us assume that $m \leq w$ holds and BSF is $O(1)$. Then the preprocessing time is $O(m + |\Sigma|)$ and the worst case complexity is clearly $O(nm)$. SVM is sublinear on the average, because at the same alignment it fetches the same text characters as the Boyer-Moore-Horspool algorithm [5] (assuming the right-to-left examining order) and can never make a shorter shift than that algorithm, which is known to be sublinear on the average. If a constant time BSF is not available, there will be an extra work of $\log m$ or $\log w$ for each alignment.

Table 2. Simulation of SVM. $P =$ ATCGA; $T =$ GCAGCTATCGAG$\cdots$; Bit-vectors C: $C[\text{A}] = 01110$, $C[\text{C}] = 11011$, $C[\text{G}] = 11101$, $C[\text{T}] = 10111$. The last fetched character has been underlined. The snapshots correspond to lines 8 and 14.

Text	S	j	$epos$	$last$
GCAG<u>C</u>TGATCGAG$\cdots$	11011	1	5	2
GCAGCT<u>G</u>ATCGAG$\cdots$	11111	1	7	5
GCAGCTGATCGA<u>G</u>$\cdots$	01110	1	12	(5)
GCAGCTGATC<u>G</u>AG$\cdots$	01110	2	12	(5)
GCAGCTGAT<u>C</u>GAG$\cdots$	01110	3	12	(5)
GCAGCTGA<u>T</u>CGAG$\cdots$	01110	4	12	(5)
GCAGCTG<u>A</u>TCGAG$\cdots$	01110	5	12	5

Search for the Lowest Zero Bit

From the previously examined characters we usually know some positions where the pattern cannot end. All these positions with reference to the end of the pattern have the corresponding bit set in the shift-vector S of SVM. The lowest bit represents the current position. To get the length of the next shift of the pattern, one has to find the rightmost zero bit in S. Alternatively one can complement the bits and search for lowest set bit.

There are several possibilities for searching of the rightmost set bit. Below we consider five alternatives: BSF-0, ..., BSF-4. If we first shift the contents of the word one position to the right and if we are using unsigned variables in C, we get zero padding and there will always exist at least one zero bit.

BSF-0. Many computer architectures have instructions for scanning bits; for example Intel's x86 has instructions for scanning both forward (*Bit Scan Forward*) and backward (*Bit Scan Reverse*). A suitable implementation can be found in Arndt's collection [1] of x86 inline asm versions of various functions as function asm_bsf. If this kind of instruction is available, using it gives the fastest performance.

BSF-1. The simplest way to seek for the lowest zero bit goes by shifting the word bit position by bit position to the right and testing the lowest bit. If lowest zero bit can be found with few iterations—e.g. when m is small—the performance is acceptable. Navarro and Raffinot [9] have used this technique in their implementation of BM_BNDM and TurboBNDM. The relative performance decreases while the average length of shift increases.

BSF-2. Search for the lowest set bit becomes easier, if we assume that at most one bit is set. This can be achieved with an expression $x \,\&\, -x$.

If at most one bit is set, it is possible to apply bit masking: we divide different sized groups in the bit-vector to an upper and lower half. If some even bit is set, then we can increase the bit number by one. If some even bit-pair is set, then we can increase the bit number by two. If some upper half of byte is set, then we can increase the bit number by four; etc. Finding the set bit this way requires $\log w$ tests with different bit masks. This idea is presented in the function lowest_bit_idx of Arndt [1].

The masking method described above requires large (i.e. w bits wide) bit masks. If they are built from smaller pieces, their construction takes considerably work.

BSF-3. This approach is similar to the previous one. Now we clear all other but the lowest set bit. If a number after shifting l positions to the right is not zero, it is obvious, that the only set bit is higher than l bits. The search goes most efficiently by halving: first $w/2$ bits, then $w/4$ bits, etc. The shifting could be made also to the left, but this way the optimizer of the compiler can produce more efficient code by reusing the results of the shifts. Examining the last byte goes faster and easier with the table lookup from precomputed constant array. Together $\log \frac{w}{8}$ shifting tests are needed. Actually the same holds also for m $\lceil \log \frac{m}{8} \rceil$ because one can tailor the routine for different pattern lengths. Relative performance improves clearly when patterns get longer.

BSF-4. We can also utilize the fact that at least one bit is set. The basic idea is that when we shift to the left and the result is zero, we can conclude that the lowest set bit was in the part that fell off. Because we try to isolate the lowest bit to smaller and smaller area, for the next step we have to shift the bit-vector to the right every time the result after shifting is zero. Examining the last byte is made with table lookup from precomputed constant array.

Typically SVM moves a couple of shorter shifts and then longer one, usually the maximum m. In our experimental tests we used the version BSF-0 utilizing the asm function.

Implementation remark. When $m = w$, the value of *last* may become w, which is too large for the shift on line 15. Then the shifting must be made in two parts. This can be made efficiently with the following changes:

13.5	$S \leftarrow S \gg 1$
14.	$last \leftarrow \mathrm{BSF}(\tilde{\ } S)$
15.	$S \leftarrow S \gg last$
16.	$epos \leftarrow epos + last + 1$

5 Experimental Results

We tested BNDM, TNDM, SBNDM and SVM together with three older algorithms TBM, GD2, and BMH4, which we know to be fast. The code of BNDM is a courtesy from G. Navarro. TBM (uf.fwd.md2) and GD2 (uf.rev.gd2) are from Hume and Sunday [6]. TBM is recommended for general purpose use [6]. The performance of GD2 [6, p. 1244] on DNA data has drawn attention quite rarely. BMH4 is a 4-gram version [11] of the Boyer-Moore-Horspool algorithm [5] tuned for DNA data. BMH4 was so poor with the English text that we do not show those figures.

BNDM and SBNDM have a skip loop that could be classified as uf1 [6]:

a while loop is skipping with m positions for characters not present in the pattern.

Our test framework is a modification of the one made by Hume and Sunday [6]. The main experiments were carried out in a Linux workstation with 256 MB (PC133A SDRAM) memory, AMD Athlon Thunderbird 1000 MHz processor, 64 KB L1 cache for both data and instructions, and 256 KB L2 cache on die. The algorithms were compiled with the GNU C compiler version 2.95.4 with optimization flag -O3. All the bit-parallel algorithms used 32 bit bit-vectors.

We ran tests with three types of texts of 1 MB: English, DNA, and binary. The English text is the beginning of the KJV bible. The DNA text is from Hume and Sunday [6].

The binary data was generated randomly. For DNA and binary we used 200 patterns of four lengths drawn from same data source as the corresponding text. So every pattern do not necessary occur in the text. For English we used 500 words of various lengths as patterns.

Table 3. Proportions of fetched characters.

Σ	m	BNDM	GD2	TBM	BMH4	TNDM	TNDMa	SBNDM	SVM
Binary	5	.868	.983	1.55	.139	.763	.763	1.05	.750
	10	.516	.732	1.63	.675	.492	.492	.647	.445
	20	.292	.520	1.55	.421	.286	.286	.343	.250
	30	.214	.453	1.55	.357	.211	.211	.243	.178
DNA	5	.445	.481	.614	.887	.425	.413	.517	.376
	10	.262	.332	.488	.428	.258	.256	.296	.217
	20	.153	.253	.473	.214	.153	.153	.167	.126
	30	.111	.212	.461	.145	.111	.111	.119	.091
English 2–16		.205	.202	.210	–	.205	.199	.213	.190

Table 3 shows the proportions of fetched characters. SVM is a clear winner. TNDM and TNDMa also inspect less characters than BNDM. TBM fetches much more characters than others in the case of small alphabets. Note that GD2 and TBM contain a skip loop (uf3), which surely worsens their results with the binary alphabet.

Table 4 shows the search times in seconds. The figures are averages of 15 runs. While repeating tests, the variation in search times was less than 2%. BMH4 is the fastest for binary and DNA data. On the English text TBM is the best. TNDM and SVM are slightly slower than BNDM.

SBNDM is on the average 10% faster than BNDM.

TNDMa (times not shown) was slightly slower than TNDM.

Table 4. Run times of the algorithms.

Σ	m	BNDM	GD2	TBM	BMH4	TNDM	SBNDM	SVM
Binary	5	3.23	2.80	3.07	1.83	3.31	2.89	3.24
	10	2.04	2.23	3.40	1.18	2.17	1.76	2.19
	20	1.30	1.79	3.26	0.99	1.49	1.10	1.56
	30	0.96	1.68	3.22	0.91	1.16	0.91	1.25
DNA	5	1.81	1.69	1.65	1.20	2.12	1.67	2.10
	10	1.28	1.39	1.45	0.85	1.55	1.12	1.53
	20	0.91	1.18	1.41	0.82	1.06	0.86	1.04
	30	0.78	1.08	1.40	0.71	0.87	0.75	0.89
English	2–16	2.69	2.45	2.39	–	2.97	2.45	3.39

It is interesting that the performance of GD2 does not seem to improve as fast as bit-parallel algorithms while patterns get longer. On GD2 the preprocessing times were 0.0013–0.0038 seconds; on all others it was less than 0.0007 seconds.

We also tested the bit-parallel algorithms with 64 bits in our workstation with AMD Athlon CPU. They are about 50% slower mainly because the machine has a 32 bit ALU and the bit operations using 64 bits need two registers.

The performance of various BSF versions depends a lot of the compiler, the computer architecture, and the size of bit-vectors. Besides AMD Athlon we tested BSF on
the following configurations:
Sun Enterprise 450
(4 UltraSPARC-II 400MHz processors,
2048 MB main memory with 4 MB Ecache, Solaris 8)
with Sun WorkShop 6 update 2 C 5.3 and gcc 3.2.1 compilers,
and
Digital Personal Workstation 433au
(Alpha 21164A-2 (EV56 433 MHz) processor, 256 MB main memory;
OSF1 V5.1 [Tru64 UNIX])
with Compaq C V6.5-011 and gcc 3.3 compilers.
Table 5 shows the
relative performance of SVM with various BSF versions on the English text, where
BSF-4 is used as a reference version (so its relative performance is 1).
Smaller values denote faster performance.
With longer patterns performance of BSF-1 got worse.
Although Ultra-Sparc-II has 64-bit instructions,
use of bit-vectors of 64 bits showed to be more than 60% slower than with 32 bits.
The Alpha Compaq C-compiler produced code
that worked rather slowly with BSF-2, BSF-3, and BSF-4.

Table 5. Relative performance of various BSF versions

CPU	AMD Athlon		UltraSPARC-II				Alpha 21164A-2	
Compiler/ w	gcc/32	gcc/64	Sun/32	gcc/32	Sun/64	gcc/64	Compaq(64)	gcc(64)
BSF-0	0.888	–	–	–	–	–	–	–
BSF-1	1.001	0.817	1.346	1.191	1.146	0.972	0.730	1.036
BSF-2	1.044	1.157	1.420	1.126	1.211	1.348	1.011	1.217
BSF-3	0.999	0.999	0.992	0.999	1.123	1.109	1.005	1.001

We compared LBNDM with the approach by Navarro and Raffinot with long patterns on computers of different kind. There was a large variation in their relative performance. LBNDM proved to be clearly faster in the English text for $m = 70, \ldots, 180$.

The basic test set was run on several other computer architectures. The results were diversed. We review some deviations. On a 500 MHz Celeron, SBNDM was 15% faster than the second best algorithm in the English test. Other Intel processors gave similar results. On 400 MHz PowerPC G4, TNDM was faster than BNDM in the DNA tests.

The compiler may affect the performance of a certain algorithm:
On the Alpha workstation both the compilers genarate equally fast code for BNDM,
but native compiler generates 30% slower code for TNBM than gcc
in the case of the English text.

6   Concluding Remarks

We introduced four bit-parallel algorithms for exact string matching: TNDM, SBNDM, LBNDM, and SVM. The algorithms are relatively compact. The algorithms can be extended to sets of strings (multiple pattern matching) and classes of characters in a similar way as BNDM [9]. It might be possible to combine SVM with Vishkin's sampling method [12]. At the monent we are working on a combination method of SBNDM and TNDM.

SBNDM showed to be the best of the new algorithms. As it often happens, algorithms with tight loops are also efficient.

SBNDM is a good candidate for implementing grep especially in Intel-based machines.

References

1. J. Arndt: Jörgs useful and ugly BIT WIZARDRY page. *URL:* http://www.jjj.de/ bitwizardry/bitwizardrypage.html.
2. R.S. Boyer and J.S. Moore: A Fast String Searching Algorithm. *Communications of the ACM,* **20**(10):762–772, 1977.

3. M. Crochemore and W. Rytter: *Text algorithms.* Oxford University Press, 1994.
4. Z. Galil: On Improving the Worst Case Running Time of the Boyer–Moore String Matching Algorithm. *Communications of the ACM,* **22**(9):505–508, 1979.
5. R.N. Horspool: Practical Fast Searching in Strings. *Software — Practice and Experience,* **10**(6):501–506, 1980.
6. A. Hume and D. Sunday: Fast String Searching. *Software — Practice and Experience,* **21**(11):1221–1248, 1991.
7. J. Kytöjoki, L. Salmela, and J. Tarhio: Tuning string matching for huge pattern sets. In *Proc CPM '03, Lecture Notes in Computer Science* **2676**:211–224, 2003.
8. G. Navarro and M. Raffinot: A Bit-parallel Approach to Suffix Automata: Fast Extended String Matching. In *Proc CPM '98, Lecture Notes in Computer Science* **1448**:14–33, 1998.
9. G. Navarro and M. Raffinot: Fast and Flexible String Matching by Combining Bit-parallelism and Suffix automata. *ACM Journal of Experimental Algorithms,* **5**(4):1–36, 2000.
10. D.M. Sunday: A Very Fast Substring Search Algorithm. *Communications of the ACM,* **33**(8):132–142, 1990.
11. J. Tarhio and H. Peltola: String Matching in the DNA Alphabet. *Software — Practice and Experience,* **27**(7):851–861, 1997.
12. U. Vishkin: Deterministic Sampling — a New Technique for Fast Pattern Matching. *SIAM Journal of Computing,* **20**(1):22–40, 1991.

Bit-Parallel Approximate String Matching Algorithms with Transposition

Heikki Hyyrö*

Department of Computer and Information Sciences
University of Tampere, Finland.
Heikki.Hyyro@cs.uta.fi

Abstract. Using bit-parallelism has resulted in fast and practical algorithms for approximate string matching under the Levenshtein edit distance, which permits a single edit operation to insert, delete or substitute a character. Depending on the parameters of the search, currently the fastest non-filtering algorithms in practice are the $O(kn\lceil m/w\rceil)$ algorithm of Wu & Manber, the $O(\lceil km/w\rceil n)$ algorithm of Baeza-Yates & Navarro, and the $O(\lceil m/w\rceil n)$ algorithm of Myers, where m is the pattern length, n is the text length, k is the error threshold and w is the computer word size. In this paper we discuss a uniform way of modifying each of these algorithms to permit also a fourth type of edit operation: transposing two adjacent characters in the pattern. This type of edit distance is also known as the Damerau edit distance. In the end we also present an experimental comparison of the resulting algorithms.

1 Introduction

Approximate string matching is a classic problem in computer science, with applications for example in spelling correction, bioinformatics and signal processing. It has been actively studied since the sixties [8]. Approximate string matching refers in general to the task of searching for substrings of a text that are within a predefined edit distance threshold from a given pattern. Let $T_{1..n}$ be a text of length n and $P_{1..m}$ a pattern of length m. In addition let $ed(A, B)$ denote the edit distance between the strings A and B, and k be the maximum allowed distance. Using this notation, the task of approximate string matching is to find from the text all indices j for which $ed(P, T_{h..j}) \leq k$ for some $h \leq j$.

Perhaps the most common form of edit distance is the Levenshtein edit distance [6], which is defined as the minimum number of single-character insertions, deletions and substitutions (Fig. 1a) needed in order to make A and B equal. Another common form of edit distance is the Damerau edit distance [2], which is in principle an extension of the Levenshtein distance by permitting also the operation of transposing two adjacent characters (Fig. 1b). The Damerau edit

---

* Supported by the Academy of Finland and Tampere Graduate School in Information Science and Engineering.

M.A. Nascimento, E.S. de Moura, A.L. Oliveira (Eds.): SPIRE 2003, LNCS 2857, pp. 95–107, 2003.

distance is important for example in spelling error applications [5]. In this paper we use the notation $ed_L(A, B)$ to denote the Levenshtein edit distance and $ed_D(A, B)$ to denote the Damerau edit distance between A and B.

During the last decade, algorithms based on bit-parallelism have emerged as the fastest approximate string matching algorithms in practice for the Levenshtein edit distance [6]. The first of these was the $O(kn\lceil m/w \rceil)$ algorithm of Wu & Manber [15], where w is the computer word size. Later Wright [14] presented an $O(mn \log(\sigma)/w)$ algorithm, where σ is the alphabet size. Then Baeza-Yates & Navarro followed with their $O(\lceil km/w \rceil n)$ algorithm. Finally Myers [7] achieved an $O(\lceil m/w \rceil n)$ algorithm, which is an optimal speedup from the basic $O(mn)$ dynamic programming algorithm (e.g. [11]). With the exception of the algorithm of Wright, the bit-parallel algorithms dominate the other verification capable[1] algorithms with moderate pattern lengths [8].

a) insertion: cat → ca**s**t   b) transposition: **ca**t → **ac**t
    deletion: **c**at → at
    substitution: ca**t** → ca**r**

Fig. 1. Figure a) shows the three edit operations permitted by the Levenshtein edit distance. Figure b) shows the additional edit operation permitted by the Damerau edit distance: transposing two adjacent characters. The transposed characters are required to be/remain adjacent in the original and the modified pattern.

In this paper we show how each of the above-mentioned three best bit-parallel algorithms can be modified to use the Damerau edit distance. Navarro [9] has previously extended the algorithm of Wu & Manber [15] for the Damerau distance. But that method adds $O(k\lceil m/w \rceil)$ work to the original algorithm, whereas the additional cost of our method is only $O(\lceil m/w \rceil)$. Our method is also more general in that its principle works with also the other two algorithms [1, 7] with very little changes.

We begin by discussing the basic dynamic programming solutions for the Levenshtein and Damerau distances. In this part we also reformulate the dynamic programming solution for the Damerau edit distance into a form that is easier to handle for the bit-parallel algorithms. Then we proceed to modify the bit-parallel algorithms of Wu & Manber [15], Baeza-Yates & Navarro [1] and Myers [7] to facilitate the Damerau edit distance. Finally we present an experimental comparison of these modified algorithms.

---

[1] Are based on actually computing the edit distance.

2 Dynamic Programming

In the following we assume that $A_{1..0} = \epsilon$, where ϵ denotes the empty string. In addition let $|A|$ denote the length of the string A. We consider first the Levenshtein edit distance. In this case the dynamic programming algorithm fills a $(|A| + 1) \times (|B| + 1)$ dynamic programming table D, where in the end each cell $D[i, j]$ will hold the value $ed_L(A_{1..i}, B_{1..j})$. The algorithm begins from the trivially known values $D[i, 0] = ed_L(A_{1..i}, \epsilon) = i$ and $D[0, j] = ed_L(\epsilon, B_{1..j}) = j$, and arrives at the value $D[A, B] = ed_L(A_{1..|A|}, B_{1..|B|}) = ed_L(A, B)$ by recursively computing the value $D[i, j]$ from the previously computed values $D[i-1, j-1]$, $D[i, j-1]$ and $D[i-1, j]$. This can be done using the following well-known Recurrence 1.

Recurrence 1

$$D[i, 0] = i, D[0, j] = j.$$
$$D[i, j] = \begin{cases} D[i-1, j-1], & \text{if } A_i = B_j. \\ 1 + \min(D[i-1, j-1], D[i-1, j], D[i, j-1]), & \text{otherwise.} \end{cases}$$

The Damerau edit distance can be computed in basically the same way, but Recurrence 1 needs a slight change. The following Recurrence 2 for the Damerau edit distance is derived from the work of Du & Chang [3]. The superscript R denotes the reverse of a string (that is, if $A =$ "abc", then $A^R =$ "cba").

Recurrence 2

$$D[i, -1] = D[-1, j] = \max(|A|, |B|).$$
$$D[i, 0] = i, D[0, j] = j.$$
$$D[i, j] = \begin{cases} D[i-1, j-1], & \text{if } A_i = B_j. \\ 1 + \min(D[i-2, j-2], D[i-1, j], D[i, j-1]), & \text{if } A_{i-1..i} = \\ & \qquad (B_{j-1..j})^R. \\ 1 + \min(D[i-1, j-1], D[i-1, j], D[i, j-1]), & \text{otherwise.} \end{cases}$$

Instead of computing the edit distance between strings A and B, the dynamic programming algorithm can be changed to find approximate occurrences of A somewhere inside B by changing the boundary condition $D[0, j] = j$ into $D[0, j] = 0$. In this case $D[i, j] = \min(ed_L(P_{0..i}, T_{h..j}), h \leq j)$ with the Levenshtein edit distance and $D[i, j] = \min(ed_D(P_{0..i}, T_{h..j}), h \leq j)$ with the Damerau edit distance. Thus, if we set $A = P$ and $B = T$, the situation corresponds to the earlier definition of approximate string matching. From now on we assume that the dynamic programming table D is filled in this manner.

Ukkonen ([12, 13]) has studied the properties of the dynamic programming matrix. Among these there were the following two, which apply to both the edit distance and the approximate string matching versions of D:

-The diagonal property: $D[i, j] - D[i-1, j-1] = 0$ or 1.
-The adjacency property: $D[i, j] - D[i, j-1] = -1, 0,$ or 1, and
$$D[i, j] - D[i-1, j] = -1, 0, \text{ or } 1.$$

Even though these rules were initially presented with the Levenshtein edit distance, it is fairly straightforward to verify that they apply also to the Damerau edit distance.

The values of the dynamic programming matrix D are usually computed by filling it in a column-wise manner for increasing j, thus effectively scanning the string B (or the text T) one character at a time from left to right. At each character the corresponding column is completely filled in the order of increasing i. This allows us to save space by storing only one or two columns at a time, since the values in column j depend only on one (Levenshtein) or two (Damerau) previous columns.

Now we reformulate Recurrence 2 into a form that is easier to use with the three bit-parallel algorithms. Our trick is to investigate how a transposition relates to a substitution. Consider comparing the strings $A = $ "abc" and $B = $ "acb". Then $D[2,2] = ed_D(A_{1..2}, B_{1..2}) = ed_D(\text{"ab"},\text{"ac"}) = 1$, where the one operation corresponds to substituting the first character of the transposable suffixes "bc" and "cb". When filling in the value $D[3,3] = ed_D(\text{"abc"},\text{"acb"})$, the effect of having done a single transposition can be achieved by allowing a free substitution between the latter characters of the transposable suffixes. This is the same as declaring a match between them. In this way the cost for doing the transposition has already been paid for by the substitution of the preceding step. It turns out that this idea can be developed to work correctly in all cases. We find that the following Recurrence 3 for the Damerau edit distance is in effect equivalent with Recurrence 2. It uses an auxiliary $|A| \times (|B| + 1)$ boolean table MT as it is convenient for bit-parallel algorithms. The value $MT[i,j]$ records whether there is the possibility to match or to make a free substitution when computing the value $D[i,j]$.

Recurrence 3

$$D[i,0] = i, D[0,j] = j, MT[i,0] = \textbf{false}.$$

$$MT[i,j] = \begin{cases} \textbf{true, if } A_i = B_j \text{ or } (MT[i-1,j-1] = \textbf{false and} \\ \qquad\qquad A_{i-1..i} = (B_{j-1..j})^R). \\ \textbf{false, otherwise.} \end{cases}$$

$$D[i,j] = \begin{cases} D[i-1,j-1], \text{ if } MT[i,j] = \textbf{true.} \\ 1 + \min(D[i-1,j-1], D[i-1,j], D[i,j-1]), \text{ otherwise.} \end{cases}$$

We prove by induction that Recurrence 2 and Recurrence 3 give the same values for $D[i,j]$ when $i \geq 0$ and $j \geq 0$.

Clearly both formulas give the same value for $D[i,j]$ when $i = 0$ or 1 or $j = 0$ or 1. Consider now a cell $D[i,j]$ for some $j > 1$ and $i > 1$ and assume that all previous cells with nonnegative indices have been filled identically by both recurrences[2]. Let x be the value given to $D[i,j]$ by Recurrence 2 and y be the

---

[2] We assume that a legal filling order has been used, which means that the cells $D[i-1,j-1]$, $D[i-1,j]$ and $D[i,j-1]$ are always filled before the cell $D[i,j]$.

value given to it by Recurrence 3. The only situation in which the two formulas could possibly behave differently is when $A_i \neq B_j$ and $A_{i-1..i} = (B_{j-1..j})^R$. In the following two cases we assume that these two conditions hold.

If $D[i-1, j-1] = D[i-2, j-2] + 1$, then $MT[i-1, j-1] =$ **false** and $MT[i, j] =$ **true**, and thus $y = D[i-1, j-1]$. Since the diagonal property requires that $x \geq D[i-1, j-1]$ and now $x \leq D[i-2, j-2] + 1$, we have $x = D[i-2, j-2] + 1 = D[i-1, j-1] = y$.

Now consider the case $D[i-2, j-2] = D[i-1, j-1]$. Because $A_{i-1} = B_j \neq A_i = B_{j-1}$, this equality cannot result from a match. If it resulted from a free substitution, then $MT[i-1, j-1] =$ **true** in Recurrence 3. As $A_i \neq B_j$, the preceding means that $MT[i, j] =$ **false**. Therefore $y = 1 + \min(D[i-1, j-1], D[i-1, j], D[i, j-1])$ and $x = 1 + \min(D[i-2, j-2], D[i-1, j], D[i, j-1])$. Because $D[i-2, j-2] = D[i-1, j-1]$, the former means that $x = 1 + \min(D[i-1, j-1], D[i-1, j], D[i, j-1]) = y$. The last possibility is that the equality $D[i-2, j-2] = D[i-1, j-1]$ resulted from using the option $D[i-1, j-1] = 1 + \min(D[i-2, j-1], D[i-1, j-2])$. As $A_{i-1} = B_j$ and $A_i = B_{j-1}$, both recurrences must have set $D[i-1, j] = D[i-2, j-1]$ and $D[i, j-1] = D[i-1, j-2]$ and therefore $D[i-1, j-1] = 1 + \min(D[i-2, j-1], D[i-1, j-2]) = 1 + \min(D[i-1, j], D[i, j-1])$. Now both options in Recurrence 3 set the same value $y = D[i-1, j-1]$, and $x = 1 + \min(D[i-2, j-2], D[i-1, j], D[i, j-1]) = 1 + \min(D[i-1, j], D[i, j-1]) = D[i-1, j-1] = y$.

In each case Recurrence 2 and Recurrence 3 assigned the same value for the cell $D[i, j]$. Therefore we can state by induction that the recurrences are in effect equivalent.   □

The intuition behind the table MT in Recurrence 3 is that a free substitution is allowed at $D[i, j]$ if a transposition is possible at that location. But we cannot allow more than one free substitution in a row along a diagonal, as each corresponding transposition has to be paid for by a regular substitution. Therefore when a transposition has been possible at $D[i, j]$, another will not be allowed at $D[i+1, j+1]$. And as shown above, this restriction on when to permit a transposition does not affect the correctness of the scheme.

3   Modifying the Bit-Parallel Algorithms

Bit-parallel algorithms are based on taking advantage of the fact that a single computer instruction manipulates bit-vectors with w bits (typically $w = 32$ or 64 in the current computers). If many data-items of an algorithm can be encoded into w bits, it may be possible to process many data-items within a single instruction (thus the name bit-parallelism) and achieve gain in time and/or space.

We use the following notation in describing bit-operations: '&' denotes bitwise "and", '|' denotes bitwise "or", '∧' denotes bitwise "xor", '~' denotes bit complementation, and '<<' and '>>' denote shifting the bit-vector left and right, respectively, using zero filling in both directions. The ith bit of the bit vector V is referred to as $V[i]$ and bit-positions are assumed to grow from right to left. In addition we use superscript to denote bit-repetition. As an example let $V = 1001110$ be a bit vector. Then $V[1] = V[5] = V[6] = 0$, $V[2] = V[3] = V[4] = V[7] = 1$, and we could also write $V = 10^2 1^3 0$.

3.1   The Bit-Parallel NFA of Wu & Manber

The bit-parallel approximate string matching algorithm of Wu & Manber [15] is based on representing a non-deterministic finite automaton (NFA) by using bit-vectors. The automaton has $(k + 1)$ rows, numbered from 0 to k, and each row contains m states. Let us denote the automaton as R, its row d as R_d and the state i on its row d as $R_{d,i}$. The state $R_{d,i}$ is active after reading the text up to the jth character if and only if $ed(P_{1..i}, T_{h..j}) \leq d$ for some $h \leq j$. An occurrence of the pattern with at most k errors is found when the state $R_{k,m}$ is active. Assume for now that $w \leq m$. Wu & Manber represent each row R_d as a length-m bit-vector, where the ith bit tells whether the state $R_{d,i}$ is active or not. In addition they build a length-m match vector for each character in the alphabet. We denote the match vector for the character λ as PM_λ. The ith bit of PM_λ is set if and only if $P_i = \lambda$. Initially each vector R_d has the value $0^{m-d}1^d$ (this corresponds to the boundary conditions in Recurrence 1). The formula to compute the updated values R'_d for the row-vectors R_d at text position j is the following:

$R'_0 \leftarrow ((R_0 << 1) \mid 0^{m-1}1) \; \& \; PM_{T_j}$
For $d = 1$ to k Do
  $R'_i \leftarrow ((R_i << 1) \; \& \; PM_{T_j}) \mid R_{i-1} \mid (R_{i-1} << 1) \mid (R'_{i-1} << 1)$

The right side of the last row computes the disjunction of the different possibilities given by Recurrence 1 for a prefix of the pattern to match with d errors. The row R_0 is different as it needs to consider only matching positions between P and the character T_j, and it also has to have its first bit set after the left-shift in order to let the first character match at the current position. When $m \leq w$, the run time of this algorithm is $O(kn)$ as there are $O(k)$ operations per text character. The general run time is $O(kn\lceil m/w \rceil)$ as a vector of length m may be simulated in $O(\lceil m/w \rceil)$ time using $O(\lceil m/w \rceil)$ bit-vectors of length w. In this paper we do not discuss the details of such a multi-word implementation for any of the bit-parallel algorithms.

Navarro [9] has modified this algorithm to use the Damerau distance by essentially following Recurrence 2. He did this by appending the automaton to have a temporary state vector T_d for each R_d to keep track of the positions where transposition may occur. Initially each T_d has the value 0^m. Navarro's formula is:

$R'_0 \leftarrow ((R_0 << 1) \mid 0^{m-1}1) \; \& \; PM_{T_j}$
For $d = 1$ to k Do
  $R'_i \leftarrow ((R_i << 1) \; \& \; PM_{T_j}) \mid R_{i-1} \mid (R_{i-1} << 1) \mid (R'_{i-1} << 1)$
    $\mid (T_i \; \& \; (B_{T_j} << 1))$
  $T'_i \leftarrow (R_{i-1} << 2) \; \& \; PM_{T_j}$

The formula adds $6k$ operations into the basic version for the Levenshtein edit distance.

Recurrence 3 suggests a simpler way to facilitate transposition. The only difference between it and Recurrence 1 is in the condition on when $D[i, j] = D[i-1, j-1]$: Instead of the condition $P_i = T_j$, Recurrence 3 sets the equal value if $MT[i, j] = $ **true** (here we again replaced A with P and B with T in the recurrence). We use a length-m bit-vector TC in storing the last column of the auxiliary table MT. The ith bit of TC is set iff row i of the last column of MT has the value **true**. When we arrive at text position j, TC is updated to hold the values of column j. Initially $TC = 0^m$. Based on Recurrence 3, the vector TC may be updated with the formula $TC' = PM_{T_j} \mid (((\sim TC) << 1)$ & $(PM_{T_j} << 1)$ & $PM_{T_{j-1}})$. Here the right "and" sets the bits in the pattern positions where $P_{i-1..i} = (T_{j-1..j})^R$, the left "and" sets off the ith bit if row $(i-1)$ of MT had the value **true** in the previous column, and the "or" sets the bits in the positions where $P_i = T_j$. By combining the two left-shifts we get the following complete formula for updating the R_d vectors:

$$TC' \leftarrow PM_{T_j} \mid ((((\sim TC) \ \& \ PM_{T_j}) << 1) \ \& \ PM_{T_{j-1}})$$
$$R_0' \leftarrow ((R_0 << 1) \mid 0^{m-1}1) \ \& \ PM_{T_j}$$
For $d = 1$ **to** k **Do**
$$\qquad R_i' \leftarrow ((R_i << 1) \ \& \ TC') \mid R_{i-1} \mid (R_{i-1} << 1) \mid (R_{i-1}' << 1)$$

Our formula adds a total of 6 operations into the basic version for the Levenshtein edit distance. Therefore it makes the same number of operations as Navarro's version when $k = 1$, and wins when $k > 1$.

3.2   The Bit-Parallel NFA of Baeza-Yates & Navarro

Also the bit-parallel algorithm of Baeza-Yates & Navarro [1] is based on simulating the NFA R. The first d states on row R_d are trivial in that they are always active. The last $m - k + d$ states will be active only if the state $R_{k,m}$ is active, and as we are only interested in knowing whether there is a match with at most k errors, having the state $R_{k,m}$ is enough. These facts enable Baeza-Yates & Navarro to include only the $m - k$ states $R_{d,d+1}..R_{d,m-k+d}$ on row R_d. A further difference is in the way the states are encoded into bit-vectors. They divide R into $m - k$ diagonals $D_1, .., D_{m-k}$, where D_i is a bit-sequence that describes the states $R_{d,d+i}$ for $d = 0..k$. If a state $R_{d,i}$ is active, then all states on the same diagonal that come after $R_{d,i}$ are active, that is, the states $R_{d+h,i+h}$ for $h \geq 1$. To describe the status of the ith diagonal it suffices to record the position of the first active state in it. If the first active state on the ith diagonal is f_i, then Baeza-Yates & Navarro represent the diagonal as the bit-sequence $D_i = 0^{k+1-f_i}1^{f_i}$. The value $f_i = k + 1$ means that $f_i \geq k + 1$, that is, that no states on the ith diagonal of R are active. A match with at most k errors is found whenever $f_{m-k} < k + 1$. The d_i bit-sequences are stored consecutively with a single separator zero-bit between two consecutive states. Let RD denote the complete diagonal representation. Then RD is the length-$(k + 2)(m - k)$

bit-sequence $0\ D_1\ 0\ D_2\ 0...0\ D_{m-k}$. We assume for now that $(k+2)(m-k) \leq w$ so that RD fits into a single bit-vector.

Baeza-Yates & Navarro encode also the pattern match vectors differently. Let PMD_λ be their pattern match vector for the character λ. The role of the bits is reversed: a 0-bit denotes a match and a 1-bit a mismatch. To align the matches with the diagonals in RD, PMD_λ has the form

$$0 \sim (PM_\lambda[1..k+1])\ \ 0\ \ \sim (PM_\lambda[2..k+2])\ \ 0...0\ \ \sim (PM_\lambda[m-k..m]).$$

Initially no diagonal has active states and so $RD = (0\ 1^{k+1})^{m-k}$. The formula for updating RD at text position j is:

$$
\begin{aligned}
x \leftarrow &\ (RD >> (k+2))\ |\ PMD_{T_j}\\
RD' \leftarrow &\ ((RD << 1)\ |\ (0^{k+1}1)^{m-k}\\
& \&\ (RD << (k+3))\ |\ (0^{k+1}1)^{m-k-1}01^{k+1}\\
& \&\ (((x + (0^{k+1}1)^{m-k}) \wedge x) >> 1)\\
& \&\ (0\ 1^{k+1})^{m-k}
\end{aligned}
$$

If $(k+2)(m-k) \leq w$, the run time of this algorithm is $O(n)$ as there is only a constant number of operations per text character. The general run time is $O(\lceil km/w \rceil n)$ as a vector of length $(k+2)(m-k)$ may be simulated in $O(\lceil km/w \rceil)$ time using $O(\lceil km/w \rceil)$ bit-vectors of length w.

Because of the different way of representing R, our way of modifying the algorithm of Wu & Manber to use the Damerau edit distance does not work here without some changes. Now we use a bit-vector TCD instead of the vector TC of the previous section. TCD has the same function as TC, but its form corresponds to the algorithm of Baeza-Yates & Navarro. First of all the meaning of the bit-values is reversed: now a 0-bit corresponds to the value **true** and a 1-bit to the value **false** in the table TR of Recurrence 3. The second change is in the way we compute the positions where $P_{i-1..i} = (T_{j-1..j})^R$. Because of the interleaving 0-bits in the pattern match vector PMD_λ, the formula $(PMD_{T_j} << 1)\ |\ PMD_{T_{j-1}}$ does not correctly set only those bits to zero that correspond to a transposable position (note that also the roles of '&' and '|' are reversed). But by inspecting the form of BPD_λ we notice that the desired effect is achieved by using the formula $(PMD_{T_j} >> (k+2))\ |\ PMD_{T_{j-1}}$. Shifting $(k+2)$ bits to the right causes the $(i-1)$th diagonal to align with the ith diagonal, and this previous diagonal handles the matches one step to the left in the pattern. The only delicacy in doing this is the fact that now the first diagonal will have no match-data. Because we need to have made a substitution before making a free substitution that corresponds to a transposition, a transposition will be possible only in diagonals $2..m-k$. Thus the missing data can be replaced with mismatches. Note that we do not need to consider the states not present in the reduced automaton of Baeza-Yates & Navarro. By similar reasoning also the previous values of TCD will be shifted $(k+2)$ bits to the right instead of 1 bit to the left, and its missing data can be replaced by '**false**' values. Initially TCD has only '**false**' values and so $TCD = (0\ 1^{k+1})^{m-k}$. The modified formula for updating RD at text position j is:

$$TCD' \leftarrow (PMD_{T_j} \& ((((\sim TCD) \mid PMD_{T_j}) >> (k+2)) \mid PMD_{T_{j-1}}))$$
$$\mid 01^{k+1}0^{(m-k-1)(k+2)}$$
$$x \leftarrow (RD >> (k+2)) \mid TCD'$$
$$RD' \leftarrow ((RD << 1) \mid (0^{k+1}1)^{m-k}$$
$$\& (RD << (k+3)) \mid (0^{k+1}1)^{m-k-1}01^{k+1}$$
$$\& (((x + (0^{k+1}1)^{m-k}) \wedge x) >> 1)$$
$$\& (0 \ 1^{k+1})^{m-k}$$

Now the number of added operations is 7, as one "extra" operation arises from having to set the missing values (second row).

3.3 Myers' Bit-Parallel Computation of D

The bit-parallel algorithm of Myers [7] is quite different from the previous two algorithms. We describe it here in a slightly simpler way than the original, even though the logic is in principle the same. The algorithm is based on representing the dynamic programming table D with vertical, horizontal and diagonal differences (see the adjacency and diagonal properties in Section 2). This is done by using the following length-m bit-vectors:

-The vertical positive delta vector VP:
  $VP[i] = 1$ at text position j iff $D[i,j] - D[i-1,j] = 1$.
-The vertical negative delta vector VN:
  $VN[i] = 1$ at text position j iff $D[i,j] - D[i-1,j] = -1$.
-The horizontal positive delta vector HP:
  $HP[i] = 1$ at text position j iff $D[i,j] - D[i,j-1] = 1$.
-The horizontal negative delta vector HN:
  $HN[i] = 1$ at text position j iff $D[i,j] - D[i,j-1] = -1$.
-The diagonal zero delta vector $D0$:
  $D0[i] = 1$ at text position j iff $D[i,j] = D[i-1,j-1]$.

In the original work of Myers the information of the vector $D0$ was represented by two separate vectors x_v and x_h.

Initially $VP = 1^m$ and $VN = 0^m$. At text position j the algorithm first computes the vector $D0$ by using the old values VP and VN and the pattern match vector PM_{T_j} (Section 3.1). Then the new HP and HN are computed by using $D0$ and the old VP and VN. Then finally the vectors VP and VN are updated by using the new $D0$, HN and HP. The complete formula for computing the updated vectors $D0', HP', HN', VN'$ and VP' at text position j is:

$$D0' \leftarrow (((PM_{T_j} \& VP) + VP) \wedge VP) \mid PM_{T_j} \mid VN$$
$$HP' \leftarrow VN \mid \sim (D0' \mid VP)$$
$$HN' \leftarrow VP \& D0'$$
$$VP' \leftarrow (HN' << 1) \mid \sim (D0' \mid HP')$$
$$VN' \leftarrow HP' \& D0'$$

The current value of the dynamic programming cell $D[m,j]$ can be updated at each text position j by using the horizontal delta vectors (the initial value is $D[m,0] = m$). A match of the pattern with at most k errors is found whenever $D[m,j] \leq k$.

If $m \leq w$, the run time of this algorithm is $O(n)$ as there is again only a constant number of operations per text character. The general run time is $O(\lceil m/w \rceil n)$ as a vector of length m may be simulated in $O(\lceil m/w \rceil)$ time using $O(\lceil m/w \rceil)$ bit-vectors of length w.

Because the algorithm of Myers uses the same pattern match vectors as the algorithm of Wu & Manber, it can be modified to use the Damerau distance by using exactly the same method as we used in Section 3.1. Thus the formula to update the vectors at text position j is simply:

$$TC' \leftarrow PM_{T_j} \mid ((((\sim TC) \ \& \ PM_{T_j}) << 1) \ \& \ PM_{T_{j-1}})$$
$$D0' \leftarrow (((TC' \ \& \ VP) + VP) \wedge VP) \mid TC' \mid VN$$
$$HP' \leftarrow VN \mid \ \sim (D0' \mid VP)$$
$$HN' \leftarrow VP \ \& \ D0'$$
$$VP' \leftarrow (HN' << 1) \mid \ \sim (D0' \mid HP')$$
$$VN' \leftarrow HP' \ \& \ D0'$$

There is again 6 added operations.

4   Test Results

We implemented and tested a Damerau edit distance -version of each of the three discussed bit-parallel algorithms. The version of the algorithm of Wu & Manber was implemented from scratch by us, and the other two were modified using the original implementations from those authors. We compared also the versions for the Levenshtein edit distance to see how our modification affects the respective performance of the algorithms. The computer used in the tests was a 600 Mhz Pentium 3 with 256 MB RAM and Linux OS. All code was compiled with GCC 3.2.1 and full optimization switched on.

The tests involved patterns of lengths 10, 20, and 30, and with each pattern length m the tested k values were $1..\lfloor m/2 \rfloor$. There were 50 randomly picked patterns for each (m,k)-combination. The searched text was a 10 MB sample from Wall Street Journal articles taken from the TREC-collection [4].

The version of the algorithm of Baeza-Yates & Navarro was the one from [10], which includes a smart mechanism to keep only a required part of the automaton active when it needs several bit-vectors. As the patterns lengths were $\leq w = 32$, the other two algorithms did not need such a mechanism.

Fig. 2 shows the results. In general the algorithms compare quite similarly to each other with and without our modification to use the Damerau edit distance. It is seen that with the Levenshtein edit distance the algorithm of Wu & Manber becomes slowest when $k \geq 4$, whereas with the Damerau edit distance it becomes slowest already at $k = 3$. The algorithm of Baeza-Yates & Navarro is typically the fastest for low error levels irrespective of which of the two distances we use. But

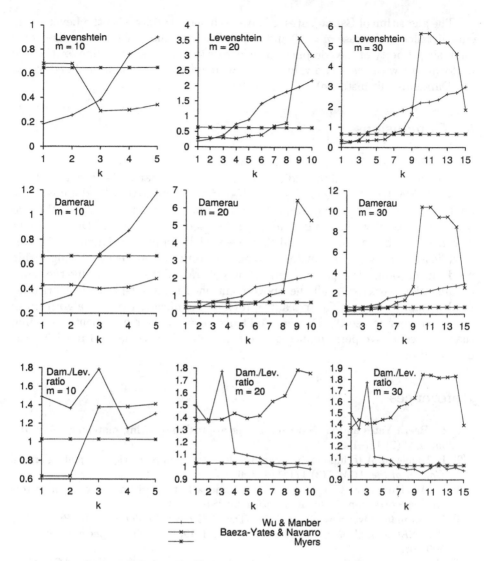

Fig. 2. The two first rows show the average time for searching a pattern from a 10 MB sample of Wall Street Journal articles taken from TREC-collection. The first row shows the results for the Levenshtein edit distance and the second row for the Damerau edit distance. The third row shows the ratio of the run times with and without the modification.

its advantage over the algorithm of Myers becomes smaller under the Damerau edit distance. The algorithm of Myers is affected very little by the modification, and it is the fastest algorithm when the error level k/m is large and the algorithm of Baeza-Yates & Navarro needs more bit-vectors in representing the automaton.

The algorithm of Baeza-Yates & Navarro behaved oddly with the Levenshtein edit distance in the case $m = 10$ and $k < 3$. We found no other reason than some intrinsic property of the compiler optimizer or the processor pipeline for the bad performance with these two values (even worse than the version modified to use the Damerau edit distance).

5   Conclusions

Bit-parallel algorithms are currently the fastest approximate string matching algorithms when Levenshtein edit distance is used. In particular the algorithms of Wu & Manber [15], Baeza-Yates & Navarro [1] and Myers [7] dominate the field when the pattern length and the error level are moderate [8]. In this paper we showed how these algorithms can be modified to use the Damerau edit distance, which is an important distance especially in natural language [5]. Our modification adds only a constant amount of work per bit-vector the algorithm needs in encoding the pattern, and it is general in that essentially the same modification works with all the above-mentioned three bit-parallel algorithms. It also improves upon Navarro's [9] previous modification of the algorithm of Wu & Manber to use the Damerau edit distance. In the experiments we found that the respective performance of the algorithms is not changed much by the modification.

References

[1] R. Baeza-Yates and G. Navarro. Faster approximate string matching. *Algorithmica*, 23(2):127–158, 1999.

[2] F. Damerau. A technique for computer detection and correction of spelling errors. *Comm. of the ACM*, 7(3):171–176, 1964.

[3] M. W. Du and S. C. Chang. A model and a fast algorithm for multiple errors spelling correction. *Acta Informatica*, 29:281–302, 1992.

[4] D. Harman. Overview of the Third Text REtrieval Conference. In *Proc. Third Text REtrieval Conference (TREC-3)*, pages 1–19, 1995. NIST Special Publication 500-207.

[5] K. Kukich. Techniques for automatically correcting words in text. *ACM Computing Surveys*, 24(4):377–439, 1992.

[6] V. Levenshtein. Binary codes capable of correcting deletions, insertions and reversals. *Soviet Physics Doklady*, 10(8):707–710, 1966. Original in Russian in *Doklady Akademii Nauk SSSR, 163(4):845–848, 1965*.

[7] G. Myers. A fast bit-vector algorithm for approximate string matching based on dynamic progamming. *Journal of the ACM*, 46(3):395–415, 1999.

[8] G. Navarro. A guided tour to approximate string matching. *ACM Computing Surveys*, 33(1):31–88, 2001.

[9] G. Navarro. NR-grep: a fast and flexible pattern matching tool. *Software Practice and Experience (SPE)*, 31:1265–1312, 2001.

[10] G. Navarro and R. Baeza-Yates. Improving an algorithm for approximate pattern matching. *Algorithmica*, 30(4):473–502, 2001.

[11] P. Sellers. The theory and computation of evolutionary distances: pattern recognition. *J. of Algorithms*, 1:359–373, 1980.

[12] Esko Ukkonen. Algorithms for approximate string matching. *Information and Control*, 64:100–118, 1985.

[13] Esko Ukkonen. Finding approximate patterns in strings. *J. of Algorithms*, 6:132–137, 1985.

[14] A. Wright. Approximate string matching using within-word parallelism. *Software Practice and Experience*, 24(4):337–362, April 1994.

[15] S. Wu and U. Manber. Fast text searching allowing errors. *Comm. of the ACM*, 35(10):83–91, October 1992.

Processing of Huffman Compressed Texts
with a Super-Alphabet

Kimmo Fredriksson[1*] and Jorma Tarhio[2]

[1] Department of CS, University of Joensuu
P.O. Box 111, FIN-80101 Joensuu, Finland
kfredrik@cs.joensuu.fi
[2] Department of CSE, Helsinki University of Technology
P.O. Box 5400, FIN-02015 HUT, Finland
tarhio@cs.hut.fi

Abstract. We present an efficient algorithm for scanning Huffman compressed texts. The algorithm parses the compressed text in $O(n\frac{\log_2 \sigma}{b})$ time, where n is the size of the compressed text in bytes, σ is the size of the alphabet, and b is a user specified parameter. The method uses a variable size super-alphabet, with an average size of $O(\frac{b}{H \log_2 \sigma})$ symbols, where H is the entropy of the text. Each super-symbol is processed in $O(1)$ time. The algorithm uses $O(2^b)$ space, and $O(b2^b)$ preprocessing time. The method can be easily augmented by auxiliary functions, which can e.g. decompress the text, or perform pattern matching in the compressed text. We give three example functions: decoding the text in average time $O(n\frac{\log_2 \sigma}{Hw})$, where w is the number of bits in a machine word; an Aho-Corasick dictionary matching algorithm, which works in time $O(n\frac{\log_2 \sigma}{b} + t)$, where t is the number of occurrences reported; and a shift-or string matching algorithm that works in time $O(n\frac{\log_2 \sigma}{b}\lceil (m+s)/w \rceil + t)$, where m is the length of the pattern and s depends on the encoding. The Aho-Corasick algorithm uses an automaton with variable length moves, i.e. it processes variable number of states at each step. The shift-or algorithm makes variable length shifts, effectively also processing variable number of states at each step. The number of states processed in $O(1)$ time is $O(\frac{b}{H \log_2 \sigma})$. The method can be applied to several other algorithms as well. We conclude with some experimental results.

1 Introduction

Huffman coding [8] is a well-known and extensively studied text compression method. It assigns for each symbol of the input a codeword, i.e. a string of bits. The more frequent the symbol is the shorter its codeword is. Huffman [8] showed how to obtain optimal *prefix codes*, i.e. no codeword is a prefix of another codeword. The entropy of the alphabet Σ is

---

* Work partially developed when the author was working in Department of Computer Science, University of Helsinki. Partially supported by the Academy of Finland.

M.A. Nascimento, E.S. de Moura, A.L. Oliveira (Eds.): SPIRE 2003, LNCS 2857, pp. 108–121, 2003.

$$H = -\sum_{c \in \Sigma} p_c \log_2 p_c,$$

where p_c is the probability of a symbol c. If the input is u bytes long, then the compressed form is approximately $n = Hu$ bytes long.

In the *string matching problem*, which is common in many applications, the task is to find all the occurrences of a given string pattern in a text. Recently the *compressed matching problem* [2] has gained much attention. The trivial method is to first decompress the text, and then perform the search operation. The preferred method is to search the compressed text directly, maybe taking advantage of its shorter representation. Researchers have proposed several efficient methods [3,9,11,12] based on Huffman coding [8] or the Ziv-Lempel family [16,17].

In the following we consider matching of multiple patterns in Huffman compressed texts. The work by Takeda et al. [13] gave motivation for this work. Our methods apply a super-alphabet, which means that several codewords can be processed at the same time. Fredriksson [7] got good results in speeding up standard string matching with super-alphabets. Our idea of utilizing super-alphabets in the context of Huffman compression is related with older approaches [6,14] to speed up decompression. In particular, we apply super-alphabets to the Aho-Corasick algorithm [1] and to the shift-or algorithm [4,15].

The Aho-Corasick automaton (the AC automaton for short) is extended to make transitions with compressed character tuples, the size of the tuple depending on the entropy H. We also extend the shift-or string matching algorithm to make variable length shifts, again the shift length depending on H. Hence the better the compression ratio is the faster the algorithms run. We first give an efficient algorithm for scanning Huffman compressed texts. The method can then be easily augmented by auxiliary functions, which can e.g. decompress the text, or perform pattern matching in the compressed text.

All the algorithms are linear in u and n, where u and n are the lengths (in bytes) of the original and compressed texts, respectively, i.e. they are $O(n) = O(u)$, but they can be said to be sublinear in the sense that the number of steps is less than n or u by a constant factor. For example, the AC automaton runs in $O(uH \log_2 \sigma/b) = O(n \log_2 \sigma/b)$ steps, where b is a user chosen (constant) parameter. We use this notion of sublinearity.

2   Preliminaries

Let a *text* $W[1..u]$ be a string in an alphabet Σ of size σ. The Huffman compressed text of W is denoted by $T[1..n]$. The number of characters in W and the number of codewords in T is u. The compressed text T occupies only $n < u$ bytes of storage. Similarly, a *pattern* $P[1..m]$ is a string in the same alphabet Σ. A *dictionary* $\mathcal{D} = \{P_1, P_2, ..., P_d\}$ is a set of d patterns. For simplicity and without loss of generality, we assume that each pattern in $\mathcal{D}$ has the same length m.

The alphabet Σ may contain symbols that do not appear in W. This is a typical situation, consider, e.g. a natural language text in the ASCII alphabet. The codewords are generated only for those symbols that appear in W. At this point one should note that if the pattern contains symbols that have no codeword, then the pattern cannot have any exact occurrences in W.

3   Basic Tools

Before describing the actual algorithms, we introduce a method for scanning the compressed text efficiently. The algorithms will process and "decode" the compressed input in blocks of b bits. Our approach is more general than that of [14], where only $b = 8$ is considered. Let us denote a block of b bits by Q. The block Q may encode several, one, or no original symbols of the original text, depending on b and on the length of the codewords. In the best case, Q encodes b symbols, each having a codeword of length 1. In addition, Q may contain a prefix of another codeword. We denote the ith bit of Q by Q_i.

We associate with Q several attributes, which are preprocessed and stored for every possible Q.

- $s(Q)$: the bit-pattern Q encodes $s(Q)$ symbols, $0 \le s(Q) \le b$.
- $r(Q)$: the number of remaining bits in Q, i.e. the length of the proper prefix of the next codeword; Q contains this prefix.
- $h(Q)$ the node in the Huffman tree after traversing the tree with the prefix $Q_{b-r(Q)+1}..Q_b$ of length $r(Q)$.

Q may have some additional attributes, depending on the algorithm. For example, if we wanted to decode the original text, we could add an attribute $c(Q)$ that stores the $s(Q)$ symbols of Σ that Q encodes.

Having this information for every Q, it is easy and efficient to traverse through the compressed file, keeping track of the codeword boundaries. Q is initialized with the first b bits of the compressed input string. Then if $s > 0$, we do whatever processing is required (e.g. dump $c(Q)$), shift the bits in Q to the right by $b-r(Q)$ bit positions, and pad Q with the next $b - r(Q)$ bits.

If $s = 0$, i.e. the whole Q was a prefix of a codeword, then we jump to the node $h(Q)$, and continue the "decoding" from there, until we reach the leaf (and e.g. dump the symbol stored in the leaf). Then we continue without the tree.

Our scanning algorithm is somewhat similar to the one given by Choueka et al. [6], but ours is simpler. Particularly, they process the remaining bits in a different way. They construct a separate look-up table of Q for each possible number of remaining bits of the previous step. Thus their approach consumes more memory than ours.

The basic scanning algorithm is given in pseudocode in Alg. 1. For simplicity of presentation, the algorithm implicitly assumes that $b = 8$, i.e. Q contains one byte, but it is trivial to modify the algorithm to use general b, while maintaining constant time updates of Q.

We use the following notation. A machine word has w bits, numbered from the least significant bit to the most significant bit. For bit-wise operations of words a C-like notation is used, & is **and**, | is **or**, and $<<$ and $>>$ are shift to left, and shift to right with zero padding.

The scanning algorithm takes an auxiliary function $A(Q, h(Q))$ as a parameter, which is called whenever at least one symbol is "decoded". If the first parameter $Q \neq 0$, then Q denotes the current bit-pattern the scanning algorithm has read, and it encodes ≥ 1 symbols of the original text. Otherwise, Q was a prefix of a code word, and the scanning algorithm traversed into a leaf of the Huffman tree bit by bit, and $h(Q)$ is a pointer to that leaf, that stores one original symbol. Otherwise we pass $h(Q) = $ NULL. Using the function A it is easy to write other algorithms that process the compressed data. For example, the decoding function is given in Alg. 2.

The time complexity of the scanning algorithm is

$$O\left(u \frac{H \log_2 \sigma}{b}\right) = O\left(n \frac{\log_2 \sigma}{b}\right),$$

as there are u characters in the original text, one codeword takes $O(H \log_2 \sigma)$ bits, where H is the entropy, and we process $O(b)$ bits at a single step.

Alg. 2 can output $\lfloor w/\log_2 \sigma \rfloor$ characters at a time. There are $O(b/(H \log_2 \sigma))$ symbols to output on average. Hence, the complexity of the decoding algorithm is

$$O\left(n \frac{\log_2 \sigma}{b} \frac{\log_2 \sigma}{w} \frac{b}{H \log_2 \sigma}\right) = O\left(n \frac{\log_2 \sigma}{Hw}\right).$$

Note that this analysis is valid only for b large enough, i.e. $b/(H \log_2 \sigma) > w/\log_2 \sigma$ should hold, i.e. $b > Hw$. Otherwise it is $O(u)$ in the worst case.

In the sequel we give functions A that perform efficient (dictionary) pattern matching in the compressed text.

Preprocessing the attributes. The attributes can be computed by generating every possible Q, in time $O(2^b)$, and then traversing the Huffman tree in time b for each generated Q. Every time we arrive into a leaf, we update the (basic) attribute information in time $O(1)$ (for some other attributes, depending on the application, the updating can take more time). Finally, $h(Q)$ is the node where we ended up after b steps. Hence, the total time is $O(b2^b)$, which is affordable for small values of b. In practice the optimal b is between 8–14, see Sec. 6. In our implementation in C, we have an array of structs for the attributes, indexed with Q.

4   Aho-Corasick Automaton

The AC automaton [1] is a finite automaton for searching a set of pattern from a text of length u in time $O(u + t)$, where t is the number of occurrences found. The automaton contains $O(dm)$ states. It can be made deterministic, so that each node has a transition for each character in the alphabet. We build directly a deterministic automaton in time $O(dm\sigma)$, and the result uses $O(dm\sigma)$ space. Our algorithm does effectively the same as the algorithm in [13], but is simpler and more efficient.

Alg. 1 $\text{Scan}(A(Q,v))$.

Input: auxiliary function $A(Q,v)$
Output: output of A

```
1        i ← 1, Q ← T[1], l ← b, v ← NULL
2        while i ≤ n                        // ANY INPUT LEFT?
3           if l < b                        // LESS THAN b BITS LEFT IN Q?
4              i ← i + 1
5              if i ≤ n
6                 Q ← Q | (T[i] << l)       // APPEND Q WITH THE NEXT b BITS
7                 l ← l + b
8           Q' ← Q & ((1 << b) − 1)         // PUT THE b FIRST BITS OF Q TO Q'
9           if v = NULL                      // TRAVERSING THE HUFFMAN TREE?
10             if s(Q') > 0                  // NO. Q' CODES ANY SYMBOL?
11                A(Q', NULL)                // YES, CALL THE AUXILIARY FUNCTION
12                s ← b − r(Q')              // s OUT OF b BITS PROCESSED
13             else                          // Q' WAS JUST A PREFIX, SO...
14                v ← h(Q')                  // JUMP TO NODE v IN THE TREE
15                s ← b                      // b BITS PROCESSED
16             Q ← Q >> s                    // REMOVE THE PROCESSED BITS
17             l ← l − s
18          else                             // TRAVERSING THE HUFFMAN TREE
19             if v is a leaf
20                A(0, v)
21                v ← NULL                   // CONTINUE W/O THE TREE
22             else
23                if Q & 1 = 0
24                   v ← left(v)
25                else
26                   v ← right(v)
27             Q ← Q >> 1                    // REMOVE THE PROCESSED BIT
28             l ← l − 1
```

Alg. 2 $\text{Dump}(Q,v)$.

Input: bit-pattern Q, leaf v of the Huffman tree
Output: the symbols coded by Q or v

```
1        if v = NULL                         // USING THE HUFFMAN TREE?
2           output(c(Q))                     // NO, OUTPUT THE SYMBOLS OF Q
3        else                                // v IS A LEAF,
4           output(v.symbol)                 // SO OUTPUT THE SYMBOL
```

Transitions with compressed character tuples. Each node node v in the automaton has transition $\delta(v,c) \to v'$, for each $c \in \Sigma$. In [7] a super-alphabet method was used to simulate deterministic automata efficiently. The basic idea is that when a *set* of characters is interpreted as one super-symbol, i.e. a catenation of the original symbols, it is possible to precompute a *shortcut* transition to the state where the original transitions would lead with that set of the original symbols. In our case, Q implicitly codes a varying length super-symbol, the length for a specific Q being $s(Q)$. We therefore precompute the shortcut transitions $\Delta(v, Q)$ for each state v of the automaton, and for each possible Q. It is also possible that this shortcut transition goes through several accepting states of the original automaton. To take this into account, we collect the output information into attribute $o(v, Q)$. The preprocessing time for a straight-forward method is $O(dm(\sigma + \frac{b}{H \log_2 \sigma}2^b) + b2^b)$, which is reasonable for small b. This can be improved to $O(dm(\sigma + 2^b) + b2^b)$ by using incremental evaluation of the shortcut transitions.

Alg. 3 gives the auxiliary function for the AC automaton. The total time of the algorithm is $O(t)$, where t is the number of matches reported, or $O(1)$, if we only count the number of matches. Hence the expected time of Alg. 1 with Alg. 3 is

$$O\left(n\frac{\log_2 \sigma}{b} + t\right),$$

which is sublinear for most reasonable choices of parameters.

Alg. 3 $AC(Q, v)$.

Input: bit-pattern Q, leaf v of the Huffman tree
Output: matches, if any

```
1      if v = NULL                           // USING THE HUFFMAN TREE?
2          state' ← Δ(state, Q)              // NO, MAKE SUPER-TRANSITION
3          if o(state, Q) has outputs
4              output the occurrences
5      else                                  // v IS A LEAF,
6          state' ← δ(state, v.symbol)       // SO MAKE A NORMAL TRANSITION
7          if o(state, v.symbol) has outputs
8              output occurrences
9      state ← state'                        // UPDATE THE CURRENT state
```

Takeda et al. [13,14] use a separate DFA to distinguish the beginning of codewords. We do not need such a DFA, because the codewords are synchronized on line.

5 Shift-or

Shift-or is a well-known bit-parallel string matching algorithm [4,15]. In [7] a super-alphabet simulation method for shift-or algorithm was given. Here we briefly review the normal shift-or algorithm, and then show how we can use Q

and variable length shifts to directly search the pattern in Huffman compressed data.

The algorithm is based on a non-deterministic finite state automaton, which is constructed as follows. The automaton has states $1, 2, \ldots, m + 1$. The state 1 is the initial state, state $m + 1$ is the final (accepting) state, and for $i = 1, \ldots, m$ there is a transition from the state i to the state $i + 1$ for character $P[i]$. In addition, there is a transition for every $c \in \Sigma$ from and to the initial state.

The preprocessing algorithm builds a table E. The table has one bit-mask entry for each character in the alphabet. For $1 \leq i \leq m$, the mask $E(c)$ has the ith bit set to 0, if and only if $P[i] = c$, and to 1 otherwise. The bit-mask table corresponds to the transitions of the implicit automaton. That is, if the bit i in $E(c)$ is 0, then there is a transition from the state i to the state $i + 1$ with character c.

We also need a bit-vector D for the states of the automaton. The ith bit of the state vector is set to 0, if and only if the state i is active. Initially each bit in the state vector is set to 1. For each new text symbol c, we update the vector as follows:

$$D \leftarrow (D << 1) \mid E(c)$$

Each state gets its value from the previous one ($D << 1$), which remains active only if the text character matches the corresponding transition ($\mid E(c)$). The first state is set active automatically by the shift operation, which sets the least significant bit to 0. If after the simulation step, the mth bit of D is zero, then there is an occurrence of P.

Clearly each step of the automaton is simulated in time $O(\lceil m/w \rceil)$, which leads to $O(n\lceil m/w \rceil)$ total time.

5.1   Super-Alphabet and Variable Length Shifts

It is possible to improve the NFA simulation by using bit-parallelism also in accessing the table E. In effect we use a variable length super-alphabet of size $\sigma^{s(Q)}$. It should be emphasized that we do *not* modify the automaton, that is, the automaton does *not* use any super-alphabet, but the super-alphabet is only used to simulate the original automaton faster.

Let $c_1, \ldots, c_{s(Q)}$ be the original symbols encoded by a block Q. We set

$$\begin{aligned}
B(Q) \leftarrow\ & ((E(c_1) \,\&\, 1^m) << (s(Q) - 1)) \\
& \mid ((E(c_2) \,\&\, 1^m) << (s(Q) - 2)) \mid \cdots \\
& \mid (E(c_{s(Q)}) \,\&\, 1^m).
\end{aligned}$$

In other words we simulate what happens in $s(Q)$ steps, which we bit-wise or into the vector D of the basic algorithm. The simulation step is

$$D \leftarrow (D << s(Q)) \mid B(Q).$$

Now $B(Q)$ pre-shifts and bit-wise ors the state transition information for $s(Q)$ consecutive original symbols, and the state vector D is then updated with this precomputation.

After the simulation step, any of the bits numbered $m \ldots m + s(Q) - 1$ may be zero in D. This indicates a pattern occurrence with an occurrence location offset of $s(Q) - 1, \ldots, 0$ corresponding to the offset of the zero bit in D.

The table B is easy to compute in time $O(b2^b)$. The bit-vectors have length $m + s - 1$, where $s = \max_Q(s(Q))$, due to the need of $s - 1$ extra bits to handle the super-alphabet. Alg. 4 gives the auxiliary function for shift-or with variable length shifts.

Alg. 4 Shift-or(Q, v).

Input: bit-pattern Q, leaf v of the Huffman tree
Output: matches, if any

```
1      if v = NULL                        // USING THE HUFFMAN TREE?
2          D ← D << s(Q) | B(Q)           // NO, MAKE A SUPER-SHIFT
3          msk ← (1 << (m + s(Q))) − 1) − (1 << (m − 2))
4          if D & msk ≠ msk               // ANY BIT m...m + s(Q) − 1 ZERO?
5              check the bits individually, and output matches...
6      else                               // v IS A LEAF,
7          D ← D << 1 | B(v.symbol)       // SO MAKE A NORMAL SHIFT
8          msk ← 1 << (m − 1)
9          if D & msk ≠ msk               // IS BIT m ZERO?
10             output match...
```

Alg. 4 runs in time $O(\lceil (m + s - 1)/w \rceil + t)$, where t is the number of matches reported, m is the length of the pattern, and w is the length of the machine word in bits (typically 32 or 64), or in time $O(\lceil (m + s - 1)/w \rceil)$, if we only count the number of matches. This is $O(1)$ for short patterns. Hence the expected time of Alg. 1 with Alg. 4 is

$$O\left(n \frac{\log_2 \sigma}{b} \lceil (m + s - 1)/w \rceil + t\right),$$

which is sublinear for most reasonable choice of parameters.

5.2 Multiple Patterns

In [5,10] the problem of searching multiple patterns is reduced to searching a single "super-imposed" pattern, using classes of characters. This approach is fairly straightforward to combine with the super-alphabet shift-or. The basic idea is that each text symbol is allowed to match to the symbol of position j in *any* of the patterns. For example, if we have patterns "Hello" and "world", then we form a super-pattern "{H,w}{e,o}{l,r}{l}{o,d}". This matches for example text strings "wello", "Horlo", and "Helld". This is obviously a filter, and thus the potential matches require verification. The bright side of this is that the algorithm is very simple; in fact it does not change at all. The only necessary thing is to alter the preprocessing. After we have computed the E_i table for each pattern $P_i \in \mathcal{D}$, we just take the union of the zero bits:

$$E \leftarrow E_1 \;\&\; E_2 \;\&\; \ldots \;\&\; E_d.$$

The E table can then in turn be used to produce the B table.

Assuming uniform, independent distribution of characters, the probability that the super-pattern matches, is

$$\left(1 - \left(1 - \frac{1}{\sigma}\right)^d\right)^m < \left(\frac{d}{\sigma}\right)^m,$$

where the inequality holds for $d < \sigma$. However, note that the assumption of uniform distribution of characters in fact contradicts with our assumption that the text is compressible. We therefore replace σ in the analysis with $1/p$, where p is the probability that two symbols match.

The filter performs well, if the number of patterns is not too large, and the patterns are reasonably long. For too long patterns ($m > w - s + 1$) we can use the suffixes of length $w - s + 1$.

As the multi-pattern shift-or is a filter, the occurrences have to be verified. For that we compress the patterns and build a binary trie of the reverse of the compressed patterns. The verification is then just a matter of scanning the compressed text backwards from the bit that triggered the verification, matching the bits against the trie until a match is found, or some bit mismatches. This requires $O(m \log_2 \sigma)$ worst case time, or

$$O\left(\log_2 d + \sum_{i=1}^{m \log_2 \sigma - \log_2 d} \left(\frac{1}{2}\right)^i\right) = O(\log_2 d)$$

average time. This holds as far as $\log_2 d < m \log_2 \sigma$, or equivalently, $d < \sigma^m$. Otherwise we replace $O(\log_2 d)$ with $O(m \log_2 \sigma)$. However, at this point the filter would not work anymore. This can be improved to $O(\log_2 d/b)$ average time by using super-alphabet. The total verification cost on average is therefore

$$\frac{u(1 - (1 - p)^d)^m \log_2 d}{b} < \frac{u(pd)^m \log_2 d}{b},$$

where p is the probability that two symbols match, and the inequality holds for $d < 1/p$.

5.3   Applying q-Grams to Shift-or

To overcome the problem of decreased filtering capability for large number of patterns (and especially with combination of small alphabets) of the previous method, we use the method suggested in [10]. That is, we apply the super-alphabet approach in a different way. We take all the consecutive non-overlapping

q-grams (substrings of length q) from the pattern(s), and build the shift-or automaton using these 'super-characters'. (Note that overlapping q-grams were used in [10].)

Consider a pattern $P =$ "qwerty", and $q = 2$. A straightforward implementation of this idea would lead to synchronization problem, only every qth position of the text would be inspected, and some matches would be lost. This automaton is illustrated in Fig. 1.

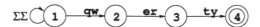

Fig. 1. Non-synchronized 2-gram automaton for $P =$ "qwerty".

We fix this problem by generating q versions, i.e. different alignments, of the pattern(s). The pattern is shifted q times to the right, one character position at a time, and for each "frame-shift", we obtain a new version of the pattern. The shifting operation introduces wild card symbols '?', which match for every character. We have to also pad each generated pattern to the length $\lceil m/q \rceil q$ with '?' symbols. For example, if $P =$ "qwerty", and $q = 2$, we obtain patterns "qwerty", and "?qwerty".

We can search all the patterns at the same time using the shift-or algorithm [4]. All the patterns can be packed in a single computer word with $(m/q)q + q - 1 = m + q - 1$ bits. The resulting automaton is illustrated in Fig. 2.

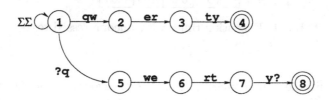

Fig. 2. Synchronized 2-gram automaton for $P =$ "qwerty".

The automaton can be simulated in $O(u\lceil (m + q - 1)/w \rceil/q)$ time for uncompressed text, which leads to

$$O\left(n\frac{\log_2 \sigma}{b}\left\lceil\left(m + \left\lceil\frac{b}{H\log_2 \sigma}\right\rceil - 1\right)/w\right\rceil + t\right)$$

time for compressed search, if we choose $q = \Theta(b/(H\log_2 \sigma))$. The (implementation) problem with this approach is that the shifts cannot be variable length now, so the shift must be delayed until at least q symbols are decoded.

Assuming again that the probability that two symbols match is p, then the probability that the q-gram super-pattern matches, is now only at most

$$(1 - (1 - p^q)^{qd})^{\lfloor m/q \rfloor - 1} < (qdp^q)^{\lfloor m/q \rfloor - 1},$$

where the inequality now holds for $qd < 1/p^q$. That is, the probability that a super-symbols matches is p^q, there are qd patterns in total, and the number of super-symbols that do not include the '?' wild card is at least $\lfloor m/q \rfloor - 1$ for each pattern. This allows much larger pattern sets, especially for small alphabets.

6   Experimental Result

We use the files bible.txt, E.coli and world192.txt in the large corpus, available in http://corpus.canterbury.ac.nz/descriptions/. The shortest file is world, which is 2473400 bytes. In able to compare the search speeds better, we truncated all three files to this length before compressing. The compression ratios (the compressed size per the original size) of the files are: world: 63.0%; bible: 54.8%; ecoli: 25.0%.

We have implemented the algorithms in C, compiled using gcc 3.1 with full optimizations. The experiments were run in 2GHz Pentium 4, with 512MB RAM, with Linux 2.4. The q-gram version of the shift-or algorithm (Sec. 5.3) has not yet been implemented. The timings are averages over 10 runs. For AC and the multi-pattern shift-or, we randomly picked 10 or 1000 patterns and for the plain shift-or one pattern. The pattern lengths were 8 characters, or more for bible and world, and 16 characters for ecoli.

time (s)	ecoli	bible	world
shift-or	0.10	0.10	0.10
AC	0.04	0.03	0.03

Table 1. Execution times with uncompressed texts.

Fig. 3 shows the search times for the shift-or algorithm and AC automaton, for varying b. As expected, the time quickly decreases with increasing b, up to a certain point. When b gets too large, the cache effects become important; the preprocessed attributes do not fit in the cache anymore, and the time begins to increase. This effect is more emphasized in the AC case, as the transition function consumes a lot of memory for large b. The results show also the predicted fact that the better the compression ratio is the faster the searching is. The preprocessing times are practically negligible (< 0.01s for $b \leq 16$) for shift-or and decompression algorithms, for AC the times rapidly grow after $b > 8$, but fortunately the AC running times for $b = 8$ are almost optimized.

For comparison, we run the basic version of the shift-or and the AC algorithm for uncompressed texts. The results are shown in Table 1. The algorithms only count the number of matches, without reporting them. The AC automaton is very simple and optimized deterministic version, containing only two lines in a for-loop. The searching times are comparable, but when adding the decompression times, the direct matching in compressed text becomes much faster. Our

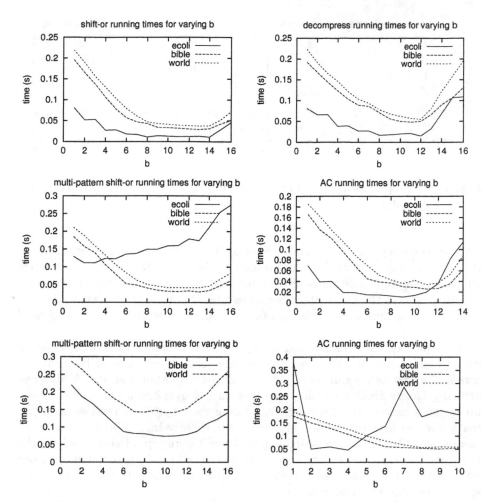

Fig. 3. Execution times in seconds for varying b. From top to bottom, left to right: shift-or (single pattern), decompression, shift-or (10 patterns), AC (10 patterns), shift-or (1000 patterns), AC (1000 patterns).

shift-or algorithm for compressed texts is extremely fast, much faster than for uncompressed texts, with the sole exception of the multi-pattern version with DNA alphabets. Even this should become competitive if the q-gram version was used.

7   Conclusions

We have presented an efficient algorithm for scanning Huffman compressed texts. The method can be augmented with many existing algorithms for non-compressed texts, resulting in fast algorithms for compressed texts. In particular,

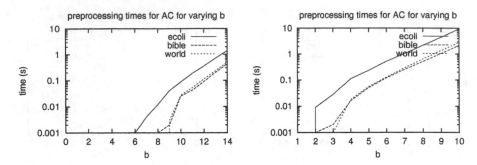

Fig. 4. AC preprocessing times in seconds for varying b. Left: for 10 patterns. Right: for 1000 patterns.

we have obtained fast string matching algorithms. The algorithms are novel in that they process variable length character tuples in constant time. The average length of the tuples depends on the entropy, and hence the better the compression ratio is the faster the algorithms are. Our experiments show that an adjustable b almost always leads to faster solutions than the fixed $b = 8$ used earlier.

One problem of Huffman coding is that the compression ratio is poor on natural language texts. However, this problem can be downgraded by using the *words* of a text as an alphabet. This was utilized by Moura et al. [11]. Instead of using binary Huffman codes, they use *tagged* byte-oriented codes to speed up decompression and searching. One bit of each byte was used as a tag to mark the the first byte of a codeword. This slightly increases the size of the compressed files but allows searching of Boyer-Moore type. Using words as the alphabet and standard binary codes (instead of byte codes), together with our approach, we can achieve even higher compression ratios with reasonably high-speed decompression and searching.

References

1. A. V. Aho and M. J. Corasick. Efficient string matching: an aid to bibliographic search. *Commun. ACM*, 18(6):333–340, 1975.
2. A. Amir and G. Benson. Efficient two-dimensional compressed matching. In *Proceedings of 2nd IEEE Data Compression Conference (DCC'92)*, pages 279–288. IEEE Computer Society Press, 1992.
3. A. Amir, G. Benson, and M. Farach. Let sleeping files lie: Pattern matching in Z-compressed files. *J. Comput. Syst. Sci.*, 52(2):299–307, 1996.
4. R. A. Baeza-Yates and G. H. Gonnet. A new approach to text searching. *Commun. ACM*, 35(10):74–82, 1992.
5. R. A. Baeza-Yates and G. Navarro. Multiple approximate string matching. In F. K. H. A. Dehne, A. Rau-Chaplin, J.-R. Sack, and R. Tamassia, editors, *Proceedings of the 5th Workshop on Algorithms and Data Structures*, number 1272 in Lecture

Notes in Computer Science, pages 174–184, Halifax, Nova Scotia, Canada, 1997. Springer-Verlag, Berlin.

6. Y. Choueka, S.T. Klein, and Y. Perl. Efficient variants of Huffman codes in high-level languages. In *Proceedings of SIGIR'85, 8th Annual International Conference of Research and Development in Information Retrieval*, pages 122–130. ACM, 1985.

7. K. Fredriksson. Faster string matching with super-alphabets. In *Proceedings of String Processing and Information Retrieval (SPIRE'02)*, Lecture Notes in Computer Science 2476, pages 44–57. Springer-Verlag, 2002.

8. D. A. Huffman. A method for the construction of minimum redundancy codes. *Proc. I.R.E.*, 40:1098–1101, 1951.

9. S.T. Klein and D. Shapira. Pattern matching in Huffman encoded texts. In *Proceedings of 11th IEEE Data Compression Conference (DCC'01)*, pages 449–458. IEEE Computer Society Press, 2001.

10. J. Kytöjoki, L. Salmela, and J. Tarhio. Tuning string matching for huge pattern sets. In *Proceedings of Combinatorial Pattern Matching (CPM'03)*, Lecture Notes in Computer Science 2676, pages 211–224. Springer-Verlag, 2003.

11. E. Moura, G. Navarro, N. Ziviani, and R. Baeza-Yates. Fast and flexible word searching on compressed text. *ACM Transactions on Information Systems*, 18(2):113–139, 2000.

12. G. Navarro, T. Kida, M. Takeda, A. Shinohara, and S. Arikawa. Faster approximate string matching over compressed text. In *Proceedings of 11th IEEE Data Compression Conference (DCC'01)*, pages 459–468. IEEE Computer Society Press, 2001.

13. M. Takeda, S. Miyamoto, T. Kida, A. Shinohara, S. Fukamachi, T. Shinohara, and S. Arikawa. Processing text files as is: Pattern matching over compressed texts, multi-byte character texts, and semi-structured texts. In *Proceedings of String Processing and Information Retrieval (SPIRE'02)*, Lecture Notes in Computer Science 2476, pages 170–186. Springer-Verlag, 2002.

14. M. Takeda, Y. Shibata, T. Matsumoto, T. Kida, A. Shinohara, S. Fukamachi, T. Shinohara, and S. Arikawa. Speeding up string pattern matching by text compression: The dawn of a new era. *Transactions of Information Processing Society of Japan*, 42(3):370–384, 2001.

15. S. Wu and U. Manber. Fast text searching allowing errors. *Commun. ACM*, 35(10):83–91, 1992.

16. J. Ziv and A. Lempel. A universal algorithm for sequential data compression. *IEEE Trans. Inf. Theory*, 23:337–343, 1977.

17. J. Ziv and A. Lempel. Compression of individual sequences via variable length coding. *IEEE Trans. Inf. Theory*, 24:530–536, 1978.

(S,C)-Dense Coding: An Optimized Compression Code for Natural Language Text Databases*

Nieves R. Brisaboa[1], Antonio Fariña[1], Gonzalo Navarro[2], and
María F. Esteller[1]

[1] Database Lab., Univ. da Coruña, Facultade de Informática, Campus de Elviña s/n,
15071 A Coruña, Spain.
{brisaboa,fari}@udc.es, mfesteller@yahoo.es
[2] Dept. of Computer Science, Univ. de Chile, Blanco Encalada 2120, Santiago, Chile.
gnavarro@dcc.uchile.cl

Abstract. This work presents (s,c)-Dense Code, a new method for
compressing natural language texts. This technique is a generalization
of a previous compression technique called End-Tagged Dense Code that
obtains better compression ratio as well as a simpler and faster encoding
than Tagged Huffman. At the same time, (s,c)-Dense Code is a prefix
code that maintains the most interesting features of Tagged Huffman
Code with respect to direct search on the compressed text. (s,c)-Dense
Coding retains all the efficiency and simplicity of Tagged Huffman, and
improves its compression ratios.

We formally describe the (s,c)-Dense Code and show how to compute the
parameters s and c that optimize the compression for a specific corpus.
Our empirical results show that (s,c)-Dense Code improves End-Tagged
Dense Code and Tagged Huffman Code, and reaches only 0.5% overhead
over plain Huffman Code.

1 Introduction

Text compression techniques are based on exploiting redundancies in the text to
represent it using less space [2]. The amount of text collections has grown in the
last years, mainly due to the widespread use of digital libraries, documental
databases, office automation systems and the Web. Current text databases
contain hundreds of gigabytes and the Web is measured in terabytes. Although
the capacity of new devices to store data grows fast and the associated costs
decrease, the size of text collections increases also faster. Moreover, CPU speed
grows much faster than that of secondary memory devices and networks, so
storing data in compressed form reduces I/O time, which is more and more
convenient even at the expense of for some extra CPU time.

Another advantage of text compression techniques is that all of them allow
(and improve) the use of *block addressing indexes*. These indexes are smaller

---

* This work is partially supported by CICYT Grant (#TIC2002-04413-C04-04),
CYTED VII.19 RIBIDI Project, and (for the third author) Fondecyt Grant 1-020831.

M.A. Nascimento, E.S. de Moura, A.L. Oliveira (Eds.): SPIRE 2003, LNCS 2857, pp. 122–136, 2003.

than standard inverted indexes because their entries point to blocks instead of exact word positions. Of course the price to pay is sequential text scanning of the pointed blocks. However, if the text is compressed with a technique that allows direct search of words in the compressed text, then not only the index and text size are reduced, but also the search inside candidate text blocks is much faster. Notice that using those two techniques together, as in [8], the index is used just as a device to filter out some blocks that do not contain the word we are looking for. This index schema was first proposed in Glimpse [13], a widely known system that uses a block addressing index. On the other hand compression techniques can be used as well to compress the inverted indexes themselves, as suggested in [8] or [10].

For these reasons, compression techniques have become attractive methods to save space and transmission time. However, if the compression scheme does not allow to search for words directly on the compressed text, the retrieval of documents will be less efficient, due to the need of decompression before the search.

Classic compression techniques, like the well-known algorithms of Ziv and Lempel [15, 16] or the character oriented code of Huffman [4], are not suitable for large textual databases. One important disadvantage of these techniques is the inefficiency of searching for words directly on the compressed text. Compression schemes based on Huffman codes are not often used on natural language because of the poor compression ratios achieved. On the other hand, Ziv and Lempel algorithms obtain better compression ratios, but the search for a word on the compressed text is inefficient. Empirical results [7] showed that searching on a Ziv-Lempel compressed text can take half the time of decompressing that text and then searching it. However, the compressed search is twice as slow as just searching the uncompressed version of the text.

In [12], they presented a compression scheme that uses a semi-static word-based model and a Huffman code where the coding alphabet is byte-oriented. This compression scheme allows the search for a word on the compressed text without decompressing it in such a way that the search can be up to eight times faster for certain queries. The key idea of this work (and others [6]) is to take the words as the symbols that compose the text (and therefore the symbols that should be compressed). Since in Information Retrieval (IR) words are the atoms of the search, these compression schemes are particularly suitable for IR.

In [3] it is shown that, although plain Huffman Code is the prefix code that gives the shortest possible output when a source symbol is always substituted by the same code, Tagged Huffman Code largely underutilizes the representation. In that paper it is shown that, by signaling the last byte instead of the first one, the rest of the bits can be used in all their combinations and the code is still a prefix code. The resulting code, called End-Tagged Dense Code, becomes much closer to the compression obtained by Plain Huffman Code. This code not only retains the ability of being searchable with any string matching algorithm, but it is also extremely simple to build (it is not based on Huffman at all) and permits a more compact representation of the vocabulary. Thus, the advantages over Tagged Huffman Code are (i) better compression ratios, (ii) same searching possibilities, (iii) simpler and faster coding and (iv) simpler and smaller vocabulary representation.

In this paper we present (s,c)-Dense Coding, a generalization of the End-Tagged Dense Code [3] that improves its compression ratio by adapting the number of terminal and non terminal symbols to the distribution of frequencies of the words in the corpus to be compressed. As a result, (s,c)-Dense Coding compresses strictly better than End-Tagged Dense Code and Tagged Huffman Code, reaching only a 0.5% overhead over Plain Huffman Code. At the same time, (s,c)-Dense Codes retain all the simplicity and direct search capabilities of End-Tagged Dense Codes and Tagged Huffman Codes. We present an efficient algorithm to build (s,c)-Dense Codes, which is so fast that it can make this an interesting alternative to Plain Huffman Codes because of speed and simplicity of construction.

2   Related Work

Huffman is a well-known coding method [4]. The idea of Huffman coding is to compress the text by assigning shorter codes to more frequent symbols. It has been proven that Huffman algorithm obtains an optimal (i.e., shortest total length) *prefix code* for a given text.

A code is called a *prefix code* (or instantaneous code) if no codeword is a prefix of any other codeword. A prefix code can be decoded without reference to future codewords, since the end of a codeword is immediately recognizable.

Plain Huffman Code [3] produces an average symbol length which is at most one extra symbol over the zero-order entropy. That is, if we call

$$E_b = \sum_{i=1}^{N} p_i \log_{2^b}(1/p_i) = \frac{1}{b} \sum_{i=1}^{N} p_i \log_2(1/p_i)$$

the zero-order entropy in base b of the text, then the average number of symbols to code a word using Plain Huffman is

$$E_b \leq H_b \leq E_b + 1$$

2.1   Word-Based Huffman Compression

The traditional implementations of the Huffman code are character based, i.e., they use the characters as the symbols of the alphabet. In [5] they use the words in the text as the symbols to be compressed. This idea joins the requirements of compression algorithms and of IR systems, as words are the basic atoms for most IR systems. The basic point is that a text is more compressible when regarded as a sequence of words rather than characters.

In [12, 17], a compression scheme that uses this strategy combined with a Huffman code is presented. From a compression viewpoint, character-based

Huffman methods are able to reduce English texts to approximately 60% of their original size, while word-based Huffman methods are able to reduce them to 25% of their original size, because the distribution of words is much more biased than the distribution of characters.

The compression schemes presented in [12, 17] use a semi-static model, that is, the encoder makes a first pass over the text to obtain the frequency of all the words in the text and then the text is coded in the second pass. During the coding phase, original symbols (words) are replaced by codewords. For each word in the text there is a unique codeword, whose length varies depending on the frequency of the word in the text. Using the Huffman algorithm, shorter codewords are assigned to more frequent words.

The basic method proposed by Huffman is mostly used as a binary code, that is, each word in the original text is coded as a sequence of bits. In [12] they modified the code assignment such that a sequence of bytes instead of bits is associated with each word in the text.

Experimental results have shown that, on natural language, there is no significant degradation in the compression ratio by using bytes instead of bits. In addition, decompression and searching are faster with byte-oriented Huffman code because no bit manipulations are necessary.

2.2   Tagged Huffman Codes

In [12] two codes following this approach are presented. In that paper, they call *Plain Huffman Code* to the one we have already described, that is, a word-based byte-oriented Huffman code.

The second code proposed is called Tagged Huffman Code. This is just like the previous one differing only in that the first bit of each byte is reserved to flag whether the byte is the first byte of a codeword. Hence, only 7 bits of each byte are used for the Huffman code. Note that the use of a Huffman code over the remaining 7 bits is mandatory, as the flag is not useful by itself to make the code a prefix code.

Tagged Huffman Code has a price in terms of compression performance: we store full bytes but use only 7 bits for coding. Hence, the compressed file grows approximately by 11%.

Tagged Huffman code, as well as Plain Huffman, is easy to analyze. It is a Huffman code over $b - 1$ bits, but using b bits per symbol, hence

$$E_{b-1} \leq T_b \leq E_{b-1} + 1$$

The addition of a tag bit in the Tagged Huffman Code permits direct searching on the compressed text by simply compressing the pattern and then using any classical string matching algorithm. On Plain Huffman this does not work, as the pattern could occur in the text and yet not correspond to our codeword. The problem is that the concatenation of parts of two codewords may form the codeword of another vocabulary word. This cannot happen in the

Tagged Huffman Code due to the use of one bit in each byte to determine if the byte is the first byte of a codeword or not.

For this reason, searching with Plain Huffman requires inspecting all the bytes of the compressed text from the beginning, while Boyer-Moore type searching (that is, skipping bytes) is possible over Tagged Huffman Code.

The algorithm to search for a single word under Tagged Huffman Code starts by finding the word in the vocabulary to obtain the codeword that represents it in the compressed text. Then the obtained codeword is searched for in the compressed text using any classical string matching algorithm with no modifications. They call this technique *direct searching* [12, 17].

Today's IR systems require also flexibility in the search patterns. There is a range of complex patterns that are interesting in IR systems, including regular expressions and "approximate" searching (also known as "search allowing errors"). See [12, 17] for more details on how Tagged Huffman Code permits these types of search.

2.3   End-Tagged Dense Codes

The End-Tagged Dense Code [3] starts with a seemingly dull change to Tagged Huffman Code. Instead of using the flag bit to signal the *beginning* of a codeword, the flag bit is used to signal the *end* of a codeword. That is, the flag bit is *0* for the first bit of any byte of a codeword except for the last one, which has a *1* in its first bit.

This change has surprising consequences. Now the flag bit is enough to ensure that the code is a prefix code regardless of the contents of the other 7 bits. To see this, consider two codewords X and Y, being X shorter than Y ($|X| < |Y|$). X cannot be a prefix of Y because the last byte of X has its flag bit in 1, while the $|X|$-th byte of Y has its flag bit in 0.

At this point, there is no need at all to use Huffman coding over the remaining 7 bits. It is possible to use *all* the possible combinations of 7 bits in all the bytes, as long as the flag bit is used to mark the last byte of the codeword.

We are not restricted to use symbols of 8 bits to form the codewords. It is possible to use symbols of b bits. The End-Tagged Dense Code is defined as follows:

Definition 1 Given source symbols with decreasing probabilities $\{p_i\}_{0 \leq i < n}$ the corresponding codeword using the End-Tagged Dense Code is formed by a sequence of symbols of b bits, all of them representing base-(2^{b-1}) digits (that is, from 0 to $2^{b-1} - 1$), except the last one which has a value between 2^{b-1} and $2^b - 1$, and the assignment is done in a completely sequential fashion.

That is, using symbols of 8 bits, the 130-th word is encoded as 00000000:10000001, the 131-th as 00000000:10000010, and so on, just as if we had a 14-bit number. As it can be seen, the computation of codes is extremely simple: It is only necessary to order the vocabulary words by frequency and then sequentially assign the codewords. Hence the coding phase will be faster than using Huffman because obtaining the codes is simpler.

In fact, it is not necessary to physically store the results of these computations: With a few operations we can obtain on the fly, given a word rank i, its ℓ-byte codeword, in $O(\ell) = O(\log i)$ time.

What is perhaps less obvious is that *the code depends on the rank of the words, not on their actual frequency.* That is, if we have four words A, B, C, D with frequencies 0.27, 0.26, 0.25 and 0.23, respectively, then the code will be the same as if their frequencies were 0.9, 0.09, 0.009 and 0.001.

Hence, there is no need to store the codewords (in any form such as a tree) nor the frequencies in the compressed file. It is enough to store the plain words sorted by frequency. Therefore, the vocabulary will be slightly smaller than in the case of the Huffman code, where some information about the shape of the tree must be stored (even when a canonical Huffman tree is used).

In order to obtain the codewords, the decoder can run a simple computation to obtain, from the codeword, the rank of the word, and then obtain the word from the vocabulary sorted by frequency. A code i of ℓ bytes can be decoded in $O(\ell) = O(\log i)$ time.

An interesting property of this code is that it can be used as a bound for the compression that can be obtained with a Huffman code. It is clear that the End-Tagged Dense Code uses all the possible combinations of all bits, except the first one, that is used as a flag as in the Tagged Huffman Code. Therefore, calling D_b the code length of an End-Tagged Dense Code that uses symbols of b bits we have

$$D_{b+1} \leq H_b \leq D_b \leq T_b \leq D_{b-1}$$

In [3] a more precise comparison on these three codes is presented. There, it is shown how the End-Tagged Dense Code provides lower and upper bounds to the compression that can be obtained by Huffman with texts in natural language where the Zipf's Law is assumed [14].

3 (S,C)-Dense Codes

As we have shown, End-Tagged Dense Code uses 2^{b-1} digits, from 0 to $2^{b-1} - 1$, for the bytes at the beginning of a codeword, and it uses the other 2^{b-1} digits, from 2^{b-1} to $2^b - 1$, for the last byte of the codeword. But the question that arises now is whether that proportion between the number of *non terminal* and *terminal* digits is the optimal one; that is, for a given corpus with a specific distribution of frequencies of words, it might be that a different number of non terminal digits (continuers) and terminal digits (stoppers) could compress better than just using 2^{b-1}. This idea has been previously pointed out in [9]. We define (s, c)- stop-cont codes as follows.

Definition 2 Given source symbols with probabilities $\{p_i\}_{0 \leq i < n}$ an (s, c) stop-cont code (where c and s are integers larger than zero) assigns to each source *symbol i a unique target code formed by a base-c digit sequence terminated by a digit between c and $c + s - 1$.*

It should be clear that a stop-cont coding is just a base-c numerical representation, with the exception that the last digit is between c and $c + s - 1$, i.e., it is a base-s number that is distinguished from previous digits by adding c. Digits between 0 and $c - 1$ are called "continuers" and those between c and $c + s - 1$ are called "stoppers". The next property clearly follows.

Property 1. Any (s, c) stop-cont code is a prefix code.

Proof. If one code were a prefix of the other, since the shorter code must have a final digit of value at least c, then the longer code must have an intermediate digit which is not in base c. This is a contradiction.   □

Among all the possible (s, c) stop-cont codes for a given probability distribution, the *dense code* is one that minimizes the average symbol length. This is because a dense code uses all the possible combinations of bits in each byte. That is, codes can be assigned sequentially to the ranked symbols.

Definition 3 Given source symbols with decreasing *probabilities* $\{p_i\}_{0 \le i < n}$, *the corresponding (s, c)-Dense Code $((s, c)$-DC$)$ is an (s, c) stop-cont code where the codewords are assigned as follows: Let k be the number of bytes in each codeword, which is always ≥ 1, then k will be such that*

$$s\frac{c^{k-1} - 1}{c - 1} \le i < s\frac{c^k - 1}{c - 1}$$

Thus, the code corresponding to source symbol i is formed by $k - 1$ base-c digits and a final digit. If $k = 1$ then the code is simply the stopper $c + i$. Otherwise the code is formed by the number $\lfloor x/s \rfloor$ written in base c, followed by $c + (x \bmod s)$, where $x = i - \frac{sc^{k-1} - s}{c - 1}$.

Example 1. The codes assigned to symbols $i \in 0 \ldots 15$ by a $(2,3)$-DC are as follows: $\langle 3 \rangle$, $\langle 4 \rangle$, $\langle 0,3 \rangle$, $\langle 0,4 \rangle$, $\langle 1,3 \rangle$, $\langle 1,4 \rangle$, $\langle 2,3 \rangle$, $\langle 2,4 \rangle$, $\langle 0,0,3 \rangle$, $\langle 0,0,4 \rangle$, $\langle 0,1,3 \rangle$, $\langle 0,1,4 \rangle$, $\langle 0,2,3 \rangle$, $\langle 0,2,4 \rangle$, $\langle 1,0,3 \rangle$ and $\langle 1,0,4 \rangle$.

Note that the code does not depend on the exact symbol probabilities, but just on their ordering by frequency. We now prove that the dense coding is an optimal stop-cont coding.

Property 2. The average length of a (s, c)-dense code is minimal with respect to any other (s, c) stop-cont code.

Proof. Let us consider an arbitrary (s, c) stop-cont code, and let us write all the possible codewords in numerical order, as in Example 1, together with the symbol they encode, if any. Then it is clear that (i) any unused code in the middle could be used to represent the source symbol with longest codeword, hence a compact assignment of target symbols is optimal; and (ii) if a less probable symbol with a shorter code is swapped with a more probable symbol with a longer code then the average code length decreases, and hence sorting the symbols by decreasing frequency is optimal.   □

Since sc^{k-1} different codewords can be coded using k digits, let us call

$$W_k^s = \sum_{j=1}^{k} sc^{j-1} = s\frac{c^k - 1}{c - 1}$$

(where $W_0^s = 0$) the number of source symbols that can be coded with up to k digits. Let us also call

$$f_k^s = \sum_{j=W_{k-1}^s+1}^{W_k^s} p_j$$

the sum of probabilities of source symbols coded with k digits by an (s, c)-DC.
Then, the average codeword length for the (s, c)-DC, $LD_{(s,c)}$, is

$$LD_{(s,c)} = \sum_{k=1}^{K^s} k f_k^s = \sum_{k=1}^{K^s} k \sum_{j=W_{k-1}^s+1}^{W_k^s} p_j$$

$$= 1 + \sum_{k=1}^{K^s-1} k \sum_{j=W_k^s+1}^{W_{k+1}^s} p_j = 1 + \sum_{k=1}^{K^s-1} \sum_{j=W_k^s+1}^{W_k^s} p_j$$

where $K^x = \lceil \log_{(2^b-x)} \left(1 + \frac{n(2^b-x-1)}{x}\right) \rceil$, and n is the number of symbols in the vocabulary.

It is clear from Definition 3 that the End-Tagged Dense Code [3] is a $(2^{b-1}, 2^{b-1})$-DC and therefore (s,c)-DC can be seen as a generalization of the End-Tagged Dense Code where s and c are adjusted to optimize the compression for the distribution of frequencies of the vocabulary.

In [3] it is proved that $(2^{b-1}, 2^{b-1})$-DC is more efficient than Tagged Huffman. This is because Tagged Huffman is a $(2^{b-1}, 2^{b-1})$ *(non dense) stop-cont* code, while the End-Tagged Dense Code is a $(2^{b-1}, 2^{b-1})$-Dense Code.

Example 2. Table 1 shows the codewords assigned to a small set of words ordered by their frequency when using Plain Huffman (P.H.), *(6,2)*-DC, End-Tagged Dense Code (ETDC) which is a *(4,4)*-DC, and Tagged Huffman (TH). Symbols of three bits are used for simplicity ($b=3$). The last four columns present the products of the number of bytes by the frequency for each word, and its addition, the average codeword length, is shown in the last row.

It is easy to see that, for this example, Plain Huffman and the (6,2)-Dense Code are better than the (4,4)-Dense Code (ETDC) and therefore they are also better than Tagged Huffman. Notice that (6,2)-Dense Code is clearly better than (4,4)-Dense Code because it takes advantage of the distribution of frequencies and of the number of words in the vocabulary. However the values $(6,2)$ for s and c are not the optimal ones since a $(7,1)$-Dense Code obtains an optimal compressed text having, in this example, the same result than Plain Huffman.

Word	Freq	P.H.	(6,2)-DC	ETDC	T.H.	Freq × bytes			
						P.H.	(6,2)-DC	ETDC	T.H.
A	0.2	[000]	[010]	[100]	[100]	0.2	0.2	0.2	0.2
B	0.2	[001]	[011]	[101]	[101]	0.2	0.2	0.2	0.2
C	0.15	[010]	[100]	[110]	[110]	0.15	0.15	0.15	0.3
D	0.15	[011]	[101]	[111]	[111][000]	0.15	0.15	0.15	0.3
E	0.14	[100]	[110]	[000][100]	[111][001]	0.14	0.14	0.28	0.28
F	0.09	[101]	[111]	[000][101]	[111][010]	0.09	0.09	0.18	0.18
G	0.04	[110]	[000][010]	[000][110]	[111][011][000]	0.04	0.08	0.08	0.12
H	0.02	[111][000]	[000][011]	[000][111]	[111][011][001]	0.04	0.04	0.04	0.05
I	0.005	[111][001]	[000][100]	[001][100]	[111][011][010]	0.01	0.01	0.01	0.015
J	0.005	[111][010]	[000][101]	[001][101]	[111][011][011]	0.01	0.01	0.01	0.015
					total compressed size	1.03	1.07	1.30	1.67

Table 1. Comparative among compression methods

The problem now consists of finding the s and c values (assuming a fixed b where $2^b = s + c$) that minimize the size of the compressed text.

4   Optimal s and c Values

Before giving the algorithm to compute the optimal s and c values, $s + c = 2^b$ and $1 \leq s \leq 2^b - 1$, we need to show that the size of the compressed text decreases when we increase s until reaching the *unique* optimal s value. After that optimal value, increments of s will produce a loss in the compression ratio. This is shown in Figure 1. Of course the value of c depends on the value of s because $c = 2^b - s$ always holds.

Although we have a formal proof of the uniqueness of the minimum, it is so technically involved that it could be an article by itself. We considered such a long proof inadequate for this conference version. So we have decided to include only an intuitive explanation in this paper, which turns out to be considerably simpler than the actual proof with all the details.

Intuitively, it is easy to see that when s is very small the number of high frequency words encoded with very few bytes (that is, one or two bytes) is also very small (s words are encoded with just one byte and $s \cdot c$ with two bytes) but in this case c is large and therefore words with low frequency will be encoded with few bytes ($s \cdot c^2$ words will be encoded with 3 bytes, $s \cdot c^3$ with 4 bytes and so on, but if c is so large, probably 3 bytes will be enough to encode the last word of the ranked vocabulary).

It is clear that, as s grows, highest frequency words will be encoded with less bytes, so we improve the compression of high frequency words. But at the same time, as s grows, lowest frequency words will need more bytes to be encoded, so we loss compression in those words.

As consequence, if we try all the possible values of s starting at $s = 1$, we will see (as in Figure 1) that, in the beginning, compression improves a lot because each increment of s produce that words with high frequency become encoded by a codeword that is one byte shorter.

When s becomes larger, for each increment of s the number of words encoded with less bytes is smaller in proportion and has lower frequency. Therefore, with each increment of s, we gain less and less compression in the highest frequency words. At the same time, we lose more and more compression in the lowest frequency words, because with each increment of s they will need more bytes to be encoded. At some point, the compression lost in the last words is larger than the compression gained in words at the beginning, and therefore the global compression ratio decreases. That point gives us the optimal s value. It is easy to see in Figure1 that, around of the optimal value, the compression is relatively insensitive to the exact value of s. This fact causes the smooth bottom of the curve.

Our algorithm takes advantage of this property. It is not necessary to check all the values of s because we know the shape of the distribution of compression ratios as a function of s. Our algorithm looks only for the direction of change the in value of s, moving towards the area where compression ratio improves.

5   Algorithm to Obtain the Optimal s and c Values

In this section, an algorithm to find the best s and consequently c for a given corpus and a given b is shown. A needed precondition is to have a list with the accumulated frequencies for all the words in the corpus, arranged in decreasing order of frequency.

The basic algorithm is presented below. It is a binary search algorithm that initially computes the size of the compressed text for two consecutive values of s: ($\lfloor 2^{b-1} \rfloor - 1$ and $\lfloor 2^{b-1} \rfloor$). As has been intuitively explained there is at most one local minimum, so the algorithm can lead the search to the point that reaches the best compression ratio. In each new iteration the search space is reduced by half and a new computation of the compression is obtained with two central points of the new interval is performed.

The process consists of two parts: The algorithm **findBestS** computes the best s and c values for a given b and a list of accumulated frequencies. This list can be obtained by sorting the words in decreasing order of frequency and computing the accumulated frequency for each position. The *size of the compressed text* (in bytes) is computed for specific s and c values by calling function **ComputeSizeS**. Finally, the s and c values that minimize the length are returned.

findBestS $(b, freqList)$
   //*Input*: b value ($2^b = c + s$).

```
//Input: A list of accumulated frequencies for words arranged on decreasing order of frequency .
//Output: The best s and c values
begin
  Lp := 1;              //Lp and Up the lower and upper
  Up := 2^b − 1;        //points of the interval being checked
  while Lp + 1 < Up do
    M := ⌊Lp+Up/2⌋;
    sizePp := computeSizeS(M − 1, 2^b − (M − 1), freqList); //size with M − 1
    sizeM := computeSizeS(M, 2^b − M, freqList);            //size with M
    if sizePp < sizeM then
        Up := M − 1;
    else Lp := M
    end if
  end while
  if Lp < Up then     //Lp = Up − 1 and M = Lp
    sizeNp := computeSizeS(Up, 2^b − Up, freqList); //size with M + 1
    if sizeM < sizeNp then
        bestS := M;
    else bestS := Up
    end if
  else bestS := Lp    //Lp = Up = M − 1
  end if
  bestC := 2^b − bestS;
  return bestS, bestC;
end
```

For any given values s and c, next algorithm computes the size of the compressed text.

```
computeSizeS (s, c, freqList)
  //Inputs: s, c, and a list of accumulated frequencies.
  //Output: length of the compressed text when using s,c
  begin
    k := 1; n := number of words in 'freqList';
    Right := min(s, n);    total := freqList[Right − 1];
    while Right < n do
        Left := Right;
        Right := Right + sc^k;
        k := k + 1;
        if Right > n then
            Right := n;
        end if
        total := total + k ∗ (freqList[Right − 1] − freqList[Left]) ;
    end while
    return total
  end
```

Notice that computing the size of the compressed text for a specific value of s costs $O(\log_c n)$, except for $c = 1$, in which case it costs $O(n/s) = O(n/2^b)$. Hence the most expensive possible sequence of calls to **computeSizeS** in a binary search is that for values $c = 2^{b-1}$, $c = 2^{b-2}$, $c = 2^{b-3}$, ..., $c = 1$. The total cost of **computeSizeS** over that sequence of c values is

$$\frac{n}{2^b} + \sum_{i=1}^{b-1} \log_{2^{b-i}} n = \frac{n}{2^b} + \log_2 n \sum_{i=1}^{b-1} \frac{1}{b-i} = O\left(\frac{n}{2^b} + \log n \log b\right)$$

The other operations of the binary search are constant, and we have also an extra $O(n)$ cost to compute the accumulated frequencies. Hence the overall cost to find s and c is $O(n + \log(n) \log(b))$. Since the maximum b of interest is such that

$b = \lceil \log_2 n \rceil$ (as at this point we can code each symbol using a single stopper), the optimization algorithm costs at most $O(n + \log(n) \log \log(n)) = O(n)$, assuming the vocabulary is already sorted. We have succeeded in making the optimization part totally negligible. Huffman algorithm is also linear once the vocabulary is sorted, but the constant is in practice larger because it involves more operations than just adding up frequencies.

6 Empirical Results

We used some large text collections from TREC-2 (AP Newswire 1988 and Ziff Data 1989-1990) and from TREC-4 (Congressional Record 1993, Financial Times 1991, 1992, 1993 and 1994). We also used a Literary Spanish corpus we created. We have compressed them using Plain Huffman, (s,c)-Dense Code, End-Tagged Dense Code and Tagged Huffman. We used the spaceless word model [11] to create the vocabulary; that is, if a word was followed by a space, we just encoded the word, otherwise both the word and the separator were encoded.

We excluded the size of the compressed vocabulary in the results (this size is negligible and similar in all cases, although a bit smaller in (s, c)-DC and ETDC because only the ranking of words is needed).

Corpus	Num words	vocabulary size	Entropy	Plain	(s,c)-DC	ETDC	Tagged
AP 1988	52,960,212	268,890	1,3032	1,4778	(189,67) 1,4908	1,5166	1,6382
Ziff 1989-90	40,548,114	237,607	1,2732	1,4500	(198,58) 1,4586	1,4909	1,6064
C.R. 1993	9,445,990	117,713	1,2950	1,4755	(195,61) 1,4874	1,5202	1,6381
F.T. 1991	3,059,634	75,687	1,2825	1,4555	(192,64) 1,4674	1,4974	1,6122
F.T. 1992	36,518,075	284,878	1,2946	1,4651	(193,63) 1,4755	1,5042	1,6275
F.T. 1993	41,772,135	291,404	1,2839	1,4474	(195,61) 1,4566	1,4891	1,6131
F.T. 1994	43,039,879	294,990	1,2843	1,4476	(195,61) 1,4569	1,4897	1,6137
Spanish Texts	18,324,100	313,977	1,3612	1,5486	(182,74) 1,5692	1,5889	1,7164

Table 2. Comparison of the Average Codeword Length

In Table 2 we present the average length of the codewords obtained with each of the compression methods, as well as the zero-order entropy of the text when words are taken as the source symbols. As it can be seen, the average codeword length in Plain Huffman and in (s, c)-Dense Code is less than 1 byte larger than the entropy. The sixth column, also gives the optimal (s, c) values found using algorithm **findBestS**.

Table 3 shows the compression ratio obtained by the aforementioned codes, as well as that corresponding to the entropy. The second column contains the original size of the processed corpus and the following columns indicate the number of words in the vocabulary, the θ parameter of Zipf's Law [14, 1], and the compression ratio for each method. Again, in the column corresponding to (s, c)-DC, the optimal (s, c) values are shown.

As it can be seen, Plain Huffman gets the best compression ratio (as expected since it is the optimal prefix code) and End-Tagged Dense Codes always obtain better results than Tagged Huffman, with an improvement of up to 2.5 points.

Corpus	Original Size	Voc. Words	θ	Entropy	P.H.	(s,c)-DC		ETDC	T.H.
AP 1988	250,994,525	241,315	1.852045	27.49	31.18	(189,67)	31.46	32.00	34.57
Ziff 1989-90	185,417,980	221,443	1.744346	27.84	31.71	(198,58)	31.90	32.60	35.13
C.R. 1993	51,085,545	114,174	1.634076	23.94	27.28	(195,61)	27.50	28.11	30.29
F.T. 1991	14,749,355	75,597	1.449878	26.60	30.19	(193,63)	30.44	31.06	33.44
F.T. 1992	175,449,248	284,904	1.630996	26.94	30.49	(193,63)	30.71	31.31	33.88
F.T. 1993	197,586,334	291,322	1.647456	27.14	30.60	(195,61)	30.79	31.48	34.10
F.T. 1994	203,783,923	295,023	1.649428	27.12	30.57	(195,61)	30.77	31.46	34.08
Spanish Texts	105,125,124	313,977	1.480535	23.71	27.00	(182,74)	27.36	27.71	29.93

Table 3. Comparison of compression ratios.

As expected, (s, c)-DC improves the results reached by $(128, 128)$-DC (ETDC). In fact, (s, c)-DC is superior to $(128, 128)$-DC and it is worse than the optimal Plain Huffman only by less than 0.5 points on average.

In Figure 1 the size of the compressed texts and the compression ratios are shown as a function of the s values, for Ziff and Spanish corpus. As shown in Table 3, the optimal s value for Ziff corpus is 198, while for the Spanish corpus the maximum compression ratio is achieved with $s = 182$. On the right we show sizes and compression ratios when s values close to the optimum are used.

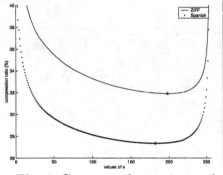

s value	ZIFF Corpus		Spanish Corpus	
	ratio	size	ratio	size
175	31.9891	59,313,463	27.3592	28,761,439
180	31.9550	59,250,251	27.3530	28,754,926
181	31.9489	59,239,066	27.3527	28,754,571
182	**31.9432**	**59,228,446**	**27.3526**	**28,754,487**
183	31.9378	59,218,406	27.3529	28,754,757
185	31.9279	59,200,048	27.3543	28,756,250
190	31.9092	59,165,319	27.3633	28,765,740
195	31.8990	59,146,488	27.3814	28,784,711
197	31.8976	59,143,905	27.3915	28,795,340
198	**31.8976**	**59,143,837**	27.3972	28,801,304
199	31.8980	59,144,550	27.4033	28,807,734
200	31.8987	59,146,012	27.4098	28,814,637

Fig. 1. Compressed text sizes and compression ratios for different s values.

7   Conclusions

We have presented (s, c)-Dense Codes, a new method for compressing natural language texts. This method is a generalization of the End-Tagged Dense Code and improves its compression ratio by adapting its (s, c) parameters to the corpus to be compressed.

We have given an algorithm that computes the optimal s, c values for a given corpus, that is, the pair that maximizes the compression ratio. Instead of sequentially computing the resulting size for each s and c value, and then choosing the best one, our algorithm uses the fact that there is a unique minimum in the size of the compressed text as a function of the s and c values, to speed up the process. In fact, our algorithm has an $O(\log n \times \log \log n)$ cost. We have presented an intuitive description of this nontrivial property of the behavior of minima as a function of s.

We have presented some empirical results comparing our method against other codes with similar features. Our new code is always better than End-Tagged Dense Code and Tagged Huffman Code, reaching only 0.5% excess from the optimal Huffman Code. It is also faster and simpler to build.

It seems that there should be some relationship between the θ of the Zipf's model (more or less biased distribution of frequencies) and the optimal s and c values. It can be shown that $s = 2^b - 2^{b/\theta}$. However, our empirical data do not confirm that. The reason is that the Zipf model is a rough approximation, possibly useless for this case. On the other hand, we found that s is always in the interval $[182, 198]$, and this information could be used to speed up, a little bit, our algorithm. In order to generalize this result we would need a model (working in practice) which, from the frequency distribution, gave us a range where the optimum s must lie.

References

[1] R. Baeza-Yates and B. Ribeiro-Neto. *Modern Information Retrieval*. Addison-Wesley Longman, May 1999.

[2] T. C. Bell, J. G. Cleary, and I. H. Witten. *Text Compression*. Prentice Hall, 1990.

[3] N. Brisaboa, E. Iglesias, G. Navarro, and J. Paramá. An efficient compression code for text databases. In *25th European Conference on IR Research, ECIR 2003*, LNCS 2633, pages 468–481, 2003.

[4] D. A. Huffman. A method for the construction of minimum-redundancy codes. *Proc. Inst. Radio Eng.*, 40(9):1098–1101, 1952.

[5] A. Moffat. Word-based text compression. *Software - Practice and Experience*, 19(2):185–198, 1989.

[6] A. Moffat and A. Turpin. On the implementation of minimum redundancy prefix codes. *IEEE Transactions on Communications*, 45(10):1200–1207, 1997.

[7] G. Navarro and J. Tarhio. Boyer-Moore string matching over Ziv-Lempel compressed text. In *Proc. 11th Annual Symposium on Combinatorial Pattern Matching (CPM 2000)*, LNCS 1848, pages 166–180, 2000.

[8] Gonzalo Navarro, Edleno Silva de Moura, Marden Neubert, Nivio Ziviani, and Ricardo Baeza-Yates. Adding compression to block addressing inverted indexes. *Information Retrieval*, 3(1):49–77, 2000.

[9] J. Rautio, J. Tanninen, and J. Tarhio. String matching with stopper encoding and code splitting. In *Proc. 13th Annual Symposium on Combinatorial Pattern Matching (CPM 2002)*, LNCS 2373, pages 42–52, 2002.

[10] F. Scholer, H. E. Williams, J. Yiannis, and J. Zobel. Compression of inverted indexes for fast query evaluation. In *Proc. 25th Annual International ACM SIGIR conference on Research and development in information retrieval*, pages 222–229, 2002.

[11] E. Silva de Moura, G. Navarro, N. Ziviani, and R. Baeza-Yates. Fast searching on compressed text allowing errors. In *Proc. 21st Annual International ACM SIGIR Conference on Research and Development in Information Retrieval (SIGIR-98)*, pages 298–306, 1998.

[12] E. Silva de Moura, G. Navarro, N. Ziviani, and R. Baeza-Yates. Fast and flexible word searching on compressed text. *ACM Transactions on Information Systems*, 18(2):113–139, 2000.

[13] Manber U. and S. Wu. GLIMPSE: A tool to search through entire file systems. In *Proc. of the Winter 1994 USENIX Technical Conference*, pages 23–32, 1994.

[14] G.K. Zipf. *Human Behavior and the Principle of Least Effort*. Addison-Wesley, 1949.

[15] J. Ziv and A. Lempel. A universal algorithm for sequential data compression. *IEEE Transactions on Information Theory*, 23(3):337–343, 1977.

[16] J. Ziv and A. Lempel. Compression of individual sequences via variable-rate coding. *IEEE Transactions on Information Theory*, 24(5):530–536, 1978.

[17] N. Ziviani, E. Silva de Moura, G. Navarro, and R. Baeza-Yates. Compression: A key for next-generation text retrieval systems. *Computer*, 33(11):37–44, 2000.

Linear-Time Off-Line Text Compression by Longest-First Substitution

Shunsuke Inenaga[1,2], Takashi Funamoto[1], Masayuki Takeda[1,2], and
Ayumi Shinohara[1,2]

[1] Department of Informatics, Kyushu University 33, Fukuoka 812-8581, Japan
{s-ine, t-funa, ayumi, takeda}@i.kyushu-u.ac.jp
[2] PRESTO, Japan Science and Technology Corporation (JST)

Abstract. Given a text, grammar-based compression is to construct a
grammar that generates the text. There are many kinds of text compression techniques of this type. Each compression scheme is categorized
as being either *off-line* or *on-line*, according to how a text is processed.
One representative tactics for off-line compression is to substitute the
longest repeated factors of a text with a production rule. In this paper,
we present an algorithm that compresses a text basing on this longest-
first principle, in linear time. The algorithm employs a suitable index
structure for a text, and involves technically efficient operations on the
structure.

1 Introduction

Text compression is one of the main stream in the area of string processing [4].
The aim of compression is to reduce the size of a given text by efficiently removing the redundancy of the text. Compressing a text enables us to save not only
memory space for storage, but also time for transferring the text since its compressed size is now smaller. It is ideal to compress the text as much as possible,
but compression in reality has to be done in the trade-off between time and space,
i.e. text compression algorithms are also required to have fast performance.

One major scheme of text compression is *grammar-based* text compression,
where a grammar that produces the text is generated. Many attempts to generate a smaller grammar have been made so far, such as in the well-known LZ78
algorithm [20] and the SEQUITUR algorithm [14, 15]. These two algorithms both
process an input text *on-line*, namely, they read the text in a single pass, and
begin to emit compressed output (production rules for a grammar) before they
have seen all of the input. Actually, the history of text compression algorithms
began with processing texts on-line, since limitation of available memory space
has until recently been a big concern. On-line algorithms run on relatively small
space by employing the idea of a sliding window, but they only generate a grammar based on replacing the repeating factors in the window that is of bounded
size. Therefore some possibilities to compress texts into smaller sizes would remain.

M.A. Nascimento, E.S. de Moura, A.L. Oliveira (Eds.): SPIRE 2003, LNCS 2857, pp. 137–152, 2003.

Due to recent hardware developments, we are now allowed to dedicate more memory space to text compression. This gives us opportunities to design *off-line* algorithms that more efficiently process an input text and give us better compression. Two strategies for seeking for repeating factors in the whole input text are possible; the *most-frequent-first* and *longest-first* strategies.

Text compression by the most-frequent-first substitution was first considered by Wolff [19]. His algorithm is, given a text, to recursively replace the most frequently occurring digram (factor of length two) with a new character, which results in a production rule corresponding the digram. Though Wolff's algorithm takes $O(n^2)$ time for an input text of length n, Larsson and Moffat [12] devised a clever algorithm, named RE-PAIR, that runs in $O(n)$ time and compresses the text by recursively substituting new characters for the most frequent digram.

In this paper we consider the other one, text compression by the longest first substitution, where we generate a grammar by substituting new characters for the longest repeating factors of a given text of length more than one. For example, from string abcacaabaaabcacbababababcaccabacabcac of length 35 we obtain the following grammar

$$S \rightarrow AaBaAbBbAcBcA$$
$$A \rightarrow \text{abcac}$$
$$B \rightarrow \text{aba}.$$

of size 24. Bentley and McIlroy [5] gave an algorithm for this compression scheme, but Nevill-Manning and Witten [16] stated that it does not run in linear time. They also claimed the algorithm by Bentley and McIlroy can be improved so as to run in linear time, but they only noted a too short sketch for how, which is unlikely to give a shape to the idea of the whole algorithm. This paper, therefor, introduces the first explicit, and complete, linear-time algorithm for text compression with the longest-first substitution. The core of our algorithm is the use of *suffix trees* [18], for they are quite useful for finding the longest repeating factors as is mentioned in [16]. Our algorithm, which is really combinatorial, involves highly technical but necessary update operations on suffix trees towards upcoming substitutions. We give a precise analysis for the time complexity of our algorithm, which results in being linear in the length of an input text string.

2   Preliminaries

2.1   Notations on Strings

Let Σ be a finite alphabet. An element of Σ^* is called a *string*. Strings x, y, and z are said to be a *prefix*, *factor*, and *suffix* of string $w = xyz$, respectively. The sets of all prefixes, factors, and suffixes of a string w are denoted by $Prefix(w)$, $Factor(w)$, and $Suffix(w)$, respectively.

The length of a string w is denoted by $|w|$. The empty string is denoted by ε, that is, $|\varepsilon| = 0$. Let $\Sigma^+ = \Sigma^* - \{\varepsilon\}$. The i-th character of a string w is denoted by $w[i]$ for $1 \leq i \leq |w|$, and the factor of a string w that begins at position i and ends at position j is denoted by $w[i : j]$ for $1 \leq i \leq j \leq |w|$. For convenience, let $w[i : j] = \varepsilon$ for $j < i$, and $w[i :] = w[i : |w|]$ for $1 \leq i \leq |w|$. For any factor x of a string w, let $BegPos_w(x)$ denote the set of the beginning positions of all occurrences of x in w.

For a non-empty factor x of a string w, $\#occ_w(x)$ denotes the possible maximum number of *non-overlapping* occurrences of x in w. If $\#occ_w(x) \geq 2$, then x is said to be *repeating* in w. We abbreviate a *longest* repeating factor of w to an *LRF* of w. Remark that there can exist more than one LRF for w.

Let $x \in \Sigma^+$. An integer $1 \leq p \leq |x|$ is said to be a *period* of x if the suffix $x[p + 1 :]$ of x is also a prefix of x, that is, $x[p + 1 :] = x[1 : |x| - p]$.

2.2   Suffix Trees

The *suffix tree* of a string w, denoted by $STree(w)$, is an efficient index structure which is defined as follows:

Definition 1. *$STree(w)$ is a tree structure such that:*

1. *every edge is labeled by a non-empty factor of w;*
2. *every internal node has at least two child nodes;*
3. *all out-going edge labels of every node begin with mutually distinct characters;*
4. *every suffix of w is spelled out in a path starting from the root node.*

Quite a lot of applications of suffix trees have been introduced so far, in the literature such as [1, 9, 8].

Assuming any string w terminates with the unique symbol \$ not appearing elsewhere in w, there is a one-to-one correspondence between a suffix of w and a leaf node of $STree(w)$. $STree(w)$ for string $ababa\$$ is shown in Fig. 1. For any node v of $STree(w)$, $label(v)$ denotes the string obtained by concatenating the labels of the edges in the path from the root node to node v. The *length* of node v, denoted $length(v)$, is defined to be $|label(v)|$. The *number* of the leaf node of $STree(w)$ corresponding to $w[i :]$ is defined to be i, for $1 \leq i \leq |w|$. The i-th leaf node of $STree(w)$ is denoted by $leaf_i$. Every node v of $STree(w)$ except for the root node has the *suffix link*, denoted $suf(v)$, such that $suf(v) = v'$ where $label(v') \in Suffix(label(v))$ and $length(v') + 1 = length(v)$.

If there exists a node v in $STree(w)$ such that $label(v) = x$ for some $x \in Factor(w)$, then we sometimes specify that x is represented by an *explicit* node. Otherwise, we say that x is represented by an *implicit* node in $STree(w)$. The implicit node is indicated by a *reference* pair $\langle s, \alpha \rangle$ of a node and string, such that $label(s) \cdot \alpha = x$.

Actually, every edge label x of $STree(w)$ is implemented by a pair $\langle i, j \rangle$ of integers such that $x = w[i : j]$, and thus occupies only constant space. Therefore, the size of $STree(w)$ is linear in $|w|$. More precisely:

Theorem 1 (McCreight [13]). *For any string $w \in \Sigma^*$ with $|w| > 1$, $STree(w)$ has at most $2|w| - 1$ nodes and $2|w| - 2$ edges.*

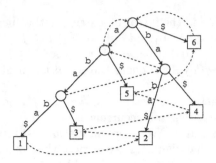

Fig. 1. *STree(w)* with $w = $ ababa$. Solid arrows represent edges, and dotted arrows are suffix links.

Moreover, on the assumption that Σ is fixed;

Theorem 2 (Weiner [18]). *For any string $w \in \Sigma^*$, STree(w) can be constructed in linear time.*

Construction of *STree(w)* has been studied in various contexts. For instance, Weiner [18] gave the first algorithm to construct *STree(w)* in linear time. Later on, McCreight [13] and Ukkonen [17] individually presented conceptionally new linear-time algorithms for construction of *STree(w)*. A merit of the two latter algorithms is that the order of the creation of a leaf node exactly corresponds to the beginning position of the suffix represented by the leaf node. Namely, the i-th created leaf node of *STree(w)* is exactly *leaf*$_i$ for any $1 \le i \le |w|$. Hereby we can easily associate each leaf node with its number, without any extra effort after the construction of *STree(w)* is completed.

3　Off-Line Compression by Longest-First Substitution

Given a text string $w \in \Sigma^*$, we here consider to replace an LRF x of w such that $|x| \ge 2$, with a new character not appearing in w. We call this operation *longest-first substitution* on w. Applying it to w as many times as possible, we can accomplish encoding of w, where we resultingly obtain a grammar consisting of the rules that produce the replaced factors. For instance, let us consider string abaaabbababb$, which has two LRFs aba and abb. Let us here choose abb for being replaced by a new character A, and then we obtain

$$S \rightarrow \text{abaa}A\text{ab}A\$$$
$$A \rightarrow \text{abb.}$$

Replacing ab by B results in a grammar consisting of the production rules

$$S \rightarrow Baa ABA\$$$
$$A \rightarrow \text{abb}$$
$$B \rightarrow \text{ab.}$$

3.1   Suffix Trees Are Useful for Longest-First Substitution

To compress w according to the above principle and in $O(|w|)$ time, we need to find in *(amortized) constant time* an LRF of w at every stage of compression. Preprocessing w is a direct and clever choice for this purpose, and concretely, we first construct $STree(w)$. We consider only the strings corresponding to the internal nodes of $STree(w)$ as candidates for LRFs. Since there can be LRFs of w that are not represented as nodes of $STree(w)$, one may think that such LRFs remain unsubstituted for, and violate our longest-first principle (e.g., see $STree(\mathtt{ababa\$})$ of Fig. 1 in which factor $\mathtt{ab}$ is an LRF of $\mathtt{ababa\$}$, but is represented only as an implicit node.). However, we can fortunately prove the following lemma which guarantees that we have only to consider the strings represented as an internal node of $STree(w)$. This lemma is essential to our algorithm for text compression with longest-first substitution.

Lemma 1. *Suppose x is an LRF of w not corresponding to a node of $STree(w)$. Then, there exists another LRF y of w that corresponds to an internal node such that $|x| = |y|$ and $\#occ_w(y) \geq \#occ_w(x) = 2$. Moreover, x is no longer present in the string after the substitution for y. (See Fig. 2.)*

Proof. Suppose the implicit node representing x is on the edge from some node s to node t of $STree(w)$. Let $u = label(t)$, and then we have $BegPos_w(x) = BegPos_w(u)$. Since x is an LRF of w and a proper prefix of u, the string u is not repeating. Let i, j be the minimum and maximum elements of $BegPos_w(u)$, respectively. It is obvious that $j - i = |x| < |u|$ and therefore the string u has a period $|x|$. Let $\ell = |u|$. The string $w[i : j + \ell - 1] = xu$ has a period $|x|$. Let p be the smallest period of the same string, and let z be the length-p prefix of x. By the periodicity lemma, we can show that $x = z^k$ for some $k \geq 1$ as in Fig.2. Let ℓ' ($\ell' \geq \ell$) be the largest integer such that the string $w[i : j + \ell' - 1]$ has a period p. It is not hard to show that $w[i : j + \ell' - 1] = z^{2k}z'$ for some prefix z' of z. Let y be the length-$|x|$ suffix of this string, and y' be the length-$|z'|$ prefix of x. Then, $w[i : j + \ell' - 1] = y'yy$. Let $a = w[j + \ell']$ and $b = w[j + \ell' - p]$. From the choice of ℓ', the characters a, b must be distinct. Since $|y| = k \cdot p$, we have $b = w[j + \ell' - p] = w[j + \ell' - |y|]$. The occurrences of y at positions $j + \ell'$ and $j + \ell' - |y|$ in w are followed by a and b, respectively, and therefore y is represented as an explicit node of $STree(w)$. Since x occurs only within the region $w[i : j + \ell' - 1]$, it cannot be present after substitution for the occurrences of y.   □

The above lemma implies that it suffices to consider the strings corresponding to the internal nodes of $STree(w)$ as candidate repeating factors for substitution. In fact, we only need to consider the LRF $\mathtt{ba}$ of $\mathtt{ababa\$}$ that is represented by an explicit internal node of $STree(\mathtt{ababa\$})$ of Fig. 1, in spite of the implicit one $\mathtt{ab}$ By sorting the internal nodes of $STree(w)$ in the order of their path lengths, we can maintain the list of such candidates. Notice that, however, the above lemma does not address every node of $STree(w)$ corresponds to a repeating factor of w. Namely, an overlapping factor x with $\#occ_w(x) = 1$ may be represented by

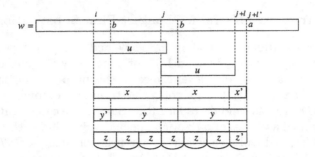

Fig. 2. An illustration for Lemma 1. An LRF x of w not corresponding to a node of $STree(w)$ implies two consecutive occurrences of x. In this case, there necessarily exists an LRF y corresponding to an internal node. The replacement of the two consecutive occurrences of y destroys the occurrences of x.

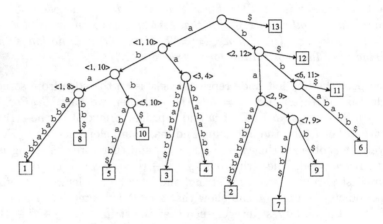

Fig. 3. Every node v of $STree(\text{abaaabbababb\$})$ shown here has got a pair $\langle i, j \rangle$, where the leftmost and rightmost occurrences of $label(v)$ are i, j, respectively.

a node of $STree(w)$. For example, see Fig. 1 displaying $STree(\text{ababa\$})$. Remark factor **aba** appears twice in the string, but $\#occ_u(\text{aba}) = 1$ since the two occurrences are overlapping. Let i, j be the beginning positions of the leftmost and rightmost occurrences of a factor x of a string w, respectively. If $|x| > j - i$, then it means that all occurrences of x are overlapping in w, and thus $\#occ_w(x) = 1$. Otherwise, we have $\#occ_w(x) \geq 2$, and therefore string x is a repeating factor of w. For any internal node s of $STree(w)$, the beginning position of the leftmost (rightmost) occurrence of $label(s)$ can be computed by a standard bottom-up traversal of the tree issuing the numbers of the leaf nodes upward. The time cost is proportional to the number of the edges in $STree(w)$, which is $O(|w|)$.

See Fig. 3, where every node v of $STree(\text{abaaabbababb\$})$ has got a pair $\langle i, j \rangle$ of integers, where i, j are the beginning positions of the leftmost and rightmost occurrences of $label(v)$, respectively.

```
 1      5      10      15      20      25      30
abaabaabaabaababaabaabababaabaaba$
```

Fig. 4. An example for a string in which some occurrences of its LRF are overlapping.

The sole remaining matter is how to construct the list of the internal nodes for substitutions, which has to be sorted by the lengths of the nodes. It can simply be done by a bin sort in linear time in the number of internal nodes in $STree(w)$, therefore in $O(|w|)$ time (according to Theorem 1).

As a result of the above discussion, it has been shown that $STree(w)$ is quite effective in providing us the list of the repeating factors of w sorted in the decreasing order of their lengths. In the following sections we will see how an LRF of w is actually replaced by a new character, and what maintenance has to be done for the suffix tree.

3.2   Substitution for Longest Repeating Factor

According to the discussion in the previous section, we have got the list of nodes candidate for longest first substitution, and now the first element of the list corresponds to an LRF x of w. If $|x| < 2$, then any substitution does not reduce the size of the string, and thus we halt here. Otherwise, we actually replace x with a new character, say A, and then create the production rule $A \rightarrow x$.

A subtle consideration reveals that every occurrence of an LRF x in w is *not* allowed to be replaced by A, if w contains some overlapping occurrences of x. Conversely, we then could have more than one choice of the occurrences of x for being replaced by A. See Fig. 4 in which the string shown contains abaabaaba as a unique LRF. For example, we can choose the occurrences of abaabaaba beginning at positions 7 and 25 for substitution. Then, no other occurrences of abaabaaba cannot be replaced since they are overlapping either of the two chosen occurrences. Notice, however, we have $\#occ_u(\text{abaabaaba}) = 3$, that is, the occurrences beginning at positions 1, 15 and 25 could be chosen to be replaced, for instance. Below we give a way to choose exactly $\#occ_w(x)$ occurrences of an LRF x of a string w for substitution.

Definition 2. Let x be a non-empty factor of $w \in \Sigma^*$. The left-first greedily selected occurrences of x in w is the sequence $i_1, \ldots, i_k$ $(k \geq 1)$ of integers satisfying:

1. $i_1 = \min BegPos_w(x)$.
2. i_ℓ is the smallest integer such that $i_\ell \in BegPos_w(x)$ and $i_{\ell-1} + |x| \leq i_\ell$, for every $\ell = 2, \ldots, k$.
3. There is no integer i such that $i \in BegPos_w(x)$ and $i_k + |x| \leq i$.

Proposition 1. Let x be a non-empty factor of $w \in \Sigma^*$. If $i_1, \ldots, i_k$ $(k \geq 1)$ is the left-first greedily selected occurrences of x in w, then $k = \#occ_w(x)$.

The above proposition states that the left-first greedy choice of occurrences of an LRF for substitutions achieves the maximum number of substitutions. What has to be considered next is how to sort the positions of occurrences of an LRF in the increasing order.

The proposition below follows from the periodicity lemma.

Proposition 2. *For any non-empty factor x of a string w and integer ℓ with $1 \leq \ell \leq |w|$, the set $S = \{i \mid i \leq \ell \leq i + |x| \text{ and } x = w[i : i + |x| - 1]\}$ forms a single arithmetic progression. If $|S| \geq 3$, then the step is the smallest period of x. All the occurrences of x at positions $i \in S$ with $i \neq \max S$ are followed by a unique character.*

Lemma 2. *For any non-repeating factor x of w, the set $BegPos_w(x)$ forms a single arithmetic progression. When $|BegPos_w(x)| \geq 3$, the step is the smallest period of x.*

Proof. Let ℓ be the maximum element of $BegPos_w(x)$. Since x is non-repeating, $i \leq \ell \leq i + |x|$ for every $i \in BegPos_w(x)$. We can apply Proposition 2 to prove the lemma. □

Remark that an arithmetic progression can be represented as a triple of the first and last elements, and the number of its elements. We store in every internal node s of $STree(w)$ the triple of the minimum element, the maximum element, and the cardinality of $BegPos_w(u)$, which is a compact representation of the set $BegPos_w(u)$ if u is non-repeating, where $u = label(s)$.

The next proposition directly follows from the definition of $BegPos$.

Proposition 3. *Let s be an internal node of $STree(w)$ having children $s_1, \ldots, s_k$. Then, the set $BegPos_w(label(s))$ is the disjoint union of the sets*

$$BegPos_w(label(s_1)), \ldots, BegPos_w(label(s_k)).$$

Lemma 3. *Suppose x is an LRF of w corresponding to an internal node s of $STree(w)$. Let $s_1, \ldots, s_k$ be the children of s. Then, $BegPos_w(x)$ is the disjoint union of $BegPos_w(label(s_1)), \ldots, BegPos_w(label(s_k))$, each of which forms a single arithmetic progression.*

Proof. Notice that the strings $label(s_1), \ldots, label(s_k)$ are non-repeating because they are longer than x that is an LRF of w. We can prove the lemma by Proposition 3 and Lemma 2. □

For finite sets S, T of integers, we write $S \prec T$ if every element of S is smaller than any of T.

Lemma 4. *Suppose x is an LRF of w corresponding to an internal node s of $STree(w)$. Let $s_1, \ldots, s_k$ be the children of s arranged in the increasing order of the minimum elements of $BegPos_w(label(s_i))$. Then,*

$$BegPos_w(label(s_1)) \prec \cdots \prec BegPos_w(label(s_k)).$$

Proof. It suffices to prove the next claim.

Claim. For any child t of s with $|BegPos_w(label(t))| \leq 2$, the node t has no sibling t' such that $BegPos_w(label(t'))$ contains an integer k with $i < k < j$, where i and j are the minimum and maximum elements of $BegPos_w(label(t))$.

Let $u = label(t)$ and let x' be the prefix of u of length $j - i$. Since x is an LRF of w and x' is repeating, x cannot be shorter than x' and thus we have $|x| \geq j - i$. Assume, for a contradiction, that t has a sibling t' such that $BegPos_w(label(t'))$ contains an integer k with $i < k < j$. Since j belongs to the intervals $[i, i + |x|]$, $[k, k + |x|]$, and $[j, j + |x|]$, we can show that $\{i, k, j\}$ is a subset of an arithmetic progression and $w[i + |x|] = w[k + |x|]$ by Proposition 2. On the other hand, the characters $w[i + |x|]$ and $w[k + |x|]$ are the first characters of the labels of the edges from s to t and t', respectively. Hence the two characters must be distinct, a contradiction. The proof of the claim is now complete. $\qquad\square$

The above lemma implies that we have only to sort the k integers that are, respectively, the minimum elements of $BegPos_w(label(s_1)), \ldots, BegPos_w(label(s_k))$. The discussion below, however, reveals that we indeed need not explicitly sort these k integers.

Recall that an edge label α in the suffix tree of a string w is represented by an ordered pair $\langle i, j \rangle$ of integers with $w[i : j] = \alpha$.

Proposition 4. *Ukkonen's suffix-tree construction algorithm guarantees that the first argument i of the ordered pair representing the label of the edge from a node s to a node t in $STree(w)$ is equal to $\min BegPos_w(label(t)) + |label(s)|$.*

The above proposition states that it suffices to arrange the out-going edges of a node s in the increasing order of the first arguments of the corresponding pairs. A short consideration reveals that this order coincides with the order of creation of the edges by Ukkonen's algorithm. Thus, all we have to do is to keep, for every node s, the list of the out-going edges of s arranged in the order of creation, which can be easily done during the suffix tree construction.

Finally, we achieve the following lemma.

Lemma 5. *For any LRF x corresponding to an internal node s of $STree(w)$ of a string w, the left-first greedily selected occurrences of x in w can be enumerated in $O(k)$ time, after an $O(|w|)$ time and space preprocessing of w, where k is the number of children of s.*

Proof. It is feasible in $O(|w|)$ time and space to build $STree(w)$ and store in each node t the triple of the minimum element, the maximum element, and the cardinality of $BegPos_w(label(t))$. By Lemma 3 and Lemma 4, we can prove the lemma. $\qquad\square$

3.3   Preparation for Next Substitution

In this section, we show how to maintain our suffix-tree based data structure after the substitution for an LRF of a string w, in order to prepare for the next LRF substitution. Let x_k denote the string being replaced with a new character, say A_k, at the k-th stage of the compression of string w with longest-first substitution. Let $w_1 = w$, and let w_{k+1} denote the string obtained by replacing every occurrence of x_k in w_k that is greedily selected in the left-first manner, with A_k which is followed by $(|x_k| - 1)$-times repetition of a special character $\bullet \notin \Sigma$. The aim of the introduction of the special character $\bullet$ is so that we have $|w_k| = |w|$ for every k. The string obtained by removing all $\bullet$'s from w_k, is denote by $\overline{w_k}$. Clearly, $\overline{w_k}$ is identical to the string obtained just after the $(k-1)$-th stage of the compression of w. By definition, x_k is an LRF of $\overline{w_k}$.

Proposition 5. *For every k, the string x_k consists only of characters from Σ.*

Proof. Assume contrarily that x_k contains a character A_j for some $j < k$, with which some occurrences of x_j have been replaced since the j-th stage. Because $\#occ_{w_k}(x_k) \geq 2$, we have $\#occ_{w_j}(x_k) \geq 2$. This implies that x_k is a longer repeating factor of $\overline{w_j}$ than x_j, and this is a contradiction.   □

We say that a position i of w_k $(1 \leq i \leq |w|)$ is *active* if $w_k[i] \in \Sigma$, and *inactive*, otherwise. Let Act_k and $Inact_k$ be the sets of the active positions and inactive positions of w_k, respectively, for every k. $Act_1 = \{1, \ldots, |w|\}$ and $Inact_k = \emptyset$ as $w_1 = w$. Due to Proposition 5, we have $Act_1 \supset Act_2 \supset \cdots$.

In the running example with **abaaabbababb$**, the sequence **abaa$A \bullet \bullet$abA$\bullet \bullet$$** is yielded after the substitution of A for the LRF **abb**, where every position assigned $\bullet$ or A is now inactive. We now have $Act_2 = \{1, 2, 3, 4, 8, 9, 13\}$ and $InAct_2 = \{5, 6, 7, 10, 11, 12\}$. After the substitution of B for the next LRF **ab**, the sequence $B \bullet$ aa$A \bullet \bullet B \bullet A \bullet \bullet$$** is yielded, which gives us $Act_3 = \{3, 4, 13\}$ and $Inact_3 = \{1, 2, 5, 6, 7, 8, 9, 10, 11, 12\}$.

The data structure we want to maintain for $k = 1, 2, \ldots$ resembles the *sparse suffix tree* [11] of w_k that represent only the suffixes beginning at the active positions of w_k. In the sequel, we present an update procedure for this data structure. It is obvious that the following lemma stands.

Lemma 6. *For any factor y of w_{k+1} with $y \in \Sigma^+$, $\#occ_{w_{k+1}}(y) < \#occ_{w_k}(y)$ if and only if an occurrence of y overlaps some occurrence of x_k in w_k.*

See Fig. 5, in which an LRF x_k beginning at position i of w_k is being replaced by a new character A. First we consider a suffix of w_k beginning at position j with $j \leq i$. The latter part of such a suffix after position i has to be modified, since its factor x_k is converted to A at position i. The number of such suffixes is proportional to i, and thus it reaches $O(|w_k|)$ in the worst case. However, the suffixes we actually have to care are only those beginning at position j with $i - |x_k| + 1 \leq j \leq i$, since in the principle of the longest-first substitution any LRF x_{k+1} cannot be longer than x_k, and all we need to know is if $\#occ_{w_{k+1}}(x_{k+1})$ becomes smaller than $\#occ_{w_k}(x_{k+1})$ and it only happens if x_{k+1} overlaps x_k in w_k (by Lemma 6). Hereby we define the *attentional zone* for x_k with respect to position i to be the region from $i - |x_k| + 1$ to i. In the right figure of Fig. 5, the suffixes in the attentional zone are light shaded.

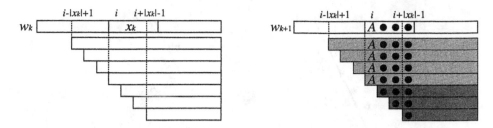

Fig. 5. Changes of the suffixes affected by the replacement of the occurrence of x_k beginning at position i of w_k during the k-th stage (from the left figure into the right figure). The occurrence of x_k in w_k is replaced with A followed by $(|x_k|-1)$-times repetition of • in w_{k+1}. In the right figure, the light-shaded region and the dark-shaded region denote the attentional and dead zones, respectively. The suffixes of w_k beginning at the positions in the attentional zone are modified accordingly, and those in the dead zone are no longer present in the sparse suffix tree for w_{k+1}.

To update our data structure for w_k to that for w_{k+1} according to the substitution for the LRF x_k, we have to check all the paths corresponding to the suffixes beginning at the positions in the attentional zone, and convert each of them accordingly. If naively traversing all these paths from the root node of the tree, then the total time cost will be $O(\#occ_{w_k}(x_k) \times |x_k|^2)$. However, we have the following lemma that reduces it to linear time.

Lemma 7. *At every k-th stage it is feasible in $O(|x_k|)$ time to maintain all paths spelling out a suffix of w_k which begins at a position in the attentional zone of w_k.*

Proof. Let $j = i - |x_k| + 1$, and $u_j = w_k[j : i-1], u_{j+1} = w_k[j+1 : i-1], \ldots, u_i = w_k[i : i-1] = \varepsilon$. Note any position in the attentional zone is in Act_k. Let s_j and t_1 be the longest nodes in the tree for w_k, such that $label(s_j) \in Prefix(u_j)$ and $label(t_j) \in Prefix(u_jx_k)$, respectively (see the left figure of Fig. 6). Note $label(s_j)$ is a prefix of $label(t_j)$. These two nodes can be found by simply traversing the path spelling out u_jx_k from the root node of the tree. Since $|u_j| + 1 = |x_k|$, the traversal can be done in $O(|x_k|)$ time (assuming $|\Sigma|$ is constant). Let $z \in \Sigma^*$ be the string such that $label(s_j) \cdot z = u_j$. If $z \neq \varepsilon$, then we create a new child node v_j of s_j such that $label(v_j) = u_j$. Otherwise, suppose $v_j = s_j$. Note that node t_j always has a unique out-going edge that is in the path spelling out u_jx_k from the root node. Let r_j be the child node of t_j connected by this edge, and let y_j be the label of this edge. We reconnect r_j to v_j with the edge labeled by A_ky, and then remove the out-going edge of v_j which no longer has a node underneath (see the right figure of Fig. 6). This operation takes only constant time.

Now we focus on u_ℓ for some $j < \ell \le i$. We need to find where nodes s_ℓ and t_ℓ in the tree such that $label(s_\ell) \in Prefix(u_\ell)$ and $label(t_\ell) \in Prefix(u_\ell)$, respectively. Remark that we have $label(suf(s_{\ell-1})) \in Prefix(s_\ell)$ and $label(suf(t_{\ell-1})) \in$

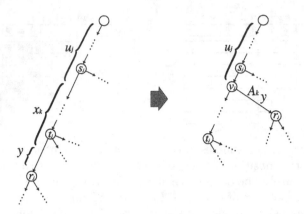

Fig. 6. Illustration for the former part of the proof of Lemma 7.

Prefix(t_ℓ), and thus we can detect them in $O(|label(s_\ell)| - |label(suf(s_{\ell-1}))| + 1)$ time and in $O(|label(t_\ell)| - |label(suf(t_{\ell-1}))| + 1)$ time, respectively, by using the suffix links. Then the total time cost for detecting s_ℓ and t_ℓ for all possible ℓ is proportional to

$$\sum_{\ell=j+1}^{i} \{(|label(s_\ell)| - |label(suf(s_{\ell-1}))| + 1) + (|label(t_\ell)| - |label(suf(t_{\ell-1}))| + 1)\}$$

$$= (|label(s_{j+1})| - |label(suf(s_j))| + 1) + (|label(t_{j+1})| - |label(suf(t_j))| + 1)$$
$$+ (|label(s_{j+2})| - |label(suf(s_{j+1}))| + 1) + (|label(t_{j+2})| - |label(suf(t_{j+1}))| + 1)$$
$$\cdots\cdots$$
$$+ (|label(s_i)| - |label(suf(s_{i-1}))| + 1) + (|label(t_i)| - |label(suf(t_{i-1}))| + 1)$$
$$= |label(s_i)| - |label(suf(s_j))| + |label(t_i)| - |label(suf(t_j))| + 4(i - j - 1) + 2$$
$$= |label(s_i)| - |label(s_j)| + |label(t_i)| - |label(t_j)| + 4(i - j)$$
$$= |\varepsilon| - |label(s_j)| + |x_k| - |label(t_j)| + 4(|x_k| - 1)$$
$$\leq |x_k| - |x_k| + 4(|x_k| - 1)$$
$$= 4(|x_k| - 1).$$

This operation for the detection is illustrated in Fig. 7. Of course, after each detection we create a new node v_ℓ for each s_ℓ, or possibly $v_\ell = s_\ell$, and reconnect to v_ℓ the out-going edge of t_ℓ leading to its certain child r_ℓ corresponding to string u_ℓ. This reconnection as well takes just constant time.   □

Secondly, we consider the suffixes of w_k beginning at position h with $i \leq h \leq i + |x_k| - 1$. As seen in Fig. 5, the beginning positions of those suffixes become inactive after the substitution of A_k for x_k occurring at position i. It means that all of them have to be removed from the tree structure. Hereby we call the region from $i + 1$ to $i + |x_k| - 1$ the *dead zone* for x_k with respect to position i. The suffixes in the dead zone are dark shaded in the right figure of Fig. 5.

Lemma 8. *At every k-th stage, it is feasible in $O(|x_k|)$ time to remove all paths spelling out a suffix of w_k which begins at a position in the dead zone of w_k.*

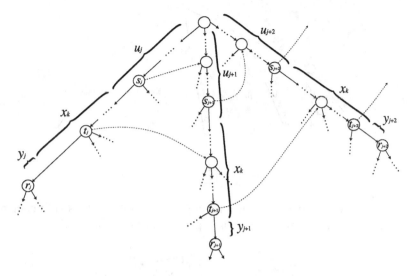

Fig. 7. Illustration for the latter part of the proof of Lemma 7.

Proof. Assume the path spelling out x_k is already converted to that spelling out a new character A_k. Remark there always exists a node v such that $label(v) = A_k$. Then, there exists $leaf_i$ in the subtree rooted at node v. It is trivial that $suf(leaf_i) = leaf_{i+1}$, and thus we can find it in constant time. By removing $leaf_{i+1}$ and its in-coming edge, we can delete the path spelling out the suffix $w_k[i+1 :]$. Similarly it takes constant time for any h with $i+1 < h \leq i+|x_k|-1$. $\square$

See Fig. 8 and Fig. 9 that show the trees after the first and second substitutions for the LRFs, respectively, with respect to string abaaabbababb$.

As stated above, we can maintain the data structure for $w_1, w_2, \ldots$. In this data structure, $BegPos_{w_k}(label(s))$ is exactly the set of leaves in the subtree rooted at node s. The sole remaining matter is, for each node s, to maintain the triple of the minimum element, the maximum element, and the cardinality of $BegPos_{w_k}(label(s))$. A short consideration reveals that we need the triples only for the nodes whose proper descendents represent non-repeating factors of w_k at the k-th stage. We can maintain the triples for such nodes only in linear time with respect to $|x_k| \cdot \#occ_{w_k}(x_k)$.

The last thing we have to clarify is how to deal with the node list from which we find the next LRF for substitution. One may think reordering the list is necessary after every substitution since some occurrences of the upcoming LRFs may disappear because of the previous LRF substitution. However, we in fact do not need to do that. If we encounter in the list a node that does not exist in the tree any more, then we just ignore it and focus on the next node in the list. Concerning the case that we encounter in the list a node s which still exists in the tree but $label(s)$ is *not* repeating any more, we do the followings. First,

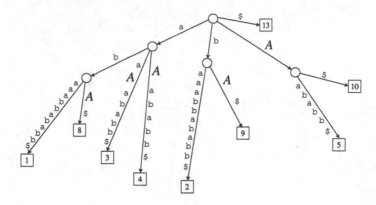

Fig. 8. The resulting tree structure for $\overline{w_2}$ = abaa$A$ab$A$\$. It is sufficient for us to find an LRF x_2. In fact, x_2 = ab is represented by an internal node.

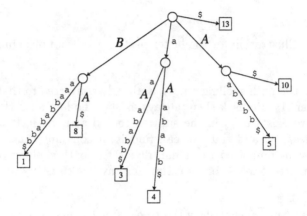

Fig. 9. The resulting tree structure for $\overline{w_3}$ = BaaABA$\$. Since there is no internal node of length more than one, the encoding of the text halts here.

we focus on the subtree rooted at the node s and see its all leaf nodes. If the remainder of subtracting the maximum leaf number from the minimum one is less than $|label(s)|$, it implies that $label(s)$ is non-repeating. We then mark node s 'dead', and focus on the upcoming LRF in the list. If in traversing the subtree rooted at s we encounter any internal node t marked 'dead', then we do not traverse the subtree rooted at t. This way we can avoid touching the leaf nodes of the subtree for t more than once. The total time cost is therefore only linear in the number of the leaf nodes, which is $O(|w|)$.

Last, recall the proof of Lemma 7 where a possibility of creation of a new node v is mentioned. If $label(v)$ is a repeating factor of length more than one, then we insert v to the bin-sorted list for LRFs. This insertion can be done in constant time. The matter is how to examine if the new node v should be in the node list or not. The length check can be done in constant time by seeing

$length(v)$. Then we see all child nodes of v and their minimum and maximum beginning positions. Since the number of the child nodes of v is at most $|\Sigma|$, we can compute the minimum and maximum beginning positions i, j of v in constant time assuming Σ is fixed. If $j - i \geq length(v)$ then v is inserted into the list, and otherwise not. Clearly this calculation takes constant time.

We now have the main result of this paper.

Theorem 3. *The text compression based on the longest-first substitution is feasible in linear time.*

Proof. The preprocessing of input string w is feasible in $O(|w|)$ time. Let N be the number of stages in the compression of w. The k-th stage of the compression takes $O(|x_k| \cdot \#occ_{w_k}(x_k))$ time. Since $|x_k| \cdot \#occ_{w_k}(x_k) \leq 2(|x_k| - 1) \cdot \#occ_{w_k}(x_k) = 2(|\overline{w_k}| - |\overline{w_{k+1}}|)$, we obtain $\sum_{k=1}^{N} |x_k| \cdot \#occ_{w_k}(x_k) \leq 2\sum_{k=1}^{N}(|\overline{w_k}| - |\overline{w_{k+1}}|) \leq 2|\overline{w_1}| = O(|w|)$.   □

4   Conclusions and Future Work

This paper introduced a linear-time algorithm to compress a given text by longest-first substitution. We employed a suffix tree in the core of the algorithm, gave some operations for updating the tree after the substitution for a longest repeating factor, and delved in the analysis of the accuracy and time complexity of the algorithm.

An interesting fact is that we can also use compact directed acyclic word graphs (CDAWGs) [6] that are smaller than suffix trees. Note that, though Proposition 4 relies on Ukkonen's suffix tree construction algorithm, the on-line algorithm of [10] could the same role for CDAWGs. However, the operation to maintain a CDAWG after the substitution for an LRF, is relatively more complicated, since it is a graph which has only one sink node. Namely, all suffixes of an input text are represented by one node, unlike the suffix tree with a one-to-one correspondence between a suffix and leaf node. However, it is possible in (amortized) constant time to simulate the suffix link traversal between two leaf nodes of a suffix tree in the corresponding CDAWG, by a technique similar to the one introduced in the latter part of the proof for Lemma 7.

The ultimate goal of off-line grammar-based text compression is to first replace the factor x of input string w with a new character, such that $\#occ_w(x) \times |x| \geq \#occ_w(y) \times |y|$ for any other $y \in Factor(w)$ [16]. Namely, the *largest-area-first* substitution mechanism. For this purpose, every node v of $STree(v)$ has to be annotated by $\#occ_w(label(v))$. It corresponds to the *minimal augmented suffix tree* (*MASTree*) of w [3, 2]. The size of $MASTree(w)$ is known to be $O(|w|)$, but there currently exists only an $O(|w| \log |w|)$-time algorithm for its construction [7]. Therefore, to achieve a linear-time algorithm for text compression by largest-area-first substitution, we first need to develop a linear-time construction algorithm for $MASTree(w)$. In addition, we need a linear-time solution for sorting nodes of the tree in the order of their 'areas', and it is also a challenging open problem.

References

[1] A. Apostolico. The myriad virtues of subword trees. In A. Apostolico and Z. Galil, editors, *Combinatorial Algorithm on Words*, volume 12 of *NATO Advanced Science Institutes, Series F*, pages 85–96. Springer-Verlag, 1985.

[2] A. Apostolico and S. Lonardi. Off-line compression by greedy textual substitution. *Proc. IEEE*, 88(11):1733–1744, 2000.

[3] A. Apostolico and F. P. Preparata. Data structures and algorithms for the string statistics problem. *Algorithmica*, 15:481–494, 1996.

[4] T. C. Bell, J. G. Cleary, and I. H. Witten. *Text Compression*. Prentice Hall, New Jersey, 1990.

[5] J. Bentley and D. McIlroy. Data compression using long common strings. In *Proc. Data Compression Conference '99 (DCC'99)*, pages 287–295. IEEE Computer Society, 1999.

[6] A. Blumer, J. Blumer, D. Haussler, R. McConnell, and A. Ehrenfeucht. Complete inverted files for efficient text retrieval and analysis. *J. ACM*, 34(3):578–595, 1987.

[7] G. S. Brødal, R. B. Lyngsø, A. Östlin, and C. N. S. Pedersen. Solving the string stastistics problem in time $O(n \log n)$. In *Proc. 29th International Colloquium on Automata,Languages, and Programming (ICALP'02)*, volume 2380 of *LNCS*, pages 728–739. Springer-Verlag, 2002.

[8] M. Crochemore and W. Rytter. *Jewels of Stringology*. World Scientific, 2002.

[9] D. Gusfield. *Algorithms on Strings, Trees, and Sequences*. Cambridge University Press, New York, 1997.

[10] S. Inenaga, H. Hoshino, A. Shinohara, M. Takeda, S. Arikawa, G. Mauri, and G. Pavesi. On-line construction of compact directed acyclic word graphs. In A. Amir and G. M. Landau, editors, *Proc. 12th Annual Symposium on Combinatorial Pattern Matching (CPM'01)*, volume 2089 of *LNCS*, pages 169–180. Springer-Verlag, 2001.

[11] J. Kärkkäinen and E. Ukkonen. Sparse suffix trees. In *Proc. 6th Annual International Conference on Computing and Combinatorics (COCOON'96)*, volume 1090 of *LNCS*, pages 219–230. Springer-Verlag, 1996.

[12] N. J. Larsson and A. Moffat. Off-line dictionary-based compression. *Proc. IEEE*, 88(11):1722–1732, 2000.

[13] E. M. McCreight. A space-economical suffix tree construction algorithm. *J. ACM*, 23(2):262–272, 1976.

[14] C. G. Nevill-Manning and I. H. Witten. Identifying hierarchical structure in sequences: a linear-time algorithm. *J. Artificial Intelligence Research*, 7:67–82, 1997.

[15] C. G. Nevill-Manning and I. H. Witten. Phrase hierarchy inference and compression in bounded space. In *Proc. Data Compression Conference '98 (DCC'98)*, pages 179–188. IEEE Computer Society, 1998.

[16] C. G. Nevill-Manning and I. H. Witten. Online and offline heuristics for inferring hierarchies of repetitions in sequences. 88(11):1745–1755, 2000.

[17] E. Ukkonen. On-line construction of suffix trees. *Algorithmica*, 14(3):249–260, 1995.

[18] P. Weiner. Linear pattern matching algorithms. In *Proc. 14th Annual Symposium on Switching and Automata Theory*, pages 1–11, 1973.

[19] J. G. Wolff. An algorithm for the segmentation for an artificial language analogue. *Britich Journal of Psychology*, 66:79–90, 1975.

[20] J. Ziv and A. Lempel. Compression of individual sequences via variable-rate coding. *IEEE Trans Information Theory*, 24(5):530–536, 1978.

SCM: Structural Contexts Model for Improving Compression in Semistructured Text Databases*

Joaquín Adiego[1], Gonzalo Navarro[2], and Pablo de la Fuente[1]

[1] Departamento de Informática, Universidad de Valladolid, Valladolid, España.
{jadiego, pfuente}@infor.uva.es
[2] Departamento de Ciencias de la Computación,
Universidad de Chile, Santiago, Chile.
gnavarro@dcc.uchile.cl

Abstract. We describe a compression model for semistructured documents, called *Structural Contexts Model*, which takes advantage of the context information usually implicit in the structure of the text. The idea is to use a separate semiadaptive model to compress the text that lies inside each different structure type (e.g., different XML tag). The intuition behind the idea is that the distribution of all the texts that belong to a given structure type should be similar, and different from that of other structure types. We test our idea using a word-based Huffman coding, which is the standard for compressing large natural language textual databases, and show that our compression method obtains significant improvements in compression ratios. We also analyze the possibility that storing separate models may not pay off if the distribution of different structure types is not different enough, and present a heuristic to *merge* models with the aim of minimizing the total size of the compressed database. This technique gives an additional improvement over the plain technique. The comparison against existing prototypes shows that our method is a competitive choice for compressed text databases. Finally, we show how to apply SCM over text chunks, which allows one to adjust the different word frequencies as they change across the text collection.

Keywords: Text Compression, Compression Model, Semistructured Documents.

1 Introduction

Compression of large document collections not only reduces the amount of disk space occupied by the data, but it also decreases the overall query processing time in text retrieval systems. Improvements in processing times are achieved thanks to the reduced disk transfer times necessary to access the text in compressed form. Since in the last decades processor speeds have increased much

* This work was partially supported by CYTED VII.19 RIBIDI project (all authors) and Fondecyt Project 1-020831 (second author).

M.A. Nascimento, E.S. de Moura, A.L. Oliveira (Eds.): SPIRE 2003, LNCS 2857, pp. 153–167, 2003.

faster than disk transfer speeds, trading disk transfer times by processor decompression times has become a better and better choice. Moreover, recent research on "direct" compressed text searching, i.e., searching a compressed text without decompressing it, has led to a win-win situation where the compressed text takes less space and is searched faster than the plain text [WMB99, ZMNBY00].

Compressed text databases pose some requirements that outrule some compression methods. The most definitive is the need for random access to the text without the possibility of decompressing it from the beginning. This rules out most adaptive compression methods such as Ziv-Lempel compression and arithmetic coding. On the other hand, semiadaptive models such as Huffman [Huf52] yield poor compression. In the case of compressing natural language texts, it has been shown that an excellent choice is to consider the words, not the characters, as the source symbols [Mof89]. Thanks to the biased distribution of words, the use of this model joined to a Huffman coder gives compression ratios close to 25%, much better than those usually obtained with the best adaptive methods. These results are barely affected if one switches to byte-oriented Huffman coding, where each source symbol is coded as a sequence of bytes instead of bits. Although compression ratios raise to 30% (which is still competitive), we have in exchange much faster decoding and searching, which are essential features for compressed text databases. Finally, the fact that the alphabet and the vocabulary of the text collections coincide permits efficient and highly sophisticated searching, both in the form of sequential searching and in the form of compressed inverted indexes over the text [WMB99, ZMNBY00, NMN⁺00, MNZB00].

Although the area of natural language compressed text databases has gone a long way since the end of the eighties, it is interesting that little has been done about considering the structure of the text in this picture. Thanks to the widespread acceptance of SGML, HTML and XML as the standards for storing, exchanging and presenting documents, semistructured text databases are becoming the standard. Some techniques to exploit the text structure have been proposed, such as *XMill* [LS00] and *XMLPPM* [Che01]. However, these are not designed to permit searching the text. Others, like *XGrind* [TH02], permit searching but do not take advantage of the structure (they just allow it).

Our goal in this paper is to explore the possibility of considering the text structure in the context of a compressed text database. We aim at taking advantage of the structure, while still retaining all the desirable features of a word-based Huffman compression over a semiadaptive model. An idea like that of XMLPPM, where the context given by the path in the structure tree is used to model the text in the subtree, is based on the intuition that the text under similar structural elements (i.e., XML tags) should follow a similar distribution. (In fact XMLPPM uses the full path, which is more powerful.) Although this compression is adaptive and does not fit our search purposes, a simplification where only the last element in the path is considered can be joined to a semiadaptive model, which is suitable for searching. The idea is then to use separate semiadaptive models to compress the text that lies inside different tags. For example, in an email archive, a different model would be used for each of the fields From:, Subject:, Date:, Body:, etc.).

While the possible gain due to this idea is clear, the price is that we have to store several models instead of just one. This may or may not pay off. In our example, coding the dates separately is probably a good idea, but coding the subjects separate from the bodies is probably not worth the extra space of storing two models (e.g., two Huffman trees). Hence we also design a technique to *merge* the models if we can predict that this is convenient in terms of compressed file length. Although the problem of finding the optimal merging seems a hard combinatorial problem, we design a heuristic to automatically obtain a reasonably good merging of an initially separate set of models, one per tag. Other related techniques can be found in [BCC+00].

In a text collection, some words can be common in some parts (with high frequency) and rather uncommon in others (low frequency). This is typical in news archives, for example, where some subjects are hot issues today and fade out in a few weeks. Considering this fact, another possiblility is to apply SCM over different text chunks. This idea allows us to adjust word frecuencies as they change across the text, improving compression rates.

This model, which we call *Structural Contexts Model*, is general and does not depend on the coder. We plug it to a word-based Huffman coder to test it. Our experimental results show significant gains over the methods that are insensitive to the structure and over the current methods that consider the structure. At the same time, we retain all the features of the original model that makes it suitable for compressed text databases.

2   Related Work

With regard to compressing natural language texts in order to permit efficient retrieval from the collection, the most successful techniques are based on models where the text words are taken as the source symbols [Mof89], as opposed to the traditional models where the characters are the source symbols.

On the one hand, words reflect much better than characters the true entropy of the text [TCB90]. For example, a semiadaptive Huffman coder over the model that considers characters as symbols typically obtains a compressed file whose size is around 60% of the original size, on natural language. A Huffman coder when words are the symbols obtains 25% [ZMNBY00]. Another example is the WLZW algorithm (Ziv-Lempel on words) [BSTW86, DPS99].

On the other hand, most information retrieval systems use words as the main information atoms, so a word-based compression eases the integration with an information retrieval system. Some examples of successful integration are [WMB99, NMN+00, MW01].

The text in natural language is not only made up of words. There are also punctuation, separators, and other special characters. The sequence of characters between every pair of consecutive words will be called a *separator*. In [BSTW86] they propose to create two alphabets of disjoint symbols: one for coding words and another for separators. Encoders that use this model consider texts as a strict alternation of two independent data sources and encode each one independently. Once we know that the text starts with a word or a separator, we know that after a word has been coded we can expect a separator and vice versa. This idea is known as the *separate alphabets model.*

A fact that the separate alphabets model does not consider is that in most cases a word is followed by a single blank space as a separator. Since at least the 70% of separators in text are single blanks [Mof89], they propose in [MNZB00] a new data model which uses a single alphabet for both words and separators, and represents the blank space implicitly. This model is known as *spaceless model.* Hence, after each word is decoded, we assume a single blank follows unless the next decoded symbol is a separator.

On the one hand we have to use a larger coding alphabet and then code lengths grow. On the other hand we do not need to code about 35% of the source symbols. It is shown in [MNZB00] that compression improves a bit using this method, although the improvement is not much.

A compression method that considers the document structure is *XMill* [LS00], developed in AT&T Labs. *XMill* is an XML-specific compressor designed to exchange and store XML documents, and its compression approach is not intended for directly supporting querying or updating of the compressed document. *XMill* is based on the *zlib* library, which combines Ziv-Lempel compression (LZ77 [ZL77]) with a variant of Huffman.

Another XML compressor is *XGrind* [TH02], which directly supports queries over the compressed files. An XML document compressed with XGrind retains the structure of the original document, permitting reuse of the standard XML techniques for processing the compressed document. It does not, however, take full advantage of the structure.

Other approaches to compress XML data exist, based on the use of a PPM-like coder, where the context is given by the path from the root to the tree node that contains the current text. One example is *XMLPPM* [Che01], which is an adaptive compressor pased on PPM, where the context is given by the structure.

3   Structural Contexts Model

Let us, for this paper, focus on a semiadaptive Huffman coder, as it has given the best results on natural language texts. Our ideas, however, can be adapted to other encoders. Let us call *dictionary* the set of source symbols together with their assigned codes.

An encoder based on the separate alphabets model (see Section 2) must use two source symbol dictionaries: one for all the separators and the other for all the words in the texts. This idea is still suitable when we handle semistructured documents —like SGML or XML documents—, but in fact we can extend the mechanism to do better.

In most cases, natural language texts are structured in a semantically meaningful manner. This means that we can expect that, at least for some tags, the distribution of the text that appears inside a given tag differs from that of another tag. In our example of Section 1, where the tags correspond to the fields of an email archive, we can expect that the From: field contains names and email addresses, the Date: field contains dates, and the Subject: and Body: fields contain free text.

In cases where the words under one tag have little intersection with words under another tag, or their distribution is very different, the use of separate alphabets to code the different tags is likely to improve the compression ratio. On the other hand, there is a cost in the case of semiadaptive models, as we have to store several dictionaries instead of just one. In this section we assume that each tag should use a separate dictionary, and will address in the next section the way to group tags under a single dictionary.

3.1 Compressing the Text

We compress the text with a word-based Huffman [Huf52, BSTW86]. The text is seen as an alternating sequence of words and separators, where a word is a maximal sequence of alphanumeric characters and a separator is a maximal sequence of non-alphanumeric characters.

Besides, we will take into account a special case of words: *tags*. A tag is a code embedded in the text which represents the structure, format or style of the data. A tag is recognized from surrounding text by the use of delimiter characters. A common delimiter character for an XML or SGML tag are the symbols '<' and '>'. Usually two types of tags exist: *start-tags*, which are the first part of a container element, '<...>'; and *end-tags*, which are the markup that ends a container element, '</...>'.

Tags will be wholly considered (that is, including their delimiter characters) as words, and will be used to determine when to switch dictionaries at compression and decompression time.

3.2 Model Description

The structural contexts model (as the separate alphabets model) uses one dictionary to store all the separators in the texts, independently of their location. Also, it assumes that words and separators alternate, otherwise, it must insert either an empty word or an empty separator. There must be at least one word dictionary, called the *default dictionary*. The default dictionary is the one in use at the beginning of the encoding process. If only the default dictionary exists for words then the model is equivalent to the separate alphabets model.

We can have a different dictionary for each tag, or we can have separate dictionaries for some tags and use the default for the others, or in general we can have any grouping of tags under dictionaries. As explained, we will assume for now that each tag has its own dictionary and that the default is used for the text that is not under any tag.

The compression algorithm written below makes two passes over the text. In the first pass, the text is modeled and separate dictionaries are built for each tag and for the default and separators dictionary. These are based on the statistics of words under each tag, under no tag, and separators, respectively. In the second pass, the texts are compressed according to the model obtained.

At the begining of the modeling process, words are stored in the default dictionary. When a start-structure tag appears we push the current dictionary in a stack and switch to the appropriate dictionary. When an end-structure tag is found we must return to the previous dictionary stored in the stack. Both start-structure and end-structure tags are stored and coded using the current dictionary and then we switch dictionaries. Likewise, the encoding and decoding processes use the same dictionary switching technique.

The following code describes the dictionary switching used for modeling, coding and decoding.

Algorithm 1 (Dictionary Switching)

current_dictionary ← *default_dictionary*
while *there are more symbols* **do**
      word ← *get_symbol*()
     if (*word is separator*)
        then *store/code/decode*(*word*, *separators_dictionary*)
         else *store/code/decode*(*word*, *current_dictionary*)
             if (*word is a start-structure tag*)
                then *push*(*current_dictionary*)
                       current_dictionary ← *dictionary*(*word*)
               else if (*word is an end-structure tag*)
                    then *current_dictionary* ← *pop*()

3.3   Considering Text Chunks

In addition to tags, we may decide to separate the text collection into a sequence of *chunks*. There will be a different dictionary for each different tag appearing in each chunk. This permits the method to adapt to word frequencies as they change across the text collections.

For each chunk we have a separate default dictionary, but still there is a unique separators dictionary for the whole collection.

There is a tradeoff regarding chunk size. Too small chunks will create too many dictionaries which will require a larger header table to find the right dictionary. Even if many dictionaries are finally merged (Section 4) and shared by many of these headers, the header table may get too large. Also, merging may become too expensive. On the other hand, too large chunks will not permit adapting fast enough to changes in text distribution.

3.4   Entropy Estimation

The entropy of a source is a number that only depends on its model, and is usually measured in *bits/symbol*. It is also seen as a function of the probability distribution of the source (under the model), and refers to the average amount of information of a source symbol. The entropy gives a lower bound on the size of the compressed file if the given model is used.

Definition 1 (Raw frequency) *Let n be the total number of terms that appear in the text. The raw frequency f_i of term i is given by*

$$f_i = \frac{occ_i}{n} \tag{1}$$

where occ_i is the number of occurrences of vocabulary term i in the text. The raw frequency is also called occurrence probability of term i.

The fundamental theorem of Shannon [Sha48] establishes that the entropy of a probability distribution $\{p_i\}$ is $\sum_i p_i \log_2(1/p_i)$ bits. That is, the optimum way to code symbol i is to use $\log_2(1/p_i)$ bits. In a zero-order model, the probability of a symbol is defined independently of surrounding symbols. Usually one does not know the real symbol probabilities, but rather estimate them using the raw frequencies seen in the text.

Definition 2 (Zero-order entropy estimation) *Let T_v be the number of vocabulary terms. Bearing in mind Shannon's theorem and assuming that a single dictionary is used to encode symbols, we estimate the zero-order entropy $\mathcal{H}$ of a text*

$$\mathcal{H} = \sum_{i=1}^{T_v} f_i \log_2 \frac{1}{f_i} \tag{2}$$

This definition lets us estimate the entropy when we have only one dictionary. If we want to estimate the entropy value when our model includes multiple dictionaries, we have to combine the entropies of each dictionary.

Definition 3 (Zero-order entropy estimation for a dictionary) *Let n^d be the total number of text terms in dictionary d. Let T_v^d be the total number of distinct terms in dictionary d. Let f_i^d be raw frequency of term i in dictionary d given by*

$$f_i^d = \frac{occ_i^d}{n^d} \tag{3}$$

where occ_i^d is the number of occurrences of vocabulary term i of dictionary d in the texts. We can reformulate equation 2 to get the entropy for terms in dictionary d:

$$\mathcal{H}^d = \sum_{i=1}^{T_v^d} f_i^d \log_2 \frac{1}{f_i^d} \tag{4}$$

Definition 4 (Zero-order entropy estimation with multiple dictionaries)
Let N be the total number of dictionaries. The zero-order entropy for all dictionaries, $\mathcal{H}$, is computed as the weighted average of zero-order entropies contributed by each dictionary ($\mathcal{H}^d, d \in 1 \ldots N$):

$$\mathcal{H} = \frac{\sum_{d=1}^{N} n^d \, \mathcal{H}^d}{n} \tag{5}$$

4   Merging Dictionaries

Up to now we have assumed that each different tag and chunk uses its own dictionary. However, this may not be optimal because of the overhead to store the dictionaries in the compressed file. In particular, if two dictionaries happen to share many terms and to have similar probability distributions, then merging both tags under a single dictionary is likely to improve the compression ratio.

In this section we develop a general method to obtain a good grouping of tags/chunks under dictionaries. For efficiency reasons we will use the entropy as the estimation of the size of the text compressed using a dictionary, instead of actually running the Huffman algorithm and computing the exact size.

Definition 5 (Estimated size contribution of a dictionary) *Let $\mathcal{V}^d$ be the size, in bits, of the vocabulary that constitutes dictionary d, and $\mathcal{H}^d$ its estimated zero-order entropy. Then the estimated size contribution of dictionary d is given by*

$$\mathcal{T}^d = \mathcal{V}^d + n^d \mathcal{H}^d \tag{6}$$

Considering the last definition we determine to merge dictionaries i and j when the sum of their contributions is larger than the contribution of their union. In other words, when

$$\mathcal{T}^i + \mathcal{T}^j > \mathcal{T}^{i \cup j} \tag{7}$$

To compute $\mathcal{T}^{i \cup j}$ we have to compute the union of the vocabularies and the entropy of that union. This can be done in time linear in the vocabulary sizes.

Definition 6 (Estimated saving of a merge) *Let $\mathcal{A}^{i \cup j}$ be the estimated saving of merging dictionaries i and j. Then*

$$\mathcal{A}^{i \cup j} = \mathcal{T}^i + \mathcal{T}^j - \mathcal{T}^{i \cup j} \tag{8}$$

Our optimization algorithm works as follows. We start with one separate dictionary per tag/chunk, plus the default dictionary for each chunk (the separators dictionary is not considered in this process). Then, we progressively merge pairs of dictionaries until no further merging promises to be advantageous. Obtaining the optimal division into groups looks as a hard combinatorial problem, but we use a heuristic which produces good results and is reasonably fast.

We start by computing $\mathcal{T}^i$ for every dictionary i, as well as $\mathcal{T}^{i \cup j}$ for all pairs i, j of dictionaries. With that we compute the savings $\mathcal{A}^{i \cup j}$ for all pairs. Then, we merge the pair of dictionaries i and j that maximizes $\mathcal{A}^{i \cup j}$, if this is positive. Then, we erase i and j and introduce $i \cup j$ in the set. This process is repeated until all the $\mathcal{A}^{i \cup j}$ values are negative.

The algorithm is depicted next. We have hidden the details on when the $\mathcal{T}$ values are precomputed and updated. Its cost is $O(VN^3)$ when there are N dictionaries and the vocabulary size is V. This can be reduced to $O(VN^2 \log N)$ by simple tricks such as recomputing savings only for the newly merged dictionaries and keeping dictionary pairs in a priority queue sorted by gain.

Algorithm 2 (Merging Dictionaries)

do *best_saving* $\leftarrow 0$
   for $1 \le i < j \le N$ **do**
       current_saving $\leftarrow \mathcal{T}^i + \mathcal{T}^j - \mathcal{T}^{i \cup j}$
       if (*current_saving* > *best_saving*)
          then *best_saving* $\leftarrow$ *current_saving*
              $bi \leftarrow i$, $bj \leftarrow j$
   if (*best_saving* > 0)
      then $d_{bi} \leftarrow$ *merge_dictionaries*(d_{bi}, d_{bj})
          $d_{bj} \leftarrow d_N$
          $N \leftarrow N - 1$
while (*best_saving* > 0)

5 Evaluation of the Model

We have developed a prototype implementing the Structural Contexts Model with a word-oriented Huffman coding, and used it to empirically analyze our model and evaluate its performance. Dictionaries are compressed using arithmetic character-based adaptive coding. Tests were carried out on the Linux Red Hat 7.2 operating system, running on a computer with a Pentium III processor at 500 MHz and 128 Mbytes of RAM.

For the experiments we selected different size collections of WSJ, ZIFF and AP, from TREC-3 [Har95]. Several characteristics of the collections are shown in Table 1. We concatenated files so as to obtain approximately similar subcollection sizes from the three collections, so the size in Mbytes is approximate.

The structuring of the collections is similar: they have only one level of structuring, with the tag <DOC> indicating documents, and inside each document tags indicating document identifier, date, title, author, source, content, keywords, etc.

When text chunks are not used, the average speed to compress all collections is around 128 Kbytes/sec. In this value we include the time needed to model, merge dictionaries and compress. Time for merging dictionaries ranges from 4.37 seconds for 1 Mb to 40.27 seconds for 100 Mb. Its impact is large for the smallest collection (about 50% of the total time), but it becomes much less significant for the largest collection (about 5%). The reason is that merging time is linear in the vocabulary size, which grows sublinearly with the collection size [Hea78], typically close to $O(\sqrt{n})$. Although merging time also depends quadratically on

Size	TREC-WSJ			TREC-ZIFF			TREC-AP		
(Mb)	#T.W.	#V.W.	Ratio	#T.W.	#V.W.	Ratio	#T.W.	#V.W.	Ratio
1	193899	18380	9.479%	161900	12924	7.982%	195915	19103	9.750%
5	874586	38750	4.430%	992067	35555	3.583%	956340	41263	4.314%
10	1669506	52218	3.127%	1821015	51094	2.805%	1721137	54058	3.140%
20	3370544	71832	2.131%	3489650	71136	2.038%	3486098	73820	2.117%
40	6690067	97190	1.452%	6970106	102737	1.473%	6985763	101480	1.452%
60	10015765	116221	1.160%	10272649	125326	1.219%	10411824	122340	1.175%
100	16672690	144701	0.867%	17289782	165113	0.954%	17252119	157376	0.912%

Table 1. Collection characteristics. For each collection we show the total number of words (#T.W.), the total number of vocabulary words (#V.W.) and the ratio between the two (Ratio).

the number of different tags, this number is usually small and does not grow with the collection size but depends on the DTD/schema.

In Table 2 we show original sizes, compressed sizes and compression ratios for each collection. It can be seen that compression ratios improve for larger collections, as the impact of the vocabulary is reduced [Hea78].

TREC-WSJ			TREC-ZIFF			TREC-AP		
Original	Compr.	Ratio	Original	Compr.	Ratio	Original	Compr.	Ratio
1221659	484575	39.66%	1021882	376180	36.81%	1185968	492832	41.55%
5516592	1793950	32.51%	6083389	1956195	32.15%	5805776	1952979	33.63%
10510481	3214613	30.58%	11164171	3480842	31.17%	10469592	3315087	31.66%
21235547	6190051	29.14%	21306059	6414762	30.10%	21219693	6371426	30.02%
42113697	11858566	28.15%	42659558	12452756	29.19%	42523572	12307072	28.94%
62963963	17498136	27.79%	62966279	18131869	28.79%	63343648	18054387	28.50%
104942941	28681879	27.33%	105709264	29972861	28.35%	105018927	29479824	28.07%

Table 2. Sizes and compression ratios for each collection.

In Figure 1 we can see a comparison, for WSJ (using up to 200 Mb this time), of the compression performance using the plain separate alphabets model (SAM) and the structural context model (SCM) with and without merging dictionaries. For short texts, the vocabulary size is significant with respect to the text size, so SCM without merging pays a high price for the separate dictionaries and does not improve upon SAM. As the text collection grows, the impact of the dictionaries gets reduced and we obtain nearly 10% additional compression. The SCM with merging obtains similar results for large collections (12.25% additional compression), but its performance is much better on small texts, where it starts obtaining 11% even for 1 Mbyte of text.

Table 3 shows the number of dictionaries merged. Column "Initial" tells how many dictionaries are in the beginning: The default and separators dictionary

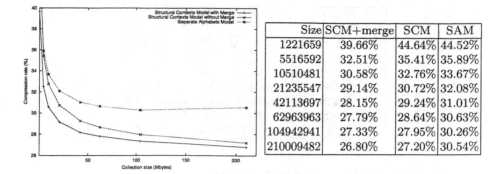

Size	SCM+merge	SCM	SAM
1221659	39.66%	44.64%	44.52%
5516592	32.51%	35.41%	35.89%
10510481	30.58%	32.76%	33.67%
21235547	29.14%	30.72%	32.08%
42113697	28.15%	29.24%	31.01%
62963963	27.79%	28.64%	30.63%
104942941	27.33%	27.95%	30.26%
210009482	26.80%	27.20%	30.54%

Fig. 1. Compression ratios using different models, for WSJ.

plus one per tag, except for <DOC>, which marks the start of a document and uses the default dictionary. Column "Final" tells how many different dictionaries are left after the merge.

For example, for small WSJ subsets, the tags <DOCNO> and <DOCID>, both of which contain numbers and internal references, were merged. The other group that was merged was formed by the tags <HL>, <LP> and <TEXT>, all of which contain the text of the news (headlines, summary for teletypes, and body). On the larger WSJ subsets, only the last group of three tags was merged. This shows that our intuition that similar-content tags would be merged is correct. The larger the collection, the less the impact of storing more vocabularies, and hence the fewer merges will occur.

Aprox.	TREC-WSJ		TREC-ZIFF		TREC-AP	
Size(Mb)	Initial	Final	Initial	Final	Initial	Final
1	11	8	10	4	9	5
5	11	8	10	4	9	5
10	11	8	10	4	9	7
20	11	9	10	6	9	7
40	11	9	10	6	9	7
60	11	9	10	6	9	7
100	11	9	10	7	9	7

Table 3. Number of dictionaries used.

The method to predict the size of the merged dictionaries from the vocabulary distributions was quite accurate: our prediction was usually 98%–99% of the final value.

Let us now consider the use of text chunks. In Table 4 we can see a comparison of the compression performance using differents chunks sizes over the same collection sizes for WSJ. The best gain obtained is around 0.03%, not really

Aprox.	Chunk size (Mbytes)				
Size(Mb)	0	2	4	8	16
1	39.66%	39.66%	39.66%	39.66%	39.66%
5	32.51%	32.51%	32.51%	32.51%	32.51%
10	30.58%	30.57%	30.57%	30.58%	30.58%
20	29.14%	29.13%	29.13%	29.13%	29.14%
40	28.15%	28.13%	28.13%	28.14%	28.14%
60	27.79%	27.76%	27.76%	27.76%	27.77%
100	27.33%	27.28%	27.28%	27.28%	27.29%

Table 4. Compression ratios using differents chunk sizes in Mbytes. Zero size shows compression ratio without using chunks.

significant. This can be due to the characteristics of WSJ: all the texts are very uniform, with similar distributions of words. In fact, all dictionaries in different chunks of tags <HL>, <LP> and <TEXT> were merged. On the other hand, the time for generating and merging dictionaries grows fast as the number of dictionaries grows. With these results, we can conclude that the use of chunks is not profitable in this case.

Finally, we compared our prototype (using merging) against other compression systems: the *MG* system, *XMill*, and *XMLPPM*. The MG system [WMB99] is a public domain software, versatile and of general purpose, which handles text and images. MG compresses structured documents by handling tags as words, and uses a variant of word-based Huffman compression called *Huffword*. On the other hand, *XMill* [LS00] is an XML-specific compressor based on Ziv-Lempel and Huffman, able to handle the document structure. XMLPPM [Che01] is also specific of XML and based on adaptive PPM over the structural context.

We compressed all the collections with the four systems[3] and averaged compression rates for each collection size. Average compression rates are shown in Figure 2. *XGrind* was not included because we could not find public code for it. *CGrep* [MNZB00] was not included because it is byte-oriented and the comparison would be unfair against it.

XMill obtains an average compression ratio roughly constant in all cases because it uses *zlib* as its main compression machinery. The compression ratio obtained is not competitive in this experiment.

XMLPPM, on the other hand, obtains the best compression. This shows that the idea of using the structural context to compress is good. The problem of XMLPPM is that its compression is adaptive, and hence it is not suitable for direct access on large compressed text databases.

Our prototype is better than MG for medium and large collection sizes, but not for small sizes. This can be due to our penalty in storing more than one dictionary. SCM starts to be better from 40 Mbytes, and for 100 Mbytes it improves over MG by 2.2%.

---

[3] XMLPPM required several changes to the sources in order to run properly, but these did not affect the compressibility of the collection.

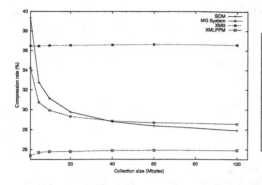

Size	SCM	MG	XMill	XMLPPM
1	39.34%	34.22%	36.46%	25.38%
5	32.76%	30.72%	36.44%	25.70%
10	31.13%	29.93%	36.49%	25.79%
20	29.75%	29.30%	36.51%	25.80%
40	28.76%	28.83%	36.55%	25.88%
60	28.36%	28.67%	36.61%	25.91%
100	27.91%	28.54%	36.56%	25.90%

Fig. 2. Comparison between SCM and other systems over WSJ, using default settings for all. The ratios shown in the table are average values for each collection size, over the different collections tested.

Note also that the difference between XMLPPM and our prototype is rather small for large collection sizes. In any case, the penalty is a rather small price for permitting direct access to the text.

6 Conclusions and Future Work

We have proposed a new model for compressing semistructured documents based on the idea that texts under the same tags should have similar distributions. This is enriched with a heuristic that determines a good grouping of tags so as to code each group with a separate model. On the other hand, the impact of the model on the retrieval performance is insignificant, in fact it is similar to the retrieval performance over compressed documents.

We have shown that the idea actually improves compression ratios by more than 10% with respect to the basic technique. We have compared our prototype against state-of-the-art compression systems, showing that our prototype obtains the best compression for medium and large collections (more than 40 Mbytes) among techniques that permit direct access to the text, which is essential for compressed text databases. On very large texts, the difference with the best prototype, which however does not permit direct text access, is no more than 7.2%. These text sizes are the most interesting for compressed text databases.

The prototype is a basic implementation and we are working on several improvements, which will make it even more competitive. We can tune our method to predict the outcome of merging dictionaries: Since we know that usually our prediction is 1%–2% off, we could add a mean value to our prediction. Also, we can try the *spaceless model* [MNZB00], which should give a small additional gain. However, the need to include the separators in all the dictionaries may make this approach unsuitable for our case.

Use of text chunks did not appear to be promising, but we plan to work on defining them more cleverly. We still have to test their effect on other collections.

With respect to the study of the method itself, we have to investigate more in depth the relationship between the type and density of the structuring and the improvements obtained with our method, since its success is based on a semantic assumption and it would be interesting to see how this works on other text collections.

References

[BCC+00]   A. L. Buchsbaum, D. F. Caldwell, K. Ward Church, G. S. Fowler, and S. Muthukrishnan. Engineering the compression of massive tables: an experimental approach. In *Symposium on Discrete Algorithms*, pages 175–184, 2000.

[BSTW86]   J. Bentley, D. Sleator, R. Tarjan, and V. Wei. A locally adaptive data compression scheme. *Communications of the ACM*, 29:320–330, 1986.

[Che01]   J. Cheney. Compressing XML with multiplexed hierarchical PPM models. In *Proc. Data Compression Conference (DCC 2001)*, pages 163–, 2001.

[DPS99]   J. Dvorský, J. Pokorný, and V. Snásel. Word-based compression methods and indexing for text retrieval systems. In *ADBIS'99*, LNCS 1691, pages 75–84. Springer, 1999.

[Har95]   D. Harman. Overview of the Third Text REtrieval Conference. In *Proc. Third Text REtrieval Conference (TREC-3)*, pages 1–19, 1995. NIST Special Publication 500-207.

[Hea78]   H. S. Heaps. *Information Retrieval - Computational and Theoretical Aspects*. Academic Press, 1978.

[Huf52]   D.A. Huffman. A method for the construction of minimum-redundancy codes. *Proc. Inst. Radio Engineers*, 40(9):1098–1101, 1952.

[LS00]   H. Liefke and D. Suciu. XMill: an efficient compressor for XML data. In *Proc. ACM SIGMOD 2000*, pages 153–164, 2000.

[MNZB00]   E. Silva de Moura, G. Navarro, N. Ziviani, and R. Baeza-Yates. Fast and flexible word searching on compressed text. *ACM Transactions on Information Systems*, 18(2):113–139, 2000.

[Mof89]   A. Moffat. Word-based text compression. *Software - Practice and Experience*, 19(2):185–198, 1989.

[MW01]   A. Moffat and R. Wan. RE-store: A system for compressing, browsing and searching large documents. In *Proc. 8th Intl. Symp. on String Processing and Information Retrieval (SPIRE 2001)*, pages 162–174, 2001.

[NMN+00]   G. Navarro, E. Silva de Moura, M. Neubert, N. Ziviani, and R. Baeza-Yates. Adding compression to block addressing inverted indexes. *Information Retrieval*, 3(1):49–77, 2000.

[Sha48]   C. Shannon. A mathematical theory of communication. *Bell Syst. Tech. J.*, 27:398–403, July 1948.

[TCB90]   Ian H. Witten Timothy C. Bell, John G. Cleary. *Text Compression*. Prentice Hall, Englewood Cliffs, N.J., 1990.

[TH02]   P. Tolani and J.R. Haritsa. XGRIND: A query-friendly XML compressor. In *ICDE*, 2002. citeseer.nj.nec.com/503319.html.

[WMB99]   I.H. Witten, A. Moffat, and T.C. Bell. *Managing Gigabytes*. Morgan Kaufmann Publishers, Inc., second edition, 1999.

[ZL77]   J. Ziv and A. Lempel. An universal algorithm for sequential data compression. *IEEE Trans. on Information Theory*, 23(3):337–343, 1977.

[ZMNBY00]   N. Ziviani, E. Moura, G. Navarro, and R. Baeza-Yates. Compression: A key for next-generation text retrieval systems. *IEEE Computer*, 33(11):37–44, November 2000.

Ranking Structured Documents Using Utility Theory in the Bayesian Network Retrieval Model

Fabio Crestani[1], Luis M. de Campos[2], Juan M. Fernández-Luna[2], and Juan F. Huete[2]

[1] Department of Computer and Information Sciences.
University of Strathclyde, Glasgow, Scotland, UK.
Fabio.Crestani@cis.strath.ac.uk
[2] Departamento de Ciencias de la Computación e Inteligencia Artificial,
E.T.S.I. Informática. Universidad de Granada, 18071 – Granada, Spain.
{lci,jmfluna,jhg}@decsai.ugr.es

Abstract. In this paper a new method based on Utility and Decision theory is presented to deal with structured documents. The aim of the application of these methodologies is to refine a first ranking of structural units, generated by means of an Information Retrieval Model based on Bayesian Networks. Units are newly arranged in the new ranking by combining their posterior probabilities, obtained in the first stage, with the expected utility of retrieving them. The experimental work has been developed using the Shakespeare structured collection and the results show an improvement of the effectiveness of this new approach.

1 Introduction and Motivations

Information Retrieval (IR) systems are powerful and effective tools for accessing documents by content [2]. A user specifies the required content using a query, often consisting of a natural language expression. Documents estimated to be relevant to the user information need expressed by the query are presented to the user through an interface. New standards in document representation require IR to design and implement models and tools to index, retrieve and present documents according to the given document structure. In fact, while standard IR treats documents as they were atomic entities, modern IR needs to be able to deal with more elaborate document representations, like for example documents written in SGML or XML, for instance. These document representation formalisms enable to represent and describe documents said to be *structured*, that is documents whose content is organised around a well defined structure that enables to represent the semantics of complex and long documents [5]. Examples of these documents are books and textbooks, scientific articles, technical manuals, educational videos, news broadcast, etc. This means that documents should no longer be considered as atomic entities, but as aggregates of interrelated semantic objects that need to be indexed, retrieved, and presented both as a whole and

M.A. Nascimento, E.S. de Moura, A.L. Oliveira (Eds.): SPIRE 2003, LNCS 2857, pp. 168–182, 2003.

separately, in relation to the user's needs. In other words, operationally, given a query an IR system must retrieve the set of document components that are most relevant to this query, not just entire documents. An example of a task that required the identification of specific structural elements is the search of a long educational video on Art Noveau for parts describing the work of Charles Rennie Macintosh. In this case, is likely that the user is not interested in the entire video or in the few frames in which Macintosh appears (identified by image analysis or word spotting on the soundtrack), but on a set of video segments (the user might not care if these are frames, scenes or large elements) which describe the work of Macintosh. In structured document retrieval this is made possible by searching with appropriate models the structured description of the video to identify the structural elements that contain the information sought.

However, the above example enables to highlight one of the problems of structured document retrieval that has not been well studied yet. Faced with a query on Charles Rennie Macintosh, a structured document retrieval system will retrieve from the educational video on Art Noveau only those structural elements (frames, scenes, etc, depending on the indexing level used) that are found to be relevant to the query. In modern IR this is achieved by ranking the structural elements based on some model that uses the weights assigned to the word (or words) "Charles Rennie Macintosh". In this way structural elements assumed to be "about" Macintosh because the query words appear in them will be ranked at the top and presented first to the user. But this might not be the best way to present the sought information to the user. In fact, using this approach the user will only see the structural elements of the video that are found to be about Charles Rennie Macintosh without their *context*.

Context is very important in structured document retrieval, but it has rarely been studied. It is easy to recognise that the context in which some information is presented is an integral component of the understanding of the information itself. In the above example, it would be of little use to the user to present him with a ranked list of frames found to be about Macintosh. Similarly, it would be of little use to retrieve the entire video or large parts of it containing much irrelevant information. What the user would like to see, we believe, is some structural elements of the video that are about Macintosh, where information about Macintosh is presented within some context, that is it is accompanied by sufficient information to enable the user to fully understand what is conveyed by the structural elements found to be relevant. This might require the retrieval of larger structural elements of the video (e.g. scenes) containing a combination of smaller structural elements (e.g. frames), some of which are highly relevant and some others being retrieved only to provide the context for the information contained in the relevant elements.

The above problem is very difficult for standard structured document retrieval and can only be tackled effectively using models that enable to fully represent the complex relationships present in a structured document among the different structural elements that compose it. This is particularly true for hierarchically structured documents where the inclusion relation between structural elements can be considered together with the proximity relation (one section following or preceding another) and the semantic similarity relation (two sections about the same topic) to fully capture the context.

Bayesian Networks (BN) are powerful tools to represent and quantify the strength of relationships between objects. As such, they are also being applied to structured document retrieval (see for example [13,8,14]). In [6] we proposed a retrieval model for structured document retrieval based on a multi-layered BN that is an extension of a previously developed model to manage standard (non-structured) documents [1,7]. However, though these models can tackle structured document retrieval (with various degrees of success), they cannot tackle the context problem explained above.

The overall objective of our work is to design a system that will enable to retrieve from a collection of structured documents elements of varying structure containing relevant information within some meaningful context, so that these structural elements can be considered self-contained informative objects that can be used on their own without reference to their documents of origin.

Until now, when the IR system decided to show a document, this decision was independent on showing any other document from the collection. But now, with structured documents, this is different because once it retrieves a piece of text, it may affect the retrieval of some others. To put into practice this previous idea, the best tool is *Decision Theory* [9], which is aimed to help making decisions, i.e., to choose an alternative among a set of them taking into account the possible consequences. In the context of this paper, the problem is to determine those parts of documents that will be shown to the users in response to a query, without showing any redundancy: if section 1.3 is more relevant than the whole chapter 1, then the IR system should only give this section to the user. But if the chapter contains more useful information, then the chapter is the text object returned and not the section, although it is also interesting. Specifically, our approach applies Utility Theory to solve this problem, i.e., the branch of Decision Theory concerned with measurement and representation of preferences. By means of *Utility Functions*, the preferences for the different decisions are described, and with them the *Expected Utility* for each alternative is computed. The alternative with the highest expected utility is considered the most preferable.

This paper is structured as follows. In section 2 we give some preliminaries to rest of the paper, including the description of the BN model for structured document retrieval. There, the assumptions that determine the network topology are considered, together with the details about the probability distributions stored in the network, and the way in which we can efficiently use the network model for retrieval, by performing probabilistic inference. Section 3 presents how decision theory can be used to capture the contextual relations between structural elements on the BN model. In Section 4 we report on some preliminary experimental results obtained with the model, using a structured document test collection [10]. Finally, Section 5 contains the concluding remarks and some directions for future research.

2 Preliminaries

In this paper we present a model called **Sride^{RB}**, which stands for *Information Retrieval System for Structured Documents based on Bayesian networks* (translated from the original name in Spanish and Italian). This model is composed of two parts: the retrieval model, which produces a ranking of all the structural units included in the documents according to the degree of relevance with respect a query, and a decision making model that will determine which units will be returned to the user in order to capture the relevant information in its context. The application of Decision Theory to Information Retrieval is a novel approach to this problem, which has been approached already with other technologies [15].

This paper addresses the issues related to the modeling of the retrieval of structured documents when the user does not explicitly specifies the structural element requested. In standard IR retrievable units are fixed, so only entire documents constitute retrievable units. The structure of documents, often quite complex, is therefore "flattened" and not exploited. Classical retrieval methods lack the possibility to interactively determine the size and the type of retrievable units that best suit an actual retrieval task or user preferences. Some IR researchers are aiming at developing retrieval models that dynamically return document components of varying complexity. A retrieval result may then consist of several entry points to a same document, corresponding to structural elements, whereby each entry point is weighted according to how it satisfies the query. Models proposed so far exploit the content and the structure of documents to estimate the relevance of document components to queries, based on the aggregation of the estimated relevance of their related components. These models have been based on various theories, like for example fuzzy logic [4], Dempster-Shafer's theory of evidence [12], probabilistic logic [3], and Bayesian inference [13]. A somewhat different approach has been presented in [15], where evidence associated with the document structure is made explicit by introducing an "accessibility" dimension. This dimension measures the strength of the structural relationship between document components: the stronger the relationship, the more impact has the content of a component in describing the content of its related components. Our approach is based on a similar view of structured document retrieval. In fact, we use a BN to model the relations between structural elements of documents. A BN is a very powerful tool to capture these relations, with particular regards to hierarchically structured document. The next subsection contains a detailed presentation of our approach.

2.1 A Multilayered Bayesian Network Model for Structured Document Retrieval

Given a document collection composed of N documents, $\mathcal{D} = \{D_1, \ldots, D_N\}$, and the set $\mathcal{T} = \{T_1, \ldots, T_M\}$ of the M terms used to index these documents (the glossary of the collection), $A(D_i)$ will denote the subset of terms in $\mathcal{T}$ that are used to index the document D_i.

172   Fabio Crestani et al.

We shall assume that each document is composed of a hierarchical structure of l abstraction *levels* $\mathcal{L}_1, \ldots, \mathcal{L}_\ell$, each one representing a structural association of elements in the text. For instance, chapters, sections, subsections and paragraphs in the context of a general structured document collection, or scenes, shots, and frames in MPEG-7 videos. The level in which the document itself is included will be noted as level 1 ($\mathcal{L}_1$), and the more specific level as $\mathcal{L}_\ell$.

Each level contains *structural units*, i.e., single elements as Chapter 4, Subsection 4.5, Shot 54, and so on. Each one of these structural units will be noted as $U_{i,j}$, where i is the identifier of that unit in the level j. The number of structural units contained in each level $\mathcal{L}_j$ is represented by $|\mathcal{L}_j|$. Therefore, $\mathcal{L}_j = \{U_{1,j}, \ldots, U_{|\mathcal{L}_j|,j}\}$. The units are organised according to the actual structure of the document: Every unit $U_{i,j}$ at level j, except the unit at level $j = 1$ (i.e., the complete document $D_i = U_{i,1}$), is related to only one unit $U_{z(i,j),j-1}$ of the lower level $j - 1$[3]. As the text (the whole set of terms) associated to $U_{i,j}$ is part of the text associated to $U_{z(i,j),j-1}$, abusing of the notation, we shall note this relation as $U_{i,j} \subseteq U_{z(i,j),j-1}$. Therefore, each structured document may be represented as a tree (Figure 1 shows an example).

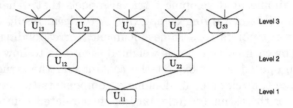

Fig. 1. A structured document.

Each term $T_k \in A(D_i)$, originally indexing a document D_i, will be assigned to those units in level $\mathcal{L}_\ell$ containing it which are associated with D_i. Therefore, only the units in level $\mathcal{L}_\ell$ will be indexed, having associated several terms describing their content (see Figure 2).

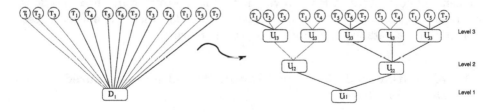

Fig. 2. From an indexed document to an indexed structured document.

---

[3] $z(i, j)$ is a function that returns the index of the unit in level $j - 1$ where the unit with index i in level j belongs to.

From a graphical point of view, our Bayesian network will contain two different types of nodes, those associated to structural units, and those related to terms, so that $V = \mathcal{T} \cup \mathcal{U}$, where $\mathcal{U} = \cup_{j=1}^{l}\mathcal{L}_j$. Each node represents a binary random variable: $U_{i,j}$ takes its values in the set $\{u_{i,j}^-, u_{i,j}^+\}$, representing that the unit is not relevant and is relevant, respectively.[4]; T_i takes its values from the set $\{t_i^-, t_i^+\}$, where in this case t_i^- stands for 'the term T_i is not relevant', and t_i^+ represents 'the term T_i is relevant'[5]. To denote a generic, unspecified value of a term variable T_i or a unit variable $U_{i,j}$, we will use lower-case letters, t_i and $u_{i,j}$. Notice that we use the notation T_i ($U_{i,j}$, respectively) to refer to the term (unit, respectively) and also to its associated variable and node.

The Bayesian network representing the structured collection has a graph topology with $l+1$ layers, where the arcs go from term nodes to structural units in level l, and from units in level j to units in level $j-1$, $j = 2,\ldots,l$. More formally, the network is characterized by the following parent sets, $Pa(.)$, for each type of node:

- $\forall T_k \in \mathcal{T},\ Pa(T_k) = \emptyset$.
- $\forall U_{i,l} \in \mathcal{L}_\ell,\ Pa(U_{i,l}) = \{T_k \in \mathcal{T} \mid U_{i,l}$ is indexed by $T_k\}$.
- $\forall j = 1,\ldots,l-1,\ \forall U_{i,j} \in \mathcal{L}_j,\ Pa(U_{i,j}) = \{U_{h,j+1} \in \mathcal{L}_{j+1} \mid U_{h,j+1} \subseteq U_{i,j}\}$.

An example of this multi-layer BN is depicted in Figure 3, for $l = 3$.

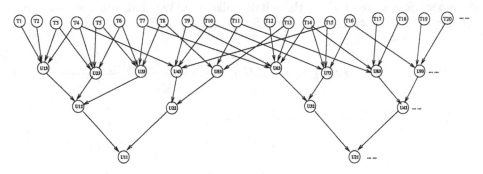

Fig. 3. Multi-layered Bayesian network for the BNR-SD model.

The following task is the assessment of the (conditional) probability distributions:

- Term nodes T_k: they store the following marginal probabilities: $p(t_i^+) = \frac{1}{M}$ and $p(t_i^-) = \frac{M-1}{M}$.

---

[4] A unit is relevant for a given query if it satisfies the user's information need expressed by means of this query.

[5] A term is relevant in the sense that the user believes that this term will appear in relevant documents.

- Structural units $U_{i,j}$: we have to assess $p(u_{i,l}|pa(U_{i,l}))$ and $p(u_{i,j}|pa(U_{i,j}))$, $j \neq l$, where $pa(U)$ denotes any configuration of $Pa(U)$, i.e., any assignment of values to all the variables in $Pa(U)$. The following canonical model is considered:

$$p(u_{i,l}^+|pa(U_{i,l})) = \sum_{T_k \in R(pa(U_{i,l}))} w(T_k, U_{i,l}), \qquad (1)$$

$$p(u_{i,j}^+|pa(U_{i,j})) = \sum_{U_{h,j+1} \in R(pa(U_{i,j}))} w(U_{h,j+1}, U_{i,j}), \qquad (2)$$

where $w(T_k, U_{i,l})$ is a weight associated to each term T_k indexing the unit $U_{i,l}$, $w(U_{h,j+1}, U_{i,j})$ is a weight measuring the importance of the unit $U_{h,j+1}$ within $U_{i,j}$, with $w(T_k, U_{i,l}) \geq 0$ and $w(U_{h,j+1}, U_{i,j}) \geq 0$. In either case $R(pa(U))$ is the subset of parents of U (terms for $j = l$, units in level $j + 1$ for $j \neq l$) that are instantiated as relevant in the configuration $pa(U)$, i.e., $R(pa(U_{i,l})) = \{T_k \in Pa(U_{i,l}) \mid t_k^+ \in pa(U_{i,l})\}$ and $R(pa(U_{i,j})) = \{U_{h,j+1} \in Pa(U_{i,j}) \mid u_{h,j+1}^+ \in pa(U_{i,j})\}$. So, the more parents of U are relevant the greater the probability of relevance of U

Before defining the weights $w(T_k, U_{i,l})$ and $w(U_{h,j+1}, U_{i,j})$ in equations (1) and (2), let us introduce some additional notation: for any unit $U_{i,j} \in \mathcal{U}$, let $A(U_{i,j}) = \{T_k \in \mathcal{T} \mid T_k$ is an ancestor of $U_{i,j}\}$, i.e., $A(U_{i,j})$ is the set of terms that are included in the unit $U_{i,j}$[6]. Let $tf_{k,C}$ be the *frequency* of the term T_k (number of times that T_k occurs) in the set of terms C and idf_k be the *inverse document frequency* of T_k in the whole collection. We shall use the weighting scheme $\rho(T_k, C) = tf_{k,C} \cdot idf_k$. We define

$$\forall U_{i,l} \in \mathcal{L}_\ell, \ \forall T_k \in Pa(U_{i,l}), \ \ w(T_k, U_{i,l}) = \frac{\rho(T_k, A(U_{i,l}))}{\sum_{T_h \in A(U_{i,l})} \rho(T_h, A(U_{i,l}))}. \qquad (3)$$

$$\forall j = 1, \ldots, l - 1, \ \forall U_{i,j} \in \mathcal{L}_j, \ \forall U_{h,j+1} \in Pa(U_{i,j}),$$
$$w(U_{h,j+1}, U_{i,j}) = \frac{\sum_{T_k \in A(U_{h,j+1})} \rho(T_k, A(U_{h,j+1}))}{\sum_{T_k \in A(U_{i,j})} \rho(T_k, A(U_{i,j}))} \qquad (4)$$

Observe that the weights in eq. (3) are only the classical tf-idf weights, normalized to sum up one. The weights $w(U_{h,j+1}, U_{i,j})$ in eq. (4) measure, in some sense, the proportion of the content of the unit $U_{i,j}$ which can be attributed to each one of its components.

The inference process that we have to carry out with this model is to obtain a relevance value for each structural unit, given a query Q. Each term T_i in the query Q is considered as an evidence for the propagation process, and its value is fixed to t_i^+. Then, the propagation process is run, thus obtaining the posterior probabilities of relevance of all the structural units, given that the

---

[6] Notice that, although a unit $U_{i,j}$ in level $j \neq l$ is not connected directly to any term, it contains all the terms indexing structural units in level l that are included in $U_{i,j}$. Notice also that $A(U_{i,l}) = Pa(U_{i,l})$.

terms in the query are also relevant, $p(u_{i,j}^+|Q)$. Later, the documents are sorted according to their corresponding probability and shown to the user. Although this computation may be difficult in a general case, in our case all the conditional probabilities have been assessed using a specific canonical model and only terms nodes are instantiated (so that only a top-down inference is required). In this context, the inference process can be carried out very efficiently, in the following way:

- For the structural units in level $\mathcal{L}_\ell$:

$$P(u_{i,l}^+|Q) = \sum_{T_k \in Pa(U_{i,l}) \cap Q} w(T_k, U_{i,l}) + \frac{1}{M} \sum_{T_k \in Pa(U_{i,l}) \setminus Q} w(T_k, U_{i,l}). \quad (5)$$

- For the structural units in level $\mathcal{L}_j$, $j \neq l$:

$$P(u_{i,j}^+|Q) = \sum_{U_{h,j+1} \in Pa(U_{i,j})} w(U_{h,j+1}, U_{i,j}) \cdot p(u_{h,j+1}^+|Q). \quad (6)$$

Therefore, we can compute the required probabilities on a level-by-level basis, starting from level l and going down to level 1.

3   Document Re-ranking Using Utility Theory

Once the probability of relevance has been computed for each structural unit, a ranking with all of them is generated. However, this ranking could show the user redundant information. Let us suppose that the top of the list of units is composed of the three subsections of a section from the same article, and the fourth item is that section. In this case, the system should detect this situation and decide to show either these three subsections or only the section, but not the four units. The problem, therefore, is to make a decision about what to retrieve, not only depending on the probability of relevance of the units but also in terms of the *usefulness* of these units for the user. One way to put into practice that idea is to use the *Decision Theory*, which would help making that decision which maximises the *Expected Utility*.

In a first step to achieve this goal, instead of deciding what to show to the user, i.e. to determine the *Best Entry Points* for a given query, the approach in this paper will be to modify the relevance value associated to each structural unit, taking into account the information involved in that decision. Taking up again the previous example, and as a consequence of this new relevance value, the section could change its position in the ranking overtaking its components.

The basis of the approach is the decision of retrieving (meaning showing it directly to the user) a structural unit, $U_{i,j}$, or not. This will be represented by introducing a decision variable, $R_{i,j}$, with possible values $r_{i,j}^+$ (retrieve $U_{i,j}$) and $r_{i,j}^-$ (do not retrieve $U_{i,j}$). The information that we shall use to make the decision is the relevance value of the own unit $U_{i,j}$ and that of the single unit, $U_{k,j-1}$, containing it (the $U_{i,j}$'s child in the network). An important element to make the corresponding decision is a *utility function*, $V(r_{ij})$, which assigns a value of utility to each possible decision $r_{i,j}$.

In our problem, the utility function $V(r_{ij})$ may be represented by means of a table that expresses the utility of making a decision, taking into account the values that both random variables, $U_{i,j}$ and $U_{k,j-1}$, could take. Therefore, for each different combination of possible units' values as well as decision's values, the values in table 1 express the corresponding user's utilities:

	$r_{i,j}^+$	$r_{i,j}^-$
$u_{i,j}^+\ u_{k,j-1}^+$	$v(r_{i,j}^+ \mid u_{i,j}^+, u_{k,j-1}^+) \equiv v_{++}^+$	$v(r_{i,j}^- \mid u_{i,j}^+, u_{k,j-1}^+) \equiv v_{++}^-$
$u_{i,j}^+\ u_{k,j-1}^-$	$v(r_{i,j}^+ \mid u_{i,j}^+, u_{k,j-1}^-) \equiv v_{+-}^+$	$v(r_{i,j}^- \mid u_{i,j}^+, u_{k,j-1}^-) \equiv v_{+-}^-$
$u_{i,j}^-\ u_{k,j-1}^+$	$v(r_{i,j}^+ \mid u_{i,j}^-, u_{k,j-1}^+) \equiv v_{-+}^+$	$v(r_{i,j}^- \mid u_{i,j}^-, u_{k,j-1}^+) \equiv v_{-+}^-$
$u_{i,j}^-\ u_{k,j-1}^-$	$v(r_{i,j}^+ \mid u_{i,j}^-, u_{k,j-1}^-) \equiv v_{--}^+$	$v(r_{i,j}^- \mid u_{i,j}^-, u_{k,j-1}^-) \equiv v_{--}^-$

Table 1. Utility function V for the decision node $R_{i,j}$, with $j \neq 1$.

For instance, $v(r_{i,j}^+ \mid u_{i,j}^+, u_{k,j-1}^+)$ is a value that represents the utility of showing unit $U_{i,j}$ to the user once that it is known that this unit is relevant and its child also is; $v(r_{i,j}^- \mid u_{i,j}^+, u_{k,j-1}^-)$ is the utility of not retrieving $U_{i,j}$ when $U_{i,j}$ is relevant and $U_{k,j-1}$ is not, and so on. To simplify the notation, the utility values will be noted as v with a $+$ or $-$ superscript depending on the semantic of the decision, and two subscripts representing the meaning of the two unit variables. We are assuming that the utility values are uniform, i.e., they do not depend on the specific unit being considered, although this restriction is not necessary.

For the structural units in level 1, that are not contained in any other, the utility function is expressed with a different table because the decision of retrieving it only depends on itself. In this case, the table is composed of two rows, one for each value that this variable may take, and two columns, representing the two possible decisions, as may be noticed in table 2. The same notation as previously explained, but only with one subscript, is used for values in that table.

	$r_{i,1}^+$	$r_{i,1}^-$
$u_{i,1}^+$	$v(r_{i,1}^+ \mid u_{i,1}^+) \equiv v_+^+$	$v(r_{i,1}^- \mid u_{i,1}^+) \equiv v_+^-$
$u_{i,1}^-$	$v(r_{i,1}^+ \mid u_{i,1}^-) \equiv v_-^+$	$v(r_{i,1}^- \mid u_{i,1}^-) \equiv v_-^-$

Table 2. Utility function V for the structural units in level $j = 1$.

The *Expected Utility* of retrieving a structural unit $U_{i,j}$ in level $j \neq 1$, given the query submitted to the IR system is computed according to the following expression:

$$EU(r_{i,j}^+ \mid Q) = \sum_{\substack{u_{i,j} \in \{u_{ij}^+, u_{ij}^-\} \\ u_{k,j-1} \in \{u_{k,j-1}^+, u_{k,j-1}^-\}}} v(r_{i,j}^+ \mid u_{i,j}, u_{k,j-1}) \cdot p(u_{i,j}, u_{k,j-1} \mid Q)$$

(7)

Alternatively, the expected utility of not retrieving this same unit is the following:

$$EU(r_{i,j}^- \mid Q) = \sum_{\substack{u_{i,j} \in \{u_{ij}^+, u_{ij}^-\} \\ u_{k,j-1} \in \{u_{k,j-1}^+, u_{k,j-1}^-\}}} v(r_{i,j}^- \mid u_{i,j}, u_{k,j-1}) \cdot p(u_{i,j}, u_{k,j-1} \mid Q)$$

(8)

Analogously, the two expected utilities for units in level 1 are the following:

$$EU(r_{i,1}^+ \mid Q) = \sum_{u_{i,1} \in \{u_{i,1}^+, u_{i,1}^-\}} v(r_{i,1}^+ \mid u_{i,1}) \cdot p(u_{i,1} \mid Q)$$
$$EU(r_{i,1}^- \mid Q) = \sum_{u_{i,1} \in \{u_{i,1}^+, u_{i,1}^-\}} v(r_{i,1}^- \mid u_{i,1}) \cdot p(u_{i,1} \mid Q)$$

(9)

From a computational point of view, obtaining the joint probability of a structural unit and its child conditioned to the query, i.e., $p(u_{i,j}, u_{k,j-1} \mid Q)$, may be a time consuming process, because of the great amount of calculations required on retrieval time. Taking into account this drawback, in this paper and as a first stage to cope with the problem, it has been considered the simplifying assumption that both units are conditionally independent given the query. Therefore, this probability distribution is computed applying the following expression:

$$p(u_{i,j}, u_{k,j-1} \mid Q) = p(u_{i,j} \mid Q) \cdot p(u_{k,j-1} \mid Q)$$

(10)

4   Experimentation

The model has been tested using a collection of structured documents, marked up in XML, containing 37 William Shakespeare's plays [10]. A play has been considered structured in acts, scenes and speeches (so that $l = 4$), and may contain also epilogues and prologues. Speeches have been the only structural units indexed using Lemur Retrieval Toolkit (available at http://www-2.cs.cmu.edu/~lemur/). The total number of unique terms contained in these units is 14019, and the total number of structural units taken into account is 32022. With respect to the queries, the collection is distributed with 43 queries, with their corresponding relevance judgments. From these 43 queries, the 35 which are content-only queries were selected for our experiments. The system evaluation has been carried out using the average precision for the eleven standard recall values.

The experimental design carried out with this model tries to determine the contribution of the use of the expected utility on the final ranking of structural units. Therefore, once the first stage in which the posterior probability of each structural unit, $p(u_{i,j}^+ \mid Q)$, has been computed, the second stage obtains the expected utility of each variable, combining these posterior probabilities and the utility function, achieving finally a second ranking.

With respect to the values contained in tables 1 and 2, and before giving values to them, it seemed to us interesting to sort them according to the utility of each value for the user. Therefore, the following ordering has been obtained using a small previous experimentation in which three users were asked to sort the values according to what they think it was more useful. All of them agreed in this ordering, being the one that has been applied in the first experiments:

$$v_{+-}^- \leq v_{--}^+ \leq v_{-+}^+ \leq v_{++}^+ \leq v_{++}^- \leq v_{-+}^- \leq v_{--}^- \leq v_{+-}^+ \tag{11}$$

From there, we could say that, for instance, to show to a user a non-relevant section in a relevant chapter (v_{-+}^+) is less useful than retrieving a relevant section in a relevant chapter (v_{++}^+), which in turns is less useful than not to present a relevant section within a relevant chapter (v_{++}^-), because in this case we would prefer to present the complete chapter and not the section). The less useful decision would be not to show a relevant section in a non-relevant chapter (v_{+-}^-), because we would definitively lose relevant information (note that the chapter would not be presented either, since it also is not relevant). The most useful decision is to retrieve a relevant section in a non-relevant chapter (v_{+-}^+). As the utility function is usually normalised in the interval [0.0, 1.0], then the limits have been assigned to $v_{+-}^- = 0.0$, and $v_{+-}^+ = 1.0$.

In the context of a usual decision problem, once the expected utilities have been calculated, we make the decision with greatest expected utility. In our case this would mean, for each structural unit $U_{i,j}$, to retrieve $U_{i,j}$ if $EU(r_{i,j}^+ \mid Q) \geq EU(r_{i,j}^- \mid Q)$ and not to retrieve $U_{i,j}$ otherwise. However, we do not only wish to decide what units to retrieve but also to give a ranking of these units. Therefore, a second important design aspect is what technique we have to use to sort these units. The first natural approach is to rank them according to the expected utility of showing a unit, $EU(r_{ij}^+ \mid Q)$. But there are two more natural options that also involve the expected utility of not showing the corresponding unit, $EU(r_{ij}^- \mid Q)$: the quotient between both expected utilities, $EU(r_{i,j}^+ \mid Q)/EU(r_{i,j}^- \mid Q)$ and the difference $EU(r_{i,j}^+ \mid Q) - EU(r_{i,j}^- \mid Q)$. These measures will be generically called Re-ranking Utility Measures (RUM) and denoted, respectively, RUM-u, RUM-q and RUM-d.

Therefore, the behaviour of this utility model depends on the utility function applied, as well as the expression of the expected utility used to rank the structural units. The aim of this experimentation has been to determine, if possible, a pattern that guarantees a good performance, by varying these two parameters.

All the re-ranking experiments with utilities are carried out using the same initial ranking of all the previously cited structural units from the test collection, obtained after performing the inference process described in subsection 2.1. The average precision for the 11 standard recall points of this running is 0.0653 [6].

Table 3 shows some representative experiments numbered in the first column (Ex.), from the great amount of tests run. In it, the measure to re-rank documents (RUM), the different utility values, as well as the average precision (AVP-11) and its corresponding percentage of change with respect to the baseline (%C) are included.

Ex.	Measure	v_{+-}^-	v_{--}^+	v_{-+}^+	v_{++}^+	v_{++}^-	v_{-+}^-	v_{--}^-	v_{+-}^+	AVP-11	%C
1	RUM-u	0.0	0.1	0.2	0.3	0.6	0.7	0.9	1.0	0.0674	3.21%
2	RUM-q	0.0	0.1	0.2	0.3	0.6	0.7	0.9	1.0	0.0684	4.75%
3	RUM-d	0.0	0.1	0.2	0.3	0.6	0.7	0.9	1.0	0.0687	5.20%
4	RUM-u	0.0	0.0	0.955	0.960	1.0	1.0	1.0	1.0	0.0735	12.57%
5	RUM-q	0.0	0.0	1.0	1.0	1.0	1.0	1.0	1.0	0.0726	11.17 %
6	RUM-d	0.0	0.0	1.0	1.0	1.0	1.0	1.0	1.0	0.0705	7.96%
7	RUM-u	0.0	0.0	0.955	0.960	1.0	1.0	1.0	1.0	0.0735	12.57%
8	RUM-q	0.0	0.0	1.0	1.0	0.5	0.0	0.4	1.0	0.0740	13.32 %
9	RUM-d	0.0	0.0	0.85	1.0	0.05	0.0	1.0	1.0	0.0733	12.25%

Table 3. Summary of experimental results.

In the first three experiments we used an increasing series of utility values according to eq. (11) with the three different RUM measures. It's noticeable a slight improvement in the performance of the system, fact that lead us to look for better combinations of utility values. By means of an intensive experimentation, where we tried many utility values, all of them satisfying the ordering restrictions imposed by eq. (11), the best results found correspond with the three next rows in table 3.

Our next objective concerned with the ordering of the utilities suggested by the users: Is the users' supposition correct? Could other different combinations of utility values that do not verify the ordering restriction obtain good or even better average precision? To find the answer other series of experiments were run, but in this case without imposing any ordering restriction. The best values obtained are shown in the last three rows of table 3.

Studying the results and the different combinations of utility values in all the experiments, it could be noted that the best performance for RUM-u is obtained when the utilities involved in the expected utility of retrieving a unit are sorted increasingly ($v_{--}^+ \leq v_{-+}^+ \leq v_{++}^+ \leq v_{+-}^+$), and are close to 1.0, except the first, which is not useful at all. The rest of utility values are not taken into account by RUM-u, and therefore their values do not matter. This behaviour of RUM-u seems to point toward a conservative strategy (probably recall-enhancing), where it is very useful to retrieve a relevant unit irrespective of the relevance of its context (v_{++}^+ and v_{+-}^+ values) and it is also quite useful to retrieve non-relevant units if their context is relevant (v_{-+}^+ value).

The other two RUM measures, RUM-q and RUM-d, also exhibit the same pattern for the utility values of retrieving a unit. Now, if we focus our attention on the other values, corresponding to the utilities of not retrieving units, v_{++}^-, v_{-+}^- and v_{--}^- (v_{+-}^- is always set to 0) for RUM-d and RUM-q, data usually shows crossed values for v_{++}^- and v_{--}^-. When in RUM-q the former is greater than the latter, in RUM-d the opposite situation occurs. Moreover, in RUM-q both values tend to be quite similar, whereas in RUM-d they are usually close to the extremes, i.e., $v_{++}^- \simeq 0.0$ and $v_{--}^- \simeq 1.0$. A surprising fact is that for both RUM measures, the utility of not retrieving a unit which is not relevant, contained in a relevant one, v^-_{-+}, is null, when our first hypothesis considered that it should be a rather high number.

Summing up, a good pattern when the RUM-u measure is being used is to follow the ordering in eq. (11), with high values for those utility values involved in the expected utility of retrieving a unit, except v^+_{+-} that is assigned to 0.0. For RUM-q and RUM-d, it is more or less the same pattern for those utility values, and for those which are used in the computation of the expected utility of not retrieving a unit, v^-_{-+} should be very low, almost 0.0. v^-_{++} and v^-_{--} should be very similar and around 0.5 for RUM-q and extreme for RUM-d. In all these cases, the performance improvement with respect to the baseline ranking obtained by using only the posterior probabilities of relevance computed from the Bayesian network, is above 12%[7].

5 Conclusions

This paper is framed as a first approach to solve a decision making problem, in which the IR system has to decide whether to retrieve or not a structural unit from a structured document collection, given a query submitted by a user. Instead of making this decision, this work presents a new way of re-ranking the structural units according to the expected utility of showing each unit, or by means of a variation in which the expected utility of not retrieving the corresponding unit is also involved.

Taking into account the experimental collection used to test the model, its performance could be described as rather good although could be clearly improved. The utility theory applied to re-rank structured documents seems to be promising. The main purpose of the experimentation has been to find patterns for the utility functions that present a good performance with the different RUM measures.

Of course we are conscious that the conclusions of this experimentation are completely related to the collection with which it has been carried out, and specially the relevance judgments, being able to change if the test bed is different. As a future work, the BN model with the utility module will be applied to other structured collections, as INEX, to test if the same patterns of utility are fulfilled.

To improve the results, one action to be taken could be to remove the simplifying assumption about the independence of a unit and the unit where it is included, given the query (eq. 10). To put it into practice, the probabilities $p(u_{ij}, u_{kj-1} \mid Q)$ have to be computed, preferably in an exact and efficient way. With this assumption, the utility model could be completely represented by means of an influence diagram [16], providing a clear semantics and a solid frame.

---

[7] We have not carried out a comparison of our results with other systems. The reason is that we only are aware of a paper containing empirical results with the same test collection [11], and there the results are obtained from a (unknown) subset containing only 25 queries from the 35 Shakespeare collection's content-only queries.

Only one utility function has been considered for all the layers in the model, although another approach could be to use a different one for each type of structural unit or layer, thus giving the possibility of assigning particularised utility values to them, modeling user's preferences.

The next stage is to use the model to determine the best entry points for a query. This task means to put into practice the whole decision making process, determining what to show to the user, and not only providing a ranking as it has been done in this paper.

Regarding the Bayesian network topology, other tasks to be done are to represent the specific textual information assigned to structural units in levels different from l (for example the title of a chapter or a section) and to allow direct relationships between units in non-consecutive levels of the hierarchy (e.g. paragraphs and chapters). Also, to permit our model to deal, not only with content-only queries, but also with structure-only and content-and-structure queries and let the queries to include, in addition to terms, also structural units.

Acknowledgments: This work has been supported by the Spanish CICYT and FIS, under Projects TIC2000-1351 and PI021147, respectively, and by the European Commission under the IST Project MIND (IST-2000-26061).

References

1. S. Acid, L.M. de Campos, J.M. Fernández-Luna, and J.F. Huete. An information retrieval model based on simple Bayesian networks. *International Journal of Intelligent Systems*, 18:251–265, 2003.

2. R. Baeza-Yates and B. Ribeiro-Nieto. *Modern Information Retrieval*. Addison-Wesley, Harlow, UK, 1999.

3. C. Baumgarten. A probabilistic model for distributed information retrieval. In *Proceedings of ACM–SIGIR Conference*, 258–266, 1997.

4. G. Bordogna and G. Pasi. Flexible representation and querying of heterogeneous structured documents. *Kibernetika*, 36(6):617–633, 2000.

5. Y. Chiaramella. Information retrieval and structured documents. *Lectures Notes in Computer Science*, 1980:291–314, 2001.

6. F. Crestani, L.M. de Campos, J.M. Fernández-Luna, and J.F. Huete. A multilayered Bayesian network model for structured document retrieval. *Lecture Notes in Computer Science*, 2711:74-86,2003.

7. L.M. de Campos, J.M. Fernández-Luna, and J.F. Huete. A layered Bayesian network model for document retrieval. *Lecture Notes in Computer Science*, 2291:169–182, 2002.

8. A. Graves and M. Lalmas. Video retrieval using an MPEG-7 based inference network. In *Proceedings of the 25th ACM–SIGIR Conference*, 339–346, 2002.

9. S. French Decision Theory. An introduction to the Mathematics of Rationality. Ellis Horwood Limited, Wiley, 1986.

10. G. Kazai, M. Lalmas, and J. Reid. The Shakespeare test collection. Available at http://qmir.dcs.qmul.ac.uk/Focus/resources2.htm

11. G. Kazai, M. Lalmas, and T. Roelleke. Focussed structured document retrieval. *Lecture Notes in Computer Science*, 2476:241–247, 2002.

12. M. Lalmas and I. Ruthven. Representing and retrieving structured documents with Dempster-Shafer's theory of evidence: Modelling and evaluation. *Journal of Documentation*, 54(5):529–565, 1998.
13. S.H. Myaeng, D.H. Jang, M.S. Kim, and Z.C. Zhoo. A flexible model for retrieval of SGML documents. In *Proceedings of the 21th ACM–SIGIR Conference*, 138–145, 1998.
14. B. Piwowarski, G.E. Faure, and P. Gallinari. Bayesian networks and INEX. In *Proceedings of the INEX Workshop*, 7–12, 2002.
15. T. Roelleke, M. Lalmas, G. Kazai, I. Ruthven, and S. Quicker. The accessibility dimension for structured document retrieval. *Lecture Notes in Computer Science*, 2291:284–302, 2002.
16. R. D. Shachter. Probabilistic Inference and Influence Diagrams. *Operations Research*, 36(5):527–550, 1988.

An Empirical Comparison of Text Categorization Methods

Ana Cardoso-Cachopo[1,2] and Arlindo L. Oliveira[1,2]

[1] Instituto Superior Técnico
Departamento de Engenharia Informática
Av. Rovisco Pais, 1
1049-001 Lisboa — Portugal
[2] INESC-ID / IST
Rua Alves Redol, 9
1000-029 Lisboa — Portugal
acardoso@gia.ist.utl.pt, aml@inesc-id.pt

Abstract. In this paper we present a comprehensive comparison of the performance of a number of *text categorization* methods in two different data sets. In particular, we evaluate the Vector and Latent Semantic Analysis (LSA) methods, a classifier based on Support Vector Machines (SVM) and the k-Nearest Neighbor variations of the Vector and LSA models.

We report the results obtained using the Mean Reciprocal Rank as a measure of overall performance, a commonly used evaluation measure for *question answering* tasks. We argue that this evaluation measure is also very well suited for *text categorization* tasks.

Our results show that overall, SVMs and k-NN LSA perform better than the other methods, in a statistically significant way.

1 Introduction

As the amount of information in written form increases, *text categorization* techniques become more necessary to find relevant information in a variety of tasks such as finding answers to similar questions, classifying news by subject or newsgroup, sorting e-mail messages, etc.

A number of approaches to *text categorization* has been proposed. The goal of *text categorization* methods is to associate one (or more) of a given set of categories to a particular document. They differ on how they represent documents and on how they decide which category to assign to a particular document. As such, a particular approach can be more suitable for a particular task, with a specific dataset, while another one is better adapted to a different setting. The measure used to quantify the performance of each approach can also influence the results.

In this paper we compare how the Vector Model, Latent Semantic Analysis (LSA), a classifier based on Support Vector Machines (SVM) and the k-Nearest Neighbors variations of the Vector and LSA models perform on two different data sets, using the Mean Reciprocal Rank as a measure of overall performance.

M.A. Nascimento, E.S. de Moura, A.L. Oliveira (Eds.): SPIRE 2003, LNCS 2857, pp. 183–196, 2003.

2   Data Description

As each model can behave differently in different settings, we have to test them in the same setting if we want to be able to compare the results. To allow for the generalization of results, we should use more than one test problem. For our study we used two different sets of data, in two different languages.

Financial Institution's Dataset The first dataset consists of messages sent by the clients of a financial institution to their help-desk and the answers they got from the help desk assistants. All these documents are in Portuguese. We had access to the collection of answered messages under a non-disclosure agreement.

We classified the data according to the type of request that was made. This dataset contains one class for each type of message that can be answered automatically and one class that comprises all the messages that need human intervention. Our complete dataset has 1391 classified messages and the respective answers. There are 37 different classes, containing from 5 to 346 messages each.

For the purpose of model comparison 10 classes were selected, containing 34 to 58 messages each, in a total of 461 messages. We will call this dataset **C10**. Table 1 lists the message types and the number of messages per type[3].

Type of message	# msgs
Incomplete data for a request of credit allowance	34
Question about the available amount of credit	36
General information about "points promotion"	42
More information on "low value payment" operation	45
Request for the receipt of an operation	46
Impossible to request checks through the internet	46
Points in the "points promotion" have disappeared	46
Impossible to buy or sell stock funds through the internet	52
How to buy or sell stocks through the internet	56
What is the price of a particular financial operation?	58
Total	461

Table 1. Number of messages of each type in C10

In this study, we will describe results that use only the client's message for training.

20 Newsgroups Dataset The second dataset is a subset of the 20 Newsgroups dataset, that can be downloaded from UCI's Knowledge Discovery in Databases Archive. Here, one thousand Usenet articles were taken from each of the 20 newsgroups in Table 2. Approximately 4% of the articles are cross-posted. The articles are typical postings and thus have headers including subject lines, signature files, and quoted portions of other articles.

---

[3] Some of these operations make sense only in Portugal's banking systems.

Group	Group
alt.atheism	rec.sport.hockey
comp.graphics	sci.crypt
comp.os.ms-windows.misc	sci.electronics
comp.sys.ibm.pc.hardware	sci.med
comp.sys.mac.hardware	sci.space
comp.windows.x	soc.religion.christian
misc.forsale	talk.politics.guns
rec.autos	talk.politics.mideast
rec.motorcycles	talk.politics.misc
rec.sport.baseball	talk.religion.misc

Table 2. Usenet groups for the 20 Newsgroups dataset

We used a subset of the 20 Newsgroups Dataset, containing a total of 100 messages from each newsgroup. Here, 18 messages were cross-posted. We will call this dataset **mini20**.

2.1   Pre-processing the Data

It is widely accepted that the way that documents and queries are represented influences the quality of the results that can be achieved. With this fact in mind, there are several proposals that aim at improving retrieval results. However, it is seldom guaranteed that they achieve their goal.

The main aim of preprocessing the data is to reduce the problem's dimensionality by controlling the size of the system's vocabulary (different index terms). In some situations, aside from reducing the complexity of the problem, this preprocessing will also unify the data in a way that improves performance.

In this work, we applied some of the filters used routinely in Information Retrieval:

- Discard words shorter than 3 or longer than 20 characters.
- Remove numbers and non-letter characters.
- Case and special character unification. Special character unification is needed in Portuguese, because there are accentuated characters and some people use them and some don't.

3   Applied Methods

In this work we are concerned with models for the categorization of natural language text. That is, models that, given a set of training documents with known categories and a new document, which is usually called the *query*, will predict the query's category.

In these models, usually based on statistical analysis, a text document is represented as a set of index terms or keywords. Each index term corresponds to a word in the initial text and has a weight associated to it, which should reflect how important this index term is, for that document and/or for the collection of documents.

For efficiency reasons, some of these models make simplifications that may not be totally justified but that have been experimentally validated. Some of these simplifications are:

1. They ignore the natural language structure of text. They do not try to fully "understand" a document, but they can use the structure that is easy to find (like HTML tags, for instance), even when they are processing large amounts of information. Besides being more efficient, this approach also has the advantage of not using domain-dependent techniques.
2. They assume that weights for the index terms are mutually independent. Although this simplification allows for a much easier treatment of the documents, weights for the index terms usually are not independent, because the fact that one of the index terms appears in the text may increase the probability of finding another term that is usually related to it, as in "computer network", for instance.
3. They ignore the order of words. This way, all the texts that are permutations of the same words are considered equal. This simplification is not always justified, but it is necessary for efficiency reasons.

In the next sections we briefly describe the methods that we compare in this paper.

Baeza-Yates and Ribeiro-Neto [1] includes a description of most Information Retrieval models and Sebastiani [19] contributed a more up-to-date survey of machine learning methods used for automated Text Categorization.

3.1   Vector Model

In the Vector Model [18, 16], documents are represented as a set of index terms which are weighted according to their importance for a particular document and for the general collection.

The index terms usually correspond to the words or tokens in the document (or query) and index term weights can be computed in several ways. The most usual is tf-idf (term frequency – inverse document frequency) [17], which increases with the number of times that the term occurs in the document and decreases with the number of times the term occurs in the collection. The weight of term t_i for document d_j is

$$w_{i,j} = \frac{freq_{i,j}}{max_l(freq_{l,j})} \times \log \frac{N}{n_i}$$

where $freq_{i,j}$ is the raw frequency of term t_i on document d_j, N the total number of documents and n_i the number of documents where term t_i appears.

For the weights of the index terms in the query, Salton and Buckley [17] suggest

$$w_{i,j} = \left(0.5 + \frac{0.5 freq_{i,j}}{max_l(freq_{l,j})}\right) \times \log \frac{N}{n_i}$$

Documents and queries are then represented as vectors in an M-dimensional space, where M is the total number of index terms.

Based on the weights of its terms, documents can be ranked by a decreasing order of similarity to the query. The similarity of each document d_j to the query q is computed as the cosine of the angle formed by the vectors that represent each of them

$$sim(d_j, q) = \frac{\vec{d_j} \cdot \vec{q}}{||\vec{d_j}|| \times ||\vec{q}||}$$

The category of the query can be determined as the category of the most similar document found.

3.2   Latent Semantic Analysis/Indexing Model

Matching documents and queries solely based on index terms can be misleading, because a document can be relevant for a query without having any terms in common with it.

The idea behind the Latent Semantic Analysis (or Latent Semantic Indexing) model (LSA/I) [11, 10] is to map each document and query vector into a lower dimensional space which is associated with concepts and retrieve the documents in this space. Arguably, retrieval effectiveness in this space will be better and it will also be computationally less costly, because it is a lower dimensional space.

LSA starts with a term-by-document rectangular matrix X which is decomposed by singular value decomposition (SVD) into the product of three other matrices: $X = T_0 S_0 D_0$, such that T_0 and D_0 have orthonormal columns and S_0 is diagonal. T_0 and D_0 are the matrices of *left* and *right singular vectors* and S_0 is the diagonal matrix of *singular values*. If the singular values in S_0 are ordered by size (and the corresponding row and column permutations applied to T_0 and D_0), the first largest k may be kept and the remaining ones set to zero. The product of the resulting matrices is a matrix $\hat{X}$ which is only approximately equal to X and is of rank k. It can be shown that the new matrix $\hat{X}$ is the matrix of rank k which is closest in the least squares sense to X. Ideally, we want a value of k that is large enough to fit all the real structure in the data, but small enough so that we do not overfit the data.

After these transformations the result can still be represented geometrically by a spatial configuration in which the cosine between vectors representing a document and a query corresponds to their similarity.

As in the Vector Model, documents can now be ranked according to their similarity to the query, and the category of the query is the category of the most similar document.

3.3   Support Vector Machines

The Support Vector Machines model or large margin classifier was introduced by Vapnik [20, 7] and was first applied for *text categorization* by Joachims [12, 13]. A thorough description can also be found in other sources [9, 3].

Support Vector Machines (SVMs) is a method for efficiently training linear classifiers. This technique is based on recent advances in statistical learning theory. They map the documents into a high dimensional feature space, and try to learn a separating hyperplane, that provides the widest margins between two different types of documents. SVMs use Lagrange multipliers to translate the problem of finding this hyperplane into an equivalent quadratic optimization problem for which efficient algorithms exist, and which are guaranteed to find the global optimum. The set of coefficients α_i^* resulting from the optimization process can then be used to construct the hyperplane that correctly classifies all the training examples with the maximum margin:

$$\vec{w} \cdot \vec{d} = \sum_{i=1}^{n} \alpha_i^* y_i (\vec{d_i} \cdot \vec{d}) \qquad \text{and} \qquad b = \frac{1}{2}(\vec{w} \cdot \vec{d_o} + \vec{w} \cdot \vec{d_\bullet})$$

This equation shows that the resulting weight vector of the hyperplane is constructed as a linear combination of the training examples. Only examples for which the coefficient α_i^* is grater than zero contribute. These are called the *support vectors*, because they have minimum distance to the hyperplane. Figure 1 illustrates these ideas.

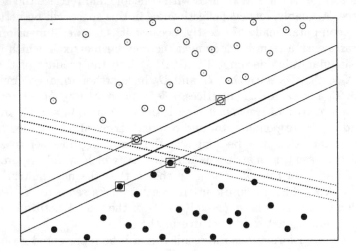

Fig. 1. Example of a two class, linearly separable problem and two possible separation hyperplanes with corresponding margins. The decision hyperplane chosen by SVMs is the bold solid line, which corresponds to the largest possible separation margins. The squares indicate the corresponding support vectors.

For sets of documents that are not linearly separable, SVMs use *convolution functions* (or kernels), that transform the initial feature space into another one, where they are able to find the hyperplane that separates the data with the widest margin.

By including several classifiers, these ideas can easily be generalized for datasets with more than two classes of documents.

3.4 k-Nearest Neighbors

The initial application of k-NN to *text categorization* was reported by Masand and colleagues [8, 15]. The idea is to determine the category of a given query based on the categories of the k documents that are nearest to it in the document space.

For this study, we first calculated each document's similarity to the query. Then, we used a voting strategy to find the query's class: each retrieved document contributes a vote for its class, weighted by its similarity to the query. The query's possible classifications will be ranked according to the votes they got in the previous step.

In this paper, we used a vector-based, distance-weighted matching function, as did Yang [22, 23], by calculating the distance using the Vector Model. We refer to it by "k-NN Vector". We also calculated the distance using the similarity obtained with LSA and called it "k-NN LSA". Because the number of examples of each class in C10 and mini20 is approximately the same, we used all the examples in each dataset as k.

4 Evaluation Measure

Evaluating the performance of computational systems is often done in terms of the resources (time and space) they need to operate, assuming that they perform the task that they are supposed to.

However, in Information Retrieval, it is not enough to retrieve a set of documents in a reasonable amount of time. The retrieved documents should also be the "right" ones, that is, the ones that are relevant for the query. Precision and recall are two measures that have been widely used to compare the performance of Information Retrieval models. *Precision* is defined as the fraction of the retrieved documents that are relevant, that is $\frac{RRD}{RetD}$ (it can be viewed as a measure of the system's soundness). *Recall* is defined as the fraction of the relevant documents that is actually retrieved, that is $\frac{RRD}{RelD}$ (it can be viewed as a measure of the system's completeness). Here, RRD means the number of retrieved documents that are actually relevant, $RetD$ means the total number of retrieved documents and $RelD$ means the total number of relevant documents.

However, to evaluate *question answering* or *answer finding* systems, the measures used to evaluate general IR systems are not very adequate [2]. We want to get the right answer, we want it only once (recall is not very important), and we want it as close to the first answer as possible. So we will be interested in a measure that takes the rank of the first correct answer into account.

The Mean Reciprocal Rank (MRR), is a measure used to evaluate submissions to the "Question Answering Track" of the TREC conferences, defined by Voorhees [21]. The idea is that its value is higher if the rank of the first correct answer is lower. We think that this measure is more adequate than the ones based on the values of precision and recall, which are more adequate for general Information Retrieval tasks. The MRR also has several advantages:

1. It is closely related to the average precision measure used extensively in document retrieval.
2. It is bounded between 0 (worst) and 1 (best), inclusive, and averages well.
3. A run is penalized for not retrieving any correct answer for a question, but not unduly so.
4. It is intuitive and easy to calculate.

The MRR can be calculated for each individual question as the reciprocal of the rank at which the first correct response was returned, or 0 if none of the first N responses contained a correct answer. The score for a sequence of questions is the mean of the individual question's reciprocal ranks.

However, the MRR also has some drawbacks:

1. The score for an individual question can take only $N + 1$ values.
2. *Question answering* systems are given no credit for retrieving multiple (different) correct answers.
3. Since the track required at least one response for each question, a system could receive no credit for realizing it did not know the answer.

In *text categorization*, we are also interested in getting the right category for a document (assuming each document has only one category), we need it only once, and the closer to the top position the better, because it gives us a measure of the system's confidence in the answer. Therefore, we decided to report the results obtained using the Mean Reciprocal Rank as a measure of overall performance. The Expected Search Lenght [6] was a good alternative, but we decided to use MRR because it is a common evaluation measure used for *question answering* tasks.

In our work, we considered the top ten categories returned by each model to calculate the MRR.

5   Experimental Setup

In our experiments we used existing implementations for each model. These implementations are freely available, and can be obtained from the authors.

For the Vector Model we used a Sourceforge project called IGLU. IGLU aims at being a software platform suitable for testing Information Retrieval models. At the time of this writing, only the Vector Model is implemented.

For LSA we used FAQO — Frequently Asked Questions Organizer [4]. FAQO is an application that was designed to help the technical support team at Unidata (University Corporation for Atmospheric Research) in the task of answering questions posed by the users of their software. It uses LSA/I to find similarities between the user's questions and questions that were previously answered by Unidata's personnel. As a result, FAQO shows a ranked list of previous questions and answers that are most similar to the present one. FAQO is an open source project released under the GPL license.

For SVMs we used a library called LIBSVM [5]. LIBSVM is an integrated software for Support Vector classification (among others) that supports multi-class classification. Their goal is to help users from other fields to easily use SVM as a tool. LIBSVM provides a simple interface that users can use to easily link it with their own programs.

LIBSVM already supports multi-class classification, returning, for each document, the (one) class it belongs to. However, to calculate the MRR, we need a ranked list of possible classes for each document, as is returned by the other models we are using. So, to determine the class of a given document, we implemented a "voting strategy", where a document's possible classes are ranked according to the number of votes that they had in a one-against-one approach, as Chang and Lin did [5].

We also used this "voting strategy", now weighted according to the similarity measure returned by the Vector or LSA models, to implement the k-NN variations of these models.

6   Results

To see if the number of terms used in the experiments influences the models' performance, the terms are ordered according to the information gain criterion [24, 12] and only the first most informative ones are selected. We performed extensive testing to determine the ideal number of terms that should be considered by each model.

For the datasets C10 and mini20, respectively, the lines in Figures 2 and 3 represent the mean of the MRR for a five-fold cross-validation test for each of the five models under evaluation, depending on the number of terms that is used.

For C10, which has a total of 2179 terms, we can see the whole range for the number of terms used in the tests. However, for mini20, which has a total of 33444 terms, we shortened the range for the number of terms, because we observed that the variation of the MRR was not interesting beyond this value. The "dots" to the right of the graphs show the value of the MRR using *all* the existing terms.

As we can observe by comparing both figures, the lines have approximately the same shape, which suggests that these results are not data-dependent. They should not depend on the language either, because each dataset is in a different language.

If we compare the performance of the Vector model with the performance of k-NN Vector, we observe that they do not show very significant differences. While the Vector Model is worse than the k-NN Vector for a smaller number of terms for C10, and improves over k-NN Vector as the number of terms increases, the opposite is true for mini20.

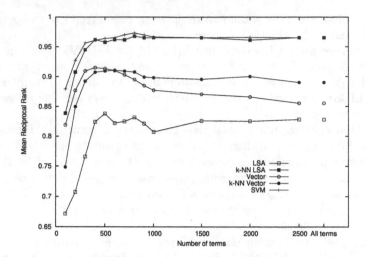

Fig. 2. MRR values for C10

However, if we compare the performance of LSA with its k-NN variation, we see that k-NN LSA behaves significantly better, and that this happens independently of the number of terms that we choose for both datasets.

While LSA is the worst performing method for C10, it performs significantly better than the Vector model and its k-NN variation for mini20. This shows that LSA performs better when it has many training examples.

The only model that has a performance comparable with k-NN LSA for C10 is the SVM-based, which even outperforms k-NN LSA for some values of numbers of features used. For mini20, SVMs are consistently above LSA.

We can also observe that, for all models, the results obtained using only a limited number of the most informative terms are not much worse than the results using all the terms in the dataset. On the contrary, in the case of the C10 dataset, the best results are obtained when we use between 400 and 800 terms. Reducing the number of terms used results in a considerable reduction in computational effort. If this is not of utmost importance for C10, it can lead to a considerable computational gain for mini20.

7   Statistical Significance Tests

To confirm if the differences observed between each pair of models are statistically significant, we performed paired t-tests for each pair of models. For each model, we chose the number of terms that provided the higher average MRR.

The values obtained for the MRR for each model, in each of the 5-folds used for cross-validation and their respective mean, are presented in Table 3 for the C10 dataset and in Table 4 for the mini20 dataset. The results of the paired t-tests between each possible pair of models are depicted in Tables 5 and 6, respectively.

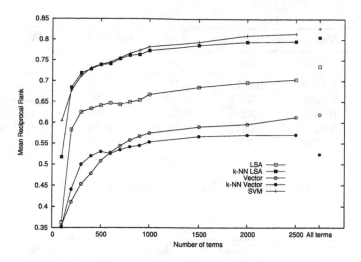

Fig. 3. MRR values for mini20 using at most 2500 terms

				C10	
	Vector	k-NN Vector	LSA	k-NN LSA	SVM, $\gamma = 0.4$
# terms	400	600	500	800	800
fold 1	0.9355	0.8922	0.8545	0.9764	0.9810
fold 2	0.8905	0.9101	0.8288	0.9602	0.9764
fold 3	0.9067	0.9184	0.8641	0.9656	0.9683
fold 4	0.9592	0.9402	0.8250	0.9837	0.9946
fold 5	0.8820	0.8907	0.8155	0.9525	0.9453
mean	0.9148	0.9103	0.8376	0.9677	0.9731

Table 3. MRR for 5-fold cross-validation for C10.

In these tables, $A \sim B$ means that the results obtained with model A are not statistically different from those obtained with model B, and $A \gg B$ means that the results obtained with model A are statistically better than those obtained with model B. In each case we present the p value, which is the significance of each paired t-test.

From the results in Table 5, we can extract a partial order among the various models, for dataset C10, when we consider only the number of terms that provide the higher MRR:

$$\{\text{k-NN LSA}, \text{SVM}\} \gg \{\text{Vector}, \text{k-NN Vector}\} \gg \text{LSA}$$

From the results in Table 6, we can extract a total order among the various models, for dataset mini20, when we consider only the number of terms that provide the higher MRR:

$$\text{SVM} \gg \text{k-NN LSA} \gg \text{LSA} \gg \text{Vector} \gg \text{k-NN Vector}$$

mini20

	Vector	k-NN Vector	LSA	k-NN LSA	SVM, $\gamma = 0.4$
# terms	18000	2500	all	12000	all
fold 1	0.6240	0.5672	0.7366	0.8040	0.8203
fold 2	0.6269	0.5341	0.7357	0.8096	0.8254
fold 3	0.6346	0.6246	0.7276	0.8198	0.8318
fold 4	0.6147	0.5571	0.7098	0.7950	0.8196
fold 5	0.6670	0.5708	0.7651	0.8274	0.8399
mean	0.6334	0.5707	0.7350	0.8112	0.8274

Table 4. MRR for 5-fold cross-validation for mini20.

c10

Model 1	t-test	Model 2	p value
Vector	$\sim$	k-NN Vector	0.7221
Vector	$\gg$	LSA	0.0038
k-NN LSA	$\gg$	Vector	0.0020
SVM	$\gg$	Vector	0.0012
k-NN Vector	$\gg$	LSA	0.0026
k-NN LSA	$\gg$	k-NN Vector	0.0007
SVM	$\gg$	k-NN Vector	0.0004
k-NN LSA	$\gg$	LSA	0.0001
SVM	$\gg$	LSA	0.0001
k-NN LSA	$\sim$	SVM	0.1581

Table 5. Results of the t-test for dataset C10.

8   Conclusions

In this paper we presented experiments using k-NN LSA, a new combination of the standard k-NN method on top of LSA that performed almost as well as the best performing methods for *text categorization* reported so far. To the best of our knowledge, there are no published results using the k-NN LSA.

We used the MRR, an evaluation measure that is very adequate for one-class *text categorization* tasks.

We showed that overall, SVMs and k-NN LSA perform better than the other methods, in a statistically significant way. As future work, we plan to investigate if the results obtained in this set of two text classification problems can be replicated in other benchmarks. We also plan to investigate if further improvements can be applied to the SVMs and k-NN LSA models. If possible, this would further enhance the superiority of these methods observed in this experiments.

mini20

Model 1	t-test	Model 2	p value
Vector	≫	k-NN Vector	0.0079
LSA	≫	Vector	0.0000
k-NN LSA	≫	Vector	0.0000
SVM	≫	Vector	0.0000
LSA	≫	k-NN Vector	0.0004
k-NN LSA	≫	k-NN Vector	0.0000
SVM	≫	k-NN Vector	0.0000
k-NN LSA	≫	LSA	0.0001
SVM	≫	LSA	0.0001
SVM	≫	k-NN LSA	0.0010

Table 6. Results of the t-test for dataset mini20.

References

[1] Ricardo Baeza-Yates and Berthier Ribeiro-Neto. *Modern Information Retrieval.* Addison-Wesley, Reading, Massachusetts, USA, 1999.

[2] Adam Berger, Rich Caruana, David Cohn, Dayne Freitag, and Vibhu O. Mittal. Bridging the lexical chasm: statistical approaches to answer-finding. In *Proceedings of the 23rd Annual International ACM SIGIR Conference on Research and Development in Information Retrieval,* pages 192–199, Athens, Greece, July 2000.

[3] Christopher J. C. Burges. A tutorial on support vector machines for pattern recognition. *Data Mining and Knowledge Discovery,* 2(2):121–167, 1998.

[4] John Caron. Experiments with LSA scoring: Optimal rank and basis. In *Proceedings of SIAM Computational Information Retrieval Workshop,* Raleigh, NC, USA, October 2000.

[5] Chih-Chung Chang and Chih-Jen Lin. *LIBSVM: a library for support vector machines,* 2001. Software available at http://www.csie.ntu.edu.tw/~cjlin/libsvm.

[6] William S. Cooper. Expected search length: a single measure of retrieval effectiveness based on weak ordering action of retrieval systems. *Journal of the American Society for Information Science,* 19(1):30–41, 1968.

[7] Corinna Cortes and Vladimir Vapnik. Support-vector networks. *Machine Learning,* 20(3):273–297, November 1995.

[8] Robert M. Creecy, Brij M. Masand, Stephen J. Smith, and David L. Waltz. Trading MIPS and memory for knowledge engineering: classifying census returns on the Connection Machine. *Communications of the ACM,* 39(1):48–63, January 1996.

[9] Nello Cristianini and John Shawe-Taylor. *An Introduction to Support Vector Machines.* Cambridge University Press, Cambridge, MA, USA, 2000.

[10] Scott C. Deerwester, Susan T. Dumais, Thomas K. Landauer, George W. Furnas, and Richard A. Harshman. Indexing by latent semantic analysis. *Journal of the American Society for Information Science,* 41(6):391–407, 1990.

[11] George W. Furnas, Scott C. Deerwester, Susan T. Dumais, Thomas K. Landauer, Richard A. Harshman, L.A. Streeter, and K.E. Lochbaum. Information retrieval using a singular value decomposition model of latent semantic structure. In *Proceedings of the 11th Annual International ACM SIGIR Conference on Research*

and Development in Information Retrieval, pages 465–480, Grassau, France, June 1988.

[12] Thorsten Joachims. Text categorization with support vector machines: learning with many relevant features. In Claire Nédellec and Céline Rouveirol, editors, *Proceedings of the 10th European Conference on Machine Learning*, pages 137–142, Chemnitz, Germany, 1998. Springer-Verlag. Published in the "Lecture Notes in Computer Science" series, number 1398.

[13] Thorsten Joachims. Transductive inference for text classification using support vector machines. In Ivan Bratko and Saso Dzeroski, editors, *Proceedings of the 16th International Conference on Machine Learning*, pages 200–209, Bled, Slovenia, 1999. Morgan Kaufmann Publishers, Inc.

[14] Karen Spark Jones and Peter Willett, editors. *Readings in Information Retrieval*. Morgan Kaufmann Publishers, Inc., Los Altos, USA, 1997.

[15] Briji Masand, Gordon Linoff, and David Waltz. Classifying news stories using memory-based reasoning. In Nicholas J. Belkin, Peter Ingwersen, and Annelise Mark Pejtersen, editors, *Proceedings of the 15th Annual International ACM SIGIR Conference on Research and Development in Information Retrieval*, pages 59–65, Copenhagen, Denmark, June 1992. ACM Press.

[16] Gerard Salton. *The SMART Retrieval System.* Prentice-Hall, Inc., New Jersey, USA, 1971.

[17] Gerard Salton and Christopher Buckley. Term-weighting approaches in automatic text retrieval. *Information Processing and Management*, 24(5):513–523, 1988. Also reprinted in [14, pages 323–328].

[18] Gerard Salton and Michael Lesk. Computer evaluation of indexing and text processing. *Journal of the ACM*, 15(1):8–36, January 1968. Also reprinted in [14, pages 60–84].

[19] Fabrizio Sebastiani. Machine learning in automated text categorization. *ACM Computing Surveys*, 34(1):1–47, 2002.

[20] Vladimir Vapnik. *The Nature of Statistical Learning Theory*. Springer-Verlag, Heidelberg, Germany, 1995.

[21] Ellen M. Voorhees. The TREC-8 question answering track report. In Ellen M. Voorhees and Donna K. Harman, editors, *Proceedings of the 8th Text REtrieval Conference*, pages 77–82, Gaithersburg, Maryland, USA, November 1999.

[22] Yiming Yang. Expert network: effective and efficient learning from human decisions in text categorisation and retrieval. In W. Bruce Croft and Cornelis J. van Rijsbergen, editors, *Proceedings of the 17th Annual International ACM SIGIR Conference on Research and Development in Information Retrieval*, pages 13–22, Dublin, Ireland, July 1994. Springer-Verlag.

[23] Yiming Yang and Xin Liu. A re-examination of text categorization methods. In Marti A. Hearst, Fredric Gey, and Richard Tong, editors, *Proceedings of the 22nd Annual International ACM SIGIR Conference on Research and Development in Information Retrieval*, pages 42–49, Berkeley, CA, USA, August 1999.

[24] Yiming Yang and Jan O. Pedersen. A comparative study on feature selection in text categorization. In Douglas H. Fisher, editor, *Proceedings of the 14th International Conference on Machine Learning*, pages 412–420, Nashville, TN, USA, 1997. Morgan Kaufmann Publishers, Inc.

Improving Text Retrieval in Medical Collections Through Automatic Categorization

Rodrigo F. Vale[1], Berthier A. Ribeiro-Neto[2], Luciano R.S. de Lima[3],
Alberto H.F. Laender[2], and Hermes R.F. Junior[1]

[1] Akwan Information Technologies
31275-050 - Belo Horizonte - MG - Brazil
{rodrigov,hermes}@akwan.com.br
[2] Computer Science Department
Federal University of Minas Gerais
31270-010 - Belo Horizonte - MG - Brazil
{berthier,laender}@dcc.ufmg.br
[3] Medical Informatics Group
Sarah Hospital Network
30510-000 - Belo Horizonte - MG - Brazil
luciano@bhz.sarah.br

Abstract. A current and important research issue is the retrieval of relevant medical information. In fact, while the medical knowledge expands at a rate never observed before, its diffusion is slow. One of the main reasons is the difficulty in locating the relevant information in the modern and large medical text collections of today. In this work, we introduce a framework, based on Bayesian networks, that allows combining information derived from the text of the medical documents with information on the diseases related to these documents (obtained from an automatic categorization method). This leads to a new ranking formula which we evaluate using a medical reference collection, the OHSUMED collection. Our results indicate that this combination of evidences might yield considerable gains in retrieval performance. When the queries are strongly related to diseases, these gains might be as high as 84%. This shows that information generated by an automatic categorization procedure can be used effectively to improve the quality of the answers provided by an information retrieval (IR) system specialized in the medical domain.

1 Introduction

Today, we observe the development of the concept of medical informatics, which presents itself as a new area in the medical field. In the broad sense, this concept is also associated with the improvement of the tasks of searching, synthesizing, organizing, and disseminating medical information to doctors, patients, and people interested in health related issues in general. These considerations indicate the great importance of combining knowledge from the medical and information sciences fields into modern information retrieval (IR) systems.

M.A. Nascimento, E.S. de Moura, A.L. Oliveira (Eds.): SPIRE 2003, LNCS 2857, pp. 197–210, 2003.
© Springer-Verlag Berlin Heidelberg 2003

The biomedical literature grows at a rate of 6% to 7% a year, doubling in size every 10 to 15 years. Most part of this literature is now available in some electronic form and frequently accessible through the Internet. Such availability facilitates the access to specialized medical information, but introduces new problems in its own. While the medical knowledge expands at a rate never observed before, its diffusion is slow. The barriers for the diffusion of the medical knowledge are many and include: the limited time for bibliographical searching, the limited access to the information sources, and the great difficulty of doctors and other medical professionals in identifying the relevant information within the vast medical collections of today [14]. In this work, we focus on this last issue, i.e., on the problem of improving the quality of the answers returned to queries focussed on medical topics.

A standard approach to this problem is to apply standard information retrieval (IR) thechniques to the medical domain. While this approach does provide a solution to the problem of finding relevant information in a large medical collection, it does not take into account any specialized information from the medical arena. This clearly seems to be a strong limitation.

An alternative approach is to develop a framework that allows combining IR techniques with knowledge from the medical domain. This is the path we follow here. We consider a specific form of medical knowledge, i.e., information on the diseases related to the documents in a medical collection. Given a medical collection, information on diseases can be generated through the assignment of ICD (International Code of Diseases) codes to the documents of the collection. This can be accomplished in fully automatic mode with great effectiveness, as we later discuss. Given the information on the diseases related to the medical documents (through ICD codes), we study the problem of how to improve the quality of the answers generated (i.e., how to improve the retrieval performance of the system).

To combine information on ICD codes with information derived from the text of the documents (which is the information used by the standard IR ranking algorithms), we adopt the framework of Bayesian networks [16]. Bayesian networks are useful because they allow combining distinct sources of evidence in a consistent fashion. Also, they provide an intuitive modeling tool that facilitates capturing (in the model) the influence of the key parameters of the problem being modeled. The bayesian framework we adopt leads to a new ranking formula that takes into account information about the text of the medical documents and information about the diseases related to the documents. Through experimentation, we show that this leads to improved retrieval performance. When only queries that are strongly related to diseases are considered, the average improvement in retrieval performance is as high as 84% (compared to a standard IR algorithm).

The paper is organized as follows. Section 2 discusses related work. Section 3 briefly describes a method for automatically categorizing medical documents we developed and that we use to assign ICD codes to the documents of the collection. Section 4 describes our ranking function based on the Bayesian network model. In

Section 5 we discuss our experimental results which are based on the OHSUMED reference collection. In Section 6 we present our conclusions.

2 Related Work

Several approaches have been proposed in the literature to address the problem of automatic categorization of medical documents. In [9, 10], the problem is treated as a classification problem which is solved by combining three classifiers based on probabilistic models [13] for the code assignment task. In [19], the problem is addressed through the usage of natural language processing techniques. Both approaches present good results in some situations but have some disadvantages. In the first case, good results depend on a large number of medical documents which have been previously classified and can be used as a training set. In the second case, an excessively complex approach is adopted to address a problem whose domain vocabulary is clearly small when compared to the vocabulary of any existing language. In addition, in both approaches the hierarchical structure of the coding standard and the knowledge of the coding specialists are completely ignored. In [12, 15], the authors propose a method for automatic categorization of medical documents that takes advantage of the hierarchical topology of coding schemes such as the International Code of Diseases (ICD) to generate high precision results.

Automatic text categorization has been used in different applications such as text classification, text filtering, and text retrieval. Applications in text retrieval, in particular, have received special attention. Methods such as decision trees [1], linear classifiers [11], context-sensitive learning [5], and learning by combining classifiers [10] have been proposed to address this problem.

Yang and Chute propose a method, known as Linear Least Square Fit (LLSF) [23], to perform automatic text categorization and text retrieval. The LLSF method uses a training set of manually categorized documents to learn word-category associations which are then applied to predict the categories of arbitrary documents. Similarly, this method uses a training set of queries and their related documents to obtain empirical associations between query words and indexing terms of documents, and then applies these associations to predict the related documents of arbitrary queries. Another method, called Expert Network [22], also needs a training set to categorize information. According to this method, the terms in a document are linked with its categories by means of a network in which there is a weight in each link. However, this method is preferable because it is simpler and computationally more efficient than the LLSF method.

Another approach, proposed in [8], also consists in a method for automatic categorization and a method for text retrieval. The categorization method derives from a machine-learning paradigm known as instance-based learning and an advanced document retrieval technique known as retrieval feedback. The text retrieval method computes two rankings: one for the free-text portion of the documents and another one for the category portion of the documents. The categories are generated according to the categorization method. The method proposes to sum both rankings and control the relative emphasis of each one through a parameter.

Our work is related to these approaches but we use different techniques for automatic categorization and text retrieval. The automatic categorization is supported by the method we proposed [12, 15] and we use Bayesian networks [16, 21] to merge the rankings generated for the free-text and category portions of the documents. Bayesian networks supply the formalism for representing, quantifying, and combining two or more sources of evidence to support a ranking for the documents in the answer set. In this work, we use this method to represent and combine concept-based and text-based evidential information in a similar way as discussed in [16, 20].

In spite of the differences in the above related works, all of them demonstrate that the categorization process, being it automatic or manual, is effective because it can be used to improve the retrieval performance when compared with a system that uses no categorization.

3   The Automatic Categorization Method

In this section, we briefly describe our method for automatic assignment of ICD codes to medical documents. The method uses the hierarchical structure of the ICD alphabetical index to guide the coding task and attains levels of precision comparable to the codification provided by medical specialists [15]. While here we focus on the ICD alphabetical index, we notice that the method can be used with other medical coding schemes such as SNOMED and MeSH.

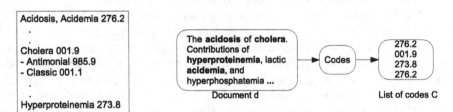

Fig. 1. An example of the term hierarchy for the ICD-9 vocabulary.

Fig. 2. Example of the categorization process.

Fig. 1 shows some fragments of the ICD version 9 (ICD-9) alphabethic index. As we can see, the code 276.2 is associated with the terms *Acidosis* and *Acidemia*, the code 001.9 is associated with the term *Cholera*, the code 985.9 is associated with the seguence of terms *Cholera + Antimonial*, and so on.

Fig. 2 illustrates the categorization process. This process can be represented by a function *codes(d)* that, given an input document *d*, returns a list of codes *C* related to *d*. This function scans the document *d* searching for terms or sequences of terms that lead to codes in the ICD-9 alphabetic index. For instance, for the document in Fig. 2 the function *codes(d)* returns the codes 276.2, 001.9, 273.8, and 276.2 which are related, respectively, to the terms *acidosis*, *cholera*, *hyperproteinemia*, and *acidemia*. For more details on our categorization method we refer the reader to [12, 15].

4   The Ranking Fusion Model

In this work, one of our main goals is to investigate whether knowledge derived from the diseases associated with a medical document (i.e., information about its ICD codes) can be used to improve retrieval performance. Our approach is to combine evidence from the vector model with evidence from the ICD categorization and to investigate whether gains in retrieval performance can be attained.

To combine these two sources of evidence, we use a framework based on Bayesian networks. Bayesian networks are useful because they allow combining distinct sources of evidence in a consistent fashion and also provide an intuitive modeling tool that facilitates capturing (in the model) the influence of the key parameters of the system. Further, they have been used successfully with various reference collections and for distinct purposes in the past [3, 4, 6, 16, 20, 21].

Here, we extend the evidence provided by the classic vector model in the Bayesian network [17, 20], to include evidence from ICD categories. Fig. 3 illustrates the extended network. The right part of the network models ICD codes

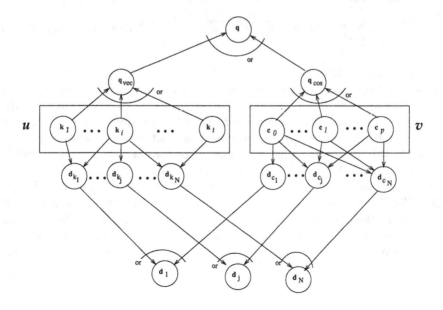

Fig. 3. Bayesian network expanded with evidence from ICD categories.

(represented by the c_l nodes) and their relationships with the query (represented by the q_{cos} node) and with the medical documents (represented by the d_{c_i} nodes). In the left part of the network, the query node is renamed as q_{vec} and the document nodes are renamed as d_{k_i} to allow distinguishing between the representations for the query and for the documents in the right and left parts of the network. An extra node q is inserted at the top of the network to represent the fact that the query now considers evidence from the vector model (through the q_{vec} node) and evidence from the ICD categories (through the q_{cos} node). Extra nodes d_j are inserted at the bottom of the network to represent the fact that a document d_j now considers evidence from the vector model (through the d_{k_j} node) or evidence from the ICD categories (through the d_{c_j} node).

Let u represent the state of the set of the k_i root nodes, and let v represent the state of the set of c_l root nodes. To allow referring to the state of each variable k_i, we define a function $g_i(u)$ that returns the value of the variable k_i according to concept u. For the k_i root nodes, we consider only the states u_i such that

$$u = u_i \iff g_i(u) = 1 \wedge g_{j \neq i}(u) = 0$$

In Fig. 3, the rank $P(d_j|q)$ associated with a document d_j is computed through basic conditioning on the root nodes and application of Bayes' rule as follows.

$$P(d_j|q) = \frac{P(d_j \wedge q)}{P(q)}$$

$$= \eta \sum_{u,v} P(d_j|u,v) \, P(q|u,v) \, P(u) \, P(v)$$

$$= \eta \sum_{u,v} [1 - (\overline{P(d_{k_j}|u)})(\overline{P(d_{c_j}|v)})] \, P(q_{vec}|u) \, P(q_{cos}|v) \, P(u) \, P(v) \tag{1}$$

where η is a normalizing constant.

Consider the situation in which two documents, d_x and d_y, contain exactly the same set of query terms. Assume that the query terms in document d_x lead to an ICD code and that this does not occur for document d_y (i.e., no codes are assigned to document d_y). Fig. 4 illustrates a situation in which this might happen. In this case, we expect document d_x to have a combined final ranking that is higher than the ranking for d_y (because $P(d_x|v) > P(d_y|v)$).

However, this is not guaranteed by Equation (1) because $P(d_x|u)$ and $P(d_y|u)$ might differ due to: (a) the frequencies of t_1 and t_2 in the two documents might differ and (b) the normalization factors $|d_x|$ and $|d_y|$ might also differ. To avoid these side effects, we adopt a ranking that considers only the idf factor of the classic vector model [18] at the left side of the network. As a result, we define the probabilities $P(q_{vec}|u)$ and $P(d_{k_j}|u)$ as follows:

$$P(q_{vec}|u) = \begin{cases} 1 \text{ if } u = u_{q_{vec}} \\ 0 \text{ otherwise} \end{cases} \tag{2}$$

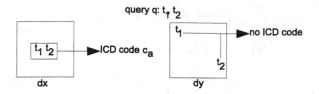

Fig. 4. Two documents, d_x and d_y, contain the query terms but only one of them d_x leads to an ICD code.

$$P(d_{k_j}|u) = \begin{cases} \sum_{k_i \in u_{qvec}} \frac{log \frac{N}{n_i}}{|d_{k_{max}}|} \times \frac{log \frac{N}{n_i}}{|q_{vec_{max}}|} & \text{if } u = u_{qvec} \\ 0 & \text{otherwise} \end{cases} \quad (3)$$

where n_i is the number of documents in which the keyword k_i appears. N is the total number of documents in the collection.

Let us now turn our attention to the right side of the network. The probability $P(q_{cos}|v)$ quantifies the relationship between the ICD categories and the query q. The larger the coverage of the query concept q provided by the ICD categories, the more related to diseases the query is. This is important because we should not expect gains in retrieval performance (i.e., in the quality of the ranking) due to ICD categories, if the query is not related to diseases. To quantify this coverage relationship, we use the number of terms in common between the query q and the ICD codes, as follows.

Let $codes(q)$ be a function that returns the set of codes generated by our coding method for the query q. Consider the 2^p possible states for the set v of root nodes. Instead of using the states in which a single node c_l is active at a time (as done for the left side of the network), we use only a single state that includes all c_l codes in the set $codes(q)$. We do so because this simplifies the computation of the coverage relationship. Define the state v_q of the set v of root nodes, as follows:

$$v = v_q \; iff \; \begin{cases} g_l(v) = 1 \; \forall l | c_l \in codes(q) \\ g_l(v) = 0 \; \text{otherwise} \end{cases} \quad (4)$$

Equation (4) defines v_q as the state of v that contains the nodes $c_l \in codes(q)$ active and the nodes $c_l \notin codes(q)$ inactive.

For each $c_l \in codes(q)$, let c_l be a vector of binary term weights, where each term weight is 1 to indicate that term is associated with the code c_l (according to the ICD hierarchy), and 0 otherwise. Also, let q_{cos} be a vector of binary term weights, where each term weight is 1 to indicate that the term occurs in the query q, and 0 otherwise. The product $c_l \bullet q_{cos}$ provides a measure of the coverage relationship between the concepts c_l and q_{cos}. We intend to identify the code c_l that best covers the query q (and thus, which is more likely to define the central disease associated with the query q). To accomplish this effect, we define:

$$P(q_{cos}|v) = \begin{cases} max_{\forall l | g_l(v)=1} \frac{c_l \bullet q_{cos}}{|c_{max}| \times |q_{cos}|} & \text{if } v = v_q \\ 0 & \text{otherwise} \end{cases} \tag{5}$$

$$P(\overline{q}_{cos}|v) = 1 - P(q_{cos}|v)$$

Notice, that we use $|c_{max}|$, instead of $|c_l|$, because we want to measure the coverage relationship with regard to the query q only.

For the probabilities $P(d_j|v)$, we are interested in a slightly distinct form of coverage relationship. Instead of simply looking at common terms, we look at the coverage relationship between the codes associated with the query q and the codes associated with a document d_j. This is an important point because a code c_l, $c_l \in codes(q)$, might have terms in common with a document d_j even if this code is not associated with d_j (as illustrated in Fig. 4). Thus, we must focus on the coverage relationship between $codes(q)$ and $codes(d_j)$. For this, we define:

v_q : vector of code weights associated with $c_l \in codes(q)$;
d_{c_j}: vector of code weights associated with $c_l \in codes(d_j)$.

The code weights here do not take into account code frequencies but do have an *idf* component (computed over the set of all codes assigned to all documents in the collection). This leads to a ranking form which yields:

$$P(d_{c_j}|v) = \begin{cases} \sum_{c_i \in q_{cos}} \frac{\log \frac{N}{C_i}}{|d_{c_{max}}|} \times \frac{\log \frac{N}{C_i}}{|q_{cos_{max}}|} & \text{if } v = v_{q_{cos}} \\ 0 & \text{otherwise} \end{cases} \tag{6}$$

$$P(\overline{d_{c_j}}|v) = 1 - P(d_{c_j}|v)$$

where C_i is the number of documents in which the code c_i appears. N is the total number of documents in the collection.

As a result of the definition of $P(q_{vec}|u)$, we have:

$$P(d_j|q) = \eta[1 - (\overline{P(d_{k_j}|u_{q_{vec}})})(\overline{P(d_{c_j}|v_{q_{cos}})})] \, P(q_{cos}|v) \, P(u) \, P(v) \tag{7}$$

Finally, the prior probabilities $P(v)$ and $P(u)$ are set to constants.

5   Experimental Results

We first present the medical reference collection we used in our experiments. Next, we discuss our results.

5.1   The Medical Reference Collection

The reference collection used in our experiments was the OHSUMED collection [7] which has been widely used for experimentation in the medical domain. The OHSUMED collection contains 348,566 references, which are derived from the subset of 270 journals found in the KF MEDLINE Primary Care session, covering the years from 1987 to 1991. The collection includes 106 example queries that were generated by actual physicians in the course of patient care. For each example query, at least one definitely relevant document is indicated. Each query is formed by a brief statement about the patient, followed by a description of the information need. The collection also includes relevance judgments for the example queries. Each relevance judgment indicates a document as definitely relevant, possibly relevant, or irrelevant. In our experiments, we used only documents with an abstract. This generated a new subcollection having 233,445 documents and 93 queries with relevant documents.

Fig. 5 quantifies the relationship between the ICD categories and each of our 93 test queries, according to Equation (5). This relationship indicates the support provided to each query by the ICD categories and is here referred to as the "query icd relation factor" (or simply, icd-relation-factor). As we can see, 24 of such queries are not related to diseases (icd-relation-factor = 0) and 69 queries have some relationship with diseases (icd-relation-factor > 0). From these 69 disease-related queries, 55 have a good focus on diseases (icd-relation-factor $\geq$ 0.5) and 10 are highly related to diseases (icd-relation-factor $\geq$ 0.8). The 69 disease-related queries are the focus of our experiments.

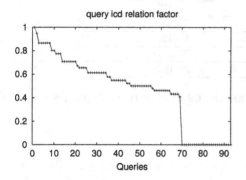

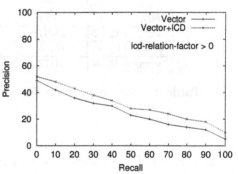

Fig. 5. Variation of the icd-relation-factor for our 93 test queries. The queries are sorted by decreasing values of the icd-relation-factor.

Fig. 6. Average precision figures for the vector and vector+ICD rankings. Only the 69 disease-related queries are considered.

5.2 Results

In this section, we present our experimental results. Fig. 6 illustrates the retrieval performance, in terms of precision-recall figures [2], for the vector and vector+ICD rankings in our Bayesian network model. We consider only the 69 example queries that are effectively related to diseases (i.e., those queries for which icd-relation-factor > 0). This is appropriate because we should not expect gains in retrieval performance due to evidence from ICD categories, whenever the query is not related to diseases.

In Fig. 6, we observe that the vector+ICD ranking is always superior for our reference collection. Table 1 details these results, which show that adding a new source of evidence, based on the ICD categorization, to the vector-based evidence leads to superior results. Another important observation is that the average recall (computed over all queries) for the vector+ICD model is 7% higher than for the vector model. This is because the ICD categories allow finding new documents, which are related to the user query, and which are not retrieved when only the term evidence is used.

Average precison figures for 69 queries(icd-relation-factor > 0			
Recall	Vector	Vector+ICD	Gain
0%	49.28	52.39	06.31%
10%	42.68	48.82	14.38%
20%	36.05	43.74	21.34%
30%	32.66	38.95	19.27%
40%	30.82	34.09	10.63%
50%	23.54	28.57	21.39%
60%	20.67	27.64	33.75%
70%	16.75	24.69	47.45%
80%	14.89	20.74	39.34%
90%	12.72	18.37	44.42%
100%	05.55	10.85	95.63%
Average	25.96	31.72	22.16%

Table 1. Average precison figures for the 69 disease-related queries.

Let us now focus on the queries that are more closely related to diseases. Fig. 7 illustrates the retrieval performance of the vector and vector+ICD rankings, when only queries with an icd-relation-factor $\geq$ 0.5 are considered (i.e., 55 example queries). Table 2 details these results. Again we observe that the vector+ICD ranking always yields higher precision figures than those obtained by the vector model. Further, the relative gain in precision is higher for these 55 queries than for the complete set of 69 disease-related queries. The reason for this better result is the higher relevance of the diseases for these 55 queries. This suggests that queries higher related to diseases will have higher improvement provided by our extended network ranking. Our following set of results confirms this interpretation.

Fig. 8 provides precision-recall figures for the 10 queries with an icd-relation-factor $\geq$ 0.8. Table 3 details these results. For these 10 queries, the vector+icd ranking yields a gain of 84,92% in the average precision, relative to the vector ranking. The average recall for the vector+ICD model is now 12,5% higher than

Average precison figures for the 55 queries			
Recall	Vector	Vector+ICD	Gain
0%	38.78	49.98	28.89%
10%	35.33	47.71	35.06%
20%	31.20	43.09	38.13%
30%	29.27	37.14	26.89%
40%	25.46	30.68	20.51%
50%	21.52	26.66	23.93%
60%	20.34	25.76	26.66%
70%	17.87	23.61	32.12%
80%	15.47	19.91	28.72%
90%	14.37	18.32	27.47%
100%	07.82	10.34	32.28%
Average	23.40	30.29	29.45%

Table 2. Average precison figures for the 55 queries (icd-relation-factor ≥ 0.5)

for the vector model. Table 4 shows the average recall figures for each of our 3 query pools (selected by the icd-relation-factor).

Average precison figures for 10 queries (icd-relation-factor ≥ 0.8)			
Recall	Vector	Vector+ICD	Gain
0%	30.52	49.91	63.56%
10%	22.77	53.75	136.02%
20%	25.35	51.29	102.29%
30%	18.39	42.10	128.88%
40%	20.45	37.46	83.20%
50%	17.60	32.08	82.25%
60%	17.25	29.64	71.80%
70%	16.16	28.49	76.37%
80%	15.08	24.95	65.46%
90%	15.13	20.71	36.89%
100%	09.84	15.22	54.68%
Average	18.96	35.05	84.90%

Table 3. Average precison figures for the 10 queries with icd-relation-factor $\geq$ 0.8.

6   Conclusions

We have described a framework for combining evidence derived from the text of medical documents with evidence provided by diseases related to these documents. The information on diseases is generated by a fully automatic catego-

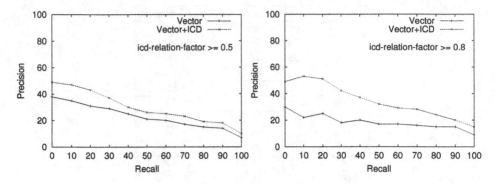

Fig. 7. Average precision figures for the vector and vector+ICD rankings, restricted to the 55 queries for which icd-relation-factor $\geq$ 0.5.

Fig. 8. Average precision figure for the vector and vector+ICD rankings, restricted to the 10 queries for which icd-relation-factor $\geq$ 0.8.

Average recall for each query pool			
icd-relation-factor	Vector	Vector+ICD	Gain
> 0.0	82.60%	88.40%	7.00%
$\geq$ 0.5	81.81%	87.27%	6.67%
$\geq$ 0.8	80.00%	90.00%	12.50%

Table 4. Average recall for each query pool.

rization method we developed, which assigns ICD codes to the documents in a medical collection.

Our framework is based on Bayesian networks. Bayesian networks are useful because they allow combining distinct sources of evidence in a consistent fashion. The Bayesian framework we propose leads to a new ranking formula that takes into account information about the text of the medical documents and information about the diseases related to these documents. Through experimentation with a medical reference collection, the OHSUMED collection, we evaluated the effectiveness of our approach. We considered 3 distinct pools of test queries: queries that mention diseases, queries related to diseases, and queries focussed on diseases. In all three cases, our new ranking formula yielded improved retrieval performance when compared to a standard IR ranking algorithm (the vector model, which we have adopted as our baseline). When only queries that are strongly related to diseases were considered, the average improvement in retrieval performance was as high as 84%. Our results show the importance of taking into account specialized medical information in medical retrieval systems.

Besides providing improved retrieval performance, our method for the automatic assignment of ICD codes generates a categorization hierarchy that includes more than 5,000 diseases (those included in the ICD hierarchy). This is a fine hierarchy which aggregates knowledge to large medical collections such as the Medline. This hierarchy can be used, for instance, to naturally design an interface based on a large directory of diseases. In the near future, we intend to experiment with such a hierarchy and evaluate its effectiveness in facilitating the access of medical information of relevance.

References

[1] C. Apte, F. Damerau, and S. M. Weiss. Automated Learning of Decision Rules for Text Categorization. *ACM Transactions on Information Systems*, 12(3):233–251, 1994.

[2] R. Baeza-Yates and B. Ribeiro-Neto. *Modern Information Retrieval*. Addison Wesley Longman, Harlow, England, 1999.

[3] J. Broglio, J.P. Callan, W.B. Croft, and D.W. Nachbar. Document retrieval and routing using the inquery system. In *Proceedings of the Third Text Retrieval Conference - TREC-3*, pages 241–256, National Institute of Standards and Technology, Gaithersburg, Maryland, USA, 1995. (NIST Special Publication 500-225).

[4] J. Callan. Document filtering with inference networks. In *Proceedings of the 19th Annual Int'l ACM SIGIR Conference on Research and Development in Information Retrieval*, pages 262–269, Zurich, Switzerland, 1996.

[5] W.W. Cohen and Y. Singer. Context-Sensitive Learning Methods for Text Categorization. In *Proceedings of the 19th Annual Int'l ACM SIGIR Conference on Research and Development in Information Retrieval*, pages 307–315, Zurich, Switzerland, 1996.

[6] D. Haines and W.B. Croft. Relevance feedback and inference networks. In *Proceedings of the 16th Annual Int'l ACM SIGIR Conference on Research and Development in Information Retrieval*, pages 2–11, Pittsburgh, PA, USA, 1993.

[7] W. Hersh, C. Buckley, T. Leone, and D. Hickam. OHSUMED: An interactive retrieval evaluation and new large test collection for research. In *Proceedings of the 17th Annual Int'l ACM SIGIR Conference on Research and Development in Information Retrieval*, pages 192–201, Dublin,Ireland, 1994.

[8] W. Lam, M. Ruiz, and P. Srinivasan. Automatic Text Categorization and its Application to Text Retrieval. *IEEE Transactions on Knowledge and Data Engineering*, 11(6):865–879, 1999.

[9] L. S. Larkey and W. B. Croft. Automatic assignment of ICD9 codes to discharge summaries. Technical report, Center for Intelligent Information Retrieval at University of Massachusetts, Amherst, Massachusetts, 1995.

[10] L. S. Larkey and W. B. Croft. Combining Classifiers in Text Categorization. In *Proceedings of the 19th Annual Int'l ACM SIGIR Conference on Research and Development in Information Retrieval*, pages 289–297, Zurich, Switzerland, 1996.

[11] D. D. Lewis, R. E Schapire, J.P. Callan, and R. Papka. Training Algorithms for Linear Text Classifiers. In *Proceedings of the 19th Annual Int'l ACM SIGIR Conference on Research and Development in Information Retrieval*, pages 298–306, Zurich, Switzerland, 1996.

[12] L.R.S. Lima, A.H.F. Laender, and B. Ribeiro-Neto. A Hierarchical Approach to the Automatic Categorization of Medical Documents. In *Proceedings of the 1998 ACM CIKM International Conference on Information and Knowledge Management*, pages 132–139, Bethesda, Maryland, USA, 1998.

[13] J. Pearl. *Probabilistic Reasoning in Intellingent System: Networks of Plausible Inference.* Morgan Kaufmann, San Francisco, California, 1988.

[14] S. L. Pestotnik. Medical informatics: Meeting the information challenges of a changing health care system. *Journal of Informed Pharmacotherapy*, 2(1), 2000.

[15] B. Ribeiro-Neto, A.H.F. Laender, and L.R.S. Lima. An experimental study in automatically categorizing medical documents. *Journal of the American Society for Information Science and Technology*, 52(5):391–401, 2001.

[16] B. Ribeiro-Neto and R. Muntz. A Belief Network Model for IR. In *Proceedings of the 19th Annual Int'l ACM SIGIR Conference on Research and Development in Information Retrieval*, pages 253–260, Zurich, Switzerland, 1996.

[17] B. Ribeiro-Neto, I. Silva, and R. Muntz. Bayesian network models for information retrieval. In *In: Soft Computing in Information Retrieval*, pages 259–291, Physica-Verlag, Heidelberg, 2000. F. Crestani & G. Pasi, editors.

[18] G. Salton and C. Buckley. Term-weighting approaches in automatic retrieval. *Information Processing & Management*, 24(5):513–523, 1988.

[19] Y. Satomura and M.B. Amaral. Automated diagnostic indexing by natural language processing. *Medical Informatics*, 17(3):149–163, 1992.

[20] I. Silva, B. Ribeiro-Neto, P. Calado, E. Moura, and N. Ziviani. Link-based and Content-based Evidential Information in a Belief Network Model. In *Proceedings of the 23rd Annual Int'l ACM SIGIR Conference on Research and Development in Information Retrieval*, pages 96–103, Athens, Greece, 2000.

[21] H. Turtle and W. B. Croft. Evaluation of an inference network-based retrieval model. *ACM Transactions on Information Systems*, 9(3):187–222, July 1991.

[22] Y. Yang. Expert Network: Effective and Efficient Learning from Human Decisions in Text Categorization and Retrieval. In *Proceedings of the 17th Annual Int'l ACM SIGIR Conference on Research and Development in Information Retrieval*, pages 13–22, Dublin, Ireland, 1994.

[23] Y. Yang and C. Chute. An Application of Least Squares Fit Mapping to Text Information Retrieval. In *Proceedings of the 16th Annual Int'l ACM SIGIR Conference on Research and Development in Information Retrieval*, pages 281–290, 1993.

A Bit-Parallel Suffix Automaton Approach for (δ, γ)-Matching in Music Retrieval

Maxime Crochemore[1,2*], Costas S. Iliopoulos[2], Gonzalo Navarro[3**], and Yoan J. Pinzon[2,4**]

[1] Institut Gaspard-Monge, Université de Marne-la-Vallée, France
mac@univ-mlv.fr
www-igm.univ-mlv.fr/~mac
[2] Dept. of Computer Science, King's College, London, England
{csi,pinzon}@dcs.kcl.ac.uk
www.dcs.kcl.ac.uk/staff/csi, www.dcs.kcl.ac.uk/staff/pinzon
[3] Dept. of Computer Science, University of Chile, Chile
gnavarro@dcc.uchile.cl
www.dcc.uchile.cl/~gnavarro
[4] Laboratorio de Cómputo Especializado,
Universidad Autónoma de Bucaramanga, Colombia

Abstract. (δ, γ)-Matching is a string matching problem with applications to music retrieval. The goal is, given a pattern $P_{1...m}$ and a text $T_{1...n}$ on an alphabet of integers, find the occurrences P' of the pattern in the text such that (i) $\forall 1 \leq i \leq m$, $|P_i - P'_i| \leq \delta$, and (ii) $\sum_{1 \leq i \leq m} |P_i - P'_i| \leq \gamma$. Several techniques for (δ, γ)-matching have been proposed. In this paper we show that a classical string matching technique that combines bit-parallelism and suffix automata can be successfully adapted to this problem. This is the first character-skipping algorithm that skips characters using both δ and γ. We implemented our algorithm and drew experimental results on real music showing that our algorithm is superior to current alternatives.

1 Introduction

The string matching problem is to find all the occurrences of a given pattern $P_{1...m}$ in a large text $T_{1...n}$, both being sequences of characters drawn from a finite character set Σ. This problem is fundamental in computer science and is a basic need of many applications, such as text retrieval, music retrieval, computational biology, data mining, network security, etc. Several of these applications require, however, more sophisticated forms of searching, in the sense of extending the basic paradigm of the pattern being a simple sequence of characters.

In this paper we are interested in music retrieval. A musical score can be viewed as a string: at a very rudimentary level, the alphabet could simply be the set of notes in the chromatic or diatonic notation, or the set of intervals that

---

* Partly supported by CNRS and NATO.
** Supported by CYTED VII.19 RIBIDI Project.

M.A. Nascimento, E.S. de Moura, A.L. Oliveira (Eds.): SPIRE 2003, LNCS 2857, pp. 211–223, 2003.

appear between notes (e.g. pitch may be represented as MIDI numbers and pitch intervals as number of semitones). It is known that exact matching cannot be used to find occurrences of a particular melody, so one resorts to different forms of *approximate* matching, where a limited amount of *differences* of diverse kinds are permitted between the search pattern and its occurrence in the text.

The approximate matching problem has been used for a variety of musical applications [15, 9, 19, 20, 6]. Most computer-aided musical applications adopt an absolute numeric pitch representation (most commonly MIDI pitch and pitch intervals in semitones; duration is also encoded in a numeric form). The absolute pitch encoding, however, may be insufficient for applications in tonal music as it disregards tonal qualities of pitches and pitch-intervals (e.g., a tonal transposition from a major to a minor key results in a different encoding of the musical passage and thus exact matching cannot detect the similarity between the two passages). One way to account for similarity between closely related but non-identical musical strings is to permit a difference of at most δ units between the pattern character and its corresponding text character in an occurrence, e.g., a C-major $\{60, 64, 65, 67\}$ and a C-minor $\{60, 63, 65, 67\}$ sequence can be matched if a tolerance $\delta = 1$ is allowed in the matching process. Additionally, we require that the total number of differences across all the pattern positions does not exceed γ, in order to limit the total number of differences while keeping sufficient flexibility at individual positions.

The formalization of the above problem is called (δ, γ)-matching. The problem is defined as follows: the alphabet Σ is assumed to be a set of integer numbers, $\Sigma \subset \mathbb{Z}$. Apart from the pattern P and the text T, two extra parameters, $\delta, \gamma \in \mathbb{N}$, are given. The goal is to find all the occurrences P' of P in T such that (i) $\forall 1 \leq i \leq m$, $|P_i - P'_i| \leq \delta$, and (ii) $\sum_{1 \leq i \leq m} |P_i - P'_i| \leq \gamma$.

Several recent algorithms exist to solve this problem [7, 10, 8, 11]. Some are based on extending well-known paradigms such as the Boyer-Moore family or the use of suffix automata. Others are based on bit-parallelism. We detail them in the next section. On the other hand, it was shown in [17, 18] that bit-parallelism and suffix automata can be nicely combined in order to obtain faster, simpler, and more flexible algorithms, which are especially robust to handle extended string matching problems (classes of characters, wild cards, regular expressions, approximate searching based on Hamming or edit distance, and so on).

In this paper we extend the bit-parallel suffix automata to handle (δ, γ)-matching: The resulting algorithm is extremely simple and much faster than the existing approaches. It is also the first truly (δ, γ) character-skipping algorithm, as it skips characters using both criteria. Existing approaches do just δ-matching and check the candidates for the γ-condition.

We use the following definitions throughout the paper. A word $x \in \Sigma^*$ is a *factor* (or substring) of P if P can be written $P = uxv$, $u, v \in \Sigma^*$. A factor x of P is called a *suffix* (*prefix*) of P if $P = ux$ ($P = xu$), $u \in \Sigma^*$. The number of bits in the computer word is denoted w.

2 Related Work

2.1 (δ, γ)-Matching

We recall three approaches that have been attempted to (δ, γ)-matching.

Bit-Parallelism consists of taking advantage of the intrinsic parallelism of the bit operations inside a computer word [1], so as to pack several values in a single word and manage to update them all in less operations than those necessary to update the values separately. In [7, 8] this approach was used to obtain an $O(n)$ search time algorithm for (δ, γ)-matching called SHIFT-PLUS. The algorithm packs m counters whose maximum value is $m\delta$, so it can pack all them in a single computer word provided $m\lceil \log_2(1 + m\delta)\rceil \leq w$. Otherwise, several computer words have to be maintained, for a total search time of $O(n\ m \log(m\delta)/w)$.

Occurrence Heuristics consist of skipping some text characters by using information on the position of some characters in the pattern. Typical algorithms of this type are those of the Boyer-Moore family [5, 21]. In [7], several algorithms of this type were proposed for δ-matching (a restricted case where $\gamma = \infty$), and they were extended to general (δ, γ)-matching in [10]. These are TUNED-BOYER-MOORE, SKIP-SEARCH and MAXIMAL-SHIFT, each of which have a counterpart in exact string matching. It is shown that these algorithms are faster than the bit-parallel ones, as they are simple and able to skip text characters.

Substring Heuristics consist of skipping some text characters by using information on the position of some pattern substrings. Typical algorithms of this type are those based on suffix automata [13, 12]. In [10, 11] three algorithms based on these ideas, called δ-BM1, δ-BM2 and δ-BM3, are proposed. They try to generalize the suffix automata to δ-matching, but they obtain only an approximation that accepts more occurrences than necessary, which have to be verified later. In classical string matching, substring heuristics perform better than character heuristics on small alphabets. This makes it probable that in this application substrings heuristics perform better for large δ and γ values.

2.2 Bit-Parallel Suffix Automata

Bit-parallelism provides a general method to use automata in their nondeterministic form rather than converting them to deterministic. The latter is the classical approach and normally involves a complex construction algorithm and lack of flexibility in the resulting scheme (see the previous comment on adapting suffix automata to δ-matching). Nondeterministic automata, on the other hand, tend to be rather simple and can be easily extended to handle new problems. Bit-parallelism permits simulating nondeterministic automata as they are, since they can handle all the active states in a single operation.

In this spirit, the algorithm BNDM was developed in [17] as a combination between Shift-Or [2] (a bit-parallel algorithm) and BDM [13] (an algorithm based on suffix automata and able to skip characters). The result is an algorithm with the best of both worlds: simple, efficient, and extensible. It is shown that it outperforms both Shift-Or and BDM, and that there is no reason for bit-parallel algorithms not to skip characters. BNDM was extended to handle classes of characters, wild cards, regular expressions, and widely used forms of approximate searching [18].

2.3   Our Work in Context

Our goal in this paper is to develop an extension of BNDM to handle (δ, γ)-matching. The algorithm turns out to be simple and very efficient. In the above categorization, it corresponds to a crossing between bit-parallel and substring-heuristic algorithms. Compared to the original bit-parallel algorithm [7, 8], it makes a better packing of values, since it needs only $m\lceil 1 + \log_2(\gamma + 1)\rceil$ bits, so the number of characters inspected has to be multiplied by $O(m\log(\gamma)/w)$. Compared to the original substring matching heuristics, the nondeterministic version is able to accept exactly the patterns that qualify, without any need of further verification. In particular, all the existing methods really do δ-matching and enforce the γ-condition in a further verification, while we are able of enforcing both conditions as we scan the text. This makes up a much more robust and efficient algorithm.

3   Searching with Suffix Automata

We describe in this section the BDM pattern matching algorithm [12, 13], which is based on a suffix automaton. A *suffix automaton* on a pattern $P_{1...m}$ (frequently called DAWG(P), for Deterministic Acyclic Word Graph) is the minimal (incomplete) deterministic finite automaton that recognizes all the suffixes of this pattern. By "incomplete" we mean that unnecessary transitions are not present. The nondeterministic version of this automaton has a very regular structure and is shown in Figure 1.

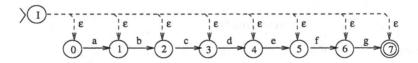

Fig. 1. A nondeterministic suffix automaton for the pattern $P = $ "abcdefg". Dashed lines represent ε-transitions (i.e. they occur without consuming any input). I is the initial state of the automaton

The (deterministic) suffix automaton is a well known structure [12]. The size of DAWG(P) is linear in m (counting both nodes and edges), and a linear on-line construction algorithm exists [12]. A very important fact for our algorithm is that this automaton cannot only be used to recognize the suffixes of P, but also factors of P: The automaton has active states as long as we have read a factor of P.

The suffix automaton structure is used in [12, 13] to design a simple pattern matching algorithm called BDM. This algorithm is $O(mn)$ time in the worst case, but optimal on average ($O(n \log_{|\Sigma|} m/m)$ time). To search for P in a text T, the suffix automaton of $P^r = P_m P_{m-1} \ldots P_1$ (i.e., the pattern read backwards) is built. A window of length m is slid along the text, from left to right. The algorithm searches the window backwards for a factor of the pattern P using the suffix automaton. During this search, if a terminal state is reached which does not correspond to the entire pattern P, the window position is recorded (in a variable *last*). This corresponds to finding a *prefix* of the pattern starting at position *last* inside the window and ending at the end of the window (since the suffixes of P^r are the reverse prefixes of P). Since we remember the last prefix recognized backwards, we have the *longest* prefix of P that is a suffix of the window. This backward search ends in two possible forms:

1. We fail to recognize a factor, i.e., we reach a character σ that does not correspond to a transition in DAWG(P^r). Figure 2 illustrates this case. In this case we shift the window to the right, its starting position corresponding to the position *last* (we cannot miss an occurrence because in that case the suffix automaton would have found its prefix in the window).

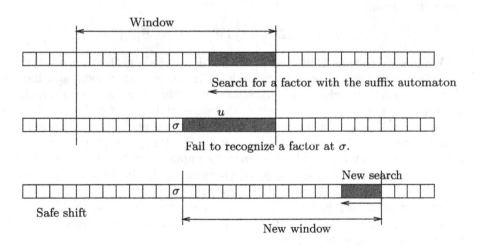

Fig. 2. Basic search with the suffix automaton

2. We reach the beginning of the window, therefore recognizing the pattern P. We report the occurrence, and shift the window exactly as in the previous case (notice that we have the previous *last* value).

4   Our Algorithm

We first describe a forward-scan version that extends Shift-And and permits us explaining the details of the bit-parallel simulation, and then a backward-scanning version that extends BNDM.

We start with some terminology. A *bit mask* of length r is a sequence of bits, denoted $b_r \dots b_1$. We use exponentiation to denote bit repetition (e.g. $0^3 1 = 0001$). We use C-like syntax for operations on the bits of computer words: "|" is the bitwise-or, "&" is the bitwise-and, " ^ " is the bitwise-xor and "~" complements all the bits. The shift-left operation, "<<", moves the bits to the left and enters zeros from the right. The shift-right, ">>" moves the bits in the other direction. Finally, we can perform arithmetic operations on the bits, such as addition and subtraction, which operate the bits as if they formed a number. For instance, $b_r \dots b_x 10000 - 1 = b_r \dots b_x 01111$.

4.1   Forward Scanning

The Shift-And algorithm first builds a table B which for each character stores a bit mask $b_m \dots b_1$. The mask in $B[c]$ has the i-th bit set if and only if $P_i = c$. The state of the search is kept in a machine word $D = d_m \dots d_1$, where d_i is set whenever $P_{1 \dots i}$ matches the end of the text read up to now. Therefore, we report a match whenever d_m is set.

We set $D = 0^m$ originally and, for each new text character T_j, update D using the formula

$$D \ \leftarrow \ ((D << 1) \mid 0^{m-1} 1) \ \& \ B[T_j]$$

We now extend the Shift-And algorithm. First of all, notice that δ-matching is trivial under the bit-parallel approach, as it can be accommodated using the ability to search for classes of characters. We define that pattern character c matches text characters $c - \delta \dots c + \delta$, therefore setting the i-th bit of $B[c]$ to 1 if and only if $|P_i - c| \leq \delta$. The rest of the algorithm is unchanged. On a uniform distribution over $\Sigma = \{1 \dots |\Sigma|\}$ we obtain $O(n \log_{|\Sigma|/\delta}(m)/m)$ time for the BNDM version, and we still need $\lceil m/w \rceil$ computer words for the simulation. However, the real challenge is to do (δ, γ)-matching. In the following we assume $\delta \leq \gamma \leq m\delta$, otherwise the formulation makes little sense.

Instead of storing just one bit d_i to tell whether $P_{1 \dots i}$ matches $T_{j-i+1 \dots j}$, we store a counter c_i to record the sum of the absolute differences between the corresponding characters. That is

$$c_i \ = \ \sum_{1 \leq k \leq i} |P_k - T_{j-i+k}|$$

In fact we are only interested in storing $\min(c_i, \gamma + 1)$, as any value larger than γ is equivalent for us. For reasons that will be clear soon, we need to represent c_i such that its highest bit is set to 1 if and only if $c_i > \gamma$. So we use $\ell = 1 + \lceil \log_2(\gamma + 1) \rceil$ bits to represent c_i, and instead of representing c_i

we represent $c_i + 2^{\ell-1} - (\gamma + 1)$. This guarantees that the highest bit is set when c_i reaches $\gamma + 1$ (as its representation reaches $2^{\ell-1}$). Hence our bit mask D needs $m\ell = m(1 + \lceil \log_2(\gamma + 1) \rceil)$ bits and our simulation needs $O(m \log(\gamma)/w)$ computer words.

We precompute a mask $B[c]$ of counters as follows. The i-th counter of $B[c]$ will store $|P_i - c|$ if and only if $|P_i - c| \le \delta$. Otherwise, the characters simply do not match, in which case we store $\gamma + 1$ for this counter. This value ensures that no match will be reported, as the global count of differences will surpass γ. Since $\delta \le \gamma$, ℓ bits suffice to store each of these counters.

The algorithm is basically the same of Shift-And, except that we add $B[c]$ to D in order to keep count of the sum of the differences between the matched characters. The overflow is avoided as follows: we remove the highest bits from the counters in D before adding those of $B[T_j]$, and then restore them in the result. Therefore, (1) overflow is impossible because we are adding two values that at most add up $2\gamma + 1$, and we have enough space to store $2^\ell - 1 \ge 2(\gamma + 1) - 1 = 2\gamma + 1$ differences; (2) if the highest bit was set before, it will stay set; (3) if the highest bit was not yet set then our operation with highest bits does not affect the sum. Note that it is not strictly true that we maintain $\min(c_i, \gamma + 1)$, but it is true that the highest bit of each counter i is set if and only if $c_i > \gamma$, and this is enough for the correctness of the algorithm.

This solution has some resemblances with that of [3] for Hamming distance.

Figure 3 depicts the forward-scanning algorithm. It is $O(n)$ time if $m \log \gamma = O(w)$, otherwise it takes time $O(nm \log(\gamma)/w)$. The preprocessing takes $O(m|\Sigma|)$ time. We remark that previous forward scanning versions [7, 8] required $O(nm \log(m\delta)/w)$ bits, which is strictly larger than our requirement. The difference is that we managed to keep the counters below 2γ instead of letting them grow up to $m\delta$.

4.2 Backward Scanning

We start by explaining the BNDM algorithm [17] and then show how to extend it. We assume $m \le w$ in the exposition for simplicity, although the scheme is general.

The BNDM algorithm moves a window over the text. Each time the window is positioned at a new text position just after pos, it searches backwards the window $T_{pos+1...pos+m}$ using the DAWG automaton, until either m iterations are performed (which implies a match in the current window) or the automaton cannot follow any transition. In this case, the bit d_i at iteration k is set if and only if $P_{m-i+1...m-i+k} = T_{pos+1+m-k...pos+m}$. Some observations follow

- Since we begin at iteration 0, the initial value for D is 1^m (recall that we use exponentiation to denote bit repetition).
- There is a match if and only if after iteration m it holds $d_m = 1$.
- Whenever $d_m = 1$, we have matched a prefix of the pattern in the current window. The longest prefix matched (excluding the complete pattern) corresponds to the next window position (variable $last$).

Forward-Scan $(P_{1...m}, T_{1...n}, \delta, \gamma)$
1.   Preprocessing
2. $\ell \leftarrow 1 + \lceil \log_2(\gamma + 1) \rceil$
3.   **For** $c \in \Sigma$ **Do**
4. $B[c] \leftarrow 0^m$
5.   **For** $i \in 1 \ldots m$ **Do**
6. $B[c] \leftarrow B[c] \mid (|c - P_i| > \delta?\gamma + 1 : |c - P_i|) << (\ell(i-1)))$
7.   Search
8. $D \leftarrow 1^{m\ell}$
9.   **For** $j \in 1 \ldots n$ **Do**
10.   **If** D & $10^{m\ell-1} = 0^{m\ell}$ **Then**
11.   **Report an occurrence at** $j - m + 1$
12. $D \leftarrow (D << \ell) \mid (2^{\ell-1} - (\gamma + 1))$
13. $H \leftarrow D$ & $(10^{\ell-1})^m$
14. $D \leftarrow ((D \ \& \ \sim H) + B[T_j]) \mid H$

Fig. 3. Forward scanning algorithm for (δ, γ)-matching

– Since there is no initial self-loop, this automaton eventually runs out of active states. Moreover, states $(m - k) \ldots m$ are inactive at iteration k.

The algorithm works as follows. Every time we position the window in the text we initialize D and scan the window backwards. For each new text character we update D. Each time we find a prefix of the pattern ($d_m = 1$) we remember the position in the window. If we run out of 1's in D then there cannot be a match and we suspend the scanning (this corresponds to not having any transition to follow in the automaton). If we can perform m iterations then we report a match.

We use a mask B which stores a bit mask for each character c. This mask sets the bits corresponding to the positions i where $P_i = c$ (just as in Shift-And). The formula to update D is

$$D \ \leftarrow \ (D \ \& \ B[T_j]) \ << \ 1$$

We now extend BNDM to (δ, γ)-matching. The main differences with respect to the representation used in forward scanning are (1) we initialize the counters of D to $c_i = 0$ because they correspond to matching empty strings; (2) after shifting D, the fresh counters that enter from the right are not important (the important ones are those present when we start scanning the window); and (3) we suspend scanning the window when all the counters exceeded γ.

Figure 4 depicts the backward-scanning algorithm. This is the first character-skipping algorithm that does not use verifications and is able to stop scanning text windows that δ-match the pattern, if they do not (δ, γ)-match the pattern.

```
Backward-Scan  (P₁...ₘ,  T₁...ₙ,  δ,  γ)
```

1.   Preprocessing
2. $\ell \leftarrow 1 + \lceil \log_2(\gamma + 1) \rceil$
3.   **For** $c \in \Sigma$ **Do**
4. $B[c] \leftarrow 0^m$
5.   **For** $i \in 1 \ldots m$ **Do**
6. $B[c] \leftarrow B[c] \mid (|c - P_{m-i+1}| > \delta ? \gamma + 1 : |c - P_{m-i+1}|) <<$
7. $(\ell(i - 1)))$
8.   Search
9. $pos \leftarrow 0$
10.   **While** $pos \leq n - m$ **Do**
11. $j \leftarrow m, \; last \leftarrow m$
12. $D \leftarrow (2^{\ell-1} - (\gamma + 1)) \times (0^{\ell-1}1)^m$
13.   **While** $D \;\&\; (10^{\ell-1})^m \neq (10^{\ell-1})^m$ **Do**
14. $H \leftarrow D \;\&\; (10^{\ell-1})^m$
15. $D \leftarrow ((D \;\&\; \sim H) + B[T_j]) \mid H$
16. $j \leftarrow j - 1$
17.   **If** $D \;\&\; 10^{m\ell-1} = 0^{m\ell}$ **Then**
18.   **If** $j > 0$ **Then** $last \leftarrow j$
19.   **Else Report an occurrence at** $pos + 1$
20. $D \leftarrow (D << \ell) \mid 10^{\ell-1}$
21. $pos \leftarrow pos + last$

Fig. 4. Backward scanning algorithm for (δ, γ)-matching. Some code optimizations are not included for simplicity

5   Experimental Results

In this section we show experimental evidence supporting the superiority of the new algorithm (THIS) compared to the (δ, γ)-Boyer-Moore algorithm (BM2) presented in [10, 11], which is currently the most competitive choice.

The time reported includes only the searching phase. Preprocessing was negligible. The tests were performed using a SUN Ultra Enterprise 300MHz running Solaris Unix with $w = 32$. We used the GNU g++ compiler version 2.95.1. Each data point represents the median of 60 trials.

We ran our experiments using both real music and random text. The music data used for this study comes from a data base of MIDI files of classic music with 1.8Mb of absolute pitches. We also make use of this music data base to measure the zero-order and one-order entropy to estimated the size of alphabet needed to emulated music using random text. Zero-order entropy was equivalent to having a random alphabet of size 17.35. One-order entropy was much smaller, 6.27. Therefore, we used random text uniformly distributed with alphabet size of 10–20 for this study. Other typical parameter values were 0–5 for δ, $1.5m$–$2.0m$ for γ, and 10–200 for m.

Figure 5 shows plots of the performance of both algorithms using random data. For the different combinations of δ and γ used in these experiments, our algorithm (THIS) was significantly faster than Algorithm BM2. As expected, the performance of the algorithm degrades with smaller alphabets. However, it also degrades as m increases, as the implementation is limited to using m/w number of computer words and skipping at most w characters. To speed-up the matching algorithm we can use an alphabet reduction method such as octave equivalence [14].

The results using real music data are shown in Figure 6. Although the difference is smaller than on synthetic data, clearly THIS algorithm performs better. As can be seen, the dependence on δ is significant to the extent that it can double (note the change of scale) the time it takes by going from $\delta = 2$ to $\delta = 4$. The dependence on γ, on the other hand, is not much significant.

In conclusion the algorithm introduced in this paper performs consistently better than previous known algorithms.

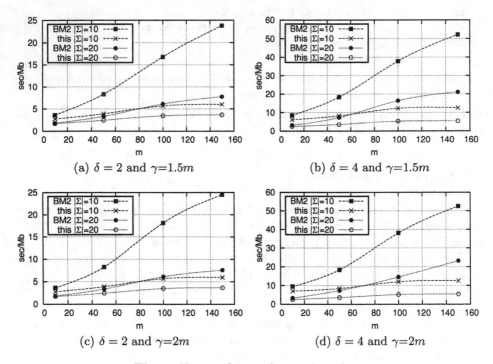

(a) $\delta = 2$ and $\gamma = 1.5m$

(b) $\delta = 4$ and $\gamma = 1.5m$

(c) $\delta = 2$ and $\gamma = 2m$

(d) $\delta = 4$ and $\gamma = 2m$

Fig. 5. Timing figures for random data

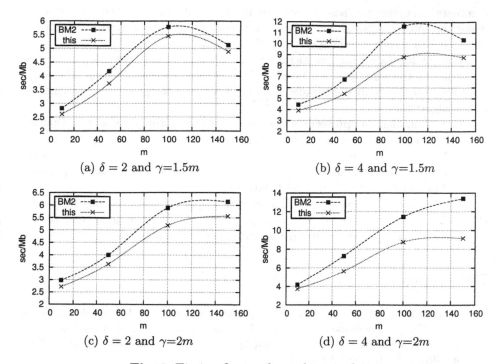

(a) $\delta = 2$ and $\gamma=1.5m$

(b) $\delta = 4$ and $\gamma=1.5m$

(c) $\delta = 2$ and $\gamma=2m$

(d) $\delta = 4$ and $\gamma=2m$

Fig. 6. Timing figures for real music data

6   Conclusions

We have presented a new bit-parallel algorithm for (δ, γ)-matching, an extended string matching problem with applications in music retrieval. Our new algorithm is a crossing between bit-parallelism and suffix automata and has several advantages over the previous approaches: it makes better use of the bits of the computer word, it inspects less text characters, it is simple and extensible.

Our algorithms is also the first truly (δ, γ) character-skipping algorithm, as it skips characters using both criteria. Existing approaches do just δ-matching and check the candidates for the γ-condition. This makes our algorithm a stronger choice for this problem.

The algorithm we have presented is useful for short pattern lengths, as it is limited by the length of the computer word. We have handled longer patterns with the naive approach of using as many computer words as needed to represent all the counters. A more sophisticated approach we are pursuing is to partition the pattern into pieces short enough to be handled with the basic algorithm. It is interesting to notice that if we partition the pattern into j pieces, then at least one of them has to match with $\gamma' = \lfloor \gamma/j \rfloor$ differences overall, so we do (δ, γ')-matching in the pieces. Moreover, if $\delta > \gamma'$ we do (γ', γ')-matching. Hence we run j searches for shorter patterns and check every match of a piece for a complete occurrence. These pieces can be grouped and searched for together using the so-called "superimposition". These ideas have been used in [4, 16] for approximate string matching, and should be useful here too.

It is not hard to design an algorithm with the same average complexity but also linear in the worst case, as done in [17]. Despite theoretically interesting, this improvement is usually disregarded because it worsens the practical performance of the algorithm.

A more challenging problem is to consider text indexing approaches, that is, preprocessing the musical strings in order to permit fast searching of patterns later. A simple solution is the use of a suffix tree of the text combined with backtracking, which yields search times which are exponential on the pattern length but independent of the text length [22].

We also plan to investigate further on more sophisticated matching problems that arise in music retrieval. For example, it would be good to extend (δ, γ)-matching in order to permit insertions and deletions of symbols.

References

[1] R. Baeza-Yates. Text retrieval: Theory and practice. In *12th IFIP World Computer Congress*, volume I, pages 465–476. Elsevier Science, September 1992.

[2] R. Baeza-Yates and G. Gonnet. A new approach to text searching. *Comm. ACM*, 35(10):74–82, October 1992.

[3] R. Baeza-Yates and G. Gonnet. Fast string matching with mismatches. *Information and Computation*, 108(2):187–199, 1994.

[4] R. Baeza-Yates and G. Navarro. Faster approximate string matching. *Algorithmica*, 23(2):127–158, 1999.

[5] R. S. Boyer and J. S. Moore. A fast string searching algorithm. *Communications of the ACM*, 20(10):762–772, 1977.

[6] E. Cambouropoulos, T. Crawford, and C. Iliopoulos. Pattern processing in melodic sequences: Challenges, caveats and prospects. In *Proc. Artificial Intelligence and Simulation of Behaviour (AISB'99) Convention*, pages 42–47, 1999.

[7] E. Cambouropoulos, M. Crochemore, C. Iliopoulos, L. Mouchard, and Y. J. Pinzon. Algorithms for computing approximate repetitions in musical sequences. In *Proc. 10th Australasian Workshop on Combinatorial Algorithms (AWOCA'99)*, pages 129–144, 1999.

[8] E. Cambouropoulos, M. Crochemore, C. S. Iliopoulos, L. Mouchard, and Y. J. Pinzon. Algorithms for computing approximate repetitions in musical sequences. *Int. J. Comput. Math.*, 79(11):1135–1148, 2002.

[9] T. Crawford, C. Iliopoulos, and R. Raman. String matching techniques for musical similarity and melodic recognition. *Computing in Musicology*, 11:73–100, 1998.

[10] M. Crochemore, C. Iliopoulos, T. Lecroq, Y. J. Pinzon, W. Plandowski, and W. Rytter. Occurence and substring heuristics for δ-matching. *Fundamenta Informaticae*, 55:1–15, 2003.

[11] M. Crochemore, C. Iliopoulos, T. Lecroq, W. Plandowski, and W. Rytter. Three heuristics for δ-matching: δ-bm algorithms. In Combinatorial Pattern Matching, CPM'2002, LNCS v. 2373, pages 178–189. Springer-Verlag, 2002.

[12] M. Crochemore and W. Rytter. *Text algorithms*. Oxford University Press, 1994.

[13] A. Czumaj, M. Crochemore, L. Gasieniec, S. Jarominek, Thierry Lecroq, W. Plandowski, and W. Rytter. Speeding up two string-matching algorithms. *Algorithmica*, 12:247–267, 1994.

[14] K Lemström and J. Tarhio. Searching monophonic patterns within polyphonic sources. In *Proc. of Content-Based Multimedia Information Access*, volume 2, pages 1261–1279, 2000.

[15] P. McGettrick. *MIDIMatch: Musical Pattern Matching in Real Time*. MSc. Dissertation, York University, U.K., 1997.

[16] G. Navarro and R. Baeza-Yates. Improving an algorithm for approximate string matching. *Algorithmica*, 30(4):473–502, 2001.

[17] G. Navarro and M. Raffinot. Fast and flexible string matching by combining bit-parallelism and suffix automata. *ACM Journal of Experimental Algorithmics (JEA)*, 5(4), 2000.

[18] G. Navarro and M. Raffinot. *Flexible Pattern Matching in Strings – Practical on-line rch algorithms for texts and biological sequences*. Cambridge University Press, 2002. ISBN 0-521-81307-7.

[19] P. Roland and J. Ganascia. Musical pattern extraction and similarity assessment. In E. Miranda, editor, *Readings in Music and Artificial Intelligence*, pages 115–144. Harwood Academic Publishers, 2000.

[20] L. A. Smith, E. F. Chiu, and B. L. Scott. A speech interface for building musical score collections. In *Proc. of the fifth ACM conference on Digital libraries*, pages 165–173. ACM Press, 2000.

[21] D. Sunday. A very fast substring searching algorithm. *Comm. ACM*, 33(8):132–142, August 1990.

[22] E. Ukkonen. Approximate string matching over suffix trees. In *Proc. 4th Annual Symposium on Combinatorial Pattern Matching (CPM'93)*, pages 228–242, 1993.

[23] S. Wu and U. Manber. Fast text searching allowing errors. *Comm. ACM*, 35(10):83–91, October 1992.

Flexible and Efficient Bit-Parallel Techniques for Transposition Invariant Approximate Matching in Music Retrieval

Kjell Lemström[1] and Gonzalo Navarro[2*]

[1] Department of Computer Science, University of Helsinki, Finland
klemstro@cs.helsinki.fi
[2] Department of Computer Science, University of Chile
gnavarro@dcc.uchile.cl

Abstract. Recent research in music retrieval has shown that a combinatorial approach to the problem could be fruitful. Three distinguishing requirements of this particular problem are (*a*) approximate searching permitting missing, extra, and distorted notes, (*b*) transposition invariance, to allow matching a sequence that appears in a different scale, and (*c*) handling polyphonic music. These combined requirements make up a complex combinatorial problem that is currently under research. On the other hand, bit-parallelism has proved a powerful practical tool for combinatorial pattern matching, both flexible and efficient. In this paper we use bit-parallelism to search for several transpositions at the same time, and obtain speedups of $O(w/\log k)$ over the classical algorithms, where the computer word has w bits and k is the error threshold allowed in the match. Although not the best solution for the easier approximation measures, we show that our technique can be adapted to complex cases where no competing method exists, and that are the most interesting in terms of music retrieval.

1 Introduction

Combinatorial pattern matching with its many application domains have been an active research field already for several decades. One of the latest such domains is *music retrieval*. Indeed, music can be encoded as sequences of symbols, i.e. as strings. At a rudimentary level this is done by taking into account exclusively the order of the starting times of the musical events (i.e., the *note ons*) together with their *pitch* information (i.e. the frequency, the perceived height of the musical event). On a more complicated level one can use several distinct attributes for each of the events (see e.g. [1,9]). Most of the interesting musical attributes used in such symbolic representations are directly available in MIDI format [13] which is a commonly used compact symbolic representation.

A straightforward application of general string matching techniques on symbolic music representation, however, does not suffice for musically pertinent

---

* Partially supported by Fondecyt Grant 1-020831.

M.A. Nascimento, E.S. de Moura, A.L. Oliveira (Eds.): SPIRE 2003, LNCS 2857, pp. 224–237, 2003.

matching queries; music has special features that have not been considered in general string matching techniques. Firstly, music is often *polyphonic*, i.e., there are several events occurring simultaneously (in a case where there exists no simultaneous events the music is said to be *monophonic*). These simultaneous events may have a collective meaning and, therefore, the polyphony has to be preserved and taken into account in the matching process. For instance, a typical music retrieval, or searching problem, is the *distributed string matching problem*: given a set t (called a *text* or a *target*) of h strings (each representing a *voice*) $t^i = t^i_1, \ldots, t^i_n$, $i \in \{1 \ldots h\}$, for some constant h and a *pattern* $p = p_1, \ldots, p_m$, we say that p occurs at position j of t if $p_1 = t^{i_1}_j, p_2 = t^{i_2}_{j+1}, \ldots, p_m = t^{i_m}_{j+m-1}$ for some $\{i_1, \ldots, i_m\} \in \{1 \ldots h\}$. The problem has been studied in [7,10].

Secondly, western people tend to listen music analytically by observing the intervals between the consecutive pitch values more than the actual pitch values themselves: A melody performed in two distinct pitch levels is perceived and recognized as the same regardless of the performed pitch level. This leads to the concept of *transposition invariance*. Formally, the *transposition invariant distributed string matching problem* is as follows. Given a monophonic pattern p and a polyphonic target t of h voices, $t^i = t^i_1 \cdots t^i_n, i \in \{1, \ldots, h\}$, the task is to find all the js such that $p_1 = t^{i_1}_j + c, p_2 = t^{i_2}_{j+1} + c, \ldots, p_m = t^{i_m}_{j+m-1} + c$ holds, for some constant c and $\{i_1, \ldots, i_m\} \in \{1, \ldots, h\}$ [10].

Thirdly, real music is often decorated, i.e., it may contain grace notes or ornamentations, for instance. The conventional procedure to overcome this problem is to allow gaps between the consecutive matching elements in found occurrences [2,6,16]. The choices are either to use parametrized gapping (as in [2,6]) or arbitrary gapping (as in [16]). As we aim at a matching method that finds all the occurrences (although it may also find spurious ones), we will use the latter approach. Instead of using the geometric approach of Wiggins et al. [16], we will use the string matching framework and apply the indel distance (the dual of LCS-matching) [5]. We claim that it is a more fruitful approach not to drop any occurrences although in some situations it may lead to a large number of spurious occurrences. The set of found occurrences may then be post-processed by musically motivated filters, for instance by those discussed in [12].

Fourthly, in a typical transposition invariant distributed string matching application the query pattern is given by humming. This kind of an application is sometimes referred as "WYHIWYG" (What You Hum Is What You Get) or "query by humming". In such a case we may expect that all the events in the hummed query pattern are relevant, but its (absolute) pitch values may be somewhat distorted. This distortion has the form of Gaussian distribution with the mean value of the correct (desired) pitch and with a relatively small variance. Therefore, in a WYHIWYG application, we would like to enable some tolerance for such errors. Here we consider two solutions for this problem, the first of which is the so-called δ-matching [3]. The pattern $p = p_1 \cdots p_m$ is said to have a δ-match in $t_1 \cdots t_n$ if $p_i \in [t_{j+i-1}-\delta, t_{j+i-1}+\delta]$ for all $i = 1, \ldots, m$. Although this approach works reasonably well in practice, it is musically more appropriate to penalize an error according to how much the pitch differs from the desired one than to allow any distortion as long it is within the allowed tolerance. Therefore, we will use a more general distance function which implements the claim above.

Although all the problems given above have been studied, no current solution can solve them all. Most relevantly, the bit-parallel algorithm by Crochemore et al. [4] can compute the LCS in $O(m^2/w)$ time, where w denotes the size of the computer word in bits. Moreover, as we discuss in Section 5, the algorithm can be extended straightforwardly to deal with polyphony, transpositions and δ matching in $O(h\sigma m^2/w)$ time (here σ denotes the number of possible transpositions). Furthermore, the same complexity is obtainable with the unit-cost edit distance by using other bit-parallel algorithms [14,8].

Our solution is also based on bit-parallelism, which is well-known for its flexibility. Our transposition invariant δ-matching algorithm for distributed string matching runs in time $O(\sigma m^2 \log(m)/w)$. Noteworthy, it is capable of applying more general and musically pertinent distance functions than the previous related solutions, e.g. those that are not based on unit costs.

2   Preliminaries

Let us start this section by a brief introduction to string combinatorics. Let Σ be a finite set of symbols, called an *alphabet*, and $\sigma = |\Sigma|$. Then any $A = (a_1, a_2, \ldots, a_m)$ where each a_i is a symbol in Σ, is a *string* over Σ. Usually we write $A = a_1 \cdots a_m$. The *length* of A is $|A| = m$. The string of length 0 is called the *empty string* and denoted λ. The set of strings of length i over Σ is denoted by Σ^i, and the set of all strings over Σ by Σ^*. If a string A is of form $A = \beta\alpha\gamma$, where $\alpha, \beta, \gamma \in \Sigma^*$, we say that α is a *factor* (substring) of A. Furthermore, β is called a *prefix* of A, and γ a *suffix* of A. A string A' is a *subsequence* of A if it can be obtained from A by deleting zero or more symbols, i.e., $A' = a_{i_1} a_{i_2} \cdots a_{i_m}$, where $i_1 \ldots i_m$ is an increasing sequence of indices in A.

To define a distance between strings over Σ^*, one should first fix the set of *local transformations* (editing operations) $T \subseteq \Sigma^* \times \Sigma^*$ and a non-negative valued *cost function* W that gives for each transformation t in T a cost $W(t)$. Each t in T is a pair of strings $t = (\alpha, \beta)$. Observing such a t as a rewriting rule, suggests a notation for t, $\alpha \to \beta$ (α is replaced by β within a string containing α), which we will use below. For convenience, if $\alpha \to \beta \notin T$, then $W(\alpha \to \beta) = \infty$.

The definition of the distance is based on the concept of *trace*, which gives a correspondence between two strings. Formally, a trace between two strings A and B over Σ^*, is formed by splitting A and B into equally many factors:

$$\tau = (\alpha_1, \alpha_2, \ldots, \alpha_p; \beta_1, \beta_2, \ldots, \beta_p),$$

where $A = \alpha_1 \alpha_2 \cdots \alpha_p$, and $B = \beta_1 \beta_2 \cdots \beta_p$, and each α_i, β_i (but not both) may be an empty string over Σ. Thus, string B can be obtained from A by steps $\alpha_1 \to \beta_1, \alpha_2 \to \beta_2, \ldots, \alpha_p \to \beta_p$.

The cost of the trace τ is $W(\tau) = W(\alpha_1 \to \beta_1) + \cdots + W(\alpha_p \to \beta_p)$. The distance between A and B, denoted $D_{T,W}(A, B)$, is defined as the minimum cost over all possible traces.

The general definition above induces, for instance, the following well-known distance measures. In *unit-cost edit distance* (or Levenshtein distance), $D_L(A, B)$, the allowed local transformations are of the forms $a \rightarrow b$ (substitution), $a \rightarrow \lambda$ (deletion), and $\lambda \rightarrow a$ (insertion), where $a, b \in \Sigma$. The costs are given as $W(a \rightarrow a) = 0$ for all a, $W(a \rightarrow b) = 1$ for all $a \neq b$, and $W(a \rightarrow \lambda) = W(\lambda \rightarrow a) = 1$ for all a. In *Hamming distance*, $D_H(A, B)$, the only allowed local transformations are of form $a \rightarrow b$ where a and b are any members of Σ, with cost $W(a \rightarrow a) = 0$ and $W(a \rightarrow b) = 1$, for $a \neq b$. Finally, the *indel distance*, $D_{LCS}(A, B)$, is defined as Levenshtein distance without the possibility to use substitutions.

It is well-known that the straightforward computation of these distances is by using recurrences like the following used for $D_{LCS}(A, B)$:

$$d_{i,0} = i; \quad d_{0,j} = j;$$

$$d_{ij} = \min \begin{cases} d_{i-1,j} + 1 \\ d_{i,j-1} + 1 \\ d_{i-1,j-1}, \text{if } a_i = b_j. \end{cases}$$

The evaluation of such a recurrence is done by *dynamic programming*, where the distances between the prefixes of A and B are tabulated. Each cell d_{ij} of the distance table (d_{ij}) stores the distance between $a_1 \cdots a_i$ and $b_1 \cdots b_j$ ($0 \leq i \leq m$, $0 \leq j \leq n$) and (d_{ij}) is evaluated by proceeding row-by-row or column-by-column using the recurrence. Finally, $d_{m,n}$ gives the distance, in this case $D_{LCS}(A, B)$.

The dual case of $D_{LCS}(A, B)$ is the calculation of the *longest common subsequence* of two strings A and B, or $lcs(A, B)$ for short. The length of $lcs(A, B)$, denoted by $LCS(A, B)$, is computed by the recurrence:

$$LCS_{i,0} \leftarrow 0; \quad LCS_{0,j} \leftarrow 0; \tag{1}$$
$$LCS_{i+1,j+1} \leftarrow \text{if } a_{i+1} = b_{j+1} \quad \text{then } 1 + LCS_{i,j}$$
$$\text{else } \max(LCS_{i,j+1}, LCS_{i+1,j}).$$

Now it is rather clear that $LCS(A, B) = \frac{|A| + |B| - D_{LCS}(A,B)}{2}$.

If we want to calculate the length of the *longest common transposition invariant subsequence*, $LCTS(A, B)$, it may be done by calculating $LCS^c(A, B)$ by all the possible $2\sigma + 1$ transpositions, and select the transposition c which gives the maximum [11]. $LCS^c(A, B)$ is defined just like $LCS(A, B)$ except that there is a match when $a_{i+1} + c = b_{j+1}$. Our idea is to simulate the computation of the (d_{ij}^c) tables, for $c = [-\sigma, \sigma]$, so that the aligned d_{ij} values are computed simultaneously in a bit vector, as long as they fit in the used computed word of w bits (see Fig. 1). Typical sizes of alphabet are, e.g., 88 (the number of keys in piano) and 127 (the number of MIDI pitch values), and 32 or 64 for the size of the current computer word. In practice, we need 3–8 bit-vectors for each d_{ij}.

Finally, the weighted edit distance that we use to make a distinction according to the amount of the local distortion is as follows:

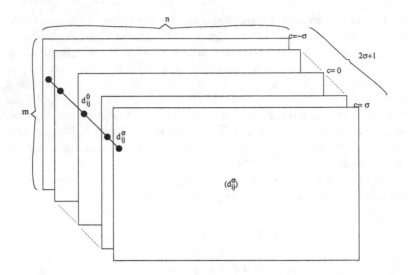

Fig. 1. We calculate in parallel $2\sigma + 1$ (d_{ij}) tables. The idea is to present the aligned nodes $d_{ij}^{-\sigma} \ldots d_{ij}^{\sigma}$ with a single bit-vector (as long as they fit in a computer word).

$$ED_{i,0} \leftarrow i \times ID; \quad ED_{0,j} \leftarrow j \times ID; \tag{2}$$
$$ED_{i+1,j+1} \leftarrow \min(|a_{i+1} - b_{j+1}| + ED_{i,j}, ID + ED_{i,j+1}, ID + ED_{i+1,j}),$$

where ID is a constant used for indel operations.

3   A Bit-Parallel Algorithm

We present a speedup technique for the computation of the $2\sigma+1$ LCS matrices. We resort to bit-parallelism, that is, to storing several values inside the same computer word. For this sake we will denote the bitwise *and* operation as "&", the *or* as "|", and the bit complementation as "~". Shifting i positions to the left (right) is represented as "$<< i$" ("$>> i$"), where the bits that fall are discarded and the new bits that enter are zero. We can also perform arithmetic operations over the computer words. We use exponentiation to denote bit repetition, e.g. $0^3 1 = 0001$, and write the most significant bit as the leftmost bit. When we write $[x]_\ell$ we mean the integer x represented in ℓ bits.

Since the values of the LCS matrix are in the range $\{0 \ldots \min(|a|, |b|)\}$, we need $\ell = \lceil \log_2(\min(|a|, |b|) + 1) \rceil$ bits to store them. This means that in a computer word of w bits we can store $\lfloor w/\ell \rfloor$ counters. For reasons that will be made clear soon, we will in fact need $\ell+1$ bits per counter, where the highest bit will always be zero, and hence we will be able to store $A = \lfloor w/(\ell+1) \rfloor$ counters.

We will divide the process of computing $LCS^c(a, b)$ for every $c \in \Sigma$ into $\lceil (2\sigma + 1)/A \rceil$ separate bit-parallel computations, each for A contiguous c values.

From now on, let us consider that we are computing in parallel $LCS^c(a, b)$ for $c \in \{C \ldots C + A - 1\}$.

The first problem to bit-parallelize Eq. (1) is its if-then-else structure. For a given c, if $a_{i+1} + c = b_{j+1}$ we have to use the value $1 + LCS^c_{i,j}$, otherwise we have to use $\max(LCS^c_{i+1,j}, LCS^c_{i,j+1})$. We solve this by using a bit-mask B of length $A(\ell + 1)$, which should have all 1's in the c values for which $a_{i+1} + c = b_{j+1}$, and zeros elsewhere. This means that we have 1's only for the value $c = b_{j+1} - a_{i+1}$. It is possible that this c value is outside our current range $\{C \ldots C + A - 1\}$. So the computation of B is as follows:

$$B \leftarrow \text{if } C \leq b_{j+1} - a_{i+1} < C + A$$
$$\begin{cases} \text{then } 0^{(A+C-1-(b_{j+1}-a_{i+1}))(\ell+1)} 1^{(\ell+1)} 0^{(b_{j+1}-a_{i+1}-C)(\ell+1)} \\ \text{else } 0^{A(\ell+1)} \end{cases}$$

Once we have computed B, we want to take the value $1 + LCS^c_{i,j}$ for the c values where B has 1's and the value $\max(LCS^c_{i+1,j}, LCS^c_{i,j+1})$ elsewhere. For the former we need to add 1 to all the counters at the same time, which is easily achieved by adding $(0^\ell 1)^A$. For the latter we need to compute $\max()$ in bit-parallel. Let us call Max this function. Hence the value we want is

$$LCS_{i+1,j+1} \leftarrow (B \mathrel{\&} (LCS_{i,j} + (0^\ell 1)^A)) \mid (\sim B \mathrel{\&} Max(LCS_{i+1,j}, LCS_{i,j+1}))$$

To compute $Max(X, Y)$, where X and Y contain several counters properly aligned, we need the aforementioned extra highest bit per counter, always zero. We precompute the bit mask $J = (10^\ell)^A$ and perform the operation $F \leftarrow ((X \mid J) - Y) \mathrel{\&} J$. The result is that, in F, each highest bit is set iff the counter of X is larger than that of Y. We now compute $F \leftarrow F - (F >> \ell)$, so that the counters where X is larger than Y have all their bits set in F, and the others have all the bits in zero. Finally, we choose the maxima as $Max(X, Y) \leftarrow (F \mathrel{\&} X) \mid (\sim F \mathrel{\&} Y)$. Also, we easily obtain $Min(X, Y) \leftarrow (F \mathrel{\&} Y) \mid (\sim F \mathrel{\&} X)$. Fig. 2 gives the code. These methods are due to [15].

Fig. 3 shows **RangeLCTS**, the bit-parallel algorithm for a range of counters $C \ldots C + A - 1$. Using this algorithm we traverse all the $c \in \Sigma$ values and compute $LCTS(a, b) = \max_{c \in -\sigma \ldots \sigma} LCS^c(a, b)$. This is done by **LCTS**.

Let us now analyze the algorithm. **LCTS** runs $(2\sigma + 1)/A$ iterations of **RangeLCTS** plus a minimization over $2\sigma + 1$ values. In turn, **RangeLCTS** takes $O(|a||b|)$ time. Since $A = w/\log_2 \min(|a|, |b|)(1 + o(1))$, the algorithm is $O(\sigma |a||b| \log(\min(|a|, |b|))/w)$ time. If $|a| = |b| = m$, the algorithm is $O(\sigma m^2 \log(m)/w)$ time, which represents a speedup of $\Omega(w/\log m)$ over the naive $O(\sigma m^2)$ time algorithm.

It is possible to adapt this algorithm to compute $\delta\text{-}LCTS(a, b)$, where we assume that two characters match if their difference does not exceed δ. This is arranged at no extra cost by considering that there is a match whenever $b_{j+1} - a_{i+1} - \delta \leq c \leq b_{j+1} - a_{i+1} + \delta$. The only change needed in our algorithm is in lines 5–7 of **RangeLCTS**, which should become:

```
Max (X, Y, ℓ)
  1.    J ← (10ℓ)^A
  2.    F ← ((X | J) − Y) & J
  3.    F ← F − (F >> ℓ)
  4.    Return (F & X) | (∼ F & Y)
```

```
Min (X, Y, ℓ)
  1.    J ← (10ℓ)^A
  2.    F ← ((X | J) − Y) & J
  3.    F ← F − (F >> ℓ)
  4.    Return (F & Y) | (∼ F & X)
```

Fig. 2. Bit-parallel computation of maximum and minimum between two sets of counters aligned in a computer word. In practice J is precomputed.

$$low \leftarrow \max(C, b_j - a_i - \delta)$$
$$high \leftarrow \min(C + A - 1, b_j - a_i + \delta)$$
If $low \leq high$ **Then**
$$B \leftarrow 0^{(A+C-1-high)(\ell+1)} 1^{(high-low+1)(\ell+1)} 0^{(low-C)(\ell+1)}$$
Else $B \leftarrow 0^{A(\ell+1)}$

4   Text Searching

The above procedure can be adapted to search for a pattern P of length m in a text T of length n under the indel distance, permitting transposition invariance. The goal is, given a threshold value k, report all text positions j such that $d(P, T_{j'...j}) \leq k$ for some j', where d is the indel distance (number of character insertions and deletions needed to make two strings equal).

Additionally, we can search polyphonic text, where there are actually h parallel texts $T^1 \ldots T^h$, and text position j matches any character in the set $\{T_j^1 \ldots T_j^h\}$.

Let us consider a new recurrence for searching. We start with a column $D_i = i$ and update D to D' for every new text position j. For every j where $D_m \leq k$ we report text position j as the end position of a recurrence. The formula for searching with indel distance using transposition c is as follows:

$$D'^c_0 \leftarrow 0$$
$$D'^c_{i+1} \leftarrow \text{if } P_{i+1} + c \in \{T_j^1 \ldots T_j^h\} \text{ then } D_i^c \text{ else } 1 + \min(D'^c_i, D_{i+1}^c)$$

RangeLCTS (a, b, C, A, ℓ)
1.   **For** $i \in 0 \ldots |a|$ **Do**
2.   **For** $j \in 0 \ldots |b|$ **Do**
3.   **If** $i = 0 \vee j = 0$ **Then** $LCS_{i,j} \leftarrow 0^{A(\ell+1)}$
4.   **Else**
5.   **If** $C \le b_j - a_i < C + A$ **Then**
6. $B \leftarrow 0^{(A+C-1-(b_j-a_i))(\ell+1)} \; 1^{(\ell+1)} \; 0^{(b_j-a_i-C)(\ell+1)}$
7.   **Else** $B \leftarrow 0^{A(\ell+1)}$
8. $LCS_{i,j} \leftarrow (B \, \& \, (LCS_{i-1,j-1} + (0^\ell 1)^A))$
                       $\mid \, (\sim B \, \& \, Max(LCS_{i-1,j}, LCS_{i,j-1})$
10.   **Return** $LCS_{|a|,|b|}$

LCTS (a, b, σ)
1. $\ell \leftarrow \lceil \log_2(\min(|a|, |b|) + 1) \rceil$
2. $A \leftarrow \lfloor w/(\ell + 1) \rfloor$
3. $c \leftarrow -\sigma$
4. $Max \leftarrow 0$
5.   **While** $c \le \sigma$ **Do**
6. $V \leftarrow$ **RangeLCTS**(a, b, c, A, ℓ)
7.   **For** $t \in c \ldots c + A - 1$ **Do**
8. $Max \leftarrow \max(Max, (V >> (t - c)(\ell + 1)) \, \& \, 0^{(A-1)(\ell+1)} 0 1^\ell)$
9. $c \leftarrow c + A$
10.   **Return** Max

Fig. 3. Computing $LCTS(a, b)$ using bit-parallelism. **RangeLCTS** computes $LCS^c(a, b)$ for every $c \in C \ldots C + A - 1$ in bit-parallel, and returns a bit mask containing $LCS^c(a, b)$ for all those c values.

where we note that we have suppressed column number j, as we will speak about the *current* column (D' or $newD$) built using the *previous* column (D or $oldD$).

Additionally, we note that, when a value is larger than k, all we need to know is that it is larger than k, so we store $k + 1$ for those values in order to represent smaller numbers. Hence the number of bits needed by a counter is $\ell = \lceil \log_2(k + 2) \rceil$.

The new recurrence requires the same tools we have already developed for the LCS computation, except for the polyphony issue and for the $k + 1$ limit. Polyphony can be accommodated by *or*-ing the B masks corresponding to the different text characters at position j. The $k + 1$ limit has to be taken care of only when we add 1 in the "else" clause of the recurrence.

The typical way to solve this requires one extra bit for the counters. We prefer instead to reuse our result for bit-parallel minimum. The recurrence can be rewritten as follows, which guarantees that any value larger than k stays at $k + 1$.

$$D'^c_0 \leftarrow 0$$

$$D'^c_{i+1} \leftarrow \text{if } P_{i+1} + c \in \{T^1_j \ldots T^h_j\} \text{ then } D^c_i \text{ else } 1 + \min(D'^c_i, D^c_{i+1}, k)$$

Finally, we have to report every text position where $D_m \leq k$. In our setting, this means that any counter different from $k+1$ makes the current text position to be reported.

Fig. 4 shows **RangeIDSearch**, which searches for a range of transpositions that fit in a computer word. The general algorithm, **IDSearch**, simply applies the former procedure to successive ranges. The algorithm is $O(h\sigma mn \log(k)/w)$ time, which represents a speedup of $O(w/\log k)$ over the classical solution.

RangeIDSearch $(P, T^1 \ldots T^h, k, C, A, \ell)$
1. $K \leftarrow [k]_{\ell+1} \times (0^\ell 1)^A$
2. $Kp1 \leftarrow K + (0^\ell 1)^A$
3.   **For** $i \in 0 \ldots k$ **Do** $D_i \leftarrow [i]_{\ell+1} \times (0^\ell 1)^A$
4.   **For** $i \in k+1 \ldots |P|$ **Do** $D_i \leftarrow Kp1$
5.   **For** $j \in 1 \ldots |T|$ **Do**
6. $oldD \leftarrow 0$
7.   **For** $i \in 1 \ldots |P|$ **Do**
8. $B \leftarrow 0^{A(\ell+1)}$
9.   **For** $g \in 1 \ldots h$ **Do**
10.   **If** $C \leq T^g_j - P_i < C + A$ **Then**
11. $B \leftarrow B \mid 0^{(A+C-1-(T^g_j-P_i))(\ell+1)} \, 1^{(\ell+1)} \, 0^{((T^g_j-P_i)-C)(\ell+1)}$
12. $newD \leftarrow (B \,\&\, oldD) \mid (\sim B \,\&\, (Min(Min(D_{i-1}, D_i), K) + (0^\ell 1)^A))$
13. $oldD \leftarrow D_i, \; D_i \leftarrow newD$
14.   **If** $newD \neq Kp1$ **Then** Report an occurrence ending at j

---

IDSearch $(P, T^1 \ldots T^h, k, \sigma)$
1. $\ell \leftarrow \lceil \log_2(k+1) \rceil$
2. $A \leftarrow \lfloor w/(\ell+1) \rfloor$
3. $c \leftarrow -\sigma$
4.   **While** $c \leq \sigma$ **Do**
5.   **RangeIDSearch**$(P, T^1 \ldots T^h, k, c, A, \ell)$
6. $c \leftarrow c + A$

Fig. 4. Searching polyphonic text with indel distance permitting any transposition.

5   A More General Distance Function

Although we have obtained important speedups with respect to classical algorithms, it turns out that there exist bit-parallel techniques that can compute the LCS in $O(m^2/w)$ time [4]. Extending these algorithms naively to deal with polyphony, transpositions and δ matching yields $O(h\sigma m^2/w)$ time. Although it has not been done, we believe that it is not hard to convert these algorithms into search algorithms for indel distance at $O(h\sigma mn/w)$ cost, which is better than ours by an $O(\log k)$ factor. The same times can be obtained if we use edit distance instead of indel distance [14,8].

The strength of our approach resides in that we are using bit-parallelism in a different dimension: rather than computing several cells of a matrix in parallel, we compute several transpositions in parallel, while the cells are computed one by one. This gives us extra flexibility, because we can handle complex recurrences among cells as long as we can do several similar operations in parallel. Parallelizing the work inside the matrix is more complex, and has been achieved only for unit-cost distances. As explained before, a weighted edit distance where the cost to convert a note into another is proportional to the absolute difference among the notes is of interest in music retrieval. We demonstrate the flexibility of our approach by addressing the computation of the weighted edit distance detailed in Eq. (2). Which follows is the search version for a given transposition c in polyphonic text, bounded by $k+1$.

$$D'^{\,c}_{\,0} \leftarrow 0$$
$$D'^{\,c}_{\,i+1} \leftarrow \min(\ \min_{g\in 1...h} |P_{i+1} + c - T^g_j| + D^c_{i-1}, ID + D'^{\,c}_{\,i}, ID + D^c_{i+1}, k+1)$$

There are two challenges to bit-parallelize this recurrence. The first is that ensuring that we never surpass $k+1$ is more difficult, because the increments are not only by 1. We choose to compute the full values and then take minimum with $k+1$, as suggested by the recurrence. However, the intermediate values can be larger. Since $ID \leq k$ (otherwise the problem is totally different), the latter terms are bounded by $2k+1$. We will manage to keep also the first term of the minimization below $2k+2$. This means that we need $\lceil \log_2(2k+3) \rceil$ bits for our counters.

The second challenge is how to compute $|P_{i+1} + c - T^g_j|$ in bit-parallel for a set of consecutive c values, with the added trouble of not exceeding $k+1$ in any counter. Depending on the range $C \ldots C+A-1$ of transpositions we are considering, these values form an increasing, decreasing, or decreasing-then-increasing sequence. For shortness, we will use $[x]$ to denote $[x]_{\ell+1}$ in this discussion. An increasing sequence of the form $I_t = [t+A-1]\ldots[t+1]\,[t]$, $t \geq 0$, is obtained simply as $I_t \leftarrow (0^\ell 1)^{A-1}[t] \times (0^\ell 1)^A$. A version bounded by $r \geq t$ is obtained as $I^r_t \leftarrow (I_t \ \& \ 0^{(A-(r-t))(\ell+1)}1^{(r-t)(\ell+1)}) \mid ([r]^{A-(r-t)}0^{(r-t)(\ell+1)})$. Similarly, a decreasing sequence $D_t = [t-A+1]\ldots[t-1]\,[t]$ is obtained as $D_t \leftarrow [t]^A - I_0$. The bounded version is obtained similarly as for increasing sequences. Finally, a decreasing-then-increasing sequence $DI_t = [A-t-1]\,[A-t-2]\ldots[2]\,[1]\,[0]\,[1]\ldots[t-1]\,[t]$ is obtained as $DI_t = (I_0 << t(\ell+1)) \mid (D_A >> (A-t)(\ell+1))$. The bounded version DI^r is obtained similarly, using I^r and D^r instead. We could even accommodate substitution costs of the form $|a_i - b_j|/q$ for integer q by multiplying by $(0^{q(\ell+1)-1}1)^A$ instead of by $(0^\ell 1)^A$. Fig. 5 gives the code to build these sequences.

I $(t,\ r,\ A,\ \ell)$
1.   If $r \le t$ Then Return $[r]_{\ell+1} \times (0^\ell 1)^A$
2. $I_t \leftarrow ((0^\ell 1)^{A-1} 0^{\ell+1} \mid [t]_{\ell+1}) \times (0^\ell 1)^A$
3.   Return $(I_t\ \&\ 0^{(A-(r-t))(\ell+1)} 1^{(r-t)(\ell+1)}) \mid ([r]_{\ell+1} \times (0^\ell 1)^{A-(r-t)} 0^{(r-t)(\ell+1)})$

D $(t,\ r,\ A,\ \ell)$
1.   If $r \ge t$ Then $r \leftarrow t$
2. $D_r \leftarrow [r]_{\ell+1} \times (0^\ell 1)^A - (0^\ell 1)^{A-1} 0^{\ell+1} \times (0^\ell 1)^A$
3.   Return $(D_r << (t-r)(\ell+1)) \mid ([r]_{\ell+1} \times 0^{(A-(t-r))(\ell+1)} (0^\ell 1)^{(t-r)(\ell+1)})$

DI $(t,\ r,\ A,\ \ell)$
1. $I \leftarrow \mathbf{I}(0, r, A, \ell)$
2. $D \leftarrow \mathbf{D}(A, r, A, \ell)$
3.   Return $(I << t(\ell+1)) \mid (D >> (A-t)(\ell+1))$

Fig. 5. Bit-parallel code to obtain increasing, decreasing, and decreasing-then-increasing sequences.

It becomes clear that we can perform approximate searching using this general distance function, permitting transposition invariance and polyphony, in $O(h\sigma mn \log(k)/w)$. This cannot be done with previous approaches and illustrates the strength of our method. Fig. 6 gives the details.

6   Experiments

We conducted a brief experiment on comparing the efficiency between our LCTS method and an algorithm based on classical dynamic programming (CDB). The experiment was run on two distinct computers, the first of which was a Sun UltraSparc-1 running SunOS 5.8 with 167 MHZ and 64 Mb RAM, and the second was a Pentium IV running Linux 2.4.10-4GB with 2 GHZ and 512 MB RAM.

Both the codes for our **RangeLCTS** algorithm and for the classical dynamic programming were highly optimized. In the experiment we used LCS matrixes of size $10,000 \times 10,000$ (the content was pitch values of musical data). We measured the CPU times spent by 1 iteration of the **RangeLCTS** (for the whole LCTS query we then calculated the required total time for a given w) and by CDB. Moreover, since both of the algorithms scale up well with n^2, we were able to estimate the running times for distinct ranges of n.

Table 1 gives results when running the two observed algorithms when executed on Sun. Note that we are better for large $n < 1,000$ (more precisely, up to $n = 510$). The reason is that our counters have to maintain the current LCS values in $w = 32$ bits, which can be as large as n.

RangeEDSearch $(P, T^1 \ldots T^h, k, C, A, \ell)$
1. $Kp1 \leftarrow [k+1]_{\ell+1} \times (0^\ell 1)^A$
2. $IDmask \leftarrow [ID]_{\ell+1} \times (0^\ell 1)^A$
3.   **For** $i \in 0 \ldots \lfloor k/ID \rfloor$ **Do** $D_i \leftarrow [i \cdot ID]_{\ell+1} \times (0^\ell 1)^A$
4.   **For** $i \in k+1 \ldots |P|$ **Do** $D_i \leftarrow Kp1$
5.   **For** $j \in 1 \ldots |T|$ **Do**
6. $oldD \leftarrow 0$
7.   **For** $i \in 1 \ldots |P|$ **Do**
8. $B \leftarrow Kp1$
9.   **For** $g \in 1 \ldots h$ **Do**
10.   **If** $T_j^g - P_i \leq C$ **Then** // Increasing sequence
11. $B' \leftarrow \mathbf{I}(C - (T_j^g - P_i), k+1, A, \ell)$
12.   **Else If** $T_j^g - P_i \geq C + A$ **Then** // Decreasing sequence
13. $B' \leftarrow \mathbf{D}((T_j^g - P_i) - C, k+1, A, \ell)$
14.   **Else** $B' \leftarrow \mathbf{DI}((T_j^g - P_i) - C, k+1, A, \ell)$
15. $B \leftarrow Min(B, B')$
16. $newD \leftarrow Min(Min(B + oldD, Min(D_{i-1}, D_i) + IDmask), Kp1)$
17. $oldD \leftarrow D_i, \ D_i \leftarrow newD$
18.   **If** $newD \neq Kp1$ **Then** Report an occurrence ending at j

EDSearch $(P, T^1 \ldots T^h, k, \sigma)$
1. $\ell \leftarrow \lceil \log_2(2k+3) \rceil$
2. $A \leftarrow \lfloor w/(\ell+1) \rfloor$
3. $c \leftarrow -\sigma$
4.   **While** $c \leq \sigma$ **Do**
5.   **RangeEDSearch**$(P, T^1 \ldots T^h, k, c, A, \ell)$
6. $c \leftarrow c + A$

Fig. 6. Searching polyphonic text with weighted edit distance permitting any transposition.

We wanted also experiment on a Pentium IV due to its very optimized pipelining, which should compromize the overhead in number of register operations due to the bit-parallelism with the fact that we have broken the if-then-else nature of the original recurrences.

Table 2 shows that in the same setting ($w = 32$) with Pentium IV. This time we are faster even for $n = 10,000$, more precisely up to $n = 65,534$. This covers virtually all cases of interest.

7   Conclusions

In this paper we have focused on music retrieval. Since we wanted to apply the general string matching framework to this particular application domain, we introduced problems that are typical to music retrieval but that are not

SUN	$n = 10$	100	1,000	10,000
LCTS	0.00049	0.07334	14.6688	1,466.88
CDP	0.00124	0.124173	12.4173	1,241.73

Table 1. Execution times (in sec) for our LCTS and CDP when running on Sun.

Pentium IV	$n = 10$	100	1,000	10,000
LCTS	0.00004644	0.006912	1.3797	137.97
CDP	0.000199	0.019929	1.9929	199.29

Table 2. Execution times for our LCTS and CDP when running on Pentium IV.

taken into account in the combinatorial pattern matching algorithms. The three distinguishing requirements are (a) approximate searching permitting missing, extra, and distorted notes, (b) transposition invariance, to allow matching a sequence that appears in a different scale, and (c) handling polyphonic music.

We introduced a flexible and efficient bit-parallel algorithm that takes into account all the requirements above, and obtains a speedup of $O(w/\log k)$ over the classical algorithms, where the computer word has w bits and k is the error threshold allowed in the match. Even though it is not the best solution when unit cost distances are applied, it performs at a comparative level. Our algorithm, however, can be adapted to complex cases where no competing method exists. Furthermore, these cases are the most interesting in terms of music retrieval.

References

1. E. Cambouropoulos. A general pitch interval representation: Theory and applications. *Journal of New Music Research*, 25:231–251, 1996.
2. M. Crochemore, C. S. Iliopoulos, Y. J. Pinzon, and W. Rytter. Finding motifs with gaps. In *First International Symposium on Music Information Retrieval (IS-MIR'2000)*, Plymouth, MA, 2000.
3. M. Crochemore, C.S. Iliopoulos, G. Navarro, and Y. Pinzon. A bit-parallel suffix automaton approach for (δ,γ)-matching in music retrieval. To appear in *Proc. SPIRE 2003*.
4. M. Crochemore, C.S. Iliopoulos, Y.J. Pinzon, and J.F. Reid. A fast and practical bit-vector algorithm for the longest common subsequence problem. *Information Processing Letters*, 80(6):279–285, 2001.
5. M. Crochemore and W. Rytter. *Text Algorithms*. Oxford University Press, 1994.
6. M.J. Dovey. A technique for "regular expression" style searching in polyphonic music. In *the 2nd Annual International Symposium on Music Information Retrieval (ISMIR'2001)*, pages 179–185, Bloomington, IND, October 2001.
7. J. Holub, C.S. Iliopoulos, and L. Mouchard. Distributed string matching using finite automata. *Journal of Automata, Languages and Combinatorics*, 6(2):191–204, 2001.

8. H. Hyyrö and G. Navarro. Faster bit-parallel approximate string matching. In *Proc. 13th Annual Symposium on Combinatorial Pattern Matching (CPM 2002)*, pages 203–224, 2002. LNCS 2373.

9. K. Lemström and P. Laine. Musical information retrieval using musical parameters. In *Proceedings of the 1998 International Computer Music Conference*, pages 341–348, Ann Arbor, MI, 1998.

10. K. Lemström and J. Tarhio. Transposition invariant pattern matching for multitrack strings. *Nordic Journal of Computing*, 2003. (to appear).

11. K. Lemström and E. Ukkonen. Including interval encoding into edit distance based music comparison and retrieval. In *Proceedings of the AISB'2000 Symposium on Creative & Cultural Aspects and Applications of AI & Cognitive Science*, pages 53–60, Birmingham, April 2000.

12. D. Meredith, K. Lemström, and G.A. Wiggins. Algorithms for discovering repeated patterns in multidimensional representations of polyphonic music. *Journal of New Music Research*, 31(4):321–345, 2002.

13. MIDI Manufacturers Association, Los Angeles, California. *The Complete Detailed MIDI 1.0 Specification*, 1996.

14. G. Myers. A fast bit-vector algorithm for approximate string matching based on dynamic programming. *Journal of the ACM*, 46(3):395–415, 1999. Earlier version in *Proc. CPM'98*, LNCS 1448.

15. W. Paul and J. Simon. Decision trees and random access machines. In *Proc. Int'l. Symp. on Logic and Algorithmic*, pages 331–340, Zurich, 1980.

16. G.A. Wiggins, K. Lemström, and D. Meredith. SIA(M): A family of efficient algorithms for translation-invariant pattern matching in multidimensional datasets. (submitted).

FindStem: Analysis and Evaluation of a Turkish Stemming Algorithm

Hayri Sever[1] and Yıltan Bitirim[2]

[1] Department of Computer Engineering
Başkent University
Ankara, 06530 Turkey
sever@baskent.edu.tr
[2] Department of Computer Engineering
Eastern Mediterranean University
Famagusta, T.R.N.C. (via Mersin 10, Turkey)
yiltan.bitirim@emu.edu.tr

Abstract. In this paper, we evaluate the effectiveness of a new stemming algorithm, FINDSTEM, for use with Turkish documents and queries, and compare the use of this algorithm with the other two previously defined Turkish stemmers, namely "A-F" and "L-M" algorithms. Of them, the FINDSTEM and A-F algorithms employ inflectional and derivational stemmers, whereas the L-M one handles only inflectional rules. Comparison of stemming algorithms was done manually using 5,000 distinct words out of which the FINDSTEM, A-F, and L-M failed on, in respect, 49, 270, and 559 cases. A medium-size collection, which is comprised of 2,468 law records with 280K document words, 15 queries in natural language with average length of 17 search words, and a complete relevancy information for each query, was used for the effectiveness of the stemming algorithm FINDSTEM. We localized SMART retrieval system in terms of a stopping list, introduction of Turkish characters, i.e., the ISO8859-9 (Latin-5) code set, a stemming algorithm (FINDSTEM), and a Turkish translation at message level. Our results based on average precision values at 11-point recall levels shows that indexing document as well as search terms with the use of FINDSTEM for stemming is clearly and consistently more effective than the one where the terms are indexed as they are (that is, no stemming at all).

1 Introduction

No matter what retrieval model is used, typically information retrieval (IR) systems are built around three basic objects: documents, terms, and user queries. The aim of information retrieval is to extract relevant documents from a collection of documents in response to queries. Terms are used to represent the contents of documents and queries. Furthermore, document terms are matched with search terms to determine the relevancy of documents to a user query. Given that it is not realistic to assume that authors and users of documents have common vocabulary in expressing their intellectual activities, to enlarge the extent of the overlap between vocabularies of these two agents becomes a sound effort. Hence, the conflation procedure to reduce variants of a word to a single

M.A. Nascimento, E.S. de Moura, A.L. Oliveira (Eds.): SPIRE 2003, LNCS 2857, pp. 238–251, 2003.

form gets into picture as a natural consequence of the rationale that similar words generally have similar meanings. The most common conflation procedure is the use of a stemming algorithm, which simply removes, in Turkish [3], inflectional variants from the word endings while keeping derivational affixes untouched. For example, *'gözlüğüm'* (my eyeglasses) and *'gözlüklüyü'* (one who wears eyeglasses) both conflates into the stem *'gözlük'* (eyeglasses), not into their root form, which is *'göz'* (eye). Similarly, all of the words *'göz'* (eye), *'gözde'* (favorite), *'gözlem'* (observation), *'gözcü'* (observer), *'gözlükçü'* (optician), *'gözetim'* (supervision) constitute to some of the stems derived from the the same root *'göz'* [4]; that is, all should be kept as they are since they have different meanings. Stemming, in other words, can be envisioned as a form of language processing [1] that consistently improves system effectiveness [2], though there is conflicting views for English text in the literature [3, 4].

As much as the stemming process might increase the effectiveness of IR systems especially in the morphologically complex languages, it also boosts up the efficiency of IR systems due to the fact that the size of the index term set will be decreased as a result of stemming. In Turkish language, the need for stemming is more dramatic, since there are approximately 23,000 stems and 350-400 roots actively used [5]; however, when the inflection of the words are included, the number is expressed in millions [6], though the number of entries in a typical Turkish dictionary is roughly about 55K. Furthermore, the index of synthesis [5] for Turkish language is found to be 2.86. There are a number of past works on Turkish stemming mostly published locally or unpublished manuscripts [8, 9, 10, 11], with the exception of the work done by Ekmekçioğlu and Willet [12]. Hence, in this article, we hold a comparative discussion of our stemming approach with the previous ones.

The organization of the paper is as follows: In section 2, Turkish stemming algorithms in the literature are discussed. Section 3 presents a stemming algorithm for Turkish, "FindStem" in detail. Section 4 considers the methods and configuration of the experiments. In section 5, experimental results for the stemming algorithms for Turkish are discussed. Finally, section 6 presents conclusions.

2 Stemming Algorithms for Turkish

We explore two stemming Algorithms [6] for Turkish in this section.

The first algorithm, developed by Kut et al. [8], and called Longest-Match (L-M), is based on the word search logic over a lexicon/dictionary that covers Turkish word stems and their possible variances (Figure 1). The authors used the L-M for indexing

---

[3] Turkish as a member of the south-western or Oghuz group of the Turkic family of languages is an agglutinative language with word structures formed by productive affixations of derivational and inflectional suffixes to the root words.

[4] There are roughly 150 stems or compound words emerging from the root *'göz'* (eye).

[5] Index of synthesis refers to the amount of affixation in a language, i.e., it shows the average number of morphemes per word in a language [7].

[6] Truncation of words has been considered as a straightforward alternative to stemming for a long time. Hence, it may be worth stating that a truncation length of 5 characters yields the best performance when compared with the those of 4, 6, 7 and 9 characters [13]

document terms and constructing a stop list, which has been in use since then and consists of 316 words.

1. Remove suffixes that are added with punctuation marks from the word. 2. Search the word in the dictionary. 3. If a matched root is found, goto step 5. 4. If the word remained as a single letter, goto step 6. Otherwise, remove the last letter from the word and goto step 2. 5. Choose the found root as a stem and goto step 7. 6. Add the searched word into unfounded records. 7. Exit.

Fig. 1. The L-M Algorithm

The second algorithm was developed by Solak and Can [10] and is referred as A-F algorithm. The algorithm works over a dictionary that keeps actively used stems for Turkish in which each record is annotated with 64 tags showing how to generate surface forms. For given a word, it is iteratively looked up in a dictionary from right to left by pruning a letter at each step. If the word matches with any of the root words, then the morphological analysis for that word is done, i.e., application of affixation rules to get the surface forms of the root word, or lexicon form. If any of the surface forms is in correspondence with the word at hand, then it is assumed that the root word [7] is an eligible stem for that word. The process is repeated until the word drops down to a single letter. The steps of the algorithm are shown in Figure 2. The algorithm provides all possible stems for a word as an output. Solak and Can [10] reported that the average word stem for Turkish words to be 1.22 [8].

Ekmekcioglu and Willett in their study of effectiveness of stemming for Turkish text retrieval choice to stem only query words in their experiments under the ground that

> Turkish word roots are generally unaffected when a suffix is added to its right-hand end. Accordingly, there is no need for the recoding procedures that are required in many other languages, and the use of a simple truncation search thus ensures that a stemmed query word is able to retrieve all of the variants in the database that are derived from it. For example, the word *enflasyonla* (with/by inflation), in one of the queries was stemmed to *enflasyon*, this resulting in matches with words such as *enflasyonu, enflasyonunu, enflasyonun, and enflasyonist, inter alia.*

---

[7] Note that Solak and Can did not distinguish a root word from a stem. This may be because the root words may be viewed as special cases of stems in the sense that the root is a stem that neither contains any morpheme nor is a compound word. From now on, we share this view as well, unless otherwise is specified.

[8] In the experimental work over the text of 533 Turkish news the A-F algorithm has enumerated 111,062 stems out of 90,912 words.

1. Remove suffixes that are added with punctuation marks from the word.
2. Search the word in dictionary.
3. If a matched root found, add the word into root words list.
4. If the word remained as a single letter, the root words list is empty then goto step 6, if root words list has at least one element then goto step 7.
5. Remove the last letter from the word and goto step 2.
6. Add the searched word into unfounded record and exit.
7. Get the root word from the root words list.
8. Apply morphological analysis to the root word.
9. If the result of morphological analysis is positive then add the root word to the stems list.
10. If there is any element(s) in root words list then goto step 7.
11. Choose the all stems in the stems list as a word stem.

Fig. 2. The A-F Algorithm

The approach described above is problematic in nature because the roots etymologically in Turkish has given rise to many other stems, e.g., the root *'göz'* (eye) is a source of derivation to roughly 150 stems which have totally different meanings indeed. The stem *enflasyon* , given as an example in the quotation, has foreign origin in the noun form, and the Turkish words having foreign origin is usually kept in noun forms which may be inflected, but not be the source of offspring to other stems. Hence, we strongly believe that stemming only search terms is a serious mistake given that the number of feasible stems per a word is between 1.2-1.5 and affixation length per word is 2.82 on average [7, 10, 11]. But we fully agree with the statement that Turkish grammar [9] makes the stemming algorithms simple. One reason behind their decision on stemming only query terms would be slowness of the tool, two-level morphological analyzer for Turkish [15], they have used. This analyzer, called PC-KIMMO [16], has been designed to generate and/or recognize words using a two-level model of word structure in a word is represented as a correspondence between its lexical level form and its surface level form. The generator component of PC-KIMMO accepts as input a lexicon form, applies the appropriate rules, and returns the corresponding surface form(s). The recognizer component accepts as input a surface form, applies the appropriate rules, consults the lexicon, and returns the corresponding the lexical form with its gloss. This way of stemming is rather slow and can analyze only about two forms per second and generate about 50 forms per second on Sun SparcStations [17]. Once more than one stem are obtained for a given search word, the smallest one is picked up by the stemming algorithm. It is reported that this choice was bounded by 17% error rate over the data set conducted for the experiment. The way of turkishizing foreign words into the language we would say the other way around: selecting the longest stem would be appropriate choice. A simpler version of the two-level morphological analyzer for Turkish for stemming (using the same lexicon) has been adapted by Solak and Can as described above by the A-F algorithm.

---

[9] For detailed information on Turkish grammar, we refer the reader to [14].

3 The FindStem Algorithm

The FindStem algorithm contains a pre-processing step that simply converts all letters of the word into their small cases and singles out the letters after the punctuation mark in the word. It has three components, namely "Find the Root", "Morphological Analysis", and "Choose the Stem" that will be explained in the remaining of this section.

3.1 Finding the Root Words in Turkish

The first step in a stemming algorithm is to find all possible roots of an examined word. Then, these roots and production rules will be used to derive the examining word.

Stemming algorithms without a lexicon ignore the word meaning and lead to a number of stemming errors [18]. As in all stemming algorithms for Turkish, the lexicon is used as an auxiliary structure for the stemming process. In lexicon, the type information [10] for every root word and possible root changes (when a root word combines with suffix) is coded for use of morphological analysis. During the root and the suffix combination in Turkish, two alteration on a root word structure would be in order: (1) change of the last vowel (e.g. ara-arıyor) or consonant letter (e.g. kitap-kitabı) of the root word and (2) drop of middle vowel letter (e.g. oğul-oğlum) [6].

The selection of possible root words from lexicon is performed by the search algorithm that uses the coded information in the lexicon. Algorithm starts with the first character of the examined word and search the lexicon for this item. Then the next character is appended to the item for which lexicon search begins. This operation continues until the item becomes equal to the examined word or until the system understands that there are no more relevant roots for the examined word in the lexicon.

3.2 Morphological Analysis

The Turkish language uses the Latin alphabet consisting of 29 letters, of which 8 are vowels and 21 are consonants, and is an agglutinative language, i.e., one in which words contain a basic root, with one or more suffixes being combined with this root in order to extend its meaning or to create other classes of words [19]. In Turkish language there are a number of rules, which are explained in the appendix, to determine the form and order of suffixation

Suffixes are divided into two main classes such as derivational and inflectional ones. Of them, the derivational suffixes are used for changing word meanings. To add the derivational suffixes to end of a word is determined by word type (this information is coded into the lexicon for every word). The derivation rules are gathered under two main titles: (a) advirable that is derivation of tense origin words and (b) de-nominal that is derivation of noun origin words. Note that it is possible to derive an advirable word from a noun origin root word or to derive a de-nominal word from a verb origin root word. For example, the advirable word "**baba**-y-dı" (he was a father) can derive

---

[10] Root words in the lexicon are divided into two main groups: nouns and verbs. The nouns are further subdivided into four groups, which are adjective, adverb, noun and pronoun. Then, this information is coded by numerical values as the type information.

from the noun origin root word **"baba"** (father). To make a derivation, all suffixes are grouped and each one is coded to be a standard method corresponding a rule defined in the appendix.

A morphological analyzer is usually required if high-quality stemming is to be achieved [12]. To show the importance of the morphological analysis step in our stemming algorithm, let us consider the word "edebilecek" as an examined word. The longest possible root words, retrieved from lexicon, are "edebi", "edep", and "ede". According to the algorithms [8, 13] that assigns a stem by matching the examined word with longest root words, these root words will be selected as output. But it is not possible to produce the examined word, "edebilecek", by using these root words merely; this result can be achieved through the morphological analysis procedure.

3.3   Selection of a Stem

In Turkish, a surface form can be generated using more than one root. For example, the word *küçücükken* (once one is very small) may conflate into either of the root *küçük* (small) or *küçücük* (very small). But, if one wonders as to which one truly represents a stem for *küçücükken*, it should be *küçücük*.

The number of application of suffixes and their types [11], at derivation, forms basis for selection operation. It is, however, worth to mention that the ambiguity in conflating Turkish words (or the way around, i.e., generation) into single terms becomes another issue for which our hands are tied for stemming. For example, assume that a word has more than one senses. In this case, let us take a look at the word "başlar" can be either plural of "baş" (head) or inflection of present tense of the verb "başlamak" (to start). To find out the actual stem of a word like the former one, a semantical reasoning about the context should be carried out [12].

If neither a possible root word is found in the lexicon for the examined word nor the production rules are successful for deriving that word from any root in the list, the word will be kept as it is and/or saved on a log file for examination without passing next steps. It is highly probable that such a word is either a foreign word or adopted into Turkish, but not yet present in the lexicon.

Putting it all together: The FindStem algorithm is shown in Figure 10.

4   The Experimental Method

For the experiments, we used localized version of SMART System. To localize the SMART system into Turkish, the Turkish characters (ğ, Ğ, ü, Ü, ş, Ş, ı, İ, ö, Ö, ç, Ç) and Turkish stopwords list are introduced to the system and the English stemming algorithm, in the system, is replaced with the FindStem stemming algorithm.

---

[11] Suffixation is divided into two main types as "derivational suffix" and "inflectional suffix", which may be also further divided into subtypes.

[12] By the context it should not automatically thought of a sentence level analysis, but it may sometimes require to go for paragraph or even for text.

1. Remove suffixes that are added with punctuation marks from the word.
2. Find all possible roots of the word in a lexicon and add them into root words list.
3. If root words list is empty, add the word into unfounded records and exit.
4. Get the root word from root words list.
5. Apply morphological analysis to the root word.
6. After morphological analysis, add the formed derivations into derivations list.
7. If there is any element(s) in root words list then goto step 4.
8. Choose the word stem by a selection between derivations in the derivations list.

Fig. 3. The FindStem Algorithm

The experiment is divided into two parts. In the first part, A-F algorithm [10] and L-M algorithm [8] are compared with FindStem algorithm and their effectiveness are investigated. In the second part, FindStem algorithm is integrated to the localized SMART system and the performance measurement of the algorithm is done by using the precision and recall parameters which can be defined for a user query as the proportion of retrieved and relevant documents over retrieval output and relevant documents, respectively.

4.1 Evaluation of the Turkish Stemming Algorithms

The A-F algorithm was used in its entirety along with its lexicon as being downloaded through private communication, and the L-M algorithm was re-coded by us with respect to the principles laid out in [8].

The algorithms were tested through a data set consisting of 5,000 words. The truth stems of each word were tagged manually. Note that there could be more than one truth stems for a given word as shown in Figure 4.1.

Searching Word	Result Stems
benzerlikten	1.benzerlik
	2.benzer
	3.benze(mek)

Fig. 4. Stems, not accepted as an error

The accuracies of three stemming algorithms over that data set were computed.

4.2 Performance Measurement

"The effectiveness of stemming algorithms has usually been measured in terms of their effect on retrieval performance with test collections" [20]. Our test collection is the set of Turkish based documents which is formed from total 2,468 law entries. The number of rows in these documents ranges between 10 and 20; the number of rows and words in total are 59,941 and 279,904 respectively. This collection was indexed twice by the localized SMART system. One was without stemming and the other was with the FindStem algorithm. As a result, two different index sets were formed in the system.

15 queries [13] have been defined with complete information about relevancy of documents. In correspondence with the document terms, the search (or query) terms were stemmed (or not stemmed). We have run each query separately and used the retrieval outputs to determine if each retrieved document was relevant or not.

We used non-interpolated precision values at 8-point recall levels (from 0.3 to 1) for effectiveness of the system with or without stemmed terms. To calculate the recall, the total number of relevant documents in the collection should be known. But this is not possible while the number of documents in the collection is approximately 2,500. Nevertheless, the cut-off point is determined as 100 documents and the assumption is made that all the relevant documents, which are related to a query, would be in the first 100 documents retrieved. The recall is accepted as 1 at the position (in the retrieval output) that the last relevant document displayed and precision values for every query are calculated for various recall parameters (1, 0.9, 0.8,..., 0.3). The formula used to calculate the precision values for various recall parameters is:

$$Precision = \frac{N \times R}{P_X}$$

where "N" is the number of relevant documents retrieved, "R" is the recall parameter (1, 0.9,..., 0.3) and P_X is the position of Xth ($X = N \times R$) relevant document in the retrieval output. For example, when the number of relevant documents is 10 out of 100 documents retrieved and the last relevant document is 85th document in the retrieval output, for recall parameter, 1, the precision value will be $10 \times 1/85 = 0.12$ and for recall parameter, 0.9, the precision value will be $10 \times 0.9/52 = 0.17$ (52 is the position of 9th (10×0.9) relevant document in the retrieval output), etc.

5   Experimental Results

5.1   Comparison and Effectiveness of Turkish Stemming Algorithms

While the FindStem and the L-M algorithms select only one root as the stem for each word, under certain conditions, the A-F algorithm can select more than one root for a word (Figure 5).

The L-M algorithm could not find 559 roots as a stem but many of them are semantically related words (such as the word "öğreti" is found to be a stem for the word "öğretilecek", instead of the word "öğret(mek)"). Because of this, only 138 of them are assumed wrong.

The FindStem algorithm has found the stems of 49 words different from manually entered stems. But actually, these roots, found by the algorithm, can be evaluated as the stem of a word (e.g. the manually entered stem word is "göz" for the word "gözden" but the algorithm finds the root word "gözde" as a stem).

---

[13] Queries are accessible online, http://cmpe.emu.edu.tr/bitirim/stemming.

Word	FindStem	A-F	L-M	Manually Entered Stem
alanında	alan	al*	alan	alan
anlatılmak	anlat	an*	anlat	anlat
aşılmıştır	aş	aş	aşı*	aş
birleşmiş	birleş	bir	birleş	birleş
belirtilmeyen	belirt	1.be*	belirti*	belirt
		2.belirt		
çekleştirdiği	çek	çekleştirdiği*	çek	çek
aksamaması	aksa	aksa	aksam*	aksa
aralıkta	ara*	aralık	aralık	aralık
eklemek	ekle	ekle	eklem*	ekle
daha	daha	1.da*	daha	daha
		2.daha		

Fig. 5. The found stems for some words by algorithms ("*" means; the word is accepted as incorrect)

The A-F algorithm is found completely wrong stems for 59 words. Furthermore, the algorithm found unsuitable roots as a stem for 270 words (such as the words "göre" and "görev" selected to be stems of the word "görevini").

Some samples of found stems for the employed algorithms are shown in Figure 5.

5.2 The Number of Documents Retrieved

The number of zero retrievals (i.e., no documents retrieved) or retrievals that contain no relevant documents (i.e., the precision ratio is zero) can be used to evaluate the retrieval performance while stemming is used or not used.

The number of relevant documents retrieved for each query is given in Table 1. The first number in the row labelled "Average" shows the average number of relevant documents retrieved and the second one (in parentheses) shows the total number of documents retrieved.

As Table 1 shows, average number of relevant documents retrieved for 15 queries over stemmed and unstemmed indexes are 23.3 and 28.4, respectively. While the total number of relevant documents retrieved over the stemmed index is 426, and 350 over the unstemmed index. Through stemming the total number of relevant documents are increased approximately by 22%.

Except in 3 of 15 queries (i.e., query 4, 10 and 14), the usage of stemming has increased the retrieval effectiveness of the system in all queries. This indicates the success of the FindStem stemming algorithm.

Table 1. Number of relevant documents retrieved

Query	Number of relevant documents	
	Stemmed index	Unstemmed index
1	66	55
2	41	32
3	68	51
4	43	43
5	28	17
6	17	12
7	46	38
8	18	16
9	8	7
10	40	40
11	9	8
12	17	11
13	13	10
14	6	6
15	6	4
Average	28.4(426)	23.3(350)

5.3   Precision Values for Various Recall Parameters

The average precision of 15 queries for various recall parameters over stemmed and unstemmed indexes are given in Table 2 [14]. The overall average of the averages are also given in Table 2.

Table 2. Average precision values when stemming is used and not used

Recall	Average Precision of 15 queries	
	w/ Stemming	w/out Stemming
1	0.415	0.283
0.9	0.508	0.316
0.8	0.534	0.415
0.7	0.586	0.490
0.6	0.625	0.547
0.5	0.681	0.589
0.4	0.781	0.644
0.3	0.818	0.664
Average	0.619	0.494

---

[14] The precision values of every query for every recall parameter (1, 0.9,..., 0.3) are accessible online, http://cmpe.emu.edu.tr/bitirim/stemming.

Table 2 shows that the precision increases while the recall decreases and when word stemming is used, better precision values are obtained. Thus the affect of stemming on the retrieval performance becomes apparent as shown in Figure 6.

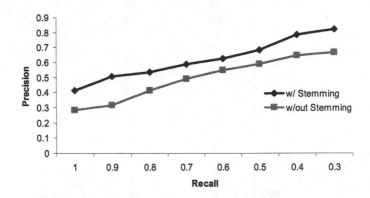

Fig. 6. Precision values for various recall parameters

The usage of stemming has increased the retrieval effectiveness of the system by approximately 25% in terms of precision.

6   Conclusions

In this article, the necessity of a morphological analysis in the Turkish stemming algorithms is described. The main idea of the algorithms, which do not use the morphological analysis, is to select the root [15] from a lexicon as the stem which increases the number of errors in word stemming. Another point is that it is possible to find more than one stem for some words, but it is not possible to decide the real stem without examining a context in which the word appears and if one of these is selected as the stem, there will be a possibility to select the wrong one and cause incorrect stemming. However, assigning all the roots that their morphological analysis result is positive as a stem, sometimes causes to find the origin beside the stem. The elimination on words, which is assigned as the stem, is a necessity to find the real stem.

A   Turkish Word Formation

In Turkish, root words and words derivated from roots are based on obvious rules such as major and minor laws of vowel harmony. These rules determine changes that are made both to root words and affixes in the formation of words.

---

[15] The root will be the longest set of characters that has compatibility with the word.

A.1   Turkish Alphabet

In the Turkish word formation, mainly the vowels and unvoiced consonants are subject to change. The vowels and voiced/unvoiced consonants, and characteristics of vowels are shown in Table 3 and Table 4.

Table 3. Vowels and their characteristics

	Unrounded		Rounded	
	Low	High	Low	High
Back	A	I	O	U
Front	E	İ	Ö	Ü

Table 4. Voiced and unvoiced consonants

Unvoiced Consonants	f,p,ş,ç,h,s,t,k
Voiced Consonants	b,c,d,g

A.2   The Possible Changes on Roots and Suffixes in Word Formation

The two important changes observed in word formation are assimilation and dropping. In addition, the character changes such as unvoiced consonants becoming voiced are observed in Turkish.

Assimilation   During the word formation process in Turkish, if the last character of a root is a vowel and if the first character of a suffix is a vowel also, then consonants such as "n", "s", "y", "ş" are used as assimilator. Some examples are:

$$
\begin{array}{lll}
\text{bahçe (garden)} & \longrightarrow + \imath & \longrightarrow \text{bahçesi (his/her/its garden)} \\
\text{komşu (neighbor)} & \longrightarrow + \text{in} & \longrightarrow \text{komşunun (neighbor's)} \\
\text{pencere (window)} & \longrightarrow + \imath & \longrightarrow \text{pencereyi (the window)} \\
\text{iki (two)} & \longrightarrow + \text{er} & \longrightarrow \text{ikişer (two each)}
\end{array}
$$

Dropping   During Turkish word formation, the loss of a letter is possible in both root word or suffix. This loss can be a vowel or a consonant.

The drop of middle vowel: The vowel of the second syllable is lost when a suffix beginning with a vowel is added. For example:

> oğul (son) $\longrightarrow$ + u $\longrightarrow$ oğlu (his/her/its son)
> burun (nose) $\longrightarrow$ + u $\longrightarrow$ burnu (his/her/its nose)
> karın (stomach) $\longrightarrow$ + im $\longrightarrow$ karnım (my stomach)

The drop of vowel at the end of a root: When some words such as *koku* (smell), *sızı* (pain), *yumurta* (egg) combine with the suffix "-le" to be derived verb, the last vowel of these words are drop. For example:

> koku (smell) $\longrightarrow$ + le $\longrightarrow$ kokla (smell it)

The drop of consonant at the end of a root There are some situations that the last consonant drop when root and suffix combine. For example:

> küçük (small) $\longrightarrow$ + cik $\longrightarrow$ küçücük (very small)
> yüksek (high) $\longrightarrow$ + (e)l $\longrightarrow$ yükselmek (to rise)

Character Change When a vowel is added to some nouns of one syllable and most nouns of more than one syllable, ending in "p", "ç", "t", "k", the final consonant changes to "b", "c", "d", or "ğ" respectively. So with the addition of suffix for the third person, "-i" as shown below:

> kitap (book) $\longrightarrow$ + ı $\longrightarrow$ kitabı (his/her/its book)
> ağaç (tree) $\longrightarrow$ + ı $\longrightarrow$ ağacı (his/her/its tree)
> armut (pear) $\longrightarrow$ + ı $\longrightarrow$ armudu (his/her/its pear)
> ayak (foot) $\longrightarrow$ + ı $\longrightarrow$ ayağı (his/her/its foot)

But there are nouns, whose final consonants are not subject to this change, when the letter "n" comes before the letter "k" at the end of a word, the letter "k" becomes "g" instead of "ğ". For example:

> renk (color) $\longrightarrow$ + ı $\longrightarrow$ rengi (his/her/its color)

In foreign origin words, if the last letter of a word is "g" and combines with the suffix where first letter is vowel, the letter "g" changes to the letter "ğ" as in the example:

> monolog (monologue) $\longrightarrow$ + ı $\longrightarrow$ monoloğu (his/her/its monologue)

The change of "g" and "ğ" is not observed for one syllable words or words which the second letter from the last one is "n". For example:

> şezlong (chaise longue) $\longrightarrow$ + ı $\longrightarrow$ şezlongu (his/her/its chaise longue)

References

[1] Irene Diaz, Jorge Morato, and Juan Lloréns. An algorithm for term conflation based on tree structures. *Journal of The American Society for Information Science and Technology*, 53(3):199–208, 2002.

[2] R. Krovetz. Viewing morphology as an inference process. *Proceeding 16th International Conference Research and Development in Information Retrieval, ACM*, pages 191–202, New York, 1993.

[3] Donna Horman. How effective is suffixing? *JASIS*, 42(1):7–15, 1991.

[4] Mirko Popovic and Peter Willett. The effectiveness of stemming for natural language access to Slovene textual data. *Journal of the American Society for Information Science*, 43:384–390, 1992.

[5] A. B. Ercilasun et al. *İmla Klavuzu*, volume 525. Atatürk Kültür ve Tarih Yüksek Kurumu, Türk Dili Kurumu Yayınları, Ankara, Turkey, 1996.

[6] T. Banguoğlu. *Türkçenin Grameri*. Atatürk Kültür ve Tarih Yüksek Kurumu, Türk Dili Kurumu Yayınları:528, Ankara, Turkey, 1995.

[7] Ari Pirkola. Morphological typology of languages for IR. *Journal of Documentation*, 57(3):330–348, May 2001.

[8] A. Kut, A. Alpkoçak, and E. Özkarahan. Bilgi bulma sistemleri için otomatik türkçe dizinleme yöntemi. In *Bilişim Bildirileri*, Dokuz Eylül University, İzmir, Turkey, 1995.

[9] A. Köksal. Tümüyle özdevimli deneysel bir belge dizinleme ve erişim dizgesi. *TURDER, TBD 3. Ulusal Bilişim Kurultayı*, pages 37–44, 6-8 April 1981. Ankara,Turkey.

[10] A. Solak and F. Can. Effects of stemming on Turkish text retrieval. Technical report BU-CEIS-94-20, Bilkent University, Ankara, Turkey, 1994.

[11] Gökmen Duran and Hayri Sever. Türkçe gövdeleme algoritmalarının analizi. In *Ulusal Bilişim Kurultayı Bildiri Kitabı*, pages 235–242, İstanbul,Turkey, September 1996.

[12] F. Çuna Ekmekçioğlu and Peter Willet. Effectiveness of stemming for Turkish text retrieval. *Program*, 34(2):195–200, April 2000.

[13] A. Köksal. *Automatic Morphological Analysis of Turkish*. PhD thesis, Hacettepe University, 1975.

[14] G. L. Lewis. *Teach Yourself Turkish*. Sevenoaks, second edition, 1989.

[15] Kemal Oflazer. Two-level description of turkish morphology. *Literary and Linguistic Computing*, 1994.

[16] E. L. Antworth. Glossing text with the pc-kimmo morphological parser. *Computers and the Humanities*, 1993.

[17] K. Oflazer and C. Guzey. Spelling correction in agglitunative languages. In *Proceedings of 4th ACL Conference on Applied Natural Language Processing*, pages 194–195, Stuttgart, Germany, October 1994.

[18] D. Hull. Stemming algorithms:A case study for detailed evaluation. *Journal of The American Society for Information Science*, 47(1):70–84, 1996.

[19] Richard Sproat. *Morphology and Computation*. Cambridge MA: MIT Press, 1992.

[20] Chris D. Paice. An evaluation method for stemming algorithms. *Proceedings of the Seventeenth Annual International ACM-SIGIR Conference on Research and Development in Information Retrieval*, pages 42–50, 3-6 July 1994.

Non-adjacent Digrams Improve Matching of Cross-Lingual Spelling Variants

Heikki Keskustalo, Ari Pirkola, Kari Visala, Erkka Leppänen, and
Kalervo Järvelin

Department of Information Studies, University of Tampere, Finland

Abstract. Untranslatable query keys pose a problem in dictionary-based cross-language information retrieval (CLIR). One solution consists of using approximate string matching methods for finding the spelling variants of the source key among the target database index. In such a setting, it is important to select a matching method suited especially for CLIR. This paper focuses on comparing the effectiveness of several matching methods in a cross-lingual setting. Search words from five domains were expressed in six languages (French, Spanish, Italian, German, Swedish, and Finnish). The target data consisted of the index of an English full-text database. In this setting, we first established the best method among six baseline matching methods for each language pair. Secondly, we tested novel matching methods based on binary digrams formed of both adjacent and non-adjacent characters of words. The latter methods consistently outperformed all baseline methods.

1   Introduction

In dictionary-based cross-language information retrieval (CLIR) a source query is typically translated word-by-word into the target language by using machine-readable dictionaries. However, due to the terminology missing from the dictionaries, untranslatable keys often appear in the queries thus posing a source for translation errors [3]. A trivial solution for handling the untranslatable keys is to use them as such in the target query. This solution succeeds sometimes, e.g., in case of some acronyms and proper names, while failing in many cases. A more advanced solution is to use approximate string matching to find the most similar word or words for the source keys from the target index, which can be placed into the target query [6].

The goal in approximate string matching is to rank or identify similar strings with respect to the given key. What is meant by similarity depends on the characteristics of the particular application. For example, human keyboard operators introduce reversal, insertion, deletion and substitution errors, while optical character recognition machines typically introduce substitution and reject errors [11]. Thus, it makes sense to consider different string pairs being similar in different usage contexts. Specifically, in case of untranslatable words in CLIR, the goal is to identify cross-lingual spelling variants. For example, by using the Spanish key *escleroterapia* we may wish to find its English variant *sclerotherapy* from

M.A. Nascimento, E.S. de Moura, A.L. Oliveira (Eds.): SPIRE 2003, LNCS 2857, pp. 252–265, 2003.

the database. It is not clear whether the similarity measures developed for other aims than CLIR are optimal for finding spelling variants. The similarity measure should take into account the special characteristics of the cross-lingual spelling variant strings.

Previous research has shown many successful applications of approximate string matching in information retrieval, see, e.g., [9] for a review of the usage of n-grams in textual information systems. Approximate matching improved proper name searching as compared to identical matching, and digrams performed best among the tested single methods among the top results in [5]. In [1] a trigram similarity measure was used for successfully identifying dictionary spellings of misspelled word forms. The study by [2] describes a multilingual retrieval system based on a vector space model in which the documents were represented by using 5-grams or 6-grams. In [12] several similarity methods for phonetic matching were tested and the best method was found to be a variant of edit distance utilizing letter groupings. Recently, [8] proposed a novel method utilizing automatically derived character transformation rules together with conventional n-grams for improving cross-lingual spelling variant matching. Also, combining evidence resulting from distinct matching methods seems to further improve the matching results [5] [12].

In this paper, we will utilize a cross-lingual research setting containing test words from five domains. Each word is expressed in seven languages (six source languages, and English as the target language). By using the words in the source languages as search keys we will compare the effectiveness of several approximate string matching methods. The main research question is to measure the effectiveness of several novel matching methods. These methods utilize non-adjacent binary digrams and we compare their effectiveness to the baseline results. The baseline matching methods include conventional n-grams of several lengths, longest common subsequence, edit distance, and exact match. The rest of the paper is organized as follows. Section 2 introduces the methodology, Section 3 presents the findings, and Section 4 contains the discussion and conclusions.

2 Preliminaries

2.1 Skip-Grams

The concept of *skip-grams* (binary digrams formed from non-adjacent letters) as a solution specifically for cross-lingual spelling variation problems was introduced in [7]. This paper contributes to the issue by testing the effectiveness of several novel skip-gram types and reporting the effectiveness of several baselines, using six source languages with respect to one target language, and by using query keys from several domains. Next, we will present a notation generalized from [7], defining how the skip-gram similarity between two strings is computed.

Let the *gram class (GC)*, expressed by a set of non-negative integers, indicate the number of skipped characters when digrams are formed from the string $S = s_1 s_2 s_3 ... s_n$. In other words, the gram class defines how one digram set *(DS)* is formed from the string S. For example, if $GC = \{0,1\}$ then for string $S = s_1 s_2 s_3 s_4$ we form the DS by skipping both zero and one characters in S when the digrams are formed, thus $DS_{\{0,1\}}(S) = \{s_1 s_2, s_1 s_3, s_2 s_3, s_2 s_4, s_3 s_4\}$. We call the largest value in GC the spanning length, e.g., for $GC = \{0,1\}$ the spanning length is one. Let the *character combination index (CCI)* be a set of gram classes enumerating all the digram sets to be produced from S. For example, if $CCI = \{\{0\}, \{1,2\}\}$ then for the string $S = s_1 s_2 s_3 s_4$ we form two digram sets, namely $DS_{\{0\}}(S) = \{s_1 s_2, s_2 s_3, s_3 s_4\}$ (by zero skipping) and $DS_{\{1,2\}}(S) = \{s_1 s_3, s_1 s_4, s_2 s_4\}$ (by skipping both one and two characters). Finally, the similarity measure *(SIM)* is defined between two strings S and T with respect to the given CCI in the following way:

$$SIM_{CCI}(S,T) = \frac{\sum_{i \in CCI} |DS_i(S) \cap DS_i(T)|}{\sum_{i \in CCI} |DS_i(S) \cup DS_i(T)|} . \tag{1}$$

For example, if $S = abcd$, $T = apcd$, and $CCI = \{\{0\},\{1,2\}\}$, we apply the set operations pairwise to digram sets $DS_{\{0\}}(S) = \{ab, bc, cd\}$ and $DS_{\{0\}}(T) = \{ap, pc, cd\}$, and then to $DS_{\{1,2\}}(S) = \{ac, ad, bd\}$ and $DS_{\{1,2\}}(T) = \{ac, ad, pd\}$, thus $SIM_{\{\{0\},\{1,2\}\}}(abcd, apcd) = (1+2)/(5+4) \approx 0.33$. The basis for the formula above is the similarity measure for two sets given in [5]. Other similarity measures could also be used analogously for a pair of sets, e.g., Dice or Overlap coefficients [9].

2.2 Cross-Lingual Spelling Variation

Cross-lingual spelling variation refers to word variation where a language pair shares words written differently but having the same origin, for example, technical terms derived from Latin or Greek, or proper names. At the string level, this variation often involves single character insertions, deletions and substitutions, or combinations of them [7]. For instance, transforming an Italian variant *ematome* into the English variant *hematoma* involves a single character insertion (h) and substitution ($e \Rightarrow a$), while transforming the corresponding Finnish variant *hematooma* involves a single character deletion (o). On the other hand, transforming Swedish variant *heksaklorid* into English *hexachloride* involves combinations of deletion and substitution ($ks \Rightarrow x$), and substitution and insertion ($k \Rightarrow ch$), and a single insertion (e). Also more complex combinations of operations occur, like between Italian and English term variants *ginecofobia* and *gynephobia*.

In [7] the effectiveness of two combinations of skip-gram classes ($CCI = \{\{0,1\}\}$ and $CCI = \{\{0\},\{1,2\}\}$) was tested in a cross-lingual setting using English, Swedish and German search keys and Finnish as the target language. In most cases the skip-grams outperformed conventional digrams. However, the performance levels of several gram class combinations were not tested. Therefore, we will next hypothesize some novel CCI values for the experimental testing by considering the properties of cross-lingual spelling variation presented above, and by associating these properties to the skip-gram classes.

2.3 Gram Classes and Spelling Variation

Cross-lingual spelling variation typically involves single character insertions, deletions and substitutions, or their two-character combinations. Therefore, in this research we restrict our attention to gram classes having spanning length two or less. The gram classes can be interpreted in the following way considering the kind of evidence they carry forward from their host string. Gram class {0} is a special case of skip-grams expressing conventional digrams formed from adjacent letters of the host string.

Gram class {1} allows one substitution, for example, substrings *gin* and *gyn* share class {1} digram *gn* although they do not share any common digrams or trigrams. This gram class is possibly meaningful from the CLIR point of view, as single character substitutions occur frequently between cross-lingual spelling variants. The gram class {0,1} allows one insertion between adjacent letters or a deletion of one letter separating two characters. For example, substrings *ic* and *isc* share class {0,1} digram *ic*.

The class {1,2} allows one insertion between letters separated by one character, or a deletion of one of the two characters separating two characters. For example, substrings *eksa* and *exa* share class {1,2} digram *ea*. Thus classes {0}, {1}, {0,1}, and {1,2} can be considered as having potential importance in CLIR. For research economical reasons, we left outside of testing some gram classes that we concluded to be less meaningful from CLIR point of view. These include the gram class {2} allowing substitution of exactly two characters, class {0,2} allowing substitution, insertion or deletion of exactly two characters, and class {0,1,2} allowing several types of combinations of substitutions, insertions and deletions.

Also negative effects may be introduced by the utilization of the novel gram classes. Hence we proceed next on running tests in order to evaluate their effectiveness in practice.

2.4 Test Data

The test data consists of three parts: the search keys, the target words, and the set of correct answers (relevance judgments).

Altogether more than 1600 search keys were used in the experiment. The search key lists were formed as follows. The first word set of 217 English words was selected from the database index and translated into the six search languages intellectually by one of the researchers. Several translation resources were used for performing this task. Thus 217 word tuples in seven languages were formed. These words were scientific terms, mostly medical or biological, called *bio* terms in the tables, or geographical place names (*geo*). As an example, the tuple *(hybridoma, hybridooma, hybridom, hybridzelle, hybridome, ibridoma, hibridoma)* contains word variants ordered by languages English, Finnish, Swedish, German, French, Italian, Spanish. We used a 26 letter alphabet augmented by letters å, ä, ö, and ü. All the translations of the first word set were checked by native speakers or advanced students majoring in each particular language. Very few corrections took place. Also, every third tuple from this set was selected as the training data to be used exclusively in the analyses performed prior to final test runs. Therefore, 72 training word tuples and 145 final test word tuples were obtained from the first word set. The second search word set was gathered by first collecting 126 supplementary English words. These were from the domains of economics (abbreviated as *econ* in the tables), technology (*tech*), and miscellaneous (*misc*) containing common foreign words. The words were translated into the six search languages by one of the researchers. Thus, altogether 271 final test word tuples were formed, each containing the English word variant and its corresponding search key variants in six languages.

The target words consisted of a list containing all words of an English full-text database index (Los Angeles Times used in CLEF 2000 experiments) [6]. It contains around 189,000 unique word forms. They are either in basic forms as recognized by the morphological analyser ENGTWOL used in indexing, or in case of unrecognised word forms, the original words as such. All words are written in monocase.

The set of relevance judgments consisted of the English word variants in the tuples. For each search key there was precisely one correct English counterpart, but in some cases there were more than one search key variants with respect to one English word. All English variants of the first search word set occurred in the original Los Angeles Times index. For the second search word set, three English keys were not found from the index list originally and they were added to the list prior to final runs.

2.5   Matching Methods

The effectiveness of each matching method was measured by calculating the average precision at 100 % recall point. Sometimes several target words gained the same similarity value with respect to the key. Therefore, we evaluated the precision by using two methods. In the worst case method we assumed the correct word to be the last word among the group of words (cohort) having the same SIM value. In the average case method we assumed the correct word to be in the middle of the cohort. In practise, these two methods gave almost the same values. This is because typically the cohorts were small. Therefore, in Tables 1-13 we report only average case results.

The following *baseline methods* were tested:

- Exact match
- Edit distance
- Longest common subsequence
- Digrams (conventional digrams, i.e., skip-grams with CCI =$\{\{0\}\}$)
- Trigrams
- Tetragrams

The exact match and edit distance were used as similarity measures as such. The longest common subsequence (*lcs*) as such would have favoured long index words, therefore, we substracted the value of lcs from the mean length of the two words compared to make the similarity measure more meaningful. The digrams, trigrams and tetragrams were utilized by applying the formula (1) to the sets of n-grams derived from the strings.

Secondly, the following *skip-gram methods* were tested:

- CCI = {{0},{1}}
- CCI = {{0},{0,1}}
- CCI = {{0},{1,2}}
- CCI = {{0},{1},{0,1}}
- CCI = {{0},{1},{1,2}}
- CCI = {{0},{0,1},{1,2}}
- CCI = {{0},{1},{0,1},{1,2}}

Formula (1) was applied for computing the skip-gram similarity. We compare the skip-gram results with several baseline results for each language pair.

Word beginnings and endings deserve special attention in approximate string matching [1]. Therefore, we used training data with conventional digrams, trigrams, and skip-grams with CCI = {{0},{1,2}} (as found to be successful in CLIR in [7]) and tested three matching variations: (i) word starts are padded with an appropriate number of special characters, (ii) both word starts and endings are padded, and (iii) no padding is performed: only the characters of the string itself are considered. The choice (ii) turned out to give the best results in most cases, although in some cases the choice (i) gave slightly better results. The choice (iii) gave consistently the worst results. On the basis of these results we decided to utilize both word start and end padding in all of the final runs.

3 Findings

Next, we will discuss the results of each language pair individually. In Sections 3.1 - 3.6 we first establish the best one of the six baseline methods for each language pair. Secondly, we present the results of the three best skip-gram methods and compare them to the best baseline method based on the average precision over all domains. This is a very conservative approach. Therefore, we also compare the effectiveness of the best skip-gram method with respect to *trigrams* in Sections 3.1 - 3.6, as a well-known method. The effectiveness of the methods is discussed also at the individual terminological domains.

3.1 Finnish-English

The best baseline method in Finnish-to-English matching was edit distance with average precision 45.9 % (Table 1). Edit distance was the best method also in each single domain, except in case of of *miscellanous words*, where the digrams slightly outperformed it. Digram based matching was in the second place, followed by our variation of the longest common subsequence. Trigrams and tetragrams performed poorly. Variation between the domain results is considerable (32.5 % to 67.7 % for edit distance). Finnish and English word variants were

Table 1. Finnish-English baseline results (Precision %).

Domain	Edit distance	Digrams	LCS	Trigrams	Tetragrams	Exact match
Bio (N=92)	67.7	61.4	54.0	49.2	45.6	0.0
Geo (N=55)	35.4	30.0	27.3	29.3	29.6	9.1
Econ (N=31)	36.5	32.2	27.5	30.7	24.8	0.0
Tech (N=36)	36.2	31.6	30.2	21.2	16.7	0.0
Misc (N=59)	32.5	33.8	31.5	28.9	26.3	0.0
Avg. (N=273)	45.9	41.9	37.6	35.0	32.0	1.8

Table 2. Finnish-English, the best baseline results (Best BL) and the results of the three best skip-gram methods (Precision %). Improvements are marked with respect to the best baseline, and with respect to the trigrams (in parantheses).

Domain	Best BL	{{0},{0,1},{1,2}}	{{0},{1,2}}	{{0},{1},{0,1},{1,2}}
Bio (N=92)	67.7	69.0 +1.9% (+40.2%)	68.6	67.3
Geo (N=55)	35.4	36.1 +2.0% (+23.2%)	36.7	36.1
Econ (N=31)	36.5	43.5 +19.2% (+41.7%)	40.0	43.7
Tech (N=36)	36.2	49.6 +37.0% (+134.0%)	49.7	48.5
Misc (N=59)	32.5	36.5 +12.3% (+26.3%)	37.5	36.5
Avg. (N=273)	45.9	49.9 +8.7% (+42.6%)	49.7+8.2%	49.2 +7.2%

rarely identical, except some *place names*, as reflected by the low precision figure (1.8 %) for exact matching. Edit distance is selected as the comparison basis for Table 2 as the best baseline method. As we can see in Table 2, the skip-gram methods outperformed the baseline methods. The best skip-gram method, using CCI = {{0},{0,1},{1,2}}, outperformed edit distance on the average by +8.7 %. In the domain of *technology* the improvement was most notable, +37.0 %, in *economics* +19.2 %, and with *miscellaneous words* +12.3 %. In case of *biological* and *geographical* terms, the improvement was inconsequential. The improvements gained by the best skip-gram method are even higher if compared to digrams (average improvement of +19.1 %), trigrams (+42.6 %) or tetragrams (+55.9 %). Thus, conventional n-grams, especially with large values of n, perform poorly with Finnish as the source language, although n-grams work well elsewhere (see French-English results). The skip-grams generally improve spelling variant matching in case of Finnish-to-English matching. The formula (1) itself allows more finegrained similarity values than edit distance or longest common subsequence. One should notice that the skip-gram methods outperformed edit distance although the conventional digrams did not. Because of this, we conclude that the evidence that the skip-grams carry forward from the host string is better suited for matching spelling variants than the evidence gained by ordinary digrams, trigrams or tetragrams (see Sections 2.2 and 2.3).

3.2   French-English

Both the general level of performance and the order of the best baseline methods are different for the French results (Table 3) as compared to the Finnish results (Table 1). The level of the average precision is much higher (73.4 %)

Table 3. French-English baseline results (Precision %).

Domain	Digrams	Trigrams	Tetragrams	Edit distance	LCS	Exact match
Bio (N=92)	88.3	87.7	87.2	89.2	87.4	41.3
Geo (N=59)	52.5	53.3	52.8	52.4	49.3	27.1
Econ (N=31)	80.1	78.1	76.3	72.3	69.7	41.9
Tech (N=36)	78.4	78.8	78.7	76.4	73.9	66.7
Misc (N=59)	64.6	64.7	64.6	62.8	60.7	37.3
Avg. (N=277)	73.4	73.2	72.7	72.2	69.9	40.8

Table 4. French-English, the best baseline results (Best BL) and the results of the three best skip-gram methods (Precision %). Improvements are marked with respect to the best baseline, and with respect to the trigrams (in parantheses).

Domain	Best BL	{{0},{0,1},{1,2}}	{{0},{1},{0,1},{1,2}}	{{0},{1},{1,2}}
Bio (N=92)	88.3	90.0 +1.9% (+2.6%)	90.0	90.0
Geo (N=59)	52.5	54.5 +3.8% (+2.3%)	54.7	55.0
Econ (N=31)	80.1	83.5 +4.2% (+6.9%)	81.9	81.6
Tech (N=36)	78.4	77.0 -1.8% (-2.3%)	77.0	78.3
Misc (N=59)	64.6	68.9 +6.7% (+6.5%)	69.2	67.3
Avg. (N=277)	73.4	75.5 +2.9% (+3.1%)	75.5 +2.9%	75.2 +2.5%

for French key matching than in case of Finnish keys (45.9 %). Also, in each domain, the results of the different methods are close to each other, except for the exact matching. The single best baseline method for French was conventional digram matching method (average precision 73.4 %), closely followed by trigrams, tetragrams, edit distance and longest common subsequence. On the basis of these results, conventional n-grams are rather well suited for French-to-English spelling variant matching. The English variant in many cases had a rather long common start with the French variant (e.g. *catalytic/catalytique; glycogen/glycogene*), whilst in case of the Finnish variant, character substitutions and insertions were typical also in the beginning and in the middle of the word (*katalyyttinen; glykogeeni*). One can notice from the exact match results that the proportion of identical spelling variants between French and English is relatively high. As the best baseline, digrams are selected as the comparison basis for the skip-gram runs below (Table 4). Also in French-to-English matching the skip-gram methods outperformed the best baseline method (Table 4), but the improvement was inconsequential (+2.9 % in the best case). The best results were again attained by using CCI={{0},{0,1},{1,2}}.

3.3 German-English

The results for the German-English baseline runs are given in Table 5. The best baseline method was again edit distance (average precision 60.8 %), closely followed by digrams (60.0 %). Also for each single domain the best results were gained by either edit distance or digrams. Compared to Finnish-English runs, trigrams and tetragrams performed rather well. The skip-gram methods out-

Table 5. German-English baseline results (Precision %).

Domain	Edit distance	Digrams	Trigrams	Tetragrams	LCS	Exact match
Bio (N=97)	76.6	77.8	75.5	71.1	73.8	15.5
Geo (N=62)	45.5	41.4	42.7	42.1	36.0	14.5
Econ (N=31)	51.1	52.6	52.3	50.6	44.9	9.7
Tech (N=36)	65.6	60.5	58.3	55.3	60.3	27.8
Misc (N=59)	53.3	54.0	52.3	51.4	50.6	22.0
Avg. (N=285)	60.8	60.0	58.9	56.5	55.9	17.6

Table 6. German-English, the best baseline results (Best BL) and the results of the three best skip-gram methods (Precision %). Improvements are marked with respect to the best baseline, and with respect to the trigrams (in parantheses).

Domain	Best BL	{{0},{1,2}}	{{0},{1},{1,2}}	{{0},{0,1},{1,2}}
Bio (N=97)	76.6	83.6 +9.1% (+10.7%)	83.6	83.9
Geo (N=62)	45.5	46.4 +2.0% (+9.1%)	46.5	47.1
Econ (N=31)	51.1	59.0 +15.5% (+12.8%)	58.9	58.9
Tech (N=36)	65.6	69.0 +5.2% (+18.4%)	69.1	67.2
Misc (N=59)	53.3	57.9 +8.6% (+10.7%)	57.1	57.1
Avg. (N=285)	60.8	65.7 +8.1% (+11.5%)	65.5 +7.7%	65.5 +7.7%

performed the baselines (Table 6). In the best case (CCI = {{0},{1,2}}) the improvement was +8.1 %. The largest domain improvements took place with *economics* and *biology* (+15.5 % and +9.1 %, respectively). The best skip-gram method for Finnish and French (CCI={{0},{0,1},{1,2}}) performed well also with the German keys (average improvement +7.7 %).

3.4 Italian-English

The results for the Italian-English baseline runs are given in Table 7. Edit distance was the best baseline method for Italian keys (average precision 53.2 %)

followed by digrams (49.9 %). The results indicate that nature of the domain terminology may have a strong impact on the selection of the appropriate matching method. For example, with *geographical terms* all matching methods perform quite alike, even the tetragrams, while on the other hand tetragrams perform very poorly, e.g., with the domain of *economics*. Edit distance is competitive in each domain. All skip-gram methods again outperformed all baseline methods

Table 7. Italian-English baseline results (Precision %).

Domain	Edit distance	Digrams	LCS	Trigrams	Tetragrams	Exact match
Bio (N=98)	67.2	62.1	57.7	56.0	50.9	6.1
Geo (N=65)	53.5	53.7	49.3	54.9	55.0	27.7
Econ (N=31)	39.4	41.3	35.4	32.7	26.7	0.0
Tech (N=36)	50.5	39.8	46.1	39.5	36.5	19.4
Misc (N=59)	38.3	35.9	39.5	35.8	33.3	10.2
Avg. (N=289)	53.2	49.9	48.3	47.1	43.8	12.8

Table 8. Italian-English, the best baseline results (Best BL) and the results of the three best skip-gram methods (Precision %). Improvements are marked with respect to the best baseline, and with respect to the trigrams (in parantheses).

Domain	Best BL	{{0},{1,2}}	{{0},{1},{1,2}}	{{0},{1},{0,1},{1,2}}
Bio (N=98)	67.2	70.2 +4.5% (+25.4%)	69.8	69.3
Geo (N=65)	53.5	60.6 +13.3% (+10.4%)	60.2	59.1
Econ (N=31)	39.4	45.1 +14.5% (+37.9%)	45.0	47.6
Tech (N=36)	50.5	48.5 -4.0% (+22.8%)	49.1	49.1
Misc (N=59)	38.3	43.5 +13.6% (+21.5%)	44.1	43.1
Avg. (N=289)	53.2	57.2 +7.5% (+21.4%)	57.2 +7.5%	56.8 +6.8%

(Table 8). The largest improvement (+7.5 %) with respect to the baseline results was gained by using CCI = {{0},{1,2}} or CCI = {{0},{1}, {1,2}}. This improvement figure for the Italian keys is of the same magnitude as the corresponding figure for Finnish (+8.7 %) and German (+8.1 %). Looking at the individual domains, for *technological* terms the performance dropped (-4.0 %) from the best baseline by using skip-grams, but it improved with all other domains, especially with the words in *economics* (+14.5 %), *miscellaneous* words (+13.6 %) and *geographical* words (+13.3 %).

3.5 Spanish-English

The results for the Spanish-English baseline runs are given in Table 9. With Spanish keys, edit distance was again the best baseline method (average precision

Table 9. Spanish-English baseline results (Precision %).

Domain	Edit distance	Digrams	Trigrams	Tetragrams	LCS	Exact match
Bio (N=94)	72.8	67.6	63.2	57.7	63.1	6.4
Geo (N=57)	54.4	55.5	54.9	55.0	51.7	31.6
Econ (N=31)	44.5	45.5	45.9	45.6	38.1	6.5
Tech (N=36)	59.5	57.5	57.9	55.9	51.3	22.2
Misc (N=59)	39.6	41.1	41.9	40.8	40.6	6.8
Avg. (N=277)	57.0	55.7	54.3	52.0	51.6	13.7

Table 10. Spanish-English, the best baseline results (Best BL) and the results of the three best skip-gram methods (Precision %). Improvements are marked with respect to the best baseline, and with respect to the trigrams (in parantheses).

Domain	Best BL	{{0},{1,2}}	{{0},{1},{1,2}}	{{0},{0,1},{1,2}}
Bio (N=94)	72.8	72.7 -0.1% (+15.0%)	72.6	72.5
Geo (N=57)	54.4	61.2 +12.5% (+11.5%)	61.8	59.4
Econ (N=31)	44.5	48.4 +8.8% (+5.4%)	48.1	48.3
Tech (N=36)	59.5	63.1 +6.1% (+9.0%)	62.1	62.0
Misc (N=59)	39.6	42.6 +7.6% (+1.7%)	42.6	42.6
Avg. (N=277)	57.0	60.0 +5.3% (+10.5%)	59.9 +5.1%	59.4 +4.2%

57.0 %), followed by digrams (55.7 %) and trigrams (54.3 %). Effectiveness of the matching methods is again sensitive to the terminological domain. For example, with *geographical* and *miscellaneous* terms, and with terms in *economics*, n-grams worked at least as well as edit distance, but for bio terms the performance level goes down as *n* increases. The best skip-gram method outperformed the best baseline by +5.3 % (Table 10). The highest average precision was gained by the method with CCI = {{0},{1,2}}. At individual domains, the performance improved especially in case of *geographical* words (+12.5 %). Other domains with notable improvement by using the Spanish keys were *economics* (+8.8 %) and *miscellaneous* words (+7.6 %). The performance improvements were remarkable also in case of Italian keys with these three domains. Moreover, the Spanish result improved also in case of *technological* words (+6.1 %), but not in the domain of *biology*.

3.6   Swedish-English

The results for the Swedish-English baseline runs are presented in Table 11. With Swedish as the source language, conventional digrams were the single best baseline method (average precision 57.5 %), closely followed by edit distance (56.0 %) and trigrams (55.3 %). Based on average precision, the skip-gram methods again outperformed the best baseline method (Table 12). The greatest improve-

Table 11. Swedish-English baseline results (Precision %).

Domain	Digrams	Edit distance	Trigrams	Tetragrams	LCS	Exact match
Bio (N=92)	73.8	68.7	69.9	66.8	62.9	10.9
Geo (N=56)	48.4	47.0	48.2	47.4	43.6	26.8
Econ (N=31)	41.7	40.2	37.5	36.9	31.4	12.9
Tech (N=36)	58.4	59.1	55.9	53.0	53.5	25.0
Misc (N=59)	48.1	51.1	48.3	47.9	44.8	27.1
Avg. (N=274)	57.5	56.0	55.3	53.6	50.3	19.7

Table 12. Swedish-English, the best baseline results (Best BL) and the results of the three best skip-gram methods (Precision %). Improvements are marked with respect to the best baseline, and with respect to the trigrams (in parantheses).

Domain	Best BL	{{0},{0,1},{1,2}}	{{0},{1},{1,2}}	{{0},{1,2}}
Bio (N=92)	73.8	79.9 +8.3% (+14.3%)	79.6	79.3
Geo (N=56)	48.4	49.2 +1.7% (+2.1%)	49.1	49.6
Econ (N=31)	41.7	46.6 +11.8% (+24.3%)	46.6	47.3
Tech (N=36)	58.4	63.6 +8.9% (+13.8%)	63.6	63.6
Misc (N=59)	48.1	53.9 +12.1% (+11.6%)	54.4	53.4
Avg. (N=274)	57.5	62.1 +8.0% (+12.3%)	62.1 +8.0%	62.0 +7.8%

ment (+8.0 %) was due to skip-grams with CCI = {{0}, {0,1},{1,2}}, but the four best skip-gram methods outperformed the best baseline by at least +7.5 %. Considering the individual domains, the biggest improvement took place with *miscellaneous* words (+12.1%) as well as with the words of *economics* (+11.8 %), *technology* (+8.9 %) and *biology* (+8.3 %).

4 Discussion and Conclusions

In this paper, we have explored cross-language spelling variant matching. We studied first the effectiveness of six baseline methods and then of seven skip-gram methods. The research setting contained more than 1600 source keys partitioned into six languages and five term domains, and about 189,000 target words in English. We found that among all tested matching methods, the skip-gram techniques were the most effective one for finding cross-lingual spelling variants in languages based on Latin alphabet.

Table 13 presents a summary of the results. Here we compare the results of skip-grams to conventional digrams. In our study, conventional digrams were always the best or the second best baseline, and they always outperformed trigrams. Even in absolute terms, the improvements gained by skip-grams were notable. As we can see in Table 13, in case of Finnish as the source language, the average precision improved from 41.9 % to 49.9 % by using CCI={{0},{0,1},{1,2}}.

Table 13. Average performance of the best skip-gram matching methods, as compared to conventional digrams (Precision %).

Source language	Digrams	{{0},{0,1},{1,2}}	{{0},{1,2}}	{{0},{1},{1,2}}
Finnish (N=273)	41.9	49.9 +19.1%	49.7 +18.6%	49.1 +17.2%
French (N=277)	73.4	75.5 +2.9%	74.7 +1.8%	75.2 +2.5%
German (N=285)	60.0	65.5 +9.2%	65.7 +9.5%	65.5 +9.2%
Italian (N=289)	49.9	56.5 +13.2%	57.2 +14.6%	57.2 +14.6%
Spanish (N=277)	55.7	59.4 +6.6%	60.0 +7.7%	59.9 +7.5%
Swedish (N=274)	57.5	62.1 +8.0%	62.0 +7.8%	62.1 +8.0%

Other large improvements took place by using CCI={{0},{1,2}} for German (60.0 % to 65.7 %) and Italian (49.9 % to 57.2 %).

Skip-grams seem to be well suited especially for some individual domains. For example, in *economics*, compared to the best baseline, an improvement of +19.2 % (Table 2), +15.5 % (Table 6), +14.5 % (Table 8), +8.8 % (Table 10), and +11.8 % (Table 12) was achieved with Finnish, German, Italian, Spanish, and Swedish, respectively, as the source languages.

In this paper, we used skip-grams to model cross-language spelling variation (Section 2.3). A comparative linguistic study on the difference in ortography between two languages may suggest *rules for spelling variation* which may be modeled by tuning the CCI value. In fact, in [8] we generate such rules automatically based on bilingual translation dictionaries. Thus, the skip-grams have a basis in linguistics (ortography).

Although a study on time and space aspects is beyond the scope of the present study, we mention that our recent implementation in C for the skip-grams (tuned presently for formula (1) using CCI = {{0,1}}) has an average response time of 0.08 seconds for finding the best match from among 189,000 words (CLEF 2000 *LA Times* collection; 1000 key word sample, average key length of 8.9 characters; Sun Ultra-10 workstation, 333 MHz, 512 MB RAM). This suggests reasonable response times also for the slightly more complex cases discussed above.

In the future, the skip-grams may be applied also in novel areas, e.g., in music retrieval based on pitch sequences [10]. One needs to infer the CCI values which could be useful in the novel domain of interest and run the tests in order to compare the different matching methods. As skip-grams are a simple technique, they are attractive in case they give good results. On the basis of this study, skip-grams do give better results in CLIR than the well-known conventional methods tested.

Our future plans include implementing the skip-gram matching as part of a real-time CLIR system and developing more advanced matching methods by utilizing, e.g., character transformation rule information [8].

Acknowledgements

This work was partly funded by *Clarity* - Proposal/Contract no.: IST-2000-25310. The target index was processed by using ENGTWOL (Morphological Transducer Lexicon Description of English): Copyright ©1989-1992 Atro Voutilainen and Juha Heikkilä. TWOL-R (Run-Time Two-Level Program): Copyright ©1983-1992 Kimmo Koskenniemi and Lingsoft Oy. We wish to thank the anonymous referees and the members of the FIRE research group for useful suggestions.

References

1. Angell, R. C., Freund, G. E., Willett, P. (1983) Automatic Spelling Correction Using a Trigram Similarity Measure, *Information Processing & Managament*, 4, 255-261.
2. Damashek, M.(1995) Gauging Similarity with n-Grams: Language-Independent Sorting, Categorization, and Retrieval of Text, *Science*, Vol. 267, Feb., 843-848.
3. Hull, D., Grefenstette, G. (1996) Querying Across Languages: A Dictionary-Based Approach to Multilingual Information Retrieval. *Proc. ACM SIGIR*, Zürich, Switzerland, 49-57.
4. Peters, C. (2002) Cross Language Evaluation Forum. [http://clef.iei.pi.cnr.it]
5. Pfeifer, U., Poersch, T., Fuhr, N. (1995) Searching Proper Names in Databases. *HIM*, 259-275.
6. Pirkola, A., Hedlund, T., Keskustalo, H., Järvelin, K. (2001) Dictionary-Based Cross-Language Information Retrieval: Problems, Methods, and Research Findings. *Information Retrieval*, 4 (3/4), 209-230.
7. Pirkola, A., Keskustalo, H., Leppänen, E., Känsälä, A-P., Järvelin, K. (2002) Targeted s-Gram Matching: a Novel n-Gram Matching Technique for Cross- and Monolingual Word Form Variants. *Information Research*, 7 (2) 2002. [Available at http://InformationR.net/ir/7-2/paper126.html]
8. Pirkola, A., Toivonen, J., Keskustalo, H., Visala, K., Järvelin, K. (2003) Fuzzy Translation of Cross-Lingual Spelling Variants. Accepted for *ACM SIGIR* 2003.
9. Robertson, A.M., Willet, P. (1998) Applications of N-Grams in Textual Information Systems. *Journal of Documentation*, 1, 48-69.
10. Salosaari, P., Järvelin, K. (1998) MUSIR - A Retrieval Model for Music. *Research Notes*, 1, Department of Information Studies, University of Tampere.
11. Ullman, J.R. (1977) A Binary n-Gram Technique for Automatic Correction of Substitution, Deletion, Insertion and Reversal Errors in Words. *Computer Journal*, 2, 141-147.
12. Zobel, J., Dart, P. (1996) Phonetic String Matching: Lessons from Information Retrieval. *Proc. ACM SIGIR*, Zürich, Switzerland, 166-173.

The Implementation and Evaluation of a Lexicon-Based Stemmer

Gilberto Silva[1] and Claudia Oliveira[2]

[1] Datasus – Centro de Tecnologia da Informação do Ministério da Saúde,
Rua México, 128, 7° andar, Rio de Janeiro, Brazil,
gilberto@datasus.gov.br
[2] Departamento de Engenharia de Computação, Instituto Militar de Engenharia,
Praça General Tibúrcio, 80, Rio de Janeiro, Brazil,
cmaria@de9.ime.eb.br

Abstract. This paper describes a stemming technique that depends principally on a target language's lexicon, organised as an automaton of word strings. The clear distinction between the lexicon and the procedure itself allows the stemmer to be customised for any language with little or even no changes to the program's source code. An implementation of the stemmer, with a medium sized Portuguese lexicon is evaluated using Paice's [16] evaluation method.

1 Introduction

One of the main functionalities of a Text Retrieval System (TRS) should be its ability to answer queries, possibly formulated by means of keywords, about the word content of documents in a collection of text documents. Exact word by word matching between the keywords and the text contents often excessively restricts the set of retrieved documents, which is the main reason for using a measure of similarity between words rather than strict equality.

In linguistics, *stem* is a form that unifies the elements in a set of morphologically similar words [4], therefore *stemming* is the operation which determines the stem of a given word. A TRS equipped with a *stemmer* extracts stems, not words, from the indexed text documents as well as the queries; results are based on stem comparisons.

The main objective of this work is to describe the implementation and evaluation of a stemming technique that depends principally on an external target language's lexicon, in contrast to procedures that embody a morphological theory of a specific language.

The validation of stemming as a beneficial text processing operation with respect to retrieval performance has been made in several studies, mostly for the English language, with conflicting conclusions. Harman [9] examined the effects of suffix stripping algorithms on test collections and found no improvements on the retrieval performance. In [12], Krovetz experiments with stemming investigated the relative effectiveness of inflexional and derivational morphology, in comparison to suffix-stripping [17] and no stemming at all, and an improvement in retrieval performance by up to 35% on some collections was reported.

M.A. Nascimento, E.S. de Moura, A.L. Oliveira (Eds.): SPIRE 2003, LNCS 2857, pp. 266-276, 2003.

Hull, in [10] provides a detailed report of the comparison between five different stemmers and no stemming. He examined not only the usual performance tables, but also some of the most influential factors on the impact of stemming over performance. Hull concludes that *"some form of stemming is almost always beneficial"* and that *"when the query is well defined and the user is only looking at a few documents, stemming provides absolutely no advantage... Stemming becomes much more valuable when queries and documents are short, as this is when it is most difficult to find term matches between query and document"*. His experiments were performed on English collections and it seems possible that highly inflected languages such as Portuguese may benefit more from stemming.

Having cast away any doubts as to whether the work presented here is relevant in the field of TRS, we are faced with the task of evaluating the algorithm. Where an IR tool is concerned, rather then a purely linguistic tool, the traditional approach is to select a standard collection of texts and measure the average improvement in precision and recall obtained by the use of the tool. As far as stemming is concerned, this approach can be very misleading. According to Fuller [7] *"...measuring average performance can mask significant changes in individual queries, and the metrics used for evaluating performance can allow the effects of stemming to seem small, if the document sets retrieved are changed significantly"*.

We chose [16] as the evaluation method, in which Paice proposes to take into account the correctness of the stemming results in order to assess the efficiency of the stemming algorithm. The stemming method is evaluated, not by its impact on query results, but by considering the adequacy and correctness of the groupings generated by the stemmer.

The paper is organised as follows: section 2 presents a brief review of the mainstream stemming methods; in section 3 we detail the proposed stemming procedure, describe the required organisation of the target language's lexicon as an automaton of word strings; in section 4 we present the evaluation method used to compare our stemmer with the Portuguese version of Porter's stemmer and describe an experiment with the set 32,000 words obtained from Porter's web page, Snowball [21], for which we have the same analysis; and in section 5 we draw some conclusions.

2 Stemming Methods

The simplest and most obvious of the stemming methods consists of storing and searching for word-stem pairs in a table. The essential feature of the *table look-up* method is the data structure, which must be extremely efficient, such as a B-tree, a hash table or an acyclic finite automaton. Its main drawback is the fact that the lexicons of natural languages are open sets. Even if all the actual words of the lexicon could be stored at a given moment, which seems to be a very unfeasible task, the table would soon be obsolete, given the dynamics of a real lexicon.

The most widely used of the stemming techniques are *affix stripping* procedures, following a model introduced by Lovins [13] known as *the iterative longest match stemmers*. The basic idea is that word endings, which are considered to be affixes in the target language, are iteratively substituted by other affixes according to predetermined rules, until the resulting word form does not contain a recognised affix. Following Lovins, other iterative longest match stemmers were proposed in [20], [5], [17] and [15]. The most widely used of these is Porter's stemmer which, possibly due to its simplicity and good performance, has become a standard in TRS systems worldwide, notwithstanding its original English specificity.

The stemming method proposed by Hafer and Weiss [8], the *successor variety* method, takes into account the number of possible letters that could follow a given prefix substring of a word, in the context of a given corpus. According to the method, a word string is analysed from left to right: the successor variety decreases as the size of the prefix increases, until it reaches the form of a word or word root, at which point the successor variety increases steeply. This prefix is considered to be the word stem. Four approaches are proposed for choosing the final stem from a set of possibilities: the cutoff method, the peak and plateau method, the complete word method and the entropy method. For further details the reader should refer to [8] or [6].

Adamson and Boreham [1] present a method called *the shared digram method*. A digram is a substring of size two in a string, which could be generalised as an n-gram, for an arbitrary size. Strictly speaking, this method does not constitute a stemming method, since the result is not a stem. Nevertheless, its purpose is the evaluation of the degree of similarity between words, therefore the method is presented here.

The main idea is that the measure of similarity between two words is calculated as a function of the numbers of distinct n-grams that they have in common. For example, considering the words *statistics* and *statistical* we observe that the former has 7 distinct digrams and the latter has 8. They share 6 digrams: *at*, *ic*, *is*, *st*, *ta*, *ti*. From this analysis, the similarity S_{ij} between two words is given by Dice's coefficient, defined as $S_{ij} = 2D_{ij} / (D_i + D_j)$, where D_i and D_j are the numbers of distinct digrams in each word and D_{ij} is the number of distinct digrams they share. In the example, the similarity between statistics and statistical is given by $(2 \times 6) \div (7 + 8) = 0.8$, or 80%.

3 The Proposed Lexicon-Based Stemming Procedure

The stemming method we propose in this work combines two of the approaches presented in section 2: affix stripping and table look-up. The affix stripping rules, as well as the exceptions to these rules, are uniformly stored in a table. This table is effectively the representation of a lexicon, stored in a minimised deterministic finite automaton, which garners two essential requirements of the stemming algorithm. Firstly, the used memory space is manageable and, even in hardware systems of modest capabilities, the lexicon can be kept in RAM, avoiding disk access. Secondly, access time is a linear function of the length of the stored string.

Our priority is the separation of the computational procedure, which is a generic language independent stemmer, from the specific lexicon representations.

3.1 The Structure of the Lexicon

Summarising the views of Aronoff and Anshem [2], morphology is the set of word formation processes, which determines the potential complex words of a given language. On the other hand, the lexicon is the inventory of existing words of a language. Therefore, morphology and the lexicon are interdependent and complementary with respect to their function of providing words with which the speaker may construct utterances.

The role of stemming is to reduce a group of words to a central form, the stem, which may carry a significant portion of the words' meanings. Even though the procedure can be seen as an implementation of some language's morphology, there are other requirements that have to be met for it to be part of a TRS. According to Porter [17], with regard to his affix stripping algorithm, "... *the affixes are being removed simply to improve IR performance, and not as a linguistic exercise*".

Although the stemming method we propose can be seen as a combination of affix stripping and table look-up, there are two important distinctions which must be made clear. First, affix stripping algorithms implement a relatively small list of very general rules, empirically created by the authors of the algorithms. In contrast, our rules are the result of semi-automatic manipulation of word lists, which normally results in an extensive set of rules.

Secondly, in affix stripping algorithms the rules are an integral part of the program. As an alternative, we chose to store the rules and the exceptions in a separate structure, where each element represents a lexical entry of the form **<left side>:<type>:<right side>,** such that:

< left side >	is a non-empty string of characters.
< type >	is one of the following characters: **l** indicating literal; **p** indicating prefix; **s** indicating suffix.
< right side >	is a string of characters, possibly empty, or one of the following: = indicating no change; or @ indicating stopword.

The **<left side>** field contains the pattern to match the input word. The matching method and the subsequent action is determined by **<type>**. The **<type>** field indicates the way in which the word should be compared with the **<left side>** pattern: if the **<type>** is **l** for literal, the match succeeds if the input word is identical to the **<left side>** pattern; if the **<type>** is **p** for prefix or **s** for suffix, the comparison is made character by character until the end of the pattern is reached. The **<right side>** complements the action indicated by **<type>**, usually indicating a substituting pattern for the **<left side>**. If the **<right side>** is empty, the **<left side>** pattern is removed from the input word; if it is the symbol = (equal sign), the input word remains unchanged; if it is the symbol @ (at sign), the input word is considered to be a stopword, and is discarded.

We list below a non-contiguous fragment of the prototype lexicon we have created. The initial sequence of entries determines the treatment that is to be given to words ending in *–seis*, but does not contain all the existing exceptions. For example, "**pusésseis:s:por**" generates the correct stem for *dispusésseis* (finite form of the verb *to dispose*) which is *dispor* (infinitive of the verb *to dispose*). By the same token, *pusésseis* (finite form of the verb *to put*) will be stemmed as *por* (preposition *by*), when the correct stem should be *pôr* (infinitive of the verb *to put*). Thus, the additional entry "**pusésseis:l:pôr**" should also be present. With the entry "**isseis:s:issar**" the word-stem pairs *aterrisseis - aterrissar* (forms of the verb *to land*) and *alunisseis - alunissar* (forms of the verb *to land on the moon*) are correctly obtained. On the other hand, *nisseis* (plural form of *first generation descendent of Japanese immigrant*) would be stemmed as **nissar* instead of *nissei* (correct singular form of *nisseis*) which requires the inclusion of the exception "**nisseis:l:nissei**".

coseis:s:coser	estivésseis:s:estar	riamente:s:@	lmente:s:@
ásseis:s:ar	ouxésseis:s:azer	plamente:s:@	omente:s:omentar
esseis:s:essar	fizésseis:s:fazer	anamente:s:@	rmente:s:rmentar
êsseis:s:er	isseis:s:issar	ramente:s:@	ormente:s:@
oubésseis:s:aber	ísseis:s:ir	osamente:s:@	smente:s:smentir
désseis:s:dar	mente:s:@	ssamente:s:@	plesmente:s:@
udésseis:s:oder	amente:s:amentar	tamente:s:@	umente:s:umentar
viésseis:s:vir	icamente:s:@	nuamente:s:@	mumente:s:@
quisésseis:s:querer	adamente:s:@	vamente:s:@	nança:s:=
dissésseis:s:dizer	idamente:s:@	emente:s:@	aço:l:=
pusésseis:s:por	gamente:s:@	gmente:s:gmentar	semi:p:
tivésseis:s:ter	nhamente:s:@	imente:s:imentar	semió:p:=

The next sequence in the sample lexicon concerns words ending in *–mente*, in a hierarchy of rules (**R**) and exceptions (**E**), which can be expressed alternatively as follows:

R: words of the form X*–mente* are stopwords[1].

    E: words of the form X-*amente* are reduced to X-*amentar*[2].

        E: words of the form X(-*icamente*, -*adamente*, -*idamente*, -*gamente*, -*riamente*, -*plamente*, -*anamente*, -*ramente*, -*osamente*, -*ssamente*, -*tamente*, -*nuamente*, -*vamente*) are stopwords.

    E: words of the form X-*gmente* are reduced to X-*gmentar*[3].

    E: words of the form X-*imente* are reduced to X-*imentar*[3].

    E: words of the form X-*lmente* are stopwords. (redundant with "**mente:s:@**")

    E: words of the form X-*omente* are reduced to X-*omentar*[3]. ("**somente:l:@**" is

                                         also required)

    E: words of the form X-*rmente* are reduced to X-*rmentar*[3].

        E: words of the form X-*ormente* are stopwords.

    E: words of the form X-*smente* are reduced to X-*smentir*[3].

        E: words of the form X-*plesmente* are stopwords.

    E: words of the form X-*umente* are reduced to X-*umentar*[3].

        E: words of the form X-*mumente* are stopwords.

Finally, the last three entries in the list may be expressed alternatively as follows:

    R: words of the form X-*nança* remain unchanged.

    R: the word *aço* remains unchanged.

    R: words of the form *semi*-X are reduced to X (i.e. the prefix *semi*- is removed).

    E: words of the form *semió*-X remain unchanged[3].

---

[1] *-mente* is an adverb forming suffix, roughly corresponding to the English suffix *–ly*, and adverbs are normally regarded as stopwords.

[2] Verbs ending in *–mentar* and *–mentir* will have a finite form in *–mente* such as *amamentar* (*to breastfeed*) and *desmentir* (*to deny*). These verbs need to be included as exceptions.

[3] To cater for words such as *semiótica* (*semiotics*).

The correctness of the stemming can be calibrated by a careful choice of lexical entries, in an iterative process that has to stop at some arbitrary moment. The lexicon fragment presented above produces results with a high degree of correctness, but errors still occur. For example, *deprimente* (*depressing*) and *dormente* (*dormant*) are adjectives, but they will be discarded as stopwords.

The choice of stopwords is also arbitrary and highly dependent on features of the target language. For Portuguese, some closed sets such as articles, conjunctions, interjections, numerals, prepositions, pronouns and auxiliary verbs have been designated as stopwords, that can be treated as literals. Adverbs are also regarded as stopwords, but, apart from a very small set of basic adverbs, they are mostly derived from adjectives by the addition of the suffix *-mente*, and therefore have to be treated likewise.

The use of deterministic finite automata (DFA) to store lexicons is common place, and with the appearance of good compression algorithms which do not compromise access speed, such as that proposed by Revuz [19], they have become increasingly used in natural language processing as shown by Pacheco [14], Kowaltolwski et al. [11] and Couto [3].

In order to illustrate the storage process of a lexicon in a DFA and its subsequent minimisation, let us consider a set of lexical entries, having the present tense of the verb *ir* (*to go*) in the indicative mood, followed by its infinitive form, *vou:ir, vamos:ir, vais:ir, ides:ir, vai:ir, vão:ir,* and the corresponding DFA, as shown in figure 1.

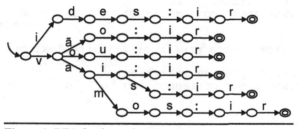

Figure 1: DFA for the verb *ir* (*to go*)

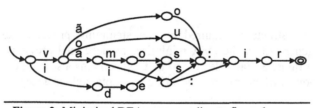

Figure 2: Minimised DFA corresponding to figure 1

The minimisation is accomplished by recognising and eliminating equivalent states in the original DFA. Initially, the DFA is partitioned into levels, such that the level of a state is defined as the length of its longest path to a final state. Two states of the same level are equivalent if they have, as successors, exactly the same set of states (same number and same variety). When two states are found to be equivalent, one of them is removed from the DFA and its incoming transitions are redirected to its remaining equivalent state. This process is carried out sequentially, starting from level zero, which includes all the final states, and working towards the initial state. Figure 2 shows the result of the minimisation of the DFA of figure 1. The resulting compression was 59% in the number of states (from 34 to 14), and 45% in the number of transitions (from 33 to 18).

3.2 Stemming Procedure

```
begin
{treat hyphenated words};
{generate the stem list};
let I := 0;
while (I < {number of strings in the stem list}) do
    begin
    {let P be the Ith string in the stem list};
    if {P is a literal in the stem list} then
        // do nothing
    else  if {P is a literal in the lexicon} then
        begin
        {delete P from the stem list};
        {include stems corresponding to P in the stem list as
                                                literals};
        end
    else  if {there is a suffix of P in the lexicon} then
        begin
        {delete P from the stem list};
        {include stems corresponding to P in the stem list as
                                                non-literals};
        end
    else  if {there is a prefix of P in the lexicon} then
        begin
        {delete P from the stem list};
        {include stems corresponding to P in the stem list as
                                                non-literals};
        end;
    I := I + 1;
    end;
{prepare the final stem list};
end.
```

The main data structures required by the stemming procedure are the array of transitions, generated by the DFA minimiser as described previously, and the stem list, shown in figure 3. Each element of that list contains a string, possibly a stem, and the information of whether or not the string was obtained via a rule of type I (literal).

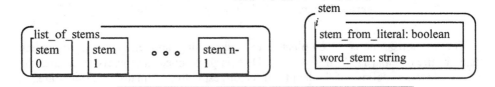

Figure 3: Structure of the stem list

In the stemming algorithm above, the input is the word to be stemmed: either a unhyphenated word or a verb form with a clitic or a hyphenated compound word.

In the first case, the whole word is included in the stem list, in the second case, the clitics are dropped, and the remaining word is included in the stem list. In the last case, all components of the word are included in the stem list. In all cases, words are initially included as non-literals.

The main cycle of the algorithm runs through the list of stems examining each in turn. If the stem is marked as a literal it will be left unchanged; otherwise it is compared with the lexical entries. In the case of a match, the stem in the list is deleted and replaced by the stem indicated in the **<right side>** field of the lexical entry. If the match was with a lexical entry of type l, the new stem is included as a literal; otherwise it is included as a non-literal and inspected during the following iteration.

Note that each stem in the list will only be treated if it is exclusively a literal, or exclusively a suffix, or exclusively a prefix. Also, a given string can match several lexical entries, thereby generating as many new stems as there are entries. Furthermore, if there is no matching lexical entry, the string remains unmodified in the stem list. The final step in the algorithm is the compilation of the remaining stems, which could be more than one.

4 An Experiment with Portuguese

The prototype lexicon, created during our research, was based on [18], an official vocabulary of approximately 103,000 words of all classes. For each verb all inflected forms were added by a specially created verb conjugator program. The resulting word list contained around 770,000 words, from which a lexicon was extracted with 15,589 entries, of which 6,240 were literals, 125 were prefixes and 9,224 were suffixes. The lexicon alone was built over a 5 month period, by far the most time consuming task in the project.

The stemming procedure, customised by the lexicon, was used as a component to build a word-clustering program. The words were clustered around the stem – if two words are reduced to the same stem, both are in the same cluster. Another similar program was built using Porter's Stemming Procedure [17].

To compare the clustering performance of both programs, we used the set 32,000 words obtained from that Porter's web page, Snowball [21], for which we have the results of Paice's evaluation method.

4.1 Paice's Evaluation Method

The standard evaluation method of a stemming algorithm is to apply it to a standard test collection and observe the effects of the algorithm on recall and precision. In [16], Paice proposes an evaluation method which looks into the groupings generated by the stemmer and verifies whether they are composed of semantically and morphologically related words. He introduced three performance indices: overstemming and understemming index and stemming weight.

For a sample of W different words partitioned into what he calls concept groups, he computes the following:

- Desired Merge Total (DMT), which is the number of different possible word form pairs in the particular group, and is given by the formula:
$$DMT_g = 0.5\ n_g\ (n_g - 1)$$
- Desired Non-merge Total (DNT), which counts the possible word pairs formed by a member and a non-member word and is given by the formula:
$$DNT_g = 0.5\ n_g\ (W - n_g)$$

where n_g is the number of words in that group.

The sum of the DMT for all groups yields the GDMT (Global Desired Merge Total) and, similarly, the sum of the DNT for all groups yields the GDNT (Global Desired Non-merge Total).

Understemming errors are considered to be the occurrence of two or more distinct stems in one group. The Unachieved Merge Total (UMT) counts the number of understemming errors for each group and is given by:
$$UMT_g = 0.5\ \sum_{i=1..s} u_i\ (n_g - u_i)$$

where s is the number of distinct stems and u_i is the number of instances of each stem.

The sum of the UMT for all groups yields the GUMT (Global Unachieved Merge Total). The understemming index (UI) is given by GUMT/GDMT.

Overstemming errors are considered to be the occurrence of distinct concepts in the same stem group. The Wrongly Merged Total (WMT) counts the number of overstemming errors for each group, considering a stem group containing n_s items which are derived from t different concept groups, and the number of representatives of these concept groups are $v_1, v_2, \ldots v_t$. The formula is given by:
$$WMT_g = 0.5\ \sum_{i=1..t} v_i\ (n_s - v_i)$$

The sum of the WMT for all groups yields the GWMT (Global Wrongly-Merged Total). The overstemming index (OI) is given by GWMT/GDNT.

A *heavy stemmer* is said to conflate words which are conceptually different into the same stem, therefore committing many overstemming errors. On the other hand, a *light stemmer* fails to conflate conceptually similar words, therefore committing many understemming errors. It should be clear that for a heavy stemmer OI should be high and UI should de low, whereas for a light stemmer the converse should be expected. The ratio between these two measurements OI/UI is said to be Stemming Weight (SW).

4.2 Comparison between the Two Stemmers

The results obtained in our experiments show that our algorithm performs better than Porter's both in terms of understemming and overstemming, according to table 1.

	UI	OI	SW
Porter stemmer for Portuguese	0.215	0.000211	0.000981
Lexicon-based stemmer	0.010341	0.00002522	0.002439

Table 1: Stemming indices

In terms of vocabulary reduction, the Portuguese version of the Porter stemmer reduces the vocabulary by 44 %; with the lexicon-based stemmer we obtained 14,209 groups, thus a very similar reduction rate.

There is one area in which our stemmer performs much better than Porter's that is for verb groups. The verb conjugator module ensures that a large number of verb exceptions are treated. In fact, even though according to traditional grammar there are only three paradigms for verb conjugation in Portuguese, and many exceptions, computational treatment of verbal inflexion has shown that less then one hundred paradigms covers the whole range of Portuguese verbs.

On the other hand, proper names are a source of many overstemming errors. It is very common to find groups of morphologically similar proper name, such as

```
beta; bete; betinho; beto;
```

that are placed in the same stem group. Recognizing proper names is a problem in itself of great relevance for TRS, since they constitute a very discriminating group of words, and ideally they would not be stemmed.

5 Concluding Remarks

Even though the unavailability of test beds for Portuguese restricted the number of comparative experiments that could be effectively carried out, we found the experimental results very promising. We are confident that, given a thoroughly compiled lexicon, our approach can produce high quality, language specific stemmers. We still regard our lexicon as a prototype, from which we generate a prototype stemmer. More work is necessary to build production-quality lexicons and experiment with them. A tool to help build such lexicons would be very welcome, because the task of selecting suffixes and prefixes is both monotonous and error-prone; on the other hand, the whole process can be almost completely automated.

In general, over the course of our research, we came to realise that the clear separation of the lexicon from the stemming procedure is an extremely positive feature of our method, because, although the construction of a robust lexicon can be extremely time consuming, it is still possible to use the stemmer at different stages during lexicon construction. Also, it is very easy to extend the stemmer to other languages without having to change the program code. Furthermore, with the expansion of the lexicon to include more linguistic information, such as part-of-speech tagging, stemming would be simply a function of the lexicon as a Natural Language Processing resource.

The natural progression of this work will be concerned mostly with the development of lexicons. First, it is necessary to implement an automatic tool to aid in the construction of the lexicon, so as to reduce to a minimum the manual labour involved, even though it is still impossible construct a lexicon without specialist human intervention. The construction of a robust lexicon for Portuguese as well as for other languages is also in order.

References

1. Adamson, G., Boreham, J.: The Use of an Association Measure Based on Character Structure to Identify Semantically Related Pairs of Words and Document Titles. Information Storage and Retrieval, vol 10 (1974)
2. Aronoff, M., Anshen, F.: Morphology and the Lexicon: Lexicalization and Productivity. In: Spencer, A., Zwicky, A. (eds.): The Handbook of Morphology. Blackwell Publishers (1998)
3. Couto, M.: Representação de Léxicos através de Autômatos Finitos. MsC Dissertation. ICMC Universidade de São Paulo, São Carlos (1999)
4. Crystal, D.: An Encyclopedic Dictionary of Language and Languages. Penguin, London (1992)
5. Dawson, J.: Suffix Removal and Word Conflation. ALLC Bulletin, Michelmas (1974)
6. Frakes, W. B.: Stemming Algorithms. In: Frakes, W. B., Baeza-Yates, R. (eds.): Information Retrieval: Data Structures & Algorithms. Prentice-Hall, Englewood Cliffs (1992)
7. Fuller, M., Zobel, J.: Conflation-based Comparison of Stemming Algorithms Proc. of the Third Australian Document Computing Symposium, Sydney, Australia (1998)
8. Hafer, M., Weiss, S.: Word Segmentation by Letter Succession Varieties. Information Storage and Retrieval. vol 10 (1974)
9. Harman, D.: How Effective is Suffixing? Journal of the American Society for Information Science, vol 42, n. 1 (1991)
10. Hull, D. A.: Stemming Algorithms: A Case Study for Detailed Evaluation. Journal of the American Society for Information Science vol 47, n. 1, 70-84 (1996)
11. Kowaltolwski, T., Lucchesi, C., Stolfi, J.: Finite Automata and Efficient Lexicon Implementation. Technical Report, Instituto de Computação, Universidade de Campinas (1998)
12. Krovetz, R.: Viewing morphology as an inference process. ACM SIGIR Conference on Research and Development in Information Retrieval, 191-202 (1993)
13. Lovins, J. B.: Development of a Stemming Algorithm. Mechanical Translation and Computational Linguistics. vol 11, n. 1 e 2 (1968)
14. Pacheco, H.: Uma Ferramenta de Auxílio à Redação. MsC Dissertation. Universidade Federal de Minas Gerais (1996)
15. Paice, C.: Another Stemmer. ACM Sigir Forum, vol 24, n. 3 (1990)
16. Paice, C.: An Evaluation Method for Stemming Algorithms. ACM SIGIR Conference on Research and Development in Information Retrieval 42-50 (1994)
17. Porter, M.: An Algorithm for Suffix Stripping. Program. vol 14, n. 3 (1980)
18. Pequeno Vocabulário Ortográfico da Língua Portuguesa. Academia Brasileira de Letras, Rio de Janeiro (1999)
19. Revuz, D.: Minimisation of acyclic deterministic automata in linear time. Theoretical Computer Science. vol 92 (1992)
20. Salton, G.: Automatic Information Organization and Retrieval. McGraw Hill (1968)
21. Snowball: http://snowball.tartarus.org.

French Noun Phrase Indexing and Mining for an Information Retrieval System

Hatem Haddad

VTT Information Technology
P.O. Box 1200, FIN-02044 VTT, Finland
Ext-Hatem.Haddad@vtt.fi

Abstract. In this paper, we present a noun phrase indexing and mining methodology for French Information Retrieval. Our assumption is that noun phrases constitute a better representation of text semantic content than single terms and can improve the effectiveness of an information retrieval system in particular when combined with a text mining process discovering associative relations with the aim of query expansion. Our experiments were conducted using two French test corpora and we compared different noun phrase indexing and mining strategies. We show that combining noun phrase indexing with associative relations can improve the information retrieval system performances, specially at low recall.

1 Introduction

Information Retrieval (IR) deals with the representation, storage and access to information. The task of an *Information Retrieval System* (IRS) is to process a set of electronic documents (called corpus), with the aim of allowing users to retrieve those whose content best matches their information need (typically a natural language declaration). An IRS includes a document indexing application. This application deals with the internal semantic content representation of the user query and the documents supposed to capture the text meaning.

Words taken directly from a document D_i are traditionally used to form a *bag-of-words* representation by measuring their weights. Whatever the information retrieval model is vectorial or probabilistic or logical, this weight is a function of the frequency of a term t_k in the document and in the collection. The IR problem seems to be resumed in a simple correspondence calculation between user query keywords set and document representation keywords set. The drawback of this approach is that single terms (STs) are often ambiguous and can, according to the contexts, refer to different concepts.

This paper represents work-in-progress towards a semantic document content representation. Specifically, we propose an approach that consists in extracting meaningful representative textual entities (single terms and noun phrases) to describe not only *aboutness* but also more detailed information such as relationships among textual entities.

M.A. Nascimento, E.S. de Moura, A.L. Oliveira (Eds.): SPIRE 2003, LNCS 2857, pp. 277–286, 2003.
© Springer-Verlag Berlin Heidelberg 2003

This paper is organised as follow: section 2 focuses on our methodology and related works, we detail in section 3 our system processing steps. In section 4, indexing strategies are explained and the experiments are studied, as well as the results obtained. We conclude in section 5.

2   Proposed Methodology and Related Works

Contrary to the majority of works analysing text in single terms, our objective is to treat the text by keeping information relating to the textual elements relations that they are the syntagmatic relations[1] and the associative relations in the documents. Our methodology is justified by the fact that these relations exist in texts and give significant information on their contents. This information restitution requires uncertainty addition if the relations are ignored during the text analysis. Indeed, this information is generally reconstituted with a thesaurus help, which introduces a certain uncertainty on the relations between the textual units because of their text context ignorance. Our methodology is based on a statistical point of view and a linguistic point of view:

The linguistic point of view relates to the units combinations on the text. It is close to the syntax level and takes into account the syntagmatic relationship between units. Our objective is not a comprehension analysis of the text but linguistic pattern recognition of textual units likely to represent the text content.

The statistical point of view relates to the distribution of textual units in the documents. It is based on the assumption that the use of units together in a document (cooccurence) suggests a semantic relation between these units [13], [19]. We use the association rules, a Text Mining technique, to discover associative relations between textual units.

2.1   Linguistic Point of View

Previous studies have shown that the use of phrases to represent a document's content can enhance the effectiveness of an automatic information retrieval (IR) system. Phrases, and specially noun phrases (NPs), have been proposed as more sophisticated representation [5], [15], [16].

The noun phrase assumption is that noun phrases are more suited to indicate semantic entities (concepts) than single terms and then constitute a better representation of the text semantic content [12]. By using a noun phrases representation, a document that contains a noun phrase used in the query would be ranked higher than a document that contains its component terms.

Both statistical and linguistic approaches are used in noun phrases extraction. The common metric used is term combination discovery, according to their appearance regularity [3], [4]. The statistical methods allow covering in an exhaustive way all the possible term combinations, in a window going from bigram

---

[1] A relation linking parts of a complex linguistic object into a construct, a more complex object [11]

to whole document. A drawback is the huge quantity of possible combinations in large unstructured corpora: some of them are valid on a statistical point of view but are not semantically correct.

Mitra and al. in [12] showed that indexing with noun phrases gives benefits at low recall. Different noun phrases indexing approaches were used in TREC campaigns showing that noun phrases can enhance retrieval performance [17], [16], [18], [20], [9]. For French text analysis, Lexter system uses linguistic method, arguing that terminological elements obey to specific rules of syntactic formation, and for the non-necessity of complete syntactical analysis, replaced by a surface grammatical analysis [2]. Lexter deals with noun phrases mainly consisting of adjectives and nouns. It analyses and parses a corpus tagged with a part-of-speech tagger.

Unlike most of the noun phrases extraction methods, our approach has to be as general as possible to handle any application domain, and particularly the Web. Thus, we based it on the most used morpho-syntactical patterns of a language (French language in our study). Given the huge information amount, an appropriate linguistic treatment should be applied. Linguistic treatment needs a robust and exhaustive language analysis, too complex for the IRS aimed objective. For this reason, we adopt a superficial analysis, which eliminates the deep structure determination and takes into account only the noun phrases extraction.

Our methodology for documents and query analysis relies upon performing partial linguistic processing based on single terms and noun phrase identification: It uses Part-Of-Speech (POS) tagger and syntactic pattern matching to extract units: single terms and noun phrases. A Text Mining process is applied to extract relationships among units.

2.2 Statistical Point of View

Text Mining, like Data Mining, attempts to discover trends, associations and deviations in large not structured textual corpora. One text mining goal is to allow looking for relationships between units in large textual collections. We use association rule mining technology to identify correlation between textual content units [7], [6]. More formally, the association rule generation is achieved from a set F of frequent itemsets in an extraction context $\mathcal{D}$, for the minimal support *minsupp*. An association rule r is a relation between itemsets of the form $r : X \Rightarrow Y$, where $X \cap Y = \emptyset$ and $X,Y \subseteq F$ in which X and Y are frequent itemsets. The itemsets X and Y are called, respectively, *antecedent* and *conclusion* of the rule r. The valid association rules are those of which the measure of confidence $Conf(r : X \Rightarrow Y) = \frac{support(X \cup Y)}{support(X)}$[2] is greater than or equal to the minimal threshold of confidence, called *minconf*. In our specific case, single terms and noun phrases are items and documents are transaction.

The intuitive meaning of $r : X \Rightarrow Y$ is that documents in the collection which contain X also tend to contain Y. Extracted association rules are used to enrich the query specification. In earlier works [6] [7] [8], preliminary results

---

[2] The number of transactions of $\mathcal{D}$ containing X: $support(X) = \frac{|t \in \mathcal{D} / Y \subseteq t|}{|t \in \mathcal{D}|}$

on interactive and automatic query expansion using association rules showed improvement of IRS results.

2.3 Noun Phrases Weighting

Typically, in an information retrieval system, weights are assigned to terms according to their frequency with the TF-IDF function. By this weight function, noun phrases are handicapped compared to the single terms by the fact that they are less frequent because of a stylistic variations (anaphors, elliptic references) and linguistic phenomena such as the lexical or syntactic variance.

To solve this problem, we can plan to solve all the linguistic phenomena (like the anaphora for example). The inconvenient of this solution is that it requires an in-depth analysis of the text and the use of semantic and paradigmatic knowledge. We propose a weighting method combining TF-IDF weighting and syntax weighting.

The syntax weighting is based on the grammatical functions to give a term more weight if it is, e.g., substantive or a proper noun. An empirical value e is given to each grammatical category and a zero value is assigned to empty words. The syntax weighting function, in which the weight s_i is assigned to a given term index t_i (simple term or noun phrase), is computed according to the following formula:

$$s_i = \sum_{c_k \in t_i} e_k$$

where c_k is a t_i component and e_k is the c_k grammatical category empirical value.

3   Processing Steps

The noun phrases extractor is based on a linguistic analysis and a noun phrase identification rules. Association rules are extracted during the Text Mining process.

3.1   Linguistic Analysis

The tokenization step constitutes the detection of sentence boundaries followed by division of sentences into words. The texts are analysed in order to assign a syntactical category to each word (noun, verb, adjective, preposition, etc.). Using several contextual rules, the contextual analysis phase processes the text further to ensure that the POS tags are disambiguated. POS stop-list is used to remove all words belonging to predetermined syntactical categories (determiners, conjunctions, etc.).

3.2   Noun Phrases Extraction

Syntactic pattern matching on the POS tags is used to extract noun phrases. Patterns describe word structures ("Noun Noun", "Noun Preposition Noun", etc.) did not require extensive linguistic knowledge. Since some of the patterns are subsets of other patterns, the longest matching pattern is used to determine the longest noun phrase. According to the linguistic principle of headedness, a noun phrase is structured into a head and a modifier [20]. Morphologic, lexical and syntactical variations are taken into account during this step [10].

3.3   Text Mining Process

Single terms and noun phrases extracted during the previous step are fed into the text mining step to compute association rules. Association rule mining algorithm operates on a data matrix to derive association rules. Since Noun phrases have a very low document frequency, more than 80% of them appear only in a single document, we used a low minimum support threshold for noun phrases and a higher value for single terms. The association rules discovered are used for the automatic expansion of the queries. For each single term or noun phrase X in a query, if there is an association rule r discovered $r : X \Rightarrow Y$ where Y can be a single term or a noun phrase then Y is added to the query. In so doing, we hope to collect relevant documents that would not be found by traditional IR approaches.

4   Experiments and Preliminary Results

Experiments were performed with the SMART system [14] using the two French collections of the Amaryllis project[3]:

- The OFIL collection that makes more that 35 MB and that contains 11016 heterogeneous articles of the newspaper *"Le Monde"* and 119434 different terms, along with 26 queries associated with 587 relevant documents as judged by human experts.
- The INIST collection that makes more that 100 MB and that contains 165431 scientific articles extracted of the bibliographic data bases and 174659 different terms, along with 30 queries associated with 1407 relevant documents as judged by human experts.

Queries are analysed and indexed as documents. The average number of noun phrases extracted from a document is more important in the case of the OFIL

---

[3] The Amaryllis project was initiated by *INIST-CNRS* (Institute for Scientific and Technical Information of National Center for Scientific Research) and co-funded by *AUPELF-UREF* (Agency for Higher Education and Research in French-speaking countries) and the French Ministry of Education and Research. Its goal is to evaluate French text information retrieval systems.

collection (15.9 noun phrases) than in the case of the INIST collection (2.26 noun phrases) where the total noun phrases number extracted from OFIL is 174950 and from INIST is 433910. The INIST collection is a scientific corpus where the sentences and documents are shorter than those of the OFIL collection.

4.1   Indexing Strategies

In addition to the traditional single terms indexing (ST), we tested the following indexing strategies:

- Strategy 1 (S_1): to index single terms and noun phrases in the same vector. The extracted noun phrases are added in the documents and in the queries like the single terms using TF-IDF[4]. For example, if the two single terms *national* and *education* form a noun phrase then they are replaced by the noun phrase *national education* . The single terms and the noun phrases are used together in an index. The document D_i index is the vector:

$$\textbf{\textit{Content}}_i = < w_{i1},\ w_{i2} \ldots w_{ij} \ldots w_{in}, p_{i1},\ p_{i2} \ldots p_{ik} \ldots p_{im} >$$

  where w_{ij} is the single term t_j weight and p_{ik} is the noun phrase weight in the document D_i.
- Strategy 2 (S_2): to index the single terms and the noun phrases separately. For each document or query, a new index is created where the extracted noun phrases are added. These noun phrases are then indexed independently of single terms using TF-IDF. That creates two under-vectors: the first corresponds to the single terms and the second with the noun phrases. The document D_i index is the vector:

$$\textbf{\textit{Content}}_i = < (w_{i1},\ w_{i2} \ldots w_{ij} \ldots w_{in}), (p_{i1},\ p_{i2} \ldots p_{ik} \ldots p_{im}) >$$

  where w_{ij} is the single term t_j weight and p_{ik} is the noun phrase p_k weight in the document D_i (only TF-IDF function is used)..
- Strategy 3 (S_3): to index the single terms and the noun phrases separately with an automatic expansion of the queries [8].
  It is about the same as Strategy 2 with an automatic query expansion by using association rules. The query expansion consists in adding, in the first query under-vector, single terms having association rules with query terms and to add noun phrases, in the second query under-vector, having association rules with query noun phrases.
- Strategy 4 (S_4): to index the single terms and the noun phrases multiplying TF-IDF weighting and syntax weighting where the empirical value e_k of a term t_k is:

$$e_k = \begin{cases} 1 & \text{if } t_k \text{ is a substantive or a proper noun} \\ 0 & \text{if } t_k \text{ is an empty word} \\ 0.5 & \text{for other grammatical function} \end{cases}$$

This choice is motivated by the fact that a noun phrase head is a substantive.

---

[4] ltc weighting formula is used [1]. It gives the best results for ST strategy over all other weighting formula

4.2 Evaluations

Results show that integrating noun phrases in the indexing process we can obtain better performances compared to the best results obtained by single terms indexing. In particular, the separation of the single terms and noun phrases in two different under-vectors gives better results than in the case of to index them together. Results show $11,5\%$ enhancement in average precision for the OFIL collection and 5.34% in the INIST case whereas this increase is 19.12% for the OFIL and 14.9% for the INIST in the case of Strategy 2 (Table 1).

Table 1. 11-point average precision

	OFIL		INIST	
	Av.Prec	Diff	Av.Prec	Diff
ST	$31,64\%$		$22,08\%$	
S_1	$35,28\%$	$+11,5\%$	$23,26\%$	$+5.34\%$
S_2	$37,69\%$	$+19.12\%$	$25,37\%$	$+14.9\%$
S_3	40%	$+26.42\%$	$26,45\%$	$+19.79\%$
S_4	$42,28\%$	$+33,62\%$	$26,66\%$	$+20.74\%$

From looking at Strategy 1 and Strategy 2 results, the number of relevant documents found is almost identical for the two strategies. What differ are the relevant documents found classification. Indeed, strategy 2 makes it possible to support the classification of these documents by putting them at the head of the list of the found documents.

Table 2. OFIL exact precision at 5, 10 15 and 30 documents

	5 doc.		at 10 doc.		at 15 doc.		at 30 doc.	
	exact.prec	Diff	exact.prec	Diff	exact.prec	Diff	exact.prec	Diff
ST	$37,69\%$		35.38%		$32,31\%$		28.72%	
S_1	40%	$+5.75\%$	38.08%	$+7.63\%$	33.59%	$+3.96\%$	27.95%	-2.68%
S_2	41.54%	$+10.21\%$	42.31%	$+19.58\%$	37.44%	$+15.85\%$	30.51%	$+6.23\%$
S_3	47.69%	$+26.53\%$	46.92%	$+32.61\%$	41.28%	$+27.76\%$	33.19%	$+15.56\%$
S_4	49.23%	$+30.61\%$	47.31%	$+33.49\%$	44.36%	$+3729\%$	33.97%	$+18.27\%$

This is reflected in the results of the average precision at 5, 10, 15 and 30 documents (Table 2 and Table 3) which confirms our assumption that the noun phrases help to increase the precision of an IRS. Strategy 3 makes it possible to increase the performances of 19.79% for INIST and 26.42% for collection OFIL. This increase is due to an increase in the number of found relevant documents what confirms the association rules use interest in an IR context.

Table 3. INIST exact precision at 5, 10 15 and 30 documents

	5 doc.		10 doc.		15 doc.		30 doc.	
	exact.prec	Diff	exact.prec	Diff	exact.prec	Diff	exact.prec	Diff
ST	47, 33%		39, 33%		37, 11%		28, 78%	
S_1	50, 67%	+7.05%	42, 00%	+6.78%	38, 22%	+2.99%	30, 11%	+4.62%
S_2	54, 67%	+15.5%	45, 67%	+16.12%	40, 89%	+10.18%	34, 22%	+18.9%
S_3	56, 00%	+18.31%	43, 67%	+11.03%	41, 33%	+11.37%	33%	+14.66%
S_4	56, 67%	+19.73%	47, 33%	+20.34%	42, 89%	+15.57%	33, 22%	+15.42%

The performances obtained by applying Strategy 4 to OFIL collection show a clear increase in average precision compared. Indeed, the average precision in 11 points of recall is of 42, 28% with 33, 62% enhancement comparing to single terms indexing. In the INIST collection case, the increase is less important with an average precision in 11 points of recall 26, 66% and 20.74% enhancement comparing to single terms indexing. This increase is due at the same time to an increase in the precision and an increase in the recall.

Indeed, this strategy makes it possible to find relevant documents which are not found with the other strategies and it makes it possible to better classify the relevant documents in order to put them in the first classified of the found documents list.

These results show that the integration of the noun phrases in documents and queries representation of the improves the performances of a SRI. These results would require additional tests making it possible more precisely to characterise noun phrases semantic importance. A finer use in the representation of the documents should also be carried out .

5   Conclusion and Ongoing Work

Our approach considers that a text is not a bag-of-words, but it is a strongly structured word set that allows communicating information of a high precision. This wealth and this complexity should be taken into account in the IRS. Our strategy for analysing information relies upon performing partial linguistic processing based on single term and noun phrase identification and text mining processing to extract correlation between them. Preliminary results showed that our system is of reasonably high quality for both noun phrases and association rules extraction.

On the other hand, the experiments were carried out within the vectorial model framework that is not adapted for noun phrase indexing. Further work includes defining a linguistic information retrieval model, which deals with noun phrases structure matching and relationships among them.

References

1. Buckley, C., Salton, G., Allan, J.: The Effect of Adding Relevance Information in a Relevance Feedback Environment. Proceedings of the 17th Annual International ACM SIGIR Conference on Research and Development in Information Retrieval (1994) 292–300
2. Bourigault, D.: LEXTER, un logiciel d'extraction terminologique. 2me Colloque international de TermNet, Avignon, France (1992)
3. Church, W.K., Hanks, P.: Word association norms, Mutual information, and Lexicography. Computational Linguistics, Vol. 16 (1990) 22–29
4. Fagan, J. L.: The effectiveness of a nonsyntactic approach to automatic phrase indexing for document retrieval. Journal of the American Society for Information Scienc Vol. 40 (1989) 115–132
5. Fagan, J. L.: Experiments in Automatic Phrase Indexing for Document Retrieval: A Comparison of Syntactic and Non-Syntactic Methods. PhD thesis, Department of Computer Science, Cornell University, Ithaca, New York (1987)
6. Gry, M., Haddad, H.: Knowledge Discovery for Automatic Query Expansion on the World Wide Web. International Workshop on the World-Wide Web and Conceptual Modeling, France (1999) 334–347
7. Haddad, H., Chevallet, J.P., Bruandet, M.F.: Relations between Terms Discovered by Association Rules. 4th European conference on Principles and Practices of Knowledge Discovery in Databases PKDD'2000, Workshop on Machine Learning and Textual Information Access, France (2000)
8. Haddad, H.: Combining Text Mining and NLP for Information Retrieval. International Conference Conference on Artificial Intelligence (IC-AI), Las Vegas, USA (2002) 434–439
9. Hull, D., Grefenstette, G., Schulze, B.M., Gaussier, E., Schutze, H., Pedersen, J.: Xerox TREC-5 Site Report. Routing,Filtering, NLP and SPANISH Track. In: Voorhees, E., Harman, D.K. (eds.): The Fifth Text REtrieval Conference (TREC-5) (1997) 167–180
10. Jacquemin, C., Tsoukermann, E.: NLP for term variant extraction: synergy between morphology, lexicon, and syntax. In: Strzalkowski, T. (eds.): Natural Language Information Retrieval. Dordrecht: Kluwer Academic Publishers (1999)
11. Khoo, C. S. G.: The Use of Relation Matching in Information Retrieval. Singapore Libraries, Vol. 26 (1997) 3–22
12. Mitra, M., Buckley, C., Singhal, A., Cardi, C.: In Analysis of Statistical and Syntactic Phrases. 5me Confrence de Recherche d'Information Assiste par Ordinateur (RIAO) (1997) 200-214
13. Van Rijsbergen, C. J.: Information Retrieval. Butterworths, London (1979).
14. Salton, G.: The SMART Retrieval System : Experiments in Automatic Document Processing. Prentice-Hall Series in Automatic Computation, New Jersey, (1971)
15. Smeaton, A., O'Donnell, R., Kelledy, F.: Indexing Structures Derived from Syntax in TREC-3: System Description. In: Harman, D.K. (eds.): The Third Text REtrieval Conference (TREC-3) (1994) 55–67
16. Strzalkowski, T., Carballo, J.P.: Natural Language Information Retrieval: TREC-4 Report. In: Harman, D.K. (eds.): The Fourth Text REtrieval Conference (TREC-4) (1995) 245–258
17. Strzalkowski, T., Carballo, J.P.: Natural Language Information Retrieval: TREC-3 Report. In: Harman, D.K. (eds.): The Third Text REtrieval Conference (TREC-3) (1994) 39–54

18. Strzalkowski, T., Lin, F., Wang, J., Guthrie, L., Leistensnider, J., Wilding, J., Karlgren, J, Straszheim, T., Carballo, J.P.: Natural Language Information Retrieval: TREC-5 Report. In: Voorhees, E., Harman, D.K. (eds.): The Fifth Text REtrieval Conference (TREC-5) (1996) 291–334
19. Xu, J., Croft, B.: Improving the effectiveness of information retrieval with local context analysis. ACM Transactions on Information Systems, Vol. 18 (2000) 79–112
20. Zhai, C., Tong, X., MilicFrayling, N., Evans, D.: Evaluation of syntactic phrase indexing - CLARIT NLP track report. In: Voorhees, E., Harman, D.K. (eds.): The Fifth Text REtrieval Conference (TREC-5) (1996) 347-358

New Refinement Techniques for Longest Common Subsequence Algorithms

Lasse Bergroth[1,3], Harri Hakonen[2,3], Juri Väisänen[2]

[1] Turku University, Department of Information Technology / Programming techniques
Ylhäistentie 2, 24280 Salo, Finland
bergroth@it.utu.fi
[2] Turku University, Department of Information Technology
Lemminkäisenkatu 14-18 A, 20520 Turku, Finland
hat@it.utu.fi, jumava@utu.fi
[3] TUCS - Turku Centre for Computer Science

Abstract. Certain properties of the input strings have dominating influence on the running time of an algorithm selected to solve the longest common subsequence (lcs) problem of two input strings. It has turned out to be difficult – as well theoretically as practically – to develop an lcs algorithm which would be superior for all problem instances. Furthermore, implementing the most evolved lcs algorithms presented recently is laborious.

This paper shows that it is still beneficial to refine the traditional lcs algorithms to get new algorithm variants that are in practice competitive to the modern lcs methods in certain problem instances. We present and analyse a general-purpose algorithm NKY-MODIF, which has a moderate time and space efficiency and can easily be implemented correctly. The algorithm bases on the so-called diagonal-wise method of Nakatsu, Kambayashi and Yajima (NKY). The NKY algorithm was selected for our further consideration due to its algorithmic independence of the size of the input alphabet and its light pre-processing phase.

The NKY-MODIF algorithm refines the NKY method essentially in three ways: by reducing unnecessary scanning over the input sequences, storing the intermediate results more locally, and utilizing lower and upper bound knowledge about the lcs. In order to demonstrate that the some of the presented ideas are not specific for the NKY only, we apply lower bound information on two lcs algorithms having a different processing approach than the NKY has. This introduces a new way to solve the lcs problem.

The lcs problem has two variants: calculating only the length of the lcs, and determining also the symbols belonging to one instance of the lcs. We verify the presented ideas for both of these problem types by extensive test runs.

KEY WORDS: longest common subsequence, string algorithms, heuristic algorithms

1 Introduction

There exist several practical applications where comparing the contents of two strings is of essential importance. For instance, in molecular biology it is important to estimate the similarity of two DNA or protein sequences. Especially for pre-selection

M.A. Nascimento, E.S. de Moura, A.L. Oliveira (Eds.): SPIRE 2003, LNCS 2857, pp. 287-303, 2003.
© Springer-Verlag Berlin Heidelberg 2003

purposes, those biological sequences can be treated as strings from an appropriate input alphabet. The degree of similarity can be measured by counting the maximal number of identical symbols existing in both input strings in the same order. Collecting these identical symbols and concatenating them produces (one of) the longest common subsequence(s) of the strings the length of which numerically describes the similarity between the strings. In order to specify some further application fields, especially text and image compression and version maintenance related problems in computer science are worth mentioning.

In this paper, we pay attention to comparing two input strings $X[1..m]$ and $Y[1..n]$ with each other. Without loss of generality it can be assumed that $m \leq n$. The elements of the input strings are from the input alphabet Σ, which consists of σ different symbols. A *subsequence* $S[1..s]$ $(0 \leq s \leq m)$ of X can be obtained by deleting arbitrarily $m\text{-}s$ symbols from X. Further, if S is also a subsequence of Y, then S is a *common subsequence* of X and Y, denoted by $cs(X,Y)$. The *longest common subsequence* of X and Y, abbreviated by $lcs(X,Y)$ (or solely lcs) is the $cs(X,Y)$ having maximal length, which will be denoted by r. The longest common subsequence need not be unique. That means that there may be several subsequences satisfying the lcs criterion for the actual problem instance. As well it is possible that the same longest common subsequence can be collected from different positions of the input strings. The following example clarifies this.

Example 1: $X[1..11]=$ '*aadddbcdacd*', $Y[1..11]=$ '*cdacbddbaab*', $\Sigma=\{$ a, b, c, d $\}$, $\sigma=4$
$\rightarrow$ $r = 5$, $lcs(X,Y) = $ '*addba*', '*dddba*' or '*cdacd*'

In example 1, three different sequences satisfying the lcs criterion can be found. Also it can be noticed that there exist several ways to build the sequence '*addba*' by alternating, which pair of symbols '*d*' lying in positions 2, 3 and 4 in X will be chosen to the $lcs(X,Y)$. Also the first character of the lcs, '*a*', can be selected freely from either of the positions 1 or 2 of X.

The lcs problem has actually two variants. Sometimes it is enough that only the length of the lcs, r, would be required, whereas in some applications the sequence itself has to be produced. The former variant will be called r-variant and the latter *lcs*-variant. Basically, every algorithm calculating r only can be modified to solve lcs also by introducing additional bookkeeping that records the algorithm progression. After r is known, the lcs can be constructed by backtracking the selections made. However, in practice, the bookkeeping causes time and space overhead, which means that the behaviour of the r-variant of a lcs algorithm may considerably differ from its *lcs*-variant. In this paper, we demonstrate how this overhead can be diminished by knowledge on the lower and the upper bound of r. To be able to understand the lcs problem properly, some additional definitions have to be declared.

The very first manageable approach to solve the lcs problem is from the year 1974. The method was based on dynamic programming technique [1]. That means that each character lying in the input string X is compared with characters from each position of Y. This leads to calculation of a lcs for all possible prefixes of X and Y. Let us denote by $r(i,j)$ the length of the lcs for the prefix pair $X[1..i]$ and $Y[1..j]$, where $0 \leq i \leq m$ and

$0 \leq j \leq n$. The following recursive rule defines the connection between the length of the lcs of two arbitrary prefix pairs, $r(i,j)$, and the immediately shorter ones, where at least one of the prefixes of X and Y has shortened exactly by one character:

$$r(i,j) = \begin{cases} 0 & \text{if } i = 0 \text{ or } j = 0 \\ r(i\text{-}1, j\text{-}1) + 1 & \text{if } i \neq 0 \text{ and } j \neq 0 \text{ and } X[i] = Y[j] \\ \max\{ r(i\text{-}1, j), r(i, j\text{-}1) \} & \text{if } i \neq 0 \text{ and } j \neq 0 \text{ and } X[i] \neq Y[j] \end{cases}$$

Considering the recursive rule it can easily be realized that $r(i,j)$ may be incremented from its earlier value only in such index pairs (i,j) where two same characters are found. Those index pairs are called *matches*. A match residing in the index pair (i,j) is assigned to a certain *class* k, where k is equivalent with the value $r(i,j)$. The k'th class contains all the matches having the $r(i,j)$ values k. In order to get the solution to the original problem by using the recursive rule, the value $r(m,n)$ has to be determined. Before being able to calculate that value, all respective values for shorter prefix pairs between X and Y have to be calculated. This means that this approach makes always mn comparisons regardless of the properties of the input strings. The calculation procedure can be illustrated by filling from top to bottom and from left to right all the cells of a *matrix*, whose row indices refer to the positions of the input string X and column indices analogically to the positions of the input string Y. The 0'th row and column are needed to the initialization of the process. The numbers in each cell denote the appropriate $r(i,j)$-values.

The fact that only those matrix cells containing a match can have contribution to r – and thus the pioneer lcs algorithm does a lot of excessive work – was detected three years later in 1977 [2, 3, 4]. That means that all the non-matching index pairs can be skipped over. To find exactly the matches without applying a linear scan repeatedly on one of input strings, it is possible to construct a case-supporting data structure called *matchlist*, which contain ordered information about the positions where the next (previous) instance of each symbol of the input alphabet can be found after (before) the current index position. When discarding the non-matching index pairs, quite a lot of excess work can be avoided. Even though the construction cost of the matchlist is linear to n, the methods basing on that technique can still be inefficient in numerous situations. When the alphabet size is small, there may exist a great number of matching index pairs, and the improvements in the running time and space complexity are thus only marginal. Most algorithms using matchlists process one row (or column) at a time. Also it is possible to search for all the matches belonging to one class at a time. Those methods are suitable for the problem instances where lcs is relatively short [2, 5, 6, 7].

In 1984, it was realized [7] that there also exist matches which need not be considered. It was proven that a match (i,j) belonging to a class k ($1 \leq k \leq m$) is important only, if there does not exist any other match (i',j') belonging to the same class k so that
$i' = i$ and $j' < j$ or alternatively $i' < i$ and $j' = j$. If such a match (i',j') cannot be found, the match (i,j) is called a *dominant match*. The lcs problem can be solved by qualifying only all the dominant matches. Auxiliary data structures, such as *closest-matrices*, assist effectively in separating all the dominant matches from the set of all matches [8, 9]. Unfortunately, the cost of building a data structure supporting direct

access during the pre-processing is $O(n\sigma)$, which means that an increase in the alphabet size quickly demolishes the advantages gained by the smarter processing [5, 8, 9].

A valuable observation contributing to the establishment of our paper was discovered in 1990, when Rick in his technical report [9] proved that if r is known beforehand, it might be possible to discard even some of the dominant matches. Let us assume to be known that $r = k + h$, and k-1 is the length of the lcs found so far. Then it would be unnecessary to register a dominant match of class k residing in index pair (i,j) where min$\{$ m-i, n-j $\}$ < h. The reason for rejecting such matches is that the amount of symbols left in X following the i'th index or in Y following the j'th index is insufficient, if a lcs of length $k + h$ should be able to be constructed. The remaining dominant matches which are potential candidates to be selected to the lcs are called *minimal witnesses*. The emphasis of this paper is that when r is not known exactly, a good approximation for it enables us to get rid of the majority of unnecessary dominant matches.

To clarify our concepts, the next example illustrates a matrix derived from the same strings as in Example 1. The values in its cells present the $r(i,j)$ values for each prefix combination. The dominant matches are surrounded by boxes and the non-dominant matches are encircled. The broken line, called a *contour*, separates two adjacent areas having different $r(i,j)$ values.

		0	1	2	3	4	5	6	7	8	9	10	11
	Y	ø	c	d	a	c	b	d	d	b	a	a	b
X													
0	ø	0	0	0	0	0	0	0	0	0	0	0	0
1	a	0	0	0	[1]	1	1	1	1	1	(1)	(1)	1
2	a	0	0	0	(1)	1	1	1	1	1	[2]	(2)	2
3	d	0	0	[1]	1	1	1	[2]	(2)	2	2	2	2
4	d	0	0	(1)	1	1	1	(2)	[3]	3	3	3	3
5	d	0	0	(1)	1	1	1	(2)	(3)	3	3	3	3
6	b	0	0	1	1	1	[2]	2	3	[4]	4	4	(4)
7	c	0	[1]	1	1	[2]	2	2	3	4	4	4	4
8	d	0	1	[2]	2	2	2	[3]	(3)	4	4	4	4
9	a	0	1	2	[3]	3	3	3	3	4	[5]	(5)	5
10	c	0	(1)	2	3	[4]	4	4	4	4	5	5	5
11	d	0	1	(2)	3	4	4	[5]	(5)	5	5	5	5

Example 2: *Graphical illustration of a matrix established by dynamic programming for input strings X = 'aadddbcdacd' and Y = 'cdacbddbaab'*

Example 2 is a visualization of our first example, where, for instance, a match at (6,11) is a match of the class 4 representing $r(X[1..6], Y[1..11])$. Because there is a 4'th class match also in the position (6,8), the match at (6,11) must be a non-dominant match. In contrary, (6,8) is a dominant match, because no *cs* of length 4 can be found when a shorter prefix from either X or Y is taken while another prefix is kept unchanged. If $r = 5$ is known in advance, a dominant match of class 3 at (4,7) is a minimal witness, because there are enough characters (at least two) in both input strings to construct a lcs of length 5 through it. Conversely, the dominant match of the 2'nd class at (2,9) does not fulfil the criterion of a minimal witness.

The majority of the lcs algorithms follows one of the following processing paradigms: either one matrix row at a time or one class at a time. But there is still one approach that could be applied – advancing one *diagonal* at a time. Almost all diagonal-wise processing algorithms have originally been developed for calculating the *edit distance* between the input strings [10, 11, 12]. The edit distance problem is closely connected with the lcs problem [5]. However, there exists one pure lcs algorithm which processes the input strings diagonal-wise. That algorithm was developed in 1980 by *Nakatsu, Kambayashi and Yajima* [13]. To our knowledge, in addition to Rick's suggestion to apply closest-matrix to that algorithm [9], neither any improvements to the NKY algorithm nor totally new diagonally processing lcs algorithms have been presented later.

In this paper, developing the NKY algorithm further is our goal. There are three reasons why to consider especially that algorithm. First, the theoretical running time of the NKY algorithm is independent of σ. In many practical applications the input alphabet may vary from small to large. So NKY would be a suitable candidate to the applications where the size of the input alphabet cannot be predicted. The second reason is that the pre-processing phase of NKY is very simple. Thus an increase in the length of the input strings does not reflect as a hardened pre-processing. A third reason is that no separate bookkeeping has to be done when new matches are found — in contrary to most lcs methods, where maintenance of the possible lcs paths requires an enormous amount of pointers. In spite of its several advantageous properties, there are still sources of inefficiency in that algorithm. Our motivation is to show that both the running time and the memory space of the NKY algorithm can remarkably be reduced. In the next section, the original NKY algorithm is described. In the third section, our suggestions for improvement will be presented. The purpose of the fourth section is to present the practical impact and to demonstrate that the presented ideas of embedding upper and lower bound information can be applied to the majority of the known and widely used lcs algorithms. Finally, the last section is reserved for conclusions and discussion.

2   The Original NKY Algorithm

The row-wise algorithms process one symbol of the shorter input string at a time, and that symbol will be compared against symbols residing in the longer input string. Depending on the degree of the refinement of the algorithm, either all matches or dominant matches for the appropriate symbol will be sought. If the processing advances, instead, one class at a time, all the (dominant) matches belonging to the current class will be determined. In both those classical paradigms it is common that the length of the lcs can increase only by one during one execution round in the outermost loop of the algorithm.

The processing manner of the NKY algorithm is rather different from any other lcs algorithm presented [13]. Both the input strings are scanned in reverse order: beginning from the last symbol towards the first. The operation mode of the algorithm is greedy. During its one execution round in the outermost loop the shorter string X will be scanned as far as all its symbols can be found in the same order in the longer string Y when scanning it towards the beginning. If the i'th symbol of X is found at position j from Y, the process continues by searching the last symbol from $Y[1..j\text{-}1]$ matching the $X[i\text{-}1]$. One round in the loop will be terminated, when either of the input strings is exhausted. That occurs when all the symbols of X have already been found in Y in the same order, or some symbol of X cannot be matched from the suffix of Y any more. New rounds will be started as long as there still are possibilities to find a longer lcs as already found. On each new round the start position in the string X shifts by one towards the beginning. That means that on the second execution round the first index of X to be inspected is $m\text{-}1$, on the third round $m\text{-}2$ etc.

The heart of the NKY algorithm builds upon the following three lemmas the proofs of which will be omitted here. The proofs can be found in the paper where the original algorithm was presented [13]. The main concept needed in those lemmas are the values $L_i(j)$, which can be interpreted as follows: "$L_i(j) = k$, where k is the last position in the string Y, such that the longest common subsequence of $X[i..m]$ and $Y[k..n]$ has length j. If no such position k exists, then $L_i(j) = 0$".

(1) $\forall i \mid i \in [1..m]: L_i(1) > L_i(2) > \ldots L_i(k)$, where $L_i(k\text{-}1)$ is the last non-zero L_i value

(2) $\forall i \mid i \in [1..m\text{-}1]: \forall j \mid j \in [1..m]: L_{i+1}(j) \leq L_i(j)$

(3) $L_i(j) = \begin{cases} \text{Max}(h, L_{i+1}(j)), \text{ where } h \text{ is the largest number such that } X[i] = Y[h] \text{ and} \\ h < range, \text{ where } range = L_{i+1}(j\text{-}1) \text{ if } j \geq 2, \text{ else } range = n + 1 \\ L_{i+1}(j), \text{ if no such } h \text{ exists} \end{cases}$

In order to save all the calculated $L_i(j)$-values, a matrix will be used. At the beginning of each execution round the left downward diagonal beginning from the cell $(1,i)$ will be filled, where i indicates the start position in X. To the initialization purposes, also the diagonal beginning at $(1,m\text{+}1)$ will be filled with zeros. On the first round, the values $L_1(m)$, $L_2(m\text{-}1)$, $L_3(m\text{-}2)$ and so on will be created, till either of the input strings exhausts. Analogically, on the second round the values $L_1(m\text{-}1)$, $L_2(m\text{-}2)$, $L_3(m\text{-}3)$ etc. will be filled. If we observe the values residing on an arbitrary row in the matrix, it can be seen that when traversing along the row from right to left, all the values either increase or remain unchanged. The increase occurs when a shorter suffix of Y is needed to produce lcs of length j with $X[i\text{-}1..m]$ than with $X[i..m]$. In Figure 1, we present the original NKY algorithm formally. Next we give a numerical example of its processing principles. In the algorithm, the input sequences are $X[1..m]$ and $Y[1..n]$, where $m <= n$. The output is a sequence $lcs[1..r]$ of pairs <index of X, index of Y>. The local variables are used in the following meaning: r is the length of the lcs so far, s is a length of the current cs, i is a traverse index of X (and j of Y, respectively), and d is an index of diagonal. Furthermore, j is bounded by $lowerY <= j < upperY$.

```
d <- m
r <- 0
while r < d do   // Main loop.
  i <- d
  s <- 1
  upperY <- n + 1

  // Diagonal loop for d.

  while i ≠ 0 and upperY ≠ 0 do
    if d = m or r < s then
       M[s][i + 1] <- 0   // Mark edge of
M.
    endif
    lowerY <- max { 1, M[s][i + 1] }
    j <- upperY - 1

    // Scanning loop.

    while lowerY <= j and X[i] ≠ Y[j]
do
       j <- j - 1
    endwhile
    if lowerY <= j then
       upperY <- j
    else
       upperY <- M[s][i + 1]
    endif
```

```
    M[s][i] <- upperY
    if upperY = 0 then
       s <- s - 1
    endif
    r <- max { r, s }   // Update r.
    i <- i - 1
    s <- s + 1
  endwhile
  d <- d - 1
endwhile

// Collect the lcs.

i <- i + 1
if upperY = 0 then
  i <- i + 1
endif
for k <- r downto 1 do
  while M[k][i] = M[k][i + 1] do
    i <- i + 1
  endwhile
  lcs[k] = <i, M[k][i]>
  i <- i + 1
endfor
```

Figure 1: *The formal description of the original NKY algorithm*

It can be noticed that the execution of the algorithm stops when the diagonal beginning at (1,6) has been fulfilled. The longest common subsequence of length 5 has already been found and the length of the next diagonal is 5. Therefore no longer common subsequences can be found. The sequence can be revealed by scanning the innermost filled diagonal, till the first non-zero value is found. If the value has duplicates on the right side on the same row, that row must be scanned till the last duplicate is detected. In Example 3, the lcs instance *'addba'* will be discovered from index pairs (3,2), (6,4), (7,5), (8,6) and (10,9). The corresponding cells are emboldened. The first index of each pair shows the actual index of the input string X, the value in cell refers to the appropriate Y-index of the selected match. The search path for collecting the lcs is shown with arrows.

The running time of the NKY algorithm is $O(m(n-r))$. Without modifications, the algorithm runs efficiently when r is long. From the matrix at most $(r+1)(m-r+1)$ cells will be visited, but indexing that data structure without any information about r is somewhat tricky. In practice, the upper left triangular part of a matrix having size $n(m+1)$ is needed. The practical space complexity of the algorithm is also $O(nm)$.

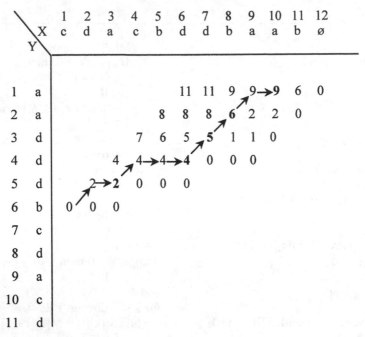

Example 3: *Solving the lcs with the NKY algorithm. For convenience, the placement of the input arrays is different from the one in previous example.*

3 Refinements to the Original NKY Algorithm

We have now considered the behaviour of the original NKY algorithm with such granularity that we are able to localize its properties, which may be generally inefficient. We propose here several suggestions how to intensify the functionality of the method. Finally, the algorithm NKY-MODIF will be presented as a sum of the gradual enhancements to the original NKY method.

3.1 Reorganizing the Matrix

As we could see from the formal algorithm description and Example 3, the cells of the matrix are addressed with a notation, which refers to the positions of the input strings. However, during the calculation of r the matrix is processed one diagonal at a time, and all the references needed to the matrix are directed to the previously handled diagonal. Then it would be more natural to enumerate the matrix in terms of diagonals instead. The outermost diagonal will be treated as the 0'th, the diagonal beginning from $(1,m)$ is the first and so on. After the modification, during one execution round of the outermost loop of algorithm the new values will be inserted in a contiguous part of the memory. All the references to the previous diagonal will now be based on the cell having index (*current_diagonal*-1, *current_lcs_length*). Each time a new loop in the algorithm begins, the variable *current_diagonal* will be incremented by one.

Although the reformation of the matrix might seem to be only cosmetic, we will later be convinced of its profitability.

3.2 Detecting Optimal Suffixes in Y

In the original NKY algorithm, on each execution round in the outermost loop the scanning of the input string Y begins from its last position n. Let us assume that X and Y have a common suffix of z characters. During the first execution round the last symbol of X will be matched with the last symbol of Y, and after that we will still find $z-1$ contiguous matches. If lcs(X,Y) is shorter than $m-1$, the outermost loop has to be repeated at least once more. Now the original algorithm tries to match $X[m-1]$ with $Y[n]$. However, the first z comparisons do not give any new information, because the values $L_{m-1}(1)$, $L_{m-2}(2)$, $L_{m-3}(3)$, ..., $L_{m-z}(z)$ cannot be improved any more. The same is true also for rest of the diagonals on the left side of the current diagonal: the first z values of them need not be calculated. In other words, the optimal suffix of Y of length z has been found. In that case, we could skip over the next $z-1$ symbols of X and select $m-z-1$ as a new start position for X. Analogically, the position, where scanning in Y begins, will be shifted with z characters towards the beginning. Embedding the control of finding optimal suffixes from Y assists us to avoid unnecessary comparisons. The contribution of this new feature to the running time is notable when there exist long common suffixes in the input strings. Only, if the last symbol of Y cannot be matched with any symbol of X, our modification is totally fruitless for the actual problem instance. To illustrate the idea, consider the match of symbols d at $(7,11)$ in Example 3. When the last symbol of Y is enough to form a lcs of length 1 with $X[7..11]$, it is not possible any more to decrease the amount of needed symbols from Y from one to zero, when a lcs of length 1 has to be produced. Clearly, the searching of lcs's of length 1 can now be terminated by ignoring the 6'th symbol of X and the 11'th symbol of Y.

3.3 Detecting Runs of Contiguous Numbers on a Diagonal

In addition to detecting optimal suffixes in Y, there exist also other situations where comparisons between symbols can be avoided. Consider again Example 3. When the values of the third diagonal have been calculated, it contains the values 9, 6, 5, 4 and 0 from top to bottom. The processing of the fourth diagonal will be started from the index pair $(1,8)$. Because the symbol b residing in $X[8]$ is not found before the 9'th position in Y, the selection of a shorter Y-suffix for lcs of length 1 could not be done. Thus the earlier value 9 will be propagated to the left. Furthermore, the symbol d in $X[7]$ is found in $Y[8]$, which compresses the needed Y-suffix for the lcs of length 2 from 9 to 8. The symbol $X[6]$, namely d, is not found until the 5'th position of Y, and the previous value for lcs of length 3, also 5, will be copied from the right. Now we can notice that on the previous diagonal the value for lcs of length 4 is only by one smaller than the value for a lcs of length 3. So the value on the previous diagonal cannot be updated on the current diagonal. If there are contiguous decreasing numbers on the previous diagonal forming a so called *run*, and a number belonging to the run has to be copied to the current diagonal, then all the later numbers belonging to the same run will be copied, too. For that reason, we can skip forward both in X and Y as many positions as the length of the run shows. In Example 3, the run consisting of 5 and 4 will be copied from the 3'rd to the 4'th diagonal. Due to that, as well X as Y index pointers will be decremented by 2 before the next comparison. In order to take advantage of detection of optimal suffixes and runs of contiguous numbers, the matrix should be initialized with zeros, if the actual lcs has to be discovered in addition to solving r. In most computer systems, the matrix initialization by zero values is well supported and does not require a noticeable increase in running time.

3.4   Utilizing A Priori Information Concerning the Length of the Lcs

The most general innovation of this paper is based on the utilization of *heuristic lower* and *upper bounds* for the lcs. When the input strings are long, solving the lcs problem by using an exact algorithm only may take an unbearably long time. In some applications it is enough that we get *a reliable approximation for r*. In such situations, a pair consisting of the upper and lower bound for the lcs can give us a guard criterion, if a more accurate investigation of the strings is needed. For those purposes, heuristic approximation algorithms for the lcs have been developed [14, 15, 16].

The idea of a lower bound heuristic is to relax the original problem. There exist several methods to get the lower bound for r (abbreviated *lbr*). This can be done, for instance, by re-mapping the original symbols onto a smaller alphabet. Some heuristics divide the original problem to smaller sub-problems and combine their results so that a legal *cs* for the original problem can be extracted. Some methods have their foundations simply on the symbol frequency information concerning the input strings. The fourth approach to calculate a lower bound is based on a greedy selection of matches. The principle of them is to process one class at a time, but only one locally viewed dominant match is selected from each class. The heuristic called *BestNext* uses this kind of a processing manner selecting such a dominant match that enables construction of the longest possible *cs* after the appropriate selection. For instance, if we had input strings of length 10, and the dominant matches of class 1 resided at (1,8), (3,5) and (7,1), the selection of (3,5) would enable constructing an lcs of length 6, because there would be five symbols left in Y and seven in X after that selection. Clearly, when choosing either of the other candidates, one of the input strings would exhaust earlier. So the point (3,5) would be locally the most economical selection. The BestNext heuristic performs in practice reliably and very fast [15, 16], so we have selected that lower bound method for this research work. The time complexity of the BestNext heuristic is $O(n + \sigma + \sigma \cdot lbr)$.

The upper bounds are harder to calculate, and there is not much research on them. The upper bound for r (abbreviated *ubr*) gives us the maximum value for r, which is worth searching for. The fastest non-trivial upper bound method is based on counting the frequencies of all symbols of Σ in both input strings and taking the sum over the minimum frequencies. This method is extremely fast and performs well, when the character distribution in the input strings is different. Unfortunately, when the distribution of symbols in both input strings is very similar, this heuristic performs poorly. In spite of its inferior performance for the similar character distributions, we selected this upper bound heuristic in the lack of adequately fast alternative methods. The running time for the selected upper bound heuristic is $O(n + \sigma)$.

If a reliable *lbr* is available, that can be used for pruning the search space of the NKY algorithm. Let us assume that *lbr* in the actual problem instance is $k + h$. Further, we will suppose that a *cs* of length *k*-1 has been found when processing the current diagonal *d*. If we do not find the *k*'th matching symbol until *h* symbols of *Y* are left, the processing of the diagonal *d* can be interrupted, because an adequately long lcs cannot be found during this round. All the additional processing along the diagonal *d* would be unnecessary. The more accurate the lower bound, the greater are the possibilities to prune the search space. In Example 3, the processing of the 1'st diagonal could be interrupted after scanning the index 3 of the input string *X*, if *lbr* were 4. Generally, numerous expensive matrix operations can be avoided by taking advantage of a reliable lower bound. Sometimes it is true that the lcs consists solely of the common suffixes of the input strings. Then a reliable upper bound could possibly interrupt the execution of the algorithm much earlier than without that information. The running time of the modified NKY algorithm is roughly $O((n(m-r)) + (n + \sigma + \sigma \cdot lbr))$, but the simulation tests showed that it practically never performs worse than the original NKY algorithm.

When the memory space need is concerned, it can be noticed that no diagonal has to be longer than *ubr*. This is an adequate length for all the diagonals from 0 to $m + 2 - ubr$. After that diagonal, the size of each diagonal diminishes by one. The execution of the algorithm will not be continued after the diagonal $m + 1 - lbr$. The maximal space need is $ubr(m + 2 - ubr) + (ubr + lbr-1) \cdot (ubr - lbr) / 2$. The formal description of the NKY-MODIF algorithm will be given next.

Input: sequences X[1..m] and Y[1..n], m <= n.
Output: sequence lcs[1..r] of pairs <index of X, index of Y>.

r = length of the lcs so far   s = length of the current cs   i = traverse index of X

j = traverse index of Y   d = index of diagonal   lowerY = lower bound for j

upperY = proper upper bound for j (upperY- 1)   lastY = upper bound for

---

```
d <- m
r <- 0
skipX <- 0
lastY <- n
rUpper <- upperBound(X[1..m], Y[1..n])
rLower <- lowerBound(X[1..m], Y[1..n])
M[0..(m + 2 - rUpper)][1..offset] <- 0
while r < min { d, rUpper - 1 } do
    i <- d - (n - lastY)
    s <- 1 + (n - lastY)
    upperY <- lastY + 1

    // Calculate M[.][.] on the diagonal d.

    while i ≠ 0 and upperY ≠ 0 do
        lowerY <-
            max { 1, M[m - d][s], rLower - s }
        upperY <-
            max { j | lowerY <= j < upperY
                and X[i] = Y[j] }
            or M[m - d][s] if no such j exist
        if upperY < rLower - s then

            // Exit diagonal loop.

            upperY <- 0
```

else
  M[m - d + 1][s] <- upperY
  if upperY = lastY **then**
    lastY <- lastY - 1
  endif
  while (1 < upperY) and
    (upperY - 1) = M[m - d][s + 1]
do

  // Run encountered.

    M[m - d + 1][s + 1] = upperY - 1
    s <- s + 1
    i <- i - 1
    upperY <- upperY - 1
  endwhile
endif
if upperY = 0 **then**
  s <- s - 1

endif
r <- max { r, s }
i <- i - 1
s <- s + 1
endwhile
  d <- d - 1
endwhile

// Recover the lcs.

d <- m - d
for k <- r downto 1 **do**
  while M[d][k] = 0 **or**
    M[d][k] = M[d - 1][k] **do**
    d <- d - 1
  endwhile
  lcs[k] = <m + 2 - (d + k),
M[d][k]>
endfor

Figure 2: *The formal description of the NKY-MODIF algorithm*

3.5   Solving Only the Length of the Lcs

We have until this point worried mainly about calculating both r and lcs. If, however, solving only r is enough, also in that case all our new features can be taken advantage of. The only, but not inferior change is the size of the needed memory space. If the lcs does not have to be collected, it is enough to maintain only the information stored in the last processed two diagonals of the matrix. That means that instead of a matrix, only two diagonal arrays are needed. The sufficient length for those arrays is *ubr*.

4   Practical Impact

In order to validate and verify the practical usefulness of the ideas presented in the previous section, numerous simulation tests were performed. All the compared algorithms were written in the C programming language. When compiling the programs, gcc version 3.2 was used with optimization –O3. The tests were run on a Pentium IV (1.8 GHz) under Red Hat Linux 8.0 3.2-7. The space allocation and de-allocation for data structures was planned carefully and fairly. The original NKY version was implemented following exactly the algorithm description of its authors. Tests were performed using both uniform and skew (Zipfian) character distribution. Further, tests runs for both problem variants were executed. The length of the input strings was held fixed — 5000 characters for both input strings. For each type of test case, 50 repetitions were made. Also the differences in the actual memory space consumption were measured. To be convinced of the usefulness of a lower bound heuristic also to other types of lcs algorithms, the influence of the lower bound heuristic was tested also on one row-wise and one column-wise processing lcs method.

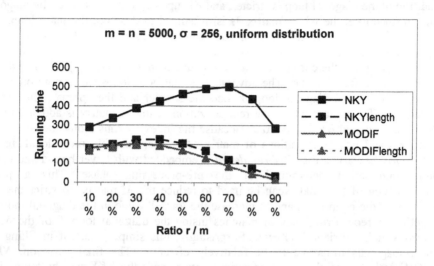

Figure 3: *Running times, when m = n = 5000, σ = 256, uniform character distribution, the ratio r / m ranges from 10 % to 90 %*

When considering Figure 3, it can be noticed that the original NKY algorithm is much slower than the NKY-MODIF variant, when the lcs is being solved. The modified *lcs*-variant outperforms even the *r*-variant of the original NKY. The difference between the two heuristic variants is amazingly small. It can be seen that the running time curves have a shape reminding a parabola. The shape of the curves is not completely in tune with the theoretical complexity of the NKY algorithm and its modified variants. The problem should become easier when the ratio *r / m* increases, but the problem seems to be hardest when the lcs ratio is near to 70 %. That phenomenon can be interpreted by taking the amount of necessary matrix operations into consideration. If the lcs is very short, several diagonals have to be processed, but this can be done with only few updates for each diagonal. When the ratio *r / m* is approximately 50-70 %, the percentage of filled matrix cells is highest. It is not problematic to believe that scanning the long string parts without stopping is faster than inspecting a little shorter string parts with more frequently repeated interrupts caused by the necessary matrix updates. In this figure, the superiority of the modified versions over the original ones can be observed. Only, when the ratio *r / m* is very low, the original and the modified *r*-variants perform approximately equally. In other words, the calculation of the upper and lower bounds does not have any significant harmful influence on the running time, although the band between the calculated lower and upper bounds could be broad, and thus the usage of the bound value information cannot be reflected as an improved running time. When a smaller alphabet size, e.g. $\sigma = 4$ is concerned, the shapes of the appropriate curves are almost similar.

In order to understand how the proposed refinements contribute to the NKY-MODIF method, we phase in six improvements one-by-one starting from the original NKY algorithm and compare their effects. We denote *NKY* the straightforward implementation of the original NKY algorithm. In the *NKY-adjusted* variant the exit condition of the diagonal loop is stricter, and r is updated only once after the diagonal loop. Furthermore, the whole matrix M is initialized to 0 before the main loop, and thus the edge marking of the diagonal loop can be discarded. The *NKY-split* variant divides the diagonal loop of the *NKY-adjusted* into two loops: a for-loop handles the definite r (length of the current lcs) cases first, and then a while-loop possibly extends this longest lcs found so far. The advantage is that both loops, from now on called diagonal loop F and diagonal loop W, become simpler and they prepare the further refinements. The variant where the reorganization of the M matrix is added into the *NKY-split*, is called *NKY-reindexed*. Because the indexing runs along the diagonals, the access and update operations of matrix M are considerably more local. In the *NKY-heuristics* variant the *NKY-reindexed* is embedded with lower bound and upper bound information determined at the pre-processing phase. This a priori approximation of the final r can be used to reduce the M matrix, to strict the exit condition of the main loop, and to increase the *lowerY* value in the diagonal loop W. Detection of reoccurring runs of matches inside the diagonal loop F of the *NKY-heuristics* yields variant *NKY-runs*. Surprisingly, this simple shortcut in filling the matrix diagonals turns out to be relatively effective. The final variation, *NKY-MODIF*, including all the proposed refinements extends the *NKY-runs* by taking into account the optimal suffixes in Y. This idea can be applied inside the both diagonal loops cost-efficiently.

Table 1 shows the results of the gradual refinements of the algorithm variations. Each row represents one algorithm variant and the values are run-time improvements from the *NKY* to that variant in percentages. The character distribution in X and Y is uniform, and σ is 256.

r/m	0.10	0.20	0.30	0.40	0.50	0.60	0.70	0.80	0.90
NKY-adjusted	13.9	13.8	13.7	13.3	14.3	13.7	12.9	11.3	8.2
NKY-split	14.1	14.4	14.6	14.6	15.4	15.3	15.7	14.3	12.3
NKY-reindexed	30.8	35.5	40.1	45.8	55.7	66.1	76.3	83.6	88.8
NKY-heuristics	29.4	34.9	41.0	48.3	58.1	68.5	78.3	84.9	89.7
NKY-runs	36.0	40.3	45.0	51.2	61.1	71.5	81.3	87.9	92.3
NKY-MODIF	37.9	42.5	47.5	53.2	63.0	72.9	82.7	88.8	93.3

Table 1: *The improvements in running times from the original NKY algorithm to the gradually refined variants of the NKY-MODIF for $\sigma = 256$, uniform character distribution*

The basic adjustments (*NKY-adjusted*) and splitting the diagonal loop (*NKY-split*) give only about 14-15% gain in run-time. However, their main contribution is a clearer algorithmic structure for further improvements. The reorganization of the matrix calculations (*NKY-reindexed*) gives the basic efficiency for the NKY-MODIF and it is the most effective single development in the refinement chain. Utilization of the lower and upper bound information (*NKY-heuristics*) causes a slight overhead for low r / m ratios, but gains 5-8 % for similar input sequences. The combination *NKY-heuristics* reinforced with runs is complemented for dissimilar inputs by recognition of the optimal *Y*-suffixes.

The utilization of a priori knowledge on the r is not specific for the NKY algorithm only. In order to demonstrate that it can be applied also into other lcs algorithms, we embedded a lower bound heuristic also into two other kinds of methods: Kuo & Cross (*KC*) [17] and Chin & Poon (*CP*) [6]. These algorithms were selected because they belong into different kinds of lcs solving approaches: the *KC* processes the input strings in a row-wise order, and the *CP* solves the lcs contour by contour. The new versions are called *KC+heur* and *CP+heur*.

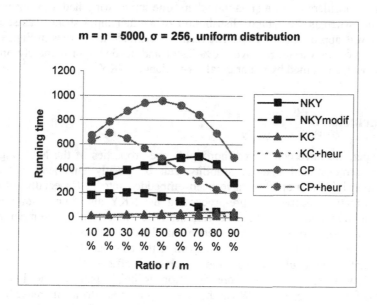

Figure 4: *Comparison of three differently processing original lcs algorithms against new, lower bound heuristic utilizing variants, $\sigma = 256$, uniform character distribution*

In Figure 4, the lower bound heuristic BestNext is embedded to three original lcs algorithms with a different processing manner. Considering each original method and its new variant with an embedded lower bound heuristic it can be noticed that the refined version using heuristic search space pruning almost always performs better. Only, when the ratio r / m is near to zero, the refined variants may perform a little bit worse than the original method, but in practice, nothing can be lost by applying a lower bound heuristic into the original algorithms. It is also worth mentioning that the benefits for the refined versions are evidently more noticeable, when the symbol distribution is skew. For such inputs, the probability for finding non-matching symbols from either input string increases, which enables the heuristic to cut the search space more effectively.

The utilization of heuristic lower and upper bounds has a remarkable effect on the space need for the NKY-MODIF algorithm. Whereas alternating the ratio r / m has no influence on the memory space need for the lcs-variant of the original NKY algorithm, the memory consumption of NKY-MODIF decreases at least by 50% compared with original NKY method, when the ratio r / m is approximately 70% or higher. The higher the value r / m increases, the more dramatically the space-efficiency of NKY-MODIF improves against the original NKY, because the lower bound prevents the allocation of surely not needed diagonals. That result is very encouraging, when long input strings having a high r / m ratio have to be handled. Also, when the ratio r / m is low and the input strings have a rather different symbol distribution, the upper bound heuristic limits effectively the maximum length of the diagonals. Only, when ubr is near to m and lbr near to 0, the heuristic bounds are totally useless.

We considered also a situation where one input string had a uniform symbol distribution, whereas the symbol distribution of another input string was skew. The ratio r / m was approximately 29%. The results resembled the curves in Figures 3 and 4: the modified lcs-variant ran over 30% faster and needed approximately only 65% of the memory consumed by the original lcs-variant of NKY.

5   Conclusions

In this paper, we have considered thoroughly the properties of the NKY algorithm. We have demonstrated that its usability can be greatly enhanced, when some intelligent additional properties have been embedded into it. Especially, utilizing a priori information received by pre-processing the NKY algorithm with lower and upper bound heuristics enables a faster running time and a shrinkage in memory space need. It was also verified that in practice that kind of pre-processing never has a negative influence on the running time, even if the calculated heuristic results were non-informative and could not prune the search space efficiently.

Nowadays, more and more attention is being paid to the linear space algorithms for the lcs problem. When the sizes of the input strings increase heavily, it can be with justice assumed that the main bottleneck in the lcs algorithms is actually the space complexity instead of the running time complexity. However, to our knowledge, there does not exist any lcs algorithm, which does not solve r before returning the sequence. So it can be for good reason claimed that especially the heuristic pre-processing could be useful even for the linear space lcs algorithms. To the class of the newest and the most sophisticated such algorithms belong e.g. the algorithms of Rick [18] and Goeman & Clausen [19]. It is worth mentioning that even those two methods need a pre-processing phase the space complexity of which is $O(n\sigma)$. When the size of input alphabet increases strongly, the possibilities for using direct access methods (closest-matrices etc.) when scanning the input strings deteriorate undoubtedly. As a crucial conclusion of this paper we can express, that the usage of heuristic methods to improve any original lcs method is a very fruitful field of research in the future.

References

1. Wagner, R. A. & Fischer, M. J.: The string to string correction problem, Journal of the Association for Computing Machinery, Vol. 21, nr 1, pages 168-173, 1974
2. Hirschberg, Daniel S.: Algorithms for the Longest Common Subsequence problem, Journal of the Association for Computing Machinery, Vol. 24, nr 4, pages 664-675, October 1977
3. Hunt, James W. & Szymanski, Thomas G.: A Fast Algorithm for Computing Longest Common Subsequences, Communications of the ACM, Vol. 20, nr 5, pages 350-353, may 1977
4. Mukhopadhyay, Amar: A Fast Algorithm for the Longest-Common-Subsequence Problem, Information Sciences 20, pages 69-82, Elsevier North Holland Inc., 1980
5. Bergroth, L & Hakonen H & Raita T: A Survey of Longest Common Subsequence Algorithms, Proceedings of SPIRE 2000, A Coruña, Spain, 2000, pages 39 to 47
6. Chin, Francis Y. L. & Poon, C. K.: A Fast Algorithm for Computing Longest Common Subsequences of Small Alphabet Size, Journal of Information Processing, Vol. 13 nr 4, pages 463-469, 1990
7. Hsu, W. J. & Du, M. W.: New Algorithms for the LCS Problem, Journal of Computer and System Sciences 29, pages 133-152, 1984
8. Apostolico, A. & Guerra, C.: The Longest Common Subsequence Problem Revisited, Algorithmica (1987) 2: pages 315-336, Springer-Verlag
9. Rick, Claus: New Algorithms for the Longest Common Subsequence Problem, Institut für Informatik der Universität Bonn, Research Report No. 85123-Cs, October 1994
10. Miller, Webb & Myers, Eugene W.: A File Comparison Program, Software — Practice and Experience, Vol. 15(11), pages 1025-1040, November 1985
11. Myers, Eugene W.: An O(ND) Difference Algorithm and Its Variations, Algorithmica (1986) 1: pages 251 – 266, Springer-Verlag
12. Wu, Sun & Manber, Udi & Myers, Gene & Miller, Webb: An O(NP) Sequence Comparison Algorithm, Information Processing Letter 35 (1990), North-Holland, pages 317-323
13. Nakatsu, Narao & Kambayashi, Yahiko & Yajima, Shuzo: A Longest Common Subsequence Suitable for Similar Text Strings, Acta Informatica 18, pages 171-179, Springer-Verlag 1982
14. Chin, F & Poon, C. K: Performance Analysis of Some Simple Heuristics for Longest Common Subsequences, Algorithmica, 12: 293-311, 1994
15. Bergroth, L. & Hakonen H. & Raita T.: New Approximation Algorithms for Longest Common Subsequences, Proceedings of SPIRE 98, Santa Cruz de la Sierra, Bolivia, September 1998
16. Johtela, T. & Smed, J. & Hakonen, H. & Raita, T.: An Efficient Heuristic for the LCS Problem, Third South American Workshop on String Processing, WSP'96, Recife, Brazil, August 1996, pp. 126-140
17. Kuo, Shufen & Cross, George R.: An Improved Algorithm to Find the Length of the Longest Common Subsequence of Two Strings, ACM SIGIR Forum, Spring / Summer 1989, Vol. 23, No. 3-4, pages 89-99
18. Rick, Claus: Simple and Fast Linear Space Computation of Longest Common Subsequences. Information Processing Letters 75(6): 275-281 (2000)
19. Goeman, H. & Clausen, M.: A New Practical Linear Space Algorithm for the Longest Common Subsequence Problem, Proceedings of the Prague Stringology Club Workshop '99

The Size of Subsequence Automaton

Zdeněk Troníček[1*] and Ayumi Shinohara[2,3]

[1] Department of Computer Science & Engineering, Faculty of Electrical Engineering
Czech Technical University, Prague
tronicek@fel.cvut.cz
[2] Department of Informatics, Kyushu University 33, Fukuoka 812-8581, Japan
[3] PRESTO, Japan Science and Technology Corporation (JST)
ayumi@i.kyushu-u.ac.jp

Abstract. Given a set of strings, the subsequence automaton accepts all subsequences of these strings. We will derive a lower bound for the maximum number of states of this automaton. We will prove that the size of the subsequence automaton for a set of k strings of length n is $\Omega(n^k)$ for any $k \geq 1$. It solves an open problem posed by Crochemore and Troníček [2] in 1999, in which only the case $k \leq 2$ was shown.

1 Introduction

A *subsequence* of a string T is any string obtainable by deleting zero or more symbols from T. Given a set P of strings, a *common subsequence* of P is a string that is a subsequence of every string in P. Motivation for study of subsequences comes from many domains, *e.g.* from molecular biology, signal processing, coding theory, and artificial intelligence.

An example of the problem with great practical impact is the longest common subsequence (LCS) problem. The problem is defined as follows: given a set P of strings, we are to find a common subsequence of P that has maximal length among all common subsequences of P. The decision version can be, for example, to decide whether a given string is a common subsequence of P. Another problem, which comes from artificial intelligence, is the problem of separating two sets of strings: given two sets P (positive) and N (negative) of strings, we are to find a string that best separates them. A string S separates sets P and N if S is a subsequence of P and simultaneously is not a subsequence of any string in N. The decision version is defined as follows: given two sets P and N of strings and a string S, we are to decide whether S separates P and N. If the problem is supposed to be answered for several strings S then it is sensible to preprocess the sets P and N. We can build the automaton accepting all common subsequences of P and the automaton that accepts any string that is a subsequence of at least one string in N. With these automata we can decide the problem in time linear in the length of S. Both automata were studied and described. The first one is called the Common Subsequence Automaton (CSA) and two algorithms for

---

* supported by GAČR grant 201/01/1433

M.A. Nascimento, E.S. de Moura, A.L. Oliveira (Eds.): SPIRE 2003, LNCS 2857, pp. 304–310, 2003.

its building, off-line [2] and on-line [6], were designed. The second automaton is known as the Directed Acyclic Subsequence Graph (DASG) and three building algorithms are available: right-to-left [1], left-to-right [2], and on-line [4].

In this paper, we investigate the number of states of the CSA. As the language accepted by the CSA is a subset of the language accepted by the DASG for the same strings, the automata are very similar. If we use the off-line or on-line algorithm, the set of states of the CSA is a subset of states of the DASG. The only previous results are, according to our knowledge, the lower bound for the maximum number of states of the DASG for two strings proved in [3] and of the CSA for two strings derived in [6]. We will prove the same lower bound for any (fixed) number of strings. The paper is organized as follows. In Section 2 we will recall the definition of the CSA from [2] and in Section 3 we will examine the asymptotic behaviour of the number of states of the CSA in the worst case.

Let Σ be a finite alphabet of size σ. A finite automaton is, in this paper, a 5-tuple $(Q, \Sigma, \delta, q_0, F)$, where Q is a finite set of states, Σ is an input alphabet, $\delta : Q \times \Sigma \to Q$ is a transition function, q_0 is the initial state, and $F \subseteq Q$ is the set of final states. Notation $\langle i, j \rangle$ means the interval of integers from i to j, including both i and j. All strings in this paper are considered on alphabet Σ, if not stated otherwise.

2   Definition of CSA

Let P denote the set of strings $T_1, T_2, \ldots, T_k$. Let n_i be the length of T_i and $T_i[j]$ be j-th symbol of T_i for all $j \in \langle 1, n_i \rangle$ and all $i \in \langle 1, k \rangle$. Given $T = t_1 t_2 \ldots t_n$ and $i, j \in \langle 1, n \rangle, i \leq j$, notation $T[i \ldots j]$ means the string $t_i t_{i+1} \ldots t_j$.

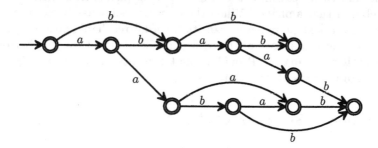

Fig. 1. The CSA for strings *ababab* and *aabaab*.

Definition 1. *We define a position point of the set P as an ordered k-tuple $[p_1, p_2, \ldots, p_k]$, where $p_i \in \langle 0, n_i \rangle$ is a position in string T_i. If $p_i \in \langle 0, n_i - 1 \rangle$ then it denotes the position in front of $(p_i + 1)$-th symbol of T_i, and if $p_i = n_i$ then it denotes the position behind the last symbol of T_i for all $i \in \langle 1, k \rangle$.*

A position point $[p_1, p_2, \ldots, p_k]$ is called *initial position point* if $p_i = 0$ for all $i \in \langle 1, k \rangle$. We denote by $ipp(P)$ the initial position point of P and by $Pos(P)$ the set of all position points of P.

Definition 2. *For a position point* $[p_1, p_2, \ldots, p_k] \in Pos(P)$ *we define the common subsequence position alphabet as the set of all symbols which are contained simultaneously in* $T_1[p_1+1 \ldots n_1], \ldots, T_k[p_k+1 \ldots n_k]$, *i.e.* $\Sigma_{cp}([p_1, p_2, \ldots, p_k]) = \{a \in \Sigma : \forall i \in \langle 1, k \rangle \exists j \in \langle p_i + 1, n_i \rangle : T_i[j] = a\}.$

Definition 3. *For* $a \in \Sigma$ *and a position point* $[p_1, p_2, \ldots, p_k] \in Pos(P)$ *we define the common subsequence transition function:*
$csf([p_1, p_2, \ldots, p_k], a) = [r_1, r_2, \ldots, r_k]$, *where* $r_i = min\{j : j > p_i$ *and*
$T_i[j] = a\}$ *for all* $i \in \langle 1, k \rangle$ *if* $a \in \Sigma_{cp}([p_1, p_2, \ldots, p_k])$, *and*
$csf([p_1, p_2, \ldots, p_k], a) = \emptyset$ *otherwise.*
Let csf^* *be reflexive-transitive closure of* csf.

Lemma 1. *The automaton* $(Pos(P), \Sigma, csf, ipp(P), Pos(P))$ *accepts a string* S *iff* S *is a subsequence of* P.

Proof. See [2]. □

The automaton from Lemma 1 is called the *Common Subsequence Automaton* (CSA) for strings $T_1, T_2, \ldots, T_k$. An example of the CSA is in Fig. 1.

Up to now, two algorithms for building the CSA have been described. The first one is off-line and uses the position points. The second one is on-line and in each step loads one input string into the automaton.

We will briefly describe the off-line algorithm. The algorithm generates step by step all reachable position points (states). At each step we process one position point. First, we will find the common subsequence position alphabet for this point and then determine the common subsequence transition function for each symbol of that alphabet. When the position point has been processed, we continue with a next point until transitions of all reachable position points are determined. The complexity of the algorithm depends on the number of states of the resulting automaton. Providing that the total number of states is $O(t)$, the algorithm requires $O(k\sigma t)$ time.

3 Number of States of CSA

We will investigate the number of states (reachable position points) of the CSA for a set of strings on binary alphabet. First, we will introduce an auxiliary structure. The *generating tree* is defined as a general tree where nodes and edges are labeled with an integer value. If the node is labeled with value v, we say that it is of order v. A node of order v has output edges labeled with $1, 2, \ldots, v$. Every edge is going to the node labeled with the same value as this edge. If the root of the tree is of order k, we say that the tree is of order k. An example of the tree of order 3 is in Fig. 2. We will use the tree to describe the set of strings. A path from the root corresponds to a string on alphabet $\{a, b\}$. All nodes but the root will contribute by b. An edge labeled with ℓ will add a^ℓ. For example, path $root \xrightarrow{4} node(4) \xrightarrow{2} node(2) \xrightarrow{1} node(1)$ corresponds to string $aaaabaabab$.

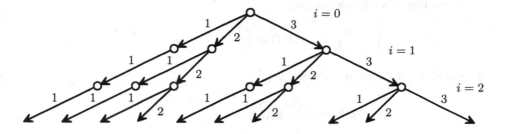

Fig. 2. The generating tree of order 3.

A node has at most one output edge for a given value, therefore no two strings generated by the tree are identical.

In the subsequent, we will consider the tree of order k and denote, for $i \in Z, i \geq 0$, by $p(k, i)$ the number of nodes on ith level of this tree. Furthermore, we will denote by $p_j(k, i), 1 \leq j \leq k$ the number of nodes on ith level which are labeled with value of j. There is just one node of order k on each level, that is $p_k(k, i) = 1$. On the 0th level, there is only one node (root). A node of order j on ith level has descendants of orders $1, 2, \ldots, j$ on $(i + 1)$th level. In other words, the node of order j on ith level is a descendant either of the node of order j or of higher order on $(i-1)$th level. The number of these nodes of higher order is the same as the number of nodes of order $j + 1$ on ith level. That is, $p_j(k, i) = p_j(k, i - 1) + p_{j+1}(k, i)$, where $i > 0$ and $1 \leq j < k$. This formula is known from combinatorics and holds for combinatorial numbers. For further discussion we will use Pascal's triangle which is a common means for expressing the relations between combinatorial numbers.

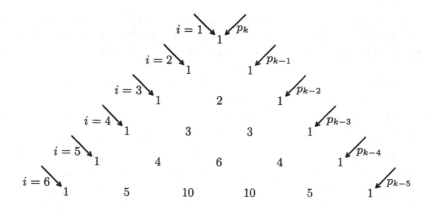

Fig. 3. The top of Pascal's triangle.

From Pascal's triangle we get:

$$p_k(k, i) = \binom{i-1}{0}, \ p_{k-1}(k, i) = \binom{i}{1}, \ldots, p_1(k, i) = \binom{i+k-1}{k-1}.$$

The number of nodes on ith level is hence

$$p(k, i) = \sum_{j=1}^{k} p_j(k, i) = \binom{i+k-1}{k-1}.$$

And the total number of nodes up to nth level is

$$p(k) = \sum_{i=1}^{n} \binom{i+k-1}{k-1} = \binom{n+k}{k}.$$

The formula for $p(k)$ determines how many strings ending with b will be generated by the tree of order k if we consider the first n levels of this tree.

Lemma 2. Let $k \in Z, k \geq 2, n_i \in Z$ for all $i \in \langle 1, k \rangle$, and $n_j \geq 2n_{j+1}$ for all $j \in \langle 1, k-1 \rangle$. Let $T_1 = (ab)^{n_1}, T_2 = (aab)^{n_2}, \ldots, T_k = (a^k b)^{n_k}, L_k = \{T_1, T_2, \ldots, T_k\}$, and δ denote the transition function of the CSA for L_k. Let M_k be the set of strings generated by the generating tree of order k. Then for all $u, v \in M_k, u \neq v$, is $\delta^*(ipp(P), u) \neq \delta^*(ipp(P), v)$.

Proof. (by induction in k): Let M_k^ℓ denote the set of strings from the ℓth level of the generating tree of order k.
1. $k = 2 : M_2^\ell = \{(ab)^\ell, aab(ab)^{\ell-1}, (aab)^2(ab)^{\ell-2}, \ldots, (aab)^\ell\}$. If two strings contain different number of b's they cannot result in shift to the same position in T_2. Therefore we can consider only the strings with the same number of b's. For given $\ell \in Z, \ell \geq 1$, all strings in M_2^ℓ have the same number of b's. But simultaneously, no such two strings have the same number of a's. Thus, the transition function will finish at the same position in T_2 and always at different position in T_1.
2. Let $n_{k+1} \in Z, n_k \geq 2n_{k+1}$. We add $T_{k+1} = (a^{k+1}b)^{n_{k+1}}$ into set L_k, that is $L_{k+1} = L_k \cup \{T_{k+1}\}$. According to the induction hypothesis the lemma holds for k. We will show that it holds for $k+1$ too by using induction in height h of the tree:
(a) $h = 1 : M_{k+1}^1 = \{ab, aab, \ldots, a^{k+1}b\}$. No two strings from this set have the same number of a's, thus the lemma holds.
(b) The hypothesis says that the lemma holds for $M_{k+1}^1, M_{k+1}^2, \ldots, M_{k+1}^h$. We will prove that it holds also for M_{k+1}^{h+1}. From the generating tree we get: $M_{k+1}^{h+1} = M_k^{h+1} \cup \{a^{k+1}bs, s \in M_{k+1}^h\}$. According to the induction hypotheses the lemma holds for M_k^{h+1} and M_{k+1}^h. Any string from M_k^{h+1} will result in shift to the $(h+1)$th b in T_k. Furthermore, $a^{k+1}b$ will make shift to the second b in T_k and because any string in M_{k+1}^h contains i symbols b, the lemma holds also for M_{k+1}^{h+1}.
□

Lemma 3. *Let $k \in Z, k \geq 2, n_i \in Z$ for all $i \in \langle 1, k \rangle$, and $n_j \geq 2n_{j+1}$ for all $j \in \langle 1, k-1 \rangle$. Let $T_1 = (ab)^{n_1}, T_2 = (aab)^{n_2}, \ldots, T_k = (a^k b)^{n_k}, L_k = \{T_1, T_2, \ldots, T_k\}$, and δ denote the transition function of the CSA for L_k. Let M_k be the set of strings generated by the generating tree of order k. Then for all $u, v \in M_k$ and all $x, y \in \{a, aa, \ldots, a^k\}, ux \neq vy$ is $\delta^*(ipp(P), ux) \neq \delta^*(ipp(P), vy)$.*

Proof. We put $\delta^*(ipp(P), u) = p$ and $\delta^*(ipp(P), v) = q$. If $p = q$ then according to Lemma 2 is $u = v$ and hence $x \neq y$. The lemma is obviously true in this case. If $p \neq q$ then either $p_k = q_k$ or $p_k \neq q_k$. If $p_k = q_k$ then either $x = y$ or $x \neq y$. For $x \neq y$ is the lemma obvious. We will consider $x = y$. From $p \neq q$ we get that there exists $\ell \in Z, 1 \leq \ell \leq k$ such that $p_\ell \neq q_\ell$. If we skip the same number of a's in T_ℓ, the positions will still differ. Hence the lemma holds in this case. For $p_k \neq q_k$ the lemma also holds because by reading any string from $\{a, aa, \ldots, a^k\}$ we will never cross b in T_k. □

The Lemma 3 shows that we can consider not only strings ending with b, *i.e.* ending in nodes of the generating tree, but we can add any string from $\{a, aa, \ldots, a^k\}$ as a suffix.

Lemma 4. *Let $k \in Z, k \geq 2, n_i \in Z$ for all $i \in \langle 1, k \rangle$ and $n_j \geq 2n_{j+1}$ for all $j \in \langle 1, k-1 \rangle$. Let $T_1 = (ab)^{n_1}, T_2 = (aab)^{n_2}, \ldots, T_k = (a^k b)^{n_k}, L_k = \{T_1, T_2, \ldots, T_k\}$ and $n = n_k$ Then the number of states of the CSA for L_k is $\Omega(n^k)$.*

Proof. The lemma directly follows from Lemma 2 and the formula for the number of strings generated by the generating tree. □

We note again that the result of Lemma 2 is applicable also for the DASG.

4   Conclusion

We checked that the maximum number of states of the subsequence automaton for k strings of length $O(n)$ is $\Omega(n^k)$. We also dealt with the problem of tight upper bound for the number of states. By exhaustive searching we found the worst cases for several lengths of input strings and verified in [5] that the sequence of the maximum numbers of the states does not form any well-known integer sequence.

References

[1] R. A. Baeza-Yates. Searching subsequences. *Theor. Comput. Sci.*, 78(2):363–376, 1991.

[2] M. Crochemore and Z. Troníček. Directed acyclic subsequence graph for multiple texts. Rapport I.G.M. 99-13, Université de Marne-la-Vallée, 1999.

[3] M. Crochemore and Z. Troníček. On the size of DASG for multiple texts. In *Proceedings of the Symposium on String Processing and Information Retrieval 2002*, pages 58–64, Lisbon, 2002.

[4] H. Hoshino, A. Shinohara, M. Takeda, and S. Arikawa. Online construction of subsequence automata for multiple texts. In *Proceedings of the Symposium on String Processing and Information Retrieval 2000*, La Coruña, Spain, 2000. IEEE Computer Society Press.

[5] N. J. A. Sloane. The on-line encyclopedia of integer sequences. http://www.research.att.com/~njas/sequences/.

[6] Z. Troníček. Common subsequence automaton. In *International Conference on Implementation and Application of Automata 2002*, Tours, France, 2002.

Distributed Query Processing Using Suffix Arrays

Mauricio Marín[1,3] and Gonzalo Navarro[2,3]

[1] Dept. of Computer Science
University of Magallanes
mmarin@ona.fi.umag.cl
[2] Dept. of Computer Science
University of Chile
gnavarro@dcc.uchile.cl
[3] Center for Web Research (www.cwr.cl)*

Abstract. Suffix arrays are more efficient than inverted files for solving complex queries in a number of applications related to text databases. Examples arise when dealing with biological or musical data or with texts written in oriental languages, and when searching for phrases, approximate patterns and, in general, regular expressions involving separators. In this paper we propose algorithms for processing in parallel batches of queries upon distributed text databases. We present efficient alternatives for speeding up query processing using distributed realizations of suffix arrays. Empirical results obtained from natural language text on a cluster of PCs show that the proposed algorithms are efficient in practice.

1 Introduction

In the last decade, the design of efficient data structures and algorithms for textual databases and related applications has received a great deal of attention due to the rapid growth of the Web [3]. Typical applications are those known as client-server in which users take advantage of specialized services available at dedicated sites [4]. For the cases in which the number and type of services demanded by clients is such that it generates a very heavy work-load on the server, the server efficiency in terms of running time is of paramount importance. As such it is not difficult to see that the only feasible way to overcome limitations of sequential computers is to resort to the use of several computers or processors working together to service the ever increasing demands of clients.

An approach to efficient parallelization is to split up the data collection and distribute it onto the processors in such a way that it becomes feasible to exploit locality by effecting parallel processing of user requests, each upon a subset of the data. As opposed to shared memory models, this distributed memory model provides the benefit of better scalability [7]. However, it introduces new problems related to the communication and synchronization of processors and

---

* Funded by Millennium Nucleus CWR, Grant P01-029-F, Mideplan, Chile.

M.A. Nascimento, E.S. de Moura, A.L. Oliveira (Eds.): SPIRE 2003, LNCS 2857, pp. 311–325, 2003.

their load balance. This paper describes strategies to overcome these problems in the context of the parallelization of suffix arrays [3]. We propose strategies for reduction of inter-processors communication and load balancing.

The advent of powerful processors and cheap storage has allowed the consideration of alternative models for information retrieval other than the traditional one of a collection of documents indexed by keywords. One such a model which is gaining popularity is the *full text* model. In this model documents are represented by either their complete full text or extended abstracts. The user expresses his/her information need via words, phrases or patterns to be matched for and the information system retrieves those documents containing the user specified strings. While the cost of searching the full text is usually high, the model is powerful, requires no structure in the text, and is conceptually simple [3].

To reduce the cost of searching a full text, specialized indexing structures are adopted. The most popular of these are *inverted lists* [3, 1, 2]. *Suffix arrays* or PAT *arrays* [3] are more sophisticated indexing structures which take space close to the text size. They are superior to inverted lists for searching phrases or complex queries such as regular expressions [3]. In addition, suffix arrays can be used to index texts other than occidental natural languages, which have clearly separated words that follow some convenient statistical rules [3]. Examples of these applications include computational biology (ADN or protein strings), music retrieval (MIDI or audio files), oriental languages (Chinese, Korean, and others), and other multimedia data files.

The suffix array uses a binary search based strategy. Processing a single T-chars-size query in a text of size N takes $O(T \log N)$ time on the standard sequential suffix array. Thus trying to reduce such time by using a P-processors distributed memory parallel computer is not very attractive in practical terms.

In this paper we assume a server site at which lots of queries are arriving per unit of time. Such work-load can be serviced by taking batches of Q queries each. Processing batches in parallel is appealing in this context as one is more interested on improving the throughput of the whole process than single operations. To achieve this goal a pragmatic (though naive) strategy would be to keep a copy of the whole text database and index in each server machine and route the queries uniformly at random among the P machines. This can be acceptable.

For very large databases, however, the non-cooperating machines are forced to keep large pieces of their identical suffix arrays in secondary memory, which can degrade performance dramatically. A more sensible approach is then to keep a single copy of the suffix array distributed evenly onto the P main memories. Now the challenge is to achieve efficient performance on a P-machines server that must communicate and synchronize in order to service every batch of queries. This is not trivial because most array positions are expected to point to text located in remote memory when naive partitioning is employed.

An important fact to consider in natural language texts is that words are not uniformly distributed, both in the text itself and in the queries provided by the users of the system. For example, in the Chilean web (www.todocl.cl) words starting with letters such as "c", "m", "a" and "p" are the most frequent ones. This fact can lead to significant imbalance in the parallel processing of queries.

The efficient index construction using parallel computing techniques has been investigated in [8, 6]. The aim was the construction of a global suffix array for the entire text collection so that queries upon that index can be performed using the standard sequential binary search algorithm. However, the problem of going further on by properly distributing the suffix array on a set of processors to efficiently support parallel processing of batches of queries has not been investigated so far. Note that in [5] a related parallel algorithm was proposed which works upon a distributed Patricia like tree that is constructed upon the suffix array. No implementation was proposed and tested. We perform parallel searching directly on the distributed suffix array with no additional data structure upon it.

In this paper we focus on such form of query processing. We propose efficient parallel algorithms for (1) processing queries grouped in batches on distributed realizations of suffix arrays, and (2) properly load balancing this process when dealing with biased collections of terms such as in natural language texts. In each case our aim is to reduce the communication and synchronization requirements. We explore alternative ways of solving those problems and our empirical results show that the proposed algorithms are efficient in practice.

A valuable feature of the algorithms we propose is that they are devised upon the bulk-synchronous model of parallel computing (BSP model) [10, 12]. This is a distributed memory model with a well-defined structure that enables the prediction of running time. We use this last feature to compare different alternatives for index partitioning by considering their respective effects in communication and synchronization of processors. The model of computation ensures portability at the very fundamental level by allowing algorithm design in a manner that is independent of the architecture of the parallel computer. Shared and distributed memory parallel computers are programmed in the same way. They are considered emulators of the more general bulk-synchronous parallel machine.

The practical model of programming is SPMD, which is realized as P program copies running on the P processors, wherein communication and synchronization among copies is performed by ways of libraries such as BSPlib [13] or BSPub [14]. Note that BSP is actually a paradigm of parallel programming and not a particular communication library. In practice, it is certainly possible to implement BSP programs using the traditional PVM and MPI libraries. A number of studies have shown that bulk-synchronous parallel algorithms lead to more efficient performance than their message-passing or shared-memory counterparts in many applications [10, 11].

2   Suffix Arrays

Suffix arrays or PAT *arrays* [3] are data structures for full text retrieval based on binary searching. Given a text collection, the suffix array contains pointers to the initial positions of all the retrievable strings, for example, all the word beginnings to retrieve words and phrases, or all the text characters to retrieve any substring.

These pointers identify both documents and positions within them. Each such pointer represents a *suffix*, which is the string from that position to the end of the text. The array is sorted in lexicographical order by suffixes as shown in Figure 1. Thus, for example, finding all positions for terms starting with "tex" leads to a binary search to obtain the positions pointed to by the array members 7 and 8 of Figure 1. This search is conducted by direct comparison of the suffixes pointed to by the array elements.

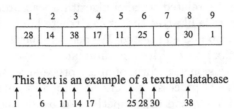

Fig. 1. Suffix array.

3   BSP and the Cost Model

In the bulk-synchronous parallel (BSP) model of computing [12, 10], any parallel computer (e.g., PC cluster, shared or distributed memory multiprocessors) is seen as composed of a set of P processor-local-memory components which communicate with each other through messages. The computation is organized as a sequence of *supersteps*. During a superstep, the processors may perform sequential computations on local data and/or send messages to other processors. The messages are available for processing at their destinations by the next superstep, and each superstep is ended with the barrier synchronization of the processors.

The total running time cost of a BSP program is the cumulative sum of the costs of its supersteps, and the cost of each superstep is the sum of three quantities: w, hG and L, where w is the maximum of the computations performed by each processor, h is the maximum of the messages sent/received by each processor with each word costing G units of running time, and L is the cost of barrier synchronising the processors. The effect of the computer architecture is included by the parameters G and L, which are increasing functions of P. These values along with the processors speed s (e.g. mflops) can be empirically determined for each parallel computer by executing benchmark programs at installation [10].

As an example of a basic BSP algorithm, let us consider a broadcast operation that will be used in this paper. Suppose a processor wants to send a copy of P chapters of a book, each of size a, to all other P processors (itself included). A naive approach would be to send the P chapters to all processors in one superstep. That is, in superstep 1, the sending processor sends P chapters to P processors at a cost of $O(P^2(a + aG) + L)$ units. Thus, in superstep 2 all P

processors have available into their respective incoming message buffers the P chapters of the book. An optimal algorithm for the same problem is as follows. In superstep 1, the sending processor sends just one *different* chapter to each processor at a cost of $O(P(a + aG) + L)$ units. In superstep 2, each processor sends its arriving chapter to all others at a cost of $O(P(a+aG)+L)$ units. Thus, at superstep 2, all processors have a copy of the whole book. Hence the broadcast of a large P-pieces a-sized message can be effected at $O(P(a + aG) + L)$ cost.

We assume a server operating upon a set of P machines, each containing its own memory. Clients request service to one or more *broker* machines, which in turn distribute them evenly onto the P machines implementing the server. Requests are queries that must be solved with the data stored on the P machines. We assume that under a situation of heavy traffic the server processes batches of $Q = qP$ queries. Processing each batch can be considered as a hyperstep composed of one or more BSP supersteps. The value of q should be large enough to properly amortize the communication and synchronization costs of the particular BSP machine.

Observe that hypersteps can be pipelined so that at any superstep we can have one or more cycles at different stages of execution. For the algorithms presented below we assume that in each superstep a new batch starts execution and its computations are performed together with those associated with the solution to previous batches. Typically processing a batch will require two supersteps, thus on average every superstep deals with queries from two different batches.

4   Global versus Local Suffix Arrays

Let us assume that we are interested in determining the text positions in which a given substring x (of length T) is located in. This means that we want all the suffixes starting with x. In the sequential suffix array this can be solved by performing two queries; one with the immediate predecesor and the other with the immediate succesor. This takes $T \log N$ time for a text of N characters. Let us call this operation *interval query*.

A suffix array can be distributed onto the processors using a *global* index approach in which a single array is built from the whole text collection and mapped evenly on the processors. A realization of this idea for the example in Figure 1 is shown in Figure 2 for 2 processors. Notice that in this global index approach each processor stands for a lexicographical interval or range of suffixes (for example, in Figure 2 processor 1 represents suffixes with first letters from "a" to "e"). The broker machine mantains information of the values limiting the intervals in each machine and route queries to the processors accordingly. This fact can be the source of load imbalance in the processors when queries tend to be dynamically biased to particular intervals.

Let us assume the ideal scenario in which the queries are routed uniformly at random onto the processors. A search for all text positions associated with a batch of $Q = qP$ queries can be performed as follows. The broker takes $QT \log P + QTG + L$ time to route the queries to their respective target pro-

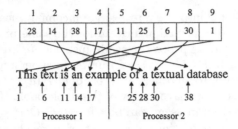

Fig. 2. A global index suffix array distributed on two processors.

cessors (note that this cost can be actually reduced to $QTG + L$ by routing uniformly at random the queries as we propose below). Once the processors get their q queries, in parallel each of them performs q binary searches. Note that for each query, with high probability $1 - 1/P$, it is necessary to get from a remote processor a T-sized piece of text in order to decide the result of the comparison and go to the next step in the search. This reading takes one additional superstep plus the involved cost of communicating T bytes per query. For a global array of size N, the binary search and the respective sending of the array positions are performed at cost $q\,T\,\log(N/P) + (q\,T\,G + L)\,\log(N/P)$. Then the q array positions per processor are received by the broker at cost $Q\,G$ to continue with the following batch and so on. However, it is not necessary to wait for a given batch to finish since in each superstep we can start the processing of a new batch. This forms a pipelining across supersteps in which at any given superstep we have, on average, $\log(N/P)$ batches at different stages of execution. The net effect is that at the end of every superstep we have the completion of a different batch. Thus the total (asymptotic) cost per batch is given by

$$[q\,PT\,\log P + q\,PTG + L] + [q\,T\,\log(N/P) + q\,T\,\log(N/P)\,G + L],$$

where the first term represents the cost of the operations effected by the broker machine whereas the second term is the (pipelined) cost of processing a Q-sized batch in the P-machines server. We call this strategy G0.

As shown in Figure 2 a binary search on the global index approach can lead to a certain number of accesses to remote memory. In BSP, one of these accesses must be done using an additional superstep; in superstep i a processor p sends a message to another processor, it receives the message in superstep $i+1$, reads the string, composes and sends to p a message containing it. In superstep $i + 2$ the processor p gets the string and performs the comparison that allows continuing the binary search. A cache scheme can be implemented in order to keep in p the most frequently referenced strings from remote memory (i.e., those close to the root of the global binary search virtual tree). A very effective way to reduce the average number of remote memory accesses is to associate with every array entry the first t characters of the suffix pointed. This technique is called *pruned suffixes*. The value of t depends on the text and usual queries. In [6] it has been shown that this strategy is able to put below 5% the remote memory references for relatively modest t values. Our experiments show rates below 1%.

In the *local* index strategy, on the other hand, a suffix array is constructed in each processor by considering only the subset of text stored in its respective processor. See Figure 3. No references to text postitions stored in other processors are made. Thus it is not necessary to pay for the cost of sending T-sized pieces of text per each binary search step.

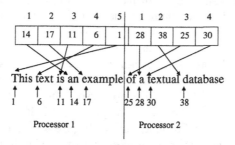

Fig. 3. Local index suffix array.

However, for every query it is necessary to search in all of the processors in order to find the pieces of local arrays that form the solution for a given interval query. As answers for interval queries, it is necessary to send to the broker $Q\,P$ pairs (a, b), Q per processor, where a/b are the start/end positions respectively of the local arrays.

The processing of a batch of Q queries is as follows. Let us charge 1 unit to the handling of each query by the broker so it first does a work proportional to $Q = q\,P$. Unfortunately, the broker now has to send every query to every processor. This broadcast operation can be effected as described in Section 3. That is, the processors get q queries from the broker and then broadcast them to all other processors at a total cost of $Q + Q\,T\,G + L$. In the next superstep, each processor performs in parallel Q binary searches and sends Q pairs (a, b) to the broker at a total cost of $q\,P\,T\,\log(N/P) + q\,P^2\,G + L$. The broker, in turn, receives $Q\,P$ queries at a cost of $q\,P^2\,G$ units of time. Thus the total cost of this strategy is given by

$$[q\,P + q\,P^2\,G] + [q\,P\,T\,\log(N/P) + q\,P^2\,G + L]\,.$$

Thus we see that the global index approach offers the potential of better performance in asymptotic terms. It is worthwhile then to focus on how to improve some performance drawbacks of the global index strategy. In the proposal we describe below we get rid of the $\log P$ factor in the broker machine by improving load balance in the P-machines server, and we reduce significantly the amount of communication ($q\,T\,\log(N/P)\,G$) performed by the server.

5   Global Multiplexed Suffix Array

One drawback of the global index approach is related to the possibility of load imbalance coming from large and sustained sequences of queries being routed to the same processor. The best way to avoid particular preferences for a given processor is to send queries uniformly at random among the processors. We propose to achieve this effect by *multiplexing* each interval defined by the original global array, so that if array element i is stored in processor p, then elements $i + 1$, $i + 2$, ... are stored in processors $p + 1$, $p + 2$, ... respectively, in a circular manner as shown in Figure 4. We call this strategy G2.

In this case, any binary search can start at any processor. Once a search has determined that the given term must be located between two consecutive entries k and $k + 1$ of the array in a processor, the search is continued in the next processor and so on, where at each processor it is only necessary to look at entry k of its own array. For example, in Figure 4 a term located in the first interval, may be located either in processor 1 or 2. If it happens that a search for a term located at position 6 of the array starts in processor 1, then once it determines that the term is between positions 5 and 7, the search is continued in processor 2 by directly examining position 6.

In general, for large P, the inter-processors search can be done in at most $\log P$ additional supersteps by performing a binary search accross processors. This increases computation and communication in an additive $\log P$ factor leaving the pipelined BSP cost of this strategy (broker + server) in

$$[q\,P + q\,P\,T\,G + L] + [q\,T\,\log(N) + q\,T\,\log(N)\,G + L].$$

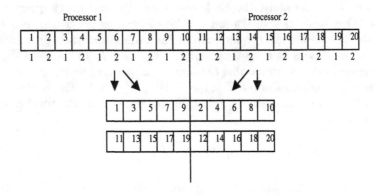

Fig. 4. Multiplexing the global index suffix array entries.

Note that the multiplexed strategy (G2) can be seen as the opposite extreme of the global index distributed lexicographically starting from processor 0 to $P - 1$, wherein each processor holds a certain interval of the suffixes pointed to by the N/P array elements (G0). The delimiting points of each interval of the G0 strategy can be kept in an array of size $P - 1$ so that a binary search conducted on it can determine to which processor to route a given query.

An intermediate strategy (G1) between G0 and G2 can be obtained by considering the global array as distributed on $V = 2^k P$ virtual processors with $k > 0$ and that each of the V virtual processors is mapped circularly on the P real processors using $i \bmod P$ for $i = 0...V$ with i being the i-th virtual processor. In this case, each real processor ends up with V/P different intervals of N/V elements of the global array. This tends to break apart the imbalance introduced by biased queries. Calculation of the array positions are trivial.

In our realization of G0 and G1 we keep in each processor an array of P (V) strings of size L marking the delimiting points of each interval of G0 (G1). The broker machine routes queries uniformly at random to the P real processors, and in every processor a $\log P$ $(\log V)$ binary search is performed to determine to which processor to send a given query (we do so to avoid the broker becoming a bottleneck). Once a query has been sent to its target processor it cannot migrate to other processors as in the case of G2. That is, this strategy avoids the inter-processors $\log P$ binary search. In particular, G1 avoids this search for a modest k whilst it approaches well the load balance achieved by G2, as we show in the experiments. The extra space should not be a burden as $N \gg P$ and k is expected to be small.

6   Global Suffix Array with Local Text

Yet another method which solves both load imbalance and remote references is to redistribute the original global array so that every element of local arrays contain only pointers to local text, as shown in Figure 5. This becomes similar to the local index strategy whilst it still keeps global information that avoids the P parallel binary searches and broadcast per query. Unfortunately we now lose the capability of performing the inter-processors $\log P$-cost binary search, since the owners of the next global array positions are unknown. We propose an $O(r\,P^{1/r})$ cost strategy to perform this search when necessary, at the cost of storing r values per suffix array cell (instead of storing a pruned suffix of t chars per cell). We call this strategy G3.

The method works for any $r \geq 1$, as follows. For $r = 1$, each cell stores the processor that owns the next cell of the global suffix array, plus the local address of that next cell inside the local suffix array of the processor owning it. Hence, given that a processor x finds the answer between its local consecutive cells i and $i + d$ (these are global addresses), it retrieves the processor y that owns cell $i + 1$, as well as the position of that cell in the local suffix array of processor y. Then x requests y to determine whether its text pointed by suffix array cell $i + 1$ is lexicographically larger than the query. If it is, then i is the right answer. If it is not, then y is now in charge of finding the right position, by finding the processor z that owns cell $i + 2$, and so on. This needs $O(d)$ supersteps because we advance cell by cell. On average $d = O(P)$ is the distance in the global suffix array between two cells that are consecutive in some local suffix array.

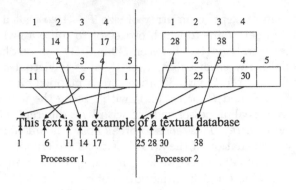

Fig. 5. Combining multiplexing with local-only references.

This can be improved for larger r as follows. The r values at cell i store the addresses of cells $i + P^{0/r}$, $i + P^{1/r}$, ..., $i + P^{(r-1)/r}$. Note that the first value is, as before, the address of cell $i + 1$. This value is essential to ensure the correctness of the algorithm, the others are just optional accelerators. Now, given that processor x finds that the answer is between cells i and $i + d$, which are consecutive in its local suffix array, it finds the largest j such that $P^{j/r} < d$. Then it finds processor y owning cell $i + P^{j/r}$. If y answers that the query is smaller than its cell, then processor x retains the problem, sets $d \leftarrow P^{j/r}$ and goes on with $j - 1$. Otherwise, processor y gets the problem, with $i \leftarrow i + P^{j/r}$ and $d \leftarrow d - P^{j/r}$. It will keep trying with the same j value.

Let us analyze the above algorithm on average, where $d = P$. We will start with $j = r - 1$. We can transfer the problem forward by $P^{(r-1)/r}$ cells at most $P/P^{(r-1)/r} = P^{1/r}$ times before the interval becomes too short for such a long skip value. At this point we set $j \leftarrow r - 2$ and the interval cannot be larger than $P^{(r-1)/r}$. By jumps of $P^{(r-2)/r}$ cells, we cannot make more than $P^{(r-1)/r}/P^{(r-2)/r} = P^{1/r}$ jumps before the interval becomes too small. This process continues until the interval is of size $P^{1/r}$ and we use the pointers to $i + 1$ to finish the search. Overall, we perform $O(r\,P^{1/r})$ steps on average. This complexity is optimized for $r = \ln P$, where the average cost becomes $O(\log P)$, just as with the multiplexed strategy G2. In practice we may not have enough space to reach this optimum. The pipelined BSP cost of this strategy (broker + server) is given by

$$[q\,P + q\,P\,T\,G + L] + [q\,T\,(\log(N/P) + P^{1/r}) + q\,T\,P^{1/r}\,G + L].$$

Strategy G3 is most useful in applications where the t-sized pruned suffixes are unable of significantly reducing the number of accesses to remote memory.

7   Experimental Results

We compared the multiplexed strategy (G2) with the plain global suffix array (G0), and the intermediate strategy (G1). For each element of the array we kept

t characters which are the t-sized prefix of the suffix pointed to by the array element. We found $t = 4$ to be a good value for our text collection.

In G2 the inter-processors binary search is conducted by sending messages with the first t characters of the query. The complete query is sent only when it is necessary to decide the final outcome of the search or when the t characters are not enough to continue the search (this reduces the amount of communication during the inter-processors search).

We use 1GB sample text from the Chilean Web search engine www.todocl.cl, treated as a single string of characters. Queries were formed in three ways: (1) by selecting at random initial word positions within the text and extracting substrings of length 16; (2) similarly but starting at words that start with the four most popular letters of the Spanish language, "c", "m", "a" and "p" ; (3) taken from the query log of www.todocl.cl, which registers a few hundred thousand user queries submitted to the web site. In set (1) we expect optimal balance, while in (2) and (3) we expect large imbalance as searches tend to end up in a subset of the global array.

The results were obtained on a PC cluster of 16 machines (PIII 700, 128MB) contected by a 100MB/s communication switch. Experiments with more than 16 processors were performed by simulating virtual processors. In this small cluster most speed-ups obtained against a sequential realization of suffix arrays were super-linear. This was not a surprise since due to hardware limitations we had to keep large pieces of the suffix array in secondary memory whilst communication among machines was composed by a comparatively small number of small strings. The whole text was kept on disk so that once the first t chars of a query were found to be equal to the t chars kept in the respective array element, a disk access was necessary to verify that the string forming the query was effectively found at that position. This frequently required an access to a disk file located in other processor, in which case the whole query was sent to that processor to be compared with the text retrieved from the remote disk.

Though we present running time comparisons below, what we considered more relevant for this paper is an implementation and hardware independent comparison among G0, G1 and G2. This came in the form of two performance metrics devised to evaluate load balance in computation and communication. They are average maxima across supersteps. During the processing of a query each strategy performs the same kind of operations, so for the case of computation the number of these ones executed in each processor per superstep suffices as an indicator of load balance for computation. For communication we measured the amount of data sent to and received from at each processor in every superstep. We also measured balance of disk accesses. In all cases the same number of supersteps were performed and a very similar number of queries were completed. In each case 5 runs with different seeds were performed and averaged. At each superstep we introduced $1024/P$ new queries in each processor.

In Table 1(1) we show results for queries biased to the 4 popular letters. Columns 2, 3, and 4 show the ratio G2/G0 for each of the above defined performance metrics (average maximum for computation, communication and disk access). The results for G2/G1 are shown in Table 1(2). These results confirm intuition, that is G0 can degenerate into a very poor performance strategy whereas G2 and G1 are a much better alternative. Noticeably G1 can achieve similar performance to G2 at a small $k = 4$. This value depends on the application, in particular on the type of queries generated by the users. G2 is independent of the application but, though well-balanced, it tends to generate more message traffic due to the inter-processors binary searches (especially for large t). The differences among G2, G1, G0 are not significant for the case of queries selected uniformly at random. G2 tends to have a slightly better load balance.

P	comp	comm	disk
2	0.95	0.90	0.89
4	0.49	0.61	0.69
8	0.43	0.45	0.53
16	0.39	0.35	0.36
32	0.38	0.29	0.24
64	0.35	0.27	0.17

(1) Ratio G2/G0.

P	comp	comm	disk
2	1.10	0.90	0.89
4	0.92	0.82	0.69
8	0.86	0.65	0.53
16	0.80	0.55	0.36
32	0.78	0.45	0.24
64	0.75	0.43	0.17

(2) G2/G1 witk $k = 4$.

P	G2/G0	G2/G1	G2/G3
4	0.68	0.87	0.41
8	0.55	0.66	0.36
16	0.61	0.67	0.31
4	0.78	0.77	0.58
8	0.78	0.73	0.45
16	0.86	0.83	0.46

(3) Running times ratios

Table 1. Comparison of search costs. The upper part of the table (3) shows results for the biased query terms (queries of type (2)) and the lower part for terms selected uniformly at random (queries of type (1)).

As speed-ups were superlinear due to disk activity, we performed experiments with a reduced text database. We used a sample of 1MB per processor, which reduces very significantly the computation costs and thereby it makes much more relevant the communication and synchronization costs in the overall running time. We observed an average efficiency (speed-up divided by the number of processors) of 0.65.

In Table 1(3) we show running time ratios for our 16 machines cluster. The biased workload increased running times by a factor of 1.7 approximately.

The results of Table 1(3) show that the G2 strategy outperformed the other two strategies, though G1 has competitive performance for the imbalanced case (first part of the table). Notice, however, that for the work-load with good load balance (second part of the table) G2 tends to lose efficiency as the number of processors increases. This is because, as P grows up, the effect of performing inter-processors binary searches becomes more significant in this very low-cost computation and ideal load balance scenario (case in which G0 is expected to achieve its best performance). G3 showed worse performance. However, this and all others were at least 3 times faster than the local index strategy.

In our computational platform we observed that the cost of broadcasts and increased number of binary searches at each processor were significant and too detrimental for the local index strategy.

Let us now further illustrate the comparative performance of G0, G1 and G2 with respect to a sequential implementation of suffix arrays, all using the same workload. This is intended to show the practicality of our algorithms.

For our cluster machines, we explored the points at which page-faults reduced performance dramatically in the sequential strategy. We found $N = 8$MB to be a reasonable maximum. Thus we decided to execute experiments for $N = 1, 2, 4$ and 8 MB in the sequential algorithm. We also performed similar experiments on 4 processors but now keeping $N/P = 1, 2, 4$ and 8 MB in each processor.

This allowed comparing the effect of communication versus the effect of disk activity, since this sequential algorithm only maintains the suffix array in main memory whereas the text database is kept in disk. For each step of the sequential binary search an access to disk must be performed in order to decide the comparison of suffixes. We retrieved t chars for t large enough so that remote memory accesses in the parallel algorithms were not significant. We tested the three types of queries, (1), (2) and (3). The results are illustrated in Figure 6.

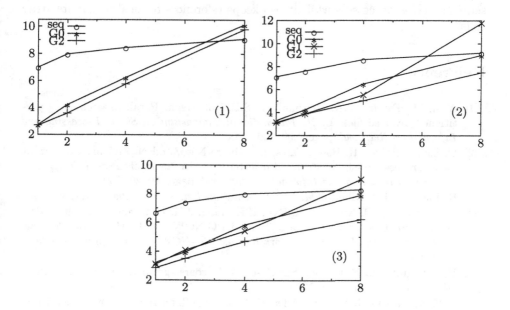

Fig. 6. Search times for (1) random balanced queries, (2) large imbalance, (3) real query log. The y-axis is running time (sec) and x-axis is DB size in MB.

The results show that the proposed algorithms are also useful in cases in which a single machine does not have enough main memory to keep in it both the text database and the index. In that case, it is more efficient to distribute the database and index on a set of machines.

8 Final Comments

We have presented a number of alternative realizations of distributed suffix arrays devised to support parallel processing of batches of queries as encountered in client-server applications. We have analyzed the algorithms by using actual implementations. Experiments were run on natural language texts.

In general, the implementation of the algorithms for G0 and G1 were simpler than that for G2. For texts and queries that are not highly biased we suggest using G1 with $k = 4$ as it is a simple strategy that achieves a reasonable load balance. Certainly the G2 strategy is the best one in cases of query patterns generating large imbalance. Note that its performance is good enough even in well-behaved (balanced) query patterns.

Strategy G3 is competitive for cases in which the t chars maintained by G0, G1 and G2 in each array cell are not able to reduce significantly the number of references to remote memory. Our results show that G3 is much more efficient than the local index strategy because it avoids completely the parallel local searches across processors while it still keeps references to local text in its array cells.

References

[1] A. A. MacFarlane, J.A. McCann, and S.E. Robertson. Parallel search using partitioned inverted files. In *7th International Symposium on String Processing and Information Retrieval*, pages 209–220, 2000.

[2] C. Santos Badue, R. Baeza-Yates, B. Ribeiro-Neto, and N. Ziviani. Concurrent query processing using distributed inverted files. In *8th International Symposium on String Processing and Information Retrieval*, pages 10–20, 2001.

[3] R. Baeza and B. Ribeiro. *Modern Information Retrieval*. Addison-Wesley., 1999.

[4] S.H. Chung, H.C. Kwon, K.R. Ryu, H.K. Jang, J.H. Kim, and C.A. Choi. Parallel information retrieval on a SCI-based PC-NOW. In *Workshop on Personal Computers based Networks of Workstations (PC-NOW 2000)*. (Springer-Verlag), May 2000.

[5] P. Ferragina and F. Luccio. String search in coarse-grained parallel computers. *Algorithmica*, 24:177–194, 1999.

[6] J. Kitajima and G. Navarro. A fast distributed suffix array generation algorithm. In *6th International Symposium on String Processing and Information Retrieval*, pages 97–104, 1999.

[7] W.F. McColl. General purpose parallel computing. In A.M. Gibbons and P. Spirakis, editors, *Lectures on Parallel Computation*, pages 337–391. Cambridge University Press, 1993.

[8] G. Navarro, J. Kitajima, B. Ribeiro, and N. Ziviani. Distributed generation of suffix arrays. In *8th Annual Symposium on Combinatorial Pattern Matching*, pages 102–115, 1997. LNCS 1264.

[9] B. Ribeiro, J. Kitajima, G. Navarro, C. Santana, and N. Ziviani. Parallel generation of inverted lists for distributed text collections. In *XVIII Conference of the Chilean Computer Science Society*, pages 149–157, 1998.

[10] D.B. Skillicorn, J.M.D. Hill, and W.F. McColl. Questions and answers about BSP. Technical Report PRG-TR-15-96, Computing Laboratory, Oxford University, 1996. Also in *Journal of Scientific Programming*, V.6 N.3, 1997.

[11] D.B. Skillicorn and D. Talia, Models and languages for parallel computation, *ACM Computing Surveys* V.20 N.2 1998.

[12] L.G. Valiant. A bridging model for parallel computation. *Comm. ACM*, 33:103–111, Aug. 1990.

[13] BSP World-wide Standard, www.bsp-worldwide.org.

[14] BSP PUB Library at Paderborn University, www.uni-paderborn.de/bsp.

BFT: Bit Filtration Technique for Approximate String Join in Biological Databases*

S. Alireza Aghili, Divyakant Agrawal, and Amr El Abbadi

Department of Computer Science,
University of California-Santa Barbara,
Santa Barbara, CA 93106
{aghili,agrawal,amr}@cs.ucsb.edu

Abstract. Joining massive tables in relational databases have received substantial attention in the past decade. Numerous filtration and indexing techniques have been proposed to reduce the curse of dimensionality. This paper proposes a novel approach to map the problem of pairwise whole-genome comparison into an approximate join operation in the well-established relational database context. We propose a novel *Bit Filtration Technique (BFT)* based on vector transformation and furthermore conduct the application of DFT(Discrete Fourier Transformation) and DWT(Discrete Wavelet Transformation, Haar) dimensionality reduction techniques as a pre-processing filtration step which effectively reduces the search space and running time of the join operation. Our empirical results on a number of Prokaryote and Eukaryote DNA *contig* datasets demonstrate very efficient filtration to effectively prune non-relevant portions of the database, incurring no false negatives, with up to 50 times faster running time compared with traditional dynamic programming, and *q*-gram approaches. BFT may easily be incorporated as a pre-processing step for any of the well-known sequence search heuristics as BLAST, QUASAR and FastA, for the purpose of pairwise whole-genome comparison. We analyze the precision of applying BFT and other transformation-based dimensionality reduction techniques, and finally discuss the imposed trade-offs.

1 Introduction

Traditional query languages and relational databases have been mainly designed for exact query search, and the problem of similarity search and the corresponding applications have been extensively studied within the past decade, especially in the context of biological databases. However, not enough advances have been made to address the need for approximate queries. In particular, mainstream database research has not paid substantial attention to the issue of approximate pairwise whole-genome similarities. Errors and modifications are observed in a variety of applications originating from typographical mistakes(*Data cleansing*),

---

* This research was supported by the NSF grants under EIA02-05675, EIA99-86057, EIA00-80134, and IIS02-09112.

M.A. Nascimento, E.S. de Moura, A.L. Oliveira (Eds.): SPIRE 2003, LNCS 2857, pp. 326–340, 2003.

inconsistent attribute design conventions(*Data integration*), or even being part of a natural mutational mechanism(*Genomics*). Each of these events may result in a series of changes on the original strings from a global point of view. The approximate search seeks the sequences close enough to a given query sequence either through dynamic programming[17, 19] or using other heuristics [3, 18, 20]. For instance, approximate sequence analysis has enabled the detection of certain strains of the *Escherichia coli(E.coli)* bacteria responsible for infant *diarrhea* and *gastroenteritis*. Similarly in large and modern enterprises, it is inevitable that different branches of the organization would need a large amount of external data, retrieved from other resources, to be integrated into the existing database. Such data would most probably use a different schema and/or tuple representation conventions, probably generated by different database engines. Integration of such data sources (approximate join to suppress the duplicates) leads to an enormous challenge since the corresponding database relations might each include hundreds of millions of records(e.g. digital libraries). Looking for pairwise whole-genome homology search or very large scale string joins, the entire database should be searched although most of the inspected strings may not actually result in the answer set. As a result, the expensive inspection of non-relevant strings impacts the performance dramatically.

The mentioned applications, motivations, and shortcomings trigger the necessity of incorporating efficient filtration techniques to leverage the complexity and scalability of the problem. In this paper we propose a novel approach to map the problem of pairwise whole-genome comparison into an approximate join operation in the well-established relational database context. Furthermore, we apply the proposed *BFT(Bit-Filtration Technique)*, and additionally, *DWT(Discrete Wavelet, Haar)* and *DFT(Discrete Fourier Transformation)* as pre-processing filtration techniques. Our simulations study the approximate join operation and the corresponding filtration efficiency gained by the proposed techniques while dealing with relations with up to 1.3 billion tuple comparisons in the worst case.

The rest of the paper is organized as follows: Section 2, discusses the background and related work. Section 3 introduces the proposed techniques. Section 4 demonstrates a concise empirical performance analysis and the simulation results, followed by section 5 which concludes the work.

2   Background, Related Work

In a typical application of approximate join, given two string datasets S and T, and range r, all the string tuples of S are compared against all string tuples of T, in search for pairs of string tuples which are at most r edit operations far from each other. However, because of the quadratic time involved, the dynamic programming[17, 19] algorithms are not feasible. Several heuristics [3, 5, 6, 13, 18] have been proposed to speed up the similarity search phase of the procedure in the case of range query and k-nearest neighbor search. Most of these heuristics need to inspect the entire database while only a very small part of it might actually be of interest. To the best of our knowledge, this study is the first effort to i) facilitate efficient filtration for approximate join queries using discrete transformation techniques, and ii) map the problem of pairwise whole-genome comparison into a relational approximate join operation in a database context.

Jin, Li, and Mehrotra[11] map the strings of database into Euclidean space and use d dimensions to represent each string in the feature space. Furthermore, a new range threshold δ for the new feature space is empirically found and all pairs of strings whose feature vector distances are greater than δ are pruned. However, i) the number of dimensions d is found empirically, which is very much data dependent, ii) range threshold δ, is found empirically by sampling random subsets of the database which results in *false negatives*. Gravano et al.[9] target the problem of approximate join in textual relational databases. They extract positional q-grams[12, 16] from each of the strings and apply count, positional, and length filtering to prune *out-of-range* string pairs. Furthermore, the SQL equivalents of the proposed operations are represented, and the work is also extended for edit distances with block shifts. Multi-Resolution index Structure(MRS)[13] uses a sliding window of size $|w|$ and extracts the first and second *Haar wavelet* coefficients of the corresponding windows. Given a range query (Q, r), MRS seeks the result set in different resolution levels of maximum postfix segments. However, i) MRS only addresses the problem of range query and k-nearest neighbor, and ii) the focus of the work is on the cost of their index structure/procedure, rather than the analysis of the filtration efficiency, and precision of the proposed approach.

Chavez and Navarro[6] translate the problem of approximate string search into a range query or proximity search in a metric space. The technique is based on picking k pivots randomly, and mapping each sequence with a k-dimensional vector, and further using triangle inequality to prune non-relevant sequences using Suffix Tree[4] as an index structure. No empirical analysis is conducted to evaluate this approach on real biological data. SST[8] uses overlapping sliding windows of size w over the database sequences and maps them into a 4^w-dimensional frequency vectors. Furthermore, SST uses k-means clustering algorithm to hierarchically cluster database sequences. Given query pattern Q, it is first divided into non-overlapping windows, pruning the database windows which are further from the given query range, and finally studying the effect of window size on search time, and error rate of input data on true positive/negative rates. Most similarly, Aghili et al.[1] provide a concise study of *Discrete Fourier Transformation(DFT)*, *Discrete Wavelet Transformation(DWT)* as pre-processing filtration techniques for approximate range query in the context of biological sequences. Finally, the authors in [21] provide a concise study of DFT and DWT transformations, but only in the context of time-series databases.

3   Proposed Techniques

The traditional database join($\bowtie$) operation is based on the *exact matching* of string tuples, while the approximate join($\bowtie$) is based on the *approximate match-*

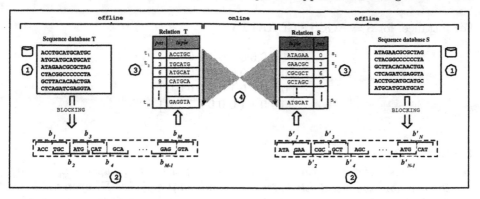

Fig. 1. The relational database conversion or block-based mapping procedure for $b = 6$

ing of the string tuples. Initially, we perform the *block-based mapping*[1] procedure as depicted in Fig. 1. Given string databases T and S: **i)** perform the block-based mapping and extract the relational equivalent of T and S: A window of size b traverses each of the databases and extracts b-sized blocks overlapped by $b/2$ characters *(Steps 1,2)*, **ii)** the extracted blocks are then represented as attribute values in a relational database with their corresponding location in the original string database as the primary key *(Step 3)*, **iii)** given range r, the *approximate join* operation seeks all the corresponding tuple pairs of T and S, which are at most r far from each other based on a well defined distance function, usually the *Edit Distance*(ED)[3] *(Step 4)*. Block-based mapping facilitates the initial step of mapping the problem of pairwise whole-genome comparison into an approximate table join.

3.1 Terminology, Formulation

The following definitions[2] introduce the steps in transforming the *original domain(set of strings)* to *frequency domain(set of feature vectors)*:

Definition 1 (frequency vector) *Let S be a string over the alphabet* $\Sigma_k = \{\alpha_1, \ldots, \alpha_k\}$, *then the frequency vector of S, called* $f(S)$ *is defined as:* $f(S) = [f_1, \ldots, f_k]$, *where each* $f_i (\geq 0)$ *corresponds to the occurrence frequency of* α_i *in S, and* $\sum_{i=1}^{k} f_i = |S| = n$.

Definition 2 (frequency quantization) *Let* $S = s_1 \ldots s_n$ *be a string from the alphabet* Σ_k. *The frequency quantization of S,* $S^F = [\xi_{s_1}, \ldots, \xi_{s_n}]$, *is a* $(|\Sigma| \times n)$ *matrix, where each orthonormal vector* ξ_{s_i} *represents the corresponding* $(|\Sigma| \times 1)$-*dimensional basis vector for* s_i *character, for* $1 \leq i \leq n$.

---

[1] Note that, in our implementation, the database designer has the freedom of choosing non-uniform blocking factors across relations.

[2] Due to space limitations more detailed definitions and proofs are provided in [2].

For instance, for S = AGGTTGCAATTA:

$$S^F = \begin{bmatrix} 1 & 0 & 0 & 0 & 0 & 0 & 0 & 1 & 1 & 0 & 0 & 1 \\ 0 & 0 & 0 & 0 & 0 & 0 & 1 & 0 & 0 & 0 & 0 & 0 \\ 0 & 1 & 1 & 0 & 0 & 1 & 0 & 0 & 0 & 0 & 0 & 0 \\ 0 & 0 & 0 & 1 & 1 & 0 & 0 & 0 & 0 & 1 & 1 & 0 \end{bmatrix}.$$

Definition 3 *(approximate join) Let $T = [a_1^T, \ldots, a_g^T]$ and $S = [a_1^S, \ldots, a_h^S]$ be two database relations with their corresponding attributes. Suppose a_i^T and a_j^S are the two non-numerical attributes over some joint alphabet Σ, upon which we would like to perform approximate join. Given range r and distance function d, approximate join of T and S, $T \bowtie_d^r S$, returns all pairs of tuples $(t, s) \in (T \times S)$ such that $d(t[i], s[j]) < r$, for $i \leq g$, and $j \leq h$.*

One way to solve the *approximate join* problem, $T \bowtie_d^r S$, is as follows: Given the relation S, compare all tuples of S against all tuples of relation T using ED as the distance measure, either through direct application of dynamic programming[17, 19] or other popular heuristics[3, 5, 18]. Although this approach is correct, it is not practical/scalable for two reasons: First, sequence databases may involve a large number of very large sequences(e.g. Chr_{22} as the smallest human chromosome[14] consists of approximately 35 million base pairs) resulting in severe performance penalty. Secondly, the prohibitive computational cost, of alignment or even heuristic-based sequence comparison, makes it impractical, specially when $|T \bowtie_d^r S| \ll |T \times S|$. A solution could involve mapping the string similarity of the ED domain($T \bowtie_{ED}^r S$) into a vector difference in an acquired *Frequency Distance (FD)*[3] domain($T \bowtie_{FD}^r S$), to benefit from much more time/space-efficient numerical methods in the literature. One way is to use a mathematical transformation to map each *string S_i*, into its corresponding *frequency vector $f(S_i)$*, and use a lower-bound frequency distance function to approximate the edit distance of the original string domain.

Definition 4 *(Frequency Distance, FD) Given two frequency vectors $U = [u_1, \ldots, u_k]$ and $V = [v_1, \ldots, v_k]$, The frequency distance $FD(U, V)$, is defined as the minimum number of (+1), (-1), and (±1) operations needed on the entries of U, to be transformed into V, or vice versa.*

Theorem 1 *(Lower bound condition)[4] Let S and T be two strings from alphabet Σ, with their corresponding frequency vectors $f(S)$ and $f(T)$. The frequency distance $FD(f(S), f(T))$, is a lower bound on the edit distance $ED(S, T)$ [13]: $FD(f(S), f(T)) \leq ED(S, T)$. Furthermore, given range r, $(FD(f(S), f(T)) > r) \Rightarrow ED(S, T) > r$.*

---

[3] We applied L_1-norm as the preferred FD when comparing DFT coefficients.

[4] For the complete proof, please refer to [2]

Theorem 1 is the main driving force behind using transformation based filtration. The calculation of distance in the frequency domain is linear in time/space, which is much more efficient compared to the calculation of the distance in the original string domain which is quadratic in time/space. Hence, approximate join is much more efficiently evaluated in the frequency domain. Given a set of strings S= $\{S_1, \ldots, S_n\}$ with their corresponding frequency vectors $f(S) = \{f(S_1), \ldots, f(S_n)\}$, and range r, let T be a relation having only one tuple t and the corresponding frequency vector $f(t)$. Suppose we want to calculate T $\bowtie_{ED}^r$ S, then all the strings S_i, for which $FD(f(t), f(S_i)) > r$ may be pruned from the answer set without the need to further calculate the edit distance. This property dramatically reduces the *computational cost*[13], and the required amount of *search space* for T $\bowtie_{ED}^r$ S, while (T $\bowtie_{ED}^r$ S) $\subseteq$ (f(T) $\bowtie_{FD}^r f$(S)). However, a very important requirement is to guarantee that the *Filtration Ratio(FR)* $= \frac{|f(T) \bowtie_{FD}^r f(S)|}{|T \bowtie_{ED}^r S|} \geq 1$, not to incur any *false negatives*. A better filtration technique should lead to a smaller filtration ratio.

3.2   Transformation-Based Filtration Techniques

Discrete Fourier and Wavelet Transformation:

Definition 5 *The kth-level Haar Wavelet Transformation(DWT) [13] of a frequency quantized string S, $\varpi_k(S)$, for $0 \leq k \leq log_2 n$, is defined as $\varpi_k(S) = [v_{k,0}, v_{k,1}, \ldots, v_{k,\frac{n}{2^k}}]$, where $v_{k,i} = [\alpha_{k,i}, \beta_{k,i}]$, for*

$$\alpha_{k,i} = \begin{cases} f(c_i) & k = 0 \\ \alpha_{k-1,2i} + \alpha_{k-1,2i+1} & 0 < k \leq log_2 n, \end{cases}$$

$$\beta_{k,i} = \begin{cases} 0 & k = 0 \\ \alpha_{k-1,2i} - \alpha_{k-1,2i+1} & 0 < k \leq log_2 n, \end{cases}$$

where for $k = log_2 n$: $\alpha_{log_2 n,0} = f(S[0 : n-1])$ and $\beta_{log_2 n,0} = f(S[0 : \frac{n}{2} - 1]) - f(S[\frac{n}{2} : n-1])$ represent the first and second Haar wavelet coefficients, respectively.

For instance, for S = AGGTTGCAATTA , the 3rd-level *Haar Wavelet* transformation of S is $\varpi_3(AGGTTGCAATTA) = \{\alpha_{3,0}, \beta_{3,0}\} = \{[4, 1, 3, 4], [-2, -1, 3, 0]\}$, represents the set of first and second wavelet coefficients.

Definition 6 *The n-point Discrete Fourier Transformation(DFT) of a sequence $S = [S_t]$, for t=0,...,n-1 is defined to be a sequence X of n complex numbers x_f of $(|\Sigma| \times 1)$-dimensional vectors, for $f = 0, \ldots, n-1$, and is given by*

$$x_f = \frac{1}{\sqrt{n}} \sum_{t=0}^{n-1} S_t e^{\frac{-j2\pi ft}{n}}, f = 0, 1, \ldots, n-1,$$

where $j = \sqrt{-1}$ is the imaginary unit. The original sequence S can be restored by the inverse transform:

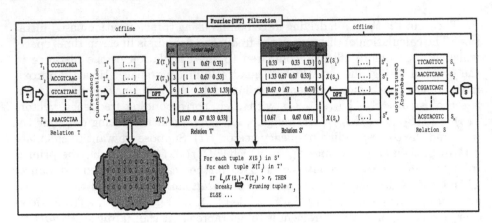

Fig. 2. The DFT filtration procedure for only one coefficient, and $b = 9$

$$S_t = \frac{1}{\sqrt{n}} \sum_{f=0}^{n-1} x_f e^{\frac{j2\pi ft}{n}}, \ t = 0, 1, \ldots, n\text{-}1,$$

where x_f is a complex number and its real and imaginary parts are $(|\Sigma| \times 1)$-dimensional vectors.

For instance, for $S' = ACCT$, the first and second DFT coefficients of S' are: $X_0(S') = [\frac{1}{2}, 1, 0, \frac{1}{2}]$ and $X_1(S') = \{[\frac{1}{2}, \frac{-1}{2}, 0, 0], [0, \frac{-1}{2}, 0, \frac{1}{2}]\}$, respectively.

The transformation-based filtration on both of DFT(Fig. 2) and DWT techniques, is identical except on the choice of transformation and the number of incorporated coefficients. The general process is shown under Algorithm 1. Given the genome databases S and T, the approximate join procedure is performed in two different stages: *offline* and *online*. In the offline stage, all the blocks/tuples S_i and T_j are extracted, and each tuple is mapped onto its corresponding feature vector(s) using DFT or DWT. Following this procedure, the S and T datasets would be mapped into S' and T' database relations, respectively. The tuple extraction procedure is very fast and needs only a single scan for each of the given databases. The actual approximate join operation is performed in the online stage. All the feature vector tuples of the relation S' are compared against their T' counterparts, and all those tuple pairs whose distance is greater than the given range r, are pruned from the resulting candidate set. Furthermore, a refinement step using dynamic programming is performed to remove the *false positives*. Additionally, a multidimensional indexing structure[7] could be built on the extracted relations for more efficient tuple pruning. However, we intend to study the impact of the various indexing schemes in our future work.

Bit Filtration Technique(BFT): Given two string databases T and S, we first construct the relational equivalent of each database as T= $\{T_1, \ldots, T_m\}$ and S= $\{S_1, \ldots, S_n\}$(Fig. 1), respectively. In the second step, the corresponding frequency vector(s), $f(T_i)(f(S_j))$, are extracted into the resulting relations T' =

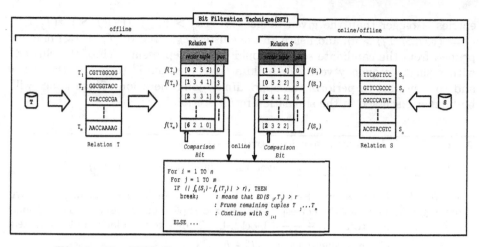

Fig. 3. The BFT filtration procedure, for blocking factor $b = 9$

$\{f(T_1), \ldots, f(T_m)\}$ and $S' = \{f(S_1), \ldots, f(S_n)\}$. The schema of $T'(S')$ has two attributes: *i)* The *index* of the tuple in the original database as the primary key, and *ii)* $|\Sigma|$-dimensional *frequency feature vector*. This process may be applied offline to the bigger relation(T'), and the smaller relation's frequency vectors may be extracted on the fly. Furthermore, the *Most Fluctuating Bit (MFB, or comparison bit)* of the frequency vector tuples of relation T' is calculated. MFB corresponds to the kth entry(column) of the frequency vector, holding the frequency of alphabet $\alpha_k \in \Sigma$, whose entry value across all frequency tuples $f(T_j)$ demonstrates the most discriminating deviation from the mean value(for $1 \le k \le |\Sigma|$ and $1 \le j \le m$).

Figure 3 depicts the steps of BFT procedure. BFT clusters the bigger relation T', on its $1^{st}, \ldots, |\Sigma|^{th}$ MFB bit, in p multiple passes, for $1 \le p \le |\Sigma|$. When the algorithm starts, the entire relation is considered as one cluster. In the first pass, the frequency tuples are clustered based on their MFB entry value, in increasing order. Given block size β, after the first pass, the relation T' would potentially be clustered into $\beta + 1$ clusters($c_0, \ldots, c_\beta$) with no special order within each cluster, typically forming clusters of size $m/(\beta + 1)$. The tuples belonging to cluster c_j, have the same value j, on their corresponding MFB entry. The second phase, subdivides each cluster into potentially $\beta + 1$ new clusters based on the values of their second MFB in an increasing order, and so on. Therefore, the maximum total number of clusters generated by BFT would be C= $\prod_1^p(\beta + 1)$, for the choice of p sequential passes. The value of p can be tuned according to the requirements of the application and the filtration threshold imposed by the user. BFT also benefits from a neighbor cluster joining mechanism to make sure that the clusters have roughly similar load of tuples. It is interesting to observe that BFT orders the frequency tuples on their MFB bits. Finally, the Algorithm 2 as the filtration step, is performed.

The intuition behind BFT is the fact that, given $f(S_i) \in c'_k$, and $f(T_j) \in c_k$ and range r, if the absolute difference between their corresponding MFB entries is bigger than the given range: $(|k' - k| > r) \Rightarrow (\text{FD}(f(S_i), f(T_j)) > r) \Rightarrow (\text{ED}(S_i, T_j) > r)$, and hence all the clusters $c_k, \ldots, c_{|\Sigma|}$ $(T_j \ldots T_m)$ may be pruned from the candidate set. We could further represent each of the clusters with a single frequency vector or build a tree index on T' to reduce the space and time needed to perform the approximate join operation. These issues will be further discussed in the simulation result section.

Algorithm 1 Approximate join processing:

Offline pre-processing phase, Given the string database, T(and S)$\in \Sigma^*$:

- (*Block-based partitioning*) Slide the blocking window of size b on the original DNA dataset T and extract the corresponding b-sized tuples, partitioning T on positions $0, \frac{b}{2}, \frac{2b}{2}, \ldots$ into a total of $\lceil \frac{|T| - b + 1}{\lfloor \frac{b}{2} \rfloor} \rceil$ blocks. Let T_j denote the block/tuple extracted from T, at position j, where $0 \leq j < |T| - b$.
- Represent the dataset with its corresponding relational representation with its tuples being the extracted blocks, and index j as the primary key of the relation.
- Perform *Frequency Quantization*(Def. 2) on each tuple T_j, constructing T_j^F,
- Use the desired *DFT* or *DWT* transformation on each *Frequency-Quantized* tuple T_j^F, and calculate the corresponding transformed vector $X(T_j^F)$ or $\varpi(T_j^F)$ coefficients in the frequency domain, respectively.
- Extract and store only a few coefficients to represent the original string tuple. For the case of *DFT*, we keep the highest *energy-concentrated* coefficients as, first, last and the second[21]. For the *DWT*, we keep the first and second coefficients.
- For each relation T, build an offline index structure, relation T'[*index#, tuple vector(s)*].

Online filtration phase, Given a distance function $d(FD$ or $L_p)$, and range r:

for all tuple vectors in S': **do**
    for all tuple vectors in T': **do**
        if $d(X(S_i) - X(T_j)) > r$ **then**
            Prune T_j from the resulting candidate set;
            Break;
        end if
    end for
end for
▷ *Refinement step:* Apply dynamic programming on the remained tuple pairs, to find the strings S_i and T_j, where $ED(S_i, T_j) < r$.

---

4   Performance Analysis

4.1   Implementation

We compared the performance of BFT, DFT, and DWT as pre-processing filtration techniques against dynamic programming [17, 19], and q-gram [9] ap-

Algorithm 2 Bit filtration procedure:

for i = 1 to n: **do**
  for j = 1 to m: **do**
    if $|(f_{MFB}(S_i) - f_{MFB}(T_j))| > r$ **then**
      // *means that* $ED(S_i, T_j) > r \Rightarrow$ *prune all remaining tuples* $T_j \ldots T_m$;
      Continue with S_{i+1};
    end if
  end for
end for

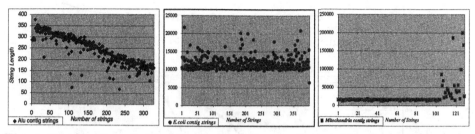

Fig. 4. Distribution of string lengths for *Alu*, *E.coli*, and *Mitochondria* datasets

proaches. Our implementation closely follows the depicted procedures of Figures 1-3. We incorporated different blocking methods for string dataset to relational database conversion procedure: *i) Consecutive* partitioning: Each of the consecutive blocks of length b, overlap by $b - 1$ residues, *ii) Half-overlapped* partitioning: Each of the consecutive blocks of length b, overlap by $b/2$ residues(Fig. 1), and *iii) non-Overlapped* partitioning, where the whole data is chopped into $l = \theta(log_{|\Sigma|}|T|)$ [16] partitions of various length. In the different block partitioning methods[5], we observed a better filtration ratio but a higher computational cost, when more blocks were extracted. This choice is a trade-off between cost versus precision. However, due to the limitation of the space, we did not include those results in this study. We implemented all the desired algorithms and transformations using *Java 1.4.1*, and ran our simulations on an *Intel Xeon 2.4GHz* processor with *2GB* of main memory.

Table 1. The statistics $(max\ b = 32)$ for the datasets used in our simulations

Dataset	A	C	G	T	Total	Block quantity	MFB
Alu	24301	18271	22192	15742	80506	4530	G
Mitocondria	1024379	647278	502392	989164	3163213	197566	A
E. coli	1148707	1184392	1181731	1147409	4662239	290779	A
imdb	N/A	N/A	N/A	N/A	788020	54000	B

---

[5] The results in the next section are based on half-overlapped partitioning.

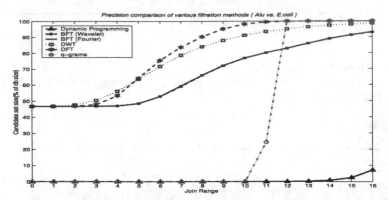

Fig. 5. Resulting candidate set of $Alu \bowtie E.coli$ for $b = 32$

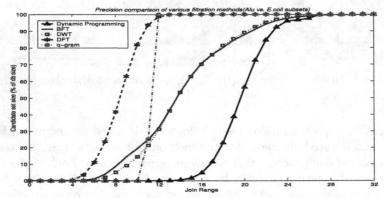

Fig. 6. Resulting candidate set of $Alu^R \bowtie E.coli^R$ for $b = 32$

4.2   Simulation Results

We ran our experiments on three Prokaryote and Eukaryote genome databases (*Alu, Escherichia coli*, and *Mitochondria*) [14], and one actor name database [10]. The Statistics of the incorporated data are depicted in Fig. 4, and Table 1. Due to the large computational cost of applying the *inner-loop-join* for the ED comparison, we had to reduce the size of each DNA database relation T into 4K tuples, named T^R, to be able to run the *all-pair-all dynamic programming*[19] in a reasonable amount of time. However, Fig. 5 demonstrates the filtration efficiency on the original files with 1.3 billion tuple comparisons. Initially, we performed block-based mapping on the DNA contig datasets to build their relational equivalents. In the blocking process, we applied a uniform tuple length($b = 32$) for all the DNA databases of choice, however, tuple lengths in the movie database[10] were variable($8 \le b \le 32$) by nature. Additionally, we could incorporate variable block lengths on our DNA datasets but, we only included the result for the uniform blocking for the sake of simplicity. We incorporated *three* coefficients($1^{st}, 2^{nd}$, and n^{th}) for DFT, and *two* coefficients (1st and 2nd)

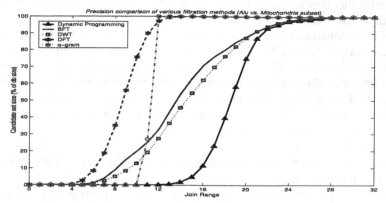

Fig. 7. Resulting candidate set of $Alu^R \bowtie Mitochondria^R$ for $b = 32$

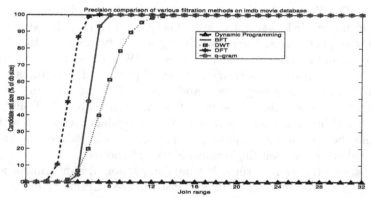

Fig. 8. Resulting candidate set of approximate join on $imdb[10]$ database

for DWT. The results of BFT were based on only using the *first* MFB, hence, only *1-pass* clustering of the relation. Due to the limitations of the space, the results of more than one MFB are not shown in this paper. Figures 5-8, demonstrate the filtration efficiency of running BFT, DWT, and DFT compared with q-gram[9], and *dynamic programming*[19] techniques on various databases.

Given two database relations S and T, let B denote the total number of tuple comparisons needed in an approximate join operation. Vertical axis demonstrates the candidate set($\propto \frac{1}{precision}$), the fraction of comparisons that is left for further refinement ($\frac{|f(S) \bowtie_d^r f(T)|}{B}\%$), as a function of join range. Smaller candidate set is the result of a higher filtration efficiency. Figures 5-8 demonstrate the filtration efficiency, out of 1.3 billion and 16 million total number of comparisons, respectively. In Fig. 5, we used two different ways of performing BFT: using the 1st coefficient of DWT versus the 1st coefficient DFT for frequency vector extraction. However, the results were identical, which can be explained by the fact that the first coefficient of DFT is identical to the first coefficient of DWT with a multiplication factor of $1/\sqrt{n}$. Therefore, for the rest of experiments, we only demonstrate the classical BFT using frequency vectors extraction. BFT, and DWT demonstrated very similar trend on the filtration ratio. Given relation S and target relation T, all the techniques except BFT, need to inspect all the tuples of the target relation T for any given tuple of S, while in contrary, BFT incorporates the pruning phase and hence, does not need to scan the entire database T. The pruning of database performed by BFT takes its best values on the lower ranges. Lower the join range, a better filtration ratio was expected and observed, while potentially a larger portion of the relation is expected to be out of range. In very low ranges, q-gram[9] provides efficient filtration, however, it needs to scan all the target tuples for a possible *within-bound* q-gram count(or positional/length filtering).

Figure 8, demonstrates the result of running our proposed techniques(for $|\Sigma| = 32$), on two disjoint subsets of $imdb$[10] movie database. DWT achieves reasonable filtration efficiency, however BFT works really bad! The reason lies in two facts: *i)* The chosen alphabet size was far too sparse and insensitive to the context, and hence MFB was not able to perform an efficient filtration on the tuples. We would need to use *words* as a finer granularity representation of name tuples rather than just single alphabet characters. We are planning to investigate this issue more in our future work *ii)* The actual portion of the database which was within the range was very small, and hence BFT had to scan the whole database to find the candidate matches. On the other hand, DFT and DWT perform efficient filtration for 0-5 range. Not surprisingly, this is the desired range within the area of data cleansing or data integration, while only very few typographical errors on each single word/block are allowed.

Table 2 shows the average running time comparison of approximate join for range $r = \{0, 1, \ldots, 8\}$. Figures 9-10, demonstrate the *"Crème de la Crème"* of applying BFT. We first applied BFT as a pre-processing filtration step to extract the candidate sets calculated from the frequency join $f(\text{S}) \bowtie^r_{FD} f(\text{T})$, incurring *no false negatives*, which is a superset of the actual result set S $\bowtie^r_{ED}$ T. Furthermore, we used local alignment, and q-gram techniques on the remaining candidate set as the next pruning step to *possibly* narrow the search space either to the actual answer set(alignment), or *possibly* a narrower candidate set(q-gram). As a result, the recall[6] of applying BFT was 100%, as expected [2](FD≤ED), hence *no false negatives* were created. Figures 9-10 show up to 50 times speed-up on the overall process, should BFT is used as a filtration pre-processing step.

Table 2. Average running time(in *milliseconds*) of approximate join, for $r = 0 \ldots 8$ and $b = 32$

	Dynamic Programming	DFT	q-gram	DWT	BFT
$Alu \bowtie^r E.coli$	109546	409156	101872	93337	4881

---

[6] $Recall = \frac{CandidateSet \cap AnswerSet}{AnswerSet}$

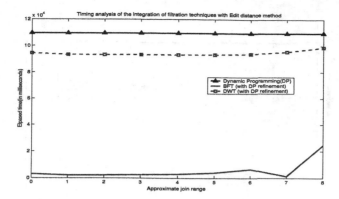

Fig. 9. Running time comparison of *Alu* ⋈ *E.coli* with the integration *BFT* on *Dynamic Programming*[19] approach as a function of approximate range, for $b = 32$

5   Conclusion

In this paper, we proposed a novel, yet simple, *Bit Filtration Technique(BFT)* for more efficient filtration of undesired tuple comparisons and studied the similar integration of DFT and DWT on biological databases and evaluated the specific problem of approximate join. BFT and other proposed transformation methods, may be applied as a pre-processing filtration step for any of the known heuristic techniques like BLAST[3], QUASAR[5], FastA[18], and even the dynamic programming sequence alignment[17, 19], and q-gram[9]. Our results show that applying the proposed techniques, a high accuracy and faster database pruning is achieved. The filtration ratio is very much data dependent and no generalization on the min/max filtration ratio or true positive rates can be suggested. However, the empirical results show promising performance behavior on the integration of BFT for very efficient filtration, incurring no false negatives, and up to 50 times faster running time.

References

[1] Aghili, S.A., Agrawal, D., El Abbadi, A.: Filtration of String Proximity Search via Transformation. *BIBE* (2003) 149–157
[2] Aghili, S.A., Agrawal, D., El Abbadi, A.: BFT: A Relational-based Bit Filtration Technique for Efficient Approximate String Join in Biological Databases (Extended Version). *UCSB Technical Report, TRCS03-12* (2003)
[3] Altschul, S., Gish, W., Miller, W., Myers, E., Lipman, D.J.: Basic Local Alignment Search tool. *J. Molecular Biology* **215** (1990) 403–410
[4] Apostolico, A.: The Myriad Virtues of Subword Trees. *Combinatorial Algorithms on Words, NATO ISI Series, Springer-Verlag* (1985) 85–96
[5] Burkhardt, S., et al.: q-gram Based Database Searching Using a Suffix Array (QUASAR). *RECOMB* (1999) 77–83

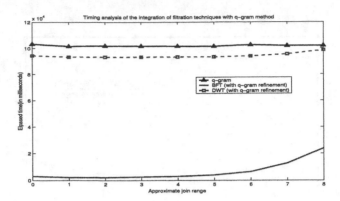

Fig. 10. Running time comparison of $Alu \bowtie E.coli$ with the integration BFT on q-gram[9] approach as a function of approximate range, for $b = 32$

[6] Chavez, E., Navarro, G.: A Metric Index for Approximate String Matching. *LATIN* (2002) 181–195
[7] Gaede, V., Günther, O.: Multidimensional Access Methods. *ACM Computing Surveys* **30** (1998) 170–231
[8] Giladi, E., Walker, M.G., Wang, J.Z., Volkmuth, W.: SST: An Algorithm for Finding Near-Exact Sequence Matches in Time Proportional to the Logarithm of the Database Size. *Bioinformatics* **18** (2002) 873–877
[9] Gravano, L., et al.: Approximate String Joins in a Database (Almost) for Free. *VLDB* (2001) 491–500
[10] Internet Movie DataBase (IMDB). *http://www.imdb.com*
[11] Jin, L., Li, C., Mehrotra, S.: Efficient Similarity String Joins in Large Data Sets. *UCI ICS Technical Report, TR-DB-02-04* (2002)
[12] Jokinen, P., Ukkonen, E.: Two Algorithms for Approximate String Matching in Static Texts. *MFCS* **16** (1991) 240–248
[13] Kahveci, T., Singh, A.K.: Efficient Index Structures for String Databases. *VLDB* (2001) 351–360
[14] National Center for Biotechnology Information(NCBI). *http://www.ncbi.nih.gov/*
[15] Navarro, G., Baeza-Yates, R.A.: A Hybrid Indexing Method for Approximate String Matching. *J. Discrete Algorithms* **1** (2000) 205–239
[16] Navarro, G., Baeza-Yates, R.A., Sutinen, E., Tarhio, J.: Indexing Methods for Approximate String Matching. *IEEE Data Engineering Bulletin* **24** (2001) 19–27
[17] Needleman, S.B., Wunsch, C.D.: General Method Applicable to the Search for Similarities in the Amino Acid Sequence of Two Proteins. *J. Molecular Biology* **48** (1970) 443–453
[18] Pearson, W.R.: Using the FASTA Program to Search Protein and DNA Sequence Databases. *Methods Molecular Biology* **25** (1994) 365–389
[19] Smith, R., Waterman, M.S.: Identification of Common Molecular Subsequences. *J. Molecular Biology* **147** (1981) 195–197
[20] Thompson, J.D., et al.: CLUSTAL W: Improving the Sensitivity of Progressive Multiple Sequence Alignment Through Sequence Weighting, Position Specific Gap Penalties and Weight Matrix Choice. *Nuc. Acids Research* **22** (1994) 4673–4680
[21] Wu, Y., Agrawal, D., El Abbadi, A.: A Comparison of DFT and DWT based Similarity Search in Time-Series Databases. *CIKM* (2000) 488–495

A Practical Index for Genome Searching

Heikki Hyyrö[1]* and Gonzalo Navarro[2]**

[1] Dept. of Comp. and Inf. Sciences, Univ. of Tampere, Finland.
helmu@cs.uta.fi
[2] Dept. of Comp. Science, Univ. of Chile.
gnavarro@dcc.uchile.cl

Abstract. Current search tools for computational biology trade efficiency for precision, losing many relevant matches. We push in the direction of obtaining maximum efficiency from an indexing scheme that does not lose any relevant match. We show that it is feasible to search the human genome efficiently on an average desktop computer.

1 Introduction

Approximate string matching [5] is a recurrent problem in many branches of computer science, with important applications to computational biology. Efficiency is crucial to handle the large databases that are emerging, so indexes are built on the text to speed up queries later [12, 8]. Although there exist several indexed search tools like BLAST and FASTA, these usually trade time for precision, losing many relevant answers [12]. In this paper we aim at building a fast index that does not lose any answer. We combine and optimize the best existing previous lossless approaches [3, 7] and focus on the simplified case of DNA search using Levenshtein distance. This case is important in the current stage of analyzing gene functionality once the genome projects are completing their first task of obtaining the DNA sequences. In particular, approximate searching in genomes is necessary to identify homologous regions, which is fundamental to predict evolutionary history, biochemical function, and chemical structure [12].

Our main result is a practical product that can be used to search the human genome on an average desktop computer. Unique features of our index are: optimized selection of pattern pieces, bidirectional text verification, and optimized piece neighborhood generation. Our tools can be generalized to more complex problem such as weighted edit distances.

2 Indexed Approximate String Matching

The problem we focus on is: Given a long text $T_{1...n}$, and a (comparatively) short pattern $P_{1...m}$, both sequences over alphabet Σ of size σ, retrieve all substrings

---

* Supported by the Academy of Finland and Tampere Graduate School in Information Science and Engineering.
** Partially supported by Fondecyt Project 1-020831.

M.A. Nascimento, E.S. de Moura, A.L. Oliveira (Eds.): SPIRE 2003, LNCS 2857, pp. 341–349, 2003.

of T ("occurrences") whose *edit distance* to P is at most k. The edit distance, $ed(A, B)$, is the minimum number of "errors" (character insertions, deletions and substitutions) needed to convert one string into the other. So we permit an "error level" of $\alpha = k/m$ in the occurrences of P.

The most successful approach to indexed approximate string matching [8] is called *intermediate partitioning* [3, 7]. It reduces the approximate search of P to approximate search of substrings of P. Their main principle is that, if P matches a substring of T, j disjoint substrings are taken from P, then at least one of these appears in the occurrence with at most $\lfloor k/j \rfloor$ errors. These indexes split P into j pieces, search the index for each piece allowing $\lfloor k/j \rfloor$ errors, and finally check whether the piece occurrences can be extended to occurrences of P. The index is designed for exact searching of pieces, so approximate searching is handled by generating the "d-neighborhood" of each piece S, $U_d(S) = \{S' \in \Sigma^*, ed(S, S') \leq d\}$, and searching the index for each $S' \in U_d(S)$.

In [3] all the text q-grams (substrings of length q), where $q = \lceil \log_\sigma n \rceil$, are stored together with their text positions. Then the pattern is recursively split into 2 or 3 pieces at each level (dividing also the number of errors permitted), until the final pieces are short enough to be searchable with the index (Fig. 1). The paper is not very explicit on how the partitioning is exactly done.

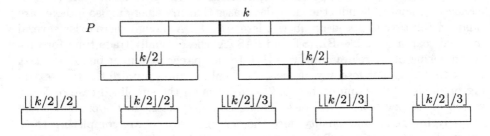

Fig. 1. The pattern is recursively split into smaller and smaller pieces, also dividing the number of errors. Above each piece we show the number of errors we permit for it.

Assume that a bottom-level piece P^i is to be searched with d_i errors. Its occurrences are found by generating its *condensed d_i-neighborhood* $UC_{d_i}(P^i)$: $A \in UC_d(B)$ iff $A \in U_d(B)$ and $A' \notin U_d(B)$ for any A' prefix of A. Any occurrence of P^i with d_i errors errors must have a prefix in $UC_{d_i}(P^i)$. Then, all these occurrences are located fast by searching the q-gram index for each string in $UC_{d_i}(P^i)$. These occurrences are then extended by going up the splitting hierarchy in stepwise manner. Each step consists of merging pieces back together and checking, with dynamic programming, whether the merged piece occurs in the text with its permitted error threshold. This recursive process is continued until either some internal node cannot be found, or we find the whole pattern.

In [7], a suffix array [2] is used instead of a q-gram index, so it can choose the partition according to optimization goals rather than guided by the constraint on the final piece lengths. They show that the optimum is $j = O(m/\log_\sigma n)$. Other differences are that text verification uses an efficient bit-parallel algorithm instead of dynamic programming, and that hierarchical verification is not used.

3   Our Proposal

The design of our index is based on the following four assumptions: (1) The indexed text is a DNA sequence. (2) The whole text is available in primary memory. (3) The index has to work efficiently on secondary memory. (4) The error level α is typically < 0.25.

The first assumption means that the alphabet size is small, $\sigma = 4$, so we can store each nucleotide in 2 bits and hence store the text in $n/4$ bytes. This permits storing the human genome in about 750 MB, which makes the second assumption more realistic in the case of the human genome. This assumption is important when evaluating the cost of accessing the text at piece verification time. The third assumption arises when one considers that the most efficient indexes take a significant amount of space, and it might not be realistic to assume that also the index will fit in main memory. Thus the index should have a suitable structure for secondary memory. The fourth assumption is based on the search parameters used in real computational biology applications. It is also very convenient because no index works well for higher α values if $\sigma = 4$.

Like [3], we use a q-gram index, d-neighborhood generation and hierarchical verification. However, we take some elements of [7] such as optimizing pattern partitioning and piece verification. We also consider secondary memory issues.

3.1   Index Structure

Our q-gram index is almost identical to that of Myers. Each q-gram is coded as a base-4 number (e.g., "agct" $\to$ 0321_4). The index has two tables, the header table and the occurrence location table. The header table H_q contains, for each q-gram, the start position of the interval in the location table L_q, which holds in ascending order all the locations of the q-gram in the text. The location table L_q holds the intervals of locations consecutively in increasing order numerical representation. Hence, the occurrences of the q-gram with numerical value x are located in $L_q[H_q[x] \ldots H_q[x+1] - 1]$.

The value of q affects the length of the pattern pieces that can be efficiently retrieved with the index. Having a large q is only a problem if the size of table H_q, $O(\sigma^q)$, becomes an issue. This is because a q-gram index can be used also in finding shorter substrings. The locations of the $(q - c)$-gram with numerical representation x are those in the interval $L_q[H_q[x\sigma^c] \ldots H_q[(x+1)\sigma^c] - 1]$. This corresponds to all q-grams having the given $(q - c)$-gram as a prefix. On the other hand, a small q may significantly degrade the performance.

Using Myers' setting $q = \lceil \log_\sigma n \rceil$ would result in the value $q = 16$ when indexing the human genome. This would result in a huge header table. Even though the index can be in secondary memory, we prefer to keep the header table in main memory (see Sec. 3.5). Hence we have opted to use $q = 12$, which results in a header table of 67 MB. With the 3 billion nucleotides human genome, the location table is roughly 12 GB, since we use 32-bit integers for all entries. It is straightforward to build this index in $O(n + \sigma^q)$ time and space.

3.2   Optimizing the Intermediate Partitioning

We employ a hierarchical partitioning that differs from [3] in that it is done bottom-up. We first determine the pieces and then build up the hierarchy. The top-down partitioning (Fig. 1) has less control over which are the final pieces.

Previous partitioning methods have assigned $d_i = \lfloor k/j \rfloor$ errors to each piece when the pattern P was partitioned into j pieces $P^1, \ldots, P^j$. However, in [8] a more accurate rule was proposed. If a string A contains no pattern piece P^i with d_i errors, then $ed(A, P) \geq \sum_{i=1}^{j}(d_i + 1) = \sum_{i=1}^{j} d_i + j$, as each piece P^i needs at least $d_i + 1$ errors to match. So we must have $\sum_{i=1}^{j} d_i + j \geq k + 1$ to ensure that no approximate occurrence of P is missed, which can be rephrased as the condition $\sum_{i=1}^{j} d_i \geq (k+1) - j$. Naturally the best choice is to allow the fewest possible errors, and thus we use the strict requirement $\sum_{i=1}^{j} d_i = k - j + 1$.

Since we have a q-gram index, we partition the pattern into pieces of length at most q. We also fix an upper bound d_M on the d_i values (see later).

We have tested two partitioning methods. A simple scheme, similar in nature to previous methods, is to partition the pattern into $j = \lceil k/d_M \rceil$ pieces, the minimum yielding $d_i \leq d_M$. Then, the pattern is split into j pieces of lengths $\lfloor m/j \rfloor$ or $\lceil m/j \rceil$, pruning pieces that are longer than q. To enforce the strict error limit $\sum_{i=1}^{j} d_i = k - j + 1$, we set $d_i = \lfloor k/j \rfloor$ for (m modulo j) + 1 pieces (giving preference to the longest pieces), and $d_i = \lfloor k/j \rfloor - 1$ for the rest.

The second, more sophisticated, approach is to precompute and store for each r-gram x, $r \in 1 \ldots q$, and for each $d \in 0 \ldots \min(d_M, \lceil 0.25 \times r \rceil - 1)$, the number of text occurrences of all the r-grams in the d-neighborhood of x. This value, $C_{x,d}$, is used to find the optimal splitting. Let us define $M_{i,t}$ as the minimum number of text positions to verify in order to search for $P_{i \ldots m}$ with t errors. Then the following recurrence holds:

$$M_{i,t} = 0, \text{ if } t < 0; \qquad M_{i,t} = \infty, \text{ if } i > m \wedge t \geq 0;$$
$$M_{i,t} = \min(M_{i+1,t}, \min_{d \in 0 \ldots \min(t,d_M), r \in 1 \ldots q} (C_{P_{i \ldots i+r-1},d} + M_{i+r,t-d-1})), \text{ otherwise.}$$

so the minimum possible verification cost is $M_{1,k}$, and we can easily retrieve from M the optimal partitioning reaching it. Once the values $C_{x,d}$ are precomputed (at indexing time), the above algorithm adds $O(qmk^2)$ to the search time, which is rather modest compared to the work it saves.

Precomputing $C_{x,d}$ is not prohibitively slow. What is more relevant is the amount of memory necessary to store $C_{x,d}$. Since the information for $d = 0$ has to be kept anyway (because it is the length of the list of occurrences of x, and it is known also for every $r \leq q$), the price is $d_M - 1$ more numbers for each different r-gram. A way to alleviate this is to use fewer bits than necessary and reduce the precision of the numbers stored, since even an approximation of the true values will be enough to choose an almost optimal strategy.

We form a hierarchy on the pattern pieces similar to that of Myers (Fig. 1). However, as we begin by optimizing the pieces at the lowest level, we form the hierarchy in bottom-up order.

Let j_h be the number of pieces and $P^{i,h}$ the ith piece at the hth level of the hierarchy. Also let $d_{i,h}$ be the number of errors associated to piece $P^{i,h}$. The top level corresponds to the whole P at the root, so $j_1 = 1$, $P^{1,1} = P$ and $d_{1,1} = k$. Assume that our optimized splitting leads to an ℓth level partitioning with j_ℓ pieces $P^{1,\ell}, \ldots, P^{j_\ell,\ell}$. In general the $(h-1)$th level is formed by pairing together two adjacent pieces from the hth level, $P^{i,h-1} = P^{2i-1,h} P^{2i,h}$. If j_h is odd, the last piece will be added to the last pair, $P^{j_{h-1},h-1} = P^{2j_{h-1}-1,h} P^{2j_{h-1},h} P^{2j_{h-1}+1,h}$. We will always have $j_{h-1} = \lfloor j_h/2 \rfloor$. This is continued until we reach level 1.

The number of errors for piece $P^{i,h-1}$ is found by locally enforcing the rule $\sum_{i=1}^{j} d_i = k-j+1$. For the piece $P^{i,h-1}$, this means $d_{2i-1,h}+d_{2i,h} = d_{i,h-1}-2+1$, which defines $d_{i,h-1}$. If piece $P^{i,h-1}$ is formed by joining three pieces, then we have $d_{i,h-1} = d_{2i-1,h} + d_{2i,h} + d_{2i+1,h} + 2$. Although the lowest level pieces may not cover P, upper level pieces are stretched to cover P. This reduces the probability of finding them in the text.

3.3   Generating d-Neighborhoods

We also use a different way of generating d-neighborhoods. Given a string A, instead of computing Myers' condensed d-neighborhood $UC_d(A)$, we compute a "length-q artificial prefix-stripped" d-neighborhood $UP_d(A)$. This is done by collecting all different strings that result from applying d errors into A in all possible combinations, with the following restrictions: (1) Errors are applied only within the window of the first q characters. (2) A character is only substituted by a different character. (3) No characters are inserted before or after the first or the last character. (4) The string is aligned to the left of the length-q window. That is, characters to the right of a deletion/insertion are moved one position to the left/right. (5) A character introduced by an insertion or substitution is not further deleted or substituted.

In practice we have noted that $UP_d(A)$ is often slightly smaller than $UC_d(A)$. For example, if $A = $ "atcg" and $d = 1$, the strings "aatcg", "tatcg", "catcg" and "gatcg" belong to $UC_d(A)$, but of these only "aatcg" belongs to $UP_d(A)$. But there are also strings in $UP_d(A)$ and not in $UC_d(A)$. For example if $B = $ "attaa" and $d = 2$, then "ataaa" is in $UP_d(A)$ but not in $UC_d(A)$, as its prefix "ataa" is in $UC_d(A)$. However, also Myers' index will fetch q-grams with prefix "ataaa" if $q \geq 5$.

The set $UP_d(A) \subseteq U_d(A)$ can be built in $O((3q\sigma)^d)$ time [11]. In our experiments with $d \leq 2$, our d-neighborhood generation was twice as fast as Myers'.

3.4   Fast Verification

In [3] they used dynamic programming approximate string matching algorithm in the stepwise merging/checking process. They also grouped into a single interval piece occurrences that were close to each other, so as to process the whole interval in a single pass and avoid checking the same text multiple times. In [7] they used a faster bit-parallel algorithm, but a more crude approach: they searched the text between the positions $j - m - k \ldots j + m + k$ whenever a piece occurrence ended at text position j. They also merged checking of adjacent occurrences.

We check each piece occurrence separately on the bottom-level of the hierarchy. We use a bit-parallel algorithm for computing edit distance [1] instead of approximate string matching. This method [6] was much faster than previous ones (Sec. 4). On the upper levels we use interval merging and a bit-parallel approximate string matching algorithm [4].

The bottom-level verification works as follows. Let $P^i = P_{i \ldots i+b}$ be a pattern piece, and let $A \in UP_d(P^i)$ occur starting from T_j. Also let substring $P^f = P_{i-u \ldots i+v}$ be the "parent" of P^i in the hierarchy, so P^f contains P^i. Initially we set $d = d_f + 1$, where d_f is the number of errors for P^f. Value d will be the number of errors in the best match for P^f found so far. If P^i is not the rightmost piece in P^f, then $ed(T_{j \ldots j+a}, P_{i \ldots i+v})$ is computed for $a = 0, 1, 2, \ldots$ until either $ed(T_{j \ldots j+a}, P_{i \ldots i+c}) \geq d$ for all $c \in [1 \ldots v]$, or we obtain $ed(T_{j \ldots j+a}, P_{i \ldots i+v}) = 0$. Whenever a value $ed(T_{j \ldots j+a}, P_{i \ldots i+v}) = d - 1$ is found, we set $d = d - 1$. This forward edit distance computation will process at most $v + d_f + 2$ characters, as after that the first stopping condition must be true. If $d = d_f + 1$ after stopping, we know that P^f does not occur. If $d \leq d_f$, we start computing the edit distance $ed(T_{j-a \ldots j-1}, P_{i-u \ldots i-1})$ for $a = 1, 2, \ldots$ similarly as above, starting with $d = d_f - d + 1$ and this time stopping as soon as $ed(T_{j-a \ldots j-1}, P_{i-u \ldots i-1}) < d$, since then we have found an occurrence of P^f with at most d_f errors.

3.5   Secondary Memory Issues

We discuss now how to handle indexes that do not fit in main memory. The biggest disadvantage of secondary memory is slow seek time. That is, although data transfer times are acceptable, performance worsens significantly if the data is not read from a moderate number of continuous locations. When using our q-gram index, queries will typically access more or less scattered positions of table L_q. When d-neighborhood generation is used, the number of q-gram lists fetched, and hence seek operations over L_d, grows exponentially with d. To limit this effect, we use bound d_M, the maximum d value. Based on practical experience we have chosen limit $d_M = 1$ in secondary memory scenarios. We also store the header table H_q in main memory to avoid an extra seek operation per q-gram. Hence the need to use a moderate q so that H_q fits in main memory.

The effects of secondary memory can also be considered when choosing the partitioning. We can weight the value $C_{x,d}$ of the occurrence table (Sec. 3.2) with an estimated cost for querying the q-gram index with the strings in $UP_d(x)$. If $C^w_{x,d}$ is the weighted cost for substring x and d errors, we use the formula

$$C_{x,d}^w = C_{x,d} \times (verification\text{-}cost + disk\text{-}transfer\text{-}cost)$$
$$+ \quad d\text{-}neighborhood\text{-}size(x,d) \times disk\text{-}seek\text{-}cost$$

normalized to the form $C_{x,d} + c \times d\text{-}neighborhood\text{-}size(x,d)$. The weight value c depends on the actual type of memory used in storing the index, and thus it should be based on empirical tests.

4   Test Results

As the test results in [7] found the index of Myers to be the best method in the case of DNA, we have compared our performance against that index. The implementation of Myers' index, from the original author, is only a limited prototype constrained to pattern lengths of the form $q \times 2^x$ and $q = \lceil \log_\sigma n \rceil$.

Fig. 2 (left) shows the results when searching the small *S. cervisiae* genome, where the index fits in main memory. We test three variants of our index, among which the clear winner is bidirectional verification of bottom-level pieces combined with our d-neighborhood generation. This is 2 to 12 (typically above 4) times faster than Myers' index. In many cases a large part of our advantage is explained by the strict rule $\sum_{i=1}^{j} d_i = k - j + 1$. This is more clear in the plots when k goes above $m/6$: at this point the index of Myers sets $d_i = 2$ for all the pieces, whereas our index increases the number of errors in a more steady manner. The difference between the search mechanisms themselves is seen when $k = m/6 - 1$ or $k = m/4 - 1$, as at these points both indexes set $d_i = 1$ or $d_i = 2$, respectively, for all the pieces. In these cases our fastest version is always roughly 4 times faster than Myers' index.

Our best combination from the above test was used for searching the human genome, where the index is on disk. We compared simple and optimized partitioning. As shown in Fig. 2 (right), in most cases using optimized partitioning had a non-negative gain, in the range 0-300%. There were also some cases where the effect was negative, but they were most probably due to the still immature calibration of our cost function. We also made a quick test to compare our disk-based index with the sequential bit-parallel approximate string matching algorithm of Myers [4]. For example in the case $m = 384$ and $k = 95$ our index was still about 6 times faster.

References

[1] H. Hyyrö. A bit-vector algorithm for computing Levenshtein and Damerau edit distances. *Nordic Journal of Computing*, 10:1–11, 2003.

[2] U. Manber and E. Myers. Suffix arrays: a new method for on-line string searches. *SIAM Journal on Computing*, pages 935–948, 1993.

[3] E. Myers. A sublinear algorithm for approximate keyword searching. *Algorithmica*, 12(4/5):345–374, Oct/Nov 1994.

[4] G. Myers. A fast bit-vector algorithm for approximate string matching based on dynamic progamming. *Journal of the ACM*, 46(3):395–415, 1999.

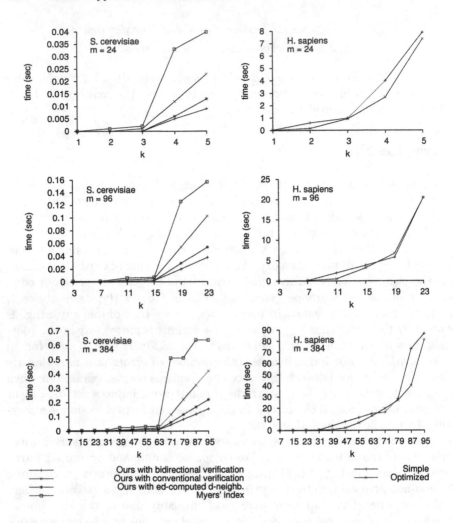

Fig. 2. On the left, Myers' index versus three variants of our index, in main memory, searching the $\approx$ 10 MB genome of *S. cerevisiae* (baker's yeast) [9]. Our variants use simple partitioning (Sec. 3.2) and $d_M = 2$. The first method uses bidirectional verification and the second conventional interval-merging combined with approximate string matching. Both of these use the d-neighborhood generation method of Sec. 3.3. The third method uses bidirectional verification combined with a d-neighborhood generation method closer to Myers' (backtracking with edit distance computation over the trie of all strings). We run on a P3 600 Mhz with 256 MB RAM and Linux OS, and compile with GCC 3.2.1 using full optimization. On the right, simple versus optimized partitioning for our index (Sec. 3.2). We use the best combination of verification/d-neighborhood generation from the tests on the left. Now the index is on disk, we use $d_M = 1$ and encode the text using 2 bits per nucleotide. The text is the Aug 8th 2001 draft of the human genome [10], of about 2.85 billion nucleotides. We run on an AMD Athlon XP 1.33 Ghz with 1 GB RAM, 40 GB IBM Deskstar 60GXP hard disk and Windows 2000 OS, and compile using Microsoft Visual C++ 6.0 with full optimization.

[5] G. Navarro. A guided tour to approximate string matching. *ACM Computing Surveys*, 33(1):31–88, 2001.

[6] G. Navarro. NR-grep: a fast and flexible pattern matching tool. *Software Practice and Experience*, 31:1265–1312, 2001.

[7] G. Navarro and R. Baeza-Yates. A hybrid indexing method for approximate string matching. *Journal of Discrete Algorithms (JDA)*, 1(1):205–239, 2000.

[8] G. Navarro, R. Baeza-Yates, E. Sutinen, and J. Tarhio. Indexing methods for approximate string matching. *IEEE Data Engineering Bulletin*, 24(4):19–27, 2001.

[9] National center for biotechnology information. http://www.ncbi.nlm.nih.gov/.

[10] Ucsc human genome project working draft. http://genome.cse.ucsc.edu/.

[11] Esko Ukkonen. Finding approximate patterns in strings. *J. of Algorithms*, 6:132–137, 1985.

[12] H.E. Williams and J. Zobel. Indexing and retrieval for genomic databases. *IEEE Trans. on Knowledge and Data Engineering*, 14(1):63–78, 2002.

Using WordNet for Word Sense Disambiguation to Support Concept Map Construction

Alberto J. Cañas[1], Alejandro Valerio[1], Juan Lalinde-Pulido[1,2], Marco Carvalho[1], Marco Arguedas[1]

[1]Institute for Human and Machine Cognition
40 South Alcaniz St., Pensacola, FL 32502
{acanas, marvalho, avalerio, marguedas}@ihmc.us
www.ihmc.us
[2]Universidad EAFIT
Medellín, Colombia
jlalinde@eafit.edu.co
www.eafit.edu.co

Abstract. The construction of a concept map consists of enumerating a list of concepts and —a more difficult task— determining the linking phrases that should connect the concepts to form meaningful propositions. Appropriate word selection, both for concepts and linking phrases, is key for an accurate knowledge representation of the user's understanding of the domain. We present an algorithm that uses WordNet to disambiguate the sense of a word from a concept map, using the map itself to provide its context. Results of preliminary experimental evaluations of the algorithm are presented. We propose to use the algorithm to (a) enhance the "understanding" of the concept map by modules in the CmapTools software that aide the user during map construction, and (b) sort the meanings of a word selected from a concept map according to their relevance within the map when the user navigates through WordNet's hierarchies searching for more appropriate terms.

1. Introduction

Concept mapping is a process of meaning-making. It implies taking a list of *concepts* – a concept being a perceived regularity in events or objects, or records of events or objects, designated by a label [1], – and organizing it in a graphical representation where pairs of concepts and linking phrases form propositions. Hence, key to the construction of a concept map is the set of concepts on which it is based. Coming up with an initial list of concepts to include in a map is really just an issue of retrieving from long-term memory. In fact, rote learners are particularly good at listing concepts. A more difficult task during concept map construction is finding the "linking phrase" that appropriately expresses the relationship between two concepts to form a meaningful proposition.

Often, while constructing a concept map, users –whether elementary school students, scientists or other professionals– pause and wonder what additional concepts they

M.A. Nascimento, E.S. de Moura, A.L. Oliveira (Eds.): SPIRE 2003, LNCS 2857, pp. 350-359, 2003.

should include in their map, or what words to use to clearly express the relationship between two concepts. Even though they know well the domain they are modeling, they cannot "remember" what other concepts are relevant, can't think of the "right word", or sometimes they need to "refresh" their knowledge about a particular sub-domain of the concept map.

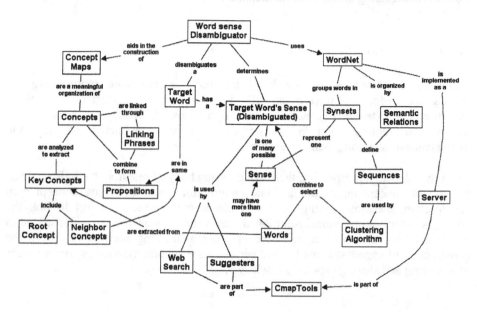

Fig. 1. A concept map on word sense disambiguating during concept map construction

At the Institute for Human and Machine Cognition (IHMC) we have developed CmapTools [2, 6], a widely-used software program that supports the construction of concept maps, as well as the annotation of the maps with additional material such as images, diagrams, video clips and other such resources. It provides the capability to store and access concept maps on multiple servers to support knowledge sharing across geographically-distant sites.

This paper describes an effort to use WordNet[13] to disambiguate the sense of words in concept maps, whether they are part of a concept or a linking phrase. By exploiting the topology and semantics of concept maps, the algorithm tries to determine which of the senses in WordNet best matches the context of the concept map. If effective, word disambiguation could then be used by the other tools to more precisely search the Web and CmapTools servers. Additionally, a WordNet server is being implemented that allows the user to lookup words and browse through the broad information that WordNet provides as an aide during concept mapping.

This paper begins with a short description of concept mapping. It then presents CmapTools, and the concept mapping aides that would take advantage of word disambiguation. Section 4 describes WordNet within the context of word disambiguation. In Section 5 we present the algorithm used to disambiguate words in a concept map. Finally, results from an experiment where we compare the word sense that the algorithm recommends with that of subjects is presented and discussed in Sections 6-8. Figure 1 shows a concept map summarizing the purpose and function of word disambiguating during concept mapping.

2. Concept Maps and Concept Mapping

Concept maps, developed by Novak [1], are tools for organizing, representing and sharing knowledge, and were specifically designed to tap into a person's cognitive structure and externalize concepts and propositions. A concept map is a two-dimensional representation of a set of concepts constructed so that the interrelationships among them are evident.

From the education perspective, there is a growing body of research that indicates that the use of concept maps can facilitate meaningful learning. During concept map construction, meaning making occurs as the learner makes an effort to link the concepts to form propositions. Additionally, concept maps have been demonstrated to be an effective means of representing and communicating knowledge during the construction of expert systems [3] and performance support systems [4] or as means of capturing and sharing experts' knowledge [5],

3. CmapTools and Concept Mapping Aides

Software programs like CmapTools make it easier for users to construct and share their knowledge models based on concept maps. In CmapTools we have extended the use of a concept maps to serve as the browsing interface to a domain of knowledge. The program facilitates the linking of a concept to other concept maps, pictures, images, audio/video clips, text, Word documents, Web pages, etc., as a means to provide access to auxiliary information on the concept. The software is based on a client-server architecture, which allows the linked media resources and concept maps to be located anywhere on the Internet.

In collaboration with D. Leake, A. Maguitman, and T. Reichherzer from Indiana University, we have developed a number of methods to aide the user during the process of construction of concept maps. These aides are based on the following observations: users often stop and wonder what other concepts they should add to the concept map they are working on; frequently, they spend time looking for the right word to use in a concept or linking phrase; they search for other concept maps that may be relevant to the one they constructing; they spend time searching through the Web for resources (Web pages, images, movies, etc.) that could be linked to their concept maps; and they search through the Web looking for additional material that could help them enhance their maps. The methods developed analyze a concept map under construction and seek useful information from both distributed concept maps and from the Web. For this, we have developed retrieval methods to exploit the semantics, topology, and context of concept maps for concept map indexing and retrieval, using methods such as topological analysis [7] to summarize structural characteristics, latent semantic analysis [8] to identify topics, and specially-developed indexing methods to capture relationships between concepts.

During concept map construction, the methods will proactively mine the web to suggest concepts that could enhance the map [9] and suggest topics for new concept maps that would complement the one being built [11], and suggest propositions and other concept maps from CmapServers that are relevant to the map being constructed [10]. Additionally, the user can, on-demand, search for concept maps, other resources, and Web pages that are relevant to the map [12].

4. WordNet

WordNet is a freely available lexical database for English whose design is inspired by current psycholinguistic theories of human lexical memory [13]. English words are organized into synonym sets, so-called synsets, and each representing one underlying lexical concept. A synset may have many words (synonyms) and one word can be a member of many synsets, one for each different sense. Relations between synsets are semantical relationships and relations between words are lexical relationships. WordNet represents both.

The literature shows that WordNet has been used successfully in word sense disambiguation algorithms in other contexts, particularly text. Li *et al.* [14] report using it as the source information for disambiguation with correct solutions up to 57% using only the sense ranked as first and 67% when considering the top two senses. Mihalcea and Moldovan[15] report better results when WordNet is combined and cross-checked with other sources, improving up to 92% when the algorithm is allowed not to give an answer when the confidence is low [16]. When using a small but representative set of words to determine the context, Nastase and Szpakowics [17] obtained an average 82% accuracy when allowing the algorithm not to give an answer.

5. Disambiguating Word Sense in Concept Maps with WordNet

The algorithm presented in this paper tries to resolve the correct sense of a polysemic (multiple meaning) word, using a concept map as its context. The selection of the appropriate words from the concept map to be used in the algorithm is crucial. The algorithm exploits the topology of the map, by including only the words of key concepts as part of the disambiguation process. Other algorithms based on text analysis (e.g. [18]) have the problem of selecting the key words, which is often difficult because there is no particular structure, and the relation between the words is not clear. We use the senses and semantic relations provided by WordNet to perform the disambiguation.

Description

The algorithm starts by selecting key concepts from the map which will be included in the process of determining the sense of a word w. Once these concepts are selected, the senses of the words within the concepts are found using WordNet after applying morphological transformations where needed.

The synsets are clustered using the hypernym distance based on WordNet's hypernym relation in such a way that only one synset per word is allowed in each cluster. Several clusters will result, each with a different weight depending on the number of words in the cluster and the hypernym distance. The cluster with the highest weight that contains a synset s of w, is the selected cluster, and s is chosen as the sense of w.

Step 1. Selection of key concepts

The topology of the map presents a strong aide in determining the key words. Based on it, these are the selected words: (a) Words in concepts with two linking phrase distance from the concept where w is found. That is, words in concepts that are in the same proposition as w; (b) Words in the root concept of the map. (The root concept of the map is usually a good representation of the overall topic of the map); (c) Other words in the concept to which w belongs. (Words within the same concept have a strong relation between them, therefore there words are included). These criteria determine the words to be used in the following steps.

Step 2. Relating words to synsets

A synset is the set of synonym words representing a concept in WordNet. Therefore, each word belongs to one or more synsets (in case of a polysemic word). In order to relate the words to the WordNet collection, we use a variation of the original morphological transformation proposed by the WordNet team in Princeton [13], making some additional validations to remove stop words and a stronger suffix and prefix analysis. At the end of this step, each word is related to the set of synsets to which it belongs.

Step 3. Hypernym sequences creation

Once the set of synsets for each word have been found, we construct all the possible hypernym sequences whose last element is a synset in one of those sets. We call a hypernym sequence an indexed collection of synsets (a list of synsets), in which the n_i element of the sequence is a hypernym of the n_{i+1} element, and n_0 is a synset with no hypernyms. The hypernym relation is transitive and asymmetrical, so it is guaranteed that there will be no repetitions and no cycles in the hypernym sequences. In

WordNet, a synset can have more than one hypernym, so there can be more than one hypernym sequence for a synset. Now we have all hypernym sequences for all words participating on the process.

Step 4. Cluster creation

For implementation purposes, an optimization is done at this point, sorting the sequences in such a way that sequences with the largest common prefix are together. This is important to reduce the cluster construction time.

With the set of sequences, the cluster creation step follows. In the context of the algorithm we define cluster as a tuple (C, l, S), where C is a hypernym sequence, l is a positive integer, S is the set of hypernym sequences belonging to the cluster and all elements of S have its first l elements equal to the first l elements of S.

For each sequence q, whose last element is a synset s that contains w, we calculate the possible clusters using q as centroid. We begin creating the first cluster which is formed by $(q, lengthOf(q), \{q\})$ and is added as to the resultant clusters. Now an iterative procedure begins: We create a new cluster grouping those sequences with $lengthOf(q)$-1 elements in common with q, then a cluster with sequences with $lengthOf(q)$-2 elements in common with q, and so forth until l is equal to 1.

Step 5. Best cluster selection

For all the clusters produced in step 4, their weight is calculated. The cluster with the highest weight is selected as the recommended one. In case two or more of them have the maximum weight, they are all selected.

The weight of each cluster is calculated as follows: Given a cluster $H = (C, l, S)$, P_i is the length of the sequence s_i, belonging to S, that is not common with C. In other words, P_i tells us in how many elements s_i differ from C, and give us a measure of distance between them. So the weight of the cluster H is $\dfrac{1}{\sum P_i}$.

Step 6. Word sense resolution

If there is only one cluster $H = (C, l, S)$ with the maximum weight, then the last synset s of C is the disambiguated sense of the word. If more than one cluster has the maximum weight, then for each of these clusters, the last synset s of C with the maximum frequency of use according to the WordNet collection is selected as the disambiguated sense of w.

An Example

To clarify the algorithm, we will use as an example the concept map in Figure 1. Let's assume the concept to disambiguate is *sense*. The algorithm first selects the words from the root concept and neighboring concepts: *words, target, synset, clustering, algorithm, disambiguator, WordNet, sequences, web, search, key, concept, suggesters, semantic,* and *relations*. Next, it checks whether any of these words does not exist in WordNet, making the morphological transformations. As the algorithm deals with nouns and the hypernym hierarchy, auxiliary WordNet relations are used to transform possible adjectives to nouns which in this case are none. To complete this step, the set of synsets for each word is determined. In the case of the word *sense*, 5 senses are found: 1-(a general conscious awareness), 2-(the meaning of a word or expression), 3-(the faculty through which the external world is apprehended), 4-(sound practical judgment), and 5-(a natural appreciation or ability). In the next step, the clusters are made using the hypernym hierarchy, resulting in 2076 paths constructed, 184 belonging to the word *sense*. This means that from 5 synsets there are 184 possible different routes from one of the *sense*'s synset to a hierarchy root. At this point, the clustering algorithm begins, resulting in 917 clusters with an average 4.9 clusters per path. The cluster with the highest weight is the one formed with paths ending with the following synsets: {*sense*(2), *word*(1), *key*(8), *wordnet*(1)} with a weight of *14.1*. This cluster is selected, with the sense *sense*(2) (the meaning of a word or expression), which is the correct sense of the word in this context.

6. Experimental Procedure

Before proceeding any further with the integration of the algorithm into CmapTools, we examined its effectiveness by running an experiment designed to compare the algorithm's designation of the sense of words from concepts in concept maps with the designation by a group of subjects. We started by asking a person with many years of experience in concept mapping to prepare a collection of 50 "relatively good" concept maps from a public CmapTools server where thousands of concept maps are stored by users from around the world. The maps needed to be in English, and "relatively good", because the server contains all kinds of "concept maps" – some of which have little resemblance to a concept map, consist of just a couple of concepts, or would be unusable for some other reason. Next, we randomly selected 10 concept maps from this set. For each of these maps, we randomly selected two of the one-word concepts in the map that had more than two senses in the WordNet collection.

For each of the 20 concepts, we printed all the senses that WordNet presents for the word in random order. We presented each concept map with the concept highlighted and the list of senses for the word, with the instructions to the subject to select the sense that was the most relevant for the word in the context of the concept map. We then refined the set of concepts by running the experiment through a small group of subjects with the only intention of eliminating those where they did not agree on the top senses for the word, to eliminate ambiguous concepts in the final selection. In this process, four concepts where dropped. The 16 concepts left where represented to each of 27 subjects, individually, asking them to select the top two senses from the list presented with each concept.

Next, we applied the algorithm to disambiguate each of the words within the context of the concept map from which it was extracted. We then compared, for each word, the sense selected by the subjects with the sense recommended by the algorithm.

7. Experimental Results

For 4 of the 16 concepts, less than 70% of the subjects agreed on the most relevant sense of the concept. These cases where dropped from the analysis because the context of the word within the concept map was not clear, and it would be impossible for the algorithm to agree with the subjects if they didn't agree among themselves..

From the 12 resulting words, the algorithm's proposed sense agreed with the sense selected by the subjects in 9 cases, giving a success rate of 75%.

The average number of concepts in the concept maps is 22.75 concepts, with a standard deviation of 9.91. The average number of concepts used by the algorithm was 9.37, with a standard deviation of 4.15.

8. Discussion

If few subjects agree on what the sense of the word is, it is impossible for the algorithm to select a sense that will be relevant to the subjects. Therefore, those words where less than 70% of the subjects agreed were excluded from the experiment. Additionally, only words with more than two senses were selected in order to eliminate the possibility of the algorithm choosing the correct sense by chance.

The results seem to indicate that it is feasible for the algorithm to obtain a result that matches the sense assigned by the subjects 75% of the time. When compared to similar efforts, the experiment's result is encouraging. Analyzing our results against previous experiments with similar conditions, Li et al. [14] obtained 57% correct solutions working over short text analysis and using 20 words as the size for the text window, compared to the 6-word average used in our algorithm. Nastase et al. [17] had 57.27% accuracy using a combined approach with Roget's Thesaurus on disambiguating nouns. Mihalcea and Moldovan [16] reported 92.2% of accuracy in nouns, but they were able to avoid suggesting a sense when the confidence level was low, which would not make sense in our intended application.

Although it is apparent that a reduced number of words can be successfully used to disambiguate the context, the correct selection of the words is crucial for the algorithm to be effective. In the case of a concept map, we exploit the topology of the map itself to define the heuristics by which the set of terms is determined.

However, the algorithm can be easily confused if the neighbor concepts are not part of the word context, which is the case in a poorly constructed map. Even though this has not been formally tested, it will most likely result on the selection of a wrong sense of the word or on constructing clusters with low coherence. Since the intended use of the algorithm always requires an answer, there is not that can be done in this case. A possible approximation that may intuitively work is returning the most common use of the word according to the WordNet collection when the weight of all clusters is under a given threshold.

We are confident that we can improve the algorithm presented by further leveraging on the map's topology and on the type of linking phrases that connect the concept to be disambiguated to other concepts. Further research on this aspect of the algorithm may improve its effectiveness.

9. Conclusions

Key to providing intelligent tools that aide the user in the construction of concept maps, is for the tools to "understand" to the extent possible the context and content of the map being constructed. Elsewhere we have reported on previous research that has shown the feasibility of using the topology and semantics of the concept map itself as the basis to find and propose new concepts, propositions, topics for new concept maps, and relevant Web pages to the user for improvement of the partially built map. In this paper, we presented the possibility of using an algorithm that exploits WordNet to disambiguate the sense of a word that is part of a concept or linking phrase in a concept map. The results shown are encouraging, and suggest more research be done to improve the algorithm. The word-disambiguating algorithm will be used within the CmapTools software suite to (a) provide context that will enhance the understanding of the concept map by other modules in the toolkit, and (b) display the most approximate sense of a word – in the context of the map being constructed-- when the user navigates through the WordNet hierarchies looking for better terms.

References

1. Novak, J. D. and D. B. Gowin, *Learning how to Learn*. NY: Cambridge Univ. Press, 1984.

2. Cañas, A. J., K. M. Ford, J. W. Coffey, T. Reichherzer, N. Suri, R. Carff, D. Shamma, G. Hill, and M. Breedy, Herramientas para Construir y Compartir Modelos de Conocimiento Basados en Mapas Conceptuales, Rev. de Inf. Educativa, Vol. 13, No. 2, pp. 145-158, 2000.

3. Ford, K. M., J. Coffey, A. J. Cañas, E. J. Andrews, C. W. Turner, *Diagnosis and Explanation by a Nuclear Cardiology Expert System*, Int. J. of Expert Systems, 9, 499-506, 1996.

4. Cañas, A. J., J. Coffey, T. Reichherzer, N. Suri, R. Carff, G. Hill, *El-Tech: A Performance Support System with Embedded Training for Electronics Technicians*, Proc. of the 11th FLAIRS, Sanibel Island, Florida, May 1997.

5. Hoffman, R.R., J. W. Coffey, and K. M. Ford, A Case Study in the Research Paradigm of Human-Centered Computing: Local Expertise in Weather Forecasting. *Unpublished Technical Report, National Imagery and Mapping Agency.* Washington, D. C., 2000.

6. Cañas, A. J., G. Hill, R. Carff, N. Suri, *CmapTools: A Knowledge Modeling and Sharing Toolkit,* Tech. Rep. IHMC CmapTools 93-01, Inst. for Human & Machine Cognition, 2003.

7. Kleinberg, J., *Authorative Sources in a Hyperlink Environment,* JACM 46(5),604-632, 1999.

8. Deerwater, S., S. T. Dumai, G.W. Furnas, T. K. Landauer, and R. Harshman, *Indexing by Latent Semantic Snalysis.* J. Am. Soc. Inf. Sci., 41(6), pp. 391-407, 1990.

9. Cañas, A. J., M. Carvalho, M. Arguedas, Mining the Web to Suggest Concepts during Concept Mapping: Preliminary Results, Proceedings of the XIII SBIE, Brazil, 2002.

10. Leake, D. B., A. Maguitman, A. J. Cañas, *Assessing Conceptual Similarity to Support Concept Mapping,* Proc. of the Fifteenth FLAIRS, Pensacola, FL (May 2002).

11. Leake, D., A. Maguitman, and T. Reichherzer, *Topic Extraction and Extension to Support Concept Mapping,* Proc. of the Sixteenth FLAIRS, 2003.

12. Carvalho, M., R. Hewett, A. J. Cañas, *Enhancing Web Searches from Concept Map-based Knowledge Models,* SCI 2001, Orlando, FL (July 2001).

13. Fellbaum, C. ed., *WordNet – An Electronic Lexical Database,* MIT Press, 1998.

14. Li X., S. Szpakowics, S. Matwin, A WordNet-based Algorithm for Word Sense Disambiguation Proceedings of IJCAI-95. Montréal, Canada, 1995.

15. Mihalcea, R., D. Moldovan, *A Method for Word Sense Disambiguation of Unrestricted Text.* Proc. of ACL '99, pp.152-158, Maryland, NY, June 1999.

16. Mihalcea, R., D. Moldovan, *An Iterative Approach to Word Sense Disambiguation,* Proc. of Flairs 2000, pp. 219-223, Orlando, FL, May 2000.

17. Nastase, V., S. Szpakowics, *Word Sense Disambiguation in Roget's Thesaurus Using WordNet,* Proc. of the NAACL WordNet and Other Lexical Resources Workshop. Pittsburgh, June 2001.

18. Fellbaum C., M. Palmer, H. Dang, L. Delfs, S. Wolf, *Manual &Z Automatic Semantic Annotation with WordNet.* Workshop on WordNet & other Lexical Resources. NAACL-01, 2001.

Memory-Adaptative Dynamic Spatial Approximation Trees*

Diego Arroyuelo[1], Francisca Muñoz[2], Gonzalo Navarro[2], and Nora Reyes[1]

[1] Depto. de Informática, Univ. Nac. de San Luis, Argentina.
{darroy,nreyes}@unsl.edu.ar
[2] Center for Web Research, Dept. of Computer Science, Univ. of Chile.
{franmuno,gnavarro}@dcc.uchile.cl

Abstract. Dynamic spatial approximation trees (*dsa–trees*) are efficient data structures for searching metric spaces. However, using enough storage, pivoting schemes beat *dsa–trees* in any metric space. In this paper we combine both concepts in a data structure that enjoys the features of *dsa–trees* and that improves query time by making the best use of the available memory. We show experimentally that our data structure is competitive for searching metric spaces.

1 Introduction

"Proximity" or "similarity" searching is the problem of looking for objects in a set close enough to a query. This has applications in a vast number of fields. The problem can be formalized with the *metric space model* [1]: There is a universe $\mathcal{U}$ of objects, and a positive real-valued distance function $d : \mathcal{U} \times \mathcal{U} \longrightarrow \mathbb{R}^+$ defined among them, which satisfies the metric properties: *strict positiveness* $(d(x,y) = 0 \Leftrightarrow x = y)$, *symmetry* $(d(x,y) = d(y,x))$, and *triangle inequality* $(d(x,z) \leqslant d(x,y) + d(y,z))$. The smaller the distance between two objects, the more "similar" they are. We have a finite database $S \subseteq \mathcal{U}$ that can be preprocessed to build an index. Later, given a *query* $q \in \mathcal{U}$, we must retrieve all similar elements in the database. We are mainly interested in the *range query*: Retrieve all elements in S within distance r to q, that is, $\{x \in S, \ d(x,q) \leqslant r\}$.

Generally, the distance is expensive to compute, so one usually defines the search complexity as the number of distance evaluations performed. Proximity search algorithms build an *index* of the database to speed up queries, avoiding the exhaustive search. Many of these indexes are based on pivots (Sec. 2).

In this paper we present a hybrid index for metric space searching built on the *dsa–tree*, an index supporting insertions and deletions that is competitive in spaces of medium difficulty, but unable of taking advantage of the available memory. This is enriched with a pivoting scheme. Pivots use the available memory to improve query time, and in this way they can beat any other structure, but too

---

* Supported in part by CYTED VII.19 RIBIDI Project and, the third author, Millenium Nucleus Center for Web Research, Grant P01-029-F, Mideplan, Chile.

M.A. Nascimento, E.S. de Moura, A.L. Oliveira (Eds.): SPIRE 2003, LNCS 2857, pp. 360–368, 2003.

many pivots are needed in difficult spaces. Our new structure is still dynamic and makes better use of memory, beating both *dsa-trees* and basic pivots.

Unlike previous work [3], (1) we use local rather than global pivots, and provide empirical evidence in favor of this decision, (2) we use pivots for free.

2 Pivoting Algorithms

Essentially, pivoting algorithms choose some elements p_i from the database S, and precompute and store all distances $d(a, p_i)$ for all $a \in S$. At query time, they compute distances $d(q, p_i)$ against the pivots. Then the *distance by pivots* between $a \in S$ and q gets defined as $\mathcal{D}(a, q) = \max_{p_i} |d(a, p_i) - d(q, p_i)|$.

It can be seen that $\mathcal{D}(a, q) \leqslant d(a, q)$ for all $a \in S$, $q \in \mathcal{U}$. This is used to avoid distance evaluations. Each a such that $\mathcal{D}(a, q) > r$ can be discarded because we deduce $d(a, q) > r$ without actually computing $d(a, q)$. All the elements that cannot be discarded this way are directly compared against q.

Usually pivoting schemes perform better as more pivots are used, this way beating any other index. They are, however, better suited to "easy" metric spaces [1]. In hard spaces they need too many pivots to beat other algorithms.

3 Dynamic Spatial Approximation Trees

In this section we briefly describe dynamic *sa–trees* (*dsa-trees* for short), in particular the version called *timestamp with bounded arity* [2], on top of which we build. Deletion algorithms are omitted for lack of space.

3.1 Insertion Algorithm

The *dsa–tree* is built incrementally, via insertions. The tree has a maximum arity. Each tree node a stores a timestamp of its insertion time, *time(a)*, and its covering radius, $R(a)$, which is the maximum distance to any element in its subtree. Its set of children is called $N(a)$, the *neighbors* of a. To insert a new element x, its point of insertion is sought starting at the tree root and moving to the neighbor closest to x, updating $R(a)$ in the way. We finally insert x as a new (leaf) child of a if (1) x is closer to a than to any $b \in N(a)$, and (2) the arity of a, $|N(a)|$, is not already maximal. Neighbors are stored left to right in increasing timestamp order. Note that the parent is always older than its children.

3.2 Range Search Algorithm

The idea is to replicate the insertion process of elements to retrieve. That is, we act as if we wanted to insert q but keep in mind that relevant elements may be at distance up to r from q, so in each decision for simulating the insertion of q we permit a tolerance of $\pm r$. So it may be that relevant elements were inserted in different children of the current node, and backtracking is necessary.

RANGE SEARCH (Node a, Query q, Radius r, Timestamp t)
1. **if** $time(a) < t \ \wedge \ d(a,q) \leqslant R(a) + r$ **then**
2.   **if** $d(a,q) \leqslant r$ **then** report a
3. $d_{min} \leftarrow \infty$
4.   **for** $b_i \in N(a)$ in increasing timestamp order **do**
5.   **if** $d(b_i, q) \leqslant d_{min} + 2r$ **then**
6. $k \leftarrow \min\{j > i, \ d(b_i, q) > d(b_j, q) + 2r\}$
7.   RANGE SEARCH$(b_i, q, r, time(b_k))$
8. $d_{min} \leftarrow \min\{d_{min}, \ d(b_i, q)\}$

Alg. 1: Range query algorithm on a *dsa–tree* with root a.

Note that, at the time an element x was inserted, a node a may not have been chosen as its parent because its arity was already maximal. So, at query time, we must choose the minimum distance to x only among $N(a)$. Note also that, when x was inserted, elements with higher timestamp were not yet present in the tree, so x could choose its closest neighbor only among older elements.

Hence, we consider the neighbors $\{b_1, \dots, b_k\}$ of a from oldest to newest, disregarding a, and perform the minimization as we traverse the list. That is, we enter into subtree b_i if $d(q, b_i) \leqslant \min(d(q, b_1), \dots, d(q, b_{i-1})) + 2r$.

We use timestamps to reduce the work inside older neighbors. Say that $d(q, b_i) > d(q, b_{i+j}) + 2r$. We have to enter subtree b_i anyway because b_i is older. However, only the elements with timestamp smaller than $time(b_{i+j})$ should be considered when searching inside b_i; younger elements have seen b_{i+j} and they cannot be interesting for the search if they are inside b_i. As parent nodes are older than their descendants, as soon as we find a node inside subtree b_i with timestamp larger than $time(b_{i+j})$ we can stop the search in that branch.

Algorithm 1 performs range searching. Note that, except in the first invocation, $d(a, q)$ is already known from the invoking process.

4   A Dsa–tree with Pivots

Pivoting techniques can trade memory space for query time, but they perform well on easy spaces only. A *dsa–tree*, on the other hand, is suitable for searching spaces of medium difficulty. However, it uses a fixed amount of memory, being unable of taking advantage of additional memory to improve query time. Our idea is to obtain a hybrid data structure that gets the best of both worlds, by enriching *dsa–trees* with pivots. The result is better than both building blocks.

We choose different pivots for each tree node, such that *we do not need any extra distance evaluations against pivots*, either at insertion or search time. Recall that, after we find the insertion point of a new element x, say $x \in N(a)$, x has been compared against all its ancestors in the tree, all the siblings of its ancestors, and its own siblings in $N(a)$. At query time, when we reach node

x, some distances between q and the aforementioned elements have also been computed. So, we can use (some of) these elements as pivots to obtain better search performance, without introducing extra distance computations. Next we present different ways to choose the pivots of each node.

4.1   H–Dsat1: Using Ancestors as Pivots

A natural alternative is to regard the ancestors of each node as its pivots. Let $\mathcal{A}(x)$ be the set of ancestors of $x \in S$. We define $P(x) = \{(p_i,\ d(x, p_i)),\ \ p_i \in \mathcal{A}(x)\}$. We store $P(x)$ at each node x and use it to prune the search.

Insertion Algorithm. We set $P(x) = \emptyset$ and begin searching for the insertion point of x. For each node a we choose in our path, we add $(a, d(x, a))$ to $P(x)$. When the insertion point of x is found, $P(x)$ contains the distances to the ancestors of x. Note that we do not perform any extra distance evaluations to build $P(x)$. Thus, the construction cost of a H–DSAT1 is *the same* of a *dsa–tree*.

Range Search Algorithm. We modify the *dsa-tree* algorithm to use the set $P(x)$ stored at each tree node x. We recall that, given a set of pivots, the distance by pivots $\mathcal{D}(a, q)$ is a lower bound for $d(a, q)$.

Consider again Alg. 1. If at step 1 it holds $\mathcal{D}(a, q) > R(a) + r$, then $d(a, q) > R(a) + r$, and we can stop the search at node a without evaluating $d(a, q)$. An element a in S is said to be *feasible* for query q if $\mathcal{D}(a, q) \leqslant R(a) + r$. That is, it is feasible that a or some element in its subtree lie within the search radius of q.

We compute $\mathcal{D}(a, q)$ at search time without additional distance evaluations. Assume we reach node p_k and want to decide whether the search must enter subtree $x \in N(p_k)$. At this point, we have computed all distances $d(q, p_i)$, $p_i \in \mathcal{A}(x)$. If $\mathcal{A}(x) = \{p_1, \ldots, p_k\}$, then these distances are $d(q, p_1), \ldots, d(q, p_k)$. In a H–DSAT1, we store $P(x) = \{(p_1, d(x, p_1)), \ldots, (p_k, d(x, p_k))\}$ at node x. Hence, all the elements needed to compute $\mathcal{D}(x, q)$ are present, at no extra cost.

The distances $d(q, p_i)$ are stored in a stack as the search goes up and down the tree. The sets $P(x)$ are also stored in root-to-x order, so that references to the pivots in $P(x)$ (first component of pairs) are unnecessary and we save space.

The *feasible neighbors* of node a, denoted $F(a)$, are the neighbors $b \in N(a)$ such that $\mathcal{D}(b, q) \leqslant R(b) + r$. The other neighbors are said to be *infeasible*.

At search time, if we reach node a, we may consider only its feasible neighbors, as other subtrees can be wholly discarded. Although they are discarded using $\mathcal{D}$, which is computed for free, it does not immediately follow that we obtain for sure an improvement in search time. The reason is that infeasible nodes still serve to reduce d_{min} in Alg. 1, which in turn may save us entering younger siblings. Hence, by saving computations against infeasible nodes, we may have to enter new siblings later. This is an intrinsic tradeoff of our method.

Alg. 2 shows the basic search approach. Note that in step 8 we run into the risk of comparing infeasible elements against q. This is done in order to use timestamp information as much as possible, but it also reduces the benefits of using pivots. The following alternatives are improvements to this weakness.

RANGE SEARCH H–DSAT1 (Node a, Query q, Radius r, Timestamp t)
1. **if** $time(a) < t \ \wedge \ d(a,q) \leqslant R(a) + r$ **then**
2.   **if** $d(a,q) \leqslant r$ **then** report a
3. $d_{min} \leftarrow \infty$
4. $F(a) \leftarrow \{b \in N(a), \ \ \mathcal{D}(b,q) \leqslant R(b) + r\}$
5.   **for** $b_i \in N(a)$ in increasing timestamp order **do**
6.   **if** $b_i \in F(a)$ **then**
7.   **if** $d(b_i,q) \leqslant d_{min} + 2r$ **then**
8. $k \leftarrow \min\{j > i, \ d(b_i,q) > d(b_j,q) + 2r\}$
9.   RANGE SEARCH H–DSAT1$(b_i, q, r, time(b_k))$
10.   **if** $d(b_i,q)$ has already been computed **then** $d_{min} \leftarrow \min\{d_{min}, \ d(b_i,q)\}$

Alg. 2: Range searching for query q with radius r in a H–DSAT1 with root a.

H–DSAT1D: *Optimizing using* $\mathcal{D}$. We use $\mathcal{D}$ not only to determine feasibility and hence prune subtrees, but also to decrease the number of infeasible elements directly compared against q in step 8. Some of those comparisons can be saved by using $\mathcal{D}$. The key observation is that $d(b_i,q) \leqslant \mathcal{D}(b_j,q) + 2r$ implies $d(b_i,q) \leqslant d(b_j,q) + 2r$, so we can conclude that b_j is not of interest in step 8 without computing $d(b_j,q)$. Although we save some distance computations and obtain the same result, still there will be infeasible elements compared against q.

H–DSAT1F: *Using Timestamps of Feasible Neighbors.* Timestamps are not essential for the correctness of the algorithm. Although the optimal choice is to use the smallest correct timestamp, any larger value would do. So we compute a safe approximation to the correct timestamp, while ensuring that no infeasible elements are ever compared against q. Note that every feasible neighbor of a node will be compared against q inevitably. So, if for $b_i \in F(a)$ it holds $d(b_i,q) \leqslant d_{min} + 2r$, then in step 8 we compute the oldest timestamp t among the reduced set $\{b_{i+j} \in F(a), \ d(b_i,q) > d(b_{i+j},q) + 2r\}$. This uses as much timestamping information as possible without considering infeasible elements.

4.2   H–Dsat2: Using Ancestors and Their Older Siblings as Pivots

We aim at using even more pivots than H–DSAT1, to improve even more the search performance. At search time, when we reach a node a, q has been compared against all the ancestors and some of the older siblings of ancestors of a. Hence, we use this extended set of pivots for each node a.

Insertion Algorithm. The only difference in a H–DSAT2 is in the $P(x)$ sets we compute. Let $x \in S$ and $\mathcal{A}(x) = \{p_1, \ldots, p_k\}$ be the set of its ancestors, where p_i is the ancestor at tree level i. Note that $p_{i+1} \in N(p_i)$. Hence, $(b, d(x,b)) \in P(x)$ if and only if (1) $b \in \mathcal{A}(x)$, or (2) $p_i, p_{i+1} \in \mathcal{A}(x) \wedge b \in N(p_i) \wedge time(b) < time(p_{i+1})$.

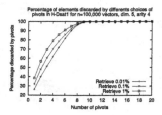 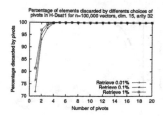

Fig. 1. Percentage of elements discarded using the latest pivots in H–DSAT1.

Range Search Algorithm. As before, to compute $\mathcal{D}(x, q)$ we need the distances between q and the pivots of x stored in a stack. But it is possible that some of the pivots of x have not been compared against q because they were infeasible. In order to retain the same pivot order of $P(x)$, we push invalid elements into the stack when infeasible neighbors are found. $\mathcal{D}$ is then computed having this in mind. We define the same variants of the search algorithm for H–DSAT2, which only differ from H–DSAT1 in the way of computing $\mathcal{D}$.

5   Limiting the Use of Storage

In practice, available memory is bounded. Our data structures use memory in a non-controlled way (each node uses as much pivots as the definition requires). This rules them out for many real-life situations. In order to adapt our structures to fit the available memory, we restrict the number of pivots stored in each node to a value k, holding a subset of the original set of pivots. As a result, the performance of our data structures may degrade at search time. A way of minimizing this effect is to choose a "good" set of pivots for each node.

We study empirically which pivots discard more elements at search time. See Sec. 6 for details on the experiments.

Good Pivots in H–Dsat1. Because of the insertion process, the latest pivots of a node should be good since they are close, and hence good representatives, of the node. We verify experimentally that most discards using pivots were due to the latter ones. Fig. 1 shows that a small number of latter pivots per node suffice. In dimension 5, about 10 pivots per node discard all the elements that can be discarded using pivots. In higher dimensions, even less pivots are needed. This alternative will be called H–DSAT1 k Latest.

Good Pivots in H–Dsat2. The ancestors of a node are close to it, but the siblings of the ancestors are not necessarily close. So we expect that using the k latest pivots (H–DSAT2 k Latest) does not perform as well as before. An obvious alternative is H–DSAT2 k Nearest, which uses the k nearest pivots, not the k latest. Fig. 2 confirms that less nearest pivots are needed to discard the same number of nodes as latest pivots. However, note that for H–DSAT2 k Nearest we

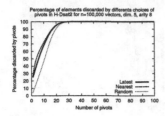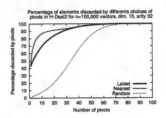

Fig. 2. Comparison between the quality of the pivots in a H–DSAT2, retrieving 0.01% of database. Unlike the others, random pivots degrade quickly as the dimension grows.

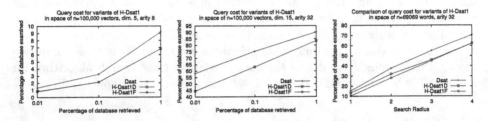

Fig. 3. Comparison of query cost for variants of H–DSAT1.

need to store the references to the pivots in order to compute $\mathcal{D}$. Hence, given a fixed amount of memory, this alternative must use less pivots per node than the others.

6   Experimental Results

We have evaluated our structures over three metric spaces. First, a dictionary of 69,069 English words under edit distance (minimum number of character insertions, deletions and substitutions to make the strings equal), of interest in spelling applications. The other spaces are real unitary cubes in dimensions 5 and 15 under Euclidean distance, using 100,000 uniformly distributed random points. We treat these just as metric spaces, disregarding coordinate information.

In all cases, we left apart 100 random elements to act as queries. The data structures were built 20 times varying the order of insertions. We tested arities 4, 8, 16, and 32. Each tree built was queried 100 times, using radii 1 to 4 in the dictionary, and radii retrieving 0.01%, 0.1%, and 1% of the set in vector spaces.

Fig. 3 shows that H–DSAT1F outperformed H–DSAT1D, clearly in the dictionary and slightly in vector spaces. The results are similar on H–DSAT2.

Fig. 4 shows that our structures are competitive, as our best versions of H–DSAT1 and H–DSAT2 largely improve upon *dsa–trees*. This shows that our structures make good use of extra memory. H–DSAT2 can use more memory than H–DSAT1, and hence its query cost is better.

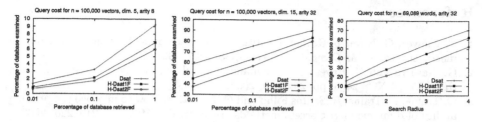

Fig. 4. Comparison of query cost among our structures.

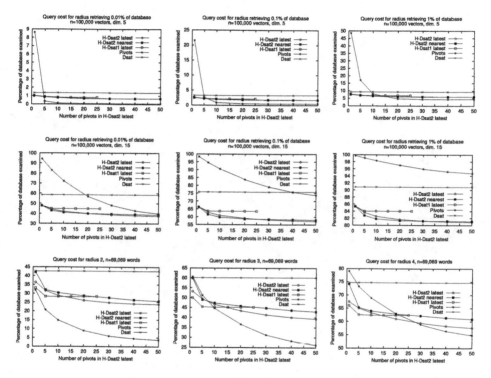

Fig. 5. Query cost of H–DSAT1F and H–DSAT2F versus a pivoting algorithm.

However, there is a price in memory usage, e.g., H–DSAT1 needs 1.3 to 4.0 times the memory of *dsa–tree*, while H–DSAT2 requires 5.2 to 17.5 times. Hence the interest in comparing how well our structures use limited memory compared to others. Fig. 5 compares against a generic pivot data structure, using the same amount of memory in all cases. We also show a *dsa–tree* as a reference point, as it uses a fixed amount of memory. In easy spaces (dimension 5 or dictionary) we do better when there is little available memory, but in dimension 15 H–DSAT2 is always the best. More pivots are needed to beat H–DSAT in harder problems

References

1. E. Chávez, G. Navarro, R. Baeza-Yates, and J. Marroquín. Proximity searching in metric spaces. *ACM Computing Surveys*, 33(3):273–321, 2001.
2. G. Navarro and N. Reyes. Fully dynamic spatial approximation trees. In *Proc. SPIRE'02*, LNCS 2476, pp. 254–270, 2002.
3. C. Traina, A. Traina, R. Santos Filho and C. Faloutsos. How to improve the pruning ability of dynamic metric access methods. In *Proc. CIKM'02*, pp. 219–226, 2002.

Large Edit Distance with Multiple Block Operations

Dana Shapira and James A. Storer

Computer Science Department Brandeis University
shapird/storer@cs.brandeis.edu

Abstract. We consider the addition of some or all of the operations *block move, block delete, block copy, block reversals,* and *block copy reversals,* to the traditional edit distance problem (finding the minimum number of insert-character and delete-character operations to convert one string to another). When all of the above operations are allowed, the problem, called the *nearest neighbors problem,* is NP hard, and the best known approximation is $O(\log n \log^* n)$, which was achieved by Muthukrishnan and Sahinalp [2000,2002a]. In this paper we show that this problem can be approximated by a constant factor of 3.5 using a simple sliding window method. When eliminating reversals, the same method reduces the best known approximation of 12, achieved by Ergun, Muthukrishnan and Sahinalp [2003], down to a factor of 4. Both constant factors are proved to be tight. Allowing only subsets of these operations does not necessarily make the problem easier. Shapira and Storer [2002] present a $\log n$ factor approximation algorithm for edit distance with block moves (which is also an NP-complete problem). Here, we show that edit distance with block deletions can be solved optimally, but edit distance with block moves and block deletions remains NP-complete and can be reduced to the problem of block moves only, keeping the same $\log n$ factor approximation.

1 Introduction

The traditional edit distance problem considers character insertions, deletions and sometimes exchanges, in order to find the minimum number of such operations required to convert a given string to another. Shapira and Storer [2002] consider the standard edit distance problem augmented with block moves, where a sequence of characters are moved from one location in the string to another with constant cost, and present a $\log n$ factor approximation algorithm to optimal (finding an optimal solution is NP-hard). The main idea is to reduce the two given strings to two new ones and perform the traditional edit distance on those. One way to model block moves is by viewing strings as linked lists, and to allow operations to apply to pointers associated with characters as well as the characters themselves; in this model both moving and deleting substrings are done in $O(1)$ processing time. In Shapira and Storer [2002], the attention is limited to only block moves. Here we consider character insertions, block deletions, block

M.A. Nascimento, E.S. de Moura, A.L. Oliveira (Eds.): SPIRE 2003, LNCS 2857, pp. 369–377, 2003.

moves, block copies, and block reversals, and prove that using a simple left to right greedy sliding window algorithm gives an approximation factor of 3.5 to optimal. We then consider block deletions with or without character insertions, character moves and block moves. These variations are shown to be solved optimally in polynomial time using dynamic programming, except when including block moves, where the problem is then NP-hard, and a *log* factor approximation algorithm can be achieved.

Muthukrishnan and Sahinalp [2002b] present a near linear time algorithm to compute the minimum number of character replacements and block reversals needed to convert a given string to another. In [2000, 2002a] they consider the edit distance with block moves, deletes, copies and reversals, and approximate this NP-hard problem, called also the nearest neighbors problem, to a factor of $O(\log n \log^* n)$, using an embedding of strings into the vector space. The same factor is achieved by Cormode and Muthukrishnan [2002], when considering the edit distance with moves only. They embed the strings into the L_1 vector space. Cormode, Paterson, Sahinalp and Vishkin [2000] consider the hamming and Levenshtein distances, and define the LZ distance, which employs block copies and block deletions, together with the usual single character operations. They consider the problem of starting from an empty string and producing one string given another, in a minimum number of operations. Here, we consider the minimum number of operations performed on a given string in order to produce the other. Ergun, Muthukrishnan and Sahinalp [2003] consider the edit distance with block moves, deletes and copies and present a polynomial time algorithm with a factor of 12 approximation to optimal. Here we show how this constant factor can be reduced to 4.

Bafna and Pevzner [1998] consider the case that S is a permutation of the integers 1 through n, and give a 1.5 approximation algorithm for minimizing the number of moves needed to transform S into another permutation T. The restriction that all characters are distinct changes the problem. Lorpresti and Tompkins [1997] compare two strings by extracting collections of substrings and placing them into the corresponding order. Tichy [1984] considers block copies and looks for the minimal covering set of one string with respect to another. In Hannenalli [1996], one can only swap a prefix or suffix of one chromosome with a prefix or suffix of another. Durand, Farach, Ravi, and Singh [1997] and Smith and Waterman [1981]) present algorithms for best string alignment.

In section 2 we consider the edit distance with block moves, block copies and block reversals, and employ a simple left-to-right greedy sliding window algorithm that achieves a constant bound approximation of 3.5 to optimal. In section 3 we present optimal algorithms for solving variations of edit distance with block deletions. In Section 4 we prove that edit distance with block moves and block deletions is NP-Hard, and present an algorithm with a *log n* approximation factor, by reducing the problem to one of moves only.

2   Block Copies, Moves, Reversals, and Deletions

Given a string S of length m, a string T of length n, and a set of operations *character insert, block delete, block move, block copy,* and *block copy reversals,* we are interested in the minimum number of operations required to transform S to T. Lopresti and Tomkins [1997] prove that finding the minimum number of edits (block moves and copies) is NP-hard, and it can be shown that it remains NP-hard when character insertions, block deletions, and block reversals are also allowed. In this section we give theoretical evidence that sliding window type compression is a good choice for approximating this problem by showing that it can be employed to compute a constant factor of 3.5 approximation to the number of operations used by an optimal algorithm that uses the minimum number of operations possible. We call this the *full window algorithm* since the window size has been made large enough so that from any point in T, a copy can reach back to the beginning of S. That is, the window starts as S and grows over time, always containing S as its initial prefix.

Full Window (FW) Algorithm:

Step 1: Form the string ST.

Step 2: Compress T with window of size $m + n$. Use unit-cost *greedy* parsing. That is, start with the first position of T, then repeatedly find the longest match/reversed-match between the incoming text and the text to the left of the current position, and replace it by a copy/copy-reversal of unit cost (or by a single character, also of unit cost, if a match of 2 or more characters cannot be found).

Step 3: Delete S.

Define a copy to be a *left-copy* if it copies a string from position i to position $j > i$, and a *right-copy* if it copies a string from position i to position $j < i$. A *left/right-copy-reversal* is defined in a similar way. X^R denotes the string obtained by reversing X. To show that FW approximates optimal by at most a constant factor, first consider the following *brute-force* method of converting S to T, that uses only left-copies and left-copy-reversals in a layered arrangement (followed by a single delete of a prefix of the generated string to obtain the final string T).

Brute-Force Method:

A. Let $(o_1, o_2, \ldots, o_k)$ be a sequence of operations (character insert, block delete, block move, block copy and block copy reversal) performed by an optimal algorithm.

B. Construct the string $X = S_0 S_1 \ldots S_k$, where $S_0 = S$, and the substring S_i is obtained from S_{i-1} via only insert-character, left-copy or left-copy-reversal operations and is the same as S_{i-1}, except with operation o_i performed. For o_i which is a *character-insert*, a single copy of all of S_i followed by a character-insert suffices. For o_i which is a *delete, move, copy* or *copy-reversal*, 2, 4, 3 or 3 copies suffice, respectively. However, for the purpose of this proof, when S_i is a right-copy or right-copy-reversal that converts $S_i = ACBD$ to $S_i = ABCBD$ (by copying the substring B to a position to its left), we use 5 copies, 4 of which copy A, the left occurrence of B, C, and D from S_i, and one that copies the right occurrence of B from the left one in S_i.

C. Perform a single block deletion to delete the prefix $S_0...S_{k-1}$, leaving $S_k = T$.

This brute force method is impractical; not only is it NP-complete to compute an optimal parsing (and why bother doing anything else once you have it), but it uses quadratic space. However, we can use it to argue an upper bound on the performance of FW. Ergun, Muthukrishnan and Sahinalp [2003] use a similar brute force construction, in conjunction with a second reduction to get a quadratic space, factor of 12 approximation. They employ a charging scheme to eliminate recursion and employ a reduction to the non-recursive case, while we directly expand each operation. Here we show how this brute force construction can be "collapsed" to just the $m + n$ space for S and T and at most a factor of 4 more operations than an optimal transformation. We first look at a left to right optimal and greedy parsing of a given string, which partitions it into blocks of reoccurring substrings. It can be proved that the number of greedy phrases of the FW algorithm is equal to the number of left to right optimal phrases.

Theorem 1 *The FW algorithm approximates the edit distance problem with character insert, block move, block delete, block copy, and block copy reversals, within a constant factor of 3.5.*

PROOF: We imagine that T is represented by a single copy of S_k and work our way from S_k down to S_1 in k stages, where we show that if T can be obtained from S_i with some number of insert-character, left-copy and left-copy-reversal operations x, then S_i can be eliminated and T can be obtained from S_{i-1} with at most $x+4$ insert-character, left-copy and left-copy-reversal operations. The key invariant at each Stage i, is that T is constructed from S_i using only character inserts, left copies or left-copy reversals with targets that lie entirely in T or entirely in S_i, and the targets in S_i do not overlap. Since T is initially a single copy from S_k, the invariant is initially true. Now inductively assume that the invariant is true prior to Stage i. Since S_i is comprised of at most 5 copies (or 1 copy and an insert-character), and hence at most 4 phrase boundaries, all copies in T can be replaced by a copy from S_{i-1}, except for at most 4, each of which can be split into two copies.

If o_i is a character-insert, at most one copy contains the inserted character, and so it can be replaced by at most two copies from S_{i-1} and a character-insert for a total of at most 2 additional operations. If o_i is a block delete, at most one copy is replaced by two copies from S_{i-1}, for a total of at most one additional operation. If o_i is a block move, (that is, for some substrings A, B, C and D, $S_{i-1} = ABCD$ is transformed to $S_i = ACBD$), at most 3 copies (the ones spanning AC, CB, and BD in S_i), are each replaced by two copies from S_{i-1}, for a total of at most 3 additional operations. If o_i is a left-copy or left-copy-reversal, (that is, $S_{i-1} = ABCD$ is transformed to $S_i = ABCBD$ for left copies and to $S_i = ABCB^R D$ for left copy-reversals), 2 copies of T (the ones spanning

CB and BD and CB^R and B^RD in S_i, respectively), become at most 4 copies, at most 2 of which copy from S_{i-1} and at most two of which are a left-copy or a left-copy-reversal contained in T (going from the rightmost of the two copies corresponding to B to the other copy/reversed-copy), for a total of at most 2 additional operations.

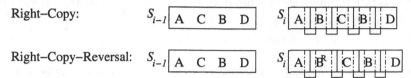

If o_i is a right-copy or right-copy-reversal, (that is, $S_{i-1} = ACBD$ is transformed to $S_i = ABCBD$ for right copies and to $S_i = AB^RCBD$ for right copy reversals), as depicted above, 4 copies of T (the ones spanning AB, BC, CB, BD and AB^R, B^RC, CB and BD, in S_i, respectively), become at most 8 copies, at most 6 of which copy from S_{i-1}, and at most two of which are a left-copy/left-copy-reversal contained in T (going from the rightmost of the two copies corresponding to B to the other copy), for a total of at most 4 additional operations.

So at the end of the k stages, the string ST remains, where T is formed by at most $4k + 1$ operations, all of which are insert-character or copies from S (the initial copy that represented T plus at most 4 operations for each stage). One additional delete of S can then remove S. Thus, S can be converted to T using just the $m + n$ space to store S and T, and with at most $4k + 2$ operations, as compared to k operations used by an optimal algorithm. Using the previous lemma, that for unit-cost sliding window compression, greedy parsing is optimal, and hence FW uses $\leq 4k + 2$ copies. To complete the proof, note that we can reverse the entire string, perform the operations, and then reverse it again if there are more left-copies and left-copy-reversals than right-copies and right-copy reversals in the reversed string. For the worst case where the number of right-copies and right-copy-reversals is equal to the number of left-copies and left-copy-reversals, $k/2$ operations cost $4(k/2)$ and the other half costs $3(k/2)$, for a total of $4(k/2) + 3(k/2) + 2 + 2 = 3.5k + 4$ (the additional 2 operations is for reversing the string). ∎

Corollary 1 *If the allowed operations are only character insert, block delete, block move and block copy, the approximation bound is 4. If, in addition, the block reversal operation is allowed the approximation bound is 3.5.*

Corollary 2 *The approximation factors of 3.5 and 4 stated in Theorem 1 and Corollary 1 are tight, even for a two symbol alphabet.*

PROOF: We first show that the bound of 4 is tight, then modify the construction for a finite alphabet, and finally use a slight variation of the construction for the factor of 3.5. Consider the following strings: $S_1 = AB_1B_2CDE$ and $T_1 = AB_1DB_2CDE$ uses a single right copy of D, but must perform 3 left copies: AB_1, D and B_2CDE. $S_2 = AB_1B_2CD_1D_2EFG$ and $T_2 = AB_1D_1FD_2B_2CD_1FD_2EFG$ uses two right copies ($\mathrm{copy}(F)$ and $\mathrm{copy}(D_1FD_2)$), but must perform 7 left copies: AB_1, D_1, F, D_2, B_2CD_1, F and D_2EFG. $S_3AB_1B_2CD_1D_2EF_1F_2GHI$ and $T_3 = AB_1D_1F_1HF_2D_2B_2CD_1F_1HF_2D_2EF_1HF_2GHI$ uses three recursive right copies (copy(H), copy(F_1HF_2) and copy($D_1F_1HF_2D_2$)), but must perform 11 left copies: AB_1, D_1, F_1, H, F_2, D_2, B_2CD_1, F_1HF_2, D_2EF_1, HF_2 and GHI. In general, n right copies are necessary in order to convert S_n to T_n, but $3 + 4(n - 1)$ left copies are required. Since $\frac{3+4(n-1)}{n} \xrightarrow[n\to\infty]{} 4$, the bound of 4 is tight for an infinite alphabet.

We now use Fibonacci codes to change the above construction to work for a binary alphabet. Fibonacci codes have the property that there are no adjacent 1's in each code word except at its end, so that 11 acts as a comma between consecutive code words. In the previous example, instead of using the ith character of the infinite alphabet, we use the ith Fibonacci code. The minimum number of left and right copies remains the same as the example since each copy that over goes a boundary, cannot include the suffix 11 of the codeword, thus still has a boundary in the codeword following the original boundary of the example.

Finally, to see that the bound of 3.5 is tight, for when block copy reversal is included in the set of operations, we use $S_i' = S_iS_i^R$ and $T_i' = T_iT_i^R$ in this construction.   ∎

3   Edit Distance with Block Deletions

In this section we consider several variations of the edit distance problem with block deletions. We show that the problem can be solved optimally, in polynomial time, when block deletions are allowed with or without character insertions, and character moves, by modifying the traditional dynamic programming method. However, adding block moves to the set of operations, changes the problem to be NP-complete. In the case of block deletions, character insertions and character moves, we show that we can apply the dynamic programming algorithm for block deletions and character insertions and modify the way we calculate the cost, even for non-uniform cost operations.

3.1   Block Deletions with or without Character Insertions

Given two strings S and T, we are interested in the smallest integer k such that S is partitioned into k blocks (substrings) and the blocks of S occur in T in the same order as in S. If $k = 1$ this is the traditional pattern matching problem, which returns whether the pattern S occurs in T or not. This problem is equivalent to finding the minimum number of block deletions to perform on T, so that T is identical to S, and can be solved in polynomial time using dynamic programming. Adding character insertions to block deletions requires small changes in the algorithm. The following algorithm deals with block deletions and character insertions, and can be easily modified to deal with block deletions only.

```
Delete_Insert(S,T)
    for (i = 0; i ≤ n ; i + +) T[i, 0] ← i
    for (j = 1; j ≤ m ; j + +) T[0, j] ← 1
```

for $(i = 1; i \leq n \; ; i + +)$
   for $(j = 1; j \leq m \; ; j + +)$ {
      if $(s_i = t_j)$
         if (during a delete process)
            $T[i,j] \leftarrow \min(T[i-1,j-1], T[i,j-1], T[i-1,j]+1)$
           else $T[i,j] \leftarrow \min(T[i-1,j-1] , T[i,j-1]+1, T[i-1,j]+1)$
        else if (during a delete process) $T[i,j] \leftarrow \min(T[i,j-1], T[i-1,j]+1)$
           else $T[i,j] \leftarrow \min(T[i,j-1]+1, T[i-1,j]+1)$}
  return $(T[n,m])$

3.2 Block Deletions with Character Moves

We are now interested in the minimum number of block deletions, character insertions and character moves applied to T in order to attain S. We use the dynamic programming algorithm introduced in the previous section taking into account character moves. A character move is an insert and a delete of the same character. Therefore, when performing dynamic programming, we try to reduce the cost by exchanging insertions and deletions with moves. If there is an optimal path that leads to a cell and consists of an insert and a delete of the same character, and these operations were not converted into a move operation yet in the current path, we reduce the cost of the cell (assuming that a move operation is cheaper than inserting and deleting). To determine the final cost of the cell, we refer to the (two) characters associated with it. We distinguish between two different cases. In the case where the character is deleted among other characters, and the same character is inserted within the same path, it is not worth to replace it by a move. The reason is that when a character is deleted among other characters within a block deletion, it is not charged an additional cost for this deletion, since all characters are deleted in a single operation. However, when converting the deletion of this character into a move operation, we must partition the block into two sub-blocks while adding another block deletion (unless it occurs at one of the block ends). This additional charge makes this case at least as expensive as the one without moves. However, the situation is different when converting a character deletion and character insertion (with the same character), both performed in the same path, to a move operation, when this character was deleted alone. In this case we should subtract the cost of an insert and a delete, and add the cost of a move to the cost of the current cell, since we have charged it while deleting it and while inserting it, but need to charge it for the move.

Shapira and Storer [2002] show that in the case of uniform costs of character insertions, character deletions and character moves, the minimal edit distance occurs in any optimal path transforming S to T of the traditional edit distance. The following generalization can be proved:

Lemma 1 *For any positive costs of character insertion, deletion, and move, the minimal edit distance including character moves occurs in any optimal path of the traditional edit-distance.*

Given the strings $T=baba$ and $S=aabb$ the dynamic programming table on the right is constructed. The bold numbers represent an optimal path, while the framed cells represent an insert and a delete of a character a. An optimal path includes 2 character moves, so the final cost for the edit distance including character moves is 2.

	ϵ	b	a	b	a
ϵ	**0**	1	1	1	1
a	**1**	**2**	1	**2**	1
a	2	3	**2**	3	2
b	3	2	3	**2**	3
b	4	3	4	**3**	**4**

The edit distance problem with block deletions, character insertions, and character moves is solved optimally as follows:

1. Compute the traditional edit distance (inserts and deletes) using dynamic programming.
2. Chose any optimal path in the constructed table, and reduce its final cost by exchanging the cost of an insert and a delete of the same character by the cost of a move.

We have shown that the edit-distance problem with block deletion with or without character insertions or character moves is solved in polynomial time using dynamic programming. However, adding block moves to the set of operations, changes the problem to be NP-Hard. In Shapira and Storer [2003b] we reduce this problem to only block moves and present a polynomial greedy algorithm with a *log n* approximation bound to optimal.

References

V. BAFNA AND P. A. PEVZNER [1998]. "Sorting by Transpositions", *SIAM Journal Discrete Mathematics* 11:2, 124–240.

V. BAFNA AND P. A. PEVZNER [1993]. "Genome Rearrangements and Sorting by Reversals", *IEEE Sym. on Foundations of Computer Science*, 148–157.

G. CORMODE, M. PATERSON, S. C. SAHINALP AND U. VISHKIN [2000]. "Communication Complexity of Document Exchange", *SODA*, 197–206.

G. CORMODE AND S. MUTHUKRISHNAN [2002]. "The String Edit Distance Problem with Moves", *SODA*, 667–676.

D. DURAND, M. FARACH, R. RAVI AND M. SINGH [1997]. "A Short Course in Computational Molecular Biology", *DIMACS Technical Report 97–63*.

F. ERGUN, S. MUTHUKRISHNAN AND S. C. SAHINALP [2003]. "Comparing Sequences with Segment Rearrangements", *DIMACS Technical Report*.

S. HANNENHALLI [1996]. "Polynomial-Time Algorithm for Computing Translocation Distance Between Genomes", *CPM*, 162–176.

D. LOPRESTI AND A. TOMKINS [1997]. "Block Edit Models for Approximate String Matching", *Theoretical Computer Science* 181, 159–179.

W. J. MASEK AND M. S. PATERSON [1980]. "A Faster Algorithm for Computing String Edit Distances", *J. Computer and System Sciences* 20, 18–31.

S. MUTHUKRISHNAN AND SAHINALP [2000]. "Approximate Nearest Neighbors and Sequence Comparison with Block Operations", *ACM STOC*, 416–424.

S. MUTHUKRISHNAN AND SAHINALP [2002a]. "Simple and Practical Sequence Nearest Neighbors with Block Operations", *CPM*, 262–278.

S. MUTHUKRISHNAN AND SAHINALP [2002b]. "An Improved Algorithm for Sequence Comparison with Block Reversals", *Latin*, 372–386.

D. SHAPIRA AND J. A. STORER [2002]. "Edit Distance with Move Operations", *CPM*, 85–98.

D. SHAPIRA AND J. A. STORER [2003a]. "In-Place Differential File Compression", *DCC*, 263–272.

D. SHAPIRA AND J. A. STORER [2003b]. "Edit Distance with Multiple Block Operations", *Technical Report* CS-03-236.

T. F. SMITH AND M. S. WATERMAN [1981]. "Identification of Common Molecular Sequences", *Journal of Molecular Biology* 147, 195–197.

W. F. TICHY [1984]. "The String to String Correction Problem with Block Moves", *ACM Transactions on Computer Systems* 2:4, 309–321.

M. VINGRON AND M. S. WATERMAN [1994]. "Sequence Alignment and Penalty Choice", *Journal of Molecular Biology*, 235, 1–12 .

Author Index

Lecture Notes in Computer Science

For information about Vols. 1–2757
please contact your bookseller or Springer-Verlag

Vol. 2806: J. Favela, D. Decouchant (Eds.), Groupware: Design, Implementation, and Use. Proceedings, 2003. XII, 382 pages. 2003.

Vol. 2807: V. Matoušek, P. Mautner (Eds.), Text, Speech and Dialogue. Proceedings, 2003. XIII, 426 pages. 2003. (Subseries LNAI).

Vol. 2810: M.R. Berthold, H.-J. Lenz, E. Bradley, R. Kruse, C. Borgelt (Eds.), Advances in Intelligent Data Analysis V. Proceedings, 2003. XV, 624 pages. 2003.

Vol. 2811: G. Karlsson, M.I. Smirnov (Eds.), Quality for All. Proceedings, 2003. XII, 295 pages. 2003.

Vol. 2812: G. Benson, R. Page (Eds.), Algorithms in Bioinformatics. Proceedings, 2003. X, 528 pages. 2003. (Subseries LNBI).

Vol. 2814: M.A. Jeusfeld, Ó. Pastor (Eds.), Conceptual Modeling for Novel Application Domains. Proceedings, 2003. XVI, 410 pages. 2003.

Vol. 2815: Y. Lindell, Composition of Secure Multi-Party Protocols. XVI, 192 pages. 2003.

Vol. 2816: B. Stiller, G. Carle, M. Karsten, P. Reichl (Eds.), Group Communications and Charges. Proceedings, 2003. XIII, 354 pages. 2003.

Vol. 2817: D. Konstantas, M. Leonard, Y. Pigneur, S. Patel (Eds.), Object-Oriented Information Systems. Proceedings, 2003. XII, 426 pages. 2003.

Vol. 2818: H. Blanken, T. Grabs, H.-J. Schek, R. Schenkel, G. Weikum (Eds.), Intelligent Search on XML Data. XVII, 319 pages. 2003.

Vol. 2819: B. Benatallah, M.-C. Shan (Eds.), Technologies for E-Services. Proceedings, 2003. X, 203 pages. 2003.

Vol. 2820: G. Vigna, E. Jonsson, C. Kruegel (Eds.), Recent Advances in Intrusion Detection. Proceedings, 2003. X, 239 pages. 2003.

Vol. 2821: A. Günter, R. Kruse, B. Neumann (Eds.), KI 2003: Advances in Artificial Intelligence. Proceedings, 2003. XII, 662 pages. 2003. (Subseries LNAI).

Vol. 2822: N. Bianchi-Berthouze (Ed.), Databases in Networked Information Systems. Proceedings, 2003. X, 271 pages. 2003.

Vol. 2823: A. Omondi, S. Sedukhin (Eds.), Advances in Computer Systems Architecture. Proceedings, 2003. XIII, 409 pages. 2003.

Vol. 2824: Z. Bellahsène, A.B. Chaudhri, E. Rahm, M. Rys, R. Unland (Eds.), Database and XML Technologies. Proceedings, 2003. X, 283 pages. 2003.

Vol. 2825: W. Kuhn, M. Worboys, S. Timpf (Eds.), Spatial Information Theory. Proceedings, 2003. XI, 399 pages. 2003.

Vol. 2826: A. Krall (Ed.), Software and Compilers for Embedded Systems. Proceedings, 2003. XI, 403 pages. 2003.

Vol. 2827: A. Albrecht, K. Steinhöfel (Eds.), Stochastic Algorithms: Foundations and Applications. Proceedings, 2003. VIII, 167 pages. 2003.

Vol. 2828: A. Lioy, D. Mazzocchi (Eds.), Communications and Multimedia Security. Proceedings, 2003. VIII, 265 pages. 2003.

Vol. 2829: A. Cappelli, F. Turini (Eds.), AI*IA 2003: Advances in Artificial Intelligence. Proceedings, 2003. XIV, 552 pages. 2003. (Subseries LNAI).

Vol. 2830: F. Pfenning, Y. Smaragdakis (Eds.), Generative Programming and Component Engineering. Proceedings, 2003. IX, 397 pages. 2003.

Vol. 2831: M. Schillo, M. Klusch, J. Müller, H. Tianfield (Eds.), Multiagent System Technologies. Proceedings, 2003. X, 229 pages. 2003. (Subseries LNAI).

Vol. 2832: G. Di Battista, U. Zwick (Eds.), Algorithms – ESA 2003. Proceedings, 2003. XIV, 790 pages. 2003.

Vol. 2833: F. Rossi (Ed.), Principles and Practice of Constraint Programming – CP 2003. Proceedings, 2003. XIX, 1005 pages. 2003.

Vol. 2834: X. Zhou, S. Jähnichen, M. Xu, J. Cao (Eds.), Advanced Parallel Processing Technologies. Proceedings, 2003. XIV, 679 pages. 2003.

Vol. 2835: T. Horváth, A. Yamamoto (Eds.), Inductive Logic Programming. Proceedings, 2003. X, 401 pages. 2003. (Subseries LNAI).

Vol. 2836: S. Qing, D. Gollmann, J. Zhou (Eds.), Information and Communications Security. Proceedings, 2003. XI, 416 pages. 2003.

Vol. 2837: N. Lavrač, D. Gamberger, H. Blockeel, L. Todorovski (Eds.), Machine Learning: ECML 2003. Proceedings, 2003. XVI, 504 pages. 2003. (Subseries LNAI).

Vol. 2838: N. Lavrač, D. Gamberger, L. Todorovski, H. Blockeel (Eds.), Knowledge Discovery in Databases: PKDD 2003. Proceedings, 2003. XVI, 508 pages. 2003. (Subseries LNAI).

Vol. 2839: A. Marshall, N. Agoulmine (Eds.), Management of Multimedia Networks and Services. Proceedings, 2003. XIV, 532 pages. 2003.

Vol. 2840: J. Dongarra, D. Laforenza, S. Orlando (Eds.), Recent Advances in Parallel Virtual Machine and Message Passing Interface. Proceedings, 2003. XVIII, 693 pages. 2003.

Vol. 2841: C. Blundo, C. Laneve (Eds.), Theoretical Computer Science. Proceedings, 2003. XI, 397 pages. 2003.

Vol. 2847: R. de Lemos, T.S. Weber, J.B. Camargo Jr. (Eds.), Dependable Computing. Proceedings, 2003. XIV, 371 pages. 2003.

Vol. 2848: F.E. Fich (Ed.), Distributed Computing. Proceedings, 2003. X, 367 pages. 2003.

Vol. 2849: N. García, J.M. Martínez, L. Salgado (Eds.), Visual Content Processing and Representation. Proceedings, 2003. XII, 352 pages. 2003.

Vol. 2850: M.Y. Vardi, A. Voronkov (Eds.), Logic for Programming, Artificial Intelligence, and Reasoning. Proceedings, 2003. XIII, 437 pages. 2003. (Subseries LNAI)

Vol. 2851: C. Boyd, W. Mao (Eds.), Information Security. Proceedings, 2003. XI, 443 pages. 2003.

Vol. 2853: M. Jeckle, L.-J. Zhang (Eds.), Web Services – ICWS-Europe 2003. Proceedings, 2003. VIII, 227 pages. 2003.

Vol. 2856: M. Smirnov, E. Biersack, C. Blondia, O. Bonaventure, O. Casals, G. Karlsson, George Pavlou, B. Quoitin, J. Roberts, I. Stavrakakis, B. Stiller, P. Trimintzios, P. Van Mieghem (Eds.), Quality of Future Internet Services. IX, 293 pages. 2003.

Vol. 2857: M.A. Nascimento, E.S. de Moura, A.L. Oliveira (Eds.), String Processing and Information Retrieval. Proceedings, 2003. XI, 379 pages. 2003.

Vol. 2859: B. Apolloni, M. Marinaro, R. Tagliaferri (Eds.), Neural Nets. Proceedings, 2003. X, 376 pages. 2003.

Vol. 2865: S. Pierre, M. Barbeau, E. Kranakis (Eds.), Ad-Hoc, Mobile, and Wireless Networks. Proceedings, 2003. X, 293 pages. 2003.